Lecture Notes in Computer Science 4215

Commenced Publication in 1973
Founding and Former Series Editors:
Gerhard Goos, Juris Hartmanis, and Jan van Leeuwen

David W. Embley Antoni Olivé
Sudha Ram (Eds.)

Conceptual Modeling – ER 2006

25th International Conference on Conceptual Modeling
Tucson, AZ, USA, November 6-9, 2006
Proceedings

Volume Editors

David W. Embley
Brigham Young University, Department of Computer Science
Provo, UT 84602, USA
E-mail: embley@cs.byu.edu

Antoni Olivé
Universitat Politècnica Catalunya
Campus Nord, Omega, 131, 08034 Barcelona, Catalonia, Spain
E-mail: olive@lsi.upc.edu

Sudha Ram
University of Arizona, Eller College of Management
Department of MIS, Tucson, AZ 85721, USA
E-mail: ram@eller.arizona.edu

Library of Congress Control Number: 2006934203

CR Subject Classification (1998): H.2, H.4, F.4.1, I.2.4, H.1, J.1, D.2, C.2

LNCS Sublibrary: SL 3 – Information Systems and Application, incl. Internet/Web and HCI

ISSN 0302-9743
ISBN-10 3-540-47224-X Springer Berlin Heidelberg New York
ISBN-13 978-3-540-47224-7 Springer Berlin Heidelberg New York

Springer is a part of Springer Science+Business Media

springer.com

Printed in Germany

Typesetting: Camera-ready by author, data conversion by Scientific Publishing Services, Chennai, India
Printed on acid-free paper SPIN: 11901181 06/3142 5 4 3 2 1 0

Preface

Conceptual modeling has long been recognized as the primary means to enable software development in information systems and data engineering. Nowadays, conceptual modeling has become fundamental to any domain in which organizations have to cope with complex, real-world systems. Conceptual modeling fosters communication between information systems developers and end-users, and it has become a key mechanism for understanding and representing computing systems and environments of all kinds, including the new e-applications and the information systems that support them.

The International Conference on Conceptual Modeling provides the premiere forum for presenting and discussing current research and applications in which the major emphasis is on conceptual modeling. Topics of interest span the entire spectrum of conceptual modeling including research and practice in areas such as theories of concepts and ontologies underlying conceptual modeling, methods and tools for developing and communicating conceptual models, and techniques for transforming conceptual models into effective implementations. Moreover, new areas of conceptual modeling broaden its application to include interdependencies with knowledge-based, logical, linguistic, and philosophical theories and approaches. The conference also makes major strides in fostering collaboration and exchange between academia and industry.

In this year's conference, research papers focused on XML, Web services, business modeling, conceptual modeling applied to human-computer interaction, quality in conceptual modeling, conceptual modeling applied to interoperability, requirements modeling, reasoning, the Semantic Web, and metadata management. The call for papers attracted 158 research papers, whose authors represent 27 different countries. The Program Committee accepted 37, for an acceptance rate of 23.4%. The authors of accepted papers come from 19 different countries.

This year, the conference celebrated its silver anniversary. In honor of 25 years of successful conferences, its founder, Peter Chen, gave the opening keynote address. The conference also featured two additional keynote addresses, 37 research papers, six industrial presentations, seven workshops (with a total of 42 additional research papers), five demos/posters, two panel sessions, and four tutorials.

We appreciate the hard work of the Program Committee and the external referees, who generously spent their time and energy reviewing submitted papers. Almost all of the 474 reviews for the 158 research papers were received, amazingly leaving only a handful for the PC chairs to do. We thank the authors who wrote high-quality research papers, and the many others who participated in the workshops, tutorials, panels, poster and demo sessions, industrial presentations, and keynote presentations. We also wish to express our sincere appreciation for the sponsorships obtained by Mohan Tanniru and Mike Grieves. Our Publicity Chair and Webmaster Huimin did a wonderful job of keeping the Web site updated promptly and publicizing the conference. Thanks are also due to Akhilesh Bajaj and Ramesh Venkataraman for organizing the demos and posters, and Len Seligman and Arnie Rosenthal for the industry track presentations. We thank John Roddick, who diligently took care of organizing the tutorials, Keng Siau and Uday Kulkarni for selecting the panels, and Bernhard Thalheim for acting as the ER Steering Committee liaison. Thanks are also due to the doctoral students from the University of Arizona who helped with various arrangements for the conference. Finally, our heartfelt thanks to Anji Seigel for taking care of registration, all local arrangements, and a myriad of other details without which the conference would not have been successful.

November 2006

David W. Embley
Antoni Olive
Sudha Ram

ER 2006 Conference Organization

Honorary Conference Chair

Peter Chen — Louisiana State University, USA

General Conference Co-chairs

Sudha Ram — University of Arizona, USA
Mohan R. Tanniru — University of Arizona, USA

Scientific Program Co-chairs

David W. Embley — Brigham Young University, USA
Antoni Olivé — Universitat Politècnica de Catalunya, Spain

Panels Co-chairs

Uday Kulkarni — Arizona State University, USA
Keng Siau — University of Nebraska,Lincoln, USA

Industrial Co-chairs

Arnie Rosenthal — Mitre Corporation, USA
Len Seligman — Mitre Corporation, USA

Tutorial and Workshop Chair

John Roddick — Flinders University, Australia

Demos and Posters Co-chairs

Akhilesh Bajaj — University of Tulsa, USA
Ramesh Venkataraman — Indiana University, USA

Steering Committee Liaison

Bernhard Thalheim, Christian-Albrechts-Universität zu Kiel, Germany

Publicity Chair and Webmaster

Huimin (Min) Zhao — University of Wisconsin-Milwaukee, USA

Local Arrangements and Registration

Anji Siegel — University of Arizona, USA

Program Committee

Alberto H. F. Laender	Federal University of Minas Gerais, Brazil
Altigran S. da Silva	Universidade do Amazonas, Brazil
Arne Solvberg	Norwegian Institute of Technology, Norway
Barbara Pernici	Politecnico di Milano, Italy
Bernhard Thalheim	University of Kiel, Germany
Bogdan Czejdo	Loyola University New Orleans, USA
Brian Henderson-Sellers	University of Technology, Sydney, Australia
Carlos Heuser	Universidade Federal do Rio Grande do Sul, Brazil
Christian S. Jensen	Aalborg University, Denmark
Christine Parent	University of Lausanne, Switzerland
Colette Rolland	University Paris 1 Panthéon-Sorbonne, France
Daniel Schwabe	PUC-Rio, Brazil
Debabrata Dey	University of Washington, USA
Diego Calvanese	Free University of Bozen-Bolzano, Italy
Dirk Draheim	Free University of Berlin, Germany
Dongwon Lee	The Pennsylvania State University, USA
Ee-Peng Lim	Nanyang Technological University, Singapore
Elisa Bertino	Purdue University, USA
Elisabeth Metais	CEDRIC-CNAM of Paris, France
Ernest Teniente	Universitat Politècnica de Catalunya, Spain
Esperanza Marcos	Rey Juan Carlos University, Spain
Gill Dobbie	University of Auckland, New Zealand
Heinrich C. Mayr	University of Klagenfurt, Austria
Il-Yeol Song	Drexel University, USA
Jan L.G. Dietz	Delft University of Technology, The Netherlands
Jean-Luc Hainaut	University of Namur, Belgium
Jeffrey Parsons	Memorial University of Newfoundland, Canada
Johann Eder	University of Vienna, Austria
John Krogstie	NTNU and SINTEF, Norway
John Mylopoulos	University of Toronto, Canada
Karen C. Davis	University of Cincinnati, USA
Klaus-Dieter Schewe	Massey University, New Zealand
Kyu-Young Whang	KAIST, Korea
Li Xu	University of Arizona South, USA
Ling Liu	Georgia Institute of Technology, USA
Lois Delcambre	Portland State University, USA
Maria E Orlowska	The University of Queensland, Australia
Mario Piattini	Universidad de Castilla-La Mancha, Spain
Mengchi Liu	Carleton University, Canada
Michael Rosemann	Queensland University of Technology, Australia
Motoshi Saeki	Tokyo Institute of Technology, Japan
Naveen Prakash	JayPee University of Information Technology, India
Nicola Guarino	ISTC-CNR, Italy
Oscar Diaz	University of the Basque Country, Spain
Oscar Pastor	Technical University of Valencia, Spain

Paolo Atzeni	Università Roma Tre, Italy
Paul Johannesson	KTH, Sweden
Peretz Shoval	Ben-Gurion University, Israel
Peri Loucopoulos	The University of Manchester, UK
Peter Scheuermann	Northwestern University, USA
Piero Fraternali	Politecnico di Milano, Italy
Qing Li	City University of Hong Kong, China
Roel Wieringa	University of Twente Netherlands
Roger Chiang	University of Cincinnati, USA
Salvatore T. March	Vanderbilt University, USA
Sandeep Purao	Penn State University, USA
S.C. Cheung	The Hong Kong University of Sci. and Technology, China
Sham Navathe	Georgia Institute of Technology, USA
Shawn Bowers	University of California, Davis, USA
Shuigeng Zhou	Fudan University, China
Silvana Castano	University of Milan, Italy
Sonia Bergamaschi	Università di Modena e Reggio Emilia, Italy
Stefan Conrad	University of Düsseldorf, Germany
Stefano Ceri	Politécnico di Milano, Italy
Stefano Spaccapietra	Ecole Polytechnique Fédérale Lausanne, Switzerland
Stephen Clyde	Utah State University, USA
Stephen W. Liddle	Brigham Young University, USA
Takao Miura	Hosei University Japan
Terry Halpin	Neumont University, USA
Tetsuo Tamai	The University of Tokyo, Japan
Ting-Peng Liang	National Sun Yat-sen University, Taiwan
Tony Morgan	Northface University, USA
Veda C. Storey	Georgia State University, USA
Vijay Khatri	Indiana University, USA
Wai Yin Mok	University of Alabama in Huntsville, USA
Wilfred Ng	The Hong Kong University of Sci. and Technology, China
Yair Wand	The University of British Columbia, Canada
Yanchun Zhang	Victoria University, Australia
Yasushi Kiyoki	Keio University, Japan

External Referees

Alexei Tretiakov
Alfio Ferrara
André Prisco Vargas
Andrea Calí
Andreas Wombacher
Asem Omari
Baoping Lin
Birger Andersson
Byron Choi
César J. Acuña
Chang Xu
Chong Wang
Christian Kluge
Christopher Popfinger
Chunyang Ye
Cristian Pérez de Laborda
Daniel Mellado
Devis Bianchini
Dolors Costal
Domenico Beneventano

Emanuele Bottazzi
Englebert Vincent
Fabio Porto
Felix Garcia
Flavio Ferrarotti
Francesco Guerra
George Abraham
Hans Mulder
Heymans Patrick
Hui Ma
James Goldman
Jan Hoogervorst
Jan Recker
João Cavalcanti
Johanna Vompras
Johannes Maria Zaha
John Horner
Jonathan Goldstein
José María Cavero
Juan A. Pereira
Jun Miyazaki
Karl Wiggisser
Ki-Jung Lee
Laura Po
Le Quang Hieu
Marco Brambilla
Marek Lehmann
Maria Bergholtz
Maria Luisa Damiani
Martin Op 't Land
Masayoshi Aritsugi
Maurice van Keulen
Maurizio Vincini
Michaël Petit
Michele Melchiori
Ming-Jun Xiao
Mireille Samia
Mirko Orsini
Nam Youn Choi
Nuno Valero Ribeiro
Ornsiri Thonggoom
Pascal van Eck
Raimundas Matulevičius
Renata de Matos Galante
Ryan Liu
Saval Germain
Sebastian Link
Sergio Mergen
Shermann S. M. Chan
Stefano Montanelli
Sven Hartmann
Tetsuji Satoh
Thomas Weishäupl
Toshiyuki Amagasa
Valeria de Castro
Xiaoling Wang
Yanan Hao
Yangfan He
Yihong Ding
Yunan Chen

Organized By

Eller College of Management at The University of Arizona

Sponsored By

The ER Institute

In Cooperation With

ACM SIGMIS
ACM SIGMOD

Table of Contents

Keynote Papers

Web Services

Quality in Conceptual Modeling

Aspects of Conceptual Modeling

Modeling Advanced Applications

XML

Semantic Web

Requirements Modeling

Aspects of Interoperability

Metadata Management

Human-Computer Interaction

Business Modeling

Reasoning

Panels

Industrial Track

Demos and Posters

Suggested Research Directions for a New Frontier – Active Conceptual Modeling

Peter P. Chen[1]

Computer Science Department, Louisiana State University
Baton Rouge, LA 70803, U.S.A
pchen@lsu.edu

Abstract. This paper discusses several research directions and challenges of a new frontier of research: active conceptual modeling. It suggests how the Entity-Relationship (ER) model may be extended to satisfy some of the needs of a new set of emerging user needs and applications.

Keywords: Conceptual Modeling, active conceptual modeling, the Entity-Relationship model.

1 Introduction

The conventional/traditional conceptual modeling concentrates on modeling the "static" views (i.e., the snapshots) of the world. Even though the static conceptual models have been used successfully in the past and will continue to do well in the foreseeable future, there is a need for make the conceptual model "active" to handle a new set of user needs and applications.

2 The Needs for Active Conceptual Modeling

There are growing needs of traceability for the evolving and changing world state. There are also increasing needs for understanding relationships among changes, which may have significance to current world state (e.g. terrorist training could have been changed since the 9-11 attack). In other words, one of the major needs today is an "advanced conceptual model" which may be useful in analyzing surprises, crises, and unconventional events (such as unconventional attacks). Some notable recent surprised incidents and events that forced us to look back the past events and changes in the world to look for clues and reasons include the following:

- The September-11 Attack of the World Trade Centers and Pentagon
- The tsunami disaster in Southeast Asia and East Africa
- The hurricane Katrina disaster.

There is a need to develop an "active conceptual Model," which will allow for continual learning and provide traceable lessons learned from past experiences,

---

[1] In the academic year of 2006-7, the author is a visiting professor at MIT, e-mail: pchen@mit.edu . Home page of the author: www.csc.lsu.edu/~chen .

D.W. Embley, A. Olivé, and S. Ram (Eds.): ER 2006, LNCS 4215, pp. 1 – 4, 2006.

including surprises. The active conceptual model may also be potentially useful for predicting future actions.

3 Problems of Existing Methodologies/Technologies

The existing methodologies (including the static conceptual models) and technologies have been proven to be very useful in the past and will continue to be so for certain applications in the foreseeable future. However, they may need to be modified in order to handle fast time-varying and time-dependent changes in world states. In particular, there are several areas that the existing technologies and methodologies need to be modified or extended:

- Current databases/knowledge-bases usually do not support information and schema changes or historical information because they usually only model the snapshots of the part of the world of interest
- Current state-of-art techniques focus on pre-defined entities of interest and their static relationships
- Virtually no constructs in the exiting conceptual models are available for modeling changes of the entity behaviors (e.g. terrorist profiles) and the dynamic and time-varying relationships among them
- Using the constructs of the existing conceptual models, it is very difficult to model a wide spectrum of situations resulting from different degrees of importance of the relationships due to different perspectives
- The Schemas of the current data models are difficult to be changed dynamically.

4 A Starting Point for Active Conceptual Modeling

After three decades of efforts of many researchers and practitioners, the conventional (static) conceptual modeling methodologies and techniques based on the Entity-Relationship (ER) model and its extensions [1-8] have being practiced daily by hundreds of thousands of professionals and developers all over the world. Now, the time is right to start a major research and development effort in active conceptual modeling. However, there are many challenging research problems which need good solutions such as:

- Time/Space: How can we model the "time" and "space"?
- Scenario: How can we describe a scenario?
- Players: Who were involved and what roles did they play?
- Cause/Effect: What is the best way to describe the cause-effect relationship?
- Event/Activity: Do we need different symbols (icons) to represent event and activity? How can we relate events with activities?

From the User/Operation Perspectives, the static ER Model needs to be extended in the following directions:

- Represent a given snapshot of the world/database by a mathematical model
- Compute the difference between the snapshots

- Represent the difference between snapshots by a "delta" model
- Identify relationships in the "delta" model and additional attributes
- Create a database for learning purposes
- Users can query this database to study the status of the world state with respect to the changes and their relationships

Some of these issues have been studied in the past, but we need coherent and integrated solutions!

Active conceptual modeling is a continual process of describing all aspects of the open world, its activities, and its changes under different perspectives, based on our knowledge and understanding. For any given time, the model can be viewed as a multilevel and multi-perspective high-level abstraction of reality. How to develop a conceptual model that can have these kinds of features and capabilities (and in a consistent and coherent way) is a great challenge!

5 Conclusion

Static conceptual models have been used successfully for at least the past 3 decades. For a set of new and emerging user needs and applications, we need an "active conceptual model." We have discussed the weaknesses of the existing static conceptual models, methodologies, and technologies in handling some of the new and emerging applications and suggested several directions to extend the Entity-Relationship (ER) model to make it an "active conceptual model." We have raised some difficult research issues and questions that need clean solutions so that the active conceptual modeling can be moved from the research stage to the development stage, and then to the practice stage. We hope the R&D community will be able to develop and perfect the active conceptual modeling methodologies and techniques quickly so that we can realize the benefits [9] of the active conceptual modeling in the not too distant future.

Acknowledgments. The author would like to express his thanks to Leah Wong and Doug Lange of U.S. Navy SPAWAR SSC San Diego for their ideas and for organizing a discussion workshop on Active Conceptual Modeling for Learning in their facility in May 2006. The research of the author was supported in part by National Science Foundation grant: ITR-IIS-0326387 and AFOSR grant: FA9550-05-1-0454.

References

1. Chen, Peter P., The Entity-Relationship Model: Toward a Unified View of Data, *ACM Transactions on Database Systems, Vol. 1,* No.1, (March 1976), pp. 9-36.
2. *Proceedings of Conceptual Modeling (ER) Conferences*, www.conceputalmodeling.org .
3. Lois M. L. Delcambre, Christian Kop, Heinrich C. Mayr, John Mylopoulos, Oscar Pastor (Eds.): Conceptual Modeling - ER 2005, 24th International Conference on Conceptual Modeling, Klagenfurt, Austria, October 24-28, 2005, Proceedings. *Lecture Notes in Computer Science 3716,* Springer 2005, ISBN 3-540-29389-2.

4. Jacky Akoka, Stephen W. Liddle, Il-Yeol Song, Michela Bertolotto, Isabelle Comyn-Wattiau, Samira Si-Said Cherfi, Willem-Jan van den Heuvel, Bernhard Thalheim, Manuel Kolp, Paolo Bresciani, Juan Trujillo, Christian Kop, Heinrich C. Mayr (Eds.): Perspectives in Conceptual Modeling, ER 2005 Workshops AOIS, BP-UML, CoMoGIS, eCOMO, and QoIS, Klagenfurt, Austria, October 24-28, 2005, Proceedings. *Lecture Notes in Computer Science 3770,* Springer 2005, ISBN 3-540-29395-7.
5. Paolo Atzeni, Wesley W. Chu, Hongjun Lu, Shuigeng Zhou, Tok Wang Ling (Eds.): Conceptual Modeling - ER 2004, 23rd International Conference on Conceptual Modeling, Shanghai, China, November 2004, Proceedings. *Lecture Notes in Computer Science 3288*, Springer 2004, ISBN 3-540-23723-2.
6. Il-Yeol Song, Stephen W. Liddle, Tok Wang Ling, Peter Scheuermann (Eds.): Conceptual Modeling - ER 2003, 22nd International Conference on Conceptual Modeling, Chicago, IL, USA, October 13-16, 2003, Proceedings. *Lecture Notes in Computer Science 2813*, Springer 2003, ISBN 3-540-20299-4.
7. Stefano Spaccapietra, Salvatore T. March, Yashiko Kambayashi (Eds.): Conceptual Modeling - ER 2002, 21st International Conference on Conceptual Modeling, Tampere, Finland, October 7-11, 2002, Proceedings. *Lecture Notes in Computer Science 2503*, Springer 2002, ISBN 3-540-44277-4.
8. Hideko S. Kunii, Sushil Jajodia, Arne Sølvberg (Eds.): Conceptual Modeling - ER 2001, 20th International Conference on Conceptual Modeling, Yokohama, Japan, November 27-30, 2001, Proceedings. *Lecture Notes in Computer Science 2224*, Springer 2001, ISBN 3-540-42866-6
9. Chen, Peter P. and Leah Wong, A Proposed Preliminary Framework for Conceptual Modeling of Learning from Surprises, *Proc. 2005 International Conference on Artificial Intelligence*, Las Vegas, June 27-30, 2005.

From Conceptual Modeling to Requirements Engineering

Colette Rolland

Université Paris1 Panthéon Sorbonne
90 Rue de Tolbiac,
75013 Paris Cedex 13
rolland@univ-paris1.fr

Motivation for the Theme of the Talk

A number of studies show [1][2][3][4] that systems fail due to an inadequate or insufficient understanding of the requirements they seek to address. Further, the amount of effort needed to fix these systems has been found to be very high [5]. To correct this situation, it is necessary to address the issue of requirements elicitation, validation, and specification in a relatively more focussed manner. The expectation is that as a result of this, more acceptable systems will be developed in the future. The field of requirements engineering has emerged to meet this expectation.

The traditional way of engineering information systems is through conceptual modelling which produces a specification of the system to be developed. This specification concentrates on what the system should do, that is, on its functionality. Such a specification acts as a prescription for system construction.

Of the assumptions on which conceptual modelling is based, we find three very important ones :

- System requirements are highly stable, i.e., they do not change with time. As a consequence the conceptualised system is itself stable.
- System requirements are given. Users have just to be questioned about their requirements. Thus, the interesting problem is that of specifying the system to meet these requirements. System analysts are the right persons to do it.
- Validation of system requirements can be done with reference to system functionality. In other words, the conceptual schema is the appropriate support for communicating, negotiating and reaching an agreement with users and system stakeholders.

It became clear in the past decade that these assumptions do not hold any longer [6]. Due to economic pressure and emergence of new technologies, organisations change much faster than before. As a consequence, expectations from information systems also change much faster which, in turn, implies that requirements are no longer stable. Understanding and recording the effect of business changes on requirements is considered as an important issue for the success of an information system development project [7]. It is also known that requirements change even as the system is being developed. Since requirements change, it is no longer possible to treat them as given. Rather, it is necessary to determine new requirements for legacy systems and to carry requirements models through the entire systems life cycle. Further the central role of system analysts is taken over by a consortium of stakeholders who bring their specific view points on what the system should do [8].

D.W. Embley, A. Olivé, and S. Ram (Eds.): ER 2006, LNCS 4215, pp. 5 – 11, 2006.

Finally, requirements validation must now be rooted in organisational change rather than in system functionality : if requirements models are to be validated then, this validation must be with reference to organisational needs rather than system functionality [9]. It is only then that computer based systems will be able to adapt to changing organisational needs [10].

In tackling these problems, the area of requirements engineering tries to go beyond the functionality based view of conceptual modelling. We highlight here two dimensions along which this attempt is made :

- Requirements engineering extends the 'what is done by the system' approach with the 'why is the system like this' view. This why question is answered in terms of organisational objectives and their impact on information systems supporting the organisation. In other words, information systems are seen as fulfilling a certain purpose in an organisation and requirements engineering helps in the conceptualisation of these purposeful systems. This has two implications (a) elicitation and validation of the requirements of a system is done with respect to their purpose in organisations and (b) only organisationally purposeful systems are conceptualised.
- Requirements engineering does not deal with the functionality of a system. Rather, it assumes that the potential users of the system provide useful and realistic view points about the system to be developed. Therefore, a detailed exploration of the various ways in which the system might be used and the activities it shall carry out is performed. This can be done, for example, by looking at typical interactions that are expected to occur with the system. This exploration leads to the identification of 'normal' and 'exceptional' activities whose integration models the full system behaviour. In this sense, the determination of what the system must do is an interesting question in requirements engineering.

To deliver the foregoing, requirements engineering must find ways to support the *conceptualisation of purposeful systems.* This implies a movement in the engineering approaches towards the 'whys' of the system To-Be. As Ross and Schoman [11] stated in their seminal paper "requirements definition must say why a system is needed, based on current and foreseen conditions, which may be internal operations or external market. It must say what a system features will serve and satisfy this context". In this movement from the 'whats' to the 'whys', it becomes mandatory to consider multiple view points of the various stakeholders, to explore alternative design choices and reason about them so as to make conceptual decisions on the basis of rationale arguments in favour and against the different alternatives. Recording these shall help to deal with changing requirements.

Content of the Talk

The talk will focus on the above issue of conceptualising purposeful systems.

(a) It first argues that the goal concept is central to resolve this issue and shall demonstrate how goal driven approaches can contribute by supporting requirements engineering activities such as requirements elicitation, specification, validation, modification, structuring and negotiation.

In the view of requirements engineering being proposed here, we consider that requirements come from two sources, users and the domain environment. The first source provides informal statements of goals and users' intentions expressed in natural language. The second source provides requirements reflecting real world facts and constraints on the designed system implied by laws of physics independently of any user's need or wish. Hence requirements may be divided into two sub-types :

1. user-defined requirements which arise from people in the organisation and reflect their goals, intentions and wishes,
2. domain-imposed requirements which are facts of nature and reflect domain laws.

This implies that the Universe of Discourse has to be partitioned into two, the *usage world* and the *subject world* [12]. The *usage world* describes the tasks, procedures, interactions etc. performed by agents and how systems are used to do work. It can be looked upon as containing the objectives that are to be met in the organisation and which are achieved by the activities carried out by agents. Therefore it describes the activity of agents and how this activity leads to useful work.

The second part of the Universe of Discourse, the *subject world*, contains knowledge of the real world domain about which the proposed system has to provide information. It contains real world objects which are to be represented in the conceptual schema.

There is a third world, the *system world* which is the world of system specifications in which the requirements arising from the two worlds must be addressed. The system world holds the modelled entities, processes, and events of the subject and usage worlds as well as the mapping from these conceptual specifications to the design and implementation levels of the software system. All these worlds are interrelated as shown in Figure 1. User-defined requirements (sub-type 1 above) are captured by the *intentional relationship*. Domain-imposed requirements (sub-type 2 above) are captured by the *representation relationship*.

The usage world provides the rationale for building a system. The purpose of developing an information system is to be found outside the system itself, in the *enterprise,* or in other words, in the context in which the system will function. The

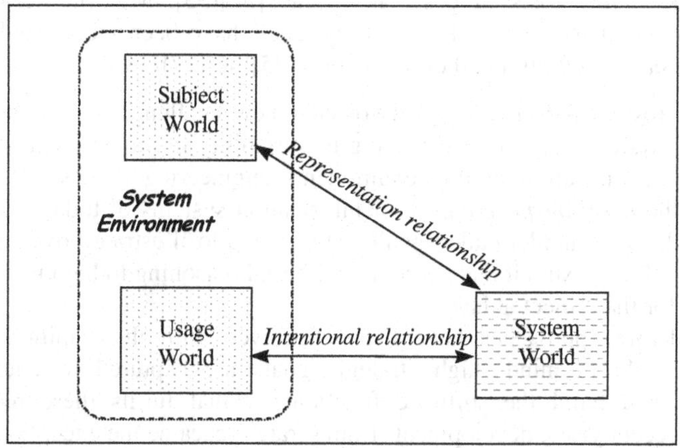

Fig. 1. Relationships between the worlds of usage, subject and system

social relationship between the usage and system world addresses the issue of the system purpose and relates the system to the goals and objectives of the organisation. This relationship explains *why* the system is developed. Modelling this establishes the conceptual link between the envisaged system and its changing environment. This suggests an augmentation of conceptual modelling to deal with the description of the context in which the system will function. In the area of requirements engineering, *goal-driven approaches* have been developed which directly model organisational objectives and relate them to system functions. These approaches address the semiotic, social link between the usage and the system world.

The talk will then elaborate on goal modeling and reasoning with goals [13] in order to demonstrate the various roles of goals in conceptualizing purposeful systems:

- Goal modeling proved to be an effective way to *elicit requirements* [14][15][16][17][18][19][20]. The assumption of goal-based requirements elicitation is that the rationale for developing a system is found outside the system itself, in the enterprise [21] in which the system shall function.
- RE assumes that the envisioned system might function and interact with its environment in many different ways. Alternative goal refinement proved helpful in the systematic *exploration of system choices* [15][21][22][23].
- *Requirements completeness* is a major RE issue. Yue [24] was probably the first to argue that goals provide a criterion for requirements completeness: the requirements specification is complete if the requirements are sufficient to achieve the goal they refine.
- Goals provide a means to ensure *requirements pre-traceability* [7][25][26]. They establish a conceptual link between the system and its environment, thus facilitating the propagation of organizational changes into the system functionality. This link provides the rationale for requirements [11][15][27][28][29] and facilitates the explanation and justification of requirements to the stakeholders.
- Stakeholders provide useful and realistic viewpoints about the system To-Be. *Negotiation* techniques have been developed to help choosing the prevalent one [30][31]. *Prioritization* techniques aim at providing means to compare the different viewpoints on the basis of costs and value [32][33]. Multiple viewpoints are inherently associated to conflicts [34] and goals have been recognized to help in the *detection of conflicts* and their resolution [35][36][37][38].

(b) In the rest of the talk, we will consider new challenges raised by emerging conditions of system development leading to variability in requirements engineering capture and customisation in the requirements engineering process. Variability is imposed by the *multi-purpose nature* of information systems of today. The talk will use a particular goal model called goal/strategy map to illustrate how a goal model can make variability explicit and support goal-based reasoning to help in selecting the right variant for the project at hand.

Goal modeling approaches have been conceived with the traditional software system life cycle in mind: high strategic goals are captured to elicit software requirements and build the software functionality that fulfils these requirements. However, in recent years, development 'from scratch' became the exception and a new context in which software systems are developed has emerged. Whereas earlier, a system met the purpose of a single organization and of a single set of customers, a system of today must be conceived in a larger perspective, to meet the purpose of several organizations and to be adaptable to different usage situations/customer sets. The former is typical of an ERP-like development situation whereas the latter is the concern of product-line development [39], [40] and adaptable software [24]. In the software community, this leads to the notion of software variability which is defined as the ability of a software system to be changed, customized or configured to a specific context [41]. Whereas the software community studies variability as a design problem and concentrates on implementation issues [39], [40], [42], we believe like Halmans [43] that capturing variability at the goal level is essential to meet the multi-purpose nature of new software systems.

Our position is that variability implies a move from systems with a *mono-facetted purpose* to those with a *multi-facetted purpose*. Whereas the former concentrates on goal discovery, the multi-facetted nature of a purpose extends it to consider the many different ways of goal achievement. For example, for the goal Purchase Material, earlier it would be enough to know that an organization achieves this goal by forecasting material need. Thus, Purchase material was mono-facetted: it had exactly one strategy for its achievement. However, in the new context, it is necessary to introduce other strategies as well, say the Reorder Point strategy for purchasing material. Purchase Material now is multi-facetted, it has many strategies for goal achievement. These two strategies, among others, are made available, for example, in the SAP Materials Management module[44].

The foregoing points to the need to balance *goal-orientation* with the introduction of *strategies for goal achievement.* This is the essence of *goal/strategy maps.*

A *goal/strategy map*, or *map* for short, is a graph, with nodes as *intentions* and *strategies* as edges. An edge entering a node identifies a strategy that can be used for achieving the intention of the node. The map therefore, shows which intentions can be achieved by which strategies once a preceding intention has been achieved. Evidently, the map is capable of expressing goals and their achievement in a declarative manner.

The talk will introduce the concept of a map [45], illustrate it with an ERP system example and discuss how the model meets the aforementioned challenges. Thereby, we consider the *customization process* implied by multi-purpose systems and discuss the way it can be handled with maps [46].

References

1. Standish Group (1995), *Chaos*. Standish Group Internal Report.
2. European Software Institute (1996), *European User Survey Analysis*, Report USV_EUR 2.1, ESPITI Project.
3. McGraw K., Harbison K. (1997), *User Centered Requirements, The Scenario-Based Engineering Process*. Lawrence Erlbaum Associates Publishers.
4. META Group (2003) *Research on Requirements Realization and Relevance,* report
5. Johnson J. (1995), *Chaos : the Dollar Drain of IT project Failures.* Application Development Trends, pp.41-47.
6. Hammer, T. F., Huffman, L. L. and Rosenberg, L. H., (1998) *Doing requirements right the first time*, Crosstalk - The Journal of Defense Software Engineering, December, pp.20-25.

7. Ramesh, B. and Jarke, M. (2001) Toward Reference Models for Requirements Traceability, *IEEE Transactions on Software Engineering*, 27(1), pp. 58-93.
8. Finkelstein A., Kramer J., Goedicke M. (1990), *ViewPoint Oriented Software Development*, Proc. Conf Le Génie Logiciel et ses Applications, Toulouse, p 337-351.
9. Bleistein S., Cox K. and Verner J. (2006), *Validating Strategic Alignment of Organisational IT Requirements using Goal Modeling and Problem Diagrams*, Journal of Systems and Software, 79 (3), pp.362-378.
10. A. Etien, C. Salinesi, (2005) *Managing Requirements in a Co-evolution Context,* Proceedings of the IEEE International Conference on Requirements Engineering, Paris, France, pp. 125-134
11. Ross D.T., Schoman K.E. (1977), *Structured Analysis for Requirements Definition*. IEEE Transactions on Software Engineering, 3(1), pp.6-15.
12. Jarke, M., and Pohl, K., (1993), *Establishing Visions in Context: Towards a Model of Requirements Processes*, Proc. 12th Intl. Conf. Information Systems, Orlando.
13. Rolland C., Salinesi C. (2005), *Modeling goals and reasoning with them,* Chap9 of the book « Engineering and Managing Requirements », A. Aurum and C. Wohlin (eds), Springer Verlag Pub, TBP 2005.
14. Potts, C., Takahashi, K., and Antòn , A. I. (1994), *Inquiry-based requirements analysis*. IEEE Software 11(2), pp. 21-32.
15. Rolland, C., Souveyet, C., and Ben Achour, C. (1998), *Guiding goal modelling using scenarios*. IEEE Transactions on Software Engineering, Special Issue on Scenario Management, 24(12), pp. 1055-1071.
16. Dardenne, A., Lamsweerde, A. v., and Fickas, S., (1993), *Goal-directed Requirements Acquisition*, Science of Computer Programming, 20, Elsevier, pp.3-50.
17. Dubois, E., Yu, E., and Pettot, M.(1998), *From early to late formal requirements: a process-control case study*. Proc. IWSSD'98 – 9th International Workshop on software Specification and design. .IEEE CS Press, pp. 34-42.
18. Anton A. I., Potts C., TakahanshiK. (1994), *Inquiry Based Requirements Analysis*, IEEE Conference on Requirements Engineering.
19. Kaindl, H. (2000), *A design process based on a model combining scenarios with goals and functions*, IEEE Trans. on Systems, Man and Cybernetic, 30(5), pp. 537-551.
20. Lamsweerde, A.v.(2001), *Goal-oriented requirements engineering: a guided tour*. RE'01 International Joint Conference on Requirements Engineering, Toronto, IEEE, pp.249-263.
21. Loucopoulos P. (1994), *The f^3 (from fuzzy to formal) view on requirements engineering*. Ingénierie des systèmes d'information, Vol. 2 N° 6, pp. 639-655.
22. Rolland, C., Grosz, G., and Kla, R. (1999), *Experience with goal-scenario coupling. in requirements engineering*, Proceedings of the Fourth IEEE International Symposium on Requirements Engineering, Limerik, Ireland, pp. 74-84.
23. Hui B., Liaskos S., and Mylopoulos J. (2003*), Requirements Analysis for Customizable Software: A Goals-Skills-Preferences Framework*. IEEE Conference on Requirements Engineering, Monterey Bay, USA, pp.117-126.
24. Yue, K., (1987), *What does it mean to say that a specification is complete?*, Proc. IWSSD-4. Four International Workshop on Software Specification and Design, Monterrey, USA.
25. Ramesh, B., Powers, T., Stubbs, C., and Edwards, M.(1995), *Implementing requirements traceability: a case study*, in Proceedings of the 2nd Symposium on Requirements Engineering (RE'95), UK, pp89-95.
26. Pohl K.(1996), *Process centred requirements engineering*, J. Wiley and Sons Ltd.

27. Bubenko, J., Rolland, C., Loucopoulos, P., De Antonellis V.(1994), *Facilitating 'fuzzy to formal' requirements modelling.* IEEE 1st Conference on Requirements Engineering, ICRE'94 pp. 154-158.
28. Sommerville, I., and Sawyer, P.(1997), *Requirements engineering.* Worldwide Series in Computer Science, Wiley.
29. Mostow, J. (1985), *Towards better models of the design process.* AI Magazine, Vol. 6, pp. 44-57.
30. Hoh P. (2002) *Multi-Criteria Preference Analysis for Systematic Requirements Negotiation* 26th Annual International Computer Software and Applications Conference, Oxford, England pp. 887
31. Boehm, B. Bose, P. Horowitz, E. Ming-June Lee, (1994) *Software requirements as negotiated win conditions*, 1rst International Conference on Requirements Engineering, USA, pp. 74-83.
32. Karlsson, J., Olsson, S., Ryan, K. (1997), *Improved Practical Support for Large-scale Requirements Prioritizing*, Journal of Requirements Engineering, Springer-Verlag, pp.51-60.
33. Moisiadis F. (2002) *The Fundamentals of Prioritising Requirements Systems Engineering*, Test & Evaluation Conference, Sydney, Australia.
34. Nuseibeh B., Kramer J., and Finkelstein A. (1994), *A framework for expressing the relationships between multiple views in requirements specification.* In IEEE Transactions on Software Engineering, volume 20, pp. 760-773.
35. Lamsweerde, A. v., and Letier, E., (2000), *Handling obstacles in goal-oriented requirements engineering.* IEEE Transactions on Software Engineering, Special Issue on Exception Handling, 26(10), pp. 978-1005.
36. Robinson W. N., Volcov S., (1996) *Conflict Oriented Requirements Restructuring*, Working Paper CIS-96-15.
37. Robinson, W.N., Volkov, S., (1998) *Supporting the Negotiation Life-Cycle*, ACM, Communications of the ACM, pp. 95-102.
38. S. M. Easterbrook (1994) *Resolving Requirements Conflicts with Computer-Supported Negotiation.* In M. Jirotka & J. Goguen (eds) Requirements Engineering: Social and Technical Issues, London: Academic Press, pp41-65.
39. Svahnberg *(2001) On the notion of variability in Software Product Lines.* Working IEEE/IFIP Conference on Software architecture, pp. 45-54.
40. Bosch (2001), *Variability issues in Software Product Lines.* 4th International Workshop on Product Family Engineering (PEE-4), Bilbao, Spain, pp. 13-21
41. Van Gurp J., (2000), *Variability in Software Systems, the key to Software Reuse.* Licentiate Thesis, University of Groningen, Sweden
42. Bachmann (2001) Managing variability in software architecture. ACM Press, NY, USA.
43. Halmans J. (2003), *Communicating the variability of a software product family to customers. Software and System Modeling*, Springer-Verlag.
44. Rolland C., Prakash N. (2000), *Bridging the gap between Organizational needs and ERP functionality.* Requirements Engineering journal 5.
45. Rolland C., Salinesi C., Etien A. (2004) *Eliciting Gaps in Requirements Change.* Requirements Engineering Journal, Vol. 9, pp1-15.
46. Rolland C. (2005), *Modeling Multi-facetted Purposes of Artifact,* SOMET Int. Conference, Tokyo, Ios Press.

A Context Model for Semantic Mediation in Web Services Composition

Michael Mrissa[1], Chirine Ghedira[1], Djamal Benslimane[1], and Zakaria Maamar[2]

[1] Université Claude Bernard Lyon 1, Villeurbanne, France
firstname.lastname@liris.cnrs.fr
[2] Zayed University, Dubai, United Arab Emirates
zakaria.maamar@zu.ac.ae

Abstract. This paper presents a context-driven approach that aims at supporting semantic mediation between composed Web services. Despite the widespread adoption of Web services by the IT community, innovative solutions are needed in order to overcome the challenging issue that relates to the semantic disparity of exchanged data. Indeed, there is a lack of means for interpreting these data according to the contextual requirements of each Web service. The context-driven approach suggests two steps. The first step consists of developing a model for anchoring context to data flowing between Web services. In the second step, we use this model to support the semantic mediation between Web services engaged in a composition.

1 Introduction

In the field of service-oriented computing, Web services are now widely used to connect business processes. The suitability of Web services for composition allows answering complex users' needs. Composition involves interacting Web services to provide value-added business processes. However, efficient description and management of semantics of data are major requirements to the success of system interoperability. Particularly, composition requires understanding the semantics of the data exchanged between Web services. The Web services protocol stack (SOAP [1], WSDL [2], and UDDI [3]) achieves application level interoperability, but does not satisfy the requirements of semantic exchange. Recent initiatives propose languages and frameworks (e.g., OWL-S [4], WSMO [5], and WSDL-S [6]) that use ontologies[1] for adding explicit semantic descriptions to Web services, which are now referred to as *semantic Web services.*

However, these initiatives towards semantic Web services do not take into consideration the *context* of exchanged data. By context, we mean the collection of implicit assumptions that are required to obtain accurate data interpretation. We advocate that a semantic concept should be interpreted differently, depending on the context it relates to. In the domain of Web services composition, context interpretation generally remains ignored, due to lack of explicit context descriptions. As a consequence, the adaptation of Web services to context

[1] An ontology is defined as a shared description of a domain knowledge in [7].

D.W. Embley, A. Olivé, and S. Ram (Eds.): ER 2006, LNCS 4215, pp. 12–25, 2006.

changes is still performed manually, which reduces their availability and reliability. Explicit context description and management are required to meet the challenges of automatic semantic interpretation and data flow handling during Web services composition.

In this paper, we aim at *presenting a context-based approach for semantic reconciliation of Web services engaged in a composition.* To this end, we develop a model that supports explicit description of context, before deploying runtime mediation mechanisms between Web services, based on the contextual annotation of WSDL input and output message parts.

This paper is organized as follows. Section 2 suggests a motivating example to back the value-added of data context management to Web services composition. Section 3 presents a context-based model for Web services, supported by the definition of *semantic object*, prior to discussing the integration of this model into the Web services protocol stack. Section 4 presents a context- and rule-based mediation architecture for Web services composition. Section 5 overviews related work on mediation and semantics for Web services and context representation. Finally, Section 6 concludes the paper and sets guidelines for future work.

2 Motivating Example

We demonstrate with a simple booking example how context impacts the interpretation of data flow between Web services. The example concerns a trip to Japan. A rate-based attractive hotel provides a Web service for bookings. To judge the affordability of this hotel for an European passenger, the following composition occurs: *hotel booking* WS_1 calculates charges based on the number of booked nights, and *banking* WS_2 manages account payment.

From a technical perspective, WS_1 sends "price-yen" parameter and WS_2 receives "price-euros" parameter. Both parameters are WSDL message parts. Although different type systems can be used, we consider for illustration purposes that "price-yen" and "price-euros" parameters are in XML Schema type system [8], and are of type "double". These details show low-level data compatibility between Web services. In addition, "price-yen" and "price-euros" parameters both have particular semantics. WS_1 delivers a value in Yens, whereas WS_2 expects a value in Euros, and both bind to a "price" semantic concept available in a common ontology. Existing approaches to semantic description and mediation of Web services, to overview in Section 5, explicitly describe the correspondence between parameters for conversion requirements. Such approaches refer to shared ontologies to address structural and semantic heterogeneities.

Now, let us inject context into these parameters. WS_1 binds to "Japanese Hotel Booking" context, in which charges have a scale factor of 1000, prices do not include Value-Added Tax (VAT), dates for conversion rates are in Japanese format (yyyy.mm.dd). WS_2 binds to "French Banking" context, where charges have a scale factor of 1, prices include VAT, and dates for conversion rates are in French format (dd.mm.yyyy). This shows context heterogeneity exists too, so an agreement on the value interpretation must be reached through context reconciliation.

Composing Web services involves dealing with many different contexts, and enabling significant interactions requires dynamic and complex transformations to adapt data to these contexts. In a semantic composition, context heterogeneity is resolved in an ad-hoc way at the receiver Web-service level, if at all. This reduces Web services adaptability and overloads them with solving context heterogeneities. To conduct context-aware composition, the context of data must be explicitly described and a mediation mechanism must handle data flow. Our proposal is to annotate WSDL so that messages parts are propelled to the level of *semantic objects*, which are described in the following.

3 A Context-Based Model for Web Services

As aforementioned, we propose a model that describes the underlying semantics of data flow between Web services. This model takes advantage of the notion of *semantic object* given in [9], and focuses on context description for data exchange in Web services composition. In this section, we define the two fundamental elements of our model: *semantic object* and *context*. Afterwards, we discuss how semantic conversion is performed between semantic objects using *conversion functions*. Finally, we define the notion of *semantic and absolute comparison* between semantic objects.

3.1 Semantic Object

In the domain of semantic Web services, concern separation between data grounding and data abstract-view is required. Listing 1.1 illustrates this separation with an OWL-S Web service input description:

```
<!-- Abstract description -->
      <process:Input rdf:ID="InputLanguage">
            <process:parameterType  rdf:datatype="&xsd;#anyURI">
                  &this;#SupportedLanguage
            </process:parameterType>
            <rdfs:label>Input Language</rdfs:label>
      </process:Input>

<!-- Grounding description-->
      <grounding:WsdlInputMessageMap>
            <grounding:owlsParameter rdf:resource="#InputLanguage"/>
            <grounding:wsdlMessagePart rdf:datatype="&xsd;#anyURI">
                  &groundingWSDL;#inputLanguage
            </grounding:wsdlMessagePart>
      </grounding:WsdlInputMessageMap>
```

Listing 1.1. OWL-S Input Description Snippet

The abstract view binds the data to a conceptual description generally using an ontology language like OWL [10]. The grounding view describes the physical representation of data which generally follows XML Schema [8]. This separation allows different physical representations of the same concept, and strengthens the role of ontologies in the abstract representation of data semantics. In the rest of this paper, we refer to concept c as an individual, or fact, defined in a domain ontology. The notion of individual is detailed in the OWL recommendation [10].

Following a similar separation of abstract and grounding descriptions, we define a semantic object as a data object, i.e., a value v that is an instance of type t with "enough" meta-data for automatic interpretation. This meta-data includes a concept c, which describes the real world phenomena that the data object refers to, and a context C represented as a tree of meta-attributes. A semantic object $SemObj$ is a 4-tuple represented as follows:

$$SemObj =< c, v, t, C >,$$

where c is the concept that the semantic object $SemObj$ adheres to, value $v \in Dom(t)$ is the physical representation of v according to the domain of representation Dom of type t, and C specifies the context of $SemObj$. This context is a tree of semantic objects called *modifiers*. Such representation of an initial semantic object with additional semantic objects makes our context-based model self-describing. A formal definition of a context C is:

$$C = \{< c_1, v_1, t_1, C_1 >, \ldots, < c_k, v_n, t_n, C_n >\}, n \in \mathbb{N} \quad ,$$

where $< c_i, v_i, t_i, C_i >, 1 \leq i \leq n$, are modifiers that describe different semantic aspects of $SemObj$. Modifiers may also have a context, described in C_i, so it is possible to use recursive descriptions and to represent context in a tree.

3.2 Static and Dynamic Modifiers

On the basis of the definition presented above, we introduce the notion of *static* and *dynamic* modifiers. Values of static modifiers have to be explicitly specified, whereas values of dynamic modifiers can be determined by a function from the values of other (static or dynamic) modifiers. In Fig. 1, "*date format*" modifier is dynamic; its value can be inferred from the value of the "*country*" modifier. The relation of inference can be described as a rule, such as "If country is *France*, then date format is *dd.mm.yyyy*". Similar rules should be used for other countries. Further details on how rules support the proposed mediation architecture are given in Section 4. Formally, being given a modifier S and a context $Ctxt$ such that $S =< c, v, t, C >\in Ctxt$, then S is *dynamic* iff:

$$\forall v \in S, \exists f : \{Dom(t) \times \ldots \times Dom(t)\} \mapsto Dom(t) \wedge \exists \{S_1, \ldots S_i, \ldots, S_n\},$$
$$s.t.\ S_i =< c_i, v_i, t_i, C_i >\in Ctxt \wedge S_i \neq S \wedge f(v_1, \ldots, v_i, \ldots, v_n) = v.$$

Figure 1 shows a semantic object to be forwarded to banking Web service of Section 2. *ns:price* attribute refers to the concept of price described in a domain ontology, *55.00* is the value of type *xsd:double* flowing between the Web services. *Context* attribute is a list of modifiers that permit explicit interpretation of the inital semantic object. Here, the semantic object is in Euro, has a scale factor of 1, and includes a VAT of 19.6%. Additional parts of the context further describe the *Currency* modifier.

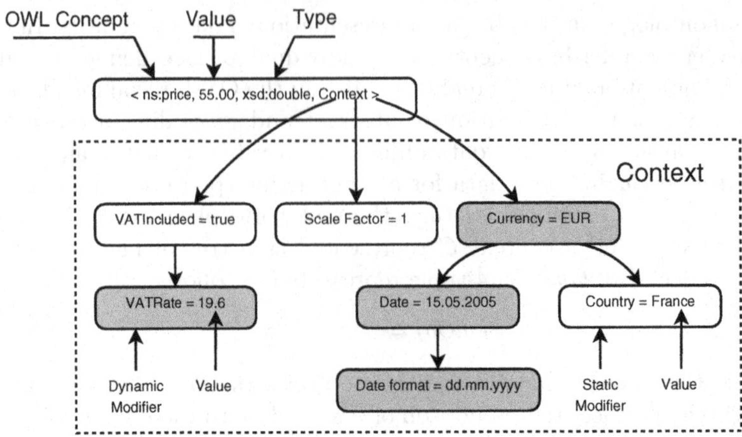

Fig. 1. Sample of a semantic object

3.3 Semantic Conversion of Semantic Objects

Adding context to data allows an explicit representation of the semantics of these data. Therefore, different semantic objects may describe the same information although they have different data and contexts. For example, let us have two simple semantic objects:

$$S_1 =< Price, 1, float, (currency = Euro) >$$
$$S_2 =< Price, 6.55957, float, (currency = French\ Francs) >$$

It is straightforward to note that S_1 and S_2 describe the same information (they are equal), because the exchange rate from French Francs to Euros is fixed at 6.55957 Francs for 1 Euro. Thus, a *conversion function* is required to change S_1 into French Francs or S_2 into Euros and show that S_1 and S_2 are equals.

Conversion functions enable mediation between semantic objects. They have several properties such as total, lossless, and order-preserving [11]. A total conversion function converts to and from any value of its domain of definition, e.g., distance unit conversion functions. An example of non-total conversion is precision conversion. Indeed, a precision conversion function can convert the value 1.25762 into a value with only one decimal of precision (1.2), but it cannot convert this result back to a better precision. In addition, a function is lossless if it can be applied several times on the same object without any loss of information. A function that compresses data files is lossless because the original content can later be extracted. However, a function that converts a BMP image into the JPEG format is lossy (loss due to image compression). A function is order-preserving when two semantic objects, once converted, conserve the order they had before. Temperature conversion functions between Celsius and Fahrenheit scales are order-preserving.

We distinguish two categories of conversion functions. *Context* and *type* conversion functions. *Context* conversion functions are related to the values that modifiers take. They change the interpretation of a semantic object and its value as well. They are stored as rules and may involve online access to other data sources. For example, currency rate conversion functions may call online currency rates providers for up-to-date rates. *Type* conversion functions only change the type t of semantic object (e.g., String2Float, Double2Integer). Such functions depend on the type system that is used to physically represent the semantic object. They can be part of a library associated with the type system, and are not prone to frequent changes.

3.4 Semantic Comparability of Semantic Objects

Since semantic objects can be converted into particular types and contexts, we introduce the notion of semantic comparability between semantic objects. Comparing semantic objects is a prerequisite to the semantic mediation to be introduced in Section 4. First, we consider two semantic objects $S_1 =< c, v_1, t_1, C_1 >$ and $S_2 =< c, v_2, t_2, C_2 >$ that refer to the same concept c. Let us have a relation ϕ (such as '<', '>' or '='), a context C (called target context), and a type t (called target type). Let us assume a conversion function $cvt(value, type, context)$ that consists of concatenating several conversions. This function converts v_1 and v_2 into type t and context C, such as $v_1' = cvt(v_1, t, C)$ and $v_2' = cvt(v_2, t, C)$. We state that S_1 and S_2 are semantically comparable with regard to type t and context C if v_1' and v_2' satisfy the relation $v_1' \, \phi \, v_2'$. Therefore, if ϕ is the equality relation '=' we verify the equality of S_1 and S_2.

Second, we show that semantic objects that do not refer to the same concept, can still be compared relatively to the semantic aspects they have in common. For example, let us compare S_1 and S_2 such as:

$$S_1 =< ns : measurePrice, 10.00, float, (currency = euro, measureUnit = kg) >$$
$$S_2 =< ns : unitaryPrice, 15.00, float, (currency = euro, scaleFactor = 1) >$$

The first concept is the price of a measure in kilograms. The second concept is the unitary price that supports different scale factors. If v_1 and v_2 are compared according to context $C = (currency = euro)$ and type $t = float$, $v_1 < v_2$ is established. This example illustrates the possibility to perform a restricted comparison of these semantic objects although they refer to different concepts. We conclude that the semantic comparability of two semantic objects depends on the target context and the possibility of casting object types.

3.5 Absolute Comparability of Semantic Objects

Another aspect that turns out relevant for semantic mediation is the absolute comparison of semantic objects. It is reached when the semantic objects always verify a relation over a target context for all the possible values of the modifiers of this context. Let us consider two semantic objects S_a and S_b. Let be a relation ϕ (such as '<', '>' or '='), a target context $C = \{S_1, \ldots, S_n\}$ and a target type t. Let us consider a conversion function $cvt(value, type, context)$ that concatenates several conversions and converts v_a and v_b into type t and context C, such as

$v'_a = cvt(v_a, t, C)$ and $v'_b = cvt(v_b, t, C)$. Then, we define S_a and S_b as absolutely comparable relatively to t and C if $v'_a \ \phi \ v'_b$ is verified, for all the possible values that the modifiers of C can take.

3.6 Context Integration into the Web Services Model

The context-based model described above meets the requirements for describing message parts of Web services as semantic objects. The concept of semantic object is intensionally described in a domain ontology, while context is extensionally described using additional meta-attributes. In addition, this model clearly distinguishes the data type t from the conceptual reference C of the semantic object. Then, existing mediation approaches to discuss in Section 5 can seamlessly adhere to our context representation. However, this model raises several questions about its integration into the Web services protocol stack.

Following Bornhövd's view [9], we advocate that a context description is always a subset of all the meaningful aspects of a concept, which are potentially infinite. However, Web service providers should be free to decide which subset of possible aspects is relevant to their application. Therefore, the vocabulary for context description cannot be added into the domain ontology. In such case the size of the latter would grow along with providers' needs. In effect, describing context as part of the domain ontology would require a specific subconcept for each possible combination of modifiers of a domain concept.

To overcome this problem, context ontologies are separated from domain ontologies so that they do not surcharge the latter. Context ontologies describe all the modifiers that Web service providers associate to a concept. Therefore, a context ontology is available for each concept of a domain ontology. Such context ontology should be extended according to Web service providers' requirements. In the following, we assume that Web service providers refer to the same context ontology when annotating Web services. Thus, our illustrative example relies on a single context ontology to put forward the importance of context.

As context ontologies provide shared vocabularies to specify structural and semantic representations of context, there is a need to extensionally specify context values into the descriptions of Web services. We propose a different solution for static and dynamic modifiers. In effect, values of static modifiers have to be specified to clarify the meaning of data. At the contrary, values of dynamic modifiers can be inferred from other parts of the semantic object. Therefore, we insert the description of static modifiers into WSDL, so that our approach is compliant with the standard Web services protocol stack. Descriptions of static modifiers provide the means for calculation of dynamic modifiers at runtime, using appropriate rules.

The use of context ontologies and WSDL annotations helps providers make explicit the context of data. It provides a scalable solution to integrate context into the Web service model. Also, it enables semantic mediation of data during the execution of a composition. In the next section, we present our solution for annotating descriptions of composed Web services, in order to make contextual

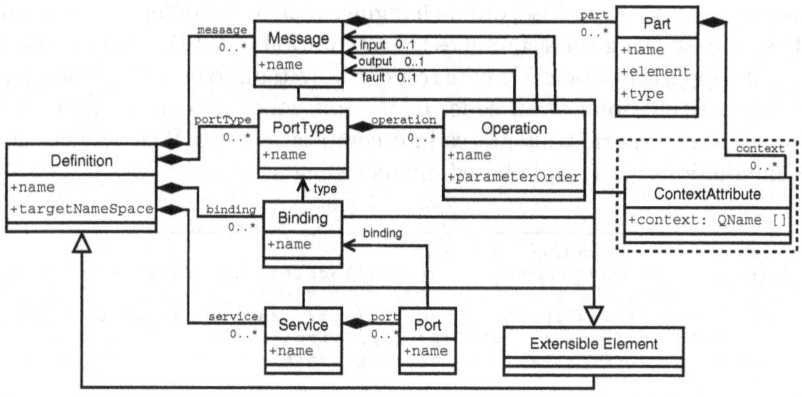

Fig. 2. Context in WSDL metamodel

information available at the execution stage of composition, before describing a service- and rule-based solution for context mediation.

4 Context Management for Web Services

4.1 Annotating WSDL with Context

The use of the model described previously requires enriching the description of Web services with context, by annotating WSDL message parts, so that they can be described as *semantic objects.*

In WSDL descriptions, `<message>` elements describe data exchanged for an operation. Each message consists of one or more `<part>` elements. We also refer to `<part>` elements as "parameters" in the rest of this paper. Each parameter has `<name>` and `<type>` attributes, and allows additional attributes. Our annotation takes advantage of such extension proposed in the WSDL specification [2], so that annotated WSDL operates seamlessly with classical and annotation-aware clients. To keep the paper self-contained, we overview a simplified structure of the WSDL metamodel including the annotation in Fig. 2.

We annotate `<part>` elements with a `context` attribute that describes the names and values of static modifiers using a list of qualified names. The first qualified name of the list specifies the ontology concept of the value (c). Additional elements refer to instances of static modifiers described in a context ontology. Listing 1.2 shows the proposed extension and corresponding namespaces in a WSDL file.

Relying on this annotation, a value v and its data type t described in WSDL are enhanced with the concept c and the modifiers necessary to define the context C, thus forming a semantic object $< c, v, t, C >$. To complete the context C, rules help infer the values of dynamic modifiers at runtime. This offers several advantages: rules are easily modifiable, making this solution adaptable to changes in the underlying semantics. Also, often-changing values of modifiers could not be statically stored, so using rules simplifies the annotation to WSDL. Furthermore, rules separate application logic from the rest of the system, so updating rules does not require rewriting application code. In the following, we detail our context mediation architecture, that integrates into composition as a Web service, and show its interactions with a rule-based inference engine.

```
<?xml version="1.0" encoding="UTF-8"?>
<wsdl:definitions targetNamespace="http://localhost.../EuroBanking.jws"
  ...
  xmlns:ctxt="http://www710.univ-lyon1.fr/~mmrissa/context/context.xsd"
  xmlns:ctxt1="http://domain.ontology.org/Price.owl"
  xmlns:ctxt2="http://context.ontology.org/context/PriceContext.owl\#">
  ...
  <wsdl:message name="checkPriceReq">
    <wsdl:part name="price" type="xsd:double"
    ctxt:context="ctxt1:Price ctxt2:France
    ctxt2:VATIncluded ctxt2:ScaleFactorOne"/>
  </wsdl:message>
  ...
  <wsdl:portType name="EuroBanking">
    <wsdl:operation name="checkPrice" parameterOrder="price">
    <wsdl:input name="checkPriceReq" message="impl:checkPriceReq"/>
    <wsdl:output name="checkPriceResp" message="impl:checkPriceResp"/>
  </wsdl:operation>
 </wsdl:portType>
  ...
</wsdl:definitions>
```

Listing 1.2. Annotated WSDL Snippet

4.2 Context Integration and Mediation

Regarding the integration of context management capabilities into composition, we adopt a decoupled approach and deploy the context mediation functionality as a Web service. This solution presents three main advantages. First, the mediator Web service can be triggered via its WSDL interface by any remote composition, so it remains independent from composition languages and engines. Second, from composition point of view, it is straightforward to handle context. Composition designers invoke the mediation Web service between every two composed Web services. Third, data mediation is performed at runtime, so the operation of conversion is not statically stored. Instead, conversion rules dynamically infer the conversion between contexts. However, the scope of the mediator Web service is limited to data types specified in its WSDL description. To work out this problem, we generate at design time adapted WSDL description for accessing the mediator Web service.

The role of the mediator Web service is to convert data from the context of the Web service it originates (called source context) into the context of the Web service it is being sent to (called target context). With each exchanged message part, the mediator Web service carries out the following operations:

1. builds and populates source and target contexts using annotated data, ontologies and rules in order to determine context modifiers and their values;

2. examines heterogeneities between these contexts and establishes how data are converted using rules;
3. converts data to target context, or generates an error message if the conversion is not possible, and sends results to the appropriate target.

The mediator Web service includes five internal components. The context reader extracts context extensibility attributes from WSDL descriptions. Two repositories for context and domain ontologies respectively identify context structures and domain concepts. The rule engine infers the values of dynamic modifiers and performs data conversion. It communicates with the rule repository that stores the rules for inferring the operations of data conversion and the values of dynamic modifiers.

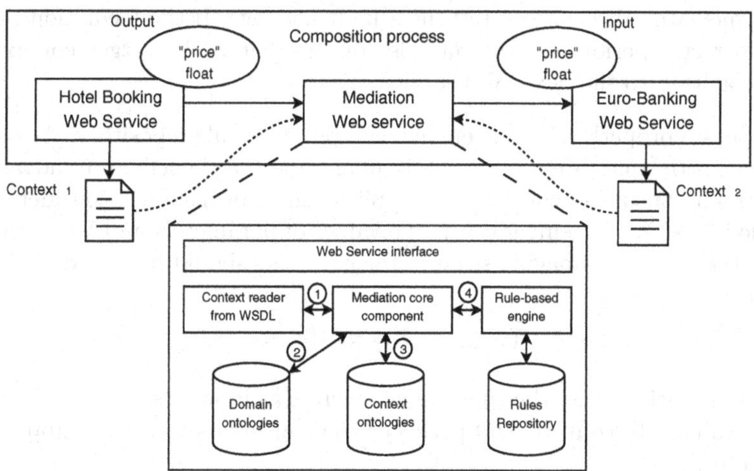

Fig. 3. Detailed View of the Mediator Web service

Figure 3 shows how the mediator Web service performs in the composition of Sect. 2. The numbers in this figure illustrate the chronology of operations that goes along the following description:

1. The mediator Web service generates an in-memory model of both WSDL descriptions and extracts context annotation for each message part concerned with the mediation process, in order to build contexts of parameters.
2. It identifies the first qualified name of each annotation as the concept of the parameter. Then, it checks that the concepts of both parameters match, i.e., that they verify a subsumption or equivalence relation. This is a simple approach to semantic matching but additional capacities can be integrated into the mediator. For a good survey on semantic integration techniques, see Noy's work [12].
3. It accesses the context ontology related to the domain concept matched, and gathers all its relative properties, as well as all its sub properties (i.e.

properties of its sub concepts in the context ontology) into a list of modifiers. With the following WSDL annotation attributes, the mediator affects values to static modifiers. Then, the values of dynamic modifiers are inferred by the rule engine, to build the context description.

4. First, the mediator determines the target context. It corresponds to the context of the banking Web service WS_2 in the example of Sect 2. For each modifier of the target context, the rule engine applies appropriate conversion to the data transmitted, so that the value of the source modifier matches the target context. If the value of the modifier is not convertible to the target context, an exception is thrown, and the mediator Web service returns a fault message. If the value of a modifier is missing, a general rule may affect a default value to this modifier. For example, a rule could set a default scale factor of 1 for prices. If such a rule is absent too, an exception is thrown, and the mediator Web service returns a fault message. If the mediation process is correctly performed, the data is converted into the target context and transmitted to the next Web service.

To operate properly, the rule engine connects to a rule repository. We assume that conversion rules are appropriately maintained, to benefit from advantages of decoupling business logic from the application[2]. For instance, considering our example in Section 2, being given V the values of parameters and SF their scale factors, the rule for managing scale factor modifiers should be stored in the rule repository as follows:

$$V_{target} = \frac{V_{source} * SF_{source}}{SF_{target}}$$

So, at execution time, the rule engine receives as input: “scalefactor”, 1000, 1 and the value v to convert, and performs the conversion to get the appropriate scale factor.

4.3 Implementation

A prototype has been developed as a proof-of-concept of the feasibility of this architecture under the Java^{TM} NetBeans environment. Figure 4 shows a snapshot of our graphical user interface to read/write context annotations from/to WSDL files. This tool enables providers or advanced users to annotate WSDL files with context, so it is possible to compose them with context-aware mediator Web services. We also developed a mediator Web service, that reads context annotation from WSDL files and converts data received from its source context to a target context. Our implementation performs at-runtime context mediation, enabling meaningful execution of composition. In the example of this paper, not only the “price” concepts match, but data is transformed at-runtime, to comply with the different scale factors, heterogeneous date formats (that allow getting up-to-date conversion rates between currencies), and different VAT rates (that also are not always included in the price), described in the context ontology.

[2] Sample rules available at http://www710.univ-lyon1.fr/~mmrissa/conversion.drl.

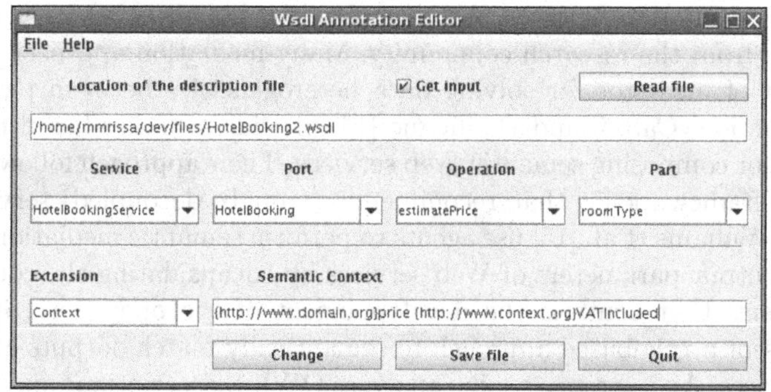

Fig. 4. Screenshot of the WSDL extension editor

Our current composition example is hosted in an Apache Tomcat container (http://tomcat.apache.org/). We also use Jena 2 (http://jena.sourceforge.net/) API and a Drools (http://www.drools.org/) rule engine, to access and manipulate OWL ontologies, infer modifier values and perform data conversion. Our prototype includes domain and context ontologies designed with Protégé (http://protege.stanford.edu/) for describing the "price" concept and context[3].

5 Related Work

This section presents different initiatives that relate to the semantic and mediation aspects of Web services, and to previous work on context description. These related works helped us build ideas, and backed our approach as they are important references of the domain.

Firstly, Semantic Web services constitute an active domain of research. Most approaches rely on ontologies to express the semantics of a domain, however, inserting semantics into Web Services involves using description languages like OWL-S [4], or extending syntactic standards with semantic features (WSDL-S) [6]. OWL-S is a subset of the OWL (ex-DAML) ontology language. It is a general ontology for building semantic Web services, and it was designed to be coupled with standard description formats like WSDL. Inspired from OWL-S, several research projects have been developed, such as ODESWS [13] that models Web services using problem-solving methods. From the DERI laboratory, WSMO [5] is a formal language and ontology that describes varied aspects of semantic Web services. It supports the development and description of semantic Web services and enables mediation as a service, so that it allows maximal decoupling between component Web services. With WSDL-S, Miller et al. annotate WSDL with several extensions related to operations and messages [6]. These extensions refer to concepts of domain models to specify semantics of messages, but also preconditions and effects of operations.

[3] Available at http://www710.univ-lyon1.fr/~mmrissa/price.owl and http://www710.univ-lyon1.fr/~mmrissa/PriceContext.owl

Secondly, mediation between Web services is a hot topic and receives a lot of attention from the research community. Many mediation approaches rely on the concept of mediator for solving data heterogeneities between participants of an interaction. Cabral and Domingue [14] provide a broker-based mediation framework for composing semantic Web services. Their approach follows WSMO conceptual framework [5] that recommends strongly decoupled, service-based mediation. Williams et al. [15] use agents to perform semantic mediation between input and output parameters of Web services by encapsulating the composition into an agent, that controls the developpement of the operation. Spencer et al. [16] present a rule-based approach to semantically match outputs and inputs of Web services. An inference engine analyzes OWL-S descriptions and generates multiple data transformation rules using a description-logic reasoning system.

Thirdly, the use of context has been studied in several domains, in order to improve the adaptability of software applications to different views on information [17]. Some approaches provides formalisms for context representation. In the domain of database interoperability, the Context Interchange approach, firstly introduced by Sciore et al. [11], is based on the notion of semantic value. It has proved to be a highly scalable, extensible and adaptable approach to semantic reconciliation of data. Goh [18] and Firat [19] presented implementations and extensions to this approach. Then, Bornhövd [9] adapted this model to the description of semi-structured data.

While mediation and semantic description of Web services in a composition are very active research fields, to the best of our knowledge, none of these works actually consider the use of explicit context description to solve semantic heterogeneities of data in Web services composition.

6 Conclusion

In this paper, we presented an approach to support the semantic mediation of data exchanged between Web services engaged in a composition. To this end, we first developed a model that leverages data to the level of semantic object, then annotated WSDL descriptions with semantic metadata for capturing contextual information, and finally proposed a context- and rule-based mediation mechanism for Web services composition.

Our future work revolves around different aspects. We envision to automatically integrate mediator Web services into the composition at-runtime, to alleviate the task of composition designers. Also, further study of ontology-based solutions for describing multiples context representations is required. Lastly, we plan to consider the possibility for successful context-based mediation as a criteria of the selection step to improve the selection of Web services.

References

1. Box, D., Ehnebuske, D., Kakivaya, G., Layman, A., Mendelsohn, N., Nielsen, H.F., Thatte, S., Winer, D.: Simple object access protocol (SOAP) 1.1. Technical report, The World Wide Web Consortium (W3C) (2000)

2. Christensen, E., Curbera, F., Meredith, G., Weerawarana, S.: Web Services Description Language (WSDL) 1.1, W3C Note. Technical report, The World Wide Web Consortium (W3C) (2001)
3. UDDI: Universal Description, Discovery, and Integration of Business for the Web. (2001) URL: http://www.uddi.org.
4. Martin, D.L., Paolucci, M., McIlraith, S.A., Burstein, M.H., McDermott, D.V., McGuinness, D.L., Parsia, B., Payne, T.R., Sabou, M., Solanki, M., Srinivasan, N., Sycara, K.P.: Bringing Semantics to Web Services: The OWL-S Approach. In Cardoso, J., Sheth, A.P., eds.: SWSWPC. Volume 3387 of Lecture Notes in Computer Science., Springer (2004) 26–42
5. Arroyo, S., Stollberg, M.: WSMO Primer. WSMO Deliverable D3.1, DERI Working Draft. Technical report, WSMO (2004) http://www.wsmo.org/2004/d3/d3.1/.
6. Miller, J., Verma, K., Rajasekaran, P., Sheth, A., Aggarwal, R., Sivashanmugam, K.: WSDL-S: Adding Semantics to WSDL - White Paper. Technical report, Large Scale Distributed Information Systems (2004) http://lsdis.cs.uga.edu/library/download/wsdl-s.pdf.
7. Gruber, T.: What is an ontology? http://www-ksl.stanford.edu/kst/what-is-an-ontology.html (2000)
8. W3C: XML Schema Part 2: Datatypes Second Edition. Technical report, W3C (2004) http://www.w3.org/TR/xmlschema-2/.
9. Bornhövd, C.: Semantic metadata for the integration of web-based data for electronic commerce. In: Int'l Workshop on E-Commerce and Web-based Information Systems (WECWIS), Santa Clara, CA. (1999) 137–145
10. Schreiber, G., Dean, M.: Owl web ontology language reference. `http://www.w3.org/TR/2004/REC-owl-ref-20040210/` (2004)
11. Sciore, E., Siegel, M., Rosenthal, A.: Using semantic values to facilitate interoperability among heterogeneous information systems. ACM Trans. Database Syst. **19**(2) (1994) 254–290
12. Noy, N.F.: Semantic integration: a survey of ontology-based approaches. SIGMOD Rec. **33**(4) (2004) 65–70
13. Corcho, Ó., Gómez-Pérez, A., Fernández-López, M., Lama, M.: ODE-SWS: A Semantic Web Service Development Environment. In Cruz, I.F., Kashyap, V., Decker, S., Eckstein, R., eds.: SWDB. (2003) 203–216
14. Cabral, L., Domingue, J.: Mediation of Semantic Web Services in IRS-III. In: First International Workshop on Mediation in Semantic Web Services (MEDIATE 2005), Amsterdam, The Netherlands. (December 12th 2005)
15. Williams, A.B., Padmanabhan, A., Blake, M.B.: Experimentation with local consensus ontologies with implications for automated service composition. IEEE Trans. Knowl. Data Eng. **17**(7) (2005) 969–981
16. Spencer, B., Liu, S.: Inferring data transformation rules to integrate semantic web services. In McIlraith, S.A., Plexousakis, D., van Harmelen, F., eds.: International Semantic Web Conference. Volume 3298 of Lecture Notes in Computer Science., Springer (2004) 456–470
17. Kwan, M.M., Balasubramanian, P.: Knowledgescope: managing knowledge in context. Decis. Support Syst. **35**(4) (2003) 467–486
18. Goh, C.H., Bressan, S., Madnick, S.E., Siegel, M.: Context interchange: New features and formalisms for the intelligent integration of information. ACM Trans. Inf. Syst. **17**(3) (1999) 270–293
19. Firat, A.: Information Integration Using Contextual Knowledge and Ontology Merging. PhD thesis, Massachusetts Institute of Technology, Sloan School of Management (2003)

Modeling Service Compatibility with Pi-calculus for Choreography

Shuiguang Deng[1], Zhaohui Wu[1], Mengchu Zhou[2], Ying Li[1], and Jian Wu[1]

[1]College of Computer Science, Zhejiang University, Hangzhou 310027, China
[2]Department of Electrical and Computer Engineering, New Jersey Institute of Technology, NJ 07102, USA
{dengsg, wzh, cnliying, wujian2000}@zju.edu.cn, zhou@njit.edu

Abstract. Service choreography has become an emerging and promising technology to design and build complex cross-enterprise business applications. Dynamic composition of services on the fly requires mechanisms for ensuring that the component services in the composition are compatible with each other. Current service composition languages provide notations for describing the interactions among component services. However, they focus only on the compatibility at the syntax and semantic level in an informal way, yet ignoring the dynamic behavior within services. This paper emphasizes the importance of the behavior in the compatibility verification between services and utilizes the -calculus to model the service behavior and the interaction in a formal way. Based on the formalization, it proposes a method based on the operational semantics of the -calculus to automate the verification of compatibility between two services and presents an algorithm to measure the compatibility degree quantitatively.

1 Introduction

Web service is emerging as the infrastructure for service-oriented architectures (SOA). It is increasingly gaining acceptance as an important method to facilitate application-to-application interactions within and across enterprises [1]. More and more enterprises are rushing to employ web services to encapsulate their business in order to accelerate the cooperation with their partners.

In general, performing complex tasks or doing cross-enterprise businesses requires a number of web services to work together. For example, to accomplish a purchase, it needs the collaboration of seller, shipping and bank service. Thus, service choreography has become one of the hottest topics in the service research area. It aims at combining different services and making these services work compatibly with each other to provide value-added functions. Many methods and prototypes are proposed to implement service choreography [2]. Moreover, several proposals such as BPEL [3] and WS-CDL [4] have been used to describe the process of collaboration among different services. However, they concern only the syntax or semantic compatibility among services. For example, they all emphasize that the message numbers and types transferred between services must be compatible.

D.W. Embley, A. Olivé, and S. Ram (Eds.): ER 2006, LNCS 4215, pp. 26–39, 2006.

As agreed by many researchers, a web service should include not only the static properties, such as interfaces, message numbers and types, but also the dynamic behavior, i.e., the supported message exchange sequences namely conversations called in such literatures as [1][7]. The static compatibility including the syntax and semantic compatibility is essential to be checked, but a more challenging problem is to check the dynamic compatibility of the service behavior. Consider two services, one for vendors and the other for customers. The former waits for payment before sending the product while the latter insists on cash on delivery. In this case, even they are syntactically and semantically compatible, the collaboration between them will lead to a deadlock as they do not negotiate well in the message exchange protocol. Thus, the dynamic behavior of web services must be taken into account when analyzing the compatibility between web services.

This paper focuses on reasoning about the behavior compatibility of web services automatically in service choreography. In order to automate the compatibility verification, it proposes a formal way to model the service behavior and the service interaction using -calculus. Based on the formal representation, it introduces a method to check whether two services are compatible with each other. It also aims at measuring the compatibility degree between services in a quantitative way.

The remainder of this paper is organized as follows. Section 2 gives a brief introduction to -calculus and then presents how to use it to model service behavior and interaction. Section 3 introduces a method to check whether two services are compatible automatically and an algorithm to calculate the compatibility degree between two services. Section 4 discusses the related work. Finally, Section 5 draws the conclusion and outlines some further research activities.

2 Formalizing Service Behavior and Interaction

-calculus is proposed by Robin Milner to describe and analyze a concurrent mobile system. Mobile systems are made up of components which communicate and change their structure as a result of interaction. A service composition is actually a concurrent system composed of several distributed and autonomous services, where services interact with others by sending and receiving messages. Hence, it is intuitive to adopt -calculus to model the service behavior and the interaction within service choreographies. Another reason for its use is that it has a series of algebraic theories, such as bisimularity and congrugence, and a number of related tools provided by many researchers to help analyzing service behavior and interaction. To introduce the -calculus in detail is beyond the scope of this paper. We only illustrate some of its necessary parts to be used later. Further details can be found in [5].

2.1 The π-Calculus

There are two core concepts in -calculus: processes and names. A -calculus process is an entity which communicates with other processes by the use of names. A name is a collective term for existing concepts like channels, pointers, and identifiers. Each name has a scope and can be unbound (global) or bound to a specific process. The scope of a bound name can be dynamically expanded or reduced during the lifetime of the system by communicating names between processes.

Syntax: The -calculus consists of an infinite set of names ranged over by $a,b,...,z$, which function as all of communication channels, variables and data values. A -calculus process can be defined as one of the following forms:

(1) 0 The Nil-process: an empty process, which performs no action.

(2) $\bar{a}<x>.P$ Output prefix: the process sends out x over the channel a and then behaves like P.

(3) $a<x>.P$ Input prefix: the process waits to read a value from the channel a. After receiving the value u, the process continues as P but with the newly received name u replacing x, denoted as $P\{u/x\}$

(4) $\tau.P$ Silent prefix: the process can evolve to P without any actions.

(5) $P+Q$ Sum: the process can enact either P or Q.

(6) $P|Q$ Parallel Composition: the process represents the combined behavior of P and Q running in parallel. P and Q can act independently, and may also communicate if one performs an output and the other an input along the same port.

(7) $(va)P$ Restriction: the process behaves like P but the name a is local, meaning that the name cannot be used for communication with other processes.

(8) *if* $x=y$ *then* P Match: the process behaves as P if x and y are the same name, and otherwise it does nothing.

Operational Semantics: it is used to describe the possible evolution of a process; more precisely, it defines a transition relation $P\xrightarrow{\alpha}P'$ meaning intuitively that "P can evolve to P' in one step through action " (where is the emission of a message, the reception of a message or a action). This relation is defined by the set of rules below, which give a precise meaning to each operator.

(1) *PREFIX* : $\dfrac{-}{\alpha.P\xrightarrow{\alpha}P}$ $\alpha\in\{\tau,x<y>,\bar{x}<y>)\}$ (2) *SUM* : $\dfrac{P\xrightarrow{\alpha}P'}{P+Q\xrightarrow{\alpha}P'}$

(3) *PAR*: $\dfrac{P\xrightarrow{\alpha}P'}{P|Q\xrightarrow{\alpha}P'|Q}$ $bn(\alpha)\cap fn(Q)=\varnothing$

(4) *COM* : $\dfrac{P\xrightarrow{a<x>}P' \quad Q\xrightarrow{\bar{a}<u>}Q'}{P|Q\xrightarrow{\tau}P'\{u/x\}|Q'}$

For instance, the *PREFIX* rule states that $\alpha.P$ can always evolve to P by performing , and the *COM* rule states that if P can evolve to P' by receiving a message from the channel a while Q can evolve to Q' by sending a message from the same channel, and $P|Q$ evolve to $P'\{u/x\}|Q'$ after an inner synchronization action (denoted as τ). A process involving a choice can evolve following one of the processes of the choice.

Structure Congrugence: it is used to identify the processes that obviously represent the same thing.

$$(1)\ P \mid 0 \equiv p \qquad (2)\ P \mid Q \equiv Q \mid P \qquad (3)\ P \mid (Q \mid R) \equiv (P \mid Q) \mid R$$

$$(4)\ P + 0 \equiv p \qquad (5)\ P + Q \equiv Q + P \qquad (6)\ P + (Q + R) \equiv (P + Q) + R$$

2.2 Modeling Service Behavior and Interaction with π-Calculus

The service behavior refers to the dynamic properties of a service including the state transitions and its supported actions and message exchange sequences. Consider the following example. Note that, here we concern only the behavior of the service while ignore other syntax and semantic aspects.

Figure 1 illustrates a vendor service that has two PortTypes named *PT1* and *PT2*, respectively and interacts with other services through five operations *Op1-5*. *Op1*, *Op4* and *Op5* are one-way-type operations which get input messages named purchase order (*PO*), cash pay (*CP*) and bank transfer pay (*BTP*), respectively. The incoming message of *PO* triggers the service to start. *Op2* and *Op3* are the notification-type operations, each of which sends out a message named delivery (*DEL*) and Refusal (*REF*), respectively. The logic of the service is described as follows: it expects to receive a *PO* message at the initial state. On a *PO* message coming, it sends out the delivery if the stock is enough; otherwise, it sends back a refusal message and ends the service. In the former case, it waits for receiving either a cash pay or bank transfer pay message after sending out the delivery. After that, the service terminates.

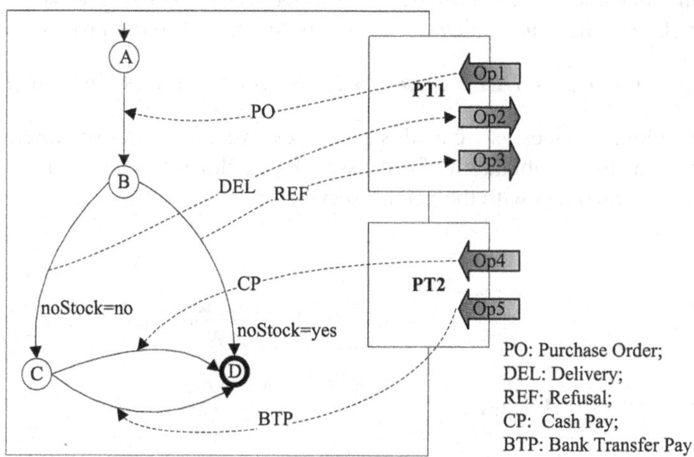

Fig. 1. A vendor service

The behavior of the service in Fig. 1 includes two aspects. From the outside of the service, it refers to the actions of receiving messages and sending messages through operations. From the inside of the service, it refers to the state transitions. Using the -calculus to model the behavior of a service, we can define the whole service as a -calculus process, in which the operations of the service are channels used to communicate with other processes. In WSDL (Web Service Definition Language), there are four types of operation, i.e., one-way, request-response, solicit-response and notification, as shown in Table 1. We use the -calculus to model each of them.

Table 1. Model Service Operation with -calculus

Service Operation Type	***Operation Example***	***-calculus Process Expression***
one-way	*< operation name = "a" >* *< input message = "m"/ >* *< / operation >*	$a<m>$
request-response	*< operation name = "a" >* *< input message = "m"/ >* *< output message = "n"/ >* *< / operation >*	$a<m>.\overline{a}<n>$
solicit-response	*< operation name = "a" >* *< output message = "m"/ >* *< input message = "n"/ >* *< / operation >*	$\overline{a}<m>.a<n>$
notification	*< operation name = "a" >* *< output message = "m"/ >* *< / operation >*	$\overline{a}<m>$

According to Table 1, we can model the vendor service as the following -calculus process which uses the channels *Op1-5* to communicate with other processes.

$$P_V = Op1 < PO > .(\overline{Op2} < DEL > .(Op4 < CP > + Op5 < BTP >) + \overline{Op3} < REF >) \quad (1)$$

After modeling services as -calculus processes, we can model the interaction between services as the combination of processes. Fig. 2 illustrates a scenario where one customer service interacts with the vendor service.

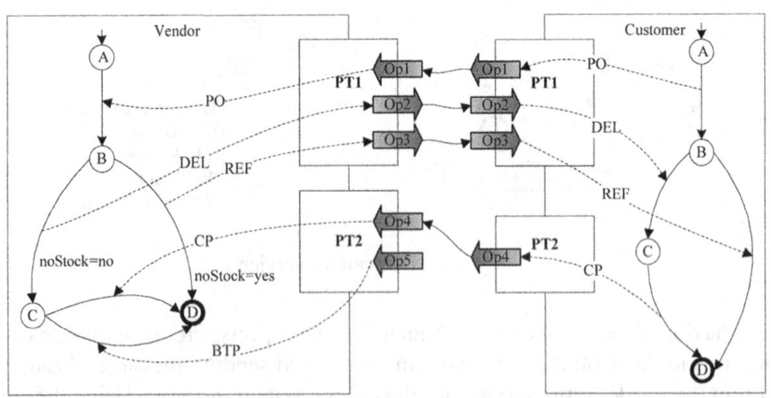

Fig. 2. Interaction between a vendor service and a customer service

The client service sends out a purchasing order and waits for a delivery or refusal message from the vendor service. If a refusal message comes, the client service ends; otherwise, it sends out a cash pay message to the vendor service and goes to an end. The customer service can be modeled as the following -calculus process.

$$P_C = \overline{Op1} < PO > .(Op2 < DEL > .\overline{Op4} < CP > + Op3 < REF >) \tag{2}$$

The interaction between the two services can be modeled as the following combination of the -calculus processes (1) and (2), which means that the interaction between them is the result of the communication carried out between the two processes.

$$\begin{aligned} & P_{Interaction(Vendor,Custom)} \\ & = P_V \mid P_C \\ & = Op1 < PO > .(\overline{Op2} < DEL > .(Op4 < CP > + Op5 < BTP >) + \overline{Op3} < REF >) \\ & \mid \overline{Op1} < PO > .(Op2 < DEL > .\overline{Op4} < CP > + Op3 < REF >) \end{aligned} \tag{3}$$

3 Reasoning About Service Compatibility

Once we have formalized the service behaviors and the interactions with the -calculus processes, we can reason about the compatibility between services formally. In this section, we introduce an automatic method to check whether two services are compatible with each other, and then propose an algorithm to measure the compatibility degree between two services.

3.1 Check Compatibility Between Two Services

Considering the aforementioned scenario, the customer service is completely compatible with the vendor service. There are two different message exchange sequences between them and each of the sequence can eventually lead to an end of the communication. For the first case, after receiving a purchase order from the customer service, the vendor service emits a refusal message due to the shortage of stock and comes to an end. The customer receives the refusal message and also terminates. This interaction leads to a failure business. For the second case, after receiving a purchase order, the vendor service sends a delivery message to the customer due to the enough stock and waits for a payment message before continuing. On receiving the delivery message, the customer service sends a cash-pay message, which will be accepted by the vendor service. After that, the communication terminates and leads to a successful business. Both of the two message exchange sequences indicate that each service has the ability to accept all the messages emitted by another and the communication between them can always terminate. Thus, the vendor service and the customer service are completely compatible with each other.

When we say two services are compatible, it means that there is at least one message exchange sequence between the two services, with which the communication of the two services can eventually come to an end. After modeling vendor and customer services as -calculus processes, the compatibility verification can be carried out formally and automatically. It is intuitive that to check whether the two services are compatible with each other, we only need to check whether the -calculus process (3) can evolve to the Nil-process after finite actions. According to the operational semantics of the -calculus process, we obtain two possible transitions of the process (3). Note that, we label each transition step with the message transferred between the two processes.

$$
\begin{aligned}
&P_{Interaction(Vendor,Customer)} \\
&= P_V \mid P_C \\
&= Op1 < PO > .(\overline{Op2} < DEL > .(Op4 < CP > + Op5 < BTP >) + \overline{Op3} < REF >) \\
&\quad \mid \overline{Op1} < PO > .(Op2 < DEL > .\overline{Op4} < CP > + Op3 < REF >) \\
&\xrightarrow{PO} (\overline{Op2} < DEL > .(Op4 < CP > + Op5 < BTP >) + \overline{Op3} < REF >) \\
&\qquad \mid (Op2 < DEL > .\overline{Op4} < CP > + Op3 < REF >) \\
&\xrightarrow{REF} 0 \mid 0 = 0
\end{aligned} \tag{4}
$$

$$
\begin{aligned}
&P_{Interaction(Vendor,Customer)} \\
&= P_V \mid P_C \\
&= Op1 < PO > .(\overline{Op2} < DEL > .(Op4 < CP > + Op5 < BTP >) + \overline{Op3} < REF >) \\
&\quad \mid \overline{Op1} < PO > .(Op2 < DEL > .\overline{Op4} < CP > + Op3 < REF >) \\
&\xrightarrow{PO} (\overline{Op2} < DEL > .(Op4 < CP > + Op5 < BTP >) + \overline{Op3} < REF >) \\
&\qquad \mid (Op2 < DEL > .\overline{Op4} < CP > + Op3 < REF >) \\
&\xrightarrow{DEL} (Op4 < CP > + Op5 < BTP >) \\
&\qquad \mid \overline{Op4} < CP > \\
&\xrightarrow{CP} 0 \mid 0 = 0
\end{aligned} \tag{5}
$$

The transition sequence (4) is in accordance with the first message exchange sequence (*PO.REF*) mentioned above, while sequence (5) is in accordance with the second one (*PO.DEL.CP*). Since each transition sequence of the parallel composition terminates at a Nil-process, it indicates that both two processes can come to an end after some message receiving and sending actions. Thus the two services are compatible with each other.

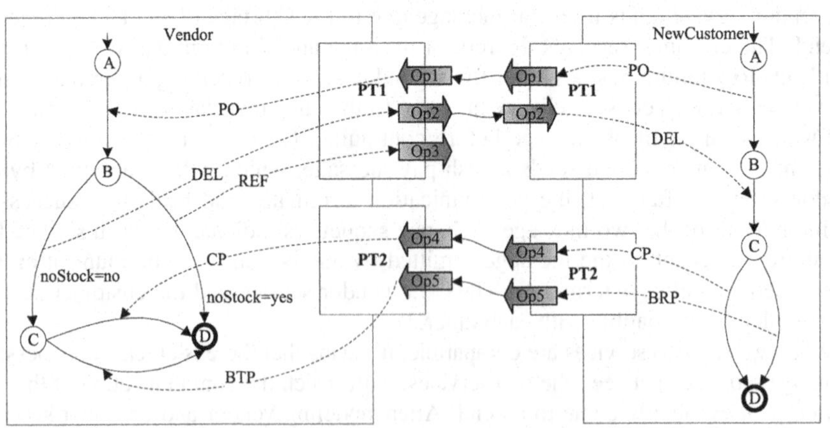

Fig. 3. Interaction between a vendor service and a new customer service

Consider another scenario shown in Fig. 3, where a new customer service interacts with the aforementioned vendor service. The new customer service sends a purchase order and then waits for a delivery from the vendor service. On receiving a delivery, it sends a cash pay message or a bank transfer pay message. The behavior of the new customer service is modeled as the following -calculus process (6).

$$P_{NC} = \overline{Op1} < PO > .Op2 < DEL > .(\overline{Op4} < CP > + \overline{Op5} < BTP >) \quad (6)$$

In fact, the new custom service is not always compatible with the vendor service. This depends on whether the stock of the vendor service is enough to satisfy the purchase order emitted from the new customer. If the stock is not enough, the vendor sends out a refusal message to the customer. However, the customer service can only accept a delivery message at the time and it is incapable of accepting the refusal message. Thus the interaction between the two services goes to a deadlock in this case. But if the stock is enough, the interaction between the two services can terminate normally. This indicates that the two services are partially compatible. For this scenario, we also check whether the parallel composition of the two -calculus processes (1) and (6) can reach the Nil-process after finite communicating actions.

As the transition sequence (7) shows, the parallel composition can lead to an end with two different message exchange sequences (*PO.DEL.CP* and *PO.DEL.BTP*). But sequence (8) leads the communication of the two services to a deadlock. This scenario shows that if two services are partially compatible, there is always at least one transition sequence with which the communication between the two services can terminate. From the analysis of the two scenarios above, we reach the following conclusion.

$$\begin{aligned}
&P_{Interaction(Vendor,NewCustomer)}\\
&= P_V \mid P_{NC}\\
&= Op1 < PO > .(\overline{Op2} < DEL > .(Op4 < CP > + Op5 < BTP >) + \overline{Op3} < REF >)\\
&\quad \mid \overline{Op1} < PO > .Op2 < DEL > .(\overline{Op4} < CP > + \overline{Op5} < BTP >)\\
&\xrightarrow{PO} (\overline{Op2} < DEL > .(Op4 < CP > + Op5 < BTP >) + \overline{Op3} < REF >)\\
&\qquad \mid (Op2 < DEL > .(\overline{Op4} < CP > + \overline{Op5} < BTP >)\\
&\xrightarrow{DEL} Op4 < CP > + Op5 < BTP > \mid \overline{Op4} < CP > + \overline{Op5} < BTP >\\
&\xrightarrow{CP\ or\ BTP} 0 \mid 0 = 0
\end{aligned} \quad (7)$$

$$\begin{aligned}
&P_{Interaction(Vendor,NewCustomer)}\\
&= P_V \mid P_{NC}\\
&= Op1 < PO > .(\overline{Op2} < DEL > .(Op4 < CP > + Op5 < BTP >) + \overline{Op3} < REF >)\\
&\quad \mid \overline{Op1} < PO > .Op2 < DEL > .(\overline{Op4} < CP > + \overline{Op5} < BTP >)\\
&\xrightarrow{PO} (\overline{Op2} < DEL > .(Op4 < CP > + Op5 < BTP >) + \overline{Op3} < REF >)\\
&\qquad \mid (Op2 < DEL > .(\overline{Op4} < CP > + \overline{Op5} < BTP >)\\
&\xrightarrow{REF}
\end{aligned} \quad (8)$$

Theorem 1. Let P_A and P_B are the -calculus processes for two services A and B, respectively. A and B are compatible in collaboration iff:

$$P_A \mid P_B \Rightarrow 0\text{, where } \Rightarrow \text{ means } (\xrightarrow{\tau})^*\text{ , i.e., zero or more } \tau \text{ transitions} \quad (9)$$

Proof: (I): If two services A and B are compatible, according to the compatible concept, it means that there is at least one message exchange sequence s, with which the communication of the two services can eventually come to an end. Thus the parallel composition of the two -calculus processes $P_A \mid P_B$ can evolve to the Nil-process under such a a transition sequence which is in accordance with s; (II) if the condition (9) is to be held, it indicates that there exist at least one transition sequence under which the communication between P_A and P_B can terminate. Due to the fact that a transition sequence represents a message exchange sequence, the two services end with a successful interaction under this message exchange sequence. Thus the two services are compatible.

To check whether two services are compatible, we only need to check whether condition (9) is satisfied. In fact, it can be done using many -calculus related tools, such as MWB (Mobility Workbench) [18] automatically. Thus, we can use -calculus tools to automatically check whether two services are compatible with each other after modeling services into -calculus processes.

3.2 Compatibility Degree Between Two Services

As two pairs of services mentioned in the aforementioned scenarios show, although they are compatible, the compatibility degree is not the same. The first pair of services is completely compatible, while the second is partially compatible. It is desired to have a method that can measure the compatibility degree between services.

Let P_A and P_B are the -calculus processes for two services A and B, respectively. The compatibility degree can be measured through computing the ratio of the successful transition sequences to all the transition sequences in $P_A \mid P_B$. A successful transition sequence is such a transition sequence that leads the parallel composition to the Nil-process. We import two notations $\xi(P_A \mid P_B)$ and $\varsigma(P_A \mid P_B)$ to represent the number of transition sequences and that of successful transition sequences, respectively. The compatibility degree, denoted as $\psi(A,B)$, between two services A and B is calculated according to the following formula.

$$\psi(A,B) = \varsigma(P_A \mid P_B)/\xi(P_A \mid P_B) \tag{10}$$

The formula implies that $0 \le \psi(A,B) \le 1$. In order to calculate the compatibility degree between two services automatically, we propose a method to compute $\xi(P_A \mid P_B)$ and $\varsigma(P_A \mid P_B)$. The values of $\xi(P_A \mid P_B)$ means the number of ways two services can follow to interact with each other. If we can change the parallel composition $P_A \mid P_B$ into the combination of several sub-processes using the sum operations, we can easily get the value of $\xi(P_A \mid P_B)$. In fact, the expansion law of the -calculus can help us to do so. It is used to change the parallel-process into the sum-process equivalently. And each of the sub-processes in a sum-process represents a possible transition sequence.

Expansion Law: Let $P = (P_1[f_1] \mid \ldots \mid P_n[f_n]) \backslash L$, with $n \ge 1$, where $\backslash L$ means the names in set L are restricted names and f_i is a renaming function. Then

$$P=\sum\{f_i(\alpha).(P_1[f_1]|\ldots|P_i'[f_i]|\ldots|P_n[f_n])\backslash L: \\ P_i\xrightarrow{\alpha}P_i', f_i(\alpha)\notin L\cup\overline{L}\} \\ +\sum\{\tau.(P_1[f_1]|\ldots|P_i'[f_i]|\ldots|P_j'[f_j]\ldots|P_n[f_n])\backslash L: \\ P_i\xrightarrow{l_1}P_i', P_j\xrightarrow{l_2}P_j', f_i(l_1)=\overline{f_j(l_2)}, i<j\}$$

Considering the parallel composition in the first scenario, according to the expansion law, we transform $P_V \mid P_C$ as follows. Note that we label each τ transition with the message transferred between the two processes. The channels Op1, Op2, Op3 and Op4 are restricted channels, i.e., $L=\{Op1, Op2, Op3, Op4\}$, because they are used to communicate between P_v and P_C only.

$$\begin{aligned}
&P_V \mid P_C \\
&=(Op1<PO>.(\overline{Op2}<DEL>.(Op4<CP>+Op5<BTP>)+\overline{Op3}<REF>) \\
&\quad \mid \overline{Op1}<PO>.(Op2<DEL>.\overline{Op4}<CP>+Op3<REF>))\backslash L \\
&=\tau_{PO}.(\overline{Op2}<DEL>.(Op4<CP>+Op5<BTP>)+\overline{Op3}<REF> \\
&\quad \mid Op2<DEL>.\overline{Op4}<CP>+Op3<REF>)\backslash L \\
&=(\tau_{PO}.\tau_{DEL}.((Op4<CP>+Op5<BTP>)\mid\overline{Op4}<CP>)+\tau_{PO}.\tau_{REF})\backslash L \\
&=\tau_{PO}.\tau_{DEL}.\tau_{CP}+\tau_{PO}.\tau_{DEL}.Op5<BTP>.\overline{Op4}<CP>+\tau_{PO}.\tau_{REF}
\end{aligned} \tag{11}$$

The result of transformation (11) has two Nil-processes and one non-Nil-process at last. Note that we must omit such a sub-process that starts with an input prefix while counting the number of transition sequences in the last sum-process. The reason is that the input prefix is a passive action, which cannot trigger the sub-process to start. So the transition represented by the sub-process does not exist indeed. Thus, the sub-process $\tau_{PO}.\tau_{DEL}.Op5<BTP>.\overline{Op4}<CP>$ is ignored. From the message flow labeled on each τ transition, we obtain two transition sequences *PO.DEL.CP* and *PO.REF*, each of which is a successful transition sequence. Thus, we have $\psi(S,C)=2/2=1$. For the second scenario, we get the transformation (12), where $L=\{Op1, Op2, Op4, Op5\}$.

$$\begin{aligned}
&P_V \mid P_{NC} \\
&=(Op1<PO>.(\overline{Op2}<DEL>.(Op4<CP>+Op5<BTP>)+\overline{Op3}<REF>) \\
&\quad \mid \overline{Op1}<PO>.Op2<DEL>.(\overline{Op4}<CP>+\overline{Op5}<BTP>))\backslash L \\
&=\tau_{PO}.((\overline{Op2}<DEL>.(Op4<CP>+Op5<BTP>)+\overline{Op3}<REF>) \\
&\quad \mid Op2<DEL>.(\overline{Op4}<CP>+\overline{Op5}<BTP>))\backslash L \\
&=\tau_{PO}.(\tau_{DEL}.((Op4<CP>+Op5<BTP>)\mid(\overline{Op4}<CP>+\overline{Op5}<BTP>)) \\
&\quad +\overline{Op3}<REF>.Op2<DEL>.(\overline{Op4}<CP>+\overline{Op5}<BTP>))\backslash L \\
&=(\tau_{PO}.\tau_{DEL}.\tau_{CP}+\tau_{PO}.\tau_{DEL}.\tau_{BTP} \\
&\quad +\tau_{PO}.\overline{Op3}<REF>.Op2<DEL>.(\overline{Op4}<CP>+\overline{Op5}<BTP>))\backslash L
\end{aligned} \tag{12}$$

The last sum-process has two Nil-processes and a non-Nil-process. Thus, we get $\psi(S,NC)=2/3$. The non-Nil-process in (12) represents such a transition sequence, in which a *REF* message is sent out on channel Op3 but not accepted. This can help us to judge when the two services cannot interact successfully.

As another example, two -calculus processes are $P_M = \overline{Op1} < M_1 > + Op2 < M_2 >$ and $P_N = Op1 < M_1 > + Op3 < M_3 >$, $P_M \mid P_N = (\overline{Op1} < M_1 > + Op2 < M_2 >) \mid (Op1 < M_1 > + Op3 < M_3 >)$ and the transformation is as follows, where $L = \{Op1\}$.

$$\begin{aligned} & P_M \mid P_N \\ & = (\overline{Op1} < M_1 > + Op2 < M_2 >) \mid (Op1 < M_1 > + Op3 < M_3 >) \setminus L \\ & = (\tau_{M_1} + Op2 < M_2 > .(Op1 < M_1 > + Op3 < M_3 >) \\ & \quad + Op3 < M_3 > .(\overline{Op1} < M_1 > + Op2 < M_2 >)) \setminus L \end{aligned} \tag{13}$$

Thus, there are three sub-processes in the last sum-process. However, the two sub-processes $Op2 < M_2 > .(Op1 < M_1 > + Op3 < M_3 >)$ and $Op3 < M_3 > .(\overline{Op1} < M_1 > + Op2 < M_2 >)$ both start with an input prefix. Thus there is only one possible transition sequence in the composition. Hence $\psi(M, N) = 1/1 = 1$.

According to the above analysis, we design the following algorithm to compute the compatibility degree between two services represented by -calculus processes. From the 3rd to 8th line, it determines the set of restricted names for the parallel composition of two processes. In fact, $L = CN_A \cap CN_B$. From the 11th to 18th line, it calculates $\xi(P_A \mid P_B)$ and $\varsigma(P_A \mid P_B)$. Using the expansion law to transform the parallel process into the sum-process is the key of the algorithm.

ALGORITHM : Calculate-Compatibility-Degree
INPUT : two π − calculus processes P_A and P_B of two services A and B
OUTPUT : $\psi(A, B)$
METHOD :

```
1:  Set P = P_A | P_B;
2:  Set L = φ;
3:  Set CN_A and CN_B as the sets of channel names in P_A and P_B, respectivley;
4:  For each channel name cn ∈ CN_A
5:      If cn ∈ CN_B Then
6:          put element cn into L;
7:      End If
8:  End For
9:  P = (P_A | P_B)\L;
10: transform P into the sum-process according to Expansion Law, thus
        P = Σ_i P_i
11: For each sub-process P_i in P
12:     If P_i = 0 Then
13:         ξ(P_A | P_B) = ξ(P_A | P_B) + 1;
14:         ς(P_A | P_B) = ς(P_A | P_B) + 1;
15:     Else If P_i starts with an output prefix Then
16:         ξ(P_A | P_B) = ξ(P_A | P_B) + 1;
17:     End If
18: End For
19: Return ψ(A, B) = ς(P_A | P_B)/ξ(P_A | P_B);
```

---

4 Related Work

There have been some published papers that discuss similarity and compatibility at different levels of abstractions of service specifications [6-11]. Due to the limited space, here we only introduce such work that adopted a formal method to the analysis. This includes the use of the Petri Net, Automata, Finite State Machine, Labeled Transition System and CCS.

Martens [6] represents a web service as a workflow module including a local process and a serial of interfaces. Petri Nets are selected to model workflow modules and compositions. Based on this formalization, the compatibility between two workflow modules can be checked by the verification of weak soundness of the composition. This work allows to reason about service compatibility very well. However, using Petri nets to model processes requires a much higher computational and space complexity. In particular, the reachability and liveness problems are non-polynomial.

Fu *et al.* [7] propose a top-down approach based on Guarded Mealy Automata to analyze the composition of web services and applies model-checking techniques to verify the conversation between two services. This approach can effectively guarantee the correctness of web services composition, but assumes that service links among peers are predetermined and established before the interaction starts. Thus, this approach cannot be used when the interactions are changing dynamically.

Wombacher *et al.* [8] extend Determined Finite State Automata by logical expressions associated to states to model web service behavior. By explicating message sequence and required messages such descriptions allow for more precise matches than the current approaches limited to matching individual messages only. However, the work is lack of quantitative analysis on business match.

Foster *et al.* [9] make use of Finite State Machine to model web service choreography and assigns semantics to the distributed process interactions. But this method is mainly for the process verification, the internal behavior of each service is not taken into account.

Bordeaux *et al.* [10] use Labeled Transition System to formalize the behavior of web services and give several definitions of compatibility at different levels. Thus compatibility checking can be automated to a large extent. However, the compatibility definitions are too strict that the service substitutability is not context-aware.

Brogi *et al.* [11] regard service compatibility as the essential reasoning tasks on service interface descriptions and use a process algebra approach to formalize one of the proposed choreography proposals. They show the benefits that can be obtained from such formalization, namely the definition of compatibility and replaceablity tests between services. This method belongs to the same category as our method. However, they discuss the test of compatibility in an informal way and focus on a very specific representation only.

Compared with the above formal methods, the main benefit of using -calculus in this work to formalize the behavior and interaction of services is its expressiveness, which is adequate to specify composition due to its compositionality property. Moreover, its texture representation is more adequate to describe real-size problems, as well as to reason on them [15].

5 Conclusion and Future Work

Determining the compatibility between Web services plays a critical role in supporting dynamic discovery and collaboration of Web services in the inherently heterogeneous web environment [12]. It is becoming well-admitted that the use of formal methods is worthy as an abstract way to deal with web service and then to tackle several issues raised in web services.

As a step toward the vision of dynamic composition of services on the fly, this paper proposes a formal approach to unambiguously model service behavior and interaction in service choreography using -calculus. The resulting formal and unambiguous characterization of -calculus processes is useful for the precise understanding of services and interactions, as well as enabling further research on automated verification of compatibility. Based on the formalizations, it proposes a method to verify service compatibility. Many existent tools can help us to do the verification automatically. This paper also gives an algorithm to measure the compatibility degree of two services. To the best of our knowledge, this is the first attempt to calculate compatibility degree based on service behavior in quantity. Using this algorithm, we can not only compute the value of compatibility degree, but also know when two services are not compatible with each other. This is very helpful for us to dynamically compose services and bind services according to the run-time information of the choreographies without introducing some flaws into the service choreography. Moreover, our compatibility checking method can help us to find replaceable services according to run-time information dynamically that can ensure that the execution of service choreography be successful.

We are currently developing a service composition framework-DartFlow [16], which as a sub-project of DartGrid (http://ccnt.zju.edu.cn/projects/dartgrid) [17] is a framework for service composition in the grid environment. It aims at providing a convenient and efficient way for the cooperation of different services from the Intelligent Transportation System (ITS) domain. We are going to implement the compatibility verification method and compatibility degree calculation algorithm in DartFlow to help us dynamically compose services and correctly replace services in choreographies.

Acknowledgement

This work is supported by Zhejiang Provincial Natural Science Foundation of China (NO. Y105463).

References

[1] B. Benatallah, F. Casati, and F. Toumani. Web Service Conversation Modeling: A Cornerstone for E-Business Automation. IEEE Internet Computing, 8(1), p46-54, 2004.

[2] S. Dustdar, W. Schreiner. A survey on web services composition, International Journal of Web and Grid Services, 1(1):1-30, 2005.

[3] BEA Systems, IBM, Microsoft, SAP, Siebel Systems: Business Process Execution Language for Web Services Version 1.1., 2003.

[4] W3C. The Web Services Choreography Description Language (WS-CDL) Version 1.0, World Wide Web Consortium, available at http://www.w3.org/TR/ws-cdl-10/, 2005.

[5] R. Milner. A Calculus of Communicating Systems, Lecture Notes in Computer Science, volume 92, Springer-Verlag, 1980.

[6] A. Martens. On compatibility of web services. Petri Net Newsletter, 65, 2003.

[7] X. Fu, T. Bultan, and J. Su. Analysis of Interacting BPEL Web Services, 13th International World Wide Web Conference (WWW), 2004.

[8] A. Wombacher, P. Fankhauser, B. Mahleko and Erich Neuhold. Matchmaking for Business Processes based on Choreographies. International Journal of Web Services Research, 1(4), p14-32, 2004.

[9] H. Foster, S. Uchitel, J. Magee, and J. Kramer. Compatibility verification for web service choreography. In Proc. International Conference on Web Service (ICWS), 2004.

[10] L. Bordeaux, G. Salaun, D. Berardi, M. Mecella. When Are Two Web Services Compatible? In Proc. of the 5th VLDB International Workshop on Technologies for e-Services (VLDB-TES), 2004.

[11] A. Brogi, C. Canal, E. Pimentel, A. Vallecillo. Formalizing Web Service Choreographies. In Proc. Of First International Workshop on Web Services and Formal Methods (WS-MF), 2004.

[12] Y. Li and H. V. Jagadish. Compatibility determination in web services. In Proc. of ICEC eGovernment Services WS, 2003.

[13] V. De Antonellis, M. Melchiori, B. Pernici, and P. Plebani. A methodology for e-service substitutability in a virtual district environment. In Proc. of Conference on Advanced Information Systems Engineering (CAISE), 2003.

[14] H. Overdick, F. Puhlmann, and M. Weske. Towards a Formal Model for Agile Service Discovery and Integration. In Proc. of the Workshop on Dynamic Web Processes (ICSOC-DWP), 2005

[15] L. Bordeaux and G. Salaün. Using Process Algebra for Web Services: Early Results and Perspectives. In the Proc. of the 5th VLDB Workshop on Technologies for E-Services (VLDB-TES), 2004.

[16] S. Deng, Z. Wu, et al. Management of Serviceflow in a Flexible Way. In Proc. of the 5th International Conference on Web Information Systems Engineering (WISE), 2004.

[17] Z. Wu, S. Tang, S. Deng. DartGrid II: A Semantic Grid Platform for ITS. IEEE Intelligent Systems, 20(3), p12-15, 2005.

[18] B. Victor, F. Moller. The Mobility Workbench - A Tool for the pi-Calculus. In the Proc. of the 6th International Conference on Computer Aided Verification (CAV), 1994.

The DeltaGrid Abstract Execution Model: Service Composition and Process Interference Handling

Yang Xiao, Susan D. Urban, and Ning Liao

Department of Computer Science and Engineering
Arizona State University
PO Box 878809 Tempe, AZ, 85287-8809 USA
{yang.xiao, susan.urban}@asu.edu

Abstract. This paper introduces the DeltaGrid abstract execution model as a foundation for building a semantically robust execution environment for concurrent processes executing over Delta-Enabled Grid Services (DEGS). A DEGS is a Grid Service with an enhanced capability to capture incremental data changes, known as deltas, associated with service execution in the context of global processes. The abstract model contains a service composition model that provides multi-level protection against service execution failure, thus maximizing the forward recovery of a process. The model also contains a process recovery model to handle the possible impact caused by failure recovery of a process on other concurrently executing processes using data dependencies derived from a global execution history and using user-defined correctness criteria. This paper presents the abstract execution model and demonstrates its use. We also outline future directions for incorporating application exception handling and build a simulation framework for the DeltaGrid system.

1 Introduction

In a service-based architecture [17], the correctness of processes composed of distributed Web/Grid services is a concern due to the challenges introduced by the loosely coupled, autonomous, and heterogeneous nature of the execution environment. Compositional serializability [16] is too strong of a correctness criterion for concurrent processes since individual service invocations are autonomous and commit before the process completes. As a result, process execution does not ensure isolation of the data items accessed by individual services, allowing dirty reads and writes to occur.

From an application point of view, dirty reads and writes do not necessarily indicate an incorrect execution, and a relaxed form of correctness dependent on application semantics can produce better throughput and performance. User-defined correctness of a process can be specified as in related work with advanced transaction models [5] and transactional workflows [20], using concepts such as compensation to semantically undo a process. But even when one process determines that it needs to execute compensating procedures, data changes introduced by compensation of a process might affect other concurrently executing processes that have either read or written data that have been produced by the failed process. We refer to this situation as *process*

D.W. Embley, A. Olivé, and S. Ram (Eds.): ER 2006, LNCS 4215, pp. 40–53, 2006.

interference. A robust service composition model should recover a failed process and effectively handle process interference based on application semantics.

This research is defining an abstract execution model for establishing user-defined correctness in a service composition environment. The research is conducted in the context of the DeltaGrid project, which focuses on building a semantically-robust execution environment for processes that execute over Grid Services. The abstract execution model, however, is general enough for use in a Web Service composition environment. Distributed services in the DeltaGrid, referred to as *Delta-Enabled Grid Services (DEGS)* [4], are extended with the capability of recording incremental data changes, known as deltas. Deltas provide the basis for backward recovery of an operation (DE-rollback) and tracking data dependencies among concurrent processes.

The focus of this paper is on the specification of the DeltaGrid abstract execution model, which is composed of a service composition model and a process recovery model. The service composition model provides multi-level protection against service execution failure and maximizes the success of a process execution using compensation, DE-rollback, and contingency. The process recovery model defines a global execution history for distributed process execution, based on which read and write dependencies can be analyzed to evaluate the applicability of DE-rollback and process interference.

The rest of this paper is organized as follows. After outlining related work in Section 2, the paper provides an overview of the DeltaGrid system in Section 3 where the DeltaGrid abstract model has been applied. Section 4 gives an overview of the DeltaGrid abstract execution model. Section 5 presents the service composition model and Section 6 presents the process recovery model. The paper concludes in Section 7 with a summary and discussion of future research.

2 Related Work

Advanced transaction models have been studied to support higher concurrency for long running transactions composed of subtransactions. Sagas [7] can be backward recovered by compensating each task in reverse order. The flexible transaction model [22] executes an alternative path when the original path fails. The backward recovery of a failed transaction causes cascaded rollback or compensation of other transactions that are read or write dependent on the failed transaction. The recent work in [12] removes transactions that are dependent on tainted data produced by a flawed transaction, using multi-version data to track read and write dependencies in a database system. These models cannot well support a service composition environment where dirty reads and writes do not necessarily indicate incorrect execution. As a result, application-dependent correctness criteria should be used.

Research projects in the transactional workflow area have adopted compensation as a backward recovery technique [6, 8, 19] and explored the handling of data dependencies among workflows [8, 19]. The ConTract model [19] compensates a process when a step failure occurs using an approach similar to sagas, and handles data dependencies through pre-/post- condition specification integrated into a workflow script. Forward recovery is not supported in ConTract. WAMO [6] supports backward and forward recovery, but process interference is not considered. CREW [8] requires a static specification on the equivalence of data items across workflows to track data dependencies. Our research maximizes the forward recovery of a process by a multi-level specification of contingency and compensation. More importantly, we build a global execution history based on which process data dependencies can be analyzed to support application-dependent correctness criteria for handling process interference.

Currently most exception handling work in service composition environments focuses on transaction model implementation and the use of active rules. Open nested transactions over Web Services are supported in [14], contingency is applied to forward recover a composite service in [18], and WS-Transaction [2] defines processes as either Atomic Transactions with ACID properties or Business Activities with compensation capabilities. Rule-based approaches are used to handle service exceptions independent of application logic, such as service availability, selection, and enactment [15, 22], or search for substitute services when an application exception occurs [11]. Our research is among the first to address process interference caused by backward recovery of a service execution failure, and establishes user-defined correctness criteria based on data dependency tracking in a service composition environment.

3 Overview of the DeltaGrid System

The DeltaGrid system, focusing on the semantically robust execution of composite services, provides an execution environment and test bed for the abstract execution model described in this paper. As the fundamental building block, a Delta-Enabled Grid Service (DEGS) is a Grid Service that has been enhanced with an interface to access the deltas that are associated with service execution in the context of globally executing processes [4]. Deltas can be used to undo the effect of a service execution through *Delta-Enabled rollback* (*DE-rollback*). Deltas, in the context of the data dependencies captured in the global process history, can also be used to analyze process interference, determining the effect that the failure recovery of one process can have on other concurrently executing processes.

The GridPML [13] is a process modeling language for the composition of Grid Services in the DeltaGrid system. The GridPML is an XML-based language that supports basic control flow constructs adopted from Web Service composition languages such as BPEL [3] and BPML [1] with features for invoking Grid Services [21]. The GridPML is used in our research to experiment with process execution history capture and has also partially implemented the service composition model [10].

4 The DeltaGrid Abstract Execution Model

The DeltaGrid abstract execution model is composed of 1) the service composition model that defines the hierarchical service composition structure and entity execution semantics, and 2) the process recovery model that tracks process data dependency and handles process interference through active rules.

Table 1 defines the execution entities of the service composition model, with the hierarchical entity composition structure presented in Fig. 1. Operation represents a service invocation and is the basic entity in the composition structure. Compensation is an operation intended for backward recovery and contingency is an operation for forward recovery. An atomic group contains an operation, an optional compensation, and an optional contingency. A composite group may contain multiple atomic groups or composite groups that execute sequentially or in parallel. A composite group can have its own compensation and contingency as optional elements. A process is defined to be a top-level composite group. The only execution entity not shown in Fig. 1 is the DE-rollback entity. DE-rollback is a system-initiated operation that uses the deltas to reverse an operation execution.

Table 1. Execution Entities

Entity Name	Definition
Operation	A DEGS service invocation, denoted as op_{ij}
Compensation	An operation that is used to undo the effect of a commited operation, denoted as cop_{ij}
Contingency	An operation that is used as an alternative of a failed operation (op_{ij}), denoted as top_{ij}
DE-rollback	An action of undoing the effect of an operation by reversing the data values that have been changed by the operation to their before images, denoted as dop_{ij}
Atomic Group	An execution entity that is composed of a primary operation (op_{ij}), an optional compensation (cop_{ij}), and an optional contingency operation (top_{ij}), denoted as $ag_{ij} = <op_{ij} [, cop_{ij}] [,top_{ij}]>$
Composite Group	An execution entity that is composed of multiple atomic groups or other composite groups. A composite group can also have an optional compensation and an optional contingency, denoted as $cg_{ik} = <ag_{ij}^{+} [,cg_{il}^{+}] [,cop_{ik}] [,top_{ik}]>$
Process	A top level composite group

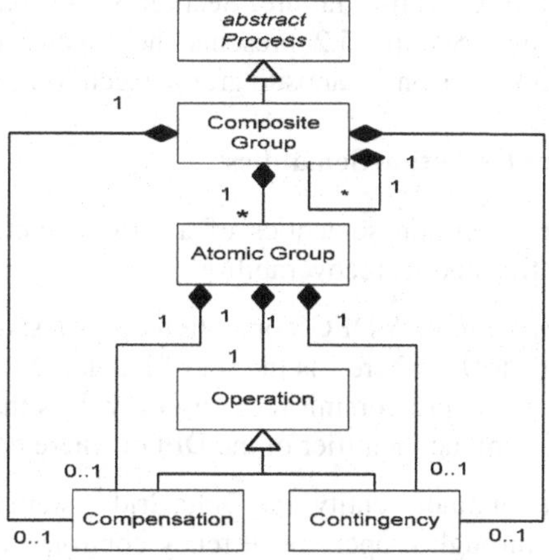

Fig. 1. The Service Composition Structure

Fig. 2 shows an abstract view of a sample process definition. A process p_1 is the top level composite group cg_0. p_1 is composed of two composite groups cg_1 and cg_2, and an atomic group ag_6. Similarly, cg_1 and cg_2 are composite groups that contain atomic groups. Each atomic/composite group can have an optional compensation plan and/or contingency plan, e.g. cg_1 has compensation cg_1.cop and contingency cg_1.top operations. Operation execution failure can occur on an operation at any level of nesting.

The purpose of the service composition model is to automatically resolve operation execution failure using compensation, contingency, and DE-rollback at different composition levels. The next section defines the execution semantics of each entity and addresses operation execution failure handling under various execution scenarios.

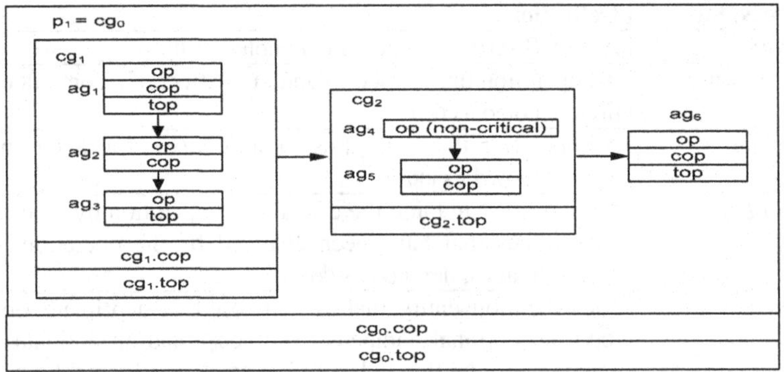

Fig. 2. An Abstract Process Definition

5 Execution Semantics of the Service Composition Model

This section presents the execution semantics of each execution entity and addresses how to resolve operation execution failure. Section 5.1 introduces the DEGS operation execution semantics. Section 5.2 presents the execution semantics of atomic groups. Section 5.3 elaborates on composite group execution semantics.

5.1 DEGS Operation Execution Semantics

Before presenting the execution semantics of a DEGS operation, this section first defines a DEGS operation and its recoverability.

Definition 1. *DEGS operation.* A DEGS operation op_{ij} is a six-element tuple, denoted as op_{ij} = <I, O, S, R, P, degsID>, where I is the set of inputs, O is the set of outputs, S is the execution state, R is the pre-commit recoverability, P is the post-commit recoverability, and degsID is a unique identifier of the DEGS where op_{ij} is executed.

Since a DEGS is an autonomous entity, the DeltaGrid system assumes a DEGS guarantees its correctness through proper concurrency control, exposing serializablity or another functionally equivalent correctness criterion to the service composition environment. A DEGS can provide different transaction semantics, supporting an operation as an *atomic* or *non-atomic* execution unit. If a runtime failure occurs, an atomic operation can automatically roll back. A non-atomic operation stays in a failed state since a service provider is incapable of performing rollback. With the delta capture capability, a DEGS can reverse the effect of an operation through DE-rollback. An operation can have different backward recovery capabilities depending on when the operation needs to be recovered.

Definition 2. *Pre-commit recoverability.* Pre-commit recoverability specifies how an operation can be recovered when an execution failure occurs before the operation completes.

Definition 3. *Post-commit recoverability.* Post-commit recoverability specifies how an operation's effect can be (semantically) undone after it successfully terminates.

Table 2 presents an operation's pre-commit and post-commit recoverability options.

Table 2. Operation Recoverability Options

Recoverability Type	Option	Meaning
Pre-commit	Automatic rollback	The failed service execution can be automatically rolled back by a service provider
	DE-rollback	The failed operation can be undone by executing DE-rollback
Post-commit	Reversible (DE-rollback)	A completed operation can be undone by reversing the data values that have been modified by the operation execution
	Compensatable	A completed operation can be semantically undone by executing another operation.
	Dismissible	A completed operation does not need any cleanup activities

Fig. 3 compares the execution semantics of a regular service operation shown in (a) with a DEGS operation shown in (b). An operation has four states: {active, successful, failed, aborted}. An operation enters the active state when it is invoked. If the execution successfully terminates, the operation enters a successful state, otherwise it enters a failed state. An atomic operation can automatically roll back to enter an aborted state. An advantage of DEGS is the use of DE-rollback to undo the effect of a failed operation, thus eliminating the failed state as an operation termination state. However, as a post-commit recovery method, DE-rollback can only be executed under valid process interleaving situations defined as semantic conditions for DE-rollback in Section 6.1.

Definition 4. *Delta.* A delta is a six-element tuple, denoted as $\Delta(oID, a, V_{old}, V_{new}, ts_n, op_{ij})$, representing an incremental value change on an attribute of an object generated by execution of a DEGS operation. A delta contains an object identifier (oID) indicating the changed object, an attribute name (a) indicating the changed attribute, the old value of the attribute (V_{old}) before the execution of the operation, the new value of the attribute (V_{new}) created by the operation, a timestamp (ts_n), and the identifier of the operation (op_{ij}) that has created this delta.

Definition 5. *Runtime context.* The runtime context of an operation is a five-element tuple, denoted as $r(op_{ij}) = <ts_s, ts_e, I, O, S>$. The runtime context of op_{ij} contains a start time (ts_s), end time (ts_e), input (I), output (O), and state (S). Similarly, the runtime context of a process $r(p_i) = <ts_s, ts_e, I, O, S>$.

Definition 6. *Operation execution history.* An operation execution history $H(op_{ij})$ is a four-element tuple, denoted as $H(op_{ij}) = <ts_s, ts_e, \delta op_{ij}, r(op_{ij})>$. ts_s and ts_e are the start and end time of op_{ij}'s execution. δop_{ij} a time-ordered sequence of deltas that are generated by execution of op_{ij}, denoted as $\delta op_{ij} = [\Delta(oID_A, a, V_{old}, V_{new}, ts_1, op_{ij}), \ldots, \Delta(oID_B, b, V_{old}, V_{new}, ts_x, op_{ij}), \ldots, \Delta(oID_D, d, V_{old}, V_{new}, ts_n, op_{ij})]$ $(ts_s< ts_1< ts_x< ts_n< ts_e)$. $r(op_{ij})$ is the runtime context of op_{ij}.

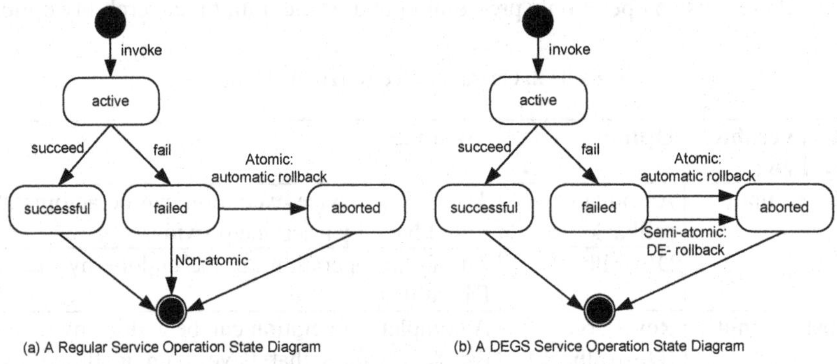

Fig. 3. DEGS Operation Execution Semantics

5.2 Atomic Group (AG) Execution Semantics

An atomic group (ag) maximizes the success of an operation execution by providing a contingency plan. If necessary, an ag can be semantically undone by post-commit recovery activity such as DE-rollback or compensation.

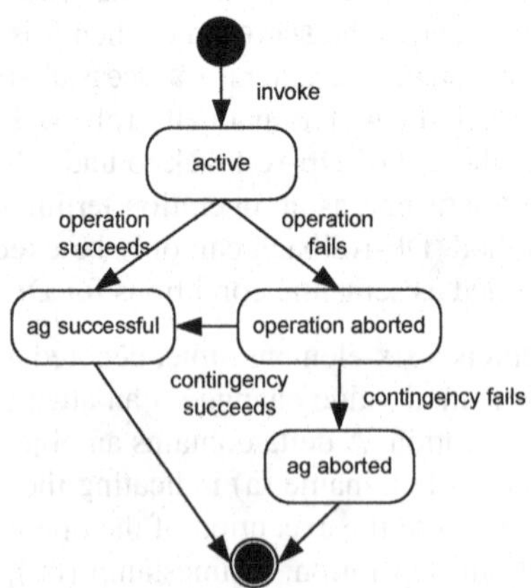

Fig. 4. Atomic Group Execution Semantics

Fig.4 describes the execution semantics of an ag. An ag has four states: {active, operation aborted, ag successful, ag aborted}. The termination states are {ag successful, ag aborted}. An ag enters the active state if the primary operation is invoked. If the primary operation successfully terminates, the ag enters the ag successful state. Otherwise the ag enters the operation aborted state, where contingency will be executed. If the contingency succeeds, the ag enters the ag successful state. Otherwise, the contingency itself is aborted, which leads the ag to the ag aborted state. Compensation and DE-rollback as post-commit recovery techniques for an atomic group are addressed in the context of a composite group execution in the next section.

5.3 Composite Group (CG) Execution Semantics

Before presenting the execution semantics of a composite group, this section first introduces concepts that are related to a composite group. This research has extended shallow/deep compensation originally defined in [9] to be used for a composite group.

Definition 7. *Critical.* An atomic/composite group is critical if its successful execution is mandatory for the enclosing composite group. The execution failure of a *non-critical* group will not impact the state of the enclosing composite group, and the composite group can continue execution. When an execution failure occurs, contingency must be executed for critical groups. Contingency is not necessary for a non-critical group. A group is critical by default.

In Fig.2, if ag_4 fails, cg_2 will continue its execution with ag_5 since ag_4 is non-critical.

Definition 8. *Shallow compensation.* Shallow compensation of a composite group invokes the composite group's compensation.

Definition 9. *Deep compensation.* Deep compensation of a composition group invokes post-commit recovery activity (DE-rollback or compensation) of each critical subgroup.

Shallow compensation is invoked when a composite group successfully terminates but needs a semantic undo due to another operation's execution failure. For example, in Fig. 2, if ag_6 fails, shallow compensation of cg_1 will be executed. When shallow compensation is not specified, a deep compensation is performed. For example, cg_2's deep compensation will be invoked when ag_6 fails since cg_2 does not have shallow compensation. A deep compensation can also be performed for a composite group cg when cg has a subgroup failure before cg completes. The service composition model currently assumes a compensation always succeeds. The model will be extended to handle compensation failure by provision of system-enforced recovery action.

The state of a composite group (cg) is determined by the combined state of the composing subgroups (sg_i), which are either atomic groups or other composite groups. A cg has states: {active, cg successful, sg_i aborted, cg aborted, cg deep compensated}. To simplify the state diagram, cg extended abort is introduced to refer to cg aborted or cg deep compensated. The termination states are: {cg successful, cg extended abort}.

Fig. 5(a) presents the execution semantics of a composite group composed of only atomic groups. A cg remains active during a subgroup's execution. If all the subgroups terminate successfully, a cg enters the cg successful state. If a subgroup ag_i fails, the cg enters the ag_i aborted state. If ag_i is the first subgroup of cg, cg enters the cg aborted state. Otherwise all of the previously executed subgroups ($ag_{1..i-1}$) will be post-commit recovered, leading cg to the cg deep compensated state. From the cg extended abort state, cg's contingency can be executed to enter the cg successful state. If cg's contingency fails, cg remains in the cg extended abort state.

Fig. 5(b) presents the execution semantics of a composite group (cg) that is composed of subgroups sg_i that can be either atomic groups or composite groups. If any subgroup sg_i fails, sg_i enters the sg_i extended abort state, according to the state transition described in Fig. 4 (if sg_i is an atomic subgroup) and in Fig. 5(a) (if sg_i is a composite subgroup). Other state transitions are the same as defined in Fig. 5(a).

In Fig.2, if ag_5 fails, cg_2's contingency gets executed since ag_4 is non-critical. If ag_6 fails, cg_2 is deep compensated by executing ag_5's compensation since ag_4 is non-critical and needs no compensation. cg_1 is shallow compensated by executing cg_1.cop.

6 The Process Recovery Model

The service composition model has elaborated on how backward recovery (DE-rollback/compensation) and forward recovery (contingency) are applied at different composition levels to maximize the successful execution of a process. After a backward recovery, the data changes introduced by backward recovery of a failed process p_f *potentially* cause a read dependent process p_r or a write dependent process p_w, to be recovered accordingly. Under certain semantic conditions, however, processes such as p_r and p_w may be able to continue running. The process recovery model addresses the applicability of DE-rollback and the handling of process interference based on data dependencies extracted from the global execution history through active rules.

This section presents the process recovery model. Section 6.1 defines process execution history and read/write dependency. Section 6.1 also presents the semantic

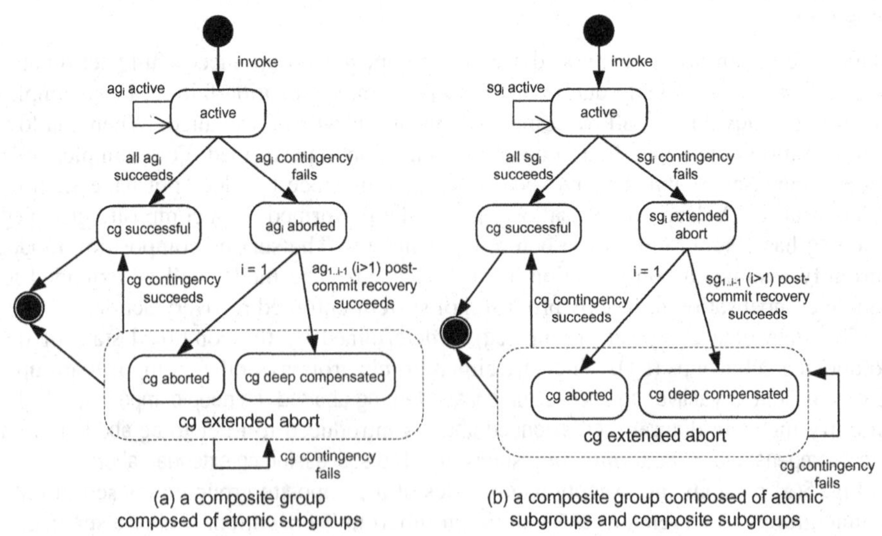

Fig. 5. Composite Group Execution Semantics

condition for DE-rollback. Section 6.2 presents process interference rule specification, and demonstrates its use through an online shopping application.

6.1 Global Execution History and Process Dependency

The global execution history is the foundation for analyzing data dependencies.

Definition 10. *Global execution history.* A global execution history GH is an integration of individual operation execution histories within a time frame, denoted as GH = <ts_s, ts_e, δg, gr>, where:

- ts_s and ts_e form the time frame of the GH.
- δg is a time-ordered sequence of deltas generated by distributed operation execution, denoted as δg = [Δ(oID_A, a, V_{old}, V_{new}, ts_1, op_{ij}),..., Δ(oID_B, b, V_{old}, V_{new}, ts_x, op_{kl}),..., Δ(oID_D, d, V_{old}, V_{new}, ts_n, op_{wz})]($ts_s < ts_1 < ts_x < ts_n < ts_e$).
- gr is the global execution context, which is a time-ordered sequence of runtime context information for operations and processes that occur within the time frame of the global execution history. The global execution context is denoted as gr = [r(en)| (en=op_{ij} or en=p_i) and (ts_s< r(en).ts_s< r(en).ts_e< ts_e)], where en represents an execution entity (either an operation op_{ij} or a process p_i). From gr, we can get a time-ordered sequence of system invocation events, denoted as E = [e(op_{ij}), ..., e(op_{wk}), ...]. E can be used to identify potential read dependencies among processes.

Data dependencies are defined based on information captured in the GH.

Definition 11. *Write dependency.* A write dependency exists if a process p_i, writes a data item *x* that has been written by another process p_j before p_j completes (i≠j).

Definition 12. *Process-level write dependent set.* A process p_j's write dependent set is a set of all the processes that are write dependent on p_j, denoted as $wd_p(p_j)$.

Definition 13. *Operation-level write dependency.* An operation-level write dependency exists if an operation op_{ik} of process p_i writes data that has been written by another operation op_{jl} of process p_j. An operation-level write dependency can exist between two operations within the same process (i = j).

Definition 14. *Operation-level write dependent set.* An operation op_{jl}'s operational-level write dependent set is a set of all the operations that are write dependent on op_{jl}, denoted as $wd_{op}(op_{jl})$.

Definition 15. *Read dependency.* A *read dependency* exists if a process p_i, reads a data item *x* that has been written by another process p_j before p_j completes (i≠j).

Definition 16. *Read dependent set.* A process p_j's read dependent set contains all the processes that are read dependent on p_j, denoted as $rd_p(p_j)$.

Write dependency can be analyzed from the global execution history GH. Suppose two operations have modified the same data item A. In GH, we observe δg = [..., Δ(oID_A, a, V_{old}, V_{new}, ts_1, op_{ij}), ..., Δ(oID_A, a, V_{old}, V_{new}, ts_x, op_{kl}), ...] ($ts_1 < ts_x$). δg indicates that at operation level, op_{kl} is write dependent on op_{ij}, denoted as $op_{kl} \in wd_{op}(op_{ij})$. At process level, if k≠i, p_k is write dependent on p_i, denoted as $p_k \in wd_p(p_i)$.

Definition 17. *DE-rollback.* DE-rollback of an operation op_{ik} is the action of undoing the effect of op_{ik} by reversing the data values that have been modified by op_{ik} to their before images, denoted as dop_{ik}.

Due to the existence of write dependency, the semantic condition of op_{ik}'s DE-rollback is: a) op_{ik}'s write dependent set is empty $wd_{op}(op_{ik}) = \Phi$, or b) op_{ik}'s write dependent set contains only operations from the same process $wd_{op}(op_{ik}) = \{op_{il}\}$ and the DE-rollback condition holds for each op_{il}. The semantic condition conforms to the traditional notion of recoverability where dirty reads and dirty writes are not allowed.

GH can also reveal potential read dependencies through runtime context. An operation op_{ik} is potentially read dependent on another operation op_{jl} if: 1) op_{ik} and op_{jl} execute on the same DEGS, denoted as $op_{ik}.degsID = op_{jl}.degsID$, and 2) op_{ik} starts after op_{jl}'s invocation, denoted as $r(op_{ik}).ts_s >= r(op_{jl}).ts_s$, or op_{ik} starts before op_{jl}'s invocation and ends after op_{jl}'s invocation, denoted as $r(op_{ik}).ts_s < r(op_{jl}).ts_s$ and $r(op_{ik}).ts_e > r(op_{jl}).ts_s$.

Assume op_{ij} is compensated. In GH, we observe an event sequence $E = [\ldots, e(op_{ij}), e(op_{km}), e(op_{xy}), e(cop_{ij})]$. E shows that op_{km} is invoked after op_{ij}, thus op_{km} is potentially read dependent on op_{ij}. At process level, if $k \neq i$ and p_k is active, p_k is potentially read dependent on p_i. A terminated process is not considered for process interference since a completed process should not be affected by ongoing changes.

Write dependencies and potential read dependencies are resolved through the use of process interference rules as defined in the next subsection.

6.3 Process Interference Rules

Process interference rules are active rules specifying how data change caused by of a process (DE-rollback or compensation) can possibly affect other active processes. This section outlines our initial phase of process interference rule specification which will be formally defined as part of future work. Fig. 6 shows that a process interference rule contains four parts: event, define, condition and action.

Event:	backward recovery event & event filter
Define:	variable declaration
Condition:	process interference evaluation
Action:	recovery command list

Fig. 6. Process Interference Rule Specification

Event contains a backward recovery event and an event filter. A backward recovery event is a DE-rollback $e(dop_{ij})$ or a compensation of an operation $e(cop_{ij})$ or process $e(cp_i)$. Compensation of a process cp_i involves compensation or DE-rollback of the process's operations. The event filter retrieves write and potential read dependent processes. Define declares variables to support condition evaluation and action invocation using the global execution history interfaces. Condition is a Boolean expression evaluating process interference based on application semantics. Action is a list of recovery commands, including backward recovery of a process (bkRecover(p_i)), and re-execution of an operation (re-execute(op_{ij})) or a process (re-execute(p_i)).

The global execution history exposes three types of interfaces: 1) $wd_p(p_i$, dependentProcessName) returns a set of active process instances of a given name (dependentProcessName) that are write dependent on p_i, 2) $rd_p(p_i$, dependentProcessName) returns a set of active process instances of given name (dependentProcessName) that are potentially read dependent on p_i, and 3) $\delta(p_i$, className) returns deltas with a given class name (className) that are generated by p_i.

The rest of the section demonstrates the use of process interference rules using an online shopping application with processes composed of DEGSs. The process placeClientOrder places client orders, decreases the inventory quantity, and possibly increases a backorder quantity. The process replenishInventory increases the inventory quantity when vendor orders are received and possibly decreases the backorder quantity. Several process instances could be running at the same time.

Write dependency scenario: Failure of a replenishInventory process could cause a write dependent placeClientOrder process to be compensated (since the items ordered may not actually be available). However, compensation of a placeClientOrder process would not affect a write dependent replenishInventory or returnClientOrder process.

Fig. 7 shows a process interference rule specifying that if a replenishInventory process (p_{ri}) is compensated, a placeClientOrder process with an inventory item that has been supplied by p_{ri} must be compensated and re-executed. In Fig. 7:

- $e(cp_{ri})$ represents the compensation of process replenishInventory.
- $wd_p(p_{ri}$, "placeClientOrder") returns a set of instances of process placeClientOrder that are write dependent on process p_{ri}. The event filter $wd_p(p_{ri}$, "placeClientOrder") $\neq \Phi$ verifies the existence of a placeClientOrder process that is write dependent on p_{ri}.
- Process p_w declares p_w as a process instance. $p_w \in wd_p(p_{ri}$, "placeClientOrder") restricts that p_w must be a placeClientOrder process that is write dependent on p_{ri}.
- $\delta(cp_{ri}$, "InventoryItem") retrieves deltas of class InventoryItem that are generated by the compensation of p_{ri}. Similarly, $\delta(p_w$, "InventoryItem") retrieves deltas of class InventoryItem that are generated by p_w. Condition $\delta(cp_{ri}$, "InventoryItem") $\cap$ $\delta(p_w$, "InventoryItem") $\neq \Phi$ evaluates if the cp_{ri} and p_w process the same inventory item.
- bkRecover(p_w) is a recovery command to backward recover p_w, based on p_w's composition structure and recoverability. re-execute(p_w) is a command to re-execute p_w.

```
Event:       e(cp_ri) & wd_p(p_ri, "placeClientOrder") ≠ Φ
Define:      Process p_w (p_w ∈ wd_p(p_ri, "placeClientOrder"))
Condition:   δ(cp_ri, "InventoryItem") ∩ δ(p_w, "InventoryItem") ≠ Φ
Action:      bkRecover(p_w);
             re-execute(p_w);
```

Fig. 7. A Sample Process Interference Rule Handling Write Dependency

As a summary, after recovery of a failed process, process interference must be identified. However write/read dependent processes *may or may not* need to be recovered, depending on the application semantics defined by a process interference rule.

7 Summary and Future Directions

This paper has presented an abstract execution model as the foundation for building a semantically robust execution environment for distributed processes over Delta-Enabled Grid services. We are developing the DeltaGrid system to support the abstract model. We have implemented several major architectural components such as DEGS [4], the GridPML [10, 13], and a process history capture system (PHCS) [21] as a logging mechanism for distributed processes. The PHCS fully implements the global execution history interfaces to evaluate the applicability of DE-rollback and process interference.

This research contributes towards establishing a semantically robust execution model for distributed processes executing over autonomous, heterogeneous resources. A unique aspect of this research is the provision for multi-level protection against service execution failure, and handling process interference based on application-dependent correctness criterion integrated with data dependency tracking through a global execution history.

Our future direction is to provide a complete support of application-dependent correctness criterion by refining the definition of process interference rules and incorporating application exceptions rules in the process recovery model. We are building a simulation framework for the DeltaGrid system to demonstrate the concepts defined in the abstract model in a distributed service composition environment.

References

1. Business Process Modeling Language, http://www.bpmi.org/specifications.esp, 2002.
2. Specification: Web Services Transaction (WS-Transaction), http://www-106.ibm.com/ developerworks/webservices/library/ws-transpec/, 2002.
3. Specification: Business Process Execution Language for Web Services Version 1.1, http://www-106.ibm.com/developerworks/webservices/library/ws-bpel/, 2003.
4. Blake, L., *Design and Implementation of Delta-Enabled Grid Services*, MS Thesis, Dept. of Comp. Sci. and Eng., Arizona State Univ., (2005).
5. de By, R., Klas, W., Veijalainen, J., *Transaction Management Support for Cooperative Applications*. 1998: Kluwer Academic Publishers.
6. Eder, J., Liebhart, W., "The Workflow Activity Model WAMO," Proc. of the *3rd Int. Conference on Cooperative Information Systems (CoopIs)*, 1995.
7. Garcia-Molina, H., Salem, K., "Sagas," Proc. of the *ACM SIGMOD Int. Conference on Management of Data*, 1987.
8. Kamath, M., Ramamritham, K., "Failure Handling and Coordinated Execution of Concurrent Workflows," Proc. of the *IEEE Int. Conference on Data Engineering*, 1998.
9. Laymann, F., "Supporting Business Transactions via Partial Backward Recovery in Workflow Management," Proc. of the *GI-Fachtagung für Datenbanksysteme in Business*, Technologie und Web (BTW'95), 1995.
10. Liao, N., *The Extened GridPML Design and Implementation*, MCS Project Report, Dept. of Comp. Sci. and Eng., Arizona State Univ., (2005).
11. Lin, F., Chang, H., "B2B E-commerce and Enterprise Integration: The Development and Evaluation of Exception Handling Mechanisms for Order Fulfillment Process Based on BPEL4WS," Proc. of the *7th IEEE Int. Conference on Electronic commerce*, 2005.

12. Lomet, D., Vagena, Z., Barga, R., "Recovery from "Bad" User Transactions," Proc. of the *ACM SIGMOD Int. Conference on Management of Data*, 2006.
13. Ma, H., Urban, S. D., Xiao, Y., and Dietrich, S. W., "GridPML: A Process Modeling Language and Process History Capture System for Grid Service Composition," Proc. of the *IEEE Int. Conference on e-Business Engineering*, 2005.
14. Mikalsen, T., Tai, S., Rouvellou, I., "Transactional Attitudes: Reliable Composition of Autonomous Web Services," Proc. of the *Workshop on Dependable Middleware-based Systems (WDMS)*, part of the *Int. Conference on Dependable Systems and Networks (DSN)*, 2002.
15. Shi, Y., Zhang, L., Shi. B., "Exception Handling of workflow for Web services," Proc. of the *4th Int. Conference on Computer and Information Technology*, 2004.
16. Singh, M.P., Huhns, M. N., *Service-Oriented Computing*. 2005: Wiley.
17. Business Service Grid: Manage Web Services and Grid Services with Service Domain Technology, http://www-128.ibm.com/developerworks/ibm/library/gr-servicegrid/, 2003.
18. Tartanoglu, F., Issarny, V., Romanovsky, A., Levy, N., "Dependability in the Web Services Architecture," Proc. of the *Architecting Dependable Systems, LNCS 2677*, 2003.
19. Wachter, H., Reuter, A., "The ConTract Model," in *Database Transaction Models for Advanced Applications*, A. Elmagarmid, Editor. 1992.
20. Worah, D., Sheth, A., "Transactions in Transactional Workflows," in *Advanced Transaction Models and Architectures*, S. Jajodia, and Kershberg,L., Editor, Springer.
21. Xiao, Y., Urban, S. D., Dietrich, S., "A Process History Capture System for Analysis of Data Dependencies in Concurrent Process Execution," Proc. of the *2nd Int. Workshop on Data Engineering Issues in E-Commerce and Services*, 2006.
22. Zeng, L., Lei, H., Jeng, J., Chung, J., Benatallah, B., "Policy-Driven Exception-Management for Composite Web Services," Proc. of the *7th IEEE Int. Conference on E-Commerce Technology*, 2005.

Evaluating Quality of Conceptual Models Based on User Perceptions

Ann Maes and Geert Poels

Faculty of Economics and Business Administration,
Ghent University, Hoveniersberg 24, 9000 Ghent, Belgium
a.maes@ugent.be, geert.poels@ugent.be

Abstract. This paper presents the development of a user evaluations based quality model for conceptual modeling applying the model of DeLone and McLean [6] for evaluating information systems in general. Given the growing awareness about the importance of high-quality conceptual models, it is surprising that there is no practical evaluation framework that considers the quality of conceptual models from a user's perspective. Human factors research in conceptual modeling is still scarce and the perception of quality by model users has been largely ignored. A first research goal is therefore to determine what the appropriate dimensions are for evaluating conceptual models from a user's perspective. Secondly, we investigate the relationships between these dimensions. Furthermore, we present the results of two experiments with 187 and 124 business students respectively, designed to test the proposed model and the generated hypotheses. The results largely support the developed model and have implications for both theory and practice of quality evaluation of conceptual models.

1 Introduction

Conceptual modeling (CM) plays an important role in information systems development (ISD) projects. Before implementing an information system (IS), a conceptual model of a real world system is developed to enhance the communication about the problem domain between designers, analysts and users. The importance of high-quality conceptual models cannot be overemphasized because they facilitate early detection and correction of errors in ISD projects. However, generally agreed quality measures still have to be developed [19]. We address this need by building a theoretical model that will support empirical evaluation of CM quality. This includes the evaluation of distinct models generated by the same modeling language as well as the quality assessment of models generated using different modeling languages. Given the call of [32] to focus future CM research more on the use of models for User-Analyst communication (as opposed to Analyst-Developer communication), we look at CM quality from an end user's perspective.

The remainder of the paper is as follows. First, we elaborate on the framework of Lindland et al. [17], which defines quality in a CM context. The next section also introduces the IS success model of DeLone and McLean [6], which provides a theoretical basis for our evaluation framework. Subsequently, the user evaluations based

D.W. Embley, A. Olivé, and S. Ram (Eds.): ER 2006, LNCS 4215, pp. 54–67, 2006.

quality model and the derived hypotheses are formulated. In the following section we describe the design of two experiments that aimed at testing the developed model. Next, the analysis of the collected data is discussed. We conclude with a short discussion of the contributions so far and an outline of future research directions.

2 Background

2.1 Understanding Quality of Conceptual Models

The Lindland et al.'s [17] framework suggests that a systematic evaluation of quality considers a model's syntax (how well does the model adhere to the rules of the modeling language?), semantics (how well does the model reflect the reality modeled?) and pragmatics (how well is the model understood and used?). In practice, syntactic quality issues in CM seem to be well controlled [23]. Therefore, the main evaluation effort is directed towards semantic and pragmatic quality.

Several instruments have been proposed for evaluating model pragmatics. For instance, when comparing alternative CM techniques or practices, resultant models have been compared with respect to how well they are understood by users. In experimental settings, measures used for comparison include comprehension task accuracy and completion time [31]. In addition, user perceptions of model pragmatics have been measured with instruments for ease of use, usefulness and user information satisfaction [4,13].

The semantic quality of a model is more difficult to evaluate as it is hard to know, externalize and agree upon reality. When evaluating semantic quality, users can only refer to their perception of reality, which is obtained through observing the 'real' focal domain of the modeling efforts. Krogstie et al. [16], therefore, extended the Lindland et al. framework with a fourth quality type, namely perceived semantic quality, which is described as the correspondence between the information that users think the model contains and the information that users think the model should contain, based upon their knowledge of the problem domain. Nevertheless, user perceptions of a conceptual model's semantic quality have been less empirically investigated than perceptions related to model pragmatics. Most studies have quantified the degree of semantic quality with respect to some reference theory or modeling benchmark, e.g. the Bunge-Wand-Weber (BWW) representational model, a reference model (like the SAP reference models) or an enterprise domain ontology, as a substitute for the 'real' domain [12]. These studies ignore the user beliefs of how well the model helps understanding the underlying reality. Even if a generally agreed reference theory or modeling benchmark could be established, it is still the user's perception of semantic quality, rather than a theoretically verified quality, that will largely determine whether benefits result from using a high-quality conceptual model during the ISD project. Therefore an empirical approach that recognizes possible differences in user perceptions of semantic quality is needed to complement more theoretically-oriented evaluation studies.

Consequently, our model is focused on the different user perceptions of CM quality since it is the user's perception of quality that will determine the effectiveness of the conceptual model to communicate IS requirements within the ISD project.

2.2 IS Success Models

For information systems, several evaluation frameworks that recognize subjective user perceptions have been proposed. Consequently, we found an appropriate basis for our model in the form of DeLone and McLean's [6] model of Information Systems Success.

Using the communications research of [30] DeLone and McLean (henceforth D&M) identify six interrelated dimensions of IS Success (figure 1): system quality, information quality, use, user satisfaction, individual impact and organizational impact. The D&M model specifies that system quality and information quality affect both use and user satisfaction, which are direct antecedents of individual impact. This will in turn have an impact on the organizational performance. Furthermore, D&M expect a two-way causal relationship between use and user satisfaction [6].

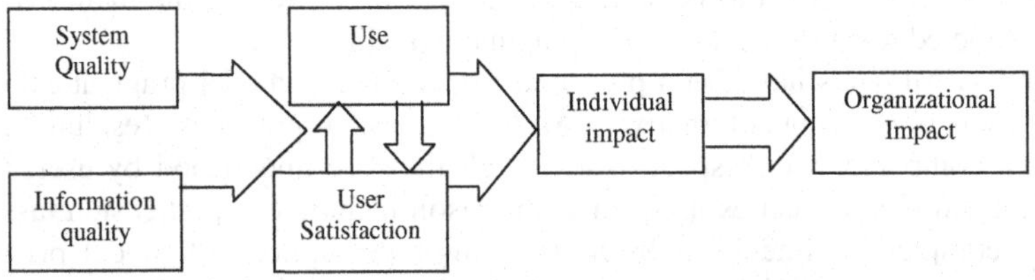

Fig. 1. DeLone and McLean's Model of IS Success ([6], Figure 2, p.87)

Empirical tests of the D&M model mostly supported the model and its relationships [7]. Seddon [26] criticizes the D&M model on combining process and causal explanations of IS success, which leads to confusing interpretations. Consequently, he [26] proposed a respecified model of IS success where the original D&M model is split into two variance sub-models (one model to predict use as a behavior and one model to assess IS success). In the IS success sub-model (figure 2), [26] retains system quality and information quality and claims their causal impact to two frequently used perceptual measures of the benefits of system use, perceived usefulness and user satisfaction. Additionally, it is postulated that perceived usefulness influences user satisfaction. Besides these perceptual measures of net benefits of system use, other net

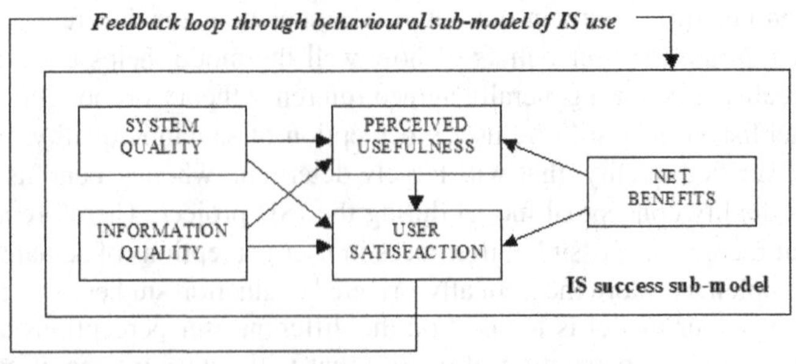

Fig. 2. Respecified model of IS Success [26]

benefits to individuals, organizations and society are represented in the model by means of the net benefits construct. These are supposed to have a direct causal connection with the perceptual measures.

3 Proposed Model

Seddon's respecified D&M IS success model, which acknowledges quality as an antecedent to system success, is used to guide the development of our user evaluations model for CM quality. We argue that there are clear parallels between the perceptual constructs of Seddon's model and perceptual conceptual model quality constructs.

3.1 Perceived Semantic Quality as Information Quality

Information Quality (IQ) concerns the quality of the information the system produces. Users assess the value of the information with respect to four IQ core dimensions : accuracy, completeness, currency and format [21]. This evaluation of the different information characteristics from a user's perspective is fairly subjective and relative to the specific context and task at hand [21].

According to [6], IQ represents a success measure at the semantic level of information in Shannon and Weaver‘s communication theory. The semantic level concerns how well the intended meaning is being conveyed to and interpreted by the receiver. Similarly as information systems, conceptual models are used to assist people in performing a particular task based on the information conveyed by the model. Users assess how well the model serves its stated purpose. If the purpose is to develop a common understanding of the problem domain, then users will evaluate the quality of the model with respect to this purpose. As a consequence, users will evaluate the conceptual model based on the quality of the information conveyed by the model. This information should be accurate, complete, up to date and presented in a format that advances users' understanding of the underlying reality when performing a certain task.

In terms of the Lindland et al. [17] framework, the IQ of a conceptual model corresponds to its semantic quality. Users will perceive the semantic quality of the model as how valid and complete it is with respect to (their perception of) the problem domain. Validity means that all information conveyed by the model is correct and relevant to the problem whereas completeness entails that the model contains all information about the domain that is considered correct and relevant [17]. Consequently, quality properties for conceptual models mapped by [17] onto their semantic quality construct include correctness, completeness and consistency.

These parallels justify the reformulation of IQ construct by the Perceived Semantic Quality (PSQ) construct when applying the respecified D&M IS success model to conceptual models.

3.2 Perceived Ease of Use as System Quality

Like IQ is concerned with the output produced by the IS, system quality (SQ) considers desired characteristics of the system that produces the output such as the consistency of the user interface, ease of use, documentation, ... [26]. The perception of system quality is formed through interaction with the system when users complete a specific task. Contrary to their IQ dimensions, the SQ dimensions of [21] are not immediately applicable to the CM context. However, SQ has several times been represented by "ease of use", which refers to the "user friendliness" of the system [25,27]. Ease of use is defined as "the degree to which a person believes that using a particular system would be free of effort" ([5], p. 320).

When users "interact" with a conceptual model, they will evaluate how well the model serves its goal in terms of semantic quality but also in terms of its pragmatic quality (i.e. how well do they understand what is modeled and how easy is it to acquire this understanding?). As mentioned before, one frequently used pragmatic quality measure for CM is Perceived Ease Of Use (PEOU), which has a similar meaning as in the IS research context. So in our evaluation model, the PEOU construct instantiates the SQ construct of the respecified D&M model.

3.3 Perceived Usefulness (PU)

Seddon [26] replaced use by "Perceived Usefulness" since it is not use but the benefits from use (e.g. usefulness) that determine whether an IS is successful. He defines Perceived Usefulness (PU) as "the degree to which a person believes that using a particular system **has** enhanced his or her job performance" (adapted from [5], p320). Users evaluate the IS with respect to its usefulness after using the IS for a certain task.

Usefulness appears to be also a valuable evaluation aspect in a CM context. After task completion, users will judge how well the model helps to 'better' understand what is modeled. In terms of the Lindland et al. [17] framework this is captured by the pragmatic quality. 'Better' model understanding can mean two things from a user's perspective: the understanding is more efficient (i.e. requiring less effort, which is reflected in the PEOU measure) or it is more effective (i.e. more accurate). Hence, users will evaluate the effectiveness or usefulness of the model, which will amongst others shape their overall quality judgment. The usefulness of conceptual models has been measured using a PU measure based on the validated instrument of [5]. This results in the third construct for our evaluation framework for CM.

3.4 User Satisfaction (US)

Seddon ([26], p. 246) defines US as "a subjective evaluation of the various consequences evaluated on a pleasant-unpleasant continuum". US is the most general perceptual measure of IS Success and is focused on overall satisfaction and effectiveness [27]. The US construct of [26] is concerned with users' overall level of satisfaction and does not include indirect measures like IQ and SQ. A measure to assess overall US directly has been constructed by [28].

"Satisfaction with Use" is also applicable to the CM context. A general evaluation towards the use of a conceptual model can be measured in terms of how satisfied users are with the model with respect to its purpose. An adaptation of the US measure of [28] has been employed in empirical comparisons of conceptual models (e.g. [10]). As such, it seems justified to include US in our CM evaluation framework.

3.5 Research Model

The adoption of Seddon's model to a CM context leads to the selection of four related but distinct evaluation aspects (PSQ, PEOU, PU, US) for our evaluation framework (figure 3). A number of relationships between these variables can be deducted. Just as SQ and IQ are independent of each other and based on their specific meaning, we argue that for conceptual models PSQ and PEOU are not related. These two evaluation aspects are likely to have an influence on US. User satisfaction is a more general concept and results from summing all the benefits [27]. A conceptual model that users perceive as easy to use will leave the user more "satisfied" about the model used. Previous research has suggested that higher perceived semantic quality may result in higher user satisfaction [9]. User satisfaction is, however, also determined by perceptions of usefulness. The better the model supports the information needs of the user performing the comprehension task, the more satisfied the user will likely be. This forms the basis for the causal relationships 1, 2 and 3 in figure 3:

- H1: Increases in PEOU will cause increases in US
- H2: Increases in PSQ will cause increases in US
- H3: Increases in PU will cause increases in US

Furthermore, evidence can be gained that PU is influenced by perceptions of ease of use and semantic quality. If two conceptual models have the same information content, the model user will find the one that is easier to use or understand more useful. Apart from evaluating the pragmatic quality of a conceptual model, users also form a perception of its semantic quality. It is plausible that this perception affects the user's perception of usefulness. If users believe that the model is invalid and/or incorrect with respect to the problem domain, they are likely to develop a less favorable perception of the model's usefulness. Of course, user perceptions of usefulness may be affected by other factors than perceived semantic quality and perceived ease of use but what we wish to investigate is the extent to which perceived usefulness is affected by these variables. Consequently, we derive the last two causal relations :

- H4: Increases in PSQ will cause increases in PU
- H5: Increases in PEOU will cause increases in PU

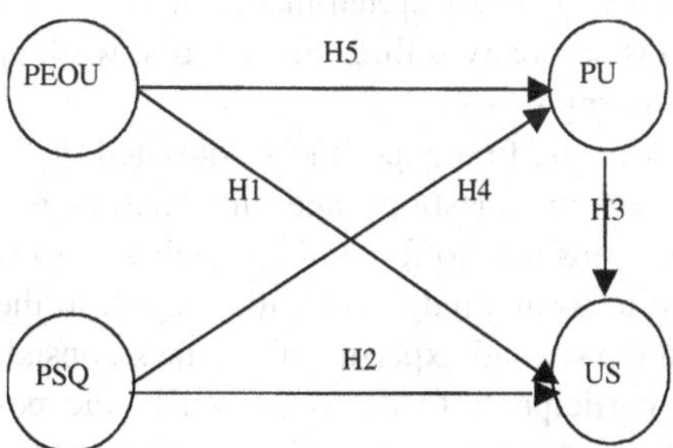

Fig. 3. User Evaluations Based Quality Model for Conceptual modeling

4 Research Method

To test the research model we conducted two experiments. The first experiment (E1) took place in november 2004 while the second experiment (E2) was conducted in november 2005. Since both experiments are similar we will present the design together but will comment on any possible differences between them.

4.1 Participants

The experiments required participants to comprehend a number of business domain models (in Entity-Relationship (ER) diagram format) for an example commercial company. The participants were 187 (E1) and 124 (E2) business students enrolled in a Management Information Systems (MIS) course. The groups of business students participating in the studies approximate representative samples of the target population of business professionals. The advantage of student participants is that they form a homogeneous group with respect to their educational background and working experience, which would not be the case if business professionals were used. Moreover, the experimental tasks did not require high levels of industrial experience, so given the recommendations in [1] experiments with students can be justified.

Acquiring CM skills and in particular being able to understand models developed by analysts, is essential for business students. Apart from studying the semantics of the ER Model, the students in the MIS course were shown examples of and learned to read ER diagrams of various domains (e.g. university personnel management, hospital operations) with the purpose of understanding the domain information conveyed by the diagrams.

4.2 Experimental Objects and Tasks

The experiments were conducted after the CM module of the course. In the experiments, each participant received one of several alternative ER diagrams depicting a structural and data view of some part of the business. Using this diagram, the participant had to answer a number of questions assessing the understanding of the part of the business modeled (based solely on the information conveyed by the diagram). The participants of E1 worked with a conceptual model of an integrated sales and acquisition process of a fictitiuos company selling surf-boards, while the model in E2 represented the hiring of consulting services.

The experimental task of the first experiment consisted of a series of questions including model comprehension questions and information retrieval questions. The main purpose of the questions was to force the participants to work with the diagram received and allow them to form a judgment with .respect to the diagram's pragmatic and semantic quality. In the second experiment, the task consisted of answering questions that required the participants to derive or verify the policies that govern the modelled process. As the diagram was the only information source available for answering the questions, participants were 'forced' to make an effort to understand the diagram.

All used questions were adapted from previously validated questionnaires (e.g. [2, 13]). Though tailored to the particular case used in the experiments, comprehension questions of the kind we used are the conventional instrument for measuring how well users understand the information conveyed by a conceptual model [22].

4.3 Operational Procedures

The two experiments were organized as class room exercises. The students were informed beforehand that the exercise was part of a research study and that additional data in the form of questionnaires would be collected. However, no information was given with respect to the research question (to avoid experimenter bias).

Participation was strictly voluntary. In order to increase the motivation to participate (and perform well), the students were explained that a similar exercise could be part of the final course exam and feedback on the performance was promised. Furthermore, in E1 optional course credits could be earned, while in E2 four prizes (i-Pod Shuffles and Nanos) were distributed to the best performers.

When students entered class, they received a sheet containing instructions and asking for their name. Next, they were given the diagram and the list of questions they had to solve. After finishing the comprehension task, they received a questionnaire measuring their perceptions and satisfaction towards the task just accomplished.

4.4 Measures

In order to evaluate the PSQ, PEOU, PU and US constructs, measures are needed. A literature search revealed the existence of validated measures for the PSQ, PEOU, PU and US constructs within the CM context. The general measurement items for each of the four constructs are shown in Table 1. These items were rephrased for the two

Table 1. Measures for PEOU, PU, US and PSQ constructs of user evaluation model

PEOU$_1$	It was easy for me to understand what the conceptual schema was trying to model.	**PU$_1$**	Overall, I think the conceptual schema would be an improvement to a textual description of business process.
PEOU$_2$	Using the conceptual schema was often frustrating.	**PU$_2$**	Overall, I found the conceptual schema useful for understanding the process modelled.
PEOU$_3$	Overall, the conceptual schema was easy to use.	**PU$_3$**	Overall, I think the conceptual schema improves my performance when understanding the process modelled.
PEOU$_4$	Learning how to read the conceptual schema was easy.	**PSQ$_1$**	The conceptual schema represents the business process correctly.
US$_1$	The conceptual schema adequately met the information needs that I was asked to support.	**PSQ$_2$**	The conceptual schema is a realistic representation of the business process
US$_2$	The conceptual schema was not efficient in providing the information I needed.	**PSQ$_3$**	The conceptual schema contains contradicting elements
US$_3$	The conceptual schema was effective in providing the information I needed.	**PSQ$_4$**	All the elements in the conceptual schema are relevant for the representation of the business process
US$_4$	Overall, I am satisfied with the conceptual schema for providing the information I needed.	**PSQ$_5$**	The conceptual schema gives a complete representation of the business process

experiments into more specific item statements according to the represented business domain. For each item statement a 7-point Likert scale with response options ranging from 'strongly disagree' to 'strongly agree' was offered.

The PSQ measure was developed by [24]. Measurement items were generated from a definition of semantic quality derived from two theoretical CM quality frameworks, i.e. the semiotics-based quality definitions of [17] and the Bunge-Wand-Weber ontology-based quality definitions of [29]. The proposed items were refined until convergent and divergent validity was deemed satisfactory. The five items of the purified PSQ measure are shown in Table 1. The PEOU items were proposed by [13] and are adapted from Moore and Benbasat's [20] PEOU measure for IT innovations. PU can be measured using Moody's [18] PU measure for method adoption (which is based on [5]) for use in the CM context. Finally, a US instrument is found in Seddon and Yip's [28] overall User Information Satisfaction measure and has been reworded by [10] for measuring satisfaction with conceptual model use.

5 Research Findings

Partial Least Squares (PLS) is an appropriate statistical analysis method for this study based on the properties of the data at hand. PLS offers an alternative for incorporating formative (causal) as well as reflective (effect) indicators in one model [8][1]. Although PLS estimates both factor loadings (i.e. measurement model) and structural paths (i.e. structural model) simultaneously we follow a two-step approach [15] in evaluating PLS models. First, the measurement model is evaluated to assess construct validity. Then, the hypothesized structural model of relationships between the four constructs is tested (hypotheses testing).

5.1 Assessing Construct Validity

In our measurement model PEOU, PU and US are, as in previous research, operationalized as reflective constructs. On the other hand, the five elements of PSQ are conceptualized as formative indicators, as PSQ results from the assessment of specific elements of semantic quality. This is consistent with the conceptual definition of [17] in which several semantic quality dimensions (e.g. correctness, completeness) have independent impacts on (or cause) the higher-order construct of semantic quality. For instance, a conceptual model can be complete with respect to the problem domain, and at the same time contain incorrect or irrelevant facts. Also, if an improvement in the correctness of the model is perceived by the model users, then PSQ will be higher, even if the completeness of the model has not changed.

---

[1] Predominantly, we think of indicators as effects of the underlying concept [3]. A change in the latent variable will result in a change in all indicators (reflective measurement perspective). An alternative perspective is based on the use of formative (causal) indicators. Here, it are the indicators "that are assumed to cause a latent variable" ([3], p. 65). Since the latent variable is formed by its indicators, a change in the latent variable is not necessarily accompanied by a change in all indicators. If any one of the indicators changes, then the latent variable will also change.

Reflective Indicators: The adequacy of the reflective measurement model (i.e. for PEOU, PU and US) is assessed by examining the individual item reliabilities and evaluating the convergent and discriminant validity of the measures. The results of the measurement model are presented in Table 2.

First, individual item reliabilities were assessed by examining the factor loadings of all items on their respective constructs. Only items with factor loadings of at least 0.50 are considered very significant and should be retained in the final measurement model [14] which is the case for all items of PEOU, PU and US. Next, the convergent validity of the different constructs was examined by computing the composite reliabilities (ICR), using the internal consistency measure developed by [11] which is similar to Cronbach's alpha. In this study composite reliability of every construct in the final measurement model was higher than 0.7, the suggested value by [11] for measures to be deemed reliable (see also Table 2).

Table 2. Assessment of reflective construct measures (measurement model)

Item	Loading		ICR		AVE	
	E1	E2	E1	E2	E1	E2
PEOU1	0.79	0.82	0.834	0.832	0.560	0,565
PEOU2	0.70	0.45				
PEOU3	0.85	0.88				
PEOU4	0.63	0.79				
PU1	0.75	0.83	0.866	0.888	0.684	0,726
PU2	0.88	0.90				
PU3	0.85	0.83				
US1	0.74	0.65	0.895	0.885	0.681	0,660
US2	0.83	0.88				
US3	0.87	0.83				
US4	0.87	0.88				

Additionally, convergent validity was investigated through the average extracted variances of the constructs (AVE). AVE is the average variance shared between a construct and its items. AVE should be higher than 0.5, meaning that at least 50 percent of measurement variance is captured by the construct [11]. The AVE of all the constructs in the measurement model were above 0.5 (Table 2).

Finally, the AVE was used for discriminant validity assessment as suggested by [11]. The test requires that the correlation between any two constructs be smaller than the average of the two root-squared AVEs meaning that the variance shared between any two constructs is less than the AVE by the constructs. For our reflective constructs there was no correlation between any two latent constructs larger than or even equal to the square root AVE of these two constructs. Consequently, discriminant validity was supported and confidence was gained that all reflective constructs in the model were indeed measuring different concepts.

Formative indicators: Because of the formative structure of the PSQ construct, traditional validity assessments can not be used. Observed correlations among the construct's measures may not be meaningful [8] and as a consequence, assessment of item reliability and convergent validity become irrelevant [15]. For the formative construct only the indicator coefficients that significantly differ from zero will be retained. As discussed above, semantic quality dimensions are used as indicators of PSQ. Indicator coefficients which are not significantly different from zero, can not be considered valid. Such indicators contain information perceived redundant by the respondents, or have high correlations with other indicators or are perceived irrelevant for the particular construct and should therefore be excluded from the model [8].

PLS analysis indicated that not all PSQ indicators have a coefficient significantly different from zero. These indicators should be deleted from the model before the structural model can be tested.

In the analysis of the first experiment, the PSQ4 (t=0.44), and PSQ5(t=0.43) indicators are not significantly related to the PSQ construct. On the other hand, the PLS analysis indicates that PSQ judgement is caused by PSQ2 (t=3.51), PSQ3 (t=4.24) and PSQ1 (t=2.21). These three PSQ elements are retained to test the hypotheses.

The construct validity assessment of the PSQ construct in the second experiment largely supports the findings of above. Here, again some PSQ indicators must be removed before testing the structural model. As in the previous assessment, not all indicator coefficients significantly differ from zero. Again, PSQ4 (t=0.00) and PSQ5 (t=0.01) are not significantly related to PSQ. Furthermore, also PSQ1 (t=0.49) will be removed when evaluating the structural model. The other two PSQ elements, PSQ2 (t=5.04) and PSQ3 (t=1.97), are relevant formative indicators of PSQ.

5.2 Hypotheses Testing

After the validity assessment of the four constructs, the structural model was tested to assess the hypothesized relationships in the proposed user evaluations based quality model (see Figure 3). Table 3 presents the structural path diagrams for the two conducted experiments with the statistically significant path coefficients and the total variance explained (R^2).

An examination of these results reveals that the variance explained of PU and US ranges from 0.42 to 0.69 and that all of the paths were statistically at least significant

Table 3. Results of research model for the two experiments (E1 &E2)

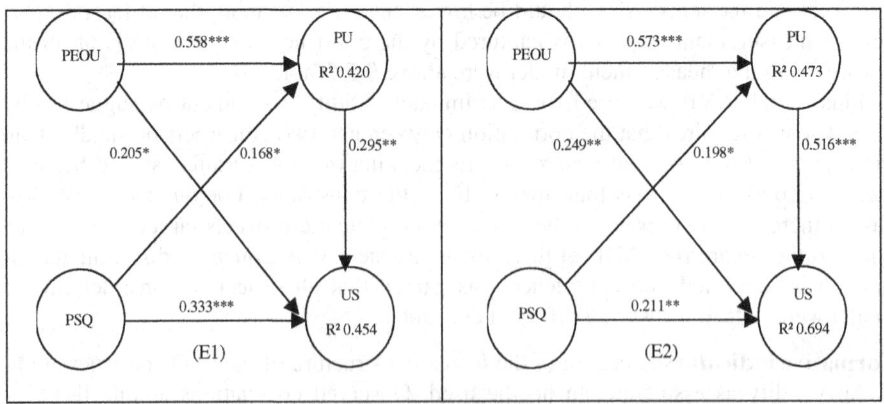

indicates significant paths : *** P< 0.001 ** P < 0.01 * P < 0.05

at the 0.05 level and as such confirm the hypothesized relationships between the four evaluation dimensions for conceptual models. The results indicate that PSQ, as was hypothesized, had a significant direct effect on US. We also found support for the relation between PSQ and PU, though this effect was not as strong than with US. More importantly in explaining PU seems PEOU since there was a highly significant and strong effect of PEOU on PU in both experiments. Together PSQ and PEOU explained 42% and 47% respectively of the variance of the PU variable. Finally, we could as in previous research also confirm the direct effects of PEOU on US and of PU on US which were more or less of equal importance. These two variables were able to explain 45% and 69% respectively of the variance of the US variable.

6 Conclusion

The research contributions of this paper are twofold: first, a new quality model and measurement instrument has been developed that is solely based on conceptual model end-user evaluations. Second, we demonstrated relationships between different quality perceptions, in particular between semantic and pragmatic quality perceptions, and also between these perceptions and the overall user satisfaction with the conceptual model. These contributions have both research and practical significance. From a research point of view, the evaluation model and instrument can serve in studies investigating the mechanisms that lead to successful CM applications. Such studies may provide insight in how to develop better conceptual models, as well as how to make sure that model end-users perceive model quality improvements.

When applied in CM practice, the proposed evaluation model (including measurement instrument) can be used as a quality assurance tool to evaluate and compare the quality of alternative conceptual models, as perceived by model end-users. As our research shows, user perceptions of model quality are an important determinant of the users' satisfaction with the conceptual model. Obtaining user satisfaction is important, given the conceptual model's role as a communication vehicle for information system requirements between analysts and future system end-users. The user evaluations based quality model may therefore supplement other (and maybe more objective) quality assurance/improvement tools, that are not directly aimed at evaluating user perceptions. Unless users perceive model quality improvements, they will not affect the users' satisfaction with the model and thus are not likely to contribute to a more successful user-analyst communication. Our evaluation model allows verifying whether model users perceive the intended effects of quality improvements actions.

Our research can be extended and improved in a number of ways. First, although the conducted experiments support the hypothesized relations of the user evaluations based quality model for CM, it is clear that the proposed model is only preliminary and needs further testing, validation and possibly reformulation to draw final conclusions and enhance external validity. More theoretical and empirical research is required to explore the relationships between the semantic and pragmatic quality measures of our model further. Furthermore, the conducted experiments were classroom experiments employing students as participants, small-scale business models (in ER format) as study objects, and relatively simple tasks to be performed. Future research might employ other tasks and models or take the form of field studies so the model is tested in different settings. Finally, the proposed model only includes perceptual measures of CM quality. Future research could extend the model with other variables of interest like theoretically established notions of semantic quality, performance-based variables of user comprehension and other model-usage factors. This should contribute to the establishment of a comprehensive model for the overall quality assessment of conceptual models.

References

1. Basili, V., Shull, F. and Lanubile, F. (1999). Building Knowledge through Families of Experiments. IEEE Transactions on Software Engineering. 25(4), 456-473.
2. Bodart, F., A. Patel, M. Sim, and R. Weber (2001). Should Optional Properties Be Used in Conceptual Modelling? A Theory and Three Empirical Tests. Information Systems Research, 12, 4 (December), 384-405.
3. Bollen, K. (1989). Structural Equations with Latent Variables, John Wiley & Sons, NY.
4. Burton-Jones, A. and Weber, R. (1999). Understanding Relationships with Attributes in Entity-Relationship Diagrams. Proc. of the 20th International Conference on Information Systems, 214-228.
5. Davis, F. (1989). Perceived Usefulness, Perceived Ease of Use, and User Acceptance of Information Technology. MIS Quarterly, 13(3), 319-339.
6. DeLone, W.H. and McLean, E.R. (1992). Information Systems Success: The Quest for the dependent variable. Information Systems Journal, 3(1), 60-95.
7. DeLone, W.H. and McLean, E.R. (2003). The DeLone and McLean model of information systems success: A ten-year update. Journal of Management Information Systems, 19(4), 9–30.
8. Diamantopoulos, A. and Winklhofer H.M. (2001). Index Construction with Formative Indicators: An Alternative to Scale Development. Journal of Marketing Research, 38(2), 269-277.
9. Dunn, C.L. and Grabski, S.V. (2000). Perceived semantic expressiveness of accounting systems and task accuracy effects. International Journal of Accounting Information Systems, 1(2), 79-87.
10. Dunn, C.L. and Grabski, S.V. (2001). An investigation of localization as an element of cognitive fit in accounting model representations. Decision Science, 32(1), 55-94.
11. Fornell, C. and Larcker, D.F. (1981). Evaluating Structural Equation Models with unobservable variables and measurement error. Journal of marketing research 18(1), 39-50
12. Gemino, A and Wand, Y. (2003) Foundations for Empirical Comparisons of Conceptual Modeling Techniques. In D. Batra, J. Parsons, and E. Ramesh (eds.), Proc. of the Second Annual Symposium on Research in Systems Analysis and Design, Miami, Florida.
13. Gemino, A. and Wand, Y. (2005). Complexity and Clarity in Conceptual Modeling: Comparison of Mandatory and Optional Properties. Data and Knowledge Engineering, 55(3), 301-328.
14. Hair, J.F., Anderson R.E. and Tatham R.L. (1987). Multivariate Data Analysis, 2nd ed.
15. Hulland, John (1999). Use of Partial Least Squares (PLS) in strategic management research: A review of four recent studies. Strategic Management Journal, 20(2), 195-204.
16. Krogstie, J., Lindland, O.I., Sindre, G. (1995). Defining quality aspects for conceptual models. In E. D. Falkenberg, W. Hesse, and A. Olive (eds.), Proc. of the 3rd IFIP8.1 Working Conference on Information Systems. Marburg, Germany, 216-231.

17. Lindland, O.I., Sindre, G., Sølvberg, A. (1994). Understanding Quality in Conceptual Modeling. IEEE Software, 11(2), 42-49.
18. Moody, D.L (2001). Dealing with Complexity: A practical Method for representing Large Entity Relationship Models, Doctoral Dissertation, University of Melbourne .
19. Moody, D.L. (2005). Theoretical and Practical Issues in Evaluating the Quality of Conceptual Models: Current state and Future directions. Data and Knowledge Engineering, 55(3), 243-276.
20. Moore, G.C. and Benbasat I. (1991). Development of an Instrument to Measure the Perceptions of Adopting and Information Technology Innovation. Information Systems Research 2(3), 192-222.
21. Nelson, R. R., Todd, P. A., Wixom, B. H. (2005). Antecedents of Information and System Quality: An Empirical Examination Within the Context of Data Warehousing. Journal of Management Information Systems, 21(4), 199-235.
22. Parsons J. and Cole L. (2005). What do the pictures mean? Guidelines for the experimental evaluation of representation fidelity in diagrammatical conceptual modeling techniques. Data & Knowledge Engineering, 55(3), 327-342.
23. Poels, G., Nelson, J., Genero, M. ,Piattini, M. (2003). Quality in Conceptual Modeling. New Research Directions. Lecture Notes in Computer Science 2784, 243-250.
24. Poels, G., Maes, A., Gailly, F., Paemeleire, R., (2005). Measuring the Perceived Semantic Quality of Information Models. Lecture Notes in Computer Science, 3770, 376-385.
25. Rai, A., Lang, S.S., Welker, R.B. (2002). Assessing the validity of IS success models: An empirical test and theoretical analysis. Information Systems Research, 13(1), 50-69.
26. Seddon, P. (1997). A Respecification and Extension of the DeLone and McLean Model of IS Success. Information Systems Research, 8(3), 240-253.
27. Seddon, P. and Kiew, M.-Y.(1994). A partial test and development of the DeLone and McLean model of IS success. In J.I. DeGross, S.L. Huff, and M.C Munro (eds,). Proceedings of the International Conference on Information Systems. Atlanta. 99-110.
28. Seddon, P. and Yip, S.-K. (1992). An Empirical Evaluation of User Information Satisfaction (UIS) Measures for Use with General Ledger Accounting Software. Journal of Information Systems, 6(1), 75-92.
29. Shanks, G., Tansley, E., Weber, R. (2003). Using ontology to validate conceptual models. Communications of the ACM, 46(10), 85-89.
30. Shannon, C.E. and Weaver, W. (1949). The Mathematical theory of Communication. University of Illinois Press, Urbana.
31. Siau, K., Wand, Y., Benbasat, I. (1997). The Relative Importance of Structural Constraints and Surface Semantics in Information Modeling. Information Systems, 22(2/3), 155-170.
32. Topi, H. and Ramesh, V. (2002). Human Factors Research on Data Modeling: A Review of Prior Research, An Extended Framework and Future Research Directions. Journal of Database Management, 13(2), 3-19.

Representation Theory Versus Workflow Patterns – The Case of BPMN

Jan Recker[1], Petia Wohed[2], and Michael Rosemann[1]

[1] Queensland University of Technology
126 Margaret Street, Brisbane QLD 4000, Australia
{j.recker, m.rosemann}@qut.edu.au
[2] Stockholm University/The Royal Institute of Technology
Forum 100, 164 40 Kista, Sweden
petia@dsv.su.se

Abstract. Selecting an appropriate process modeling language forms an important task within business process management projects. A wide range of process modeling languages has been developed over the last decades, leading to an obvious need for rigorous theory to assist in the evaluation and comparison of the capabilities of these languages. While academic progress in the area of process modeling language evaluation has been made on at least two premises, Representation Theory and Workflow Patterns, it remains unclear how these frameworks relate to each other. We use a generic framework for language evaluation to establish similarities and differences between these acknowledged reference frameworks and discuss how and to what extent they complement respectively substitute each other. Our line of investigation follows the case of the popular BPMN modeling language, whose evaluation from the perspectives of Representation Theory and Workflow Patterns is reconciled in this paper.

1 Introduction

Improving and managing business processes continues to be on the top of the agenda for chief executives [1]. This strong momentum has, over time, led to the development of a wide range of solutions and approaches for Business Process Management. One prominent example in this context is the increased popularity of business process modeling [2]. Recently, "yet another" process modeling language has entered the BPM domain, the Business Process Modeling Notation (BPMN) [3]. The conformity with emerging Web Services standards, its reasonably intuitive notation and the promise of becoming an official process modeling industry standard, have boosted the popularity of BPMN. The attention that BPMN has been receiving since its first release, however, had at the time of release not been balanced by a critical analysis of its actual and perceived capabilities. Quite contrary indeed, the proliferation of arbitrary approaches to process modeling has led to a need for rigorous theory to assist in the evaluation and comparison of process modeling languages. Van der Aalst [4] points out

D.W. Embley, A. Olivé, and S. Ram (Eds.): ER 2006, LNCS 4215, pp. 68–83, 2006.

that many of the available 'standards' for process and workflow specification lack critical evaluation. Along similar lines, Moody [5] states a concern about lacking evaluation research with respect to the conceptual modeling of the dynamics of information systems. In fact, the large selection of currently available process modeling languages stands in sharp contrast to the paucity of evaluation frameworks that can be used for the task of evaluating and comparing those modeling languages. However, while there is un-fortunately not one single framework that facilitates a comprehensive analysis of all facets of a process modeling language (*e.g.*, expressive power, consistency and correctness of its meta model, perceived intuitiveness of its notation, available tool sup-port), reasonably mature research has emerged over the last decade with a focus on the representational capabilities and expressive power of modeling languages. In academia two examples, Representation Theory [6,7,8] and the Workflow Patterns Framework [9,10,11], have emerged as well-established evaluation frameworks in the field of process modeling. What remains unclear, however, is how these frameworks relate to each other. Are they complementary in their approaches and are their results comparable? What types of insights into expressive power and shortcomings of a process modeling language can be obtained from them? These and related questions can be traced back to Moody's [5] argument that a proliferation of different quality measurement proposals is counterproductive to research progress; in fact, the existence of multiple competing proposals is a sign of an immature research field. What is needed is a reconciliation and synthesis of available proposals in order to establish consensus on a common understanding of conceptual modeling quality [5, p. 258]. Taking together the ongoing proliferation of prospective standard languages for process modeling and the need for a reconciliation of quality frameworks, our paper seeks to contribute to the body of knowledge on at least two premises. First, we apply a framework for language evaluation to both Representation Theory and Workflow Patterns Framework in order to establish commonalities and differences between these two quality proposals. As a second contribution we use the example of the most recent and prominent candidate for a process modeling standard, BPMN, as a language that is evaluated by both frameworks; thereby we are able to reconcile the analyses of BPMN and give a comprehensive picture of its capabilities and shortcomings.

We proceed as follows. First we briefly introduce our selected example, BPMN, and discuss studies related to our research (section 2). We then establish a framework for language evaluation and apply it to the frameworks in question (section 3). Section 4 presents and discusses our reconciliation of the frameworks, and also gives a synthesis of the analyses of BPMN. We close in section 5 by summarizing our work and outlining future research opportunities.

2 Background and Related Work

2.1 Overview of the Process

In the remainder of this paper we will refer to previous analyses of the Business Process Modeling Notation (BPMN) as examples for our elaborations. In this section we briefly introduce BPMN in order to give the reader sufficient background for understanding our subsequent argumentations.

BPMN was developed by the Business Process Management Initiative and adopted by OMG for standardization purposes in February 2006 [3]. The development of BPMN stemmed from the demand for a graphical notation that complements the BPEL4WS standard for executable business processes. Although this gives BPMN a technical focus, it has been the intention of the BPMN designers to develop a modeling technique that can be applied for typical business modeling activities as well. The complete BPMN specification defines thirty-eight language constructs plus attributes, grouped into four basic categories of elements, *viz.*, Flow Objects, Connecting Objects, Swimlanes and Artefacts. *Flow Objects*, such as events, activities and gateways, are the most basic elements used to create Business Process Diagrams (BPDs). *Connecting Objects* are used to inter-connect Flow Objects through different types of arrows. *Swimlanes* are used to group activities into separate categories for different functional capabilities or responsibilities (*e.g.*, different roles or organizational departments). Finally, *Artefacts* may be added to a diagram where deemed appropriate in order to display further related information such as processed data or other comments. Refer to the specification [3] for further information on BPMN.

2.2 Related Work

Work related to our study can broadly be differentiated into (a) research on the evaluation of process modeling languages in general and of BPMN in particular, and (b) research on the comparison of evaluation techniques for conceptual models. We briefly recapitulate such related work in this section and will, where appropriate, refer to it in the later sections of this paper.

In the area of evaluation of process modeling languages, only little research has tried to compare process modeling languages based on an established theoretical model. The most prominent example for an evaluation framework that has deductively been derived from established theory is the Bunge-Wand-Weber (BWW) representation model [6,7,8] that forms the core of Representation Theory. The BWW representation model, which will be discussed in more detail in section 3.1 of this paper, has a strong track record in the area of process modeling, for instance in the evaluation of Petri Nets, EPCs, BPMN, ebXML and others. A comprehensive annotated overview is given in [12].

A second example of a theoretical sound quality proposal is the Workflow Patterns framework [9,10,11], which will also be considered in more detail in this paper later on. Since its establishment, the framework that has inductively been derived from observable practice in workflow management has been widely used both as a benchmark for analysis and comparison of languages. A comprehensive annotated overview is given in [13].

Besides these two established proposals it is worthwhile to mention the semiotic quality framework [14], which is a well-discussed framework for evaluating the quality of conceptual models in general. However, it has so far only sparingly been applied to the domain of process modeling [15]. Research related directly to the evaluation of BPMN is still limited due to the recency of its release. The semiotic quality framework [14] has been used to evaluate BPMN with respect to the criteria domain appropriateness, participant language knowledge appropriateness, knowledge externalizability appropriateness, comprehensibility appropriateness, and technical actor interpretation appropriateness analytically [16] and empirically [17]. Both studies conclude that BPMN particularly excels in terms of comprehensibility appropriateness due to its construct specializations and type aggregations, is overall well-suited for the domain of business process modeling but achieves rather modest results in domain appropriateness. In preparation for this study, the Workflow Patterns framework was used to evaluate BPMN [13]. The results from this evaluation show that BPMN performs well in terms of capturing the control flow and handling data in a process but is limited in expressing resources and the work distribution of activities among them. Also, in preparation for this study, was BPMN analyzed as per Representation Theory [18]. The analysis proposed, and empirically confirmed, shortcomings related to organizational modeling due to unclear specifications of the Pool and Lane constructs. Also, representational shortcomings were found, amongst others, in the specification of business rules. Both analyses will be further discussed in section 4 of this paper.

Regarding related work on comparing evaluation techniques, Siau and Rossi [19] provide a classification of evaluation approaches for modeling methods and differentiate multiple proposals into analytical and empirical approaches. They discuss analyses based on the BWW model, however, an evaluation based on workflow pat-terns does not fit into their classification scheme. We see a reason for this in the scope of Siau and Rossi's study, which focused modeling *methods* rather than modeling *languages*. Similarly, Recker [20] proposes a comparison framework that comprises the facets *model perception*, *evaluation perception* and *quality perception*, in order to assess the suitability of modeling language evaluation approaches in various research contexts. He argues that the suitability of any evaluation approach is determined by the conformity of its underlying epistemological viewpoints to the overall presuppositions of the research context.

3 Evaluating Process Modeling Languages - A Theoretical Perspective

3.1 Framework for Language Evaluation

Before we compare Representation Theory and the Workflow Patterns framework it is necessary to appreciate the theoretical analysis model that underlies research on language evaluation. The purpose of the current section is to define a framework for language evaluation under which existing approaches can be subsumed.

In order to establish this framework we draw on the generally acknowledge objective of conceptual modeling, which is to build a representation of a selected domain of interest for the purpose of understanding and communication among stakeholders in the process of requirements engineering for Information Systems analysis and design [21]. These stakeholders are confronted with the need to represent the requirements in a conceptual form, *viz.*, an underlying conceptual structure is needed on which conceptual models can be based [22]. As such underlying conceptual structures are dependant on, *inter alia*, modeling purpose and the preferences of the involved modeling participants, they cannot be equated for anyone. They merely denote potentially valid modeling references that hold true in certain but not all modeling contexts. The overall lack of such underlying conceptual structures for conceptual modeling motivated research on reference frameworks for conceptual models in given domains, against which modeling languages can be assessed as to their compliance with the framework, leading to statements about the 'goodness' of the resulting model in light of the selected framework. Fig. 1 explicates these relations.

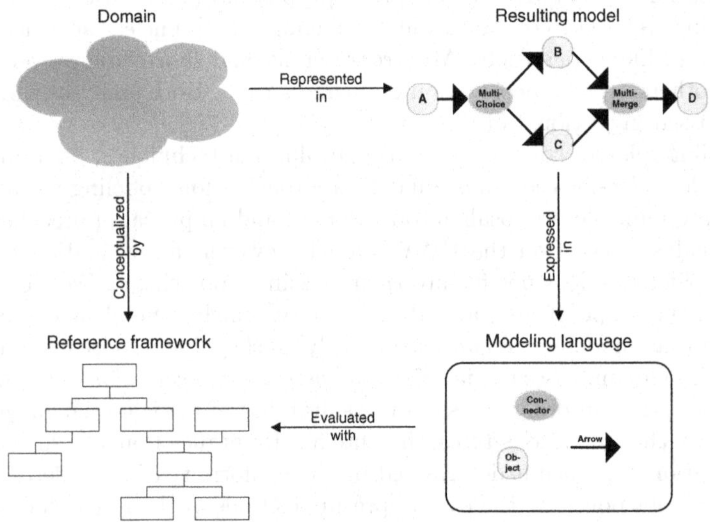

Fig. 1. Relations between domain, reference framework, modeling language and model

According to Fig. 1, a modeling reference framework, such as the BWW representation model or the Workflow Patterns framework, can be used as a heuristic specification of the domain to be modeled. As an example, the Workflow Patterns framework conceptualizes the domain of processes in form of atomic chunks of workflow semantics, differentiated in the perspectives of control flow, data and resources. In order to assess whether a given modeling language is 'good' with respect to its capability to represent relevant aspects of the domain, the reference framework serves as a theoretical benchmark in the evaluation and comparison of available modeling languages. The assumption of this type of research is that capabilities and shortcomings of a conceptual modeling language in light of the reference framework in use ultimately affect the quality of the model produced.

Taking these elaborations into account, the process of evaluating modeling languages against a reference framework consists of a pair wise bi-directional mapping between the constructs specified in the reference framework against the constructs specified in the modeling language. For example, the Workflow Patterns framework assesses which of the specified patterns can be expressed by a given language. The basic assumption is that any deviation from a 1-1 relationship between the corresponding constructs in the reference framework and the modeling language leads to situations of deficiency and/or ambiguity in the use of the language, thereby potentially diminishing the quality of the model produced.

Formally, the relationships between what can be represented (constructs of the modeling language) and what is represented (constructs of the reference framework as a heuristic for the domain being modeled) can be specified as follows (see Fig. 2)[1].

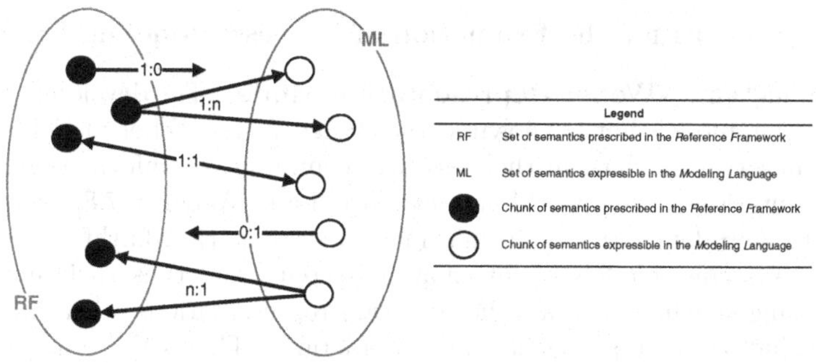

Fig. 2. Framework for language evaluation

- *Equivalence*: The construct prescribed by the reference framework can unequivocally be mapped to one and only one construct of the modeling language (1:1 mapping).
- *Deficiency*: The construct prescribed by the reference framework cannot be mapped to any construct of the modeling language (1:0 mapping).
- *Indistinguishability*: The construct prescribed by the reference framework can be mapped to more than one construct of the modeling language (1:n mapping).

[1] Note that the framework for language evaluation presented here draws on previous work in related disciplines. Weber [23], for instance uses a similar albeit not identical framework to explain the two situations of ontological completeness and clarity of a language. Guizzardi [24] argues along similar lines in the context of structural specifications. Gurr [25] uses similar mapping relations to analyze diagrammatic communication. We do not claim to supersede the works of these authors but merely build upon their works to explain in general the research type of language evaluation.

- *Equivocality*: More than one construct prescribed by the reference framework can be mapped to one and the same construct of the modeling language (n:1 mapping).
- *Overplus*: Not one construct prescribed by the reference framework can be mapped to the construct of the modeling language (0:1 mapping).

Having defined hypothetical relationships that may occur in a pair wise bi-directional mapping between a reference framework and a given modeling language we can now turn to existing frameworks in the research field of process modeling in order to investigate which of these potential constellations are covered in the respective evaluation approach. For the purpose of this study we selected the Bunge-Wand-Weber representation model, which forms the core of Representation Theory, and the Workflow Patterns framework as indications for available reference frameworks in the domain of process modeling. Subsequently, we will briefly introduce both approaches.

3.2 Frameworks for the Evaluation of Process Modeling Languages

The Bunge-Wand-Weber Representation Model. The development of the representation model that is known as the Bunge-Wand-Weber model stemmed from the observation that, in their essence, computerized information systems are representations of real world systems. Wand and Weber [6,7,8] suggest that in order to help define and build information systems that faithfully represent real world systems, models of information systems and thus their underlying modeling language must contain the necessary representations of real world constructs including their properties and interactions. The BWW representation model contains four clusters of constructs that are deemed necessary to faithfully model information systems: things including properties and types of things; states assumed by things; events and transformations occurring on things; and systems structured around things [23,12]. The BWW model defines a *theory of representation* that has been developed deductively from philosophical research, in particular an ontology defined by Bunge [26].

The BWW model allows for the evaluation of modeling languages with respect to their capabilities to provide complete and clear descriptions of the IS domain being modeled [23]. Referring to the five types of relations specified above (see Fig. 2, the completeness of a description can be measured by the degree of *construct deficit*, *i.e.*, deficiency. The clarity of a description can be measured by the degrees of *construct overload*, *i.e.*, equivocality, *construct redundancy*, *i.e.*, indistinguishability, and *construct excess*, *i.e.*, overplus. Although implicitly being measured by the extent of deficiency, we were not able to locate any previous analysis based on the BWW model that explicitly documented equivalence of a modeling language.

The Workflow Patterns Framework. The development of the Workflow Patterns framework was triggered by a bottom-up analysis and comparison of workflow management software. Provided during 2000 and 2001, this analysis included the evaluation of 15 workflow management systems, with focus being given to their underlying modeling languages. The goal was to bring insights into the expressive power of the underlying languages and hence outline similarities and differences between the analyzed systems. During the work 20 *control-flow patterns* [9] were inductively derived. These patterns in the control-flow context denote atomic chunks of behavior capturing some specific process control requirements. The identified patterns span from simple to complex control-flow scenarios and provide a taxonomy for the control-flow perspective of processes.

Recently, the Workflow Patterns framework was extended to also cover pattern constructs for the data and the resource perspectives of workflows. While the control-flow perspective focuses extensively on the ordering of the activities within a process, the data perspective focuses on the data representation and handling in process-aware information systems. The resource perspective further complements the approach with focusing on describing the various ways in which work is distributed amongst and managed by the resources associated with a business process. In 2005, a set of 43 *resource patterns* [10] and a set of 40 *data patterns* [11] were added to the framework. All control-flow, resource and data pattern constructs are grouped into various clusters.

Referring back to the five types of relations specified above (see Fig. 2, evaluations using the Workflow Patterns framework focus on the identification of potential representations within a given modeling language for each of the patterns (*i.e.*, on identification of equivalence). The non-identification of a representation for a pattern denotes a deficiency of the language. The identification of alternative representations of a pattern denotes indistinguishability. Previous analyses based on this framework have not explicitly taken into consideration the constellations of overplus and equivocality. While the performed analysis can be used to partially reveal some equivocality, it is not sufficient to identify and reason about overplus.

4 Reconciling the Evaluation Frameworks - The Case of BPMN

Based on the elaborations in section 3.1 we argue that it is possible to pair wise compare the findings obtained from analyses using Representation Theory and Workflow Patterns by using the framework for language evaluation defined in Fig. 2. In preparation for this study we analyzed BPMN against the BWW model [18] and the Workflow Patterns framework [13]. In the following we reconcile these analyses in order to extract similarities and differences in the reference frameworks. This allows us to address both objectives of this paper, *viz.*, delivering a comprehensive evaluation of the capabilities of BPMN and studying to what extent the two frameworks under observation complement respectively substitute each other.

4.1 Evaluation Frameworks Synthesis

In previous studies we have used the frameworks in questions to evaluate BPMN individually. Due to space restrictions we cannot outline the individual analyses here but refer to our previous studies described in [18] and [13]. We fitted the results of these analyses into Table 1, structured in accordance to the framework for language evaluation (see Fig. 2)[2]. Subsequently we pair wise compare the findings derived from each analysis for each of the five mapping relations.

In conducting the pair wise comparison two researchers first individually cross-evaluated the findings from each analysis, then met to defend their evaluation. A second, joint draft of the pair wise comparison was then presented to, and discussed with, a third member of the research team. By reaching a consensus over the third, joint draft of the comparison we feel that we have displayed sufficient reliability and validity of our evaluation.

Equivalence. From Table 1 it can be observed that from a Representation Theory perspective, there is not a single language construct in BPMN that is unambiguously and unequivocally specified. While this finding per se is problematic as the usage of any given construct potentially causes confusion in the interpretation of the resulting model (for empirical support for this proposition refer, for instance, to [18]), the Workflow Patterns framework shows that the atomic constructs provided in BPMN can nevertheless be arranged in a meaningful, unambiguous manner to arrange a series of control-flow, data and resource patterns. This indicates that it may not be sufficient to analyze languages solely on a construct level, but it is moreover required to assess the modeling context in which the language constructs are used to compose "chunks" of model semantics. In this regard, the Workflow Patterns framework appears to be an extension in the level of analysis of Representation Theory as it transcends the construct level by specifically taking into consideration the capability of a language to compose atomic language constructs to sets of preconceived domain semantics such as control-flow patterns.

Deficiency. Table 1 strongly suggests a lack of capability of BPMN to model state-related aspects of business processes. Both analyses reveal that BPMN is limited in modeling states assumed by things [18] and state-based patterns [13], respectively. Here, the two frameworks complement each other and together make a strong case for a potential revision and extension of the BPMN specification in order to advance its capability of modeling state-related semantics.

[2] For the Workflow Patterns-based evaluation, note that CP7, CP9 and CP17 have partial representations, *i.e.*, they present solutions that are not general enough to hold for all potential scenarios but may be used in some cases. Also note that, for the cluster equivocality, the differences between the solutions are captured though advanced attribute settings. The attribute settings can indeed be graphically captured through text annotations, however, such text annotations lie in our opinion outside the graphical notation of a language.

Table 1. Comparison of analysis results. Extracted from [13] and [18], respectively

Relation	Workflow Patterns	Representation Theory
1:1 Mapping *Equivalence*	The following Workflow Patterns can unequivocally be expressed in BPMN: *CP1, CP11-14, CP19; RP11, RP14, RP19, RP36, RP39, RP42; DP1, DP2, DP5, DP10i, DP10ii, DP11i, DP11ii, DP15-18, DP27, DP28, DP31, DP34, DP36, DP38-40*	There is no construct in the BWW model that can unequivocally be mapped to a single BPMN construct.
1:0 Mapping *Deficiency*	The are no representations in BPMN for the following Workflow Patterns: *CP7, CP9, CP15, CP17, CP18; RP3-10, RP12, RP13, RP15-18, RP20-35, RP37, RP38, RP40, RP41, RP43; DP3, DP4, DP6, DP7, DP8, DP12-14, DP19-26, DP29, DP30, DP32, DP33, DP35, DP37*	There are no representations in BPMN for the following BWW constructs: *State, Stable State, Unstable State, Conceivable State Space, State Law, Lawful State Space, Conceivable Event Space, Lawful Event Space, History, Property (in particular, hereditary, emergent, intrinsic, mutual: non-binding, mutual: binding, attributes).*
1:n Mapping *Indistinguishability*	The following Workflow Patterns have multiple representations in BPMN: *CP2-6, CP10, CP16, CP20; RP1, RP2; DP9*	The following BWW constructs have multiple representations in BPMN: *Thing, Property (in general), Class, Event, External Event, Internal Event, Well-defined Event, Poorly-defined Event, Transformation, Lawful Transformation (including Stability Condition, Corrective Action), Acts On, Coupling, System, System Decomposition, System Composition, System Environment, Subsystem, Level Structure.*
n:1 Mapping *Equivocality*	The following Workflow Patterns have the same graphical representations in BPMN: *CP4 and CP6; CP9, CP12, CP13 and CP14*	The following BPMN constructs represent many BWW constructs: *Lane (Thing, Class, Kind, System, System Decomposition, System Composition, System Environment, Subsystem, Level Structure); Pool (Thing, Class, System, System Decomposition, System Composition, System Environment, Subsystem, Level Structure); Message Flow (Acts On, Coupling); Start Event (Internal Event, External Event); Intermediate Event (Internal Event, External Event); End Event (Internal Event, External Event); Error (Internal Event, External Event); Cancel (Internal Event, External Event); Compensation (Internal Event, External Event);*
0:1 Mapping *Overplus*	Workflow Patterns analysis does not lead to statements about a possible overplus of patterns, which a language may be able to represent but which are not included in the framework.	The following BPMN constructs do not map to any BWW construct: *Link, Off-Page Connector, Gateway Types, Association Flow, Text Annotation, Group, Activity, Looping, Multiple Instances, Normal Flow, Event (super type), Gateway (super type)*

Another interesting deficiency of BPMN is the lack of means to describe some of the data patterns. In particular, data interaction to and from multiple instances tasks (DP12 and DP13) cannot comprehensively be described, which is mostly credited to a lack of attributes in the specification of the language constructs. This finding aligns with the BWW-based finding that BPMN lacks mechanisms to describe properties, especially property types that *emerge* or are *mutual* due to couplings of things, or those that characterize a component thing of a composite thing (*hereditary*).

Furthermore, the Workflow Pattern analysis reveals deficiency in BPMN's support for the majority of the resource patterns. This finding can also be supported by the BWW-based analysis that found that the constructs in BPMN dedicated to modeling an organizational perspective, *viz.*, Lane and Pool, are considerably unclear in their specification (see next paragraph). Hence it appears that a language specification containing unclear definitions on a construct level lead to deficiencies in composing these constructs to meaningful sets of constructs.

Indistinguishability. The Workflow Pattern-based evaluation reveals that while BPMN is capable of expressing all basic control-flow patterns (CP1-5), it contains multiple representations for them, thereby potentially causing confusion as to which representation for a pattern is most appropriate in a given scenario. This aligns with the finding in [18] that BPMN contains a reasonably high degree of construct overload. Especially, in terms of modeling essential concepts of process modeling, such as things, events and transformation, it appears that BPMN is considerably overloaded. This complements the finding that the modeling of the most basic workflow patterns is doubled and thereby unnecessarily complex.

The BWW-based analysis furthermore reveals that the Lane and Pool constructs are extensively overloaded, allowing for representation of various domain aspects (in the case of the Lane construct for example things, classes of things, systems, kinds of things etc.). This complements the statement from the analysis in [13] that the resource patterns RP1 and RP2 use the same graphical notation, relying mostly on Lanes and Pools, for representing two different patterns.

Equivocality. The notion of equivocality reveals an interesting facet in the comparison of the two reference frameworks. The findings from the two frameworks do not seem to match with each other. As an example, the control flow patterns 9, 12, 13 and 14 were found to use the same graphical notation, with the differences between the solutions for these patterns only readable from the attribute settings. These solutions rely on the Multiple Instances construct, which the BWW-based analysis classified as overplus. On the other hand, the BWW-based analysis proposes that the different event types in BPMN are redundant. This finding, however, is not supported by the Workflow Pattern-based analysis. It is interesting to note that our own empirical findings related to the BWW-based analysis have, in fact, led to the conclusion that BPMN's differentiation of event constructs has been perceived as very helpful for modeling by BPMN users [18].

Overplus. The perspective of language overplus denotes yet another interesting comparison aspect. It proposes that the Workflow Patterns framework can be used as a means of reasoning for explaining why a particular language contains some constructs that, from a Representation Theory perspective, seem to be unnecessary for capturing domain semantics. In particular, throughout the whole process modeling domain, control flow mechanisms such as logical connectors, selectors, gateways and the like are repeatedly proposed as overplus as they do not map to any construct of the BWW model [12]. However, the Workflow Patterns framework suggests that these constructs nevertheless are central to modeling control-flow, based on the understanding that these mechanisms essentially support the notion of being "in between" states or activities [9].

It must be stated that the Workflow Patterns framework so far has not been used to identify potential overplus of workflow patterns that may be supported in a given language. However, in principle it is possible to apply overplus analysis to the framework for a limited number of language construct involved in a model chunk. It may even be worthwhile investigating how language constructs that the BWW representation model considers as overplus may, in composition, constitute patterns of workflows that have not yet been identified. In this regard the BWW analysis appears to extend the scope of the Workflow Patterns analysis.

4.2 Synopsis

While in the previous section we used the case of BPMN to discuss the complementary and/or substitutive nature of the two reference frameworks under observation, in this section we seek to establish similarities and differences between statements derivable from the analyses of process modeling languages based on different reference framework in a more general fashion.

Fig. 3 presents a simple set model that illustrates potential relationships between two reference frameworks (Representation Theory *BWW* and Workflow Patterns *WP*) and the modeling language under observation (*BPMN*)[3]. Note that in the following we will abstract from the specific relationship types (1:1, 1:0, 0:1, 1:m, m:1) that may occur in a mapping.

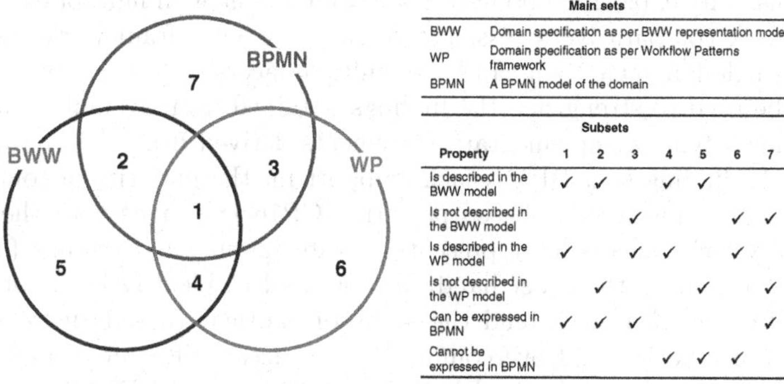

Main sets	
BWW	Domain specification as per BWW representation model
WP	Domain specification as per Workflow Patterns framework
BPMN	A BPMN model of the domain

Property	Subsets 1	2	3	4	5	6	7
Is described in the BWW model	✓	✓		✓	✓		
Is not described in the BWW model			✓			✓	✓
Is described in the WP model	✓		✓	✓		✓	
Is not described in the WP model		✓			✓		✓
Can be expressed in BPMN	✓	✓	✓				✓
Cannot be expressed in BPMN				✓	✓	✓	

Fig. 3. Set model showing relationships between reference frameworks and modeling language

From Fig. 3 it can be observed that seven hypothetical constellations may in principle occur.

- A set of constructs is provided by both of the reference frameworks and it is found that the modeling language is able to express this set of constructs (subset 1).

[3] We use these indications merely to illustrate our point. The approach itself is in principle applicable to any given combination of two (or even more) reference frameworks and a modeling language.

- A set of constructs is provided by only one of the reference frameworks and it is found that the modeling language is able to express this set of constructs (subsets 2 and 3, respectively).
- A set of constructs is provided by both of the reference frameworks and it is found that the modeling language is not able to express this set of constructs (subset 4).
- A set of constructs is provided by only one of the reference frameworks and it is found that the modeling language is not able to express this set of constructs (subsets 5 and 6, respectively).
- A set of constructs is not provided by any of the reference frameworks but it is found that the modeling language is able to express this set of constructs (subset 7).

Besides the fact that the set model given in Fig. 3 allows for the specification of a ranking of constellations that may occur in the evaluation of modeling languages (*e.g.*, a mapping to subset 1 is of higher relevance than a mapping to subset 3), it also allows us to conclude about the comparison and assessment of modeling languages and reference frameworks in general. As shown, language evaluation by means of reference frameworks has two facets. On the one side, reference frameworks provide a filtering lens that facilitates insights into potential issues with a modeling language. On the other side, any evaluation is restricted to that lens, only exploring potential issues of a language in light of the selected framework. A comparative assessment of such reference frameworks using the case of a single language then can have multiple facets.

It can be used to strengthen the findings obtained from an individual evaluation by identifying complementary statements derived from the analyses. For instance, the finding that BPMN lacks support for the majority of control-flow patterns in the cluster state-based patterns (CP16-18) aligns with the finding that BPMN lacks means for representing states assumed by things (subset 1 in Fig. 3). It can, on the other hand, also be used to identify facets of a given reference framework that extend the scope of another, thereby increasing the focus of an evaluation and overcoming the restricting filter of a single framework. As an example, while the BWW-based evaluation of BPMN shows that BPMN does not contain a single construct that is unambiguously equivalent to any construct of the BWW model, the Workflow Patterns-based analysis reveals that the (potentially ambiguous) atomic BPMN constructs can be arranged to a set of constructs that, as a set, unequivocally equals a number of workflow patterns (subset 3 in Fig. 3). Or, the BWW-based evaluation classifies BPMN connector types as an overplus unnecessary to model IS domains. The Workflow Patterns-based analysis on the other hand suggests that the connector types are in fact essential for the description of control-flow convergence and divergence. However, as subset 7 in Fig. 3 indicates, there may be aspects of a modeling language that are not found to map to any aspect of any of the reference framework used. This scenario can lead to two findings. On first sight, such aspects of a modeling language may in fact unnecessary, ambiguous and/or potentially confusing for modeling the given domain and their usage should therefore be avoided or at least better specified. On the other hand, such a finding may also contribute to the further development of the selected theoretical bases as it indicates that the reference frameworks in use potentially lack relevance or scope for the given domain and thus should be refined or extended. For instance, in an earlier study we discussed the potential lack of relevance of the BWW model for the domain of process modeling [12]. In the case of the Workflow Patterns framework it can by no means be guaranteed that the identified set of patterns is complete.

This brief discussion indicates a need for researchers to carefully observe and scrutinize the findings they derive from their evaluations with respect to the extent to which their findings are rooted in an actual shortcoming of the artifact being evaluated or in a limitation of the selected theoretical reference framework(s) used for the evaluation.

5 Contributions and Future Research

This paper presented the first comprehensive study that compares evaluation frameworks for process modeling languages based on an analysis of the principles of language evaluation.

We do not consider this research complete. In particular, we look to further extend our assessment of evaluation frameworks to incorporate other levels of analysis such as the ones identified in [20]. In particular, we seek to use the principles of presupposition analysis in order to establish differences between evaluation approaches that are imposed by underlying paradigms, for instance in terms of methodology (inductive vs. deductive) or epistemology (constructionist vs. realist). Also, we seek to further populate our set model given in Fig.řeffigthree by comparatively assessing the findings from the evaluations of other process modeling languages such as BPEL4WS (evaluated in [27] and [28], respectively).

In spite of some limitations of our study, *e.g.*, we have not obtained an empirical perspective towards our evaluation and we have not fully taken into consideration the differences in terms of analysis granularity (atomic notation elements versus compositions of notation elements), we see first evidence for the usefulness of our approach. Our research hopefully motivates practitioners and researchers to converge (rather than diverge) their use of theoretical bases for process modeling. A combination of the principles of both Representation Theory (for the specification of the language constructs) and the Workflow Patterns framework (for the specification of the relationships of language constructs to form meaningful composites) may ultimately lead to the design of process modeling languages that not only provide complete and clear descriptions of real-world domains but also provide sophisticated support for advanced workflow concepts.

We further see potential of generalizing our research to related domains. While our comparative assessment was restricted to process modeling languages and reference frameworks for process modeling languages, we spent considerable effort on defining a generic analysis level that allows for wider uptake. For instance, our research might motivate other researchers to conduct a similar study on reference frameworks for data or object-oriented modeling languages.

Acknowledgement. The authors would like to express their gratitude towards the fruitful contributions of Marta Indulska and Peter Green from the University of Queensland to the evaluation of BPMN by means of Representation Theory.

References

1. Group, G.: Delivering ITs Contribution: The 2005 CIO Agenda. Gartner EXP Premier Reports January2005, Gartner, Inc (2005)
2. Davies, I., Green, P., Rosemann, M., Indulska, M., Gallo, S.: How do Practitioners Use Conceptual Modeling in Practice? Data & Knowledge Engineering **58** (2006) 358–380
3. BPMI.org, OMG: Business Process Modeling Notation Specification. Final Adopted Specification (2006)
4. van der Aalst, W.M.P.: Don't Go with the Flow: Web Services Composition Standards Exposed. IEEE Intelligent Systems **18** (2003) 72–76
5. Moody, D.L.: Theoretical and Practical Issues in Evaluating the Quality of Conceptual Models: Current State and Future Directions. Data & Knowledge Engineering **15** (2005) 243–276
6. Wand, Y., Weber, R.: An Ontological Model of an Information System. IEEE Transactions on Software Engineering **16** (1990) 1282–1292
7. Wand, Y., Weber, R.: On the Ontological Expressiveness of Information Systems Analysis and Design Grammars. Journal of Information Systems **3** (1993) 217–237
8. Wand, Y., Weber, R.: On the Deep Structure of Information Systems. Information Systems Journal **5** (1995) 203–223
9. van der Aalst, W.M.P., ter Hofstede, A.H.M., Kiepuszewski, B., Barros, A.P.: Workflow Patterns. Distributed and Parallel Databases **14** (2003) 5–51
10. Russell, N., van der Aalst, W.M.P., ter Hofstede, A.H.M., Edmond, D.: Workflow Resource Patterns: Identification, Representation and Tool Support. In Pastor, O., Falcao e Cunha, J., eds.: Advanced Information Systems Engineering - CAiSE 2005. Volume 3520 of Lecture Notes in Computer Science. Springer, Porto, Portugal (2005) 216–232
11. Russell, N., ter Hofstede, A.H.M., Edmond, D., van der Aalst, W.M.P.: Workflow Data Patterns: Identification, Representation and Tool Support. In Delcambre, L.M.L., Kop, C., Mayr, H.C., Mylopoulos, J., Pastor, O., eds.: Conceptual Modeling - ER 2005. Volume 3716 of Lecture Notes in Computer Science. Springer, Klagenfurt, Austria (2005) 353–368
12. Rosemann, M., Recker, J., Indulska, M., Green, P.: A Study of the Evolution of the Representational Capabilities of Process Modeling Grammars. In Dubois, E., Pohl, K., eds.: Advanced Information Systems Engineering - CAiSE 2006. Volume 4001 of Lecture Notes in Computer Science. Springer, Luxembourg, Grand-Duchy of Luxembourg (2006) 447–461
13. Wohed, P., van der Aalst, W.M.P., Dumas, M., ter Hofstede, A.H.M., Russell, N.: On the Suitability of BPMN for Business Process Modelling. In: 4th International Conference on Business Process Management, Vienna, Austria, Springer (2006) forthcoming

14. Lindland, O.I., Sindre, G., Sølvberg, A.: Understanding Quality in Conceptual Modeling. IEEE Software **11** (1994) 42–49
15. Krogstie, J., Sindre, G., Jørgensen, H.D.: Process Models Representing Knowledge for Action: a Revised Quality Framework. European Journal of Information Systems **15** (2006) 91–102
16. Wahl, T., Sindre, G.: An Analytical Evaluation of BPMN Using a Semiotic Quality Framework. In Castro, J., Teniente, E., eds.: CAiSE'05 Workshops. Volume 1. FEUP, Porto, Portugal (2005) 533–544
17. Nysetvold, A.G., Krogstie, J.: Assessing Business Process Modeling Languages Using a Generic Quality Framework. In Castro, J., Teniente, E., eds.: CAiSE'05 Workshops. Volume 1. FEUP, Porto (2005) 545–556
18. Recker, J., Indulska, M., Rosemann, M., Green, P.: How Good is BPMN Really? Insights from Theory and Practice. In Ljungberg, J., Andersson, M., eds.: 14th European Conference on Information Systems, Goeteborg, Sweden (2006)
19. Siau, K., Rossi, M.: Evaluation of Information Modeling Methods – A Review. In Dolk, D., ed.: 31st Hawaii International Conference on System Sciences, Big Island, Hawaii, Computer Society Press (1998) 314–322
20. Recker, J.: Evaluation of Conceptual Modeling Languages. An Epistemological Discussion. In Romano, N.C., ed.: 11th Americas Conference on Information Systems, Omaha, Nebraska, Association for Information Systems (2005) 329–337
21. Siau, K.: Informational and Computational Equivalence in Comparing Information Modeling Methods. Journal of Database Management **15** (2004) 73–86
22. Floyd, C.: A Comparative Evaluation of System Development Methods. In Olle, T.W., Sol, H.G., Verrijn-Stuart, A.A., eds.: Information System Design Methodologies: Improving the Practice. North-Holland, Amsterdam, The Netherlands (1986) 19–54
23. Weber, R.: Ontological Foundations of Information Systems. Coopers & Lybrand and the Accounting Association of Australia and New Zealand, Melbourne, Australia (1997)
24. Guizzardi, G.: Ontological Foundations for Structural Conceptual Models. Volume 015 of Telematica Instituut Fundamental Research Series. Telematica Instituut, Enschede, The Netherlands (2005)
25. Gurr, C.A.: Effective Diagrammatic Communication: Syntactic, Semantic and Pragmatic Issues. Journal of Visual Languages and Computing **10** (1999) 317–342
26. Bunge, M.A.: Treatise on Basic Philosophy Volume 3: Ontology I - The Furniture of the World. Kluwer Academic Publishers, Dordrecht, The Netherlands (1977)
27. Green, P., Rosemann, M., Indulska, M., Manning, C.: Candidate Interoperability Standards: An Ontological Overlap Analysis. Technical report, University of Queensland (2004)
28. Wohed, P., van der Aalst, W.M.P., Dumas, M., ter Hofstede, A.H.M.: Analysis of Web Services Composition Languages: The Case of BPEL4WS. In Song, I.Y., Liddle, S.W., Ling, T.W., Scheuermann, P., eds.: Conceptual Modeling - ER 2003. Volume 2813 of Lecture Notes in Computer Science. Springer, Chicago, Illinois (2003) 200–215

Use Case Modeling and Refinement: A Quality-Based Approach

Samira Si-said Cherfi[1], Jacky Akoka[2], and Isabelle Comyn-Wattiau[3]

[1] CEDRIC-CNAM, 292 Rue Saint Martin, F-75141 Paris Cedex 03
[2] CEDRIC-CNAM and INT
[3] CEDRIC-CNAM and ESSEC
sisaid@cnam.fr, akoka@cnam.fr, wattiau@cnam.fr

Abstract. In this paper, we propose a quality-based use case refinement approach. It consists of a step by step refinement process that combines quality metrics with use case transformation rules. We propose several quality metrics, based on complexity concepts, aimed at measuring the complexity of use cases. Starting from an initial use case, we apply successively a set of transformation rules and measure the resulting use case based on the quality metrics. Our approach is embedded in a general framework allowing us to guide software designers by the mean of quality metrics.

Keywords: use case modelling, modularization, complexity, quality criteria.

1 Introduction

The principle of non-separation-of-concerns asserts that software development should not be decomposed in such a way that the quality "concern" is solved as a separate process from the design and development process. We believe that associating quality concerns with design aspects could play an important role in the successful implementation of the system. In this paper, we propose a quality-based approach for use case design and refinement. We present an extension to UML use case meta-model incorporating quality criteria. The refinement process is based on quality measurements using a set of decomposition and restructuring rules applied to the initial use case diagram as well as a set of quality metrics. This refinement process, based on guidelines principles, can be partially automated.

This paper is structured as follows. Section 2 gives an overview of quality measurements in information systems. Section 3 describes our quality driven approach. It gives guidelines for the systematic refinement of use case diagrams. Section 4 is devoted to the definition of quality metrics derived from entropy and cohesion concepts. In Section 5, we define and motivate the decomposition and restructuring rules proposed to the designer in order to improve the use case quality values. The illustration of our approach on an example is described in Section 6. Finally, the last section presents some concluding remarks and an overview of future work.

D.W. Embley, A. Olivé, and S. Ram (Eds.): ER 2006, LNCS 4215, pp. 84–97, 2006.

2 A Brief State of the Art

Quality assessment aims at three different objectives leading to three main streams: 1) Helping in predicting effort in software projects, 2) Estimating maintenance effort and guiding design choices in order to decrease maintenance cost, 3) Evaluating design components such as UML class diagrams, UML use cases, etc. in order to provide the designer with quality indicators.

In the first stream, cost models are defined to help in predicting human resources and time needed for a software project. COCOMO and Function Point (FP) Analysis are the most popular effort prediction models. In the context of object-oriented (OO) systems, specific cost models such as Class Point have been defined. This FP-like approach, based on the number of external methods and the number of services requested, defines the complexity level of a class, hence allowing the project manager to estimate the initial size estimation [1]. In [2] authors have experimented common cost modeling techniques on a large set of projects in order to evaluate the generalizability of these techniques. They conclude that ordinary least-squares regression is sufficient to help predicting development effort. The Use Case Point approach is a FP-like approach based on use case analysis to predict effort [3].

In the second stream, quality measures are used to estimate maintenance costs. They can be used to choose between different design alternatives. For example, several coupling criteria were proposed to predict fault-proneness. Intuitively, the more objects and/or classes are coupled, the more maintenance will be necessary. A large survey was conducted in [4] in order to compare different coupling measures. Large empirical studies have been conducted in order to assess the predictive properties of these measures. However, their conclusions are not easy to interpret due to the quality attributes definition. Arisholm et al. [5] go beyond these coupling measures by defining and assessing dynamic coupling metrics. They argue that static coupling measurement is not adequate since it does not take into account polymorphism and dynamic binding. They suggest to predict this coupling using interaction diagrams. Entropy is another criterion used for estimating maintenance effort. Based on the principle that systems which undergo frequent change tend toward disorder, entropy is a measure of disorder used in all branches of science. Several papers define metrics based on the entropy concept and experiment it in the OO context [6]. [7] defines quantitative subclassing criteria and an algorithm allowing the designer to minimize the entropy by a correct subclassing. Dependencies are a generic concept for OO design quality metrics proposed in [8]. Dependencies between parts of design are not desired since each single change has heavy impact.

In the third stream, numerous approaches deal with quality based design and development. They define quality criteria relevant to conceptual schema evaluation. Authors in [9] have presented a set of automatically computed metrics for evaluating ER diagram complexity. We have defined a framework allowing the designer to choose between several UML diagrams based on quality criteria. These criteria are automatically computed and inserted in a CASE tool [10].

In each stream, many metrics have been defined. A survey of OO metrics can be found in [11]. Baig [12] compares cohesion and coupling metrics. His experiments conclude that not all cohesion and coupling measures are correlated. Quality criteria are also applied to requirements engineering [13]. To the best of our knowledge, no previous approach deals with use case quality measurement aiming at improving design. Let us mention [14] which compares use case diagrams to deal with non-functional requirements. Authors in [15] have developed a method and a tool for refactoring use case models. However, no quality measure is mentioned. The rest of this paper is devoted to the description of a quality based approach for use case design and refinement.

3 A Quality Based Approach for Use Case Refinement

Software metrics are used to assess several software quality attributes (complexity, coupling, cohesion etc.). They provide designers with assistance during the development process. In this section, we describe an approach where quality measurement is used as a mean to assess and improve use case models during the development process. The improvement is quality-directed and is performed by a set of decomposing and restructuring rules in order to increase use case modularity.

3.1 A Use Case Meta-Model

This section describes a UML use case meta-model, derived from CWM [16], and adapted in order to meet our requirements. UML suggests describing use case content using textual expression. The organization of this content could be guided using templates. However, our approach requires a more formal and structured use case definition. Hence, the textual form is not convenient. Many authors proposed extensions to the use case semantics to make it more precise. [17] identifies four dimensions to use case descriptions: *purpose, content, plurality,* and *structure*. Each of these dimensions has an enumerated domain value. Amyot et al. [18] proposed an extension of the UML with UCM (Use Case Maps [19]) semantics for reactive systems modeling. Regnell et al. [20] proposed a use case extension for requirements engineering and Rui et al. [21] proposed an adaptation of this meta-model for use case refactoring. In order to meet robustness properties, our approach requires formally structured use cases. Therefore, we propose the following use case meta-model extension as a mean to provide a precise vocabulary. We use the CWM UML meta-model as a starting point. We do not redefine concepts but we enrich the meta-model with new concepts. Fig.1 presents our extended use case meta-model. Grey boxes represent the new concepts added to the CWM proposal. A use case has three components, namely a structure, a behavior and a quality value: **i) A structure** describes the static content of a use case. It is composed of a set of action descriptions locally defined within the use case and a set of relationships (extend and include relationships). An action has a name and a textual description. The latter defines the goal to be achieved by the action execution. **ii) A behavior** describes the dynamics of the use case. It is composed of a set of scenarios. A scenario is a sequence of use case actions performed to yield an observable result. It is defined as a use case instance. **iii) A quality value** is a value resulting from the computation of quality metrics applied to use case structure and behavior characteristics. The quality metrics are not part of the UML meta-model extension. They are presented in Section 3.2. Due to space limitations, the formal meta-model on which our approach relies is not described.

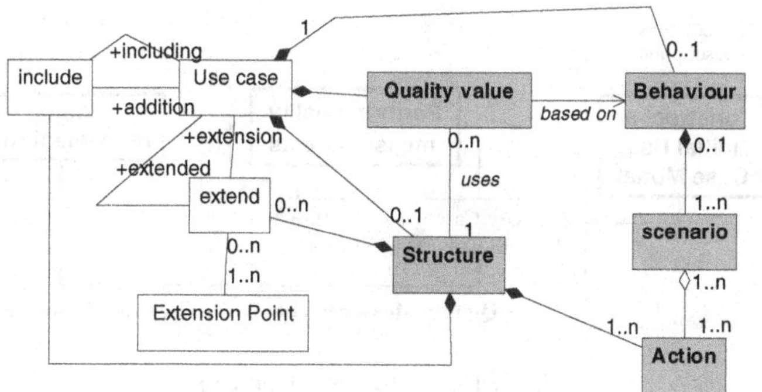

Fig. 1. Extension of the UML use case meta-model

3.2 The Quality-Based Approach

Our approach is based on an incremental process performing use case diagrams improvement. It is composed of a set of refinement actions that are successively and iteratively executed (Fig 2). The central concept underlying the refinement process is the modularity applied to the use case construct. Modularity respects the separation-of-concerns principle. According to this principle, software should be decomposed in such a way that different "concerns" of the problem are solved in well-separated modules or parts of the software. Indeed, modular systems 1) are easier to maintain as changes are likely to be applied to limited sub systems and not to propagate through the rest of the system, 2) are easier to upgrade by adding or replacing modules without affecting deeply the other parts, 3) are more reliable since easier to validate by testing parts of systems and not entire systems, 4) could be implemented incrementally and even implemented through reusable components. As use case modeling is widely adopted as a starting point in object-oriented projects, we believe that their modularity impacts heavily the modularity of the final system.

The input of the refinement process is an initial use case diagram elaborated by the designer. The improvement process is designer directed: the approach is presented as a set of decomposition and restructuring rules and a set of quality measurement metrics, available to the designer. The approach provides him/her with the quality measurements determining whether the transformation improves or not the quality of the use case model specification. He/she can further decide whether he/she applies the transformation. We have adopted this loose guidance since we believe that absolute quality values have no readable semantics. The computed quality value is useful only if the designer can compare it with other quality values in similar contexts. Therefore, we recommend to iteratively and alternatively apply "quality measurement" and "use case refinement" activities. In the two following sections, we describe the quality measurement and the use case refinement activities. In this paper we concentrate on two quality metrics, namely entropy and lack of cohesion described below.

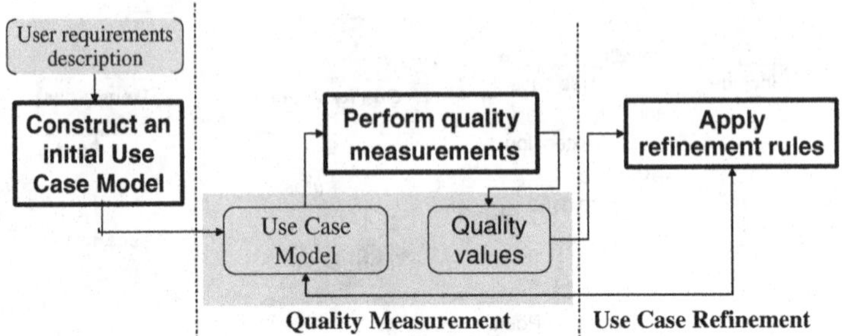

Fig. 2. The quality-driven process

4 Use Case Quality Metrics

We define below a set of metrics for use case quality assessment and improvement. Our contribution is twofold. First, we provide a formal definition of the metrics thus facilitating their evaluation. Second, we link them to quality criteria that support use case improvement. The objective of our use case refinement is to decrease their complexity and consequently decrease the complexity of the whole system. We believe that decreasing complexity improves systems quality. The concept of modularity is defined by G. Booch as "the property of a system that has been decomposed into a set of cohesive and loosely coupled modules". He argued that complex systems constructed from scratch never work. Hence, lack of modularity leads to more complexity. Our guidance approach for use case refinement approach is based on complexity measurement [22, 23, 3]. Complexity measurement is a relevant technique for use case quality evaluation since it provides information on the effort needed to understand, specify and implement a use case. Based on the literature, we have selected and analyzed OO metrics dealing with complexity and we have adapted the two more relevant ones in our context. They are based respectively on entropy and cohesion concepts.

4.1 Use Case Entropy Metric

In this section, we define and apply an entropy-based metric.

4.1.1 Entropy Measurement

The concept of entropy has first been introduced in information theory by Shannon [24]. A measure of the information contained in an outcome is given by:

$$I(x_i) = -\log_2(p\{x_i\})$$

Where p{x_i} is the probability of x_i. The entropy of an information source X with an alphabet A={x_1, x_2,.., x_n} and probability distribution P_x={p_1, p_2,.., p_n } is defined as:

$$H(x_i) = -\sum_{i=1}^{n} p_i \log_2(p_i)$$

This means that the entropy of an information source grows with the uncertainty of the source outcome. Within the context of object-oriented systems analysis and design, entropy has been adopted as a measure of complexity [25]. Harisson proposed to compute code entropy in procedural programs using empirical distribution of operators (reserved words, function calls, etc.). Bansiya et al. [26] propose to use "name strings" (user defined names for classes, data declarations, methods and parameters in class definitions) as information source in the measure of class entropy at a design level. They define a Class Design Entropy (CDE) metric as follows:

$$CDE = -\sum_{1}^{n1} (f_i / N_1) \log_2 (f_i / N_1)$$

Where n1 is the number of unique string names, N1 is the total number of non-unique string names, and f_i the frequency of occurrence of the ith string name.

4.1.2 Definition of Use Case Entropy Metric

As our concern is use case modularization throughout their restructuring, we are interested in use case complexity. Hence, we propose a use case entropy metric.

Let <UC, A, S> be a use case definition, where UC is a use case name, A= $\{a_1, a_2,.., a_n\}$ a set of actions describing the structure of the use case and S=$\{ s_1, s_2,.., s_m\}$ a set of scenarios describing the instances of UC. As the overall use case behavior is described by its related scenarios, and as scenarios are defined upon use case actions, the amount of information conveyed by each action a_i grows when the probability of using this action grows i.e. its occurrence within use case scenarios. According to the entropy theory, the amount of information I_i contained in a_i with an occurrence probability p_i is:

$$I(a_i) = -\log_2 (p_i)$$

We define the probability p_i of an action a_i as its frequency within use case scenarios. It is defined as follows:

$$p_i = n_i / N$$

where n_i is the number of a_i occurrences and N the total number of use case actions occurrences.

[25] proved that information is additive. Thus information contained in two actions is the sum of information held individually by each action. Therefore the entropy of a use case is defined as the average value of information held by each of its actions:

$$UC\_E = -\sum_{i=1}^{n} (p_i \log_2 p_i)$$

where n is the number of actions within a use case.

Note that when n increases, entropy increases. This implies that a larger number of actions describing a use case makes it more complex. Note also that our objective is to use the entropy measures in order to compare two versions of the same use case specification within the iterative refinement process.

To illustrate this metric, let us consider a use case representing the "withdraw cash" problem for the ATM system cash dispenser (Table 1).

Table 1. Example of use case description

Action \ scenario	S1	S2	S3	S4	S5	S6
a1: Card validation	X	X	X	X	X	X
a2: Code validation	X	X	X	X		X
a3: Amount validation	X	X	X	X		
a4: Eject card	X	X	X	X	X	
a5: Dispense cash	X	X	X			
a6: Print receipt	X					
a7: Disclaim cash			X			
a8: Disclaim card				X		X

Table 1 expresses the six following cash withdrawal scenarios:

- S1:withdraw cash with receipt,
- S2:withdraw cash without receipt,
- S3:cash not taken after a few seconds,
- S4:card not taken after a few seconds,
- S5:card is not valid,
- S6:code validation failed

The amount of information conveyed by action a1 = 6/27 as it occurs 6 times and the sum of all actions occurrences is 27. As a consequence, the value of entropy for the whole "withdraw cash" use case is **2.77**

4.2 Lack of Cohesion Measurement

We define below the cohesion concept and its application in the refinement process.

4.2.1 Lack of Cohesion Concept

Cohesion is defined as an attribute characterizing modules and describing the extent to which the individual module components are needed to perform the same task [27]. Thus the cohesion of a component is high if it implements a single logical function. In order to obtain an inverse measure of cohesion, [28] define the concept of Lack of Cohesion in Methods (LCOM). This metric is based on sharing of instance variables. It is defined as the number of pairs of methods in the class using no instance variables in common. Several versions of this metrics have been defined in the literature. [29] proposed another version:

$$LCOM^* = \left(\frac{1}{a}\sum_{j=1}^{n}\mu(A_j)\right) - m \Big/ (1-m)$$

where n is the number of attributes, a is the number of instance variables, m is the number of methods, $\mu(A_j)$ is the measure which yields 0 if each method in the class references all attributes, and 1 if each method in a class references only one single attribute. A class is said to be the most cohesive (LCOM*=1, i.e. LCOM* is minimal) when all of its methods use all of its attributes.

4.2.2 Definition of Use Case Lack of Cohesion Metric

As an adaptation of Henderson-Sellers's LCOM metric, let us consider a use case UC as a module with a set of variables constituted by its associated actions A= $\{a_1, a_2,.., a_n\}$, and S=$\{s_1, s_2,.., s_m\}$ a set of scenarios describing the instances of UC. Intuitively, the cohesion of a use case reflects the degree of cohesion between the functionalities that the use case supports. If we apply the μ function as it is defined at the class level by Henderson-Sellers, we consider that for a given action a_i, μ(ai) = 1 if ai is required for all scenarios and 0 otherwise. However, this is too restrictive for use cases since we should accept use case definitions with alternate and exception courses. For this reason we redefine the μ function as follows.

μ(ai,sj) holds 1 if the scenario sj requires action ai, and 0 otherwise.

In this case, the lack of cohesion of a given scenario is defined as:

$$\mu(ai,sj) = 1 \text{ if } m = 1 \text{ and } \mu(ai,sj) = \left(\frac{1}{n}\sum_{i=1}^{n}\mu(ai,sj)\right) - m \Big/ (1-m) \quad \text{if } m \neq 1$$

The Use Case Lack of Cohesion (UC_LC) metric is then defined as the average value of the Lack of Cohesion of all the scenarios:

if m=1 then UC_LC=1; else $UC\_LC = \left(\frac{1}{n}\sum_{i=1}^{n}\left(\sum_{j=1}^{m}\mu(a_i, s_j) \Big/ m\right)\right) - m \Big/ (1-m)$

where a_i is an action, s_j is a scenario, m is the number of scenarios and n the number of actions. Note that if all scenarios require all actions, UC_LC equals 1 and thus respects the definition given by LCOM*. If we consider the example given in Table 1, the value of UC_LC is **1.09.** Based on the entropy and the lack of cohesion metrics defined on use cases, our approach allows the designer to refine use cases using the decomposition and restructuring rules described below.

5 Use Case Refinement

Use case refinement activity is based on a set of predefined decomposition and restructuring rules that the designer can apply to a use case model. The objective is to decrease use case model complexity. Object oriented approaches propose three principles to deal with complexity: decomposition, abstraction and hierarchy:

- Our approach provides the designer with a set of restructuring rules that decompose use cases into smaller and more cohesive ones.
- We rely on our definition of use case entropy which promotes use cases having a tight correlation with user requirements to construct the right abstraction.
- We propose some rules to organize use cases into hierarchies.

We present below our refinement rules. The refinement process encompasses two major phases namely use case decomposition and use case restructuring.

5.1 Use Case Decomposition Rules

The decomposition rules objective is to decrease use case complexity and to increase its cohesion. The principle is to extract a set of functionalities from use case description. These functionalities are described in the scenarios. The following rules are triggered by the refinement process which relies on the quality values in order to propose the adequate decomposition, as explained below.

R1: Having a use case <UC;A;S> specified by the set of actions A={a1,..,an} and a set of scenarios S={s1,..,sm}. Let's assume s∈S, and s implying a set of actions {ai,..,aj} ⊂ A, and ∃{ak,..,ap} ⊆ {ai,..,aj} having no occurrence in S-{s} (i.e.{ak,..,ap} occurs exclusively in s).
Decomposing UC according to s produces two use cases UCa and UCb standing respectively for <UCa;{a1,..,an}-{ak,..,ap};S-{s}> and <UCb;{ai,..,aj};{s}>

To illustrate this rule, let us consider again the "withdraw cash" use case defined by <"withdraw cash" ; {a1,..,a8};{S1,..,S6}>. Let us suppose also that we want to decompose "withdraw cash" according to S3. This will produce two use cases UC1 and UC2 where UC1 stands for <UC1;{a1,a2,a3,a4,a5,a6,a8}; {S1,S2,S4,S5,S6}> and UC2 stands for <UC2;{a1,a2,a3,a4,a5,a7}; {S3}>. Note that UC1 and UC2 contain redundant actions. This will be addressed by the restructuring rules described below. The second rule is the generalization of rule R1:

R2: Having a use case <UC;A;S> specified by the set of actions A={a1,..,an} and the set of scenarios S={s1,..,sm}. Let's assume S1 ⊂ S, and S1 contains p scenarios implying respectively t sets of actions A'1, A'2,…, A't and ∃{a_k,..a_p} ⊆ {ai,..,aj} and having no occurrence in S-S1.
Decomposing UC according to S1 produces two use cases UCa and UCb where UCa stands for <UCa; {a1,..,an}-{ak,..,ap};S-S1} and Ucb stands for < UCb; A'1 ∪A'2 ∪…∪A't}; S1 >

For example if we decompose "withdraw cash" according to {S3,S4} we will obtain two use cases UC3 and UC4 where UC3 stands for <UC3;{a1,a2,a3, a4, a5,a6,a8}; {S1,S2,S5,S6}> and UC4 stands for <UC4;{a1,a2,a3,a4,a7,a8}; {S3,S4}>

5.2 Use Case Restructuring Rules

The restructuring performed by the following rules aims to achieve minimality in the requirements model specification. A model is said to be minimal when every aspect of the requirements appears only once. In other words, non-minimality is due to a lack of factorization.

R3: Having two use cases <UC1;A={a1,..,an},S={s1,..sm}> and <UC2;B={b1,..,bk},T={t1,..,tp}>.
If ∃ {ai,..,aj}⊆ A ∩ B and {ai,..,aj} occurring in all scenarios s1,..sm, t1,..,tp Then {UC1, UC2} is equivalent to {UCa,UCb,UCc,R} where UCa stands for <UCa; {a1,..,an}-{ai,..,aj}, S-S1> where S1 is a set of scenarios from S defined only on {ai,..,aj}, and UCb stands for <UCb;{b1,..,bk}- {ai,..,aj}, T-T1> where T1 is a set of scenarios from T defined only on {ai,..,aj}, and UCc stands for <UCc;{ai,..,aj}, S1∪T1> and R = {Ra, Rb} where Ra (resp. Rb) is an "include" relationship from UCa to UCc (resp. UCb to UCc)

Applying this rule on the result of rule R1 ({UC1,UC2}) will produce:

<UC1';{a2,a3,a4,a5,a6,a8};{S1,S2,S4,S5,S6}>
<UC2';{a2,a3,a4,a5,a7};{S3}> and <UC3;{a1}>
and UC1' includes UC3 and UC2' includes UC3.

Since UC3 has no associated scenario, it can be used only throughout other scenarios.

R4: Having two use cases <UC1; A={a1,..,an},S={s1,..sm}> and <UC2;B={b1,..,bk},T={t1,..,tp}>.
If ∃ {ai,..,aj} ⊆ A ∩ B and {ai,..,aj} occurring in a set of scenarios V where V ⊂ S ∩T Then {UC1, UC2} is equivalent to {UCa,UCb,UCc,R} where UCa stands for <UCa; {a1,..,an}-{ai,..,aj}, S-S1> where S1 is a set of scenarios from S defined only on {ai,..,aj}, UCb stands for <UCb; ={b1,..,bk}- {ai,..,aj}, T-T1> where T1 is a set of scenarios from T defined only on {ai,..,aj},UCc stands for <UCc; {ai,..,aj}, S1∪T1>, R ={Ra, Rb} where Ra (resp. Rb) is an "extend" relationship from UCc to UCa (resp. UCc to UCb)

As an illustration, let us consider the following use cases obtained after applying R2:

<UC3;{a1,a2,a3,a4,a5,a6,a8}; {S1,S2,S5,S6}>, and
<UC4;{a1,a2,a3,a4,a7,a8}; {S3,S4}>

Let us now apply R4, we will obtain:

<UCa;{a1,a2,a3,a4,a6},{S1,S2,S5,S6}>
<UCb;{a1,a2,a3,a4,a7},{S3,S4}> and <UCc;{a5,a8}, { }>

Note again that UCc has no associated scenario, thus meaning that it could be used only throughout other scenarios. This also means that UCc lacks coherence and will probably be decomposed after a new iteration of the decomposition rules.

The last restructuring rule deals with inheritance among use cases. This rule could be applied when a use case is similar to another use case apart a variant. In such a situation the two use cases are related to each other by an inheritance relationship.

R5: Having two use cases <UC1; A={a1,..,an},S={s1,..sm}> and <UC2; B={b1,..,bk}, T={t1,..,tp}>.
If B ⊂ A and T ⊂ S Then {UC1 ; UC2} is equivalent to {UC1, UC2', R} where R is an inheritance relationship directed from UC2' to UC1 and UC2' stands for <UC2';{b1,..,bk}-(A ∩ B),T}>.

6 Applying the Approach: On Line Bookstore Case Study

In order to illustrate our quality driven approach, we use an online bookstore web application allowing registered and unregistered customers to i) Browse the book catalogue organized into categories, ii) Search for a given book using several search criteria (title, author, keywords, etc.), iii) Select books and add them to a shopping cart that could be transformed into an order. To order books, customers must log in, using a user-id and a password. Other functionalities such as accessing recent orders, modifying account's data, etc., are also available through the registered access.

6.1 Initial Use Case Diagram Construction

An initial use case model is established by the designer. For lack of space we consider only the "use registered access" use case summarized in Table 2.

Table 2. "Use registered access" structure and behavior summary

use case actions	SC	SC	SC	SC	SC	S
a)login	X	X	X	X	X	X
b)create order	X	X	X			
c)select shipping method	X	X	X			
d)create account	X					X
e)display account details	X					X
f)access recent orders				X	X	
g)display order details	X	X	X	X	X	
h)cancel order			X	X		

The lines (use case actions) exhibit the activities performed by the system. The columns describe the system functions. They are scenarios described as flows of actions. For example SC1 expresses the following flow of actions:

1.the customer chooses to create an order 2.the system asks for identification 3.the customer enters login and password 4.the system verifies login and password 5. the system creates a candidate order	6.the system asks for a shipping method 7.the customer enters a shipping method 8.the customer asks to see order details 9.the system displays order details 10. the customer validates the order 11. the system creates a validated order

In the current version, this is performed manually. We are working on a semi automated process enabling extraction of flows of actions from scenario descriptions.

6.2 Initial Use Case Model Quality Measurement

We compute the values of use case entropy and Lack of Cohesion, by applying UC-E and UC-LC metrics. The overall values obtained are **UC_E =2.86 and UC_LC =1.01**

We suggest a new iteration in order to check whether these quality values can be improved.

6.3 Applying Use Case Decomposition

In order to apply use case decomposition rules we need the values of the scenario Lack of Cohesion given in Table 3. Based on this table, we assert that scenarios SC5 and SC6 having the highest Lack of Cohesion values and thus contribute more than the others. Therefore, we propose to decompose the initial use case according to {SC5, SC6}.

Table 3. Scenarios Lack of Cohesion values

use case scenarios	SC1	SC2	SC3	SC4	SC5	SC6
Scenario lack of cohesion	1.05	1.1	1.07	1.1	1.125	1.125

By applying the decomposition rule R2, we generate two new use cases namely UC1 and UC2 sketched in Table 4 and Table 5 below.

Table 4. Use case UC1description

actions	SC1	SC2	SC3	SC4
a)	X	X	X	X
b)	X	X	X	
c)	X	X	X	
d)		X		
e)		X		
f)				X
g)	X	X	X	X
h)			X	X

Table 5. Use caseUC2 description

actions	SC5	SC6
a)	X	X
d)		X
e)		X
f)	X	
g)	X	

6.4 Applying Use Case Restructuring Rules

We will now apply restructuring rules on the use cases obtained at the end of the decomposition phase. Note that both R3 and R4 could apply in this case.

Table 6. Use case UC1 after R3 and R4

actions	SC1	SC2	SC3	SC4
a)	X	X	X	X
b)	X	X	X	
c)	X	X	X	
d)		X		
e)		X		
f)				X
g)	X	X	X	X
h)			X	X

Table 8. Use case UC2 after applying R3 and R4

actions	SC5	SC6
a)	X	X
d)		X
e)		X
f)	X	
g)	X	

Table 7. New use case generated by R3

actions		
a)		

Table 9. New use case created by applying R3 and R4 on UC2 and UC1

actions	SC6
a)	X
d)	X
e)	X

We obtain the use cases sketched in Tables 6, 7, 8 and 9. After refinement, we can associate relevant names for the resulting use cases: Table 6: "order books", Table 7: "login"; Table 8: "track recent orders"; Table 9: "register". The result is sketched in Fig. 3 as a UML use case diagram. The quality values computed for the use cases of Fig. 3 are summarized in Table 10. The last three use cases have a minimal value for Lack of Cohesion. The entropy value difference is due to the number of actions that impact complexity (entropy).

Note that the use case "order books" could be refined to increase its quality. A further iteration of the process would lead to UC_LC=1 and to UC_E=1. For space considerations, we do not describe this iteration. Finally, let us note that the case

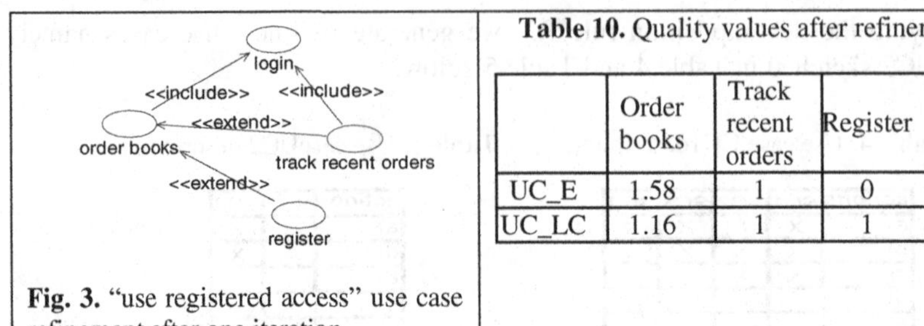

Fig. 3. "use registered access" use case refinement after one iteration

Table 10. Quality values after refinement

	Order books	Track recent orders	Register	Login
UC_E	1.58	1	0	1
UC_LC	1.16	1	1	1

study aims mainly at illustrating the approach on a readable example. The interest of the refinement process is more significant if we consider large scale uses cases.

7 Conclusion and Future Work

In this paper, we describe a quality based approach allowing designers to improve an initial design model. It is mainly built on a use case meta-model extension providing a relevant basis suited for use case refinement. It proposes an incremental process for use case diagram improvement. It is a quality driven process performing iteratively use case diagram refinement according to quality measurement. Designers can apply on demand decomposition and restructuring rules. Some steps can be performed in a semi-automatic way. Our approach is applied to an example. An important next step is to extend the existing prototype to enable visualization of the use case diagrams at each step. In addition, a CASE tool supporting our approach is planned, enabling a large scale empirical validation. Further work will be done on use case quality measurement, especially enlarging use case quality metrics, such as correctness as well as enriching the decomposition and restructuring rule set.

Acknowledgements. We would like to sincerely thank the anonymous referees for the useful comments.

References

1. G. Costagliola, F. Ferrucci, G. Tortora, G. Vitiello, Class Point: An Approach for the Size Estimation of Object-Oriented Systems, IEEE Transactions on Software Engineering, 31(1), 2005.
2. L. Briand, T. Langley, I. Wieczorek, A Replicated Assessment and Comparison of Common Software Cost Modeling Techniques, International Software Engineering Network Technical Report ISERN-99-15.
3. S. Kusumoto, F. Matukawa, K. Inoue, S. Hanabusa, .Y. Maegawa: Estimating Effort by Use Case Points: Method, Tool and Case Study, In 10th IEEE International Symposium on Software Metrics (METRICS'04).
4. L. Briand, J. Daly, J. Wüst, A Unified Framework for Coupling Measurement in OO Systems, ISERN-96-14.
5. E. Arisholm, L. Briand, A. Foyen, Dynamic Coupling Measurement for OO Software, IEEE Transactions on Software Engineering, 30(8), 2004.

6. A. Chatzigeorgiou, G. Stephanides, Entropy as a Measure of Object-Oriented Design Quality, (BCI'2003), Thessaloniki, Greece.
7. J. Dvorak, Conceptual Entropy and Its Effect on Class Hierarchies, IEEE Computer, June 1994.
8. R. Martin, OO Design Quality Metrics – An Analysis of Dependencies, http://www.objectmentor.com/resources/articles/oodmetrc.pdf
9. Metrics for Software Conceptual Models, edited by Marcela Genero, Mario Piattini & Coral Calero, Imperial College Press, January 2005.
10. S. Si-Saïd, J. Akoka, I. Comyn-Wattiau, Conceptual Modeling Quality - From EER to UML Schemas Evaluation, Proceedings of ER2002, Tampere (Finland).
11. K. El Emam, Object-Oriented Metrics: A Review of Theory and Practice, NRC-CNRC 44190, National Research Council Canada.
12. I. Baig, Measuring Cohesion and Coupling of OO Systems, Master Thesis, School of Engineering, Ronneby, Sweden, 2004.
13. M. Azuma, Applying ISO/IEC 9126-1 Quality Model to Quality Requirements Engineering on Critical Software, Proceedings of the Third International Workshop on Requirements for High Assurance Systems (RHAS 2004).
14. H. Kaiya, A. Osada, K. Kaijiri, Identifying Stakeholders and Their Preferences about NFR by Comparing Use Case Diagrams of Several Existing Systems, 12th IEEE International Requirements Engineering Conference (RE'04), 2004.
15. W. Yu, J. Li, G. Butler, Refactoring Use Case Models on Episodes, Proceedings of the 19th International Conference on Automated Software Engineering (ASE04).
16. www.omg.org
17. A. Cockburn: Writing Effective Use Cases, Addison-Wesley, 2001
18. D. Amyot, Mussbacher, G., On the Extension of UML with Use Case Maps Concepts. *<<UML>>2000,*. LNCS 1939, 16-31.
19. R.J.A. Buhr, R.S. Casselman, Use Case Maps for Object-Oriented Systems, Prentice Hall, 1999.
20. B. Regnell, P. Beremark, O. Eklundh, A Market-Driven Requirements Engineering Process Results from an Industrial Process Improvement Programme, CEIRE´98 - Journal of Requirements Engineering, Vol. 3, no. 2, pp 121-129, 1998.
21. K. Rui ,G. Butler, Refactoring use case models: the metamodel. In Proc. Twenty-sixth Australasian computer science conference on Conference in research and practice in information technology, pages 301–308. Australian Computer Society, Inc., 2003.
22. B. Henderson-Sellers, D. Zowghi , T. Klemola , S. Parasuram: Sizing Use Cases: How to Create a Standard Metrical Approach, In Proceesding of the 8th International Conference on Object-Oriented. Information Systems, OOIS 2002, Montpellier, France, September 2-5, 2002.
23. B. Anda, H. Dreiem, D. Sjøberg, M. Jørgensen Estimating Software Development Effort Based on Use Cases - Experiences from Industry, I, In Proceedings of (UML2001), Toronto, Canada, October 1-5, 2001
24. C. Shannon A mathematical theory of communication, Bell System Technical Journal.
25. W. Harisson An entropy base measure of software complexity, IEEE Transaction on Software Engineering, 1992, 18(11):1025-1029.
26. J. Bansiya, C. Davis, and L. Etzkorn. An entropy-based complexity measure for object-oriented designs. Theory and Practice of Object Systems, 5, 1999.
27. Norman E. Fenton, Shari Lawrence Pfleeger, "Software Metrics: A Rigorous and PracticalApproach", PWS Publishing Company, 1998.
28. S. Chidamber and C. Kemerer, "A metrics suite for OO design", IEEE Trans. Software Eng.,20 (1994) 476–493.
29. Henderson-Sellers, B. (1996). Object-Oriented Metrics measures of Complexity. Prentice Hall.

Ontology with Likeliness and Typicality of Objects in Concepts

Ching-man Au Yeung and Ho-fung Leung

Department of Computer Science and Engineering
The Chinese University of Hong Kong
Shatin, Hong Kong
{cmauyeun, lhf}@cse.cuhk.edu.hk

Abstract. Ontologies play an indispensable role in the Semantic Web by specifying the definitions of concepts and individual objects. However, most of the existing methods for constructing ontologies can only specify concepts as crisp sets. However, we cannot avoid encountering concepts that are without clear boundaries, or even vague in meanings. Therefore, existing ontology models are unable to cope with many real cases effectively. With respect to a certain category, certain objects are considered as more representative or typical. Cognitive psychologists explain this by the prototype theory of concepts. This notion should also be taken into account to improve conceptual modeling. While there has been different research attempting to handle vague concepts with fuzzy set theory, formal methods for measuring typicality of objects are still insufficient. We propose a cognitive model of concepts for ontologies, which handles both likeliness (fuzzy membership grade) and typicality of individuals. We also discuss the nature and differences between likeliness and typicality. This model not only enhances the effectiveness of conceptual modeling, but also brings the results of reasoning closer to human thinking. We believe that this research is beneficial to future research on ontological engineering in the Semantic Web.

1 Introduction

Ontology [14] is becoming increasingly important and is identified as it plays an important role in enabling information retrieval, information exchange and agent communications [5]. It is also expected to provide semantics to resources on the Web in the emerging Semantic Web [2]. Ontology is usually defined as an explicit specification of conceptualization [13]. Currently, there are several standards for specifying an ontology, such as OWL (Web Ontology Language) [20]. One problem of the existing approaches is that ontologies cannot handle concepts which are vague or without clear boundaries, because concepts in these ontologies are represented as crisp sets of individuals.

However, it is obvious that many concepts we encounter are vague and have no clear boundaries, such as "hot", "tall" and "far". In addition, cognitive psychologists also suggest another type of uncertainty in judging membership of objects, which is called "typicality" [24,25]. Typicality reflects how typical or

D.W. Embley, A. Olivé, and S. Ram (Eds.): ER 2006, LNCS 4215, pp. 98–111, 2006.

representative an individual is with respect to a concept [18]. For example, to most English-speaking people, robins are more typical birds than penguins [24]. In this paper, we explain that fuzzy membership grade, which reflects the varying degree of certainty of an individual's membership in concepts (we give this kind of measure the name of *likeliness*), and *typicality*, which reflects the representativeness of an individual with respect to a concept, are two different kinds of measure. When asked whether a penguin is a bird, no one will doubt that the answer is positive, and there is no fuzziness involved. However, many people tend to think that penguin is a less typical bird when compared to other birds, this is the psychological effect that typicality measures.

In this paper, we argue that both likeliness and typicality should be modeled in an ontology to give a clearer picture of an object's membership as well as representativeness with respect to a concept. Modeling typicality in ontology allows reasoning to be more realistic and closer to human thinking. Existing ontology models do not have the mechanisms to determine likeliness and typicality of objects in concepts, and are therefore not able to provide the best and most accurate answers to human users in the reasoning process. With likeliness and typicality, ontologies are able to determine how likely or how typical an object is, and present these results in a way that is more compatible to the expectation of human users. Therefore, we propose a model of concept for constructing ontologies, which is inspired by the Prototype Theory in cognitive psychology, to handle both likeliness and typicality of individual objects.

This paper is structured as follows. Section 2 gives background on ontology and the Prototype Theory in cognitive psychology. Related works are presented in Section 3. Section 4 provides a detail description of the new model of concepts. Section 5 gives an example to illustrate how the model can be used. A discussion of the properties of the model is given in section 6. Finally section 7 mentions future work and concludes the paper.

2 Preliminaries

2.1 Ontology

Ontology is originally a philosophical discipline which deals with the study of being and existence. The term is borrowed to computer science and defined as an explicit specification of conceptualization [13], which specify the set of concepts that will be used in a particular system as a basis for communication or sharing of information. In particular, ontology is an important component in the Semantic Web [2].

An ontology generally consists of a taxonomy of concepts, a set of relations, a set of individuals (representing real objects), and possibly a set of inference rules for discovering of implicit knowledge [2]. In this paper, we formally define an ontology O as a four-tuple $O = (C, P, I, R)$, where C is a set of concepts, P is a set of properties, I is a set of data instances, representing real objects in the domain of interest, and lastly R is a set of rules, propositions or axioms that specify the relations between concepts and properties.

Research on ontology is not limited to the specification or construction of ontology, other aspects such as ontology matching [3,33], ontology learning [10,27] and using ontology to assist information retrieval [15,22] are also the foci of ontology researchers. The thorough review paper by Ding [5,6] can be referred to for a more detailed discussion of ontology development.

2.2 The Prototype Theory

One of the major areas of research in cognitive psychology is how concepts and categories are represented in the human mind [9]. Until the 1970s, the general view of concept held commonly among psychologists suggested that concepts are defined by singly necessary and jointly sufficient properties. This view is now referred to as the *classical view* [28]. Instances of concepts must meet a set of pre-defined conditions in order to be considered as a member of a concept.

Although the classical view sounds reasonable and intuitive, it has contradicted many empirical findings. Rosch found that people judged different members of a category as varying in representativeness [23,25]. For example, people consider a robin as a better example of bird than others such as ostrich, even though these are all classified as birds. These findings have motivated the development of the *Prototype Theory* of concepts [24]. According to this theory, a concept is represented by a prototype (an abstraction of the concept) in human mind. The prototype of a concept consists of all the salient properties, which are properties that appear frequently in instances classified to this concept. The properties defining the prototype are not limited to necessary properties but also non-necessary ones. This is to model the fact that people use both necessary and non-necessary properties to judge the representativeness of an instance.

The theory explains the existence of varying representativeness of instances by the similarity between the instances and the concept prototype, and use the term *typicality* to refer to the degree of representativeness. It has been found that typicality of an instance can be determined by the number of properties that match between the instance and the prototype. For example, since most birds can fly, the property "*can-fly*" will probably appear in the prototype of the concept "*Bird*". Hence, birds that can fly will be judged as more *typical* than those that cannot. Moreover, further studies also suggest that properties in the prototype may not be of equal importance [25]. Some of the properties are considered more significant or important to the concept while others are considered less important. Thus, properties are weighted according to their importance in the prototype of a concept.

2.3 Likeliness and Typicality of Objects in Concepts

When one learns that concepts have a graded structure (individuals have different membership grades in a concept), one tends to think of fuzzy set theory [34] when they try to model vagueness and uncertainty of concepts, because the theory is a well-known generalization of crisp sets with a characteristic function assigning membership grades to individuals. However, there are in fact differences between likeliness grades and typicality value.

Armstrong, Gleitman and Gleitman [1] point out that typicality effects occur even in some concepts such as *odd number*, which has clear boundaries and definitions. They suggest that one should distinguish membership from prototypicality (typicality). Kamp and Partee [18] also address the distinction between the two, and use c^e to represent the degree of membership in the extension of a concept (e stands for goodness of example), and c^p to represent the degree of typicality (p stands for prototypicality). While c^e measures whether or not and to what degree an instance is classified to a concept, c^p measures how representative or typical is an instance in a concept. It seems that typicality is rather a psychological measure than an objective decision of an individual's membership, because typicality effect is observed even in well-defined concepts.

From a logical perspective, it can also be seen that fuzzy set theory does not capture the essence of the Prototype Theory. As suggested in [24,25], non-necessary properties are involved in determining typicality of instances. Instances that do not possess some of these properties are judged as less typical, but are not judged as non-member. Fuzzy set theory, though a generalization of crisp sets, still requires an element to attain membership greater than zero in each conjuncts in order to attain an overall non-zero membership grade.

In summary, while fuzzy set theory is necessary to model concepts which are vague and has no clear or well-defined boundaries, we need a new mechanism if we want to model typicality of objects in concepts.

3 Related Works

Currently, ontologies are constructed by defining concepts and properties using one of the ontology languages. The concepts in these ontologies are interpreted as crisp sets. An individual is either considered as an instance of a concept or it is not. As the theoretical counterpart of ontologies, Description Logics are also restricted to handle crisp concepts [8].

A number of research works apply fuzzy set theory to enhance ontologies. For example, Cross and Cross [4] present fuzzy ontologies to facilitate the retrieval of multilingual documents. Parry [21] introduces fuzzy set theory into ontologies by adding degrees of membership to indicate how likely each term is found in certain locations. Widyantoro and Yen [32] devise a method to construct a fuzzy ontology automatically from a corpus and use the notion of fuzzy narrower term relation to assist querying in a personalized search engine. These works mainly use fuzzy set theory to deal with uncertainty within a taxonomy or a hierarchy of terms, which is less related to definition of concepts and properties.

On the other hand, there are also different works which concern extending Description Logics, the theoretical counterpart of ontologies, to handle fuzziness and uncertainty in concepts. For example, Koller [19] proposes a probabilistic version of Description Logics. On the other hand, Straccia [29,30] combines fuzzy set theory and Description Logics and introduces fuzzy $\mathcal{ALC}$, in which concepts are interpreted as fuzzy sets. Straccia also develops a reasoning procedure and an algorithm for deciding satisfiability in fuzzy $\mathcal{ALC}$. Others further extend the expressiveness of fuzzy Description Logics such as by introducing fuzzy hedges, such as "very" and "quite", as concept modifiers [17].

There are also projects which try to model typicality. For example, [7] describes a frame-based object-centered representation (O.C.R) which incorporates fuzzy set theory to model concepts. The frame slots include information of the typical range of values. With a similar approach, [31] presents an ontology model which represents semantic information about concepts more explicitly. It introduces three characterizations of properties, namely attribute behaviour over time, modality and prototypicality. The model is able to specify whether the value of a property of a concept is typical. However, the framework does not provide mechanisms for calculating an individual object's typicality in a concept.

Most of the works do not directly address the problem of modeling typicality of instances. The introduction of fuzzy set theory allows handling of fuzzy concepts such as "tall" and "expensive". These concepts can be represented by a fuzzy set with an appropriate membership function. However, when we consider common concepts such as birds, fishes and furniture, we cannot simply use fuzzy set to model typicality. This is because typicality depends on the properties possessed by the objects, and fuzzy set does not provide the appropriate mechanism to determine typicality.

4 Fuzzy Ontology with Likeliness and Typicality

It is clear that the problems that previous works tried to solve by introducing fuzzy set theory into ontologies are quite different from the psychological effect described in the Prototype Theory. Therefore, we are motivated to develop a better model for ontologies which can handle both likeliness grade and typicality of individuals. To handle likeliness, we extend the traditional model of ontologies by using fuzzy set theory. We further extend such model by constructing concept prototypes for the calculation of typicality of individuals.

4.1 Concepts and Properties

An ontology is expected to give a formal specification of different concepts in a particular domain. Hence, although we use ideas of the Prototype Theory, we still treat each concept as characterized by a set of necessary properties. This model will be extended to handle both likeliness and typicality. The properties serve as the requirements for being considered as an instance of a concept. A weight is associated with each property in a concept to indicate the importance of that property. For individuals, each of them possesses a set of properties and a value is also associated with each property to indicate the degree to which the individual possesses the property.

Definition 1. *A* ***concept*** $x \in C$ *is a fuzzy subset of* I*, with a membership function* μ_x *assigning each instance* $a \in I$ *a membership grade in this concept.*

To formally represent concepts and properties, we propose two mathematical notations. Firstly, a *characteristic vector* of a concept is defined as a vector of real number in the range of 0 to 1, in which each element corresponds to the weight of a different property.

Definition 2. *A* ***characteristic vector*** $\mathbf{c}_x$ *of a concept* x *is a vector of real numbers,*

$$\mathbf{c}_x = (c_{x,1}, c_{x,2}, ..., c_{x,n}), 0 \leq c_{x,i} \leq 1$$

where n *is the total number of properties.*

For an individual, a value of 1 of an element in the characteristic vector means that the property is essential to the concept, while a value of 0 means that the property is not required. Secondly, we define *property vector* of an individual as a vector of real number in the range of 0 to 1, in which each element corresponds to the degree to which the individual possesses a property.

Definition 3. *The* ***property vector*** $\mathbf{p}_a$ *of an individual* a *is a vector of real numbers,*

$$\mathbf{p}_a = (p_{a,1}, p_{a,2}, ..., p_{a,n}), 0 \leq p_{a,i} \leq 1$$

where n *is the total number of properties.*

Concepts in an ontology are generally arranged in a hierarchy such as in OWL [20], and subsumption of concepts are determined by examining whether the set of properties of one concept is a subset of that of another. In this model, we generalize this idea and subsumption of concepts can be determined by comparing the weights in the characteristic vector. For a concept to be considered as subsumed by another concept, it should be characterized at least by all the properties of the latter, and with higher weights for each of these properties.

Definition 4. *For two concepts* x *and* y, x *is said to be* ***subsumed by*** y, *denoted by* $x \sqsubseteq y$, *if and only if* $c_{x,i} \geq c_{y,i}$ *for all* $i = 1, 2, ..., n$.

This definition implies two situations that one concept x can be considered as a sub-concept of another concept y. In the first case, two concepts are defined by the same set of properties, but x weights some properties higher than y does. In the second case, x has a larger set of defining properties than y. Both situations are intuitive, because a sub-concept should impose more requirements of properties on an individual than its super-concept.

In addition, we define the notion of sub-concepts, super-concepts, defining properties and possession of properties as follows.

Definition 5. *If* $x \sqsubseteq y$, *then* x *is said to be a* ***sub-concept*** *of* y, *and* y *is said to be a* ***super-concept*** *of* x.

Definition 6. *The set of properties* P_x *that includes all properties having a weight greater than zero in the characteristic vector of a concept* x *is said to be the set of* ***defining properties*** *of* x, *or* x *is said to be* ***defined by*** *the set* P_x.

Definition 7. *The set of properties* P_a *that includes all properties having a degree greater than zero in the property vector of an individual* a *is said to be the set of* ***properties possessed by*** a.

4.2 Likeliness of an Individual in a Concept

The first type of uncertainty we want to address is fuzzy membership grade of individuals. We call this degree of membership *likeliness.* The measure of likeliness of an individual determines whether or not and to what degree an individual is classified to a concept according to the defining properties.

Definition 8. *In an ontology $O = (C, P, I, R)$,* ***likeliness*** *of an individual object a in a concept x is determined by a function which returns the degree to which a is considered as an instance of x: $\lambda_x : I \longrightarrow [0,1]$.*

To determine the likeliness of an individual in a concept, a membership function is required. While it is possible to have different functions for likeliness, we argue that likeliness should satisfy the following axioms.

Axiom 1. *An individual a has a degree of likeliness of 1 in a concept x if and only if $c_{x,i} > 0 \rightarrow p_{a,i} = 1$ for all $i = 1, 2, ..., n$.*

Axiom 2. *An individual a has a degree of likeliness of 0 in a concept x if and only if $c_{x,i} > 0$ and $p_{a,i} = 0$ for some $i \in [1, n]$.*

Axiom 3. *For a concept x, and two individuals a and b, if for some j such that $c_{x,j} > 0$, $p_{a,j} > p_{b,j}$ and $p_{a,i} = p_{b,i}$ for all $i \neq j$, then $\lambda_x(a) > \lambda_x(b)$.*

Axiom 4. *For two concepts x and y, and an individual a, if for some j such that $c_{x,j} \geq c_{y,j} > 0$, $1 > p_{a,j} > 0$, $c_{x,i} = c_{y,i}$, $p_{a,i} > 0$ for all $i \neq j$, then $\lambda_y(a) \geq \lambda_x(a)$.*

Axiom 5. *For two concepts x and y, and an individual a, if for some j such that $c_{x,j} \geq c_{y,j} > 0$, $p_{a,j} = 1$, $c_{x,i} = c_{y,i}$, and $p_{a,i} > 0$ for all $i \neq j$, then $\lambda_y(a) = \lambda_x(a)$.*

Axioms 1 and 2 state the boundary conditions for the degree of likeliness. An individual must possess all the properties with non-zero weight in the characteristic vector in order to be an instance of the concept. To have a likeliness of one, the degree of a property in the property vector should be one whenever that is a defining property of the concept. On the other hand, if the individual does not possess one or more of the defining properties, its likeliness will be zero.

Axioms 3 to 5 state how the degree of likeliness is varied when degrees of possession and property weights change. If one individual possesses a property that the concept assumes non-zero weight to a degree higher than another individual does, then the former will attain a higher degree of likeliness than the latter. This is justified by the fact that the first individual satisfies the requirement to a higher degree. Axiom 4 states that an individual should achieve a higher degree of likeliness in a concept that places lower weights on properties that the individual possesses than another concept that places higher weights on the properties. This axiom is justified because when a property is given higher weight, it is considered as more important and thus there is a more strict requirement on an individual, and therefore the likeliness of an individual is lowered.

Lastly, an exception is described in Axiom 5, which is when the degree of the property in question in the property vector is equal to 1. In this case, since the individual already possesses the property to a full extent, it does not matter how important a property is to the definition of the concept, hence it makes no differences between the degree of likeliness of the individual in the two concepts.

Here, we present a possible function that can be used as the membership function of a concept to determine the degree of likeliness of an individual.

$$\lambda_x(a) = \min_i \{l_i\} \tag{1}$$

where

$$l_i = \begin{cases} p_{a,i} + (1 - c_{x,i}) \times (1 - p_{a,i}) & \text{if } c_{x,i} > 0, p_{a,i} > 0 \\ 0 & \text{if } c_{x,i} > 0, p_{a,i} = 0 \\ 1 & \text{if } c_{x,i} = 0 \end{cases}$$

Since $p_{a,i}$ is in the range of [0,1], $\lambda_x(a)$ is also in the range of [0,1]. The idea of this function is to scale the degrees ($p_{a,i}$'s) in the property vector of an individual by using the property weights ($c_{x,i}$'s) in the characteristic vector of the concept. The function of likeliness can be used as the membership function of a concept to determine the extent to which an individual object is considered as an instance of a concept: $\mu_x(a) = \lambda_x(a)$.

4.3 Prototype Vector and Typicality

As suggested by cognitive psychologists [24,18], *typicality* is a measure of how representative or typical is an individual in a particular concept. Typicality is measured based on the number of properties shared by most of the individuals of the concept, which usually include non-necessary properties of a concept [28]. In other words, the characteristic vector alone is not enough to handle typicality because it only contains information of necessary properties of a concept. Therefore, we introduce here a new notation called *prototype vector*.

As typicality of an individual is determined by its similarity to the prototype of a concept [25], we need to first construct a prototype for the concept. According to [28], properties in the prototype "*are salient ones that have a substantial probability of occurring in instances of the concept*", in other words, weights of the properties in the prototype depend on the saliency of the properties in the instances. In this model, we construct the prototype of a concept based on this idea. However, we rely on weights of properties in the sub-concepts instead of using the saliency of properties. The reason is twofold. Firstly, information is probably be stored in a distributive manner and instances may be scattered in different ontologies. If the weights are dependent on the instances, then the prototypes in different ontologies will tend to be different to a large extent. Moreover, weights of properties in the sub-concepts indicate the importance of the properties, which imply that representative objects will possess properties of higher weights. This also gives us information of the saliency of properties. Therefore, we define the prototype of a concept as follows.

Definition 9. *The* ***prototype vector*** $\mathbf{t}_x$ *of a concept* x *is a vector of real numbers,* $\mathbf{t}_x = (t_{x,1}, t_{x,2}, ..., t_{x,n}), 0 \leq t_{x,i} \leq 1$*, and is determined by the following equation:*

$$\mathbf{t}_x = \frac{1}{|S|} \sum_{s \in S \cup \{x\}} \mathbf{c}_s \qquad (2)$$

where S *is the set of sub-concepts of* x *as determined by Definition 4.*

Typicality is determined by a "*weighted feature (property) sum*" [28], which means that typicality is reflected by the summation of the weights of the properties that the individual possesses. In our model, this involves first matching the properties in the prototype vector of a concept and the property vector of an individual. We denote the typicality function of a concept by τ_x:

Definition 10. *For an ontology* $O = (C, P, I, R)$*,* ***typicality*** *of an individual object* a *in a concept* x *is determined by a function which returns the degree to* a *is considered as a typical instance of* x *according to the prototype of* x*:* $\tau_x : I \longrightarrow [0, 1]$.

In general, typicality is a function of the prototype vector of the concept and the property vector of the object. We formulate the following axioms which a function for typicality should follows.

Axiom 6. *An individual* a *has a degree of typicality of* 1 *in a concept* x *if and only if* $t_{x,i} > 0 \rightarrow p_{a,i} = 1$ *for* $i = 1, 2, ..., n$.

Axiom 7. *An individual* a *has a degree of typicality of* 0 *in a concept* x *if and only if* $t_{x,i} > 0 \rightarrow p_{a,i} = 0$ *for* $i = 1, 2, ..., n$.

Axiom 8. *For a concept* x*, and two individuals* a *and* b*, if for some* j *such that* $t_{x,j} > 0$*,* $p_{a,j} > p_{b,j} \geq 0$ *and* $p_{a,i} = p_{b,i}$ *for all* $i \neq j$*, then* $\tau_x(a) > \tau_x(b)$.

Axiom 9. *For two concepts* x *and* y*, and an individual* a*, if for some* j *such that* $t_{x,j} > t_{y,j} > 0$*,* $p_{a,j} > 0$ *and* $t_{x,i} = t_{y,i}$ *for all* $i \neq j$*, then* $\tau_y(a) > \tau_x(a)$.

Axioms 6 and 7 specify the boundary cases of typicality. According to the Prototype Theory [28], there are two major issues in determining the typicality of an individual in a concept: (1) an individual does not need to possess all the properties in the prototype, and (2) an individual is considered as more typical if it has more properties of the concept prototype. Hence, an individual's typicality will only be zero when it does not possess any of the properties in the prototype.

Axiom 8 states the influence of degrees in the property vector on typicality. If two individuals possessing the same set of properties, and one possesses the properties which appear in the prototype to a higher degree than the other, then the former will attain a higher typicality than the latter. Moreover, if the first individual possesses more properties in the prototype than the other, the former individual should attain a higher typicality. This axiom is justified to be in line with the Prototype Theory because in both cases the former individual is considered as more similar to the concept prototype.

The last axiom states that an individual should achieve a higher degree of typicality in a concept that places less weights on properties that the individual possesses than another concept that places more weights on the properties. This is justified because when a property is given more weights, it is more important in the prototype, thus an individual will attain lower typicality in such concept than in another concept which does not consider that property to be that important.

Similar to the discussion on likeliness, we present a possible function for calculating an individual's typicality in a concept. The typicality of an individual a of a concept x, denoted by $\tau_x(a)$ is given by:

$$\tau_x(a) = \frac{\boldsymbol{p}_a \cdot \boldsymbol{t}_x}{\sum_{i=1}^{n} t_{x,i}} \tag{3}$$

5 Illustrating Example

To illustrate how the proposed model of concepts can measure both likeliness and typicality of objects in concepts, and to provide a more formal and detail demonstration, we present the following example which involves an ontology of birds. [1] Firstly, we assume the following properties in the ontology.

A	Animal	B	Has-Wings	C	Has-Feathers	D	Can-Fly
E	Eat-Seed	F	Has-Curved-Beak	G	Can-Sing	H	Can-Run

We then assume that the following concept are defined using the above properties in the ontology.

$$\begin{aligned}
\mathsf{Bird} &: [\mathsf{A}]_1 \quad [\mathsf{B}]_1 \quad [\mathsf{C}]_1 \\
\mathsf{Sparrow} &: [\mathsf{A}]_1 \quad [\mathsf{B}]_1 \quad [\mathsf{C}]_1 \quad [\mathsf{D}]_1 \quad [\mathsf{E}]_{0.8} \\
\mathsf{Parrot} &: [\mathsf{A}]_1 \quad [\mathsf{B}]_1 \quad [\mathsf{C}]_1 \quad [\mathsf{D}]_1 \quad [\mathsf{F}]_1 \\
\mathsf{Robin} &: [\mathsf{A}]_1 \quad [\mathsf{B}]_1 \quad [\mathsf{C}]_1 \quad [\mathsf{D}]_1 \quad [\mathsf{G}]_{0.8} \\
\mathsf{Ostrich} &: [\mathsf{A}]_1 \quad [\mathsf{B}]_1 \quad [\mathsf{C}]_1 \quad [\mathsf{H}]_{0.9}
\end{aligned}$$

The above statements define the five concepts (Bird, Sparrow, Parrot, Robin and Ostrich) by using the eight properties listed above. For examples, the concept *Bird* is defined by three properties, namely *is-an-animal*, *has-wings* and *has-feathers*. The numbers written immediately next to each property is the weight of that property. Since there are a total of eight properties, the characteristic vectors of the concepts and the property vectors of the individuals contain eight elements, presumably in the order listed above.

[1] This ontology is only for illustration and is not meant to be a precise definition of the birds.

Furthermore, we assume that we have two individuals, a sparrow s and an ostrich o, in the ontology representing two real birds. Let the property vectors of the two individuals be

$$\boldsymbol{p}_s = (1, 1, 1, 0.9, 1, 0, 0, 0), \quad \boldsymbol{p}_o = (1, 1, 1, 0, 0, 0, 0, 0.8).$$

The property vector of the individual s indicates that s possesses properties A, B, C and E to a degree of 1 and property D to a degree of 0.9, and that of the individual o indicates that o possesses properties A, B, C to a degree of 1 and property H to a degree of 0.8. With these information, it is possible to calculate the likeliness and typicality of both individuals. Firstly, we have to obtain the characteristic vectors of the concepts *Sparrow* and *Ostrich*.

$$\boldsymbol{c}_{\mathsf{Sparrow}} = (1, 1, 1, 1, 0.8, 0, 0, 0), \quad \boldsymbol{c}_{\mathsf{Ostrich}} = (1, 1, 1, 0, 0, 0, 0, 0.8).$$

Using equation (1), we can then calculate the degree of likeliness of s in the concept *Sparrow* and that of o in the concept of *Ostrich*:

$$\lambda_{\mathsf{Sparrow}}(s) = \min(1, 1, 1, 0.9, 1, 1, 1, 1) = 0.9$$
$$\lambda_{\mathsf{Ostrich}}(o) = \min(1, 1, 1, 1, 1, 1, 1, 0.82) = 0.82$$

In addition, since both individuals possess all the required properties in the concept *Bird*, it is obvious that their degrees of likeliness in the concept *Bird* are both equal to 1: $\lambda_{\mathsf{Bird}}(s) = 1$, $\lambda_{\mathsf{Bird}}(o) = 1$.

The degrees of typicality of the two individuals in the concept *Bird* can be obtained by using the typicality function. Firstly, from the characteristic vectors of the four sub-concepts, the prototype vector of *Bird* can be obtained by using equation (2):

$$\boldsymbol{t}_{\mathsf{Bird}} = (1, 1, 1, 0.75, 0.25, 0.25, 0.25, 0.225)$$

Using this prototype vector of the concept *Bird*, we can obtain the degrees of typicality of s and o by applying the typicality function (4):

$$\tau_{\mathsf{Bird}}(s) = 0.836, \quad \tau_{\mathsf{Bird}}(o) = 0.673.$$

Hence, judging from the typicality of the two individuals, the result suggests that the sparrow s is a more typical bird than the ostrich o.

6 Discussions

6.1 Comparing Likeliness and Typicality

Likeliness is used to model the measure c^e mentioned by Kamp and Partee [18], which deals with whether or not and to what extent an individual is classified to a particular concept. Typicality, on the other hand, models the measure c^p, which measures how representative or typical is an individual in a particular concept. As mentioned before, typicality is a less logical and more psychological measure, because it involves judgement based not only on the necessary and sufficient properties, but involves also non-necessary properties as influenced by its sub-concepts and instances.

Consider the example of birds mentioned in the previous section. Once an individual satisfies the requirements of a concept, it attains a positive value in likeliness. Therefore the two individuals s and o both attain a degree of 1 in likeliness in the concept *Bird*. And it is true that they are classified as birds and no one will object to this. However, psychologically, people tend to think of certain birds as more typical. The measure of typicality reflects this phenomenon. As the result of the example suggests, a sparrow is a more typical bird than an ostrich. This is due to the fact that most birds (concepts) in the ontology are defined by the property *can-fly*. As this is a very common property in birds, birds that do not possess this property are likely to be considered as atypical. This result also agrees with findings in cognitive psychology, which suggests that atypical examples are those that are not similar to the prototype of the concept.

From this example, we can see that an individual may attain high degree of likeliness as it fulfils the requirements of the concept, yet still attain a low degree of typicality because it is not similar to the prototype of the concept. The following property summarize this characteristic of the model.

Property 1. Assume that two individuals a and b, with their property vectors $\boldsymbol{p}_a$ and $\boldsymbol{p}_b$, have the same degree of likeliness in a concept x, i.e. $\lambda_x(a) = \lambda_x(b)$. Let P_t be the set of properties which assume non-zero weights in the prototype vector of x. If some properties in P_t is weighted higher in $\boldsymbol{p}_a$ than in $\boldsymbol{p}_b$ while other properties are weighted the same in both vectors, then we have $\tau_x(a) > \tau_x(b)$.

6.2 Choosing Between Likeliness and Typicality

Since likeliness and typicality concern different aspects in concepts and categorization, it is also worth to discuss which of the two we should use under different situations. Basically, likeliness is an extension of the traditional way of modeling concepts as crisp sets. As we move on to model vague concepts or concepts without clear boundaries, likeliness provides a measure which more clearly reflects the degree to which the data instances in the ontology are classified to these concepts. For example, we may be interested in "senior employees who have worked in the company for a long period of time", "flowers with large petals and red in color", or "restaurants that are close to the railway station and not expensive". All these concepts – *long period of time*, *large*, *red*, *close*, *expensive* – imply that likeliness is essential in giving us an account of how each data instance in the ontology satisfies these requirements.

On the other hand, typicality provides an alternative mechanism to sort the individuals in a way that is closer to human thinking and psychological belief. Consider again the example of birds, since every individual birds will be classified as birds, it is not possible to sort or rank the individuals by their degrees of likeliness in the concept *Bird*. However, we may sort the individuals based on their typicality ratings, and such order will be similar to what a human user would expect to see. Take searching in the Semantic Web as an example, when a user searches for birds, it will be a very good idea to present first the data instances that are thought to be more representative or typical. It is also possible that such idea can be further extend to handle more complex concepts.

7 Conclusions and Future Work

We presented a novel model of concepts for the construction of ontologies. The model allows both measures of likeliness and typicality of objects in a concept to be represented. We also discuss the nature and differences between likeliness and typicality. A set of axioms which the likeliness function and the typicality function should satisfy is proposed. The model extends traditional ontologies by using fuzzy sets and ideas from cognitive psychology, it provides a mechanism of defining concepts by properties with different weights, and provides a formal method to handle concept prototypes and typicality of objects.

We note that constructing an ontology requires substantial effort, and one challenge of the proposed model is that determining the weights of the properties in the concepts puts extra burden on constructing an ontology. One of our future research directions is to investigate how property weights can be determined more efficiently. For instance, [16] proposes a method for constructing Bayesian networks by combining knowledge from domain expert and information from a small data collection. Similar method may be useful in ontology learning. In addition, the model has much potential in being further developed in different aspects. One of these aspects is context sensitivity. It is mentioned that context is an important issue in knowledge representation [12,11]. Cognitive psychologists also point out that typicality is context-dependent [26]. Hence, we will further investigate how context sensitivity can be incorporated into our ontology model.

References

1. S. L. Armstrong, L. R. Gleitman, and H. Gleitman. What some concepts might not be. *Cognition*, 13(3):263–308, 1983.
2. T. Berners-Lee, J. Hendler, and O. Lassila. The semantic web. *Sci. Am.*, 284(5):34–43, 2001.
3. V. Cross. Uncertainty in the automation of ontology matching. In *4th International Symposium on Uncertainty Modelling and Analysis*, 2003.
4. V. Cross and C. R. Voss. Fuzzy ontologies for multilingual document exploitation. In *Proceedings of the 1999 Conference of NAFIPS*, pages 392–397, 1999.
5. Ying Ding and Schubert Foo. Ontology research and development part 1 – a review of ontology generation. *Journal of Information Science*, 28(2), 2002.
6. Ying Ding and Schubert Foo. Research and development: Part 2 – a review of ontology mapping and evolving. *Journal of Information Science*, 28(4), 2002.
7. D. Dubois, H. Prade, and J. P. Rossazza. Vagueness, typicality, and uncertainty in class hierarchies. *International Journal of Intelligent Systems*, 6:167–183, 1991.
8. Franz Baader et al., editor. *The Description Logic Handbook: Theory, Implementation, and Applications.* Cambridge University Press, 2003.
9. Kathleen M. Galotti. *Cognitive Psychology In and Out of the Laboratory.* Belmont, CA: Wadsworth, third edition, 2004.

10. Asunción Gómez-Pérez and David Manzano-Macho. An overview of methods and tools for ontology learning from texts. *Knowl. Eng. Rev.*, 19(3):187–212, 2004.
11. D. Grossi, F. Dignum, and J-J. Ch. Meyer. Contextual taxonomies. In *Proceedings of Fifth Internationanal Workshop on Computational Logic in Multi-Agent Systems*, 2004.
12. D. Grossi, F. Dignum, and J-J. Ch. Meyer. Context in categorization. In *Workshop on Context Representation and Reasoning*, 2005.
13. Thomas R. Gruber. A translation approach to portable ontology specifications. *Knowledge Acquisition*, 5(2):199–220, 1993.
14. Nicola Guarino. Formal ontology and information system. In *Proceedings of the Formal Ontology and Information System*, 1998.
15. R. Guha, R. McCool, and E. Miller. Semantic search. In *WWW '03: Proceedings of the 12th int. conf. on World Wide Web*, pages 700–709, 2003.
16. E. M. Helsper, L. C. van der Gaag, A. J. Feelders, W. L. A. Loeffen, P. L. Geenen, and A. R. W. Elbers. Bringing order into bayesian-network construction. In *Proceedings of Third International Conference on Knowledge Capture*, 2005.
17. Steffen Hölldobler, Tran Dinh Khang, and Hans-Peter Störr. A fuzzy description logic with hedges as concept modifiers. In *IPMU*, 2004.
18. H. Kamp and B. Partee. Prototype theory and compositionality. *Cognition*, 57:129–191, 1995.
19. D. Koller, A. Levy, and A. Pfeffer. P-classic: A tractable probabilistic description logic. In *Proceedings of the 14th National Conference on AI*, pages 390–397, 1997.
20. Deborah L. McGuinness and Frank van Harmelen. OWL web ontology language overview. *http://www.w3.org/TR/owl-features/*, 2004.
21. David Parry. A fuzzy ontology for medical document retrieval. In *CRPIT*, pages 121–126, 2004.
22. C. Rocha, D. Schwabe, and M. de Aragao. A hybrid approach for searching in the semantic web. In *WWW'04*, pages 374–383, 2004.
23. E. H. Rosch. On the internal structure of perceptual and semantic categories. In T. E. More, editor, *Cognitive Development and the Acquisition of Language*. New York: Academic Press, 1973.
24. E. H. Rosch. Cognitive represerntations of semantic categories. *Journal of Exp. Psy.*, 104:192–233, 1975.
25. Eleanor Rosch and Carolyn B. Mervis. Family resemblances: Studies in the internal structural of categories. *Cognitive Psychology*, 7:573–605, 1975.
26. E. M. Roth and E. J. Shoben. The effect of context on the structure of categories. *Cognitive Psychology*, 15:346–378, 1983.
27. Mehrnoush Shamsfard and Ahmad Abdollahzadeh Barforoush. Learning ontologies from natural language texts. *Int. J. Hum.-Comput. Stud.*, 60(1):17–63, 2004.
28. E. E. Smith and D. L. Medin. *Categories and Concepts*. Harvard University Press, 1981.
29. Umberto Straccia. A fuzzy description logic. In *AAAI*, pages 594–599, 1998.
30. Umberto Straccia. Reasoning within fuzzy description logics. *Journal of Artificial Intelligence Research*, 14:137–166, 2001.
31. V. Tamma and T.J.M. Bench-Capon. An ontology model to facilitate knowledge sharing in multi-agent systems. *Knowledge Engineering Review*, 17(1):41–60, 2002.
32. D. H. Widyantot and J. Yen. Using fuzzy ontology for query refinement in a personalized abstract search engine. In *Proceedings of IFSA and NAFIPS*, 2001.
33. Floris Wiesman and Nico Roos. Domain independent learning of ontology mappings. In *AAMAS*, pages 846–853, 2004.
34. L.A. Zadeh. Fuzzy sets. *Information and Control*, 8:338–353, 1965.

In Defense of a Trope-Based Ontology for Conceptual Modeling: An Example with the Foundations of Attributes, Weak Entities and Datatypes

Giancarlo Guizzardi[1,2], Claudio Masolo[1], and Stefano Borgo[1]

[1] Laboratory for Applied Ontology (ISTC-CNR), Trento, Italy
{guizzardi, masolo, borgo}@loa-cnr.it
[2] Computer Science Department,
Federal University of Espirito Santo,
Vitoria-ES, Brazil

Abstract. In recent years, there has been a growing interest in approaches that employ foundational ontologies as theoretical tools for analyzing and improving conceptual modeling languages. However, some of these approaches do not always make explicit their ontological commitments. This leads to situations where criticisms resulting from the specific ontological choices made by a particular approach are generalized to the enterprise of ontology as a whole. In this paper we discuss an example of such a case involving the BWW approach. First, we make explicit the ontological commitments underlying that approach by relating it to other possible philosophical alternatives. Second, we construct an ontological theory which commits to a different philosophical position. Third, we show how the ontology proposed here can be used to provide real-world semantics and sound modeling guidelines for the modeling constructs of Attributes, Weak Entities and Datatypes. Finally, we compare the ontology proposed here with BWW, thus demonstrating its benefits.

1 Introduction

In recent years, there has been a growing interest in the use of foundational ontologies for: (i) evaluating conceptual modeling languages; (ii) developing guidelines for their use; (iii) providing real-world semantics for their modeling constructs (e.g., [5,7,18]).

A well-known example of a foundational ontology in the conceptual modeling/information systems area is the *Bunge-Wand-Weber (BWW)* ontology proposed by Wand and Weber in a series of articles (e.g., [5,20]) on the basis of the original metaphysical theory developed by Bunge in [2]. Recently, this ontology has received a number of criticisms in the literature, mainly due to the contrast between the modeling rules proposed by the BWW ontology, on one side, and what is prescribed by linguistic and cognitive studies as well as empirical sessions with practitioners, on the other (e.g., [8,15,16]). One of the strong points of disagreement between BWW and these approaches is the BWW-rule that states that intrinsic properties (roughly attributes) and associations should never be modeled as entity types in an ontologically correct conceptual model.

D.W. Embley, A. Olivé, and S. Ram (Eds.): ER 2006, LNCS 4215, pp. 112 – 125, 2006.

In a series of papers, Veres and colleagues (e.g., [8,15,16]) offer a detailed analysis and criticism of the general assumptions of the BWW approach. More specifically, in [16], they provide empirical evidence to support a case against the BWW treatment of associations. The danger in many of these criticisms is that they are formulated as general criticisms to ontology, not as specific criticisms to BWW. In other words, criticisms which are consequent of specific choices made in that ontology are generalized to the whole enterprise of ontological foundations for conceptual modeling. However, in the case of Veres et al., the criticisms cannot be against ontology *per se*, since the authors themselves state that they "describe an ontology of conceptual structure" or "psychologically motivated ontology" for the same purpose.

The purpose of this article is three fold. First, we want make explicit some ontological choices made by the BWW approach, and to show that the specific theory of universals underlying this approach is only one among many other philosophically correct theories. Second, we want to propose an alternative foundational theory, and to show how it can be used to provide an ontological interpretation for some conceptual modeling fundamental constructs. In particular, we want to create an ontology that countenances the existence of property instances, and a derived approach for conceptual modeling that accepts the representation of both attributes and associations as classes. Third, we intend to demonstrate that a trope-based ontology such as the one proposed here leads to better results as a foundational theory for conceptual modeling from philosophical, cognitive and practical points of view.

In section 2, we discuss different theories of universals and make explicit the BWW choices regarding these theories. In section 3, we propose a trope-based ontology, which is used in section 4 to provide ontological semantics for the conceptual modeling constructs of *attribute*, *weak entity* and *datatype*. In section 5, we compare the results of section 4 with the approach proposed in [5] that uses the BWW ontology as a foundation for UML as a conceptual modeling language. Section 6 presents some final considerations.

2 Universals, Tropes and Properties

Properties, their interpretation and nature have been discussed at length in the western philosophical tradition giving rise to subtle distinctions and disparate characterizations. Here, we introduce and discuss two general views, namely *universalism* and *trope theory*, and a third position that merges both universals and tropes. The discussion of these theories requires a terminological clarification so our first goal is to introduce a few concepts.

We use the term *particular* to refer to entities that have no instances, that is, entities that cannot be predicated of others; for instance the Tour Eiffel or the Mars planet. Contrast this notion with the notion of *universal* which, on the contrary, characterizes any entity that can have instances, e.g. the color Red or the car model Ferrari 250 GTO. Roughly, the properties (and the relations) used in a language are generally taken to correspond to universals since they are attributed to other entities. The notion of class is generally taken as a formal counterpart of the notion of universal. However, this may be misleading. By universal we mean a characterizing qualification of entities like "a Ferrari 250 GTO", i.e., a property that an entity may satisfy. The corresponding class is the collection of entities that satisfy that property. Another important notion we need to include is the notion of *trope*. Intuitively, a trope is an instance of a property (i.e., the instance of an objectified property) of a specific entity: the redness of John's T-shirt is a trope that *inheres* to John's T-shirt (the host).

Both John's T-shirt and the redness of John's T-shirt are particulars. However, they are particulars of very different natures. Tropes are particulars which can only exist in other individuals, i.e., they are *existentially dependent* on other individuals in the way, for instance, the color of an apple *a* depends on *a*, and the electric charge of a conductor *c* depends on *c*. In contrast, particulars such as John, the apple *a*, and the conductor *c* do not inhere in other individuals and, hence, are not existentially dependent entities in this sense. In this article, we give the name *Object* to the latter type of particular.

This brief and rough discussion of objects, universals, classes and tropes tells us that these concepts correspond to different categories of entities. However, which of these entities as well as the relations between them which are countenanced in one's ontology depend very much on one's philosophical position w.r.t. the so-called *Problem of Universals* [1,7]. This problem can be summarized as follows: We know that proper names (e.g., Noam Chomsky or Spot) refer to individual entities, but what do general terms (or universal properties) refer to (if anything at all)? We classify objects as being of the same type (e.g., person) and use the same predicate or general term (e.g., red) to different objects. What exactly *is the same* in different objects that justify their belonging to the same category?

Figure 1 illustrates three different representations of the fact: "the particulars a and b share the property being red". *Universalism* claims that a and b both *instantiate* (I) the being red (Red) universal, i.e. the universal being red is a spatiotemporal independent entity which is somehow wholly present in both a and b (fig.1-left). The trope theory denies the existence of universals as repeatable entities, and considers only tropes and classes of tropes. An important feature that characterizes all tropes is that they can only exist in other individuals, named their *bearers*. A formal relation of *inherence* symbolized as *i(x,y)* is defined to hold between a trope x and its bearer y. Inherence is an irreflexive, asymmetric and intransitive type of existential dependence relation. Moreover, it satisfies the *non-migration principle* [7]. This means that it is not possible for a trope *p* to inhere in two different individuals *a* and *b*. In other words, if we have two particulars *a* (a red apple) and *b* (a red car), and two tropes a_{red} (particular redness of *a*) and b_{red} (particular redness of *b*), we consider a_{red} and b_{red} to be different individuals, although perhaps qualitatively indistinguishable. What does it mean then to say that *a* and *b* have the *same* color? Due to the non-migration principle, sameness here cannot refer to strict (numerical) identity, but only to a qualitative one (i.e., equivalence in a certain respect). In standard Trope theory, a relation of *resemblance* (≈) is defined between tropes. Hence, tropes can resemble each other to a certain degree and, as in the example above, if they are qualitatively indistinguishable, we say that they exactly resemble each other. This way, Trope theory does not have to commit to the existence of universals as a separate category of abstract entities, since equivalence classes of resembling tropes are enough for predication: a and b have the common property of *being red* because there are two red tropes a_{red} and b_{red} both belonging (∈) to the red class ($|red|_{\approx}$) of tropes that inhere in a and b, respectively. If on the one hand by accepting tropes one does not have to accept universals, on the other hand, these two theories are not incompatible and, actually, they can be merged: a and b have the property being red because the a_{red} trope and the b_{red} trope both are instances of the universal Red. In this case, universals exist but they are instantiated only by tropes.

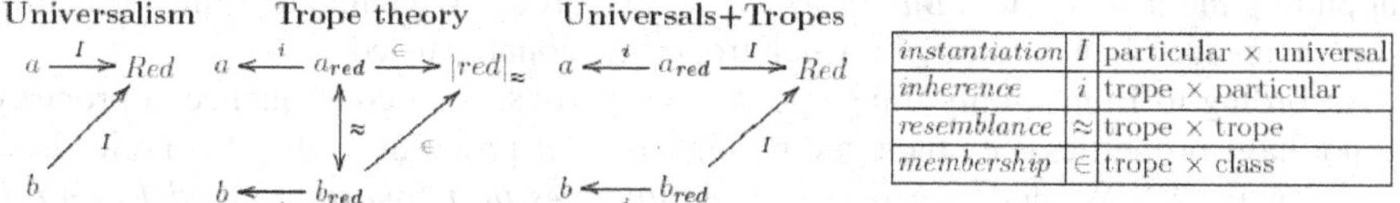

instantiation	I	particular × universal
inherence	i	trope × particular
resemblance	$\approx$	trope × trope
membership	$\in$	trope × class

Fig. 1. Different philosophical positions on Universals

2.1 Making Explicit the Ontological Position Behind BWW

In BWW, we have a fundamental dichotomy between the notions of *substantial individual* (or *thing*) and *substantial property*. A thing is defined as a substantial individual with all its substantial properties: *"a thing is what is the totality of its substantial properties"* [2, p.111]. Despite of apparently equating a thing which the sum of its properties, Bunge himself does not embraces a type of universalism named the *Bundle of Universals* theory. In fact, he explicitly rejects this theory and, instead, holds another (universalist) position that can be better identified with the *substance-attribute* view [1].

In short, in the former type of theory, particulars are taken as *bundles of universals*, i.e., as aggregates of properties which themselves are repeatable abstract entities. An exemplar theory of this type was proposed by Russel in [12]. For details on this theory as well as for a discussion on the many problems related to it one should refer to [1]. In fact, among the universalist theories, [1] considers the bundle theory of universals to be the weakest one from a philosophical point of view. The *substance-attribute* view makes an explicit distinction between a thing and the properties that the thing has. As a consequence, the theory countenances the existence for every individual of a propertyless *substratum* or *bare particular*. The notion of substratum is strongly associated with the British empiricist philosopher John Locke [1] and due to its mysterious nature it has been the target of strong criticism throughout history. Nonetheless, Bunge claims that as a *"theoretical fiction"* it solves some of the philosophical problems existing in the *bundle of universals* theories [2, p.57]. Hence, for Bunge a thing is a bare particular endowed by all its substantial properties, i.e., he commits to the substance-attribute sort of universalism and, as consequence, denies the existence of *particularized properties*.

In principle, it seems that a thing in BWW could be directly associated to the concept of object in a trope-based theory (figs. 1.center and 1.right). However, there are some important differences between the two. Whilst a BWW-thing can be thought as a substratum instantiating a number of properties (as repeatable abstract entities), objects in a trope-based approach are particulars that bear other particularized properties, or to borrow Simons' phrase, *"particulars in particular clothing"*[14]. Thus, in a trope-theoretical approach, one does not have to make any ontological commitment w.r.t. the nature of the *substratum*. In particular, if necessary, one can dispense with a substratum of a mysterious nature. An example of such a view is the one of Simons' *Nuclear Theory* (ibid.). This approach has the benefits of the substance-attribute view, without having to accept its problems, since the nucleus is akin to a substratum, only not a mysterious one. In BWW, the mysterious substratum cannot be eliminated without putting the theory into a *Bundle of Universals* group. We claim that this flexibility is an advantage of an ontology in which tropes are countenanced.

According to Bunge, only things possess properties. As a consequence, a property cannot have properties, i.e., there are no higher-order properties. This dictum leads to the following BWW modeling principle: *entity types in a conceptual model of a domain should only be used to represent substantial universals* [5]. This principle proscribes the representation of types whose instances are particularized properties, including relations. This claim is not only perceived as counterintuitive by conceptual modeling practitioners (as shown by [8,16]), but it is also controversial from a metaphysical point of view. For instance, Armstrong [1], who as much as Bunge embraces scientific realism as a theory of universals, claims that higher-order properties are *necessary* to represent the concept of a *law*. For Armstrong, a law such as Newton's F = MA describes a second-order relation between the three universals involved. Strangely enough, Bunge also defines the concept of a *Law* (quite a central notion is his approach) as a relation between properties, which makes it a second-order relation [2, p.77]. The view that there are, in fact, material higher-order universals is also shared by other approaches (e.g., [4]). Even simple higher-order relations between universals such as "*Redness is more like Orange than it is like yellow*" cannot be dealt with in the current version of the BWW framework. In contrast, in a trope-based approach, if one wants to dispense with higher-order properties of this kind, this relation can be expressed in terms of first-order inexact resemblance relations between tropes. In fact, in such an approach, traditional properties of properties such as the *hue of a certain color* or the *graveness of a certain symptom* can be modeled in terms of first-order inherence relations between tropes (see fig.4).

If one subscribes to Bunge's theory, however, there is a much stronger reason to argue against the representation of non-substantial universals as types: since Bunge denies the existence of *particularized properties*, one could simply state that properties should not be represented as entity types because they should not be allowed to have instances. However, it is important to emphasize that to accept the claims: (c1) *there are instances of properties*, as well as (c2) *properties can have properties* does not amount to an ontologically incorrect position. The claims (c1) and (c2) are only incompatible with the very specific ontological choices made for the BWW framework. As mentioned above, even if one embraces universalism, (c2) can be accepted. Moreover, the denial of (c1) puts BWW in a singular position among the foundational ontologies developed in the realm of computer science (e.g., [4, 7, 9, 13]). As pointed out by [13], there is solid evidence for (c1) in the literature. On the one hand, in the analysis of the content of perception, particularized properties such as colors, sounds, runs, laughter and singings are the immediate objects of everyday perception. On the other hand, the idea of tropes as *truthmakers* underlies a standard event-based approach to natural language semantics, as initiated by [3] and [11].

3 A Trope-Based Ontology

Figure 2 illustrates the main categories that constitute the ontology proposed in this article. The category of particulars comprises both Objects and Tropes. The relation of inherence is defined between tropes and other particulars, which are not necessarily objects. In other words, we admit that tropes can inhere in other tropes. We also consider the categories of *object kind* and *trope kind* as two possible sorts of *kinds*. We use the term kind here in a broader sense than the term universal, without necessarily committing to the existence of universals, i.e., without choosing *a priori* between position (b) or (c) in figure 1. A kind thus can be considered here simply as something (i) which can be predicated of other entities and (ii) that can potentially be represented in language by *predicative terms*. We also use the relation :: of classification between particulars and kinds. Likewise, classification can be interpreted as instantiation or membership depending on the ontological commitment which is made.

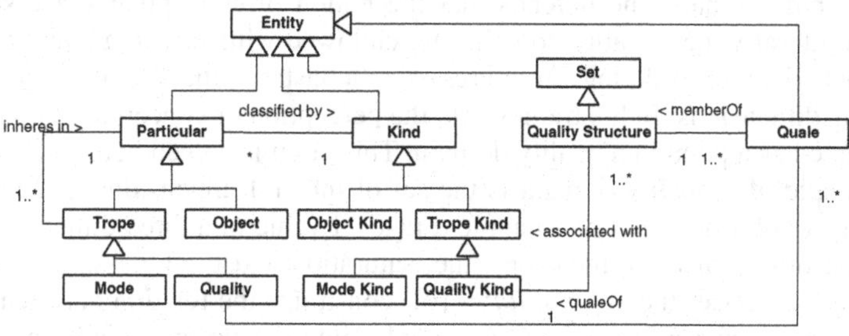

Fig. 2. The Categories composing a simple trope-based ontology

Object Kinds classify objects and Trope Kinds classify tropes. Examples of object kinds include Apple, Person and Ferrari 250 GTO. Examples of trope kinds include Color, Electric Charge and Headache. This distinction is also present in Aristotle's original differentiation between what is *said of a subject* (*de subjecto dici*), denoting classification and what is *exemplified in a subject* (*in subjecto est*), denoting inherence. Thus, the linguistic difference between the two meanings of the copula "is" reflects an ontological one. For example, the ontological interpretation of the sentence "Jane is a Woman" is that the object Jane is classified by the object kind Woman. However, when saying that "Jane is tall" or "Jane is laughing" we mean that Jane *exemplifies* the trope kind Tall or Laugh, by virtue of her specific height or laugh.

Here, we capture the intension of a kind by means of an axiomatic specification, i.e., a set of axioms that may involve a number of other kinds representing its essential features. A particular form of such a specification of a kind *U* is called an *elementary specification* (ES). An ES of a kind *U* consists of a number of trope kinds $T_1,\ldots,T_n$ and the inherence relation which attaches instances from the T_i to instances of *U*, expressed by the following schema: $\forall a(a :: K \rightarrow \exists t_1 \ldots t_n \bigwedge_{i \leq n}(t_i :: T_i \wedge i(t_i, a)))$. The relation between a kind U and the trope kinds in its elementary specification is one of *characterization*: A kind U is characterized by a trope kind T iff every instance of K exemplifies T, i.e., iff $\mathbf{\forall x\ (x::U \rightarrow \exists y\ y::T \wedge i(y,x))}$.

An attempt to model the relation between properties and their representation in human cognitive structures is presented in the theory of *conceptual spaces* introduced in [6]. The theory is based on the notion of *quality dimension*. The idea is that for several perceivable or conceivable trope kinds there is an associated quality dimension in human cognition. For example, height and mass are associated with one-dimensional structures with a zero point isomorphic to the half-line of nonnegative numbers. Other properties such as color and taste are represented by multi-dimensional structures.

Gardenfors [6] distinguishes between *integral* and *separable* quality dimensions: "certain quality dimensions are integral in the sense that one cannot assign an object a value on one dimension without giving it a value on the other. For example, an object cannot be given a hue without giving it a brightness value (...) Dimensions that are not integral are said to be separable, as for example the size and hue dimensions." He then defines a *quality domain* as "a set of integral dimensions that are separable from all other dimensions" and a *conceptual space* as a "collection of one or more domains" (ibid.). Finally, he defends that the notion of conceptual space should be understood literally, i.e., quality domains are endowed with certain geometrical structures (topological or ordering structures) that constrain the relations between its constituting dimensions. In his framework, the perception or conception of a trope can be represented as a point in a quality domain. This point is named here a *quale* [9].

An example of a quality domain is the set of integral dimensions related to color perception. A color quality *c* of an apple *a* takes it value in a three-dimensional color domain constituted of the dimensions hue, saturation and brightness. The geometric structure of this space (the *color splinter* [6]) constrains the relation between some of these dimensions. In particular, saturation and brightness are not totally independent, since the possible variation of saturation decreases as brightness approaches the extreme points of black and white, i.e., for almost black or almost white, there can be very little variation in saturation. A similar constraint could be postulated for the relation between saturation and hue. When saturation is very low, all hues become similarly approximate to grey.

We adopt in this work the term *quality structures* to refer to quality dimensions and quality domains, and we define the formal relation of *association* between quality structure and a trope kind. Additionally, we use the terms *quality kinds* for those trope kinds that are associated with a quality domain, and the term *quality* for a trope classified under a quality kind. We also assume that quality structures are always associated with a unique quality kind, i.e., a quality structure associated with the kind Weight cannot be associated with the kind Color.

Following [9], we take that whenever a quality kind Q is related to a quality domain D, then for every individual quality x::Q there are *indirect qualities* inhering in x for every quality dimension associated with D. For instance, for every particular quality c instance of Color there are quality individuals h, s, b which are instances of quality kinds Hue, Saturation and Brightness, respectively, and that inhere in c. The qualities h, s, b are named *indirect qualities* of c's bearer. Qualities such as h, s, b are named *simple qualities*, i.e., qualities which do not bear other qualities. In contrast, a quality such as c, is named a *complex quality*. Since the qualities of a complex quality x::Q correspond to the quality dimensions of the quality domain associated with Q, then we have that no two distinct qualities inhering a complex quality can be of the same type. For the same reason, since there are not multidimensional quality dimensions, we have that complex qualities can only bear simple qualities. Moreover, we use predicate *ql(x,y)* to represent the formal relation between a quality individual y and its quale x.

Finally, we make a distinction between qualities and another sort of trope named here *modes*. Modes are tropes whose kinds are not directly related to quality structures. Gardenfors [6] makes the following distinction between what he calls *concepts* and *properties*: "Properties…form as special case of concepts. I define this distinction by saying that a *property* is based on *single domain*, while a *concept* may be based on *several domains*". We claim that only trope kinds that are conceptualized w.r.t. a single domain, i.e., quality kinds, correspond to properties in Gardenfors sense. However, there are trope kinds that as much as object kinds can be conceptualized in terms of multiple separable quality dimensions. Examples include beliefs, desires, intentions, perceptions, symptoms, skills, among many others. Like objects, modes can bear other tropes, and each of these tropes can refer to separable quality dimensions. However, since they are tropes, differently from objects, modes are necessarily existentially dependent of some particular.

4 A Foundation for Attributes, Weak Entities and Datatypes

Suppose that we have an object kind *Apple* whose elementary specification contains the trope kind *Weight*. Thus, for an instance *a* of Apple there is an instance *w* of the quality kind Weight inhering in *a*, i.e., $\forall \mathbf{a}\ (\mathbf{a::Apple} \rightarrow \exists \mathbf{w}\ (\mathbf{w::Weight} \land \mathbf{i(w,a)}))$.

Associated with the quality kind Weight we have a quality dimension **WeightDim** and, hence, for every instance *w* of Weight there is a quale *c* denoting a particular weight value, i.e., a point in the weight quality dimension such that *ql(c,w)* holds. We take here the weight quality domain to be a one-dimensional structure isomorphic to the half-line of non-negative numbers, which can be represented by a set. The mapping between a substantial *a* and its weight quale can then be represented by the function: **weight: Ext(Apple) → WeightDim** such that $\mathbf{weight(x) = y} \mid \exists \mathbf{z}\ \mathbf{z::Weight} \land \mathbf{i(z,x)} \land \mathbf{ql(y,z)}$, and **Ext(Apple)** represents the set extension of the kind Apple.

In general, let K be a (object or trope) kind and let $Q_1,\ldots,Q_n$ be a number of quality kinds. Let E be an elementary specification characterizing the kind U: $\forall \mathbf{x}\ (\mathbf{x::U} \rightarrow \exists q_1,\ldots,q_n \bigwedge_{i\leq n} (\mathbf{q_i::Q_i} \land \mathbf{i(q_i,x)}))$. If D_i is a quality domain directly *associated with* Q_i, we can define the function $\mathbf{Q_i: Ext(U) \rightarrow D_i}$ (named an *attribute function* for quality universal Q_i) such that for every x::U we have that $\mathbf{Q_i(x) = y \mid y \in D_i \land \exists q::Q_i \land i(q,x) \land ql(y,q)}$.

Let us suppose for now a situation in which every Q_i present in the elementary specification of a kind U is a simple quality kind i.e., Q_i is associated to a one-dimensional quality domain. In this simplest case, the quality kinds appearing in the elementary specification of *U* can be represented in a conceptual model via their corresponding *attribute functions* and associated *quality dimensions* in the following manner: **[Principle 1:** Every attribute function derived from the elementary specification of the kind U may be represented as an attribute of the class C_U (representation of the kind U) in a conceptual model; every *quality dimension* which is the co-domain of one of these functions may be represented as data types of the corresponding attributes in this conceptual model. Finally, relations constraining and informing the geometry of a quality dimension may be represented as constraints in the corresponding data type].

In UML "a data type is a special kind of classifier, similar to a class, whose instances are values (not objects)... A value does not have an identity, so two occurrences of the same value cannot be differentiated" [10, p.95]. A direct representation of Apple's elementary specification in UML according to principle 1 maps the attribute function **weight: Ext(Apple)→WeightDim** to an attribute weight with data type WeightValue in class Apple (figures 3.a-b).

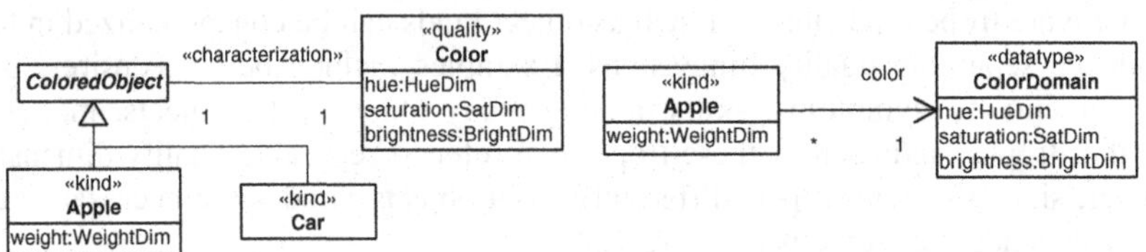

Fig. 3. (a, left) - Representing Quality Universals and Indirect Qualities; (b) Representing Qualia in a Multi-Dimensional Quality Domain

Suppose now that we have the following extension of the elementary specification of the kind Apple: **∀a (a::Apple → ∃c∃w (c::Color ∧ i(c,a)) ∧ (w::Weight ∧ i(w,a)))**. In order to model the relation between the quality c (color) and its quale, there are other issues to consider. As previously mentioned, the Color quality kind can be associated with a tri-dimensional quality structure composed of quality dimensions hue, saturation and brightness. These dimensions can be considered to be indirect quality kinds exemplified in an apple *a*, i.e., there are quality individuals h, s, b which are instances of quality universals Hue, Saturation and Brightness, respectively, that inhere in the color quality c (which in turn inheres in object *a*). The elementary specification of quality universal Color could then be specified as follows: **∀c (c::Color → ∃h∃s∃b (h::Hue ∧ i(h,c)) ∧ (s::Saturation ∧ i(s,c)) ∧ (b::Brightness ∧ i(b,c)))**. In this case, we can derive the following attribute functions from the features in this specification: **hue: Ext(Color) → HueDim**; **saturation: Ext(Color) → SatDim**; **brightness: Ext(Color) → BrightDim**. Together these functions map each quality of a color c to its corresponding quality dimension. One possibility for modeling this situation is a direct application of principle 1 to the Color kind specification. In this alternative, depicted in figure 3.a, the UML class Color directly represents the quality universal color and, its attribute functions hue, saturation and brightness.

Another modeling alternative is to use directly the construct of a data type to represent a quality domain and its constituent quality dimensions (figure 3.b). That is, we can define the quality domain associated with the universal Color as the set **ColorDomain ⊂ HueDim × SatDim × BrightDim**. Then, we can define the following *attribute function* for the object kind Apple: **color: Ext(Apple) → ColorDomain** such that **color(x) = {⟨h,s,b⟩ ∈ ColorDomain | ∃c::Color i(c,x) ∧ (h = hue(c)) ∧ (s = saturation(c)) ∧ (b = brightness(c))}** where hue, saturation and brightness are the attribute functions previously defined. In figure 3.b, we use the UML construct of a *structured datatype* to model the **ColorDomain**. In this representation, the *datatype fields* hue, saturation, brightness are placeholders for the coordinates of each of the (integral) quality dimensions forming the color domain. In this way the "instances" (members) of ColorDomain are quale vectors ⟨x,y,z⟩ where $x \in$ HueDim, $y \in$ SatDim and $z \in$ BrightDim. The *navigable end name* ***color*** in the association between Apple and ColorDomain represents the attribute function ***color*** described above.

The two forms of representation exemplified in figures 3.a and 3.b do not convey the same information, which we highlight by the use of different stereotypes. In figure 3.a, color instances are one-sidedly existentially dependent on the particulars they are related to via an *inherence* relation. These instances are genuine individuals with a definite numerical identity. In contrast, the members of the ColorDomain are *pure values* that represent points in a quality domain. These values can qualify a number of different objects but they exist independently of them in the sense that a color tuple is a part of quality domain even if no object "has that color".

Both representations are warranted in the sense that ontologically consistent interpretations can be found in both cases. Notwithstanding, we believe that some guidelines could be anticipated regarding which alternative should be pragmatically more suitable in different cases. In situations in which the tropes of a trope all take their values (qualia) in a single quality domain, the latter alternative (shown in figure 3.b) should be preferred due to its compatibility with the modeling tradition in conceptual modeling and knowledge representation. This is the case with quality kinds. Additionally, since the conceptualization of these tropes depends on the combined appreciation of all their quality dimensions, we claim that they should be mapped in an integral way to a quale vector in the corresponding n-dimensional quality domain.

In the sequel, we observe the following principle between quality domains and their representation in terms of data types: [**Principle 2:** Every quality dimension D directly associated to a quality kind Q may be represented as a datatype DT in a conceptual model; Relations constraining and informing the geometry of a quality dimension D may be represented as operators in the corresponding datatype DT. A collection of integral dimension $D_1 \ldots D_n$ (represented by data types $DT_1 \ldots DT_n$) constituting a quality domain QD can be grouped in structured datatype W representing quality domain QD. In this case, every quality dimension D_i of QD may be represented by a field of W of type DT_i. Moreover, the relations between the dimensions D_i of QD may be represented by constraints relating the fields of data type W].

Principle 2 is a generalization of principle 1 in order to account for quality domains. In summary, every quality kind Q that is associated to a quality domain in an elementary specification of kind U can be represented in a conceptual model via attribute functions mapping instances of U to quale vectors in the n-dimensional domain associated with Q. The n-dimensional domains should be represented in a conceptual model as an n-valued structured data type.

Now, let us consider a case where one of the trope kinds M that characterizes a kind U in its elementary specification is a mode kind. We defend here that these are the cases in which we want to explicitly represent a trope kind in a conceptual model. An example of such a situation is depicted in Figure 4, which models the relation between a Hospital, its Patients, and a number of symptoms reported by these patients. Suppose that an individual patient John is suffering from headache and influenza. John's headache and influenza are modes inhering in John. Even if another patient, for example Paul, has a headache that is qualitatively indistinguishable from that of John's, John's headache and Paul's headache are two different particulars. Instances of Symptoms can bear tropes themselves (such as duration and graveness) and can participate in relations of, for example, causation or precedence.

In figure 4, the mode kind Symptom is represented by a class construct decorated with the «mode» stereotype. The formal relation of «characterization» between Symptom and Patient is mapped to the inherence relation in the instance level, representing the existential dependence of a Symptom on a Patient. In other words, for an instance s of Symptom there must be a specific instance p of Patient associated with s, and in every situation that s exists p must exist and the inherence relation between the two must hold. A mode kind such as Symptom in figure 4 can be seen as the ontological counterpart of the concept of *Weak entities types* in EER diagrams, which has been lost in the UML unification process [17].

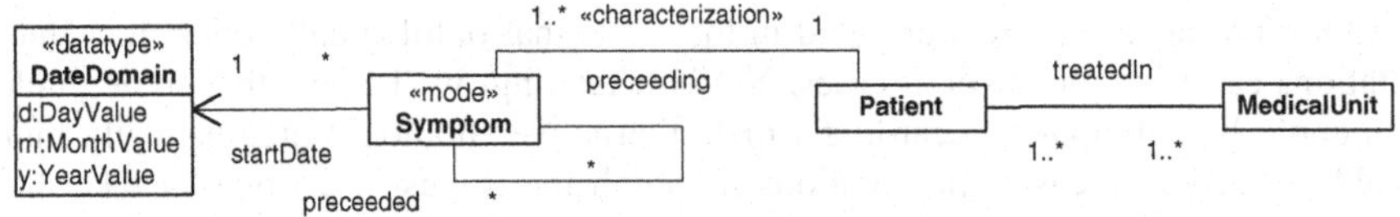

Fig. 4. Representing Object and Mode Kinds and Quality Structures

To summarize this section we can provide the following procedure to represent in conceptual modeling the elementary specification of kinds and their associated trope kinds and quality structures: Take an object kind U with its associated elementary specification E. For every trope kind Q characterizing U do: (1) If Q is a simple quality kind then principle 1 can be applied; (2) If Q is a complex quality kind then principle 2 can be applied; (3) If Q is a mode kind then it should be explicitly represented and should be related to U in a model via a *characterization* relation. Moreover, this procedure can be re-applied to the elementary specification of each trope kind Q in E.

5 A Comparison with the BWW Approach

One of the most defended principles of the BWW approach is the one that states that *"properties cannot have properties"*. So, a question that comes to the mind is: how would one model in the BWW approach situations such as the ones depicted in figures 3 and 4? Take for example, the model in figure 3. In [5], Color is one of the examples used for a property. However, if both Color and Hue (Saturation, Brightness) are properties, how can this conceptualization be modeled in an approach that proscribes the representation of properties of properties?

According to [5], in BWW, the intrinsic (as opposed to relational) properties of a thing *must* be modeled as attributes of the type instantiated by that thing. Since, only substantial types can have attributes, we have that intrinsic properties must be modeled as attributes of substantial types. Thus, a solution to the problem mentioned above is to consider Hue, Saturation and Brightness to be direct properties of Apple, not of Color. The latter, in turn, is then considered to be a conjunction of these three properties, i.e., to instantiate a specific super-determinate shade of red is to instantiate the specific values of Hue, Saturation and Brightness that compose this color. However, in order to be complete, such a solution must also account for the constraints that restrict the possible values that these three dimensions together can assume.

In BWW, a type is represented by a model named a *functional schema.* A functional schema comprises a finite sequence of functions $F = \langle F_1..F_n \rangle$, such that each function F_i (named an *attribute*) represents a property shared by the members of the type described by the functional schema. For every attribute F_i there is a co-domain V_i of values. Bunge defines a function $F(t)$ as the *state function* of the thing, such that $F(t') = \langle F_1(t')..F_n(t') \rangle$ is said to represent the *state of a thing* at time t'. The set $V_1 \times \ldots \times V_n$ is termed the *state space of a thing*. Now, there are certain sorts of types named *Natural Kinds* whose instances have properties which are lawfully related. For these types, it is not the case that the coordinates of the state vectors representing their properties can vary freely. The subset of $V_1 \times \ldots \times V_n$ constrained by the laws of that type being described is named by Bunge the *lawful state space* of a thing. In other words, the lawful state space associated with a natural kind defines all possible states that instances of that kind can assume.

Compared to the approach advocated in this article, we claim that the solution just discussed has two drawbacks. First, as exemplified in figure 3.a, the constraints relating the properties of Hue, Saturation and Brightness are not intrinsic to the type Apple but to the geometry of the Color quality structure and, thus, are reflected in all colored objects. Moreover, these properties form a closure set w.r.t. to mutual dependence and, thus, define a quality domain. In other words, these properties are *integral* and one *"cannot assign an object a value on one dimension without giving it a value on the other"*. For these reasons, we claim that the proposal advanced here of explicit representation of quality domains as datatypes provides the following modeling benefits: (i) a further degree of structuring on lawful state spaces by acknowledging that the co-domains V of attribute functions can also be multidimensional. In fact, this allows for the representation of richer conceptual structures such as the one modeled in figure 5 in which the same Color trope can be measured (take its value) in alternative quality domains; (ii) a structured datatype representing a quality domain can reinforce (via its constructor method) that its tuples will always have values for all its integral dimensions, and only values which obey the constraints imposed by the geometry of that domain; (iii) it also allows for a potential reuse of specifications of multidimensional value co-domains. In this example, once the constraints representing the geometry of the color domain are captured in the specification of the ColorDomain datatype, this specification can be consistently re-used for all colored objects.

The second problem with the solution previously discussed can be defined as follows. If Hue, Saturation and Brightness and its relating constraints are represented in the specification of all types whose instances are colored objects, then by the BWW definition of a natural kind, we can define a natural kind whose instances are all particulars that exemplify the lawfully related properties of Hue, Saturation and Brightness. This allegedly natural kind would be analogous to the type *ColoredObject* depicted in figure 3.a. However, the typical notion of natural kinds in philosophy implies that [7]: (i) they are rigid designators, i.e. that they classify necessarily (in the modal sense) their instances; (ii) that they afford the best inductive generalizations, i.e., that knowing that a particular x is of a kind A also imply knowing that x has all essential properties which are common to instances of A; (iii) that they are associated with a criterion of individuation. These characteristics (i-iii) can all be found in *Apple* but none of them in *ColoredObject*.

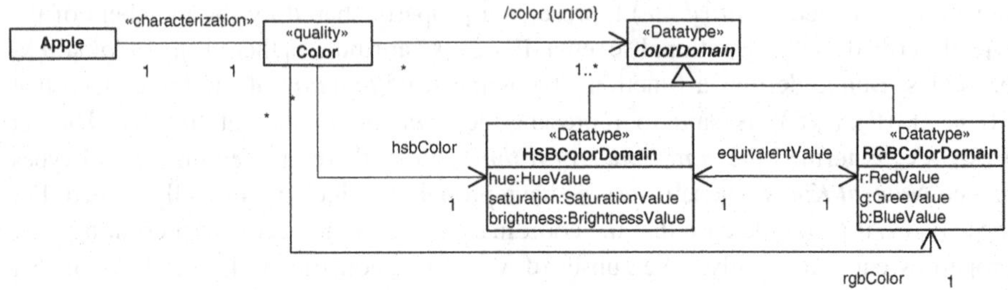

Fig. 5. Explicitly representing quality universals and quality spaces

Let us now consider the case depicted in figure 4. Here, once more, the trope kind symptom can be modeled by having its properties ascribed directly to the type Patient. However, take the property of graveness. "Being grave" is not a property of a particular Patient but a property of a symptom of that patient. Suppose that graveness can be valued in a range 0-5. It is still possible to represent the values in this range as different sets of values of other attributes of symptom, but the introduction of a graveness-space is conceptually clearer. The latter is only possible with a reification of symptom, as illustrated in figure 4 using tropes.

A similar case regards the expression of relations between tropes as the relation of precedence (but also causality) between symptoms depicted in figure 4. According to this model, a symptom such as headache or fever can be caused by another one, for example, influenza. However, differently from the cases mentioned above, these relations cannot be described in general terms; they are indeed relations between instances of these properties. To put it differently, it is John's fever which has been caused by his influenza of a certain graveness. Paul's fever in turn has been caused by his pneumonia.

6 Final Considerations

Despite the perceived usefulness of ontologically well-founded principles and tools for the practice of conceptual modeling, a number of recent results have pointed out the incongruence between what is prescribed by the BWW ontology, on one side, and what is indicated by cognitive and linguistically motivated theories, as well as empirical results of experiments with conceptual modeling practitioners, on the other. The position defended in this paper is in line with some of these criticisms to the BWW ontology. In particular, we reject the BWW-rule that in conceptual modeling only substantial universals should be represented as classes. However, as we have pointed out, it is a mistake to generalize these criticisms to the enterprise of ontology-based conceptual modeling as a whole. As we have shown in the paper, the modeling principles advocated by the BWW framework are a consequence of the very particular type of ontological theory sponsored by its proponents, and their ontological view is only one among many other alternatives.

Furthermore, in this paper we have proposed an alternative ontology which has been used as a foundation for the conceptual modeling primitives of attribute, datatype and weak entities. The ontology presented here is only a fragment of a larger theory which has been extended elsewhere to account for other modeling constructs, such as, classifiers (kinds. roles, phases, mixins), association, part-whole relations, among others [7]. In particular, as demonstrated there, when relational properties are considered, a trope-based approach such as this one not only escapes the criticisms pointed out in [8,15,16], but it also brings a number of additional benefits from a modeling point of view.

References

1. Armstrong, D.M. 'Universals: An Opinionated Introduction', Westview Press, 1989.
2. Bunge M.: Treatise on Basic Philosophy. Vol. 3. Ontology I. The Furniture of the World. D. Reidel Publishing, New York, 1977.
3. Davidson, D. 'The Logical Form of Action Sentences', Essays on Actions and Events, Oxford University Press, 1980.
4. Degen, W., Heller B., Herre H., Smith, B. GOL: 'Towards an axiomatized upper level ontology'. Proc. of FOIS'01, Maine, USA, ACM Press, 2001.
5. Evermann J., Wand Y.: Towards ontologically based semantics for UML constructs, Proceedings of ER 2001, pages 354–367. Springer-Verlag, 2001.
6. Gärdenfors, P. 'Conceptual Spaces: the Geometry of Thought', MIT Press, USA, 2000.
7. Guizzardi, G. 'Ontological Foundations for Structural Conceptual Models', PhD Thesis, University of Twente, The Netherlands, 2005.
8. Hitchman, S. "An interpretive study of how practitioners use entity-relationship modeling in a ternary relationship situation",Communications of the Association for Information Systems, 2003, 11, 451-485.
9. Masolo, C., Borgo, S., Gangemi, A., Guarino, N., Oltramari, A. 'Ontology Library', WonderWeb Deliverable D18, 2003.
10. Object Management Group, 'UML 2.0 Superstructure Specification', ptc/03-08-02, 2003.
11. Parsons, T. 'Events in the Semantics of English: A Study in Subatomic Semantics'. Cambridge/MA: MIT Press, 1990.
12. Russel, B. 'Human Knowledge, its Scopes and Limits', Allen and Unwin, 1948.
13. Schneider, L. 'Formalised Elementary Formal Ontology', ISIB-CNR Technical Report 03/2002, [online: http://www.loa-cnr.it/Publications.html], 2002.
14. Simons, P. Particular in Particular Clothing: Three Trope theories of Substance', Philosophy and Phenomenological Research, 54, 553-576, 1994.
15. Veres, C.; Hitchman, S, 'Using Psychology to Understand Conceptual Modeling', 10th European Conference on Information Systems (ECIS 2002), Poland.
16. Veres, C.; Mansson, G., 'Cognition and Modeling: Foundations for Research and Practice', Journal of Information Technology Theory and Application, v.7, n.1, 93-10, 2005.
17. Vigna, S. 'ERW: The Manual', [online: http://erw.dsi.unimi.it/ERW/index.html], 2004.
18. Wand Y.,Storey V.C., Weber R.: An ontological analysis of the relationship construct in conceptual modeling. ACM Transactions on Database Systems, 24(4):494–528, December 1999.

Explicitly Representing Superimposed Information in a Conceptual Model

Sudarshan Murthy, Lois Delcambre, and David Maier

Department of Computer Science, Portland State University
PO Box 751 Portland, OR 97207 USA
{smurthy, lmd, maier}@cs.pdx.edu
http://sparce.cs.pdx.edu

Abstract. *Superimposed information* (SI) refers to new information such as annotations and summaries overlaid on fragments of existing *base information* (BI) such as web pages and PDF documents. Each BI fragment is referenced using an encapsulated address called a *mark.* Based on the widespread applicability of SI and wide range of superimposed applications (SAs) that can be built, we consider here how to represent marks explicitly in a conceptual model for an SA. The goal of this work is to facilitate the development of SAs by making it easy to model SI (including the marks) and to exploit the middleware and query capability that we have developed for managing marks and interacting with the base applications. The contribution of this paper is a general-purpose framework to make marks explicit in a conceptual (ER) model. We present conventions to associate marks with entities, attributes, and relationships; and to represent that an attribute's value is the same as the excerpt obtained from a mark. We also provide procedures to automatically convert ER schemas expressed using our conventions to relational schemas, and show how a resulting relational schema supports SQL queries over the combination of SI, the associated marks and the excerpts associated with the marks.

1 Introduction

Over the last decade, our research group has been developing the notion of *superimposed information* (SI) consisting of information placed over arbitrary *base information* sources to support new applications and new purposes [11]. SI can be represented in any data model appropriate for the *superimposed application* (SA). The key feature of SI is that it can contain *marks* [7], which are encapsulated addresses to bits of base information at fine granularity as demonstrated in Figure 1, in addition to data that is defined and created directly in the superimposed layer. The mark is an *explicit* construct that crosses from one layer of information to another. The *superimposed layer* contains the SI, including marks, and the *base layer* consists of all documents that can be referenced, using marks, from the SI. Each referenced base information source can use a distinct data model and schema; to date, we have relied on existing base applications (BAs) to manage and manipulate the base information.

Our first SA is a superimposed scratchpad tool [14], called *Sidepad* (earlier called RIDPad and SLIMPad), that uses a simple hierarchical model in the superimposed layer that can reference selections in a number of base source types including

D.W. Embley, A. Olivé, and S. Ram (Eds.): ER 2006, LNCS 4215, pp. 126–139, 2006.

Microsoft® Word, PowerPoint®, Excel®, PDF, XML, HTML, and several audio and video formats. Figure 1 shows a Sidepad document instance with five *items*: `Query Optimizer`, `Goal`, `Model`, `Definition`, and `SchemaSQL`. An item has a name (shown underlined in Figure 1), a comment, and an encapsulated mark to a selection in a base document. For example, the item `Goal` contains a mark into a selection in a PDF document. The boxes labeled `Garlic` and `Schematic Heterogeneity` are *groups* of items. The result of activating the PDF selection that the `Goal` item references is shown on the right side in Figure 1.

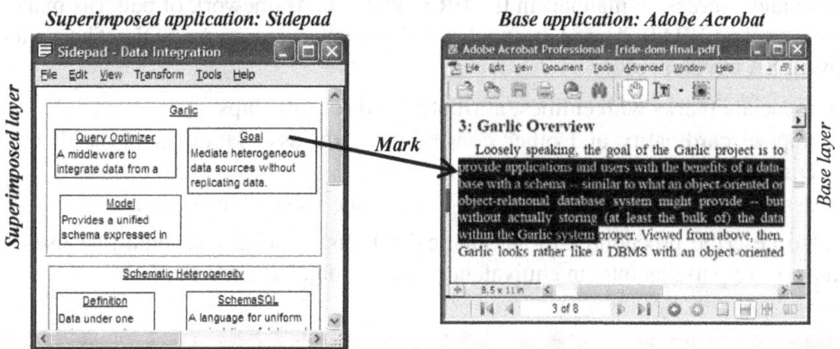

Fig. 1. Superimposed information (left) created using *Sidepad*, a superimposed application. The `Goal` *item* in the Sidepad document has an associated *mark* that encapsulates the address of the PDF excerpt shown on the right side of the figure. A mark is activated in Sidepad by double-clicking on an item.

To aid SA implementation, we have developed the middleware architecture called the *Superimposed Pluggable Architecture for Contexts and Excerpts* [14] (SPARCE) that manages mark *descriptors* in an XML repository. SPARCE assigns each mark a unique ID represented as a string. SAs need to incorporate only mark IDs in their SI. To operate on a mark (for example, to activate it), an SA passes a mark ID to SPARCE to obtain a mark *object* at run time.

SPARCE relies on plug-ins for base applications to create marks and uses wrappers called *context agents* to interact with underlying base applications to activate marks and to retrieve content or *excerpts* from marks. We have used SPARCE and the context agents to materialize and query *bi-level information* (an SI source, with its associated marks and their respective excerpts) and to transform it into alternative representations [13]. For example, Figure 2 shows a portion of the Sidepad document of Figure 1 transformed into an HTML document via XML. The text labeled 'Comment' is the descriptive text associated with an item. The text labeled 'Excerpt' is the text excerpt retrieved from the mark encapsulated in the corresponding item.

Several other SAs have been developed, including a *Superimposed Schematics Browser* [3] with an Entity-Relationship (ER) model in the superimposed layer that provides structured browsing of underlying document content. In general, SI allows bits of information, at small granularity, from a wide variety of base information sources to be selected, integrated, elaborated, structured, and mixed with arbitrary additional information in an SA.

Over the last decade, we have seen increasing interest in SI in general, and in particular in the SAs we have developed. Some of our research partners have also begun using SPARCE to build new SAs (for example, see http://si.dlib.vt.edu). Our experience in designing SI has highlighted the need to model SI beyond what is possible in traditional modeling frameworks such as ER. Since the mark abstraction, by design, explicitly crosses from one information source to another, we seek to model marks explicitly at the conceptual level. Specifically, we seek to identify the modeling constructs with which marks may be associated, and to capture the semantics of such associations. We present in this paper a set of patterns for representing marks, in a flexible and expressive manner, in the ER model. The framework of patterns makes it easy to exploit SPARCE and it enables bi-level querying using SQL. The patterns allow an SA developer to:

- associate marks with entities, attributes, and relationships,
- impose cardinality and other constraints when associating marks with model constructs, and
- assign the excerpt obtained from a mark as the value of an attribute.

We also describe procedures to automatically translate an ER schema that uses this framework of patterns into an equivalent relational database schema.

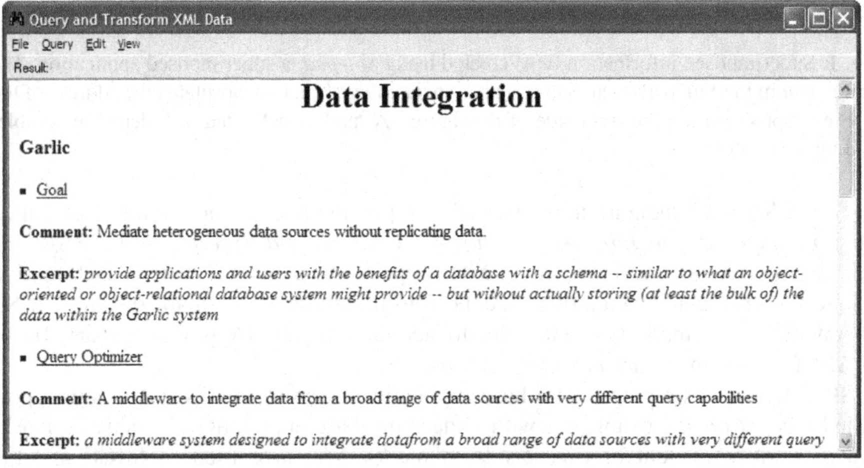

Fig. 2. Sidepad document of Figure 1 transformed to an HTML document

We assume that the SA developer cannot alter the information model of any base application, and that the developer incorporates selected aspects of base information into the SI model (using marks). The SA developer need not be aware of the underlying information model in the base source; the mark abstraction encapsulates the references to the selected base information element of interest. The set of patterns to represent marks and the examples we present demonstrate the ability to superimpose new models over existing information in combination with modeling SI for a particular SA.

Our approach to modeling SI and incorporating parts of base information models is different from the approach to information integration in systems such as MIX and

Garlic [2, 4] which require the schema of integrated sources to be described *a priori*. Our approach does not alter base information or replicate it, and there is no need to describe the schema of any base source.

The rest of this paper is organized as follows. In Section 2 we introduce an SA for browsing information related to desktop computers with an associated superimposed ER schema. Section 3 introduces our enhanced ER framework with examples from the SA introduced in Section 2. Section 4 presents our procedures for generating a relational schema for an arbitrary enhanced ER schema. Bi-level queries expressed in SQL are presented in Section 5. The paper concludes with a discussion of related work in Section 6, and conclusions and future work in Section 7.

2 The Superimposed System-Information Browser

Our latest superimposed application, the *Superimposed System-Information Browser* (*SSIB*), allows users to browse information such as operating system (OS) updates, and application and OS events for a collection of computers. System administrators can use this application to browse information resident on networked computers for diagnostic purposes.

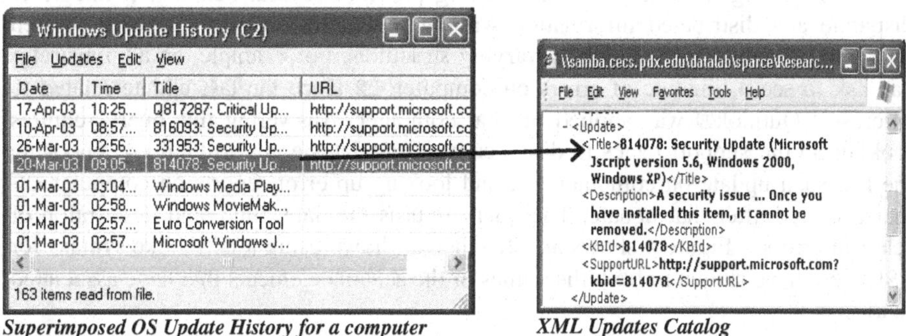

Superimposed OS Update History for a computer ***XML Updates Catalog***

Fig. 3. Operating-System Update information displayed in SSIB on the left, with a mark into an XML document on the right

Figure 3 shows OS-Update information displayed in SSIB. The window with the caption 'Windows Update History (C2)' displays a table structure superimposed on OS update information for computer C2. The highlighted row shows the details of one OS update applied on that computer, excerpted from a set of marks. For example, the title of this update is retrieved using a mark into a shared catalog of available updates (called the *Updates Catalog*) stored on the network, shown on the right side of Figure 3. Though not shown in the figure, the highlighted row also contains support details such as a reason for the update and the cause of the underlying problem that necessitated the update. These details are retrieved using marks into support pages on the web. Table 1 describes these and other sources that SSIB uses to display system information. SSIB uses SPARCE to interact with appropriate base applications.

Table 1. Base sources that SSIB consults

Info. Kind	Doc. Type	Location	Description
Event log	MS Excel	Distributed	Records OS and application events, typically one event per row. Obtained using the *Event Log Viewer* built into MS Windows.
Error reports	MS Word	Distributed	Records OS and application errors. Obtained using the *System Information Viewer* built into MS Office; reformatted for demo purposes.
Update log	Text	Distributed	Contains one line per OS update applied. Not all available updates might be applied on a computer.
Updates Catalog	XML	Network, shared	Contains one Update element per available update (see Figure 1).
Support details	HTML	Web	Describes symptoms, cause, and resolution related to a problem along with a list of affected applications. Typically one page per update. Available from Microsoft Support.

Superimposing information in this setting provides several benefits. It integrates disparate and distributed information without replication. It also allows structured querying over base information of varying structures. For example, an administrator can ask to see a timeline of errors on computer C2 since the last update related to Microsoft Outlook® was applied on that computer. Answering this query requires looking up the support pages to discover which updates apply to Outlook, choosing the last such update on computer C2, and looking up error reports on computer C2 that occurred after that update. The query returns the date, time, and description of relevant errors. Figure 4 shows an ER schema (drawn using a UML-like syntax) for SSIB. We have shown in **bold** the names of the schema elements that have associated marks.

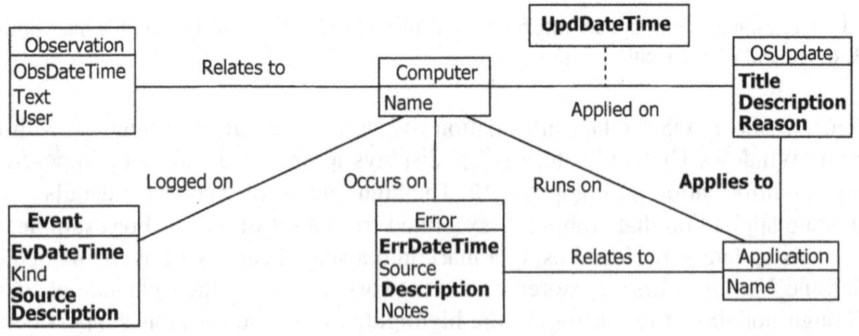

Fig. 4. An ER schema for SSIB. Names in bold indicate constructs with associated marks. All relationships are many-to-many; all entities have a key attribute named ID (not shown).

The representation of marks in an ER model raises several questions. Can a mark be associated with an attribute? How many marks can be associated with a given entity, relationship, or attribute? Is the excerpt for a mark associated with an attribute treated as the value for the attribute? We present next a series of patterns that allow these kinds of details to be specified.

3 Representing Marks in ER

Our framework for representing marks explicitly in superimposed ER schemas is based on a general framework for *relationship patterns* [12] (recurring problems, solutions, or needs in establishing data relationships). We define an entity Mark to model the mark abstraction. It has a key attribute named ID. (We omit describing its other attributes for brevity.) We show the use of marks in the ER schema using relationships involving the Mark entity. We define a relationship pattern for each type of schema element with which marks can be associated: entity, entity attribute, relationship, and relationship attribute. Finally, deriving attribute values from the text excerpt of a mark forms another pattern.

The patterns we define have the following informal signature: <pattern>:<type> (<parameters>), where <pattern> is the name of the pattern, <type> is the name of the relationship type as chosen by the developer, and <parameters> indicate attribute names, when they are needed by the pattern. All relationship patterns we define in this section relate entities of the Mark type to entities of non-Mark (that is, regular) types. We call such regular entity types in an SI ER model *SI entity types*. Regular ER relationships are allowed among regular SI entities, as usual. The examples we use in this section and the next section are based on the ER schema in Figure 4.

3.1 Associating Marks with Entities

The EMark pattern associates marks with regular entities. Figure 5(a) shows the use of this pattern where a mark is associated with an Event entity. EMark is the name of the relationship pattern, EventDetail is the relationship type. Note that Logged on is a regular ER relationship type.

Signature: EMark:<type>. A relationship of EMark pattern has no parameters.

Semantics: The EMark pattern associates marks with *entire* entities, not with any particular set of entity-attributes. Instead, the developer interprets this association. For example, the developer might incorporate the excerpt extracted from the mark in the user interface.

Constraints: The developer can choose the cardinality constraints on EMark relationships. The schema in Figure 5(a) restricts the cardinality of EventDetail to 1 because each event has just one associated mark in the SSIB application.

3.2 Associating Marks with Entity Attributes

The AMark pattern associates marks with attributes of an entity. Figure 5(b) shows two relationship types that associate marks with attributes. The relationship type Error

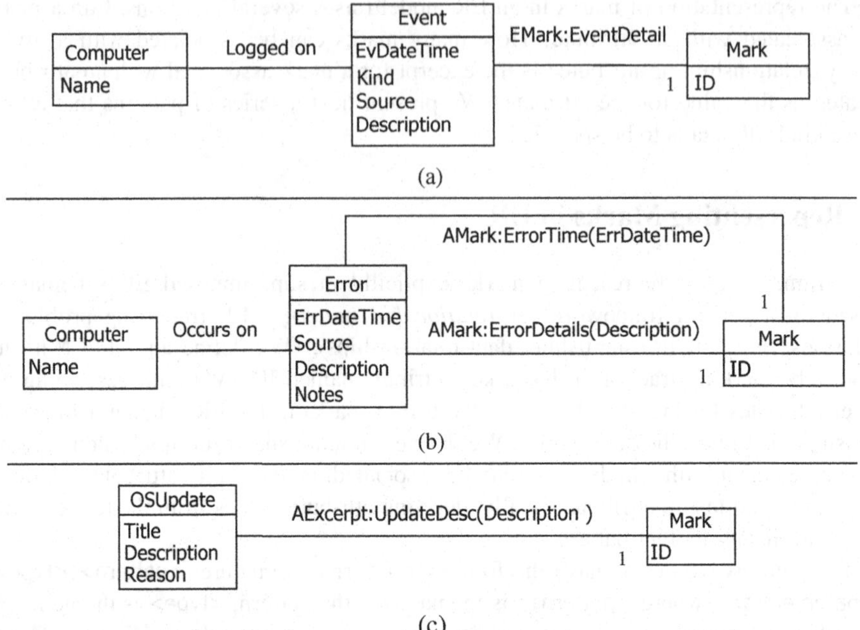

Fig. 5. (a) Associating marks with an entity (b) Associating marks with entity attributes (c) Deriving an entity attribute's value from a mark's excerpt

Details associates the attribute Description with a mark. The relationship type ErrorTime associates the attribute ErrDateTime with a mark. Occurs on is a regular ER relationship type.

Signature: AMark:<type>(a_1, a_2, ..., a_n), where a_1, a_2, ..., a_n ($n>0$) are distinct attributes of an SI entity.

Semantics: All attributes specified are associated with the same mark (or the same set of marks if cardinality is greater than one). Associating a mark with an attribute does *not* mean its value is obtained using the mark. Rather, it allows an SA to access and display the excerpt of the associated mark(s), e.g., as a "tool tip" displayed upon mouse rollover, in addition to having an attribute value stored in the superimposed layer. An SA might also use the associated mark for navigation to the base layer.

Constraints: An AMark relationship type is always a binary relationship between an SI entity type and the Mark entity type. At least one attribute must be listed; the AMark pattern also allows for a single mark or a set of marks to be associated with several attributes. The SSIB schema in Figure 5(b) restricts the cardinality of relationships ErrorDateTime and ErrorDetails to exactly one mark.

3.3 Deriving Attribute Values from Excerpts

We define the pattern AExcerpt to derive an attribute's value from the excerpt of a mark. Figure 5(c) shows a relationship type in the AExcerpt pattern to set the value of the attribute Description as the excerpt of a mark.

Signature: AExcerpt:<type>(a), where a is an attribute of an SI entity.

Semantics: The value of the attribute associated with a mark using this pattern is a function of the text excerpt obtained from the mark. We assume appropriate type conversion is provided by an `excerpt` function that retrieves the excerpt from a mark. The context agents SPARCE uses to interact with base applications implement the `excerpt` function.

Constraints: Like an AMark relationship type, an AExcerpt relationship type is always binary: between an SI entity type and the Mark entity type. The attribute in an AExcerpt relationship type can be associated with at most one mark (because we assume that attributes in the ER model are single-valued).

3.4 Associating Marks with Relationships

We use the RMark pattern to associate marks with relationships. Figure 6(a) shows a relationship type of this pattern associating zero or more marks with relationships of type Applies to. We first aggregate the relationship type Applies to (indicated by a dashed rectangle around the relationship type [15]) to clarify that marks are associated with a relationship. We use the term *anchored relationship* [3] to refer to the relationship with which marks are associated. In Figure 6(a), the relationship Applies to is anchored.

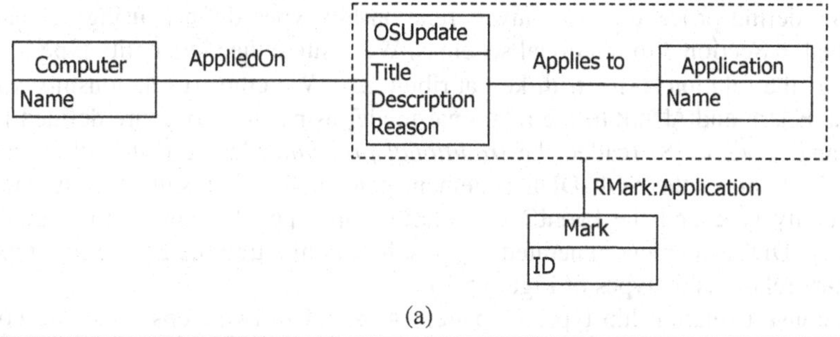

(a)

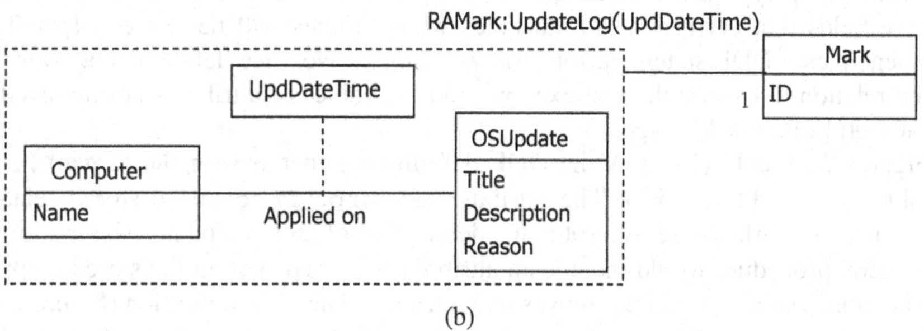

(b)

Fig. 6. (a) Associating marks with a relationship (b) Associating marks with a relationship attribute

Signature: RMark:<type>. A relationship of RMark pattern has no parameters.

Semantics: The RMark pattern associates marks with entire relationships.

Constraints: A relationship of any type may be anchored. There are no constraints on the degree of the anchored relationship type, but an RMark relationship itself is always binary (that is, it relates an aggregated relationship type with the Mark entity type). There are no constraints on the cardinality of either relationship type. Both relationship types may define attributes.

3.5 Associating Marks with Relationship Attributes

The RAMark pattern associates marks with attributes of a relationship. Figure 6(b) shows a relationship type that associates marks with the attribute UpdDateTime of an Applies to relationship. We aggregate the anchored relationship type Applied on to clarify that marks are associated with a relationship's attribute.

Signature: RAMark:<type>(a_1, a_2, a_n), where a_1, a_2, ..., a_n ($n>0$) are distinct attributes of a relationship.

Semantics and Constraints: The RAMark pattern imposes the same constraints as the RMark pattern. The semantics of the RAMark pattern are similar to that of the AMark pattern.

4 Generating Relational Schemas

We now define procedures to convert relationship types defined using the patterns described in Section 3 to relational schemas. We assume the Mark entity type is represented as the relation `Mark` with key attribute `ID`. We convert relationship types of patterns EMark and AMark to the relational model using the procedure defined by Elmasri and Navathe [8] (called the *traditional procedure* in the rest of this section). Figure 7(a) shows the SQL-DDL statement generated as a result of converting the Event entity type and the EventDetail relationship type of Figure 5(a). Figure 7(b) shows the DDL statement generated as a result of converting the Error entity type and the AMark relationship types of Figure 5(b).

We convert relationship types of pattern AExcerpt in two steps. First, we convert the relationship type and the related entity types using the traditional procedure and *remove* fields that correspond to attributes whose values will be text excerpts. This step generates a DDL statement for a *stored relation*. Next we define a *view* over this stored relation to expose the text excerpts and the values of attributes not involved in the AExcerpt relationship type.

Figures 7(c) and 7(d) show the DDL definitions generated for the AExcerpt relationship type of Figure 5(c). The attribute `AExcerpt_Desc` in the stored relation represents the mark whose excerpt is the description of an OS Update. The traditional conversion procedure would include an attribute `Description` in the stored relation, but our conversion procedure removes that attribute. The view definition (Figure 7(d)) includes a call to a function `excerpt` to retrieve the text excerpt from the mark. We implement this function as a user-defined function, a facility typically available in RDBMSs. The user-defined function invokes the function `excerpt` of the appropriate SPARCE context agent.

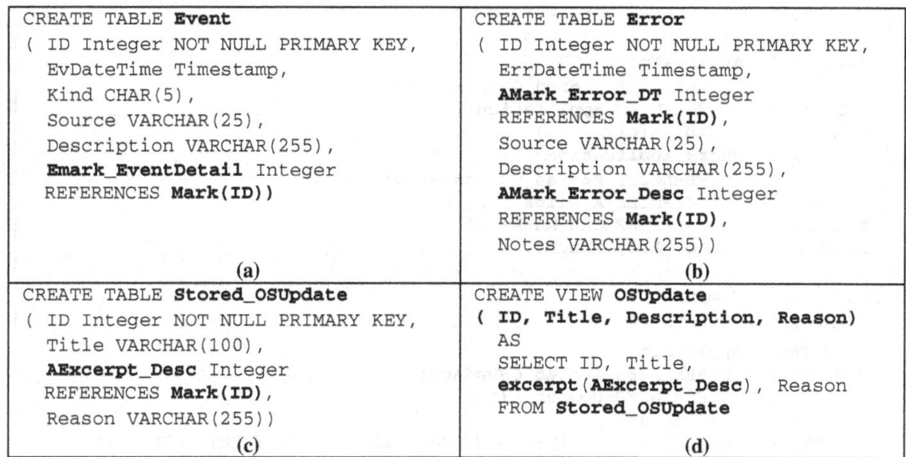

CREATE TABLE **Event** (ID Integer NOT NULL PRIMARY KEY, EvDateTime Timestamp, Kind CHAR(5), Source VARCHAR(25), Description VARCHAR(255), **Emark_EventDetail** Integer REFERENCES **Mark(ID)**) **(a)**	CREATE TABLE **Error** (ID Integer NOT NULL PRIMARY KEY, ErrDateTime Timestamp, **AMark_Error_DT** Integer REFERENCES **Mark(ID)**, Source VARCHAR(25), Description VARCHAR(255), **AMark_Error_Desc** Integer REFERENCES **Mark(ID)**, Notes VARCHAR(255)) **(b)**
CREATE TABLE **Stored_OSUpdate** (ID Integer NOT NULL PRIMARY KEY, Title VARCHAR(100), **AExcerpt_Desc** Integer REFERENCES **Mark(ID)**, Reason VARCHAR(255)) **(c)**	CREATE VIEW **OSUpdate** **(ID, Title, Description, Reason)** AS SELECT ID, Title, **excerpt(AExcerpt_Desc)**, Reason FROM **Stored_OSUpdate** **(d)**

Fig. 7. Example relational schemas for (a) EMark (b) AMark; (c) Stored relation for AExcerpt (d) View definition for AExcerpt

To convert a relationship type of pattern RMark, we first convert the anchored relationship type using an appropriate procedure: that relationship could be a regular ER relationship between SI entities, or it could be a relationship of any of the five patterns described in Section 3. For example, we use the traditional procedure to convert the relationship type Applies To in Figure 6(a). If more than one mark is allowed for an RMark relationship, we create a new relation and perform the following actions.

1. Add the key attributes of the relation that captures the anchored relationship type; define the attributes as a foreign key.
2. Add a foreign key attribute that references the attribute `Mark.ID`.
3. Add attributes of the RMark relationship.
4. Define the primary key as the set of foreign key attributes.

If the RMark relationship can have at most one mark, we perform only Actions 2 and 3 but with the relation that corresponds to the anchored relationship type.

Figure 8(a) shows the DDL definitions generated for the RMark relationship type of Figure 6(a). The relation `Stored_OSUpdate` referenced in the definitions is shown in Figure 7(c). The relation `AppliesTo` captures the AppliesTo relationship type (generated using the traditional procedure). The relation `RMark_Application` captures the RMark relationship type. This relation is required because the example schema allows many marks to be associated with each Applies To relationship.

Converting RAMark relationship types is similar to converting RMark relationship types. Figure 8(b) shows the schema generated for the RAMark relationship type of Figure 6(b). The relation `AppliedOn` captures the Applied On relationship type (generated using the traditional procedure). An additional relation is not needed to capture the RAMark relationship type because the example schema allows at most one mark to be associated with each Applied On relationship.

```
CREATE TABLE Application
(ID Integer NOT NULL PRIMARY KEY, Name
  VARCHAR(256))
CREATE TABLE AppliesTo
( UID Integer REFERENCES Stored_OSUpdate(ID),
  AID Integer REFERENCES Application(ID),
  PRIMARY KEY (UID, AID))
CREATE TABLE RMark_Application
( UID Integer REFERENCES Stored_OSUpdate(ID),
  AID Integer REFERENCES Application(ID),
  RMarkID Integer REFERENCES Mark(ID),
  PRIMARY KEY (UID, AID, RMarkID))
```

(a)

```
CREATE TABLE Computer
(ID Integer NOT NULL PRIMARY KEY, Name VARCHAR(256))
CREATE TABLE AppliedOn
( UID Integer REFERENCES Stored_OSUpdate(ID),
  CID Integer REFERENCES Computer(ID),
  UpdDateTime As Timestamp,
  RAMark_UpdateLog Integer REFERENCES Mark(ID), PRIMARY KEY (UID, CID))
```

(b)

Fig. 8. Relational schemas for (a) RMark relationship type and (b) RAMark relationship type

5 Bi-level Querying

We now demonstrate the ability to express bi-level queries over the relational schema automatically generated from the conceptual schema expressed using our framework. The example queries we show demonstrate the ability to express structured queries over combined SI and base information, though base information might be heterogeneous, possibly not even in a database, and distributed.

Query 1: List all updates related to security.

```
SELECT * FROM OSUpdate WHERE Description LIKE 'Security%'
```

The descriptions of OS Updates are *automatically* obtained from the base layer when the view `OSUpdate` is built, because the view definition includes calls to the user-defined function `excerpt` (see Figure 7(d)).

Query 2: List errors related to the application MS Word (see Figure 7(b)).

```
SELECT ErrDateTime, Source, Description, Notes
FROM Error
WHERE excerpt(AMark_Error_Desc) LIKE '%word.exe%'
```

This query uses the function `excerpt` at query-execution time to get the text excerpt from the mark associated with the `Description` attribute. It returns the stored attribute values if the excerpt retrieved contains the string `'word.exe'`.

The explicit use of the function `excerpt` is avoided (as in Query 1) if the `Description` attribute is conceptually modeled using the AExcerpt pattern instead of the AMark pattern.

Query 3: Show a timeline of errors on computer `C2` since the last update related to MS Outlook was applied on that computer. (A query we first presented in Section 2.)

Assuming the relation `OccursOn` represents the relationship type Occurs On, the required SQL query would be as follows:

```
SELECT ErrDateTime, Description
FROM Error JOIN OccursOn JOIN Computer C
WHERE C.Name = 'C2' AND ErrDateTime > ANY (
  SELECT MAX(UpdDateTime)
  FROM OSUpdate JOIN AppliesTo JOIN Application A
  JOIN AppliedOn
  WHERE C.ID = AppliedOn.CID AND A.Name LIKE '%Outlook%'
)
```

This query returns the date, time, and description of errors as it is stored in the relation `Error`. Instead, one could use the function `excerpt` to retrieve those values from the base layer. Again, if these attributes are modeled using the AExcerpt pattern, the query shown (as is) would automatically return excerpts from the base layer.

6 Related Work

A *superimposed schematic* [3], our first SA with an ER-like schema, supports navigation through base documents, based on the superimposed ER model. Each entity and relationship in the superimposed schematic can be *anchored* but only with at most one mark. Relationships are restricted to be binary and to have no attributes. Marks associated with an attribute are always assumed to take their value from the corresponding excerpt. Our approach here generalizes the model used for superimposed schematics by removing the limitations on cardinality, allowing relationship attributes, and by allowing marks to be associated with attributes. We also allow the SA developer to choose whether or not the excerpt is to be used as the attribute value of the attribute(s) with which the mark is associated.

Marks associated with ER schema elements are similar to the "hinges" of Feyer and Thalheim [9]. In their model, a hinge relates concepts in the "association dimension" of a schema. Marks represented using the AExcerpt pattern could be seen as "cooperation hinges" as they enable cooperative views; marks of other patterns could be seen as "full hinges" as they only establish references from the SI layer to the base layer. Conceptually, marks are "mono-directional hinges" in the latter case, but as shown in Query 2 in Section 5, an SA can explicitly invoke functions in context agents to obtain context information back from the base layer.

The hypertext modeling community has considered modeling structure, navigation and presentation aspects of hypertext. The work presented in this paper can be related to *structure sub-models* that Casanova and others [5] have described. The mark abstraction and its use to reference base selections from SI is similar to the concept of *anchors* and *links* that Garzotto and others [10] have described.

The framework presented in this paper extends the ER model. Many other researchers have extended the ER model to make it more expressive. For example, Elmasri and Navathe [8] have extended it to support generalization and specialization; Tanaka and others [16] have extended it to capture application semantics; Cysneiros and others [6] have extended it to capture non-functional requirements; and Thalheim [17] and others have done extensive work defining and formalizing the Higher-Order

Entity Relationship (HERM) model for database design. But, to the best of our knowledge, none of these efforts consider extensions to support marks in SI.

UML associations can model EMark relationship types. And UML *Derived Attributes* in conjunction with invariants specified in the Object Constraint Language [1] can model AMark and AExcerpt relationship types, but they are not as concise as our solution for ER.

7 Conclusions and Future Work

We have presented a framework to explicitly represent marks in ER schemas using a set of conventions to augment the semantics of existing ER model constructs. A superimposed application that uses an ER schema with these conventions can easily access the excerpt (and associated context) for mark; can invoke base applications to navigate to marks, as desired; and can readily express SQL queries over an SI source and all of the associated, marked base information. Using SQL as the bi-level query language is appropriate for SI expressed in an ER model.

Currently, we use a single entity type Mark to represent marks. We would like to investigate the potential for additional typing of marks, according to either the base type or domain-specific types. Domain-specific types can abstract over base types, yet support additional semantics (and additional behavior) specific to a domain. For example, marks into patent applications can be defined as a domain-specific type, such as *claim*, regardless of the format (such as HTML or PDF) of the patent documents. We also plan to explore the introduction of marks into other conceptual models and development of additional means to query and navigate SI and its associated BI.

References

1. UML 2.0 OCL Specification. 2005. Object Management Group, Inc.
2. Baru, C., Gupta, A., Ludäscher, B., Marciano, R., Papakonstantinou, Y., Velikhov, P., Chu, V. XML-Based Information Mediation with MIX. In proceedings of SIGMOD 1999. 1999. Philadelphia, PA. p. 597-599.
3. Bowers, S., Delcambre, L., Maier, D. Superimposed Schematics: Introducing E-R Structure for In-Situ Information Selections. In proceedings of ER 2002. 2002. Tampere, Finland. p. 90–104.
4. Carey, M.J., Haas, L.M., Schwarz, P.M., Arya, M., Cody, W.F., Fagin, R., Flickner, M., Luniewski, A.W., Niblack, W., Petkovic, D., Thomas, J., Williams, J.H., Wimmers, E.L. Towards heterogeneous multimedia information systems: The Garlic approach. 1994.
5. Casanova, M.A., Tucherman, L., Lima, M.J.D., Netto, J.L.R., Rodriguez, N.R., Soares, L.F.G. The Nested Context Model for Hyperdocuments. In proceedings of Hypertext 1991. 1991. San Antonio, Texas. p. 193-201.
6. Cysneiros, L.M., Leite, J.C., Neto, J.M. A Framework for Integrating Non-Functional Requirements into Conceptual Models. In Requirements Engineering. 2001. 6(2). p. 97-115
7. Delcambre, L., Maier, D., Bowers, S., Weaver, M., Deng, L., Gorman, P., Ash, J., Lavelle, M., Lyman, J. Bundles in Captivity: An Application of Superimposed Information. In proceedings of ICDE 2001. 2001. Heidelberg, Germany. p. 111-120.

8. Elmasri, R., Navathe, S.B. Fundamentals of Database Systems. 4th ed. 2003: Addison-Wesley. ISBN: 0321122267.
9. Feyer, T., Thalheim, B. Many-Dimensional Schema Modeling. In proceedings of Proceedings of the 6th East European Conference on Advances in Databases and Information Systems. 2002. p. 305-318.
10. Garzotto, F., Mainetti, L., Paolini, P. HDM2: Extending the E-R Approach to Hypermedia Application Design. In proceedings of ER '93. 1993. Arlington, Texas. p. 178-189.
11. Maier, D., Delcambre, L. Superimposed Information for the Internet. In proceedings of WebDB 1999. 1999. Philadelphia, PA. p. 1-9.
12. Murthy, S., Maier, D. A Framework for Relationship Pattern Languages. *Unpublished.* 2005. Portland State University. http://sparce.cs.pdx.edu/pubs/relationshipPatternLanguages.pdf.
13. Murthy, S., Maier, D., Delcambre, L. Querying Bi-level Information. In proceedings of 7th International Workshop on the Web and Databases. 2004. Paris, France. p. 7-12.
14. Murthy, S., Maier, D., Delcambre, L., Bowers, S. Putting Integrated Information in Context: Superimposing Conceptual Models with SPARCE. In proceedings of First Asia-Pacific Conference of Conceptual Modeling. 2004. Dunedin, New Zealand. p. 71-80.
15. Ramakrishnan, R., Gehrke, J. Database Management Systems. Third ed. 2003: McGraw Hill. ISBN: 0072465638.
16. Tanaka, A.K., Navathe, S.B., Chakravarthy, S., Karlapalem, K. ER-R: An Enhanced ER Model with Situation-Action Rules to Capture Application Semantics. In proceedings of 10th International Conference on Entity-Relationship Approach (ER'91). 1991. San Mateo, California. p. 59-75.
17. Thalheim, B. Entity-Relationship Modeling, Foundations of Database Technology. 2004: Springer. ISBN: 3540654704.

Preference Functional Dependencies for Managing Choices*

Wilfred Ng

Department of Computer Science and Engineering
The Hong Kong University of Science and Technology
Hong Kong
wilfred@cse.ust.hk

Abstract. The notion of user preference in database modeling has recently received much attention in advanced applications, such as personalization of e-services, since it captures the human wishes on querying and managing data. The paradigm of preference-driven choices in the real world requires new semantic constraints in modelling. In this paper, we assume preference constraints can be defined over data domains and thus the assumption gives rise to preference relations as a special case of ordered relations over schemas consisting of the preference, preference-dependent and preference-independent attributes. We demonstrate that Lexicographically Ordered Functional Dependencies (LOFDs) can be employed to maintain the consistency of preference semantics embedded in preference database, since prioritized multiple preferences can be represented. We thus define a useful semantic constraint in terms of a set of LOFDs, called Preference Functional Dependencies (PFDs), in order to capture the semantics of the preference ranked data. We exhibit a sound and complete axiom system for PFDs, whose implication problem is shown to be decidable in polynomial-time. We also confirm the existence of Armstrong preference relations for PFDs, a fundamental result related to the practical use of PFDs in database design.

1 Introduction

Preference is natural in real world. When searching for items to be purchased over the internet, customer wishes and preferences are important, since they relate to managing of goods and developing selling tactics of a business corporation. It is a frustrating experience if one encounters many times some query results like “no match” or “sorry, try again with some other choices”. The traditional constraints like functional dependencies model an exact world where the semantics capture the hard fact only, rather than the constraints specified by a list of user preferences. We share the same idea with [5,6] that the fundamental nature of different preferences in the form of “I like A better than B” can be modelled by a set of orderings defined over data.

* This work is partially supported by RGC CERG under grant number HKUST6185/03E.

D.W. Embley, A. Olivé, and S. Ram (Eds.): ER 2006, LNCS 4215, pp. 140–154, 2006.

We assume here that the data domains of the relational data model are linearly ordered and call the extended model the ordered relational model [11,12]. Within the model, we have formalised the notion of *Lexicographically Ordered Functional Dependencies* (LOFDs) being satisfied in an ordered database and tackled their implication problem in [10]. The semantics of LOFDs are defined by means of the *lexicographical orderings* on the domains associated with the involved attributes, which resemble the way that words are arranged in a dictionary. For example, the LOFD $\langle POST\_RANK, WORKING\_YEARS\rangle \rightsquigarrow SALARY$ can capture the preference constraint that in a company the higher salary is preferably given for those employees who are in higher post rank, or if they are at the same rank but are more experienced. Here there are two preferences are involved, namely, $POST\_RANK$ and $WORKING\_YEARS$; the former preference is considered more important than the latter. The left-hand side attributes capture the notion of *prioritized preference* (cf. Definition 6 in [5]), i.e. $POST\_RANK$ is considered more important than $WORKING\_YEARS$ and $WORKING\_YEARS$ is respected only where $POST\_RANK$ is the same.

In this paper we apply LOFDs in the context of preference relations and view preference relations as a special class of ordered relations. The underlying idea is that *preference* is inherent to the ordering relationship between the data projected onto the *preference* (e.g. $POST\_RANK$ and $WORKING\_YEARS$) and *preference-dependent* (e.g. $SALARY$) attributes is important to the design of preference databases. We classify the attributes in a preference relation schema according to their preference nature into three categories of the *preference*, *preference-dependent* and *preference-independent* attributes. Such a classification of attributes allows us to express the semantics of a Preference Functional Dependency (PFD) in terms of the satisfaction of a corresponding set of LOFDs in a relation, each of them with its left-hand side restricted to a sequence of prioritized preference attributes and its right-hand side restricted to a single preference-dependent attribute in the canonical form.

A PFD is a semantic constraint that arises naturally from preference relations, since most preference data is dependent on preference in a monotonic manner. For example, the PFD $\langle PRICE, CATEGORY, POWER, MILEAGE\rangle \mapsto MIDDLE\_CLASS$ states the fact that when some middle class customers choose a second-hand car in a market, the complex preference can be prioritized in terms of the sequence of selling price, category, engine power, and used mileage. Note that the order of the attributes here may not follow the alphabetical or numerical order. For example, the engine power preference may be defined as $\{3500cc <_p 1500cc <_p 3000cc <_p 2000cc\}$, where $<_p$ captures the meaning of "is preferable to".

The main result of this paper is fundamental. We establish a simple, sound and complete axiom system for PFDs and show that the implication problem for PFDs is decidable in polynomial-time. This result is significant because it implies that, in principle, by using our established system all possible PFDs being logically implied by a given set of PFDs can be effectively generated in polynomial-time. The simplicity of the system for PFDs is also important from the point of view of *usability*, since it provides different categories of database users with impetus for accepting and applying PFDs in preference data modelling. In addition, the axiom system provides us with a basis to find a more efficient algorithm for solving the implication problem of PFDs.

In order to incorporate PFDs into preference database design, we tackle the problem whether Armstrong relations exist for PFDs. The importance of Armstrong relations for FDs in the process of database design is well-recognised in conventional database design [9,2]. In our case, Armstrong preference relations exist and can also be served as *example relations* in the design process. They help the database designers to gain a better insight of PFDs needed in modelling the preference data in an enterprise.

The rest of the paper is organised as follows. In Section 2 we review some related work. In Section 3 we clarify the notion of the extension of linear order to the Cartesian product of linearly ordered sets and then define the ordered relational model. In Section 4 we present the chase rules for LOFDs and, using an extended notion of tableaux for LOFDs, show that the chase is sound and complete for LOFDs. In Section 5 we illustrate the uses of LOFDs and formally define PFDs in preference relations. A sound and complete axiom system is then presented for PFDs. We also show that Armstrong relations exist for PFDs. In Section 6 we give our concluding remarks.

2 Related Work

There are a number of different approaches for defining constraints as a fundamental component in databases. Functional Dependencies (FDs) [2] are essentially the kinds of *equality generating dependencies.* It is worth mentioning that in [3,4] the axiom system for partial order dependencies is co-NP, which limits the usability of such kind of *order comparison dependencies.* However, we impose a preference partial order to override a linearly ordered domain whenever there is a conflict and thus, the linear order assumption simplify most of the complex results.

Comparing to the body of work on data dependencies in databases in literature [2,7,8], we believe that our definition of PFDs are a novel constraint that is useful in preference relations for three main reasons. First, in our data model we consider the fundamental feature that linear ordering is an integral part of simple preference domains from which to derive complex preferences in a relation in a straightforward manner. Second, a PFD captures the semantics of ordering relationships that arises naturally from the interaction between preference and preference-dependent data. Third, the concept of PFDs is founded on the formal notion of lexicographical ordering on preference domains, which paves the way to develop more advanced preference constraints.

Soft constraints in the form of numerical preferences have been used in many database and information retrieval applications [1,8]. Basically, the usual numerical order are used for ranking preference items. For example, in the area of full-text searching [1,13], where keywords can be understood as implicit score preferences indicating their relevance. The combining function for ranking is typically some scalar product taking the cosine function commonly used in the vector space model from information retrieval [13]. Preferences are receiving attention as DBMSs need to provide better information service. Preference SQL [6] has been extended by a "preferring" clause that allows user to specify soft constraints reflecting complex preferences.

3 The Ordered Relational Model

We assume throughout that sequences consist only distinct attributes. For any two sequences X and Y, $X \sim Y$ denotes the fact that X and Y have the same elements. XY denotes the *concatenation* of X and Y, where $XY = X(Y - X)$. A *prefix* of X, denoted by *pre*(X), is a sequence of the form $\langle A_1, \ldots, A_{m_1} \rangle$, where $X = \langle A_1, \ldots, A_m \rangle$ and $1 \leq m_1 \leq m$. A *shuffle* of X and Y, denoted by *shu*(X, Y), is defined as a sequence of the form $\langle C_1, \ldots, C_{m+n} \rangle$, where there exists two subsequences of attributes $\langle C_{i_1}, \ldots, C_{i_m} \rangle = X$ and $\langle C_{j_1}, \ldots, C_{j_n} \rangle = Y$, and the order of the attributes in X and Y is preserved in *shu*(X, Y).

As usual a *linear ordering* $\leq$ on a set S is a binary relation on S which satisfies the conditions of *reflexivity, anti-symmetry, transitivity* and *linearity*. A *linearly ordered set* (or simply an ordered set) is a structure $\langle S, \leq \rangle$. We assume the usual predicates, $=$ and $<$, still applies to ordered sets. We let $D_1, \ldots, D_n$ be n ordered sets, t be an element in the Cartesian product $S = D_1 \times \cdots \times D_n$, and $t[i]$ be the ith coordinate of t. We now define *lexicographical ordering* in order to capture the semantics of data.

Definition 1. (Lexicographical Ordering) Let $t_1, t_2 \in S$. A *lexicographical ordering* on S is a linear ordering $\leq_S^{lex}$ (or simply $\leq_S$ whenever it is clear from the context) such that $t_1 \leq_S t_2$ if either (1) there exists k with $1 \leq k \leq n$ such that $t_1[k] <_{D_k} t_2[k]$, and for all $1 \leq i < k$, $t_1[i] = t_2[i]$, or (2) for all $1 \leq i \leq n$, $t_1[i] = t_2[i]$.

Lexicographical ordering is a fundamental property of many primitive data types, for example the alphabetical ordering over the domain of characters. It is easy to see that the preference of "the earlier the better" can be modelled as an ordering of the domain *DATE*, which is called a *chronological ordering*.

Let D be a countably infinite set of constant values and $\leq_D$ be an ordering on D. We assume that all attributes share the same domain D. A *relation schema* $R = \{A_1, \ldots, A_m\}$, is a non-empty finite subset of a countably infinite set of attributes U. A *database schema* $\mathbf{R}$ is a non-empty finite set of relation schemas. A *tuple* t over R is a member of D^m and $t[A_i]$ denotes the ith coordinate of t, i.e. the *projection* of t onto the attribute A_i. A *relation* r defined over R is a finite set of tuples over R. An *database* over $\mathbf{R} = \{R_1, \ldots, R_n\}$ is a finite set of relations $d = \{r_1, \ldots, r_n\}$ where by convention r_i is a relation over R_i.

We also make two assumptions in our model.

First, given a data domain, $D = \{a, b, c\}$, there is a *background ordering* (linear ordering) such as alphabetical ordering or numerical ordering on the domains associated with the attributes present in the underlying schema. In this case we have the background ordering $\{a <_{bg} b <_{bg} c\}$ over D.

Second, apart from the standard ordering assumption, according to the preference (modelled as a set of *irreflexive* and *transitive* ordered pairs) such as $P = \{c <_p a, c <_p b\}$ used in an application, we can declare one or more *preference orderings* which override the default standard ordering. A preference ordering is also a linear ordering formed by imposing all the preference on the background ordering. For example, if the background ordering of $\leq_{bg}$ is used, then the preference ordering arising from P is given by $\{c <_p a <_p b\}$ in which $(a <_p b) \notin P$ is derived from $a <_{bg} b$.

These two assumptions are found to be useful in many database applications. The second assumption simplify some technical complications in our subsequent discussion, since all comparison is defined. From the application view point, in most cases we also need to present the ranked (i.e. linearly ordered) result according to user preferences. (Readers may refer to [11,12] for more detailed discussion of various notions of orderings in our model and their applications.)

4 Lexicographically Ordered Functional Dependencies

In this section, we present lexicographically ordered functional dependency and a chase procedure to maintain its consistency over an ordered relation.

The semantics of a Lexicographically Ordered Functional Dependency (LOFD) with two or more attributes on either the left- or right-hand side is defined according to lexicographical orderings on the Cartesian product of the underlying domains of the attributes in the LOFD.

Definition 2. (Lexicographically Ordered Functional Dependency) A *lexicographically ordered functional dependency* (or simply an LOFD) over a relation schema R, is a statement of the form $R : X \leadsto Y$ (or simply $X \leadsto Y$ whenever R is understood from the context), $X, Y \subseteq R$ are sequences of attributes and $X \neq \emptyset$. An LOFD, $X \leadsto Y$, is satisfied in a relation r over R, denoted by $r \models X \leadsto Y$, if for all $t_1, t_2 \in r$, $t_1[X] \leq_X^{lex} t_2[X]$ implies that $t_1[Y] \leq_Y^{lex} t_2[Y]$.

We denote $min(a, b)$ and $max(a, b)$ the minimum and maximum of the values a and b, respectively. For any two distinct tuples $t_1, t_2 \in r$ and some $A \in R$, the *equate* of t_1 and t_2 on A, denoted as $equate(t_1[A], t_2[A])$, is defined by replacing both $t_1[A]$ and $t_2[A]$ by $min(t_1[A], t_2[A])$; the *swap* of t_1 and t_2 on A, denoted as $swap(t_1[A], t_2[A])$, is defined by replacing $t_1[A]$ by $min(t_1[A], t_2[A])$ and $t_2[A]$ by $max(t_1[A], t_2[A])$. We now extend the classical chase defined over conventional relations with respect to FDs [2] to ordered relations with respect to LOFDs.

Definition 3. (Chase Rules for LOFDs) Let t_1 and t_2 be two tuples in r such that $t_1[X] \leq_X^{lex} t_2[X]$ but $t_1[Y] \not\leq_Y^{lex} t_2[Y]$, A be the first attribute in X such that $t_1[A] \neq t_2[A]$, if such an attribute exists, and B be the first attribute in Y such that $t_1[B] \neq t_2[B]$, then the *chase rules* for the LOFD $X \leadsto Y$ is defined by the following two rules:

1. **Equate rule:** if $t_1[X] = t_2[X]$ but $t_1[B] \neq t_2[B]$, then $equate(t_1[B], t_2[B])$;
2. **Swap rule:** if $t_1[A] < t_2[A]$ but $t_2[B] < t_1[B]$, then $swap(t_1[B], t_2[B])$, or if $t_2[A] < t_1[A]$ but $t_1[B] < t_2[B]$, then $swap(t_1[A], t_2[A])$.

The said chase rules cater for all of the possible cases when there are two tuples in a relation violating $X \rightsquigarrow Y$ (see [10] for details). We now give the pseudo-code of an algorithm designated $CHASE(r,\mathrm{F})$, which applies the chase rules given in Definition 3 to R for as long as possible, and returns the resulting relation r over R.

Algorithm 1 ($CHASE(r, \mathrm{F})$)

---

begin
    Result := $r = \langle t_1, \ldots, t_n \rangle$;
    Tmp:= $\emptyset$;
    while Tmp $\neq$ Result **do**
        Tmp := Result;
        if $\exists X \rightsquigarrow Y \in \mathrm{F}$, $\exists\, t_p, t_q \in$ Result such that $t_p[X] \leq_X^{lex} t_q[X]$
        but $t_p[Y] \not\leq_Y^{lex} t_q[Y]$
        then apply the appropriate chase rule to Result with
        $t_1 = t_{min(p,q)}$ and $t_2 = t_{max(p,q)}$;
    end while
    return Result;
end.

It is easy to verify that $CHASE(r,\mathrm{F})$ in Algorithm 1 satisfies F, which can be computed in preference polynomial in the sizes of r and F. In order to provide a proof procedure for LOFDs, we need to define the notion of *ordered variable domains* as follows. The *variable domain* of a relation schema R, denoted by $vdom(R)$, is the finite set $\{l_1, \ldots, l_m, h_1, \ldots, h_m\}$, where $m = \mid R \mid$. The variables l_i and h_i with $i \in \{1, \ldots, m\}$ are called *low ordered variables* and *high ordered variables*, whose ordering is given by $l_i < h_i$.

Definition 4. (Template Relations for an LOFD) Let f be the LOFD $X \rightsquigarrow Y$ over R with $\mid X \mid = n$ and $\mid R \mid = m$. We use two shorthand symbols, u_i and v_i, to represent one of the following three cases: (1) $u_i = l_i$ and $v_i = l_i$, (2) $u_i = l_i$ and $v_i = h_i$, or (3) $u_i = h_i$ and $v_i = l_i$. A *template relation* (or simply a *template*) with respect to f, denoted as r_f, is a relation consisting of two tuples, t_1 and t_2, whose underlying domain is $vdom(R)$, such that it is equal to either Γ_0 or Γ_k shown in Figure 1 , where $pre(X) = \langle x_1, \ldots, x_k \rangle$ for $1 \leq k \leq n$.

We remark that in Definition 4, the symbols u_i and v_i represent three possibilities of combinations of l_i and h_i; it is easy to verify that the order of the upper bound of the number of templates is $O(3^m)$, where m is the number of attributes in R. Note that m is usually small for a relation schema in practice. We will also show

$\Gamma_0 =$

	X	$R-X$
t_1	$l_1 \cdots l_n$	$u_{n+1} \cdots u_m$
t_2	$l_1 \cdots l_n$	$v_{n+1} \cdots v_m$

$\Gamma_k =$

	$x_1 \cdots x_{k-1}$	x_k	$R-pre(X)$
t_1	$l_1 \cdots l_{k-1}$	l_k	$u_{k+1} \cdots u_m$
t_2	$l_1 \cdots l_{k-1}$	h_k	$v_{k+1} \cdots v_m$

Fig. 1. Template relations for an LOFD

in Theorem 3 that the complexity of chasing all the templates can be greatly reduced when the templates are applied for PFDs.

A template can be viewed as a relation instance consisting of two tuples by mapping values in D to ordered variables. We define *tableaux*, denoted by Γ_f, to be the set of all template relations in Definition 4. The tableaux in our case is different from that for FDs, which requires just a single template for FDs (see Theorem 4.2 in [2]). The chase of Γ_f, denoted as $CHASE(\Gamma_f, F)$, is defined by $CHASE(\Gamma_f, F) = \{CHASE(r_f, F) \mid r_f \in \Gamma_f\}$. $CHASE(\Gamma_f, F)$ satisfies $X \rightsquigarrow Y$, denoted by $CHASE(\Gamma_f, F) \models X \rightsquigarrow Y$, if for all $r_f \in \Gamma_f$, $CHASE(r_f, F) \models X \rightsquigarrow Y$. Furthermore, $CHASE(\Gamma_f, F)$ satisfies F, denoted by $CHASE(\Gamma_f, F) \models$ F, if for all $X \rightsquigarrow Y \in$ F, $CHASE(\Gamma_f, F) \models X \rightsquigarrow Y$. We now re-state the main theorem for LOFDs (c.f. see the proof of Theorem 9, page 550 in [10]), which shows that the chase procedure is a decidable, sound and complete inference algorithm for LOFDs.

Theorem 1. Let F be a set of LOFDs over R and f be a LOFD $X \rightsquigarrow Y$. Then $CHASE(\Gamma_f, F) \models f$ if and only if F $\models f$. □

5 Applications of LOFDs in Preference Relations

In this section we discuss the applications of LOFDs in preference relations. We define a novel constraint called Preference Functional Dependencies (PFDs) and establish a corresponding set of axiom system that tackle the implication problem of PFDs.

We adopt a natural view of a user preference, which is perceived as being a declaration of a set of *irreflexive* and *transitive* ordered pairs specified by users [5,6]. The specification includes non-numerical and numerical ranking methods. This view affords us a general way to define preference as a sequence of ordered domains of preference related attributes (or simply preference domains) and further classify preference domains into *simple* and *complex* ones.

Definition 5. (Simple and Complex Preference Domains) A preference domain is said to be *simple* if its data elements (i.e. preference items) are *atomic*, meaning that the elements in such a domain are indivisible as far as the DBMS is concerned. A *complex* preference domain is defined as a sequence of more than one simple preference domain. The ordering of a complex preference domain is defined according to the lexicographical ordering on the Cartesian product of the involved simple preference domains.

Some examples of commonly used simple preference domains related to second handed cars are $PRICE\_RANGE = \{(1000-2000) < (2001-3000) < \cdots <$

$(9001 - 10000)\}$ and $ENGINE\_POWER = \{1500cc < \cdots < 3000cc\}$. We can also make use $I(n) = \{1, \ldots, n\}$ as simple domains to construct a complex preference domain, which provides a convenient way to model a complex preference system as well as to define an arbitrary preference granularity (cf. the formation of complex preference in [6]).

We assume that there is a partition on the countably infinite set of attributes U, which forms the three distinguished classes of the *preference* (PE), the *preference-dependent* (PD), and the *preference-independent* (PI) attributes. Under this classification, preference is specified by choosing only the attribute names defined in PE. Furthermore, we are able to differentiate the data elements that represent preference (such as $PRICE\_RANGE$ or $ENGINE\_POWER$), that are dependent on preference (such as $FAMILY\_CHOICE$ or $BUSINESS\_CHOICE$), and that are invariant with respect to preference (such as $PAYMENT\_METHOD$ or $SALES\_MANAGER$).

Definition 6. (Preference Relation Schema and Preference Relation) Let PE, PD and PI be three distinguished non-empty subsets of U such that they are pairwise disjoint. A *preference relational schema* R is a schema which satisfies $R \subseteq PE \cup PD \cup PI$ and $R \cap PE \neq \emptyset$. A *preference relation* is a relation r over R. For simplicity in notation, we denote $R \cap PE = R^{PE}$, $R \cap PD = R^{PD}$ and $R \cap PI = R^{PI}$. We call r a *PE relation* when $R = R^{PE}$.

The following example illustrates that LOFDs are employed to maintain the consistency of the data elements in different preference domains.

Example 1. Suppose a customer preference relation is defined by the preference attributes $PRICE\_RANGE$, $ENGINE\_POWER$ and $MILEAGE$. The following LOFD, $\langle PRICE\_RANGE,\ ENGINE\_POWER,\ MILEAGE\rangle \rightsquigarrow YOUTH\_CHOICE$, asserts the preference specification defined by $PRICE\_RANGE$, $ENGINE\_POWER$ and $MILEAGE$, such that the rank of $YOUTH\_CHOICE$ (the choice of young customers) increases with first the price range and then the engine power and finally the car milage. In addition, we use the PREFERRING clause in [5] to express the preference terms, which essentially impose the preference order over their corresponding data domains given by (1) LOWEST(price), (2) HIGHEST(power) and (3) mileage AROUND 30000km.

A preference relation which is described by the preference attributes $PRICE\_RANGE$ and $ENGINE\_POWER$, where $YOUTH\_CHOICE = I(5)$ (i.e. 5 possible ranks are used for labelling the preference of the second-hand cars) is used for defining the overall preference ranking, as shown in Figure 2. Note that some attributes are abbreviated in the table due to width limit. The attributes $SALES\_MANAGER$ and $PAYMENT\_METHOD$ are preference-independent attributes.

For the choice from middle class customers, we may need to change the preference terms, which give rise to a different consistent preference relation as shown in Figure 3. The preference order is (1) price AROUND \$4000-\$5000, (2) HIGHEST(power) and (3) LOWEST(mileage).

Next, we define an interesting class of LOFDs, called Preference Functional Dependencies (PFDs), to order to capture the ordering semantics between the two sets of values projected onto the preference and preference-dependent attributes. A PFD is essentially an LOFD that has a sequence of the preference attributes in the left-hand side, constituting a simple or a compound preference domain, and the preference-dependent attributes in the right-hand side, capturing the semantics of preference-dependent data.

Finally, for the choice of pensioner customers, we may have another set of preference terms and also need to impose the new LOFD, $\langle PRICE\_RANGE, MILEAGE, ENGINE\_POWER\rangle \rightsquigarrow PENSIONER\_CHOICE$, which give rise to a different consistent preference relation shown in Figure 4. The preference order is (1) LOWEST(price), (2) mileage BETWEEN 20000km AND 30000km, and (3) power AROUND 2000cc.

PRICE	*ENGINE*	*MILEAGE*	*YOUTH*	*MANAGER*	*PAYMENT*
1001-2000	1500*cc*	20000*km*	1	Jane	Installment
4001-5000	3000*cc*	30000*km*	2	Jane	Installment
4001-5000	2000*cc*	20000*km*	3	Ken	Installment
4001-5000	1500*cc*	10000*km*	4	Ken	Installment
5001-6000	3000*cc*	10000*km*	5	Larry	Installment

Fig. 2. An example showing $\langle PRICE\_RANGE, ENGINE\_POWER, MILEAGE\rangle \rightsquigarrow YOUTH\_CHOICE$ in a second-hand car preference relation

PRICE	*ENGINE*	*MILEAGE*	*MIDDLE_CLASS*	*MANAGER*	*PAYMENT*
1001-2000	1500*cc*	20000*km*	5	Jane	Installment
4001-5000	3000*cc*	30000*km*	1	Jane	Installment
4001-5000	2000*cc*	20000*km*	2	Ken	Installment
4001-5000	1500*cc*	10000*km*	3	Ken	Installment
5001-6000	3000*cc*	10000*km*	4	Larry	Installment

Fig. 3. An example showing $\langle PRICE\_RANGE, ENGINE\_POWER, MILEAGE\rangle \rightsquigarrow MIDDLECLASS\_CHOICE$ in a second-hand car preference relation

PRICE	*ENGINE*	*MILEAGE*	*PENSIONER*	*MANAGER*	*PAYMENT*
1001-2000	1500*cc*	20000*km*	1	Jane	Installment
4001-5000	3000*cc*	30000*km*	3	Jane	Installment
4001-5000	2000*cc*	20000*km*	2	Ken	Installment
4001-5000	1500*cc*	10000*km*	4	Ken	Installment
5001-6000	3000*cc*	10000*km*	5	Larry	Installment

Fig. 4. An example showing $\langle PRICE\_RANGE, MILEAGE, ENGINE\_POWER\rangle \rightsquigarrow PENSIONER\_CHOICE$ in a second-hand car preference relation

Definition 7. (Preference Functional Dependency) A *Preference Functional Dependency* (PFD) over a preference relation schema R, denoted as $R : T \mapsto X$ (or simply $T \mapsto X$ whenever R is understood from the context), $T \subseteq R^{PE}$ is a sequence of the preference attributes and $X \subseteq R^{PD}$ is a sequence of the preference-dependent attributes. A PFD, $T \mapsto X$, is satisfied in a preference relation r over R, if and only if, for all $A \in X$, $r \models T \leadsto A$.

From now on, we use $F' = \{T \mapsto A \mid T \mapsto X \in \mathrm{F} \text{ and } A \in X\}$ to represent the set of *unary* PFDs corresponding to F. The following proposition immediately follows from Definition 7, which justifies the equivalence in semantics between F and F'.

Proposition 1. $r \models \mathrm{F}$ if and only if $r \models F'$. □

An *axiom system* $\mathcal{A}$ for F is a set of inference rules (or simply rules) that can be used to *derive* PFDs from F over R. We denote by $\mathrm{F} \vdash f$ the fact that f is *derivable* from F by a specified axiom system [2,10].

Definition 8. (Inference Rules for PFDs) Let F be a set of PFDs over R and T_1, T_2 be subsets of R^{PE}. The inference rules for PFDs are defined as follows:

(PFD1) *Shuffle*: If $\mathrm{F} \vdash T_1 \mapsto X$ and $\mathrm{F} \vdash T_2 \mapsto X$, then $\mathrm{F} \vdash shu(T_1, pre(T_2)) \mapsto X$.
(PFD2) *Left Expansion*: If $\mathrm{F} \vdash T_1 \mapsto X$, then $\mathrm{F} \vdash T_1T_2 \mapsto X$.
(PFD3) *Decomposition*: If $\mathrm{F} \vdash T_1 \mapsto X$, then $\mathrm{F} \vdash T_1 \mapsto Y$, where $Y \subseteq X$.
(PFD4) *Union*: If $\mathrm{F} \vdash T_1 \mapsto X$ and $\mathrm{F} \vdash T_1 \mapsto Y$, then $\mathrm{F} \vdash T_1 \mapsto XY$.

We remark that the axiom system comprising these rules is *minimal*, since the four rules given in Definition 8 are primitive. The *reflexivity* rule is not applicable for PFDs, since the preference attributes exist only in the left-hand side of LOFDs. We still need the following inference rule to deal with the sequences of attributes in the right-hand side of LOFDs, which can be derived from the inference rules PFD3 and PFD4.

Proposition 2. The following inference rule is sound.

(PFD5) *Permutation*: If $\mathrm{F} \vdash T_1 \mapsto X$, then $\mathrm{F} \vdash T_1 \mapsto X'$, where $X \sim X'$. □

We now show in next theorem that the axiom system comprising the inference rules in Definition 8 is sound and complete for PFDs, holding in preference relations. The underlying idea in this proof is first to assume that a PFD $T \mapsto A$ cannot be inferred from the axiom system, and then to present a relation as a counter-example in which all the PFDs of F' hold except $T \mapsto A$ (c.f. see Theorem 3.21 in [2]). The result is significant since it indicates that the axiom system can be employed as a theorem-proving tool for PFDs.

Theorem 2. The axiom system comprising from PFD1 to PFD4 is sound and complete for PFDs.

Proof. It is easy to show that the inference rules from PFD1 to PFD4 are sound. We now establish the completeness by showing that if $F' \nvdash T \mapsto A$, then $F' \not\models T \mapsto A$. Equivalently for the latter, it is sufficient to exhibit a relation as a counter-example r^c, such that $r^c \models F'$ but $r^c \not\models T \mapsto A$. Assuming that for all $Q \subseteq R^{PE}$, P is the largest prefix of T such that $F' \vdash PQ \mapsto A$. Let us call this the *P-assumption.* There are two cases to consider.

In the first case, we assume $P = T$. We consider the relation r^c shown in Figure 5, where $A \in R^{PD}$ and $Z = R^{PD}R^{PI} - A$. Obviously, we have $r^c \not\models T \mapsto A$. It remains to show that $r^c \models F'$. Assume to the contrary that $r^c \not\models F'$. So $\exists f \in F'$ such that $r^c \not\models f$. Let $f = T' \mapsto A'$. By the construction of r^c, we have $T' \subseteq T$ and $A' = A$. By the P-assumption and PFD1, it follows that $F' \vdash PT' \mapsto A$. So we have $F' \vdash P \mapsto A$, which is a contradiction, since we derive $T \mapsto A$ from F'.

	T	$R^{PE} - T$	A	Z
t_1	$0 \cdots 0$	$0 \cdots 0$	0	$0 \cdots 0$
t_2	$0 \cdots 0$	$1 \cdots 1$	1	$0 \cdots 0$

Fig. 5. A counter-example relation r^c used in the case of $P = T$

	P	B	$R^{PE} - BP$	A	Z
t_1	$0 \cdots 0$	1	$0 \cdots 0$	0	$0 \cdots 0$
t_2	$0 \cdots 0$	0	$1 \cdots 1$	1	$0 \cdots 0$

Fig. 6. A counter-example relation r^c used in the case of $P \neq T$

In the second case, we assume $P \neq T$. Let $T = PBQ$ where $B \notin P$ and $BQ \subseteq R^{PE}$. We construct the relation r^c shown in Figure 6, in which $r^c \not\models T \mapsto A$.

We now show that $r^c \models F'$. Assuming to the contrary that $\exists f \in F'$ such that $r^c \not\models f$, where $f = T' \mapsto A'$. By the construction of r^c, we have $A' = A$ and the following two possible cases concerning T'.

(Case of $T' \subseteq P$). By PFD2, we expand f by attaching the attribute B on its left-hand side. It follows that $F' \vdash T'B \mapsto A$. By the P-assumption and PFD1, it follows that $F' \vdash PT'BQ \mapsto A$. So we have $F' \vdash PBQ \mapsto A$. But PB is the prefix of T and strictly contains P. This leads to a contradiction, since we violate the P-assumption.

(Case of $T' \nsubseteq P$). Let $T' = VBW$ where $V \subseteq P$ and $W \subseteq R^{PE}$. By the P-assumption and PFD1, it follows that $F' \vdash PT' \mapsto A$. So we have $F' \vdash PBW \mapsto A$. But PB is the prefix of T. This leads to the same contradiction, since we violate the P-assumption. □

As we discussed in Section 3, the number of possible templates used in $CHASE(\Gamma_f, F)$ is $O(3^m)$. We now show that the complexity of applying the chase for PFDs is much better than exponential-time. Let $T = \langle B_1, \ldots, B_n \rangle$ (i.e. a sequence of n preference attributes for some positive integer n) and $f = T \mapsto A$. For $k \in \{0, \ldots, n\}$, we define the *k-th reduced form* of a given set of PFDs F with respect to f by $\Delta_k(F) = \{T' \mapsto A \in F \mid T' \subseteq T\}$ when $k = 0$, and $\Delta_k(F) = \{T' \mapsto A \in F \mid T' = pre(WB_kQ)$ such that $W \subseteq \{B_1, \ldots, B_{k-1}\}$ and $Q \subseteq R^{PE}\}$ when $n \geq k > 0$.

Theorem 3. Let F be a set of PFDs and $f = T \mapsto A$ where $\mid T \mid = n$. Then $\Delta_k(F) \neq \emptyset$ for all $k \in \{0, \ldots, n\}$ if and only if $CHASE(\Gamma_f, F) \models T \mapsto A$.

Proof. (*IF:*) Let $A \in R^{PD}$ and $Z = R^{PD}R^{PI} - A$. From Definition 4, a template r_f in Γ_f can be equal to either Γ_0 or Γ_k with $n \geq k > 0$, which give rise to the following two cases.

($k = 0$). Consider the following template r_f that is derived from Γ_0.

$r_f =$

	T	$R^{PE} - T$	A	Z
t_1	$l_1 \cdots l_n$	$l_{n+1} \cdots l_p$	l_{p+1}	$l_{p+2} \cdots l_m$
t_2	$l_1 \cdots l_n$	$h_{n+1} \cdots h_p$	h_{p+1}	$l_{p+2} \cdots l_m$

By the assumption of $CHASE(\Gamma_f, F) \models T \mapsto A$, it follows that $CHASE(r_f, F) \models T \mapsto A$. Clearly, there exists at least one application of a chase rule in order to fix the violation of $T \mapsto A$ in r_f. From the construction of r_f, it can check that the only possible way to initialise the chase is to have some $T' \mapsto A$ in F such that $T' \subseteq T$. So $\Delta_0(F) \neq \emptyset$.

($n \geq k > 0$). Consider the following template r_f derived from Γ_k, where $P = \langle B_1, \ldots, B_{k-1} \rangle$.

$r_f =$

	P	B_k	$R^{PE} - PB_k$	A	Z
t_1	$l_1 \cdots l_{k-1}$	l_k	$h_{k+1} \cdots h_p$	h_{p+1}	$l_{p+2} \cdots l_m$
t_2	$l_1 \cdots l_{k-1}$	h_k	$l_{k+1} \cdots l_p$	l_{p+1}	$l_{p+2} \cdots l_m$

Again, by the given assumption, it follows that $CHASE(r_f, F) \models T \mapsto A$. Thus, there exists at least one application of a chase rule in order to fix the violation of $T \mapsto A$ in r_f. From the construction of r_f, it can check that the only possible way to initialise the chase is to have some $T' \mapsto A$ in F such that one of the following conditions holds: (i) $T' = W$, (ii) $T' = WB_k$, or (iii) $T' = WB_kQ$, where $W \subseteq P$ and $Q \subseteq R^{PE}$. It follows that $T' = pre(WB_kQ)$. So $\Delta_k(F) \neq \emptyset$.
(*ONLY IF:*) It follows from the antecedent that, for all $k \in \{0, \ldots, n\}$, there exists a PFD $f' = T' \mapsto A \in \Delta_k$ in F such that f' is violated in the templates derived from Γ_k. From Definition 4, there are two cases concerning the templates in Γ_f to consider.

First, if a template r_f is derived from Γ_0, then we have $t_1[T] = t_2[T] = \langle l_1, \ldots, l_n \rangle$ in r_f, whose equality will not be changed by any chase rules. So we have $t_1[A] = t_2[A] = l_p$ in $CHASE(r_f, F)$. It follows that $CHASE(r_f, F) \models f$. Second, if a template r_f is derived from Γ_k where $n \geq k > 0$, then we have $t_1[PB_k] = \langle l_1, \ldots, l_{k-1}, l_k \rangle$ and $t_2[PB_k] = \langle l_1, \ldots, l_{k-1}, h_k \rangle$ in r_f. The relative ordering $t_1[PB_k] <^{lex} t_2[PB_k]$ will not be changed by any chase rules, since the attributes in PB_k exists in the left-hand side of an PFD. So we have $t_1[A] = l_p$ and $t_2[A] \in \{l_p, h_p\}$ in $CHASE(r_f, F)$. It follows that $CHASE(r_f, F) \models f$.

The result thus follows, since $f = T \mapsto A$ is satisfied in $CHASE(\Gamma_f, F)$. □

We now formally state the result concerning the complexity of $CHASE(\Gamma_f, F)$. The next corollary follows from Algorithm 1 and Theorem 3.

Corollary 1. Let F be a set of PFDs over R and f be a PFD. Then $CHASE(\Gamma_f, F)$ can be computed in polynomial-time in the sizes of R and F.

Proof. Let $f = T \mapsto A$ and $T = \mid n \mid$. It is easy to check that the decision of whether $\Delta_k(F)$ being empty for a given $k \in \{0, \ldots, n\}$ depends linearly on the number of PFDs in F. Consider that the maximum size of n is equal to $\mid R \mid$. The result is then followed by Algorithm 1 and Theorem 3. □

In order to incorporate PFDs into preference database design, we now tackle the problem whether Armstrong relations exist for PFDs. The importance of such relations for standard FDs in the process of database design is well-recognised [9,2]. Essentially, Armstrong relations can be served as *example relations* in the design process. They help the designers to gain a better insight of the data dependencies needed in modelling the data in an enterprise. We now give the definition of Armstrong relations in the context of preference relations.

Definition 9. (**Armstrong Preference Relation**) Let F^* be the set of all PFDs that are logically implied by a given set of PFDs F over R. An *Armstrong preference relation* for F is a preference relation r^{Arm} over a preference schema R such that $r^{Arm} \models T \mapsto X$ if and only if $T \mapsto X \in F^*$.

We will use $poss(R)$ in Lemma 1 and Theorem 4 to represent the set of all PFDs that can be defined over a schema R.

Lemma 1. Given preference relations r_1 and r_2 over R. Then there exists a preference relation r_3 over R such that $F_3 = F_1 \cap F_2$, where $F_i = \{f \mid r_i \models f\}$ for $i = 1, 2, 3$.

Proof Sketch. We start by assuming that all the attributes share with a common (ordered) domain of integers. Let $r_1 = \{t_1, \ldots, t_m\}$ and $r_2 = \{s_1, \ldots, s_n\}$ where $1 \leq m, n$. We define the *active domain* of a relation r over R by $adom(r) = \{v \mid \exists A \in R, \exists t \in r \text{ such that } t[A] = v\}$. We define the *safe distance* of two relations r_1 and r_2 over R by $sdist(r_1, r_2) = max(adom(r_1)) - min(adom(r_2)) + 1$. Intuitively, *sdist* guarantees that the satisfaction of a PFD in a relation can be preserved under the union operation. For each tuple $s_i \in r_2$, we define t'_i as follows: $t'_i[A] = s_i[A] + sdist(r_1, r_2)$ for each $A \in R$. We construct $r_3 = r_1 \cup r_4$, where $r_4 = \{t'_1, \ldots, t'_n\}$ being a preference relation over R. Then we can show that $F_3 = F_1 \cap F_2$ by establishing the fact that $F_3 \subseteq F_1 \cap F_2$ and $F_3 \supseteq F_1 \cap F_2$. □

We now show that Armstrong preference relations exist. Our construction is essentially to adapt the classical techniques in [9,2] for constructing Armstrong relations in our context.

Theorem 4. Given a set of PFDs F over R. There exists an Armstrong preference relation for F.

Proof. Let $F^* = \{f \mid F \models f\}$ and $\bar{F} = \{f \in poss(R) \mid f \notin F^*\}$. We now construct a preference relation r^{Arm} such that $r^{Arm} \models f'$ if and only if $f' \in F^*$. For the "if" case we let $f \in \bar{F}$. We then have a preference relation $r_f \models F$ but $r_f \not\models f$. Let $F_f = \{f \mid r_f \models f\}$. By repeated application of Lemma 1 running for all $f \in \bar{F}$, we have a relation r^{Arm} such that $r^{Arm} \models \bigcap_{f \in \bar{F}} F_f$. Since $F^* \subseteq F_f$, we have $F^* \subseteq \bigcap_{f \in \bar{F}} F_f$. It thus follows that $r^{Arm} \models F^*$. It remains to show the "only if" case. Let $f \notin F^*$. Then $f \in \bar{F}$. So there exists F_f such that $f \notin F_f$. It follows that $f \notin \bigcap_{f \in \bar{F}} F_f$. Thus, $r^{Arm} \not\models f$. □

6 Concluding Remarks

We consider preference handling in relations in order to express the daily and business preferences in practice. Within the context of preference relations, we discussed the applications of LOFDs in the areas of (1) maintaining the consistency of preference data, and (2) capturing the semantics of the ordering relationship between preference and preference-dependent data. In order to establish an in-depth study for the latter case, we defined PFDs in Definition 7 based on the notions of LOFDs and ordered relations, and presented a sound and complete axiom system for PFDs in Theorem 2. We showed in Theorem 3 that the complexity of chasing the tableaux given in Definition 4 is equivalent to decide whether all the reduced forms of a given set of PFDs are empty. As a result, the complexity of the implication problem for PFDs is found to be polynomial-time in the sizes of the relation schema and the given set of PFDs. We also showed in Theorem 4 that Armstrong relations exist for PFDs, an important result for incorporating PFDs into the process of database design in practice. We remark that the issues related to the interaction between PFDs and FDs is an interesting area to explore. For example, if $r \models \{T \mapsto X, T \mapsto Y\}$, then an equivalence class s in a partition of r, whose tuples have the same value of $t[T]$ for some $t \in r$, satisfies the FD $X \rightarrow Y$. In order to enhance the expressive power of our PFDs we are considering to generalise PFDs to incorporate vagueness semantics [8] in complex preference in the future work. Another more challenging issue is to explore the possibilities of efficient evaluating preference SQL [5] by using PFDs. The motivation is that, if PFDs can be applied to maintain a preference view of data then it may help some commercial web sites to give a more effective and efficient answer when facing a heavy load of preference SQL queries.

References

1. S. Amer-Yahia et al. *Structure and Content Scoring for XML.* In: Proc. of VLDB, (2005).
2. P. Atzeni and V. De Antonellis. *Relational Database Theory.* Benjamin/ Cummings Publishing Company, Inc., (1993).
3. S. Ginsburg and R. Hull. Order Dependency in the Relational Model. *Theoretical Computer Science* **26**(1-2), pp. 149-195, (1983).
4. S. Ginsburg and R. Hull. Sort Sets in the Relational Model. *Journal of the Association for Computing Machinery* **33**(3), pp. 465-488, (1986).
5. W. Kießling and G. Köstler. Preference SQL - Design, Implementation, Experiences. In: *Proc. of VLDB*, (2002).
6. W. Kießling and G. Köstler. Foundations of Preference in Database Systems. In: *Proc. of VLDB*, (2002).
7. M. Levene and G. Loizou. *A Guided Tour of Relational Databases and Beyond.* Springer-Verlag, London, (1999).

8. A. Lu and W. Ng. *Vague sets or intuitionistic fuzzy sets for handling vague data: Which one is better?* Proc of ER 2005. LNCS Vol 3716, pp. 401–416,(2005).
9. H. Mannila and K-J Raiha. *The Design of Relational Databases.* Addison-Wesley, (1992).
10. W. Ng. Ordered Functional Dependencies in Relational Databases. *Information Systems* **24**(7), pp. 535-554, (1999).
11. W. Ng and M. Levene. The Development of Ordered SQL Packages to Support Data Warehousing. Journal of Database Management **12**(4), pp. 27-49, (2001).
12. W. Ng. An Extension of the Relational Data Model to Incorporate Ordered Domains. *ACM Transactions on Database Systems* **26**(3), (2001).
13. Q. Tan et al. *Applying Co-training to Clickthrough Data for Search Engine Adaptation.* In: Proc. of DASFAA, LNCS Vol 2973, pp. 519-532, (2004).

Modeling Visibility in Hierarchical Systems*

Debmalya Biswas[1] and K. Vidyasankar[2]

[1] IRISA-INRIA, Campus Universitaire de Beaulieu
Rennes, France 35042
dbiswas@irisa.fr

[2] Dept. of Computer Science, Memorial University of Newfoundland
St. John's, NL, Canada A1B 3X5
vidya@cs.mun.ca

Abstract. We consider hierarchical systems where nodes represent entities and edges represent binary relationships among them. An example is a hierarchical composition of Web services where the nodes denote services and edges represent the parent-child relationship of a service invoking another service. A fundamental issue to address in such systems is, for two nodes X and Y in the hierarchy whether X can see Y, that is, whether X has visibility over Y. In a general setting, X seeing Y may depend on (i) X wishing to see Y, (ii) Y wishing to be seen by X, and (iii) other nodes not objecting to X seeing Y. The visibility could be with respect to certain attributes like operational details, execution logs, security related issues, etc. In this paper, we develop a generic conceptual model to express visibility. We study two complementary notions: *sphere of visibility* of a node X that includes all the nodes in the hierarchy that X sees; and *sphere of noticeability* of X that includes all the nodes that see X. We also identify the dual properties, coherence and correlation, that relate the visibility and noticeability notions. We propose elegant methods of constructing the spheres with these properties.

Keywords: Visibility, Noticeability, Hierarchical Systems, Hierarchical Web Services Compositions, Coherence, Correlation.

1 Introduction

Hierarchical systems are prevalent everywhere. While hierarchical systems provide an elegant mechanism to analyze the system functionality at different levels of abstraction, most of them allow interaction only between adjacent (parent-child) layers. Such restricted means of communication are often not sufficient for real-life scenarios. For example, in a supply chain management system, [1] states the need for visibility across levels as follows: "The information required by downstream entities are mainly material and capacity availability information from their suppliers. The information acquired by an upstream entity is information about customer demand and orders. The depth of information penetration can be specified in various degrees, e.g., isolated,

* Debmalya Biswas's work is supported by the RNRT (French ministry of research) project SWAN, decision No. 03 S 481. K Vidyasankar's work is supported in part by the Natural Sciences and Engineering Research Council of Canada Discovery Grant 3182.

D.W. Embley, A. Olivé, and S. Ram (Eds.): ER 2006, LNCS 4215, pp. 155–167, 2006.

upward one tier, upward two tiers, downward one tier, downward two tiers, and so forth". Also, non-functional aspects such as transactions, monitoring, user-interaction, etc. call for nodes having visibility over their ancestors, descendents and siblings. On the other hand, allowing arbitrary interaction among the hierarchical entities, without any restrictions, may not be an acceptable solution either. In a dynamic and heterogeneous environment, issues such as trust and autonomy force an entity to be selective in the interactions it has with others. The situation is worse for large scale systems where the number of involved entities may be in hundreds. We encountered the above issues while studying hierarchical Web Services compositions [2]. However, we believe that the proposed solutions are applicable for most hierarchical systems in general.

Thus, we need a model to capture the "visibility" aspect. For a pair of nodes X and Y in the hierarchy, we would like to capture whether X can see Y, that is, whether X has visibility over Y. In a general setting, X has visibility over Y if

- X wishes to see Y: X may be interested in Y due to functional or non-functional requirements.
- Y does not have any objection to X seeing it: As mentioned earlier, security, privacy, confidentiality, etc. issues play an important role in determining the visibility allowed by a provider.
- Remaining nodes in the hierarchy do not have any objections to X seeing Y: Contractual agreements between Y and another node Z may have a bearing on X seeing Y.

The requested visibility is usually with respect to some attribute of the nodes in the hierarchy. Examples of possible attributes (in a Web Services context are) are: provider details (URI, physical address), service details (pre-conditions, input, output and effects) and execution details (execution state, history). Roughly, provider details are required to invoke an operation of the provider, service and execution details for non-functional aspects such as recovery, monitoring, auditing, and other.

The main contribution of this paper is to propose a generic conceptual model to express visibility. Towards this end, we introduce the complementary notions of (i) *Sphere of Visibility* (SoV), and (ii) *Sphere of Noticeability* (SoN). For a node X, SoV of X reflects X's visibility over others, while SoN of X reflects the visibility others' have over X. We also identify two dual properties, coherence and correlation, that relate the visibility and noticeability notions. We propose elegant methods of constructing the spheres with these properties.

The rest of the paper is organized as follows: In section 2, we provide an informal introduction to SoV with the help of an e-shopping scenario. The formal definitions of SoV, coherence and correlation properties are given in Section 3. Section 4 introduces SoN and the relationship between the visibility and noticeability notions. Section 5 is dedicated to implementation details including algorithms to construct the SoV's and SoN's of the nodes in a hierarchy. Section 6 discusses some related work and section 7 concludes the paper.

2 An Informal Introduction to SoV

The Sphere of Visibility (SoV) of a node X (SoV_X) consists of nodes visible to X in the hierarchy. The visibility is with respect to some attribute A such as provider, service and execution details (discussed earlier). The visibilities of a provider corresponding to different attributes are mutually exclusive, that is, a provider Y might have visibility over X's provider details only, service details only, execution details only or any combination of the above. The visibility of each provider may be determined based on (a) the functional and non-functional requirements of the provider, (b) security, privacy and anonymity characteristics of the providers, whose visibility is sought, and (c) the global policies and constraints imposed by the environment.

For example, let us consider an e-shopping scenario (Fig. 1). A customer U orders a few goods from a store S. S splits the order into two parts and sends them to suppliers S-A and S-B. Supplier S-B uses supplier S-C to fulfil part of the order. S-A and S-B use courier companies C-A and C-B respectively to ship the goods to the customer. The store uses a financial service P for processing payment for the goods. This involves charging a credit card, by the credit card company H, and awarding bonus air miles, by another service B. The store also uses a monitor/auditor M to keep track of the service execution.

Taking the attribute A as service details, the visibility of some of the providers over other providers in the hierarchy of Fig. 1 are as follows. In the illustration of visibility of X over Y, X is represented in double ovals, Y is represented in thick oval, and the other nodes, if any, are represented in thin ovals.

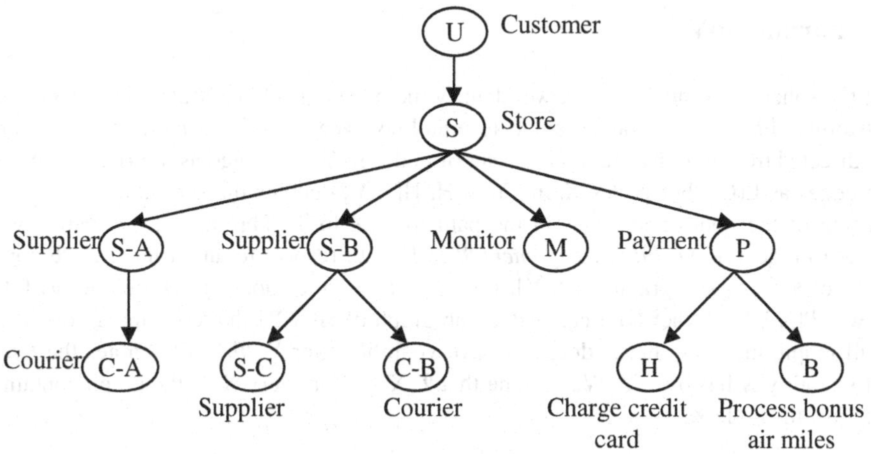

Fig. 1. A hierarchical composition graph H corresponding to an e-shopping scenario

- The store S has visibility over its parent and all its children. It does not have visibility over the next level descendents (Fig. 2a).
- The bonus air miles processing unit B has visibility over only the credit card company H and the customer U (Fig. 2b). It is only concerned with the customer's credit card number and the purchase amount *without any need to know the context*, namely the goods purchased and the store. We call the visibilities of B over H and U as *weak visibilities (or weak references)*, whereas the visibilities of S over U,

S-A, S-B, M and P, described above, are referred to as *strong visibilities (or strong references)*, meaning that the "structures" of the nodes S-A, S-B, M and P, relative to S, in the hierarchy are also visible to S.

- The courier company C-A has strong visibility over supplier S-A and weak visibility over customer U (Fig. 2c).
- The (strong) visibility of the courier company C-B over S-B, S and U (Fig. 2d).
- The visibilities of U over S, S-A, H and B, are described in Fig. 2e. They have the following characteristics: (a) The visibilities over S and S-A are strong, while the last one (over B) is a weak visibility. (b) The third visibility is of "intermediate strength". We call this *partially strong visibility (or reference)*. We interpret this as U gets the service details of H directly (by weak reference to H), or from P (by weak reference to P) which gets the details from H. (c) U does *not* have visibility over the service details of P. Thus, U can get the service details of H from P, but not the service details of P itself.
- Visibilities need not be symmetric. For example, S does not have visibility over C-B (Fig. 2a), but C-B has visibility over S (Fig. 2d).
- Visibilities of the providers in the hierarchy need not be related. For example, U has (weak) visibility over B (Fig. 2e), but U's child S does not have visibility over B (Fig. 2a).

3 Formal SoV

In the sphere of visibility of X, we identify the nodes visible to X and their "type" of visibility. First, we introduce some terminology. We consider a hierarchy H as an undirected tree. For any graph G, the set of nodes in G is denoted as V(G), and the set of edges as E(G). For nodes X and Y in H, H[X,Y] denotes the sub-graph of H consisting of the nodes and edges in the path from X to Y. Throughout this paper, we refer to a generic *visibility assignment* $\mathcal{V}$ in H with respect to an attribute A. $\mathcal{V}$ consists of a set of sub-graphs $\mathcal{V}$[X,Y], for all pairs X, Y of nodes in H, defined as follows: $\mathcal{V}$[X,Y] is either (i) a connected sub-graph of H[X,Y] that contains Y, or (ii) a null graph, meaning that X does not have visibility over Y. $\mathcal{V}$[X,Y] denotes the *type* of visibility X has over Y. We assume that $\mathcal{V}$[X,X], for every X, is the graph containing just the node X.

Definition. The *Sphere of Visibility* of a node X in hierarchy H, denoted SoV_X, and also as $\mathcal{V}_X$, is (V_X, $\mathcal{VS}_X$), where V_X is the set of nodes Y in V(H) for which $\mathcal{V}$[X,Y] is non-null, and $\mathcal{VS}_X$ is the set of sub-graphs $\mathcal{V}$[X,Y], for Y in V_X.

A node in V_X will be referred to as a node in SoV_X also, and similarly, a sub-graph $\mathcal{V}$[X,Y] in $\mathcal{VS}_X$ will be referred to as an element of SoV_X also. We say that X has a *weak* reference to any node Y that is visible to X. If $\mathcal{V}$[X,Y] has some edges then we say that X has a *partial strong* reference to Y. If $\mathcal{V}$[X,Y] is H[X,Y], that is, it has all the nodes and edges in the path from X to Y in H, then we say that X has a *strong* reference to Y.

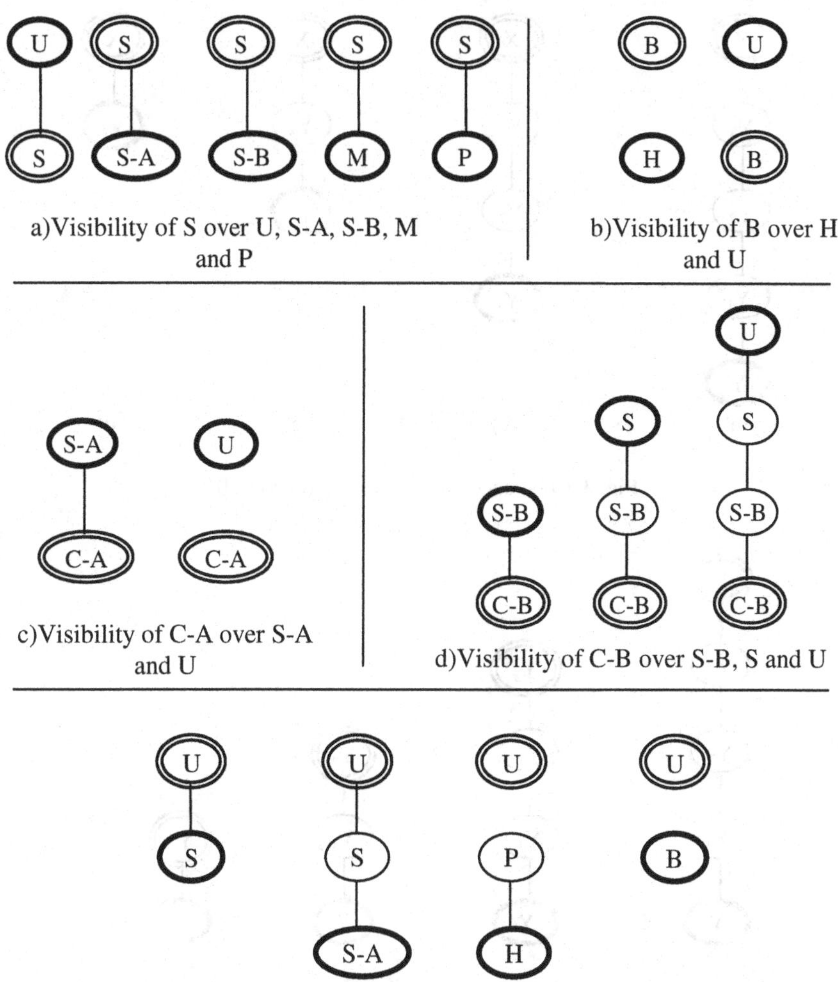

Fig. 2. SoV's of some of the providers in hierarchy H of Fig. 1

In the following, we define two special properties of visibility assignments: coherence and correlation. We first illustrate these properties with a strong reference $\mathcal{V}$[X,Y], in Fig. 3 and Fig. 4. Here, H[X,Y] = (X, Y_3, Y_2, Y_1, Y) is the path from X to Y through nodes Y_3, Y_2, and Y_1.

- (Fig. 3) Coherence refers to the property that $\mathcal{V}$[X,Y] is H[X,Y] implies (i) $\mathcal{V}[X,Y_1]$ is $H[X,Y_1]$, (ii) $\mathcal{V}[X,Y_2]$ is $H[X,Y_2]$, and (iii) $\mathcal{V}[X,Y_3]$ is $H[X,Y_3]$.
- (Fig. 4) Correlation refers to the property that $\mathcal{V}$[X,Y] is H[X,Y] implies (i) $\mathcal{V}[Y_3,Y]$ is $H[Y_3,Y]$, (ii) $\mathcal{V}[Y_2,Y]$ is $H[Y_2,Y]$, and (iii) $\mathcal{V}[Y_1,Y]$ is $H[Y_1,Y]$.

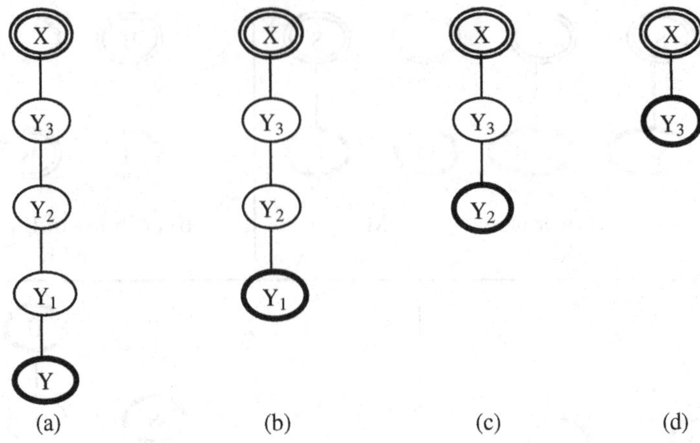

Fig. 3. Coherence: (a) implies (b), (c) and (d)

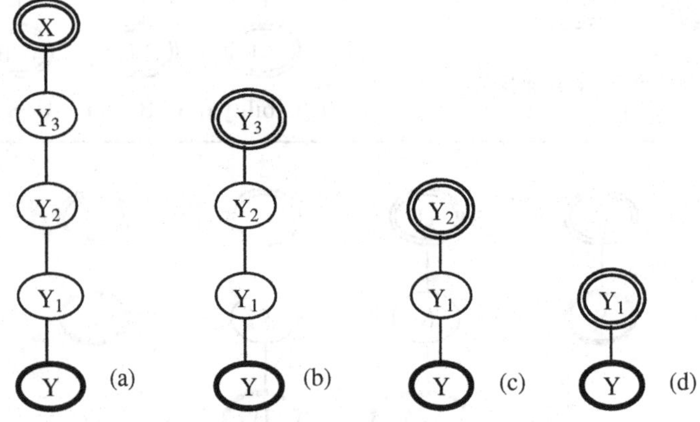

Fig. 4. Correlation: (a) implies (b), (c) and (d)

3.1 Coherence

Definition. A visibility assignment $\mathcal{V}$ is *coherent* if for each pair of nodes X and Z, $\mathcal{V}$[X,Z] is either (i) null or (ii) for every node Y in the path from X to Z in H, $Y \neq X$ and $Y \neq Z$, $\mathcal{V}[X,Z] \cap H[X,Y]$ is a sub-graph of $\mathcal{V}$[X,Y].

Fig. 5 describes several instances of $\mathcal{V}$[X,Z] and $\mathcal{V}$[X,Y] in coherent and non-coherent visibility assignments. Informally, coherence means that the strength of visibility of X over Y is at least as much as the strength used for visibility of X over Z: $\mathcal{V}$[X,Z] intersection H[X,Y] refers to the strength of visibility of X over Y "used" for visibility over Z, whereas $\mathcal{V}$[X,Y] is simply the strength of visibility of X over Y; coherence means the latter is at least as much as the former.

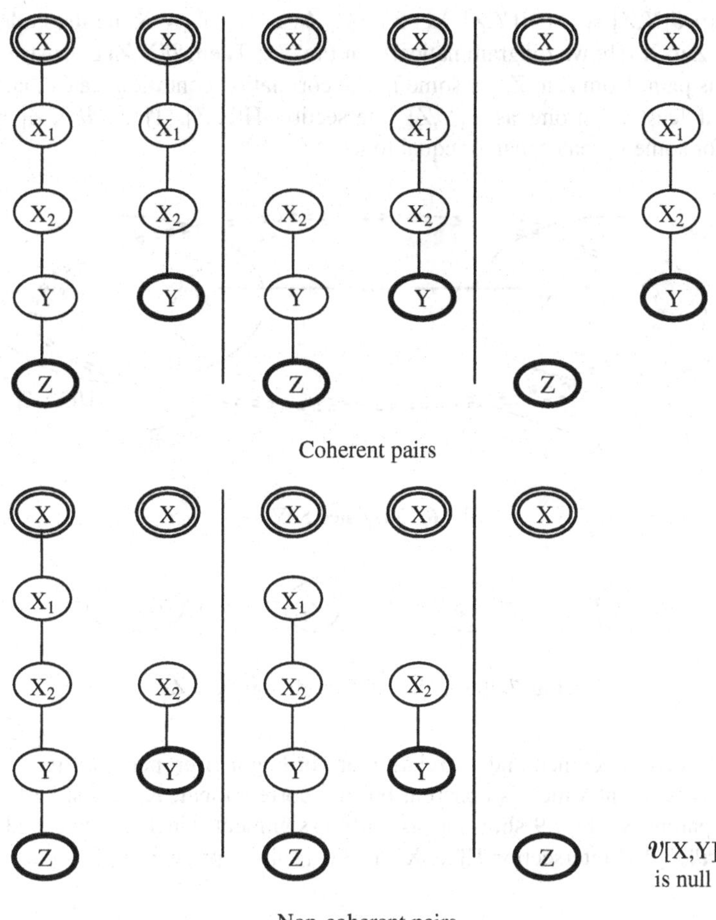

Fig. 5. Coherent property illustration

3.2 Correlation

For a pair of nodes X and Y in the hierarchy H, on deleting the edges and the intermediate nodes in the path from X to Y, we get one component containing X, one component containing Y, and possibly some more components. We refer to the first component as H[X;Y] and the second as H[Y;X].

Definition. A visibility assignment $\mathcal{V}$ is *correlated* if for every pair of nodes X and Y in H, (i) for each Z in ($V_Y \cap$ H[X;Y]), ($\mathcal{V}$[Y,Z] $\cap$ H[X;Y]) is a sub-graph of $\mathcal{V}$[X,Z], and (ii) for each W in ($V_X \cap$ H[Y;X]), ($\mathcal{V}$[X,W] $\cap$ H[Y;X]) is a sub-graph of $\mathcal{V}$[Y,W].

A diagrammatic representation of the first part of the correlation definition appears in Fig. 6. There are two possibilities: (a) $\mathcal{V}$[Y,Z] is H[Y,Z]. Then, $\mathcal{V}$[X,Z] should be

H[X,Z]. (b) $\mathcal{V}$[Y,Z] is not H[Y,Z]. Let Z_0 = Z, Z_1, Z_2, ..., Z_m = X, be the nodes in the path from Z to X (shown diagrammatically in Fig. 7). Then, $\mathcal{V}$[Y,Z] consists of a sub-path of this path, from Z to Z_i for some i. The correlation condition states that $\mathcal{V}$[X,Z] must be at least as strong as $\mathcal{V}$[Y,Z] intersection H[X,Z]. Thus, $\mathcal{V}$[X,Z] must be H[Z,Z_j], for some j greater than or equal to i.

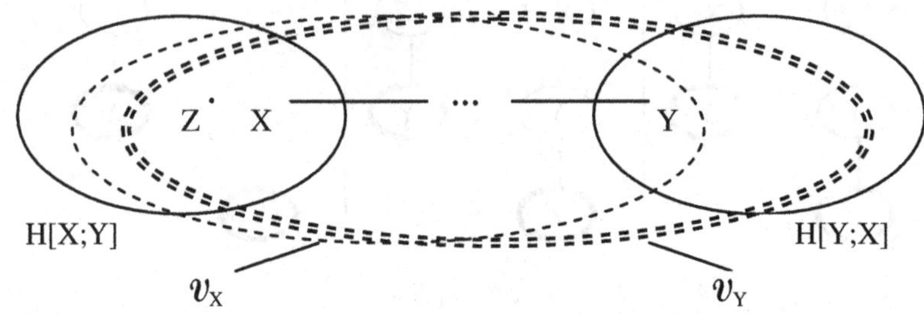

Fig. 6. Correlated SoV's

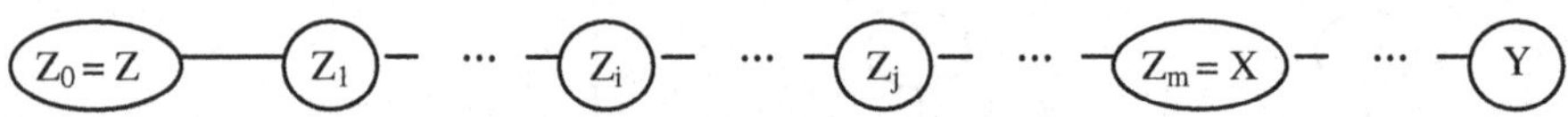

Fig. 7. Illustration of the path from X to Z

We note that coherence and correlation are orthogonal properties. Fig. 8 shows a visibility assignment which is coherent but not correlational: X_1 is visible to X_4, but not to its parent X_3. Fig. 9 shows a visibility assignment which is correlated but not coherent: $\mathcal{V}$[X_4,X_1] intersection H[X_4,X_2] is not a sub-graph of $\mathcal{V}$[X_4,X_2].

4 Sphere of Noticeability (SoN)

For a node X, the Sphere of Noticeability notion in intended to capture: (i) which nodes have visibility over X; and (ii) what type of visibility they have of X. First we define noticeability independent of, but in a way analogous to the definition of, visibility. We refer to a general *noticeability assignment* $\mathcal{N}$ in H with respect to an attribute A. $\mathcal{N}$ consists of a set of sub-graphs $\mathcal{N}$[X,Y], for all pairs X, Y of nodes in H, defined as follows: $\mathcal{N}$[X,Y] is either (i) a connected sub-graph of H[X,Y] that contains X, or (ii) a null graph. $\mathcal{N}$[X,Y] denotes the *type* of noticeability, that is, the type of visibility Y has over X. In the last case, X is not noticed by Y. We assume that $\mathcal{N}$[X,X], for every X, is the graph containing just the node X. Note that since visibility and noticeability notions are complementary, $\mathcal{V}$ and $\mathcal{N}$ definitions are also complementary. That is, for $\mathcal{N}$ that "corresponds to" a $\mathcal{V}$, for X and Y, $\mathcal{N}$[X,Y] is the same as $\mathcal{V}$[Y,X]. We use $\mathcal{N}$[X,Y] most of the time in the definitions and discussions in this section, though $\mathcal{V}$[Y,X] could also be used instead.

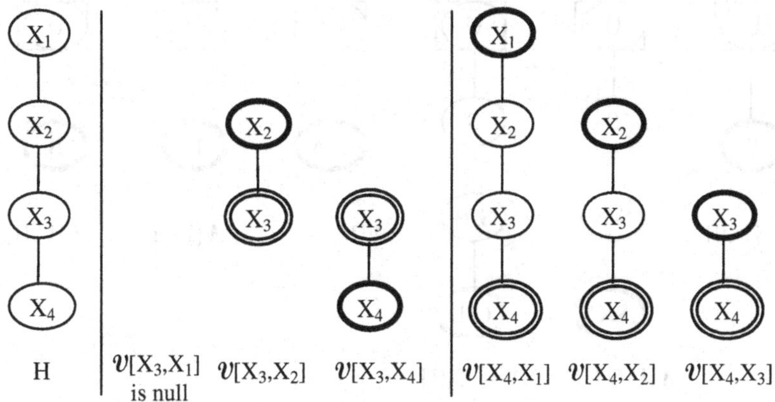

Fig. 8. Illustration of coherent, but not correlated, SoV's

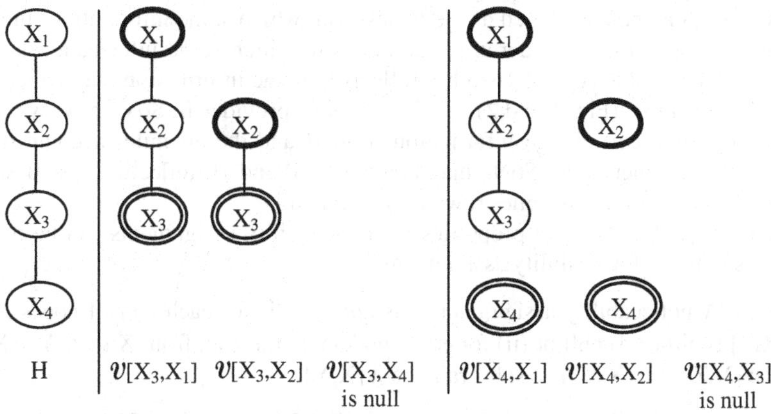

Fig. 9. Illustration of correlated, but not coherent, SoV's

Definition. The *Sphere of Noticeability* of a node X in hierarchy H, denoted SoN_X, and also as $\mathcal{N}_X$, is (N_X,$\mathcal{NS}_X$), where N_X is the set of nodes Y in V(H) for which $\mathcal{N}$[X,Y] is non-null, and $\mathcal{NS}_X$ is the set of sub-graphs $\mathcal{N}$[X,Y], for Y in N_X.

Note that, for a specific node X, SoV_X is the set of $\mathcal{V}$[X,Y]'s for different Y's, whereas SoN_X is the set of $\mathcal{V}$[Y,X]'s for different Y's.

For provider U in Fig.1, $\mathcal{NS}_U$ is illustrated in Fig. 10. In each figure, the node whose SoN is illustrated is indicated by a rectangle enclosing the oval representing the node.

An obvious application of SoN is for change management. For example, a provider X notifying the providers, who have visibility over X, when there is some change in the provider URI (provider details), metrics used to compute the service (service details), log format (execution details), etc. An interpretation of the relationship between

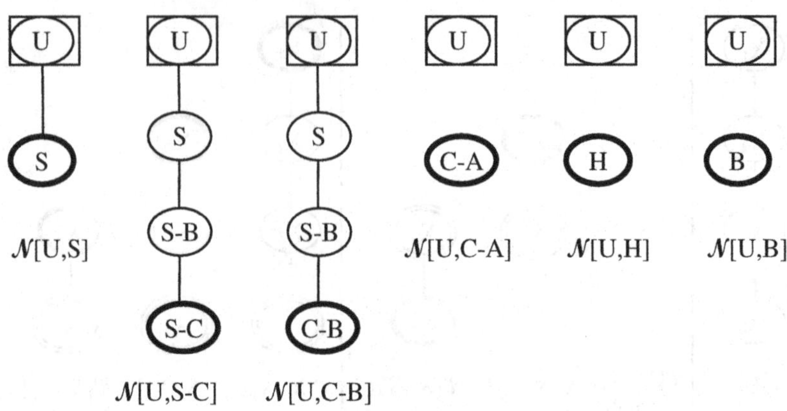

Fig. 10. $\mathcal{N}S_U$ for provider U in Fig. 1

SoV and SoN using the e-shopping scenario introduced earlier (Fig. 1) follows. For a node X, SoV_X can be considered as the nodes from which some information (input) is expected. SoN_X can be considered as the nodes to which some information is to be sent. In both cases, the type of visibility reflects how the information may be received or sent. For example (Fig. 1 and 2), for the air miles provider B, SoV_B conveys that B is expecting the credit charge information from H and the air miles account details from U. On the other hand, SoN_B may contain U, P and H, reflecting that B should send confirmation of the air miles reward to U, P and H.

Coherence and correlation properties for noticeability assignments can be defined analogous to those for visibility assignments.

Definition. A noticeability assignment $\mathcal{N}$ is *coherent* if for each pair of nodes X and Z, $\mathcal{N}$[X,Z] is either (i) null or (ii) for every node Y in the path from X to Z, Y $\neq$ X and Y $\neq$ Z, $\mathcal{N}[X,Z] \cap H[X,Y]$ is a sub-graph of $\mathcal{N}$[X,Y].

SoN_U, given in Fig. 10, is not coherent as $\mathcal{N}$[U,C-B] intersection H[U,S-B] is not a sub-graph of $\mathcal{N}$[U,S-B] (which is null).

Definition: A noticeability assignment $\mathcal{N}$ is *correlated* if for every pair of nodes X and Y in H, (i) for each Z in ($N_Y \cap H[X;Y]$), ($\mathcal{N}[Y,Z] \cap H[X;Y]$) is a sub-graph of $\mathcal{N}$[X,Z], and (ii) for each W in ($N_X \cap H[Y;X]$), ($\mathcal{N}[X,W] \cap H[Y;X]$) is a sub-graph of $\mathcal{N}$[Y,W].

Again, there are two possibilities: (a) if $\mathcal{N}$[Y,Z] is H[Y,Z] itself then $\mathcal{N}$[X,Z] should also be H[X,Z]. (b) Here also, let $Z_0 = Z, Z_1, Z_2, ..., Z_m = X$, be the nodes in the path from Z to X (shown diagrammatically in Fig. 7). Then, in the case $\mathcal{N}$[Y,Z] is not H[Y,Z], it will be a connected sub-graph containing Y, $H[Y,Z_j]$, for j between 1 and m. Then, the correlation condition states that $\mathcal{N}$[X,Z] should also contain at least this path. That is, if it is $H[X, Z_i]$, then i should be less than or equal to j.

Property. In a hierarchy H, a visibility assignment is coherent if and only if the corresponding noticeability assignment is correlated, and vice versa.

Proof: First we consider the "only if" part. For nodes X and Y in H, we need to show that (i) for each Z in ($N_Y \cap$ H[X;Y]), ($\mathcal{N}$[Y,Z] $\cap$ H[X;Y]) is a sub-graph of $\mathcal{N}$[X,Z], and (ii) for each W in ($N_X \cap$ H[Y;X]), ($\mathcal{N}$[X,W] $\cap$ H[Y;X]) is a sub-graph of $\mathcal{N}$[Y,W]. Since $\mathcal{N}$[Y,Z] is $\mathcal{V}$[Z,Y], and $\mathcal{N}$[X,Z] is $\mathcal{V}$[Z,X], and by coherence of $\mathcal{V}$, ($\mathcal{V}$[Z,Y] $\cap$ H[Z,X]) is a sub-graph of $\mathcal{V}$[Z,X], the assertion (i) follows. Assertion (ii) follows similarly. The rest of the proof is also similar.

5 Implementation

Consider a static hierarchy H where each node X in H has an initial set of visibility requirements and noticeability restrictions. Note that the "initial" set of X only reflects the intended set, that is, visibility as X would like. By abuse of notation, we use the spheres, Sphere of Intended Visibility of X ($SoIV_X$) and Sphere of Intended Noticeability of X ($SoIN_X$), to refer to X's intended visibility and noticeability respectively. $SoIV_X$ ($SoIN_X$) may not be the same as the final assigned $\mathcal{V}_X$ ($\mathcal{N}_X$) due to negotiations/conflicts between the SoIV's and SoIN's. For example, let us consider a path from X1 to Xn in H. Let the nodes in the path be X1, X2, X3, ..., Xn. Suppose Xn is in $SoIV_{X1}$ but X1 is not in $SoIN_{Xn}$. Given this, there are two options: (i) Xn's restriction cannot be overruled and so X1 cannot have visibility over Xn ($SoIV_{X1} \neq \mathcal{V}_{X1}$), and (ii) X1's requirement has higher priority leading to negotiation of Xn's restrictions and X1 finally having visibility over Xn ($SoIN_{Xn} \neq \mathcal{N}_{Xn}$). Note that this argument applies to visibility of any strength.

In addition to the individual SoIV's and SoIN's, visibility may be restricted by the SoIV's and SoIN's of other nodes in H, and desired coherence and correlation properties, as well. Often (in a Web Services context), it is not the service provider itself but some higher level logical entity or an agent acting on behalf of the provider which is responsible for regulating the visibility of a provider. For example (Fig. 1), let us assume that S-A would like to have visibility over the courier companies (such as C-B) used by other suppliers to find the cheapest option. On the same lines, S-B (a higher level provider) might like to keep the details of its courier company C-B hidden due to competitive reasons and should be in a position to reject S-A's request for visibility over C-B.

We outline a simple scheme for adjusting SoV's (and SoN's) of the existing nodes dynamically, each time a node Y is added to the hierarchy. We consider the changes required at an existing node X due to the addition of Y. Let Y = Y_0, Y_1, Y_2, ..., Y_i, ..., Y_j, ..., Y_k, ..., Y_n, Y_{n+1} = X, be the nodes in the path from Y to X such that $k \geq j \geq i$ (shown diagrammatically in Fig. 11). We denote the path from X to Y as X-Y, the path from X to Y_1 as X-Y_1, etc. We also denote $\mathcal{V}$[X,Y] as Y_j-Y, or $\mathcal{V}$[X,Y] is null. And, $\mathcal{V}$[X,Y] is $\mathcal{N}$[Y,X]. Note that Y_j-Y and Y-Y_j refer to the same path, that is, we do not consider direction of the path.

Steps to define $\mathcal{V}$[X,Y], that is, determining j in Y_j-Y:

1. $\mathcal{V}$[X,Y] could be null. In the following, we consider non-null options.
2. For coherent $\mathcal{V}$, if $\mathcal{V}$[X,Y_1] is null, then $\mathcal{V}$[X,Y] has to be Y-Y, that is, (weak reference to) just the node Y; otherwise, $\mathcal{V}$[X,Y_1] must be Y_k-Y_1, that is, $j \leq k$. This will also give correlated $\mathcal{N}$.
3. For correlated $\mathcal{V}$, if $\mathcal{V}$[Y_n,Y] is null, then $\mathcal{V}$[X,Y] must be null too; otherwise, $\mathcal{V}$[Y_n,Y] must be Y_k-Y, that is, $j \leq k$. This will also give coherent $\mathcal{N}$.

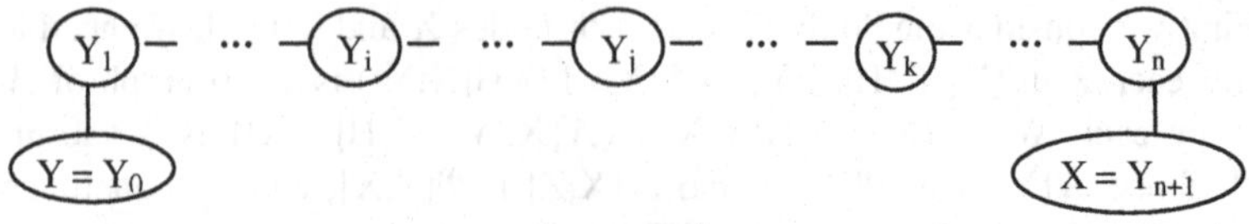

Fig. 11. Illustration of the path from Y to X

Steps to define $\mathcal{V}$[Y,X], that is, determining j in Y_j-X:

1. $\mathcal{V}$[Y,X] could be null. In the following, we consider non-null options.
2. For coherent $\mathcal{V}$, if $\mathcal{V}$[Y,Y_n] is null, then $\mathcal{V}$[Y,X] has to be X-X, that is, (weak reference to) just the node X; otherwise, $\mathcal{V}$[Y,Y_n] must be Y_i-Y_n, that is, $i \leq j$. This will also give correlated $\mathcal{N}$.
3. For correlated $\mathcal{V}$, if $\mathcal{V}$[Y_1,X] is null, then $\mathcal{V}$[Y,X] must be null too; otherwise, $\mathcal{V}$[Y_1,X] must be Y_i-X, that is, $i \leq j$. This will also give coherent $\mathcal{N}$.

Such adjustments need to be made for every existing node X.

6 Related Works

The notion of spheres is based on the concept of Spheres of Control (SoC) [3]. A Sphere of Control encapsulates entities sharing a similar set of properties or having a dependency relation. The dependency relations considered in [3] are atomicity, commitment, resource allocation, recovery, auditing, consistency, etc. SoV and SoN logically group the nodes (and their attributes) visible to another node in a hierarchy. Also, [3] considers homogeneous and non-autonomous systems where visibility is not an issue. Thus, our work can be considered as complementary to the work in [3] to heterogeneous and autonomous systems. Later works have extended the initial concept of SoC to Spheres of Atomicity [4] and Commitment [5]. [4] utilizes the properties of the processes (pivot, compensatable and retriable) in a Sphere of Atomicity to determine if the sphere, as a whole, guarantees atomicity. [5] applies the concept of SoC to Multi-Agent Systems (MAS) to structure agents based on their commitment guarantees. However, the above works are not directly related to the work presented in this paper and we mention them for the sake of completeness. No other work (that we are aware of) has attempted to formalize the visibility aspect for hierarchical systems. Some of the works which have touched upon this aspect are the following. [6] identifies real-life scenarios where there might be a need to deviate from the inheritance of access rights upwards through the hierarchy in a role-based access control. [7] discusses the visibility aspect with respect to the visibility of the results of a subtransaction in a nested transactional system. Basically, [7] advocates the provision to be able to expose the results to a particular ancestor to improve performance. [8] proposes a formal model based on π-calculus to capture the behaviour of nested long running transactions in a Web services context. Of particular interest are the different modes of failure propagation: up-propagation, down-propagation, down-specific propagation and non-propagation.

In a previous work [9], we had introduced the SoV concept with respect to hierarchical Web Services compositions and shown its application in the context of performing compensation under visibility constraints. However, [9] only considers vertical visibility (that is, visibility over ancestors and descendents) as compared to the more generalized notion of visibility in this paper (visibility over siblings, uncles, cousins, etc.). The notion of SoN and discussion with respect to the properties (coherence and correlation) are novel contributions of this paper.

7 Conclusion

The main contribution of this paper starts with a formalization of the visibility notion. The SoV definition is intuitive and encompasses "strong", "weak" and a variety of partially strong notions. The SoN definition follows naturally from that of SoV. We have identified (i) the properties of coherence and correlation, which can be defined uniformly for both visibility and noticeability assignments, and (ii) how these properties relate the two assignments in interesting ways. We have shown how the interrelationship can be exploited in associating meaningful visibility characteristics to the nodes of a hierarchy. It will be interesting to look for other nice visibility properties that can be applied to all hierarchical systems or at least to special cases. From an implementation perspective, we would also like to consider dynamic hierarchies (structure of the hierarchy itself may change). We are also considering its practical applications with respect to non-functional aspects, such as, transactions, monitoring, security, etc.

Acknowledgments. We would like to thank the referees for their comments which helped to improve the presentation.

References

[1] Fu-Ren Lin, Gek Woo Tan, and M.J. Shaw, "Modeling Supply-Chain Networks by a Multi-Agent System", In proceedings of the 31st Annual Hawaii International Conference on System Science (HICSS), 1998, pp. 105-114.

[2] G. Alonso, F. Casati, H. Kuno, and V. Machiraju, "Web Services: Concepts, Architecture and Applications", Springer Verlag 2004, ISBN: 3540440089.

[3] C. Davies, Jr, "Data processing spheres of control", IBM Systems Journal, 17(2), 1978, pp. 179-198.

[4] Gustavo Alonso, and Claus Hagen, "Exception Handling in Workflow Management Systems", IEEE Transactions on Software Engineering, vol. 26, no. 10, Oct 00, pp. 943-958.

[5] Munindar P. Singh, and Pinar Yolum, "Commitment Machines", Revised Papers from the 8th International Workshop on Intelligent Agents VIII, Aug 01, pp. 235-247.

[6] J. D. Moffet, "Control principles and role hierarchies", In proceedings of the 3rd ACM Workshop on Role-Based Access Control (RBAC), 1998, pp. 63-69.

[7] Qiming Chen, and U. Dayal, "A Transactional Nested Process Management System", In proceedings of the 12th International Conference on Data Engineering (ICDE), 1996, pp. 566-573.

[8] Laura Bocchi, "Compositional Nested Long Running Transactions", In proceedings of the 7th International Conference on Fundamental Approaches to Software Engineering (FASE), 2004, LNCS 2984, pp. 194-208.

[9] D. Biswas, and K. Vidyasankar, "Spheres of Visibility", In proceedings of the 3rd IEEE European Conference on Web Services (ECOWS), 2005, pp. 2-13.

A Model for Anticipatory Event Detection

Qi He, Kuiyu Chang, and Ee-Peng Lim

School of Computer Engineering,
Nanyang Technological University, Singapore 639798, Singapore
qihe@pmail.ntu.edu.sg, kuiyu.chang@pmail.ntu.edu.sg, aseplim@ntu.edu.sg

Abstract. Event detection is a very important area of research that discovers new events reported in a stream of text documents. Previous research in event detection has largely focused on finding the first story and tracking the events of a specific topic. A topic is simply a set of related events defined by user supplied keywords with no associated semantics and little domain knowledge. We therefore introduce the Anticipatory Event Detection (AED) problem: given some user preferred event transition in a topic, detect the occurence of the transition for the stream of news covering the topic. We confine the events to come from the same application domain, in particular, mergers and acquisitions. Our experiments showed that classical cosine similarity method fails for the AED task, whereas our conceptual model-based approach, through the use of domain knowledge and named entity type assignments, seems promising. We show experimentally that an AED voting classifier operating on a vector representation with name entities replaced by types performed AED successfully.

1 Introduction

Anticipatory Event Detection (AED)[1] refers to the problem of detecting the occurrence of a user-specified anticipatory event (AE). AED is a very hard problem since it requires a basic understanding of the AE semantics, which can vary by event type. Current news alert systems such as Google News Alerts[2] typically produce abysmal results for AED. For example, the search terms "China attacks Taiwan" (describing an AE that has not happened as of this writing) will generate numerous false alarm articles from Google News Alerts.

One way to look at AED is to think of it as finding the transition between two adjacent events in an *event transition graph* whose events are represented by news articles covering the event transition graph before and after a particular transition has consummated. Figure 1 shows an *event transition graph* with n events and $n-1$ transitions for $topic_i$ (e.g. eBay buys Skype). A user may only be interested in receiving a notification when a particular transition has fired, and not be bothered about the remaining transitions. If sufficient number of news articles can be collected for each of the events, it would be theoretically possible to detect any of the $n-1$ transitions. In order to learn a particular transition, a model will have to be trained to classify articles as occurring "before" or "after"

D.W. Embley, A. Olivé, and S. Ram (Eds.): ER 2006, LNCS 4215, pp. 168–181, 2006.

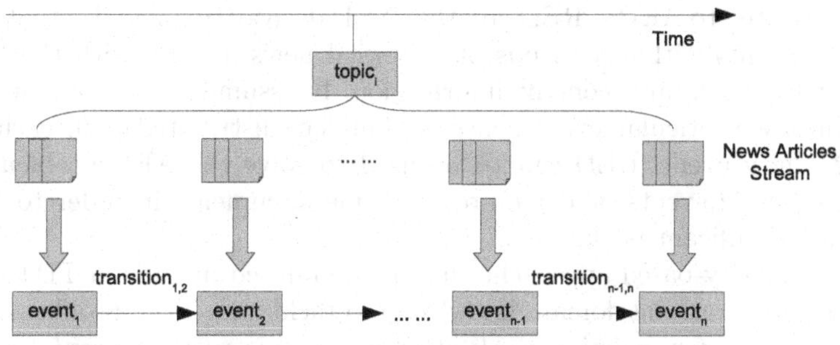

Fig. 1. Anticipatory event transition graph

the transition. For example, given $transition_{1,2}$ in the *event transition graph* of Figure 1, we would like to detect the first story of $event_2$.

In this paper, we report new results on modeling the AED problem. To simplify the problem, we assume that 1) the topic is constrained to a particular domain, i.e. mergers and acquisitions, 2) the *event transition graph* is created manually, 3) we only detect a single event transition within the *event transition graph.*

2 Related Work

AED was previously proposed and tackled using a sentence classification approach [1] for detecting final scores of basketball matches. Moreover, AED falls under the broader family of problems collectively known as Topic Detection and Tracking (TDT), which includes traditionally, New Event Detection (NED), Topic Tracking (TT), and Retrospective Event Detection (RED), etc. TDT defines a evaluation paradigm that addresses event-based organization of broadcast news[3], with a significant focus on NED and TT for news [4][5][6][7][3][8][9][10]. AED differs from typical TDT tasks like NED/TT/RED primarily in two ways: 1) AED is concerned only with one particular user-predefined anticipatory event; 2) AED will return a hit if and only if the user-anticipated transition has consummated for that specified event genre. For example, suppose NED or RED is set up to return alerts for mergers and acquisitions events, then any news describing a new rumor or latest developments related to acquisition could result in one or more NED/RED hits. On the other hand, AED could be configured to return a hit if and only if a particular acquisition such as some company buying Skype is formally announced.

Morever, NED was shown empirically to be a very hard problem if only simple vector space representation was used [6]. Yang et al.[8] reported a substantial performance gain by first classifying news articles into different topics, followed by applying 1NN to detect new events (NED). Kumaran et al.[10] applied text classification techniques and extracted named entities, but for detecting *all* new events of a particular category (using a model trained threshold) instead of finding the transition of a user-specified AE. Unlike AED, non of the above uses classification to detect *new* events.

Closely related to AED is RED, another NED derivative. Li et al.[11] attempts to identify events within a corpus of historical news articles with the help of time, user feedback, and content information. It assumes that the news event histogram of a particular event genre is Gaussian-distributed with each burst denoting a new event. RED cannot be used to solve the AED problem since it detects generic events, and requires multiple documents in order to form a statistically significant peak.

While similarity-based approaches had made limited inroads in TDT, others have tried incorporating domain knowledge to tackle the TDT problem[12][13]. Moreover, only a few existing work attempt to construct an *event transition graph*[14], which is the prerequisite for representing transitions between events in AED. Specific to news alerts, there has been previous work on presenting news to users in a meaningful and efficient manner[15][16].

Nallapati et al.[16] used interdependencies between news events to build an unsupervised relational structure similar to AED's *event transition graph*, but which was not used for AED. Another related work is Kleinberg's model for online change detection in data streams [17], which assumes that the points (news articles) in the stream are independently emitted by some underlying probability distribution; its goal is to detect any changes in distribution. Like NED, it requires more than one document to identify a significant change.

3 AED Model

Our proposed AED system first retrieves a set of *generic* acquisition news articles from Google News Alerts based on the user supplied list of domain specific keywords. The articles are then manually labelled as positive or negative with respect to a single transition, and fed into a classifier for training. To test this AED model, we manually created and labelled a separate and independent dataset comprising seven acquisition topics. For each topic, we use the trained generic AED classifer to detect the earliest news article published after the AE (in this case the announcement of an acquistion) has consummated.

3.1 Anticipatory Event Representation

An AED user preference is defined as a single transition in the event transition graph. In practice, topics of the same type (e.g. US Presidential elections) often involve a typical set of event transitions (e.g. nomination of party's Presidential candidates, nomination of party's Vice-Presidential candidates, election of party's Presidential team, election of Presidential team). Thus, it is reasonable to train an AED model using news about past-occurences of a similar nature.

Creating an event transition graph automatically based on arbitrary user specifications is extremely difficult. In our model, we assume that an event transition graph is already available, along with generic articles representing the "pre" and "post" states of a user preferred transition (preference). Our problem is thus reduced to applying *online AED* to a live stream of news articles with the goal of identifying the first story after a user-specified transition.

Figure 2 shows an example event transition graph describing typical states shared by most company acquisition topics. Suppose a user is interested in the event transition, $transition_{2,3}$ from $event_2$ ("In talk to acquire") to $event_3$ ("Announce acquisition"). As there are usually multiple news articles associated with the "Announce acquisition" event, AED will try to detect the first story among these. The complete AED framework is shown in Figure 3.

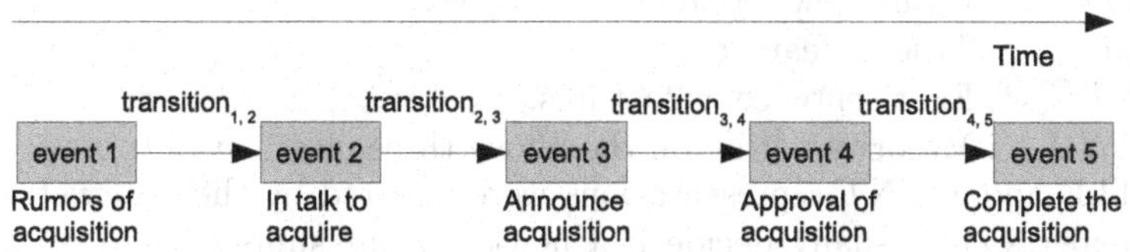

Fig. 2. Event transition graph for the "acquisition" topic

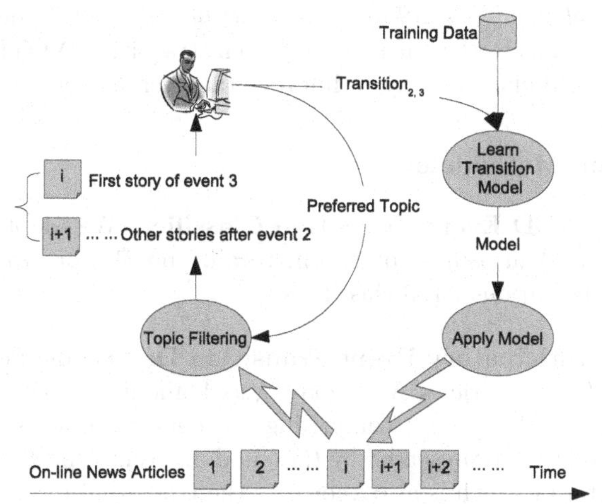

Fig. 3. Online AED system framework

3.2 Named Entities and Text Classification in AED

Named Entities Analysis in AED. In news stories, named entities of different types help provide essential context information. For example, company names involved in a merger and acquisition topic clearly helps to distinguish a particular topic from other topics. However, within a specified topic, named entities alone are not sufficient to determine an event transition boundary. As a matter of fact, we found experimentally that verbs and their senses actually carry more valuable information for determining a transition.

In our experiments, we use BBN's Identifinder[18] to identify 24 types of named entities, including *Animal*, *Contact info*, *Disease*, *Event*, *Facility*, *Game*,

Geo-political entities, *Language*, *Law*, *Location*, *Nationality*, *Organization*, *Person*, *Plant*, *Product*, *Substance*, *Work of art*, *Date*, *Time*, *Cardinal*, *Money*, *Ordinal*, *Percentages*, and *Quantity*. Extracted named entities are then replaced in line by one of the 24 named entity types.

Classification Methods. We tried three different feature representation methods and one classifier combining strategy to train the AED classifier, as follows:

CONTENT : Entire news content as features.
TITLE : Title as features.
1SENT : First sentence as features.
VOTING : Majority voting on the above three classifier outputs.

The TITLE and 1SENT representations were inspired by the observation that human experts can usually decide if a news is a hit simply based on its first sentence and/or title. Moreover, the TITLE and 1SENT representation of a news article may not always carry useful features, and the AED decision will have to fall back to the CONTENT representation. For example, the first sentence "*Signature Control Systems is off to a busy start in early 2006*" does not contain features really relevant to the "acquisition" event transition. VOTING was thus used as a simple and effective way to improve the overall accuracy.

3.3 Evaluation Methodology

Evaluating the AED Event Transition Classifier. We adopt the standard information retrieval measures, precision, recall, and f1-score to evaluate the performance of the various AED classifiers.

Evaluation of Anticipatory Event Transition Detection. Suppose we are given a set of N news articles $X = \{x_1, ..., x_N\}$ about a topic, and an event transition graph $E = \{e_1, ..., e_n\}$ comprising n events. Each news x_i is assigned a publication date/time represented by $t(x_i)$ and an event type in E represented by $e(x_i)$, the latter of which is also known as the true event of x_i.

We assume that all news articles in X are sorted in time ascending order, i.e. $t(x_i) \leq t(x_j)\ \forall i < j$, and all events in E are sorted in time ascending order, i.e. $t(e_i) \leq t(e_j)\ \forall i < j$.

By applying our trained AED classifier on a news article x_i, we obtained its assigned event denoted by $s'(x_i)$. Given a $transition_{k-1,k}$ (i.e. user preference), the objective of AED is therefore to find the news article x_m that satisfies:

$$x_m = \arg\min \{t(x_i) \mid \forall x_i\ where\ \ s'(x_i) = e_k\}$$

To make the time comparison easier between the detected first story x_m and the event e_k, we also define the *true time* of e_k, $t(e_k)$, as follows:

$$t(e_k) = \min \{t(x_i) \mid \forall x_i\ where\ \ e(x_i) = e_k\}$$

Once the first story x_m of the anticipatory event e_k is determined by the AED classifier, all subsequent news articles, x_j, $j = (m+1), \ldots, N$ will be assigned to event(s) e_k post $transition_{k-1,k}$. Occasionally, the first story identified by AED may be prematured, delayed, or undefined (never found). Accordingly, we define four evaluation criteria as follows:

Accurate Alarm : $t(x_m) = t(e_k)$. First story of e_k found successfully.
Delayed Alarm : $t(x_m) > t(e_k)$. First story found was too late.
False Alarm : $t(x_m) < t(e_k)$. First story found was prematured.
Miss : $t(x_m) = undefined$. No x_i in X has $s'(x_i) = e_k$. AED fails to even identify the event!

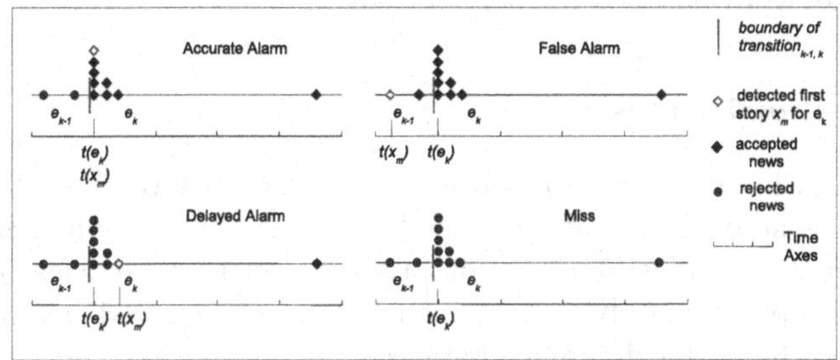

Fig. 4. An evaluation example for *Transition Detection* in AED

Figure 4 graphically depicts each of the four evaluation criteria for AED *Transition Detection*. In Section 5 we will use the same type of graph to illustrate and analyze our experimental results. Specifically, we simply tally the total number of *false alarms*, *delayed alarms*, *accurate alarms*, and *misses* to evaluate the AED performance on a given set of events. For news alerts, an *accurate alarm* is the most desirable, followed by a *delayed alarm*. Otherwise, a *miss* is generally preferred over a *false alarm*.

4 Testbed

Two datasets were created specifically for evaluating the AED problem. For quality assurance purposes, each document in the two datasets was scrutinized and annotated by at least two people.

4.1 *Google Acquisition* Dataset

In order to learn an anticipatory event transition such as $transition_{2,3}$ in Figure 2, we manually created the generic *Google Acquisition* dataset. This dataset contains 346 as-it-happens news articles returned by Google News Alerts using the keywords “announce acquisition”, which corresponds to *event*3 in Figure 2, during the two-month period from Dec 19, 2005 to Feb 19, 2006.

Each article in *Google Acquisition* is manually labelled as one of two possible events, i.e. “pre” or “post” $transition_{2,3}$. Unfortunately, some articles can appear ambiguous even to a human expert. One general rule-of-thumb is to label the document based on overall context. For example, if the primary theme of an article revolves around the announcement/agreement/completion of an acquisition, we label it as post-$transition_{2,3}$; otherwise, it is labelled as pre-$transition_{2,3}$. We note that the latter case could also include irrelevant documents completely unrelated to acquisition.

To ensure consistency in labelling, a set of guidelines and rules was established, based on which 178 documents were labelled as positive and 168 as negative, which means that Google News Alerts returned 168 (48.6%) outright false alarms for the subscribed keywords "announce acquisition". This is a typical result from a simplistic keyword-based news alert system.

4.2 *Acquisition7* Dataset

We created another dataset, *acquisition7*, which covers seven recent acquisition topics as the test data for our proposed online AED solution. Each acquisition news topic in *acquisition7* is comprised of 20 news articles returned by Google News, approximately half of each (10) were reported before and after $transition_{2,3}$. The major difference between this dataset and the *Google Acquisition* dataset is that each document is not generic but instead tied to a specific acquisition. Further, there are no irrelevant documents in this dataset; a document occurs either before or after $transition_{2,3}$ for a specific acquisition.

The 7 acquisition news topics are listed in Table 1, where $t(e_3)$ refers to the true occurrence date for $event_3$ in Figure 2. The annotation of *Acquisition7* follows the same criteria as defined in Section 4.1.

Table 1. Make up of the *Acquisition7* dataset

Acquisition Topics	$t(e_3)$
Adobe acquires Macromedia	Apr 18, 2005
CNPC acquires PetroKazakhstan	Oct 26, 2005
eBay acquires Skype	Sep 12, 2005
Lenovo acquires IBM PC Division	Dec 08, 2004
Oracle acquires PeopleSoft	Dec 13, 2004
Oracle acquires Siebel	Sep 12, 2005
SBC acquires AT&T	Jan 31, 2005

5 Simulation Results

5.1 Experiment Setup

Lucene 1.4.3 was used to tokenize the news text content with stop word removal to create the corresponding document-word vector. In order to preserve time-sensitive past/present/future tenses of verbs, no stemming was done other than the removal of a few articles.

We used a normalized (unit length) binary document vector representation because we observed that co-occurrences of terms are far more important than the raw term frequency and inverse document frequency for AED. The normalized binary document-word vectors are than fed into SVM-light [19] for training and classification. SVM cost factors[20] were used to offset the slight imbalance in numbers between the positive and negative documents.

5.2 AED Via Cosine Similarity

As a baseline, we evaluated AED performance using simple cosine similarity on the *Acquisition7* dataset. Standard TFIDF document representation was used with the following variations [10]: all terms (All Terms), all terms without named entities (No NE), and name entities only (NE only).

Each incoming news article is compared to *all* existing news articles (assumed to be negative or pre-transition) from all 7 topics. If the cosine similarity between this news and its nearest neighbor falls below a threshold, the incoming news is considered to have consummated the transition; otherwise it is classified as a negative news.

The similarity approach generated largely false alarms and misses, except for one accurate alarm, using various values of similarity threshold. Figure 5 shows the ratio of misses to false alarms for all 3 vector representations versus a gradually increasing similarity threshold. From Figure 5, we observe that starting from a low similarity threshold, the system was initially very strict (incoming news must be significantly different, i.e. has low cosine similarity compared to all existing news), resulting in high percentage of misses. As the similarity threshold is gradually increased, the system was able to detect some news, but almost all prematuredly as false-alarms, except for one accurate alarm detected by the "no NE" representation. Our results clearly show that similarity based approaches, which does not use a conceptual model, are too simplistic to detect a transition leading to a user-desired AE.

5.3 AED Via Event-Conditioned Novelty Detection

Event-conditioned 1NN novelty detection [8], essentially a topic-constrained cosine similarity approach, first classifies a news into a known topic before applying cosine similarity comparison between it and its nearest neighbor. To model this approach, we applied cosine similarity AED to all news within the same topic to obtain the results listed in Table 2. Clearly, event-conditioned novelty detection failed the AED task miserably as it generated all but one false alarms. This shows that even with topical constraints, similarity approaches still cannot perform AED reliably.

5.4 Validating the *Google Acquisition* Dataset

In order to validate the generic $transition_{2,3}$ trained model, we conducted two-fold cross-validated experiments using the four text classification approaches of

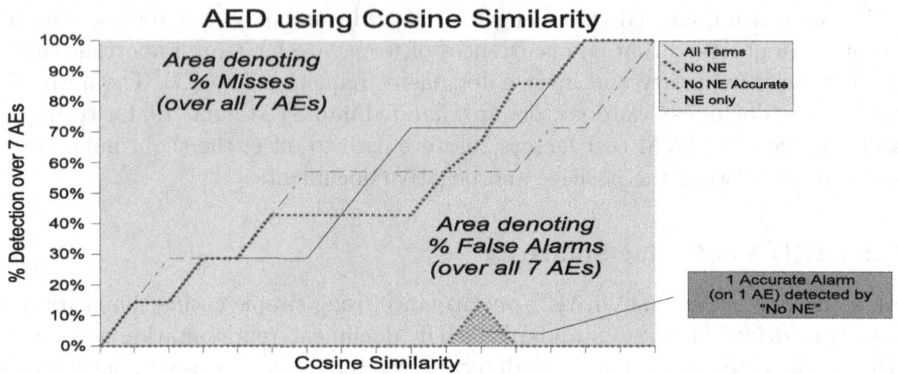

Fig. 5. AED using cosine similarity on Acquisition7 Dataset

Table 2. AED results on *Acquisition7* using event-conditioned novelty detection

Alarms:	*Accurate*	*Delayed*	*False*	*Miss*
Adobe acquire Macromedia			√	
CNPC acquires PetroKazakhstan			√	
eBay acquires Skype	√			
Lenovo acquires IBM PC Divison			√	
Oracle acquires PeopleSoft			√	
Oracle acquires Siebel			√	
SBC acquires AT&T			√	

Section 3.2 on the *Google Acquisition* dataset. The dataset is first split along the timeline into two equal parts: 1) news articles dating from Dec 19, 2005 to Jan 19, 2006, and 2) news articles dating from Jan 20, 2006 to Feb 19, 2006. One part was used for training with the other part used for testing and vice-versa.

From the test results summarized in Figure 6 and Table 3, we see that the VOTING strategy is the overall best performer with the least number of false alarms, while the CONTENT method gives a slightly higher recall at the expense of almost twice as many false alarms. The main problem with the CONTENT method is that it is easily affected by a few transition-alluding sentences in negative documents, such as "*Additionally, Magazine Acquisition announced that Morgan Stanley Real Estate and Onex Real Estate will be partnering with Sawyer Realty Holdings LLC ("Sawyer") in the TCT acquisition*", which understandably appears positive to a classifier. This is because the mere occurrence of the words "acquisition" and "announced" is sufficient to trigger the trained model, which uses a binary bag-of-words representation. The VOTING strategy thus combines the best results from CONTENT, TITLE, and 1SEN methods.

Apart from deciding the best classification strategy, one other significance of this experiment is that it increased the precision of Google's returned news alerts from 51.4% to 85.7%, a more than 33% improvement! All in all, the high precision and recall figures confirmed that the *Google Acquisition* dataset is

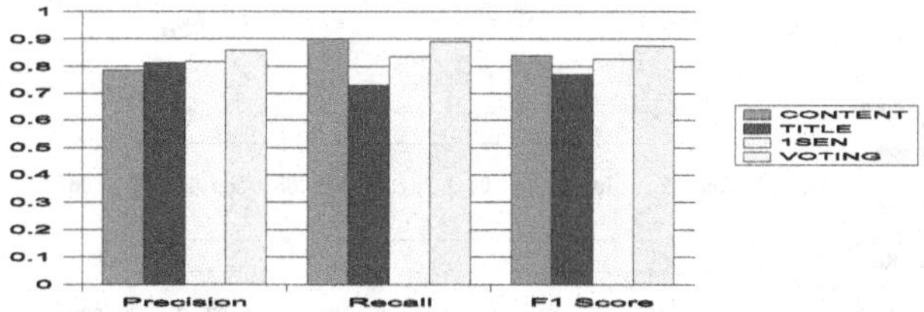

Fig. 6. Average test results of the four text classifiers on *Google Acquisition*

Table 3. Average test results on *Google Acquisition.* Best results are shown in bold.

Average	*CONTENT*	*TITLE*	*1SEN*	*VOTING*
False Alarms	22.5	15.5	17	**13.5**
Misses	**9**	24.5	15	10
Precision	0.7847	0.8110	0.8172	**0.8571**
Recall	**0.9011**	0.7308	0.8352	0.8901
F1	0.8389	0.7688	0.8261	**0.8733**

indeed suitable for modelling $transition_{2,3}$ for subsequent AED evaluations in Section 5.5.

5.5 AED Via Classification

In this section, we test the generic AED classifier trained by *Google Acquisition* on the *Acquisition7* dataset. Figure 7 shows the true $transition_{2,3}$ boundaries for each of the 7 *Acquisition7* topics distributed along a timeline. Three AED outcomes are shown in Figures 8-10. Note that once the "first" story of e_3 has been identified by AED, all subsequent news articles are labelled post-$transition_{2,3}$.

Table 4. AED results on *Acquisition7* using the VOTING method

Alarms:	*Accurate*	*Delayed*	*False*	*Miss*
Adobe acquires Macromedia	√			
CNPC acquires PetroKazakhstan	√			
eBay acquires Skype	√			
Lenova acquires IBM PC Division			√	
Oracle acquires PeopleSoft			√	
Oracle acquires Siebel	√			
SBC acquires AT&T		√		

Table 4 gives a summary of the overall performances, which shows that AED based on the VOTING method generated 4 accurate alarms, 1 delayed alarm, 2 false alarms, and 0 misses. This means that the model trained by *Google Acquisition* was able to cover the main characteristics of all 7 acquisition topics.

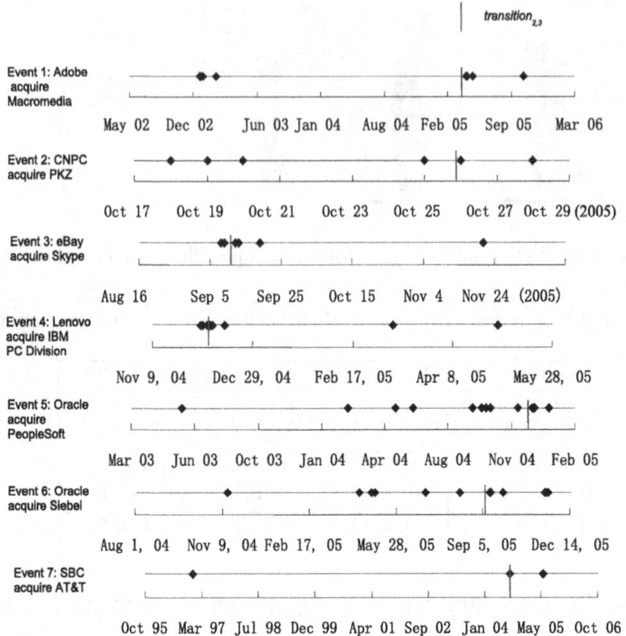

Fig. 7. $transition_{2,3}$ boundaries in *Acquisition7*

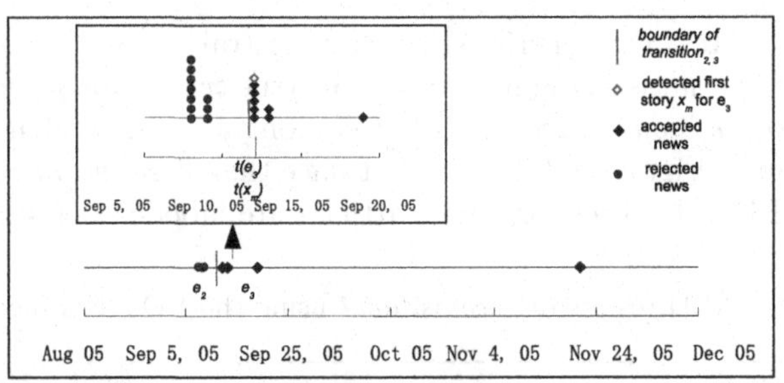

Fig. 8. Online AED of "eBay acquires Skype" found an accurate alarm, $t(x_m) = t(e_3)$

Moreover, comparing this result with that of the CONTENT method as shown in Table 5, we found that the AED evaluation for Acquisition7 dataset is inconsistent with the two-fold cross-validation results for *Google Acquisition* dataset with respect to false alarms. In *Google Acquisition*, the VOTING method reduces false alarms, with the CONTENT method yielding the highest recall. The situation is completely reversed for *Acquisition7*. Based on the analysis in Section 5.4, we are inclined to trust the evaluation results for *Google Acquisition* better because the inconsistencies could simply be caused by the relatively small size of the *Acquisition7* dataset.

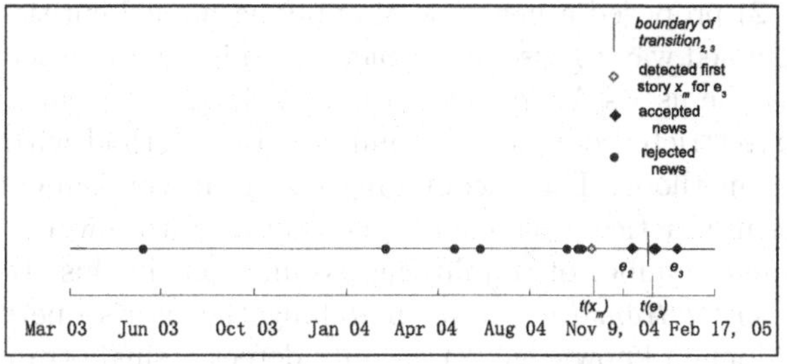

Fig. 9. Online AED of "Oracle acquires PeopleSoft" found a false alarm, $t(x_m) < t(e_3)$

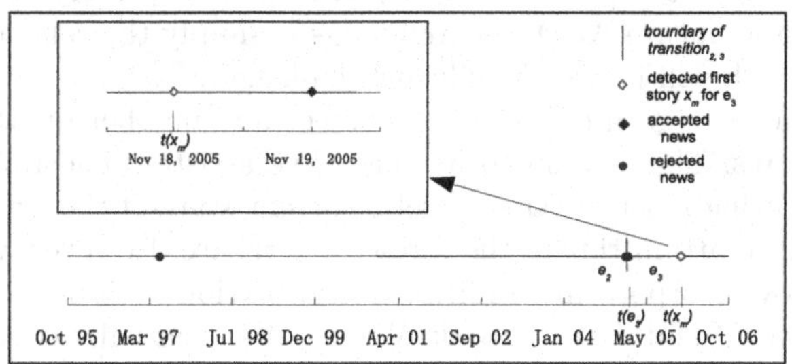

Fig. 10. Online AED of "SBC acquires AT&T" found a delayed alarm, $t(x_m) > t(e_3)$

Table 5. AED results on *Acquisition7* using the CONTENT method

Alarms:	*Accurate*	*Delayed*	*False*	*Miss*
Adobe acquires Macromedia	√			
CNPC acquires PetroKazakhstan	√			
eBay acquires Skype	√			
Lenovo acquires IBM PC Division				√
Oracle acquires PeopleSoft		√		
Oracle acquires Siebel	√			
SBC acquires AT&T		√		

Nevertheless, in spite of the above inconsistencies, AED results achieved by both the VOTING and CONTENT methods were leaps and bounds ahead of the cosine similarity results (Figures 5) and event-conditioned novelty detection results (Table 2). This is actually a very encouraging outcome for a preliminary investigation into AED, and thus provides strong support and credibility to our AED model and solution.

6 Conclusion

We have made five main contributions in this paper: 1) we formally defined and formulated a conceptual model for the AED problem and identified its associated research issues, 2) proposed a new way of applying named entities for AED, 3) proposed a principled way to assemble generic training data for learning one AE transition, using the user's AE preferences, 4) verified the feasibility of AED in practice for one restricted domain, 5) compared our method with two classical cosine similarity methods. The encouraging results in this paper showed AED to be applicable in practice, thus paving the way for future work.

We have made a number of simplifying assumptions in this study: 1) we assumed that an *event transition graph* matching the user's query is available, based on some domain knowledge, 2) we only detect a single transition, among many other possible transitions in the graph, and we claim the transition corresponds to the user specified list of keywords (i.e. user preferences), 3) we constrained our testbed to a particular genre of AE, that of mergers and acquisitions. One possible future AED research focus is simply the relaxation of these assumptions, which will involve significant challenges.

Naturally, the holy grail of AED is to detect any number of AE transitions of arbitrary genres. This is akin to having a live assistant constantly scanning newsfeed monitoring a set of AEs. Surely, current state-of-the-art technologies will not be able to attain this in the foreseeable future. However, we could still improve AED by incorporating additional information such as frequency/time of documents/words and user feedback. We hope to eventually come up with an effective and practical AED system, perhaps initially for some restricted domain, and which overcomes limitations of existing systems like Google News Alerts.

References

1. He, Q., Chang, K., Lim, E.P.: Anticipatory event detection via sentence classification. In: IEEE SMC Conf. (2006) to appear
2. Google: (Google news alerts, http://www.google.com/alerts.)
3. Allan, J.: Topic Detection and Tracking. Event-based Information Organization. Kluwer Academic Publishers (2002)
4. Allan, J., Jin, H., Rajman, M., Wayne, C., Gildea, D., Lavrenko, V., Hoberman, R., Caputo., D.: Topic-based novelty detection: Final report. In: DARPA Broadcast News Transcription and Understanding Workshop. (1999)
5. Jin, H., Schwartz, R., Sista, S., Walls, F.: Topic tracking for radio, tv broadcast, and newswire. In: DARPA Broadcast News Workshop. (1999) 199–204
6. Allan, J., Lavrenko, V., Jin, H.: First story detection in tdt is hard. In: 9th ACM CIKM Conf. (2000) 374–381
7. Stokes, N., Carthy, J.: Combining semantic and syntactic document classifiers to improve first story detection. In: 24th ACM SIGIR Conf. (2001) 424–425
8. Yang, Y., Zhang, J., Carbonell, J., Jin, C.: Topic-conditioned novelty detection. In: 8th ACM SIGKDD Conf. (2002) 688–693
9. Brants, T., Chen, F., Farahat, A.: A system for new event detection. In: 26th ACM SIGIR Conf. (2003) 330–337
10. Kumaran, G., Allan, J.: Text classification and named entities for new event detection. In: 27th ACM SIGIR Conf. (2004) 297–304
11. Li, Z., Wang, B., Li, M., Ma, W.Y.: A probabilistic model for retrospective news event detection. In: 28th ACM SIGIR Conf. (2005) 106 – 113

12. Fukumoto, F., Suzuki, Y.: Event tracking based on domain dependency. In: 23rd ACM SIGIR Conf. (2000) 57–64
13. Maguitman, A., Leake, D., Reichherzer, T., Menczer, F.: Dynamic extraction topic descriptors and discriminators: towards automatic context-based topic search. In: 13th ACM CIKM Conf. (2004) 463 – 472
14. Mei, Q., Zhai, C.: Discovering evolutionary theme patterns from text: an exploration of temporal text mining. In: 11th ACM SIGKDD Conf. (2005) 198–207
15. Allan, J., Wade, C., Bolivar, A.: Retrieval and novelty detection at the sentence level. In: 26th ACM SIGIR Conf. (2003) 314–321
16. Nallapati, R., Feng, A., Peng, F., Allan, J.: Event threading within news topics. In: 13th ACM CIKM Conf. (2004) 446–453
17. Kifer, D., Ben-David, S., Gehrke, J.: Detecting change in data streams. In: 30th VLDB Conf. (2004)
18. Bikel, D.M., Schwartz, R., Weischedel, R.M.: An algorithm that learns what's in a name. In: Machine Learning. (1999) 34(1–3):211C231
19. Joachims, T.: (Svm-light, http://svmlight.joachims.org/)
20. Morik, K., Brockhausen, P., Joachims, T.: Combining statistical learning with a knowledge-based approach - a case study in intensive care monitoring. In: 16th ICML Conf. (1999) 268–277

A Framework for Integrating XML Transformations

Ce Dong and James Bailey

NICTA Victoria Laboratory
Department of Computer Science and Software Engineering
The University of Melbourne, VIC 3010, Australia
{cdong, jbailey}@csse.unimelb.edu.au

Abstract. XML is the de facto standard for representing and exchanging data on the World Wide Web and XSLT is a primary language for XML transformation. Integration of XML data is an increasingly important problem and many methods have been developed. In this paper, we study the related and more difficult problem of how to integrate XSLT programs. Program integration can be particularly important for server-side XSLT applications, where it is necessary to generate a global XSLT program, that is a combination of some initial XSLT programs and which is required to operate over a newly integrated XML database. This global program should inherit as much functionality from the initial XSLT programs as possible, since designing a brand new global XSLT program from scratch could be expensive, slow and error prone, especially when the initial XSLT programs are large or/and complicated. However, it is a challenging task to develop methods to support XSLT integration. Difficulties such as template identification, unmapped template processing and template equivalence all need to be resolved. In this paper, we propose a framework for semi-automatic integration of XSLT programs. Our method makes use of static analysis techniques for XSLT and consists of four key steps: i) Pattern Specialization, ii) Template Translation, iii) Lost Template Processing and iv) Program Integration. We are not aware of any previous work that deals with integrating XML transformations.

1 Introduction

XML [6] is rapidly emerging as a dominant standard for data representation and exchange on the Web [11]. The eXtensible Stylesheet Language Transformations (XSLT) standard [8, 26] is a primary language for transforming, reorganizing, querying and formatting XML data. In particular, server-side XSLT [23] is an extremely popular technology for processing and presenting results in response to user queries issued to a server side XML database. An XSLT program consists of a set of templates. Execution of the program is by recursive application of individual templates to the source XML document.

The availability of large amounts of homogeneous Web databases necessitates XML integration [5, 7, 12, 15, 20, 22, 27, 29], e.g. when two organizations which have similar XML information databases are amalgamated. Such XML integration is

D.W. Embley, A. Olivé, and S. Ram (Eds.): ER 2006, LNCS 4215, pp. 182 – 195, 2006.

typically DTD-directed, that is, the integration task is constrained by a predefined DTD, to which the target XML document is required to conform [11]. A set of mapping rules between the initial DTDs and the global DTD must be provided.

However, when databases are amalgamated, it is not just static information which needs to be combined. XML repositories will often have associated dynamic aspects as well, such as XSLT programs or stylesheets, that have been designed to transform or present the XML information. When repositories are combined, so too must be the dynamic aspects. In other words, we require a new (global) XSLT program to access the integrated XML database. It is likely that this program will be required to inherit much of the functionality that was present in the initial XSLT programs, which operated over the original XML repositories.

Different from the language XQuery [4], an XSLT program consists of templates, which can be regarded as the basic program unit for building the global XSLT program during integration. Also, different from static XML data or schema integration [5, 7, 12, 15, 20, 22, 27, 29], XSLT integration is additionally challenging, because it must deal with the dynamic aspects. Some difficulties are faced: 1) A specific XSLT template might match, by means of selection patterns, multiple XML elements. This can cause confusion when mapping the template from the initial XSLT program to the global XSLT program, using the element mapping rules. 2) Two initial templates (from different initial programs) which match the same XML element, will need to be combined together within the global XSLT program. However, it is difficult to identify the conflicts and relationships (equivalence, containment and intersection) between their functionalities, when generating the global template body. 3) Some initial templates might not be mapped to and included in the global XSLT program, based on the element mapping rules. However, their absence might strongly affect the execution result and thus they must be properly combined within the global XSLT program. 4) Some templates contain functionality which is valid for an initial XSLT program, but which is no longer useful or even invalid for the global XSLT program. This needs to be detected and reconciled.

The integration framework proposed in this paper has four main components: 1) *Pattern Specialization* is used to specialize the template selection patterns and construction patterns and consequently lessen element reference ambiguity; 2) *Template Translation* is used to translate template selection patterns and construction patterns to conform to the global DTD; 3) *Lost Template Processing* is used to process the templates which match XML elements not existing in the mapping rule list; 4) *Program Integration* is used to generate the global XSLT program and mark any problematic templates for further consideration by the program designer.

The problem of XSLT integration is a new and challenging research issue. We are not aware of any other similar work that addresses this topic.

The remainder of this paper is organized as follows. We first review some basic concepts in section 2. Then, in section 3 we introduce XML integration approaches and related terminology. Next, in section 4, we propose the XSLT integration framework step by step. Related work is surveyed in section 5 and finally in section 6, we conclude our research and give the discussion of future work.

2 Background

We begin by briefly reviewing some concepts regarding DTDs, XSLT and XPath, assuming the reader already has basic knowledge in these areas.

2.1 DTDs and DTD-Graph

An XML DTD [6, 19] provides a structural specification for a class of XML documents and is used for validating the correctness of XML data. Based on the DTD, we can create a data structure to summarize the hierarchical information within a DTD, called the DTD-Graph. It is a rooted, node-labeled graph, where each node represents either an element or an attribute from the DTD and the edges indicate element nesting. The DTD-Graph developed in our previous work [10] is similar to the Dataguide structure described by Goldman and Widom in 1997[13]. It is an important data structure used to validate the XPath expressions (selection patterns and construction patterns) of XSLT programs during XSLT integration.

2.2 XSLT and Functionality Blocks

XSLT is a recursive XML transformation language [8, 16, 17, 18]. An XSLT program can be thought of as an ordered collection of templates. Each template has an associated pattern (selection pattern) and contains a nested set of construction rules. A template processes XML-tree [8] nodes that match the selection pattern and constructs output according to the construction rules [23].

An XSLT program is also an XML document, with a corresponding tree structure, having a 'root element' node of *<xsl:stylesheet>* that has *<xsl:template>* child nodes. We refer to the sub-trees which are children of the *<xsl:template>* nodes as "functionality blocks".

2.3 XPath

The primary purpose of XPath is to address parts of an XML document using path expressions. It also provides basic facilities for manipulation of strings, numbers and booleans.[28]. A *location path* is an XPath expression which selects a set of nodes relative to the context node. If we remove 'predicate(s)' from the location path, we can get an XPath expression consisting of 'axes', 'steps' and '/', called a *distinguished* XPath [2] expression. The selection patterns and construction patterns in an XSLT program are expressed using XPath. Selection patterns can only use the axes of 'child' and 'attribute', whereas construction patterns may be full XPath expressions. XPath expressions starting with '/' or '//' are called *absolute* XPath expressions. Otherwise (e.g. starting with '.' or 'node name'), they are called *relative* XPath expressions. *Simple* XPath (similar to [2]) is a fragment of XPath which disallows the use of any 'function', 'predicate' and 'axes' other than 'child', 'self', and 'descendant-or-self'. Oppositely, XPath expressions which contain 'functions' or 'predicates' or 'axes' other than those above, we will term *rich* XPath. Our XSLT integration framework can deal with simple XPath expressions automatically and handles rich XPath expressions via human interaction (to be discussed in section 4).

We further define *full-absolute* XPath expressions to be those starting with '/', followed by a sequence of node names separated by '/' (e.g. '/a/b/c/d'). We define *full-relative* XPath expressions to be those starting with './' or 'node name', followed by a sequence of node names separated by '/' (e.g. './b/c/d' and 'b/c/d'). These concepts are important for supporting the descriptions of the XSLT integration framework in section 4.3 and 4.4.

2.4 The Template and Association Graph (TAG) of an XSLT Program

XSLT syntactic structure gives rise to calling relationships between templates [14, 17]. In our previous work [10], we designed a *Template and Association Graph* (TAG), which is a rooted node-labeled directed graph used to describe the calling relationships between XSLT templates. The TAG can be used to analyze an XSLT program and help to find bugs in XSLT program design [10]. In this paper, we use the TAG to eliminate unreachable templates, missing templates and invalid calling relationships [10], that are generated as 'side-effects' during the XSLT integration process.

2.5 Server-Side XSLT

Server-side XSLT [23] is a popular solution for data exchange and querying on the Web. It is often deployed in e-commerce, e-publishing and information services applications. Transforming the content on the server has advantages such as providing convenience for business logic design and code reuse, cheaper data access and security and smaller client downloads [18]. XSLT integration is more meaningful for server-side XSLT (as opposed to client side XSLT), since a global XSLT program must be constructed after the server XML databases are merged.

3 XML Integration

Suppose we have XML databases associated with a server-side XSLT system. There are then two major different approaches which can be used for XML integration [3, 22, 24]. One is *virtual* integration, where no physically integrated XML needs to be built. Specifically, *virtual* integration publishes a global XML schema (e.g. a DTD) which is 'integrated' from the initial distributed XML database schemas. A user query over the global schema passed to the system is then re-written into distributed queries (i.e. parameters to distributed XSLT programs) to access the distributed XML databases (initial XMLs). A combined result is returned to the user. Another kind of XML integration is called *instance* integration, since a global XML is physically built. Specifically, based on a predefined global XML schema, the data of the initial XMLs is merged into the global XML. A user query based on the global DTD is evaluated directly over the integrated XML database. Our XSLT integration framework is designed to integrate the initial XSLT programs according to instance based integrated XML. Hereafter, when we refer XML integration, this should be understood to mean instance based XML integration. In the following definitions, Doc_XML1 and Doc_XML2 denote the initial XMLs and Doc_XML3 denotes the global XML.

- **Mapping rule:** A pair containing an initial element and a global element. It indicates that the initial element describes the same object as the global element. The XML elements are expressed using full-absolute XPath expressions. For example, (*'/a/b/c'*, *'/X/Y/Z'*) denotes that the 'c' node of parent node 'b' and grand parent node 'a' under the 'root' in the initial XML is mapped to the 'Z' node of parent node 'Y' and grand parent node 'X' under the 'root'. XML integration refers to two sets of mapping rules: i) MAP1 contains all the mapping rules from Doc_XML1 to Doc_XML3, ii) MAP2 contains all the mapping rules from Doc_XML2 to Doc_XML3.
- **Name Change:** This term refers the situation when the name of element of an initial XML element is mapped to a different name in the global XML, based on the mapping rules (e.g. initial element 'c' is mapped to global element 'Z').
- **Structure Change:** This term is used to refer the situation when a parent-child relationship between elements in the initial XML doesn't exist between their mapped elements in the global XML, based on the mapping rules.
- **Lost Element:** This term is used to refer to an element in an initial XML document which doesn't have a corresponding (mapped) element in the global XML document, according to the mapping rules.

4 XSLT Integration

XSLT program integration concerns not only schema mapping, but also comparisons between template selection patterns and the relationships between template bodies (functionality). We now define some terminology that will be useful when we discuss comparison of templates.

Definition_1: *Potentially Conflicting Template Pair* is used to refer a pair of XSLT templates, each from different *initial* XSLT programs that are awaiting integration, and which have the same *distinguished* XPath selection pattern.

Definition_2: *Rich Template* is used to refer to templates whose selection pattern or/and construction pattern(s) are *rich* XPath expressions.

We also have some restrictions and assumptions on our model.

- The initial XSLT programs are well-formed and valid (error free).
- The output of the XSLT transformations is HTML or XML (the most popular cases used in XSLT transformations).
- The template(s) for the *'root'* (*'/'*) and *'root element'* must exist (XSLT program traverses the XML-tree from the top).

For simplicity, in this paper, the DTD-Graphs of Doc_XML1, Doc_XML2 and Doc_XML3 are denoted by DG1, DG2 and DG3 respectively. XSL1, XSL2 and XSL3 denote two initial XSLT programs and the global XSLT program respectively. Their corresponding Template and Association Graphs are denoted by TAG1, TAG2 and TAG3 respectively. *<T m='selection pattern'>* denotes XSLT element *<xsl:template match='selction pattern'>* and *<A s='construction pattern'>* denotes *<xsl:apply-templates select='construction pattern'>*.

4.1 Overview of XSLT Integration

Our framework addresses the XSLT integration task in four principal steps.

Step_1: Pattern Specialization: The system converts all selection patterns and absolute construction patterns into full-absolute XPath and specializes the relative construction patterns containing '*' and/or '//' into full-relative XPath expressions. Human interaction is required for processing 'rich' templates.

Step_2: Template Translation: This step translates all XPath expressions that conformed to the initial DTD-Graphs (DG1 and DG2) into corresponding XPath expressions conforming to the global DTD-Graph (DG3), based on mapping rules (MAP1 and MAP2). Human interaction is also required to handle some special situations of element mapping.

Step_3: Lost Template Processing: This follows the template translation step and invokes special processing for templates or construction statements which refer to lost elements. Human interaction is asked before applying the default processes.

Step_4: Program Integration: The pre-processed initial XSLT programs are integrated into the global XSLT program XSL3, by means of integration algorithms. Human interaction is required for *rich* templates and static analysis.

Finally, all problematic templates in XSL3 are detected and marked based on TAG3, which can then be used as support for program further revision.

We use human interaction as a supplement to our XSLT integration framework. A completely automatic method is clearly impossible, due to the undecidable nature of much of the analysis required. This is also in line with the requirement of human interaction for static and schema integration [5, 7, 12, 15, 20, 22, 27, 29]. The overall aim of our framework though, is to alleviate the burden on the designer as much as possible, presenting them with a clear set of choices which need to be made. Furthermore, different methods and static analysis techniques can be 'plugged in' to the framework, according to their availability.

4.2 XSLT Integration Example

An XSLT integration example is provided here to help explain our method. It includes i) two synthetic initial server-side XSLT programs (XSL1 and XSL2), ii) the corresponding DTD-Graphs (DG1 and DG2) and iii) the corresponding mapping rules (MAP1 and MAP2). The scenario is based on integration between two XML employee information databases. We omit the XMLs, since it is the structure of the data which determines the XSLT integration workflow, not the data values.

Firstly, the initial DTD-Graphs (DG1 and DG2) and the global DTD-Graph (DG3) are shown in figures 1 (a), (b) and (c) respectively.

Secondly, the sets of mapping rules of MAP1 (map from DG1 to DG3) and MAP2 (map from DG2 to DG3) are listed respectively in tables 1 and table 2. For example, the second row of table 1 shows that DTD-Graph node '/Factory/Name' of DG1 is mapped as node '/Factory/FN' in the global DTD-Graph). From figure 1 and tables 1 and table 2 we can see that the underlying XML integration covers scenarios of 'name change', 'structure change' and 'lost element'.

Thirdly, we show the initial XSLT programs to be integrated (i.e. XSL1 and XSL2). Their functionality is for retrieving and displaying the information about factory employees. Due to the space restrictions, we only show fragments of the programs (figures 2 (a) and (b)).

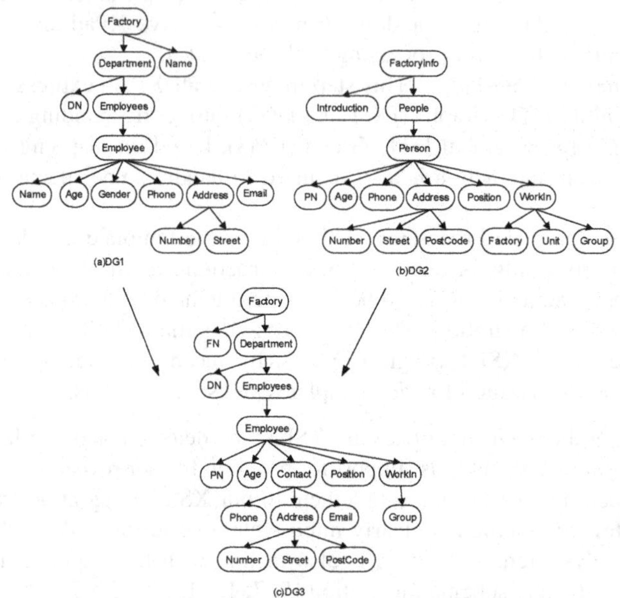

Fig. 1. DTD-Graphs of Doc_XML1, Doc_XML2 and Doc_XML3

Table 1. The fragment of mapping rules between DG1 and DG3

('/Factory', '/Factory')
('/Factory/Name', '/Factory/FN')
('/Factory/Department', '/Factory/Department')
('/Factory/Department/DN', '/Factory/Department/DN')
('/Factory/Department/Employees/Employees', '/Factory/Department/Employees/Employees')
('/Factory/Department/Employees/Employees/Employee', '/Factory/Department/Employees/Employees/Employee')
('/Factory/Department/Employees/Employee/Name', '/Factory/Department/Employees/Employee/PN')
...

Table 2. The fragment of mapping rules between DG2 and DG3

('/FactoryInfo', '/Factory')
('/FactoryInfo/Introduction', '')
('/FactoryInfo/People', '/Factory/Department/Employees')
('/FactoryInfo/People/Person', '/Factory/Department/Employees/Employee')
('/FactoryInfo/People/Person/WorkIn', '/Factory/Department/Employees/Employee/WorkIn')
('/FactoryInfo/People/Person/WorkIn/Factory', '/Factory/Name')
('/FactoryInfo/People/Person/WorkIn/Unit', '/Factory/Department/DN')
...

Next, based on the example shown above, we explain the details of our XSLT integration framework step by step.

4.3 Pattern Specialization

Selection patterns in XSLT can be either full-absolute or non-full-absolute XPath expressions. A full-absolute XPath expression uniquely identifies a DTD-Graph node (i.e. the mapping relationship between a full-absolute XPath expression and a DTD-Graph node is 1 to 1), while a non-full-absolute XPath expression may identify multiple

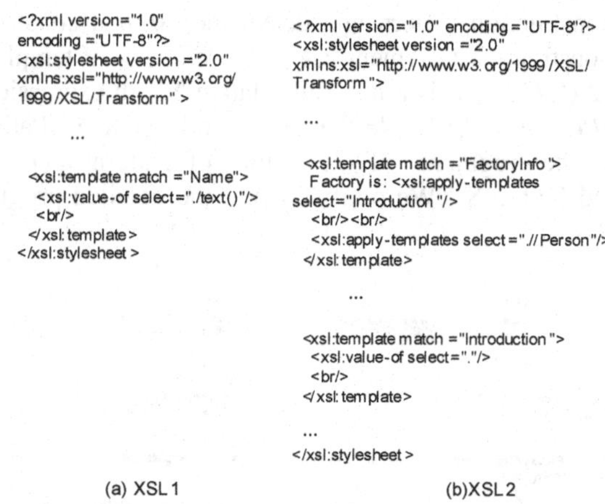

Fig. 2. Fragments of the initial XSLT programs to be integrated

DTD-Graph nodes (i.e. the mapping relationship between a non-full-absolute XPath expression and a DTD-Graph node is 1 to N (N>=1)). Thus, when a template selection pattern is a non-full-absolute XPath expression, we might not sure which mapping rules should be chosen for translating the corresponding template from the initial DTD based XSLT program into the global DTD based XSLT program (step_2) and, consequently, can not continue the integration step to build global XSLT XSL3 (step_4). For example, consider the XSL1 fragment shown in figure 2 (a). The selection pattern of template *<T m='Name'>* can refer to the node of '/Factory/Name' and also the node of *'/Factory/Department/Employees/Employee/Name'* according to DG1 (show in figure 1 (a)). It is not clear whether 'Name' should be mapped to *'/Factory/FN'* or to *'/Factory/Department/Employees/Employee/PN'* according to MAP1 (shown in table 1), during the translation from the initial structure (DG1) to the global structure (DG3). Wrong translation can result in an integrated XSLT program which deviates from the original intentions of the initial XSLT program designers.

We choose to handle this ambiguity using a direct approach, which specialises the non-full-absolute selection patterns in XSL1 and XSL2 into full-absolute XPath expressions. This is called *pattern specialization.* In the case of a single template selection pattern matching multiple DTD-Graph nodes, we create new templates, one for each possible corresponding full-absolute selection pattern, and we then delete the original template. Let's examine the example of *<T m='Name'>* again - the template will be replaced by two new templates: *<T m='/Factory/Name'>* and *<T m='/Factory/Department/Employees/Employee/Name'>*, each with the same body as the original *<T m='Name'>*.

For the same reason and in the same way as for selection pattern specialization, e specialize construction patterns if i) they are absolute XPath expressions but not full-absolute XPath expression or ii) they are relative XPath expressions, but not full-relative XPath expressions. In the former case, the construction patterns are specialised into full-absolute XPath expressions and, in the latter case, the construction patterns are specialised into the full-relative XPath expressions. When a construction pattern indicates multiple nodes of DG1 (or DG2), we create a new construction statement for each specialized construction pattern and delete the original construction statement. For example, the construction statement *<A s='.//Person'>* of template *<T m= 'FactoryInfo'>* in XSL2 ('.//Person' is a non-full-relative XPath expression) is specialized to *<A s='./People/Person'>* (*'./People/Person'* is a full-relative XPath expression).

Figure 3 shows the fragments of the output of pattern specialization process, named XSL1_S and XSL2_S. We omit showing the detailed programs here due to the space restrictions.

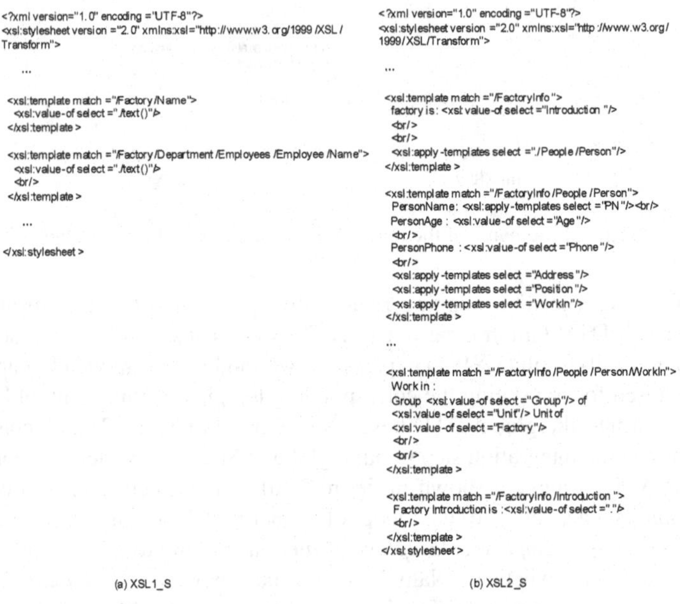

Fig. 3. Fragments of the XSLT programs output after pattern specialization

This kind of automatic resolution is not feasible for *rich* templates and human interaction is needed to guide the process. Specifically, the designer is asked by the system to give a new XPath expression based on the global DTD, to replace the XPath expression based on the initial DTD. Then, these templates with new selection pattern(s) and/or construction pattern(s) will be marked and the subsequent processing steps of template translation and lost template processing need not be applied.

Pattern specialization is a direct way to determine accurately the DTD-Graph node to which the selection pattern refers. However, it might generate some redundant templates which could cause unreachable template(s), missing template(s) and invalid template calling relationship(s) because i) the 'new' template selection pattern may not be harmonious with its inner construction pattern (invalid template calling relationship); ii) the created template which uses the 'new' full-absolute selection pattern might never be called by another construction statement during XSLT execution (unreachable template); iii) The newly created construction pattern might call a non existent template (missing template). These possible 'side-effects' can be detected and eliminated by using Template Association Graph (TAG) [10].

4.4 Template Translation

After pattern specialization, XPath expressions next need to be translated so that they use the vocabulary of the global DTD (DG3).

Let's see an example. The mapping rule at row 4 of table 2 shows that XPath expression *'/FactoryInfo/People/Person'* over the initial schema is mapped to the XPath expression *'/Factory/Department/Employees/Employee'* over the global schema. Thus, the corresponding template *<T m='/FactoryInfo/People/Person'>* in XSL2_S (figure 3) will be translated into *<T m='/Factory/Department/Employees/Employee'>*.

Similar to the selection patterns, the construction patterns also need to be translated. The construction pattern using a full-absolute XPath expression can be translated based on the mapping rules directly. A construction pattern that uses a full-relative XPath expression implies a relationship between the *nodes* located by the selection and construction patterns in that template. E.g. suppose *nodes* 'a' and 'b' are in an *ancestor-descendant* relationship in one of the initial DTD-Graphs. Suppose the nodes that each maps to in the global DTD-Graph are 'A' and 'B'. We then have two situations: 1) 'B' is a 'descendant' or 'sibling' or 'preceding' node of 'A'; 2) 'B' is an 'ancestor' of 'A'. In the former case, our method translates the initial construction pattern automatically into a full-relative XPath expression of the context node. In the latter case, human interaction is required to build the new template manually. Specifically, if 'B' is the 'descendant' node of 'A', the construction pattern is translated to the full-relative XPath expression based on the context node 'A'. For example, the ancestor-descendant relationship between the selection pattern of *<T m= 'FactoryInfo'>* and the construction pattern of *<A s='./People/Person'>* in XSL2_S (figure 3) based on DG2 (figure 1 (b)) is preserved in their mapped nodes *'/Factory'* and *'/Factory/Department/Employees/Employee'* based on DG3 (figure 1 (c) and table 2). So, *<A s='./People/Person'>* is translated as *<A s='Department/ Employees/Employee'>*. If 'B' is 'sibling' or 'preceding' node of 'A', and if there exists node 'C', the closest common ancestor node of both 'A' and 'B' in the global DTD-Graph, the translated construction pattern is an XPath expression which starts with *'ancestor::C'*, followed by the full path from 'C' to 'B'. For example, in XSL2_S (figure 3 (b)), template *<T m='WorkIn'>* contains a construction statement *<A s='Unit'>* and node 'WorkIn' is the parent node of 'Unit' in DG2. Based on MAP2, they are mapped to 'WorkIn' and 'DN' in DG3 and 'DN' is the 'preceding' node of 'WorkIn' node. Thus, we find 'Department', the common and closest ancestor node of 'DN' and 'WorkIn', and then create the construction statement *<A s='ancestor::Department/ DN'>* during the template translation step.

However, if 'B' is the ancestor of 'A', human interaction is required to do the translation, due to the high degree of change in structure. The designer is asked to i) provide the new XPath expression(s) for the selection pattern or construction pattern(s) or both or; ii) provide a new template to replace the original one.

4.5 Lost Template Processing

During XSLT integration, there may be initial XSLT templates whose selection pattern refers to XML elements which do not get mapped to any element in the global

DTD. This causes a problem when translating this initial template into a global template. The same problem happens for construction patterns too. Looking back at table 2 and figure 1 (b) of the XSLT integration example in section 4.2, the node indicated by *'/FactoryInfo/Introduction'* based on DG2 doesn't have any mapped to node in DG3. The corresponding template *<T m=' FactoryInfo/Introduction'>* has become a lost template in XSL2_S as a result of doing the translation. We need to correct such lost templates during the integration process.

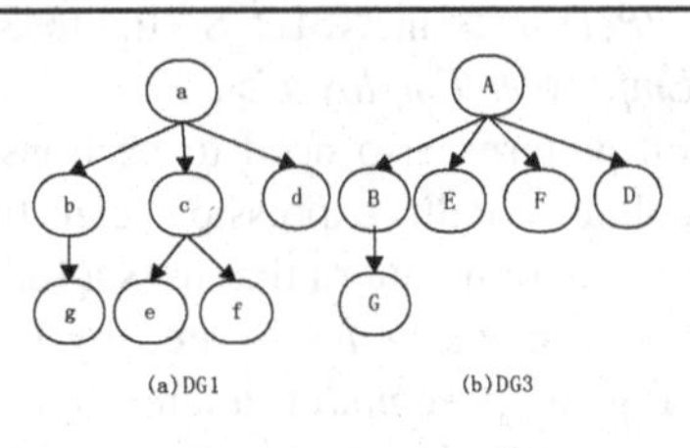

Fig. 4. The example of mapping lost

We cannot simply delete the lost template or construction statement, since i) the body of the lost template might contain valuable data processing, or ii) the inner construction statement of the *lost* template might be the only caller of another existing template, and in this case, deleting the lost template will cause a new missing template.

The integration system detects any lost templates and informs the designer, who then has the task of deciding whether to delete the lost template, or whether to provide a new XPath expression for its selection pattern and, consequently, confirm each element inside this template (i.e provide a new construction pattern for that element or create a new element to replace that element or just delete that element).

Some kinds of lost template cases (shown in figure 4) can be processed automatically based on the integration framework. Looking at figure 4, (a) is an initial DTD-Graph DG1, and (b) is a corresponding global DTD-Graph DG3. Nodes 'a', 'b', 'd', 'e', 'f', 'g' in DG1 are mapped to 'A', 'B', 'D', 'E', 'F', 'G' in DG3. Obviously, the non-terminal element node 'c' is lost during the integration. Moreover, the children nodes of 'c' (i.e. 'e' and 'f') are mapped to children nodes ('E' and 'F') of node 'A' in DG3. This is a common situation for data structure mapping in XML integration and indeed it is reasonable to expect that a parent element covers all concepts of its descendant element. Suppose the template that locates the lost element node 'c' is *<T m='/a/c'>*, lost template processing replaces the selection pattern '/a/c' with its prefix selection pattern '/a', and then, *<T m='/a'>* is translated into *<T m='A'>* in XSL1_T (or XSL2_T) if there is no *<T m='A'>* already existing in XSL1_T (or XSL2_T). If *<T m='A'>* exists in XSL1_T (or XSL2_T), the system only translates the body of *<T m='/a/c'>* and appends it at the end of the existing template *<T m='A'>*. Based on the example shown in figure 4, if template *<T m='/a/c'>* contains a construction statement *<A s='./e'>*, it will be translated to *<A s='./E'>* and appended at the end of template *<T m='A'>*.

The output XSLT programs, after the template translation and lost template processing steps have been performed, are termed as XSL1_T and XSL2_T (we omit these two programs due to the restrictions of space).

4.6 Program Integration

Following the steps of pattern specialization, template translation and lost template processing, our XSLT integration framework applies the program integration step to generate the global XSLT XSL3, based on XSL1_T and XSL2_T.

The templates among XSL1_T plus XSL2_T can be classified into two classes: i) *Unique* templates, whose *distinguished* XPath selection pattern is unique among all templates; ii) *Potentially conflicting template*s (recall Definition_1).

A unique template will be moved to XSL3 directly, without any modification, since it is the only choice of template for a specific XML node or set of nodes.

For a potentially conflicting template pair, the framework (or designer) must make its choice when generating the global template in XSL3. If one or both template(s) has a '*rich*' selection pattern or construction pattern, human interaction is required. The designer needs to decide i) what new template needs to be generated for XSL3, ii) what the template functionality should be.

The templates of potentially conflicting template pair that both use '*simple*' XPath expression(s) as selection pattern(s), can be integrated semi-automatically. We now discuss how to deal with this case.

Suppose <T1> is a template in XSL1_T with body B1 and <T2> is a template in XSL2_T with body B2 and <T1> and <T2> are a pair of *potentially conflicting templates*. Each body B is assumed to be a set of functionality blocks. There a number of possible relationships between B1 and B2. Loosely speaking, these are: 1) B1=B2 (the two templates are guaranteed to give exactly the same result), 2) $B1 \subset B2$ or $B1 \supset B2$ (the output of one template is subsumed by the output of the other), 3)$B1 \cap B2 = \phi$ (the templates are independent), 4) $B1 \cap B2 \mathrel{!=} \Phi$ (the output of the templates may overlap).

Precisely determining the relationships between template bodies is undecidable. We can develop tests based on *syntactic criteria* (e.g. do a pairwise comparison between the statements in each template body). This may be effective when the components of template body are simple. More complex tests may be based on *semantic criteria*□which concerns the data retrieved from XML source tree and ignores the constant data (strings) and data format (the data order and display styles) of template output. The work in [25] describes a technique where tests for template equivalence are performed by translating the template logic into an XML query algebra [25] and then judging if two templates yield the same result by applying the evaluation rules. Different analysis techniques could also be used.

Based on the different relationships between the functionality (bodies) of the potentially conflicting template pair, our integration approach builds the functionality of the global template according to the rules described in table 3. Human interaction is required in when the static analysis is too difficult or yields imprecise results.

Table 3. Building the new functionality of the global template

Relationship	Process
B1= B2	B1 is chosen as the global functionality
$B1 \supset B2$	B1 is recommended as the global functionality.
$B1 \subset B2$	B2 is recommended as the global functionality.
$B1 \cap B2 = \Phi$ or $B1 \cap B2 \mathrel{!=} \Phi$	The designer is asked to decide.

Finally, the unreachable templates, missing templates and invalid template calling relationships are marked (based on checking TAG3) as referential information for possible further action and modification by the designer.

5 Related Work

To the authors' knowledge, no other work has been done on XSLT integration.

A number of integration systems have been developed for semi-structured data and XML. One major kind of XML integration method is view/schema based XML integration (virtual integration) [21, 25]. Another major method is called instance based XML integration [5, 7, 12, 27].

An XSLT template call-graph was described in [14] as part of a translation scheme from XSLT to SQL.

Testing equivalence of XSLT templates is examined in [25]. This work presents a powerful XML query algebra TAX and provides a collection of template equivalence rules. Based on the approach, XSLT templates are automatically translated into TAX and they are judged to be equivalent if they satisfy certain evaluation rules.

XPath analysis and XPath based XML query optimization have been considered in a large number of papers [1, 9, 21]. Any such analysis techniques can in principle be used within our framework.

6 Conclusions and Future Work

In this paper, we have proposed a novel framework for XSLT integration. Our approach is applicable for instance based XML integration methods, where server-side XSLT applications are being used. It consists of four major parts: 1) Pattern Specialization, 2) Template Translation, 3) Lost Template Processing and 4) Program Integration. We believe this new framework can be a significant aid to the designer in integration scenarios. Importantly, our framework is extensible. A variety of analysis techniques can be plugged in to provide enhanced precision.

As part of future work, we would like to investigate methods for handling further XSLT syntax, such as the use of functions and other XPath axes automatically. We also plan to investigate and extend our algorithm to provide more flexible mechanisms for the designer, as part of the global template generation process.

Acknowledgement

This work is partially supported by National ICT Australia. National ICT Australia is funded by the Australian Government's Backing Australia's Ability initiative, in part through the Australian Research Council.

References

[1] S. Abiteboul and V. Vianu.: Regular path queries with constraints. In *Proc.of 16th ACM SIGACT-SIGMOD-SIGSTART Symposium on Principles of Database Systems,*Tucson, AZ, US (1997) 122-133

[2] J. Bailey, A. Poulovassilis, P. T. Wood.: An Event-Condition-Action Language for XML *Proc.Conf. WWW2002,* Honolulu, Hawaii, USA (2002) 486-495

[3] E. Bertino and E, Ferrari.: XML and Data Integration. Internet Computing, IEEE (2001)

[4] S. Boag et al.: XQuery 1.0: An XML Query Language W3C Candidate Recommendation 3 November 2005. http://www.w3.org/TR/xquery/
[5] P. Bohannon, S. Ganguly, H. Korth, P. Narayan, and P. Shenoy.: Optimizing view queries in ROLEX to support navigable result tree. *In VLDB,* HongKong, China (2002) 119-130
[6] T. Bray, et al.: W3C Recommendation. Extensible Markup Language (XML) 1.0 (2000)
[7] M. J. Carey, D. Florescu, Z. G. Ives, Y. Liu, J. Shanshanmugsundaram, E. J. Shekita, and S. N. Subramanian.: XPERANTO: Publishing object-relational data as XML. In *Proc.of WebDB* (2000) 105-110
[8] J. Clark.: W3C Recommendation. XSL Transformations (XSLT) version 1.0 (1999)
[9] A. Deutsch and V. Tannen. Containment and integrity constraints for XPath. Proc. *KRDB 2001, CEUR Workshop Proceedings 45* (2001)
[10] C. Dong and J. Bailey.: The static analysis of XSLT programs. In *Proc.of The 15th Australasian Database Conference*, Vol.27, Pages 151-160, Dunedin, New Zealand (2004)
[11] W. Fan, Minos Garofalakis, Ming Xiong, Xibei Jia.: Composable XML integration grammars. In *Proc.of ACM CIKM*, Washington, D.C., USA (2004) 2-11
[12] F. M. Fernandez, A. Morishima, and D. Suciu.: Efficient evaluation of XML middle ware queries. *In SIGMOD 2001.*
[13] R. Goldman and J. Widom.: DataGuides: Enabling query formulation and optimization in semi-structured database. Proc. *Int'l Conf on VLDB*, Athens, Greece (1997) 436-446
[14] S. Jain, R. Mahajan and D. Suciu.: Translating XSLT Programs to Efficient SQL Queries. In *Proc.of WWW 2002*, 616-626
[15] Euna Jeong and Chun-Nan Hsu.: Induction of integrated view for XML data with heterogeneous DTDs. In *Proc.of CIKM*, Atlanta, Georgia, USA (2001) Pages: 151 – 158
[16] M. Kay.: Anatomy of an XSLT Processor. (2001)
[17] M. Kay.: Saxon XSLT Processor. http://saxon.sourceforge.net/
[18] C. Laird.: XSLT powers a new wave of web, 2002. http://www.linuxjournal.com/article/5622
[19] D. Lee, W. Chu.: Comparative analysis of six XML schema languages. *ACM SIGMOD Record archive Volume 29, Issue 3*. ACM Press, New York, NY, USA (2000) 76–87
[20] M. L. Lee, L. H. Yang, W. Hsu, X. Yang.: XClust: clustering XML schemas for effective integration. In *Proc.of CIKM* (2002) 292-299
[21] Q. Li, B. Moon.: Indexing and querying XML data for regular path expressions. *Proc. Int'l Conf on VLDB*, Roma, Italy (2001) 361-370
[22] http://dx.doi.org/10.1007/11603412_7H. Ma, K. Schewe, B. Thalheim, J. Zhao.: View Integration and Cooperation in Databases, Data Warehouses and Web Information Systems. *Data Semantics IV* (2005)
[23] S. Maneth and F. Neven.: Structured document transformations based on XSL. In Proc.of DBPL'99, Kinloch Rannoch, Scottland (1999)
[24] K. Passi, L. Lane, S. Madria, B. Sakamuri, M. Mohania, S. Bhowmick.: A model for XML schema integration. In *Proc.of The third International Conference on E-Commerce and Web Technologies*, Aix-en-Provence, France (2002) 193 - 202
[25] A. Trombetta and D. Montesi.: Equivalences and optimizations in an expressive XSLT fragment. In *Proc.of IDEAS 2004*, Coimbra, Portugal (2004) 171-180
[26] W3C. XSL transformations (XSLT) version 2.0. http://www.w3.org/TR/xslt20/.
[27] Wanxia Wei, Mengchi Liu, and Shijun Li.: Merging of XML documents. *In 23rd Intenational Conference on Conceptual Modelling*, ShangHai, China, November 2004
[28] W3C.: XML Path Language(XPath) Recommendation. http://www.w3.org/TR/xpath.
[29] C. Yu, L. Popa.: Constraint-based XML query rewriting for data integration, In *Proc.of The 2004 ACM SIGMOD international conferenc onference on management of data* (2004).

OXONE: A Scalable Solution for Detecting Superior Quality Deltas on Ordered Large XML Documents

Erwin Leonardi and Sourav S. Bhowmick

School of Computer Engineering, Nanyang Technological University, Singapore
{pk909134, assourav}@ntu.edu.sg

Abstract. Recently, a number of relational-based approaches for detecting the changes to XML data have been proposed to address the scalability problem of main memory-based approaches (e.g., X-Diff, XyDiff). These approaches store the XML documents in the relational database and issue SQL queries (whenever appropriate) to detect the changes. In this paper, we propose a relational-based *ordered* XML change detection technique (called OXONE) that uses a *schema-conscious* approach as the underlying storage strategy for XML data. Previous efforts have focused on detecting changes to ordered XML in an *schema-oblivious* storage environment. Although the schema-oblivious approach produces better *result quality* compared to XyDiff (a main memory-based ordered XML change detection approach), its performance degrade with increase in data size and is slower than XyDiff for smaller data set. We propose a technique to overcome these limitations. Our experimental results show that OXONE is up to 22 times faster and more scalable than the relational-based schema-oblivious approach. The performances of OXONE and XyDiff (C version) are comparable. However, more importantly, our approach is more scalable compared to XyDiff for larger datasets and has much superior the result quality of deltas than XyDiff.

1 Introduction

Detecting changes to XML data is an important research problem. Recently, a number of main memory-based techniques for detecting the changes to XML data has been proposed. XyDiff [1] is an approach for detecting the changes to *ordered* XML documents. In an *ordered* XML, both the parent-child relationship and the left-to-right order among siblings are important. Wang et al. proposed X-Diff [8] for computing the changes to *unordered* XML documents. In *unordered* XML, the parent-child relationship is significant, while the left-to-right order among siblings is not important. All these algorithms suffer from scalability problem as they fail to detect changes to large XML documents due to lack of main memory.

In [3,4], we have addressed this scalability problem in the context of unordered XML documents by leveraging on the relational technology. In this approach, given the old and new versions of an XML document, we store both documents in a relational database. Next, we issue a set of SQL queries (wherever appropriate) to detect the changes. Efficient and accurate change detection in such a relational environment is largely determined by the underlying storage structure. Particularly, there are two major approaches for storing XML documents in a relational database [7]. In *schema-conscious approach*, a relational schema is created based on the DTD/schema of the

D.W. Embley, A. Olivé, and S. Ram (Eds.): ER 2006, LNCS 4215, pp. 196–211, 2006.

XML documents. In the *schema-oblivious approach*, a fixed schema used to store XML documents is maintained. The basic idea is to capture the tree structure of an XML document. This approach does not require existence of an XML schema/DTD. In [2,3], we have used schema-oblivious approach to detect changes to both *ordered* and *unordered* XML documents. Whereas, in [4], we proposed a schema-conscious driven approach for detecting changes to *unordered* XML data.

In this paper, we present a relational-based approach, called OXONE[1] (schema-c**O**nscious **X**ML-enabled **O**rdered cha**N**ge d**E**tection), for detecting the changes to *ordered* XML data using a *schema-conscious approach* (Shared-Inlining [6] in our case). Our effort is motivated by the following observations. First, a growing body of work suggests that schema-conscious approaches perform better than majority of the schema-oblivious approaches as far as XML query processing is concerned [7]. Second, our recent effort for detecting changes to *unordered* XML data in [4] using schema-conscious approach shows encouraging results. In particular, we have shown that the schema-conscious driven approach is significantly more scalable and faster than not only X-Diff [8] but also relational-based schema-oblivious approach such as XANDY [3].

At this point one may question the justification of this work as we have already explored the feasibility of using schema-conscious storage approach for detecting changes to XML data. However, the work reported in this paper is important for the following reasons. First, in [4] we have focused on change detection to *unordered* XML whereas in this paper we focus on *ordered* XML data. Although some of the SQL queries introduced in [4] can be used for detecting changes to ordered XML with minor modifications, as we shall see later, the very nature of ordered XML pose new challenges. For instance, unlike unordered change detection, ordered XML change detection has additional *move* operation that needs to be detected accurately. Second, the characteristics of schema-conscious approach raise certain challenges. Unlike schema-oblivious approaches, the underlying relational schema is DTD-dependent. Consequently, the challenge is to create a general framework for change detection so that the framework is independent of the structural heterogeneity of various XML documents. Third, it has been shown in [8] that XyDiff is significantly faster than X-Diff. However, the *result quality* of XyDiff is significantly poorer compared to X-Diff [8]. In [2,3], we have shown that it is possible to generate superior quality deltas for both ordered and unordered XML change detection problem using relational-based approach. However, due to the underlying storage strategy, the relational-based approach in [2] is significantly slower than XyDiff and does not scale well with large data. *Consequently, is it possible to design a relational-based ordered XML change detection system that is more scalable and generates superior quality results, yet have response time which is at least comparable to XyDiff if not better?* In this paper, we propose OXONE to address these challenges.

In our approach, we first store two versions of an XML document, namely, T_1 and T_2, in a relational database whose underlying storage scheme is based on *modified* Shared-Inlining approach [6]. Then, OXONE can be used to detect the changes to T_1 and T_2 in a bottom-up fashion. Our approach consists of two phases: *finding best matching subtrees* phase and the *change detection* phase. The objective of the first phase is to find the most similar subtrees in T_1 and T_2. In order to find the most similar subtrees, we need to

[1] pronounced as "ozone".

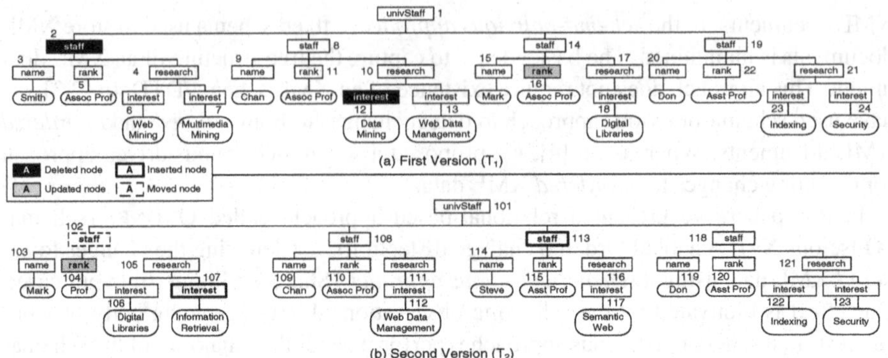

Fig. 1. Two versions of XML documents

match subtrees in T_1 to ones in T_2. Note that a subtree in T_1 can be matched to more than one subtree in T_2, and vice versa. In addition, we need to measure the similarity of each matching by calculating the *similarity score*. The most similar matching subtrees are called *best matching subtrees*. In our approach, we issue SQL queries (whenever appropriate) to find the best matching subtrees. We shall elaborate on this phase in Section 3. Having determined the best matching subtrees between T_1 and T_2, in the second phase OXONE issues SQL queries (whenever appropriate) to detect different types of changes. The types of changes that can be detected by OXONE are similar to the one in [1]. The detected changes are stored in several relations. We shall elaborate on this phase in Section 4.

We have implemented the prototype of OXONE on top Microsoft SQL Server 2000 using Java. We compared OXONE to XANDY–O [2], a published schema-oblivious ordered XML change detection system, and XyDiff [1]. Our results show that OXONE has comparable response time with XyDiff for large XML documents. However, it is more scalable and has superior *result quality* compared to XyDiff. Particularly, XyDiff fails to detect changes to XML documents containing around 356,000 nodes or more. Also, OXONE outperforms XANDY–O by up to 22 times and is more scalable. In addition, for larger data sets, OXONE is up to 44 times faster than X-Diff [8]. X-Diff is unable to detect the changes on XML documents that have more than 5000 nodes due to lack of main memory. We shall elaborate on the experimental results in Section 5. Note that

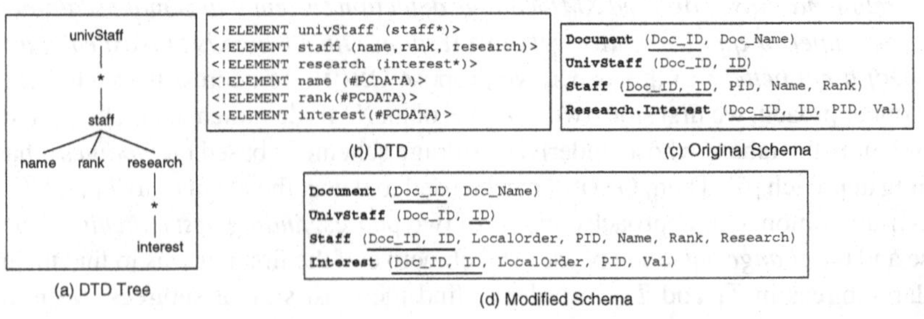

Fig. 2. DTD Tree, DTD, and Relational Schema

the framework discussed in this paper is only for XML documents whose schemas do not contain recursive elements.

2 Background

In this section, we first define some terms that we shall use subsequently to facilitate exposition. Then, we discuss how the Shared-Inlining schema is modified to support ordered XML change detection. We use the two versions of XML document in Figure 1 as running example throughout the paper.

2.1 Terminology

Let T be a tree representation of an XML document D. The root node of T is denoted by $root(T)$. Let $\mathcal{L}(T) = \{\ell_1, \ell_2, ..., \ell_n\}$ be a set of leaf nodes in XML tree T. The textual content of a leaf node ℓ is denoted by $value(\ell)$. A set of internal nodes in T is denoted by $\mathcal{I}(T)$, and i denotes an internal node, where $i \in \mathcal{I}$. The name and level of node n are denoted by $name(n)$ and $level(n)$, respectively. Then, $path(n)$ denotes the path from $root(T)$ to node n. The parent node, child node, and ancestor node of node n are denoted as $parent(n)$, $child(n)$, and $ancestor(n)$, respectively. In ordered XML, the left-to-right position of a node among its siblings is significant. Hence, $pos(n)$ denotes the left-to-right position of node n among its siblings if D is an *ordered* XML. Note that we use T_1 and T_2 as depicted in Figures 1(a) and 1(b), respectively, as our running example in the later discussion.

Let $\ell_{1_x} \in \mathcal{L}(T_1)$ and $\ell_{2_y} \in \mathcal{L}(T_2)$ be two leaf nodes in the first and second versions of an XML tree respectively. Then, ℓ_{1_x} and ℓ_{2_y} are *matching leaf nodes* (denoted as $\ell_{1_x} \leftrightarrow \ell_{2_y}$) if $name(\ell_{1_x}) = name(\ell_{2_y})$, $level(\ell_{1_x}) = level(\ell_{2_y})$, $path(\ell_{1_x}) = path(\ell_{2_y})$, and $value(\ell_{1_x}) = value(\ell_{2_y})$. For example, leaf nodes ℓ_{13} and ℓ_{112} are matching leaf nodes ($\ell_{13} \leftrightarrow \ell_{112}$) because they satisfy the above conditions. Note that a leaf node in T_1 can be matched to more than one leaf node in T_2, and vice versa. Leaf node ℓ_{110} in T_2 can be matched to node ℓ_4, ℓ_{10}, and ℓ_{16} in T_1 as they satisfy the above conditions. Note that if ℓ_1 and ℓ_2 are not matching leaf nodes, then they are denoted by $\ell_1 \not\leftrightarrow \ell_2$.

We classify the matching leaf nodes into two types, namely, *fixed matching leaf nodes* and *shifted matching leaf nodes*. This classification is important in the context of ordered change detection as if the left-to-right position among siblings of a node is changed, then it is possible that this node is moved among its siblings. Formally, let $\ell_1 \leftrightarrow \ell_2$. If $pos(\ell_1) = pos(\ell_2)$, then ℓ_1 and ℓ_2 are *fixed matching leaf nodes*. Otherwise, they are *shifted matching leaf nodes*. For example, leaf nodes ℓ_{18} and ℓ_{106} are fixed matching leaf node as $\ell_{18} \leftrightarrow \ell_{106}$ and $pos(\ell_{18}) = pos(\ell_{106})$. Leaf nodes ℓ_{13} and ℓ_{112} are shifted matching leaf node as $\ell_{13} \leftrightarrow \ell_{112}$ and $pos(\ell_{13}) \neq pos(\ell_{112})$.

Next, we define the notion of *matching leaf node groups*. Let $\mathcal{G}_1$ and $\mathcal{G}_2$ be two sets of leaf nodes whose parent nodes are i_1 and i_2, respectively, where $i_1 \in \mathcal{I}(T_1)$ and $i_2 \in \mathcal{I}(T_2)$. Then, $\mathcal{G}_1$ and $\mathcal{G}_2$ are *matching leaf node groups* (denoted as $\mathcal{G}_1 \Leftrightarrow \mathcal{G}_2$) iff $\exists \ell_x \exists \ell_y$ such that $\ell_x \leftrightarrow \ell_y$, where $\ell_x \in \mathcal{G}_1$ and $\ell_y \in \mathcal{G}_2$. For example, suppose $\mathcal{G}_{17} = \{\ell_{18}\}$ and $\mathcal{G}_{105} = \{\ell_{106}, \ell_{107}\}$ are two sets of leaf nodes in T_1 and T_2 whose parent nodes are nodes 17 and 105, respectively. We observe that $\mathcal{G}_{17} \Leftrightarrow \mathcal{G}_{105}$ as $\ell_{18} \leftrightarrow \ell_{106}$, $\ell_{18} \in \mathcal{G}_{17}$, and $\ell_{106} \in \mathcal{G}_{105}$.

Next, we define *matching subtrees*. The root nodes of two matching subtrees are called *matching internal nodes*. From a set of matching subtrees, we determine the most similar subtrees to be *best matching subtrees*. Similar to X-Diff [8] and XyDiff [1], we only match two subtrees at the same level. Formally, the *matching subtrees* are defined as follows. Let t_1 and t_2 be two subtrees rooted at nodes $i_1 \in \mathcal{I}(T_1)$ and $i_2 \in \mathcal{I}(T_2)$, respectively. Then, t_1 and t_2 are *matching subtrees* (denoted by $t_1 \hat{=} t_2$) if $name(i_1) = name(i_2)$, $level(i_1) = level(i_2)$, $path(i_1) = path(i_2)$, and $\exists p\ \exists q$ such that $p \leftrightarrow q$, where $i_1 = ancestor(p)$, $i_2 = ancestor(q)$, $p \in \mathcal{L}(T_1)$, and $q \in \mathcal{L}(T_2)$. For instance, the subtrees rooted at node 8 in T_1 and node 108 in T_2 are matching subtrees ($t_8 \hat{=} t_{108}$) as they have three matching leaf nodes ($\ell_9 \leftrightarrow \ell_{109}$, $\ell_{10} \leftrightarrow \ell_{110}$, and $\ell_{13} \leftrightarrow \ell_{112}$). If t_1 and t_2 are not matching subtrees, then they are denoted by $t_1 \not\hat{=} t_2$. We use the terms of *matching subtrees* and *matching internal nodes* interchangeably.

Having found a set of matching subtrees, we need to measure the degree of similarity between two matching subtrees. We now define a metric called *similarity score* to measure how similar two subtrees are. The similarity score $\Re$ of two subtrees t_1 and t_2 that are in T_1 and T_2, respectively, is as follows: $\Re(t_1, t_2) = \frac{2|A|+|B|}{|t_1|+|t_2|}$ where $|t_1|$ and $|t_2|$ are the total numbers of leaf nodes in t_1 and t_2, respectively, $|A|$ and $|B|$ are numbers of nodes of fixed and shifted matching leaf nodes in t_1 and t_2, respectively and $A \cap B = \emptyset$. For example, the similarity score of t_8 in T_1 and t_{108} in T_2 is $\Re(t_8, t_{108}) = 0.714$. The value of similarity score is between 0 and 1. Two subtrees are more similar if the similarity score is higher. Based on the similarity score, we classify the subtrees into two types as follows. If $0 < \Re(t_1, t_2) \leq 1$, then the subtrees are *matching subtrees* and they have at least one matching leaf node. Otherwise, the subtrees are *unmatching subtrees* and they do not have matching leaf nodes ($\Re(t_1, t_2) = 0$).

Next, based on the above concepts, the *best matching subtrees* are formally defined as follows. Let $\mathcal{T}_1$ and $\mathcal{T}_2$ be two sets of subtrees that are in T_1 and T_2, respectively. Let $t \in \mathcal{T}_1$ be a subtree and $P \subseteq \mathcal{T}_2$ be a set of subtrees. Also t and $t_i \in P$ are matching subtrees $\forall\, 0 < i \leq |P|$. Then, t and t_i are *best matching subtrees* (denoted by $t \Bumpeq t_i$) iff $(\Re(t, t_i) > \Re(t, t_j))\ \forall\, 0 < j \leq |P|$ and $i \neq j$. For example, subtree t_{14} can be matched to subtrees t_{102} and t_{108}. Observe that $\Re(t_{14}, t_{102}) = 0.571$ and $\Re(t_{14}, t_{108}) = 0.333$. Consequently, subtrees t_{14} and t_{102} are best matching subtrees ($t_{14} \Bumpeq t_{102}$). Note that if t_1 and t_2 are not best matching subtrees, then they are denoted by $t_1 \not\Bumpeq t_2$.

2.2 Extension of Shared-Inlining Approach

Recall that the OXONE approach is based on the Shared-Inlining storage strategy. For instance, given a DTD depicted in Figure 2(b), Shared-Inlining approach generates a relational schema as depicted in Figure 2(c). In [6], Shared-Inlining approach does not explicitly store the local order of nodes which is important in ordered XML documents. As this information is critical for our change detection process, we need to extend the relational schema generated by Shared-Inlining approach.

Before we discuss the extensions, let us present some notations that will be used in later discussion. Given a DTD tree $\mathcal{H}_U$ that is tree representation of DTD U, the nodes in $\mathcal{H}_U$ are classified as *inlined* and *non-inlined* nodes. An *inlined node* is one that is not below "$*$" or "$+$" node. There are two types of inlined nodes, namely, *inlined leaf nodes* (denoted by $\mathbb{I}_\ell$) and *inlined internal nodes* (denoted by $\mathbb{I}_i$). For example, consider

```
Input
  U : DTD of the XML documents
  Two versions of an XML document
      stored in RDBMS
Output
  the Matching table
  /* --- STEP 1 --- */
  for all ℓ in ℕℓ(U) do
    tbName ← rℓ ; tempTb ← Mℓ ;
    findMatchingLeafNodesGroups(tbName, tempTb);
  end for
  /* --- STEP 2 --- */
  maxLevel = maximum level at which there is i in 𝕀i(U)
  /* bottom-up matching */
  for lev = maxLevel down to 1 do
    for all i ∈ 𝕀i(U) at level lev do
      childNode ← child( i );
      tempMChild ← M_childNode;
      tbName ← ri ; tempTb ← Mi ;
      /* --- STEP 2.1 --- */
      findMatchingInternalNodes(tbName, tempTb, tempMChild);
      /* --- STEP 2.2 --- */
      maximizeScore(ωx);
    end for
  end for
  /* --- STEP 3 --- */
  root is the root node of U
  Queue Q ← {root}
  while (Q is not empty) do
    q = Q.get();
    Q ← the child internal
            nodes of q in U;
    nodeName ← name(q); tempTb ← rq;
    parentNode ← parent(q);
    parentNodeName ← name(parentNode);
    attrName ← attribute(q);
    retrieveMatching(nodeName, tempTb, parentNodeName, attrName);
  end do
```

Fig. 3. The *findBestMatchingSubtrees* Algorithm

a DTD tree as depicted in Figure 2(a). An inlined node will be stored as an attribute in the relation of its parent nodes. For example, the parent nodes of node *name* and *research* are node *staff*. The information on nodes *name* and *research* is stored in the *Name* attribute in the `Staff` table (Figure 2(c)). A *non-inlined* node is one that is below "$*$" or "$+$" node. There are also two types of non-inlined nodes, namely, *non-inlined leaf nodes* (denoted by $\mathbb{N}_\ell$) and *non-inlined internal nodes* (denoted by $\mathbb{N}_i$). An non-inlined node will be stored in a separate relation. For example, nodes *interest* and *staff* are a non-inlined leaf node and a non-inlined internal node whose information are stored in the `Interest` and `Staff` tables (Figure 2(c)), respectively.

Let us now elaborate on the extensions of relational schema generated by Shared-Inlining approach. We add the *LocalOrder* attribute to the corresponding relations of non-inlined nodes. We store the information on inlined internal nodes as a `BOOLEAN` attribute (e.g., *research* attribute) in its parent relation. The extended relational schema is depicted in Figure 2(d). The *PID* in the figure refers to the parent node id.

3 Finding Best Matching Subtrees Phase

The *findBestMatchingSubtrees* algorithm is depicted in Figure 3. Note that "`[param]`" in the SQL queries (Figures 4 and 7) used in the later discussion will be replaced the parameter *param* defined in the algorithm. Also, due to space constraints, in our subsequent discussions we will not elaborate on queries and algorithms that are similar to the ones discussed in [4]. Rather, we shall highlight the differences (if any).

3.1 Finding Matching Leaf Nodes Groups Phase

The *findMatchingLeafNodesGroups* algorithm for finding matching leaf nodes groups works as follows. First, the *findMatchingLeafNodesGroups* algorithm determines the *fixed matching leaf nodes* by using the SQL query in Figure 4(a). Lines 10–11 are used to ensure that fixed matching leaf nodes have the same values and local orders. Next, we determine the *matching leaf nodes groups* from a set of fixed matching leaf nodes. The SQL query in Figure 4(b) is used to determine matching leaf nodes groups from a set of fixed matching leaf nodes. The idea behind this SQL query is to group the fixed matching leaf nodes by their *PID1* and *PID2* attributes (line 4, Figure 4(b)). Observe

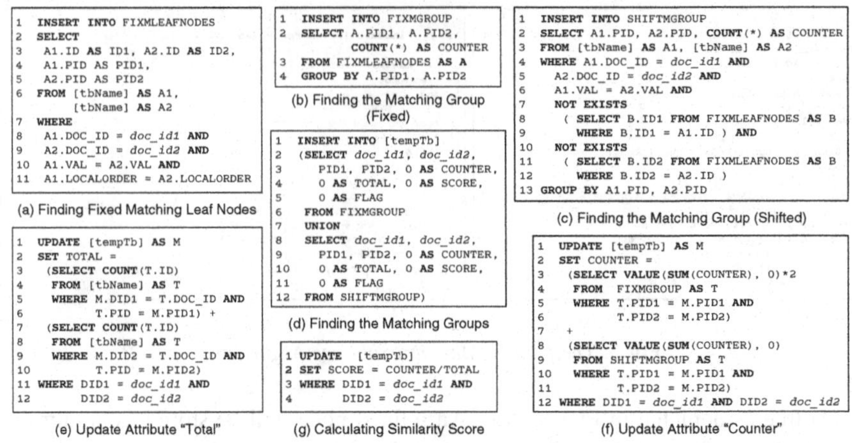

```
1  INSERT INTO FIXMLEAFNODES
2  SELECT
3   A1.ID AS ID1, A2.ID AS ID2,
4   A1.PID AS PID1,
5   A2.PID AS PID2
6  FROM [tbName] AS A1,
        [tbName] AS A2
7  WHERE
8   A1.DOC_ID = doc_id1 AND
9   A2.DOC_ID = doc_id2 AND
10  A1.VAL = A2.VAL AND
11  A1.LOCALORDER = A2.LOCALORDER
```

(a) Finding Fixed Matching Leaf Nodes

```
1  INSERT INTO FIXMGROUP
2  SELECT A.PID1, A.PID2,
          COUNT(*) AS COUNTER
3  FROM FIXMLEAFNODES AS A
4  GROUP BY A.PID1, A.PID2
```

(b) Finding the Matching Group (Fixed)

```
1  INSERT INTO SHIFTMGROUP
2  SELECT A1.PID, A2.PID, COUNT(*) AS COUNTER
3  FROM [tbName] AS A1, [tbName] AS A2
4  WHERE A1.DOC_ID = doc_id1 AND
5    A2.DOC_ID = doc_id2 AND
6    A1.VAL = A2.VAL AND
7    NOT EXISTS
8     ( SELECT B.ID1 FROM FIXMLEAFNODES AS B
9       WHERE B.ID1 = A1.ID ) AND
10   NOT EXISTS
11    ( SELECT B.ID2 FROM FIXMLEAFNODES AS B
12      WHERE B.ID2 = A2.ID )
13 GROUP BY A1.PID, A2.PID
```

(c) Finding the Matching Group (Shifted)

```
1  INSERT INTO [tempTb]
2  (SELECT doc_id1, doc_id2,
3     PID1, PID2, 0 AS COUNTER,
4     0 AS TOTAL, 0 AS SCORE,
5     0 AS FLAG
6   FROM FIXMGROUP
7   UNION
8   SELECT doc_id1, doc_id2,
9     PID1, PID2, 0 AS COUNTER,
10    0 AS TOTAL, 0 AS SCORE,
11    0 AS FLAG
12  FROM SHIFTMGROUP)
```

(d) Finding the Matching Groups

```
1  UPDATE [tempTb] AS M
2  SET TOTAL =
3   (SELECT COUNT(T.ID)
4    FROM [tbName] AS T
5    WHERE M.DID1 = T.DOC_ID AND
6          T.PID = M.PID1) +
7   (SELECT COUNT(T.ID)
8    FROM [tbName] AS T
9    WHERE M.DID2 = T.DOC_ID AND
10         T.PID = M.PID2)
11 WHERE DID1 = doc_id1 AND
12       DID2 = doc_id2
```

(e) Update Attribute "Total"

```
1 UPDATE  [tempTb]
2 SET SCORE = COUNTER/TOTAL
3 WHERE DID1 = doc_id1 AND
4       DID2 = doc_id2
```

(g) Calculating Similarity Score

```
1  UPDATE [tempTb] AS M
2  SET COUNTER =
3   (SELECT VALUE(SUM(COUNTER), 0)*2
4    FROM  FIXMGROUP AS T
5    WHERE T.PID1 = M.PID1 AND
6          T.PID2 = M.PID2)
7   +
8   (SELECT VALUE(SUM(COUNTER), 0)
9    FROM SHIFTMGROUP AS T
10   WHERE T.PID1 = M.PID1 AND
11         T.PID2 = M.PID2)
12 WHERE DID1 = doc_id1 AND DID2 = doc_id2
```

(f) Update Attribute "Counter"

Fig. 4. SQL Queries for Finding Matching Leaf Nodes

DID1	DID2	PID1	PID2	Counter	Total	Score
1	2	2	2	1	3	0.333
1	2	3	1	2	3	0.666
1	2	4	4	4	4	1.000

(a) M_Interest Table

DID1	DID2	ID1	ID2	LO1	LO2	PID1	PID2	Counter	Total	Score	Flag
1	2	1	1	1	1	*null*	*null*	17	29	0.586	0

(c) M_univStaff Table

DID1	DID2	ID1	ID2	LO1	LO2	PID1	PID2	Counter	Total	Score	Flag
1	2	1	2	1	2	1	1	2	8	0.250	0
1	2	2	2	2	2	1	1	5	7	0.714	0
1	2	3	1	3	1	1	1	4	7	0.571	0
1	2	3	2	3	2	1	1	2	6	0.333	0
1	2	4	3	4	3	1	1	2	7	0.286	0
1	2	4	4	4	4	1	1	8	8	1.000	0

(b) M_Staff Table

DID1	DID2	ID1	ID2	LO1	LO2	PID1	PID2	Score	Name
1	2	1	1	1	1	*null*	*null*	0.586	univStaff
1	2	2	2	2	2	1	1	0.714	staff
1	2	3	1	3	1	1	1	0.571	staff
1	2	4	4	4	4	1	1	1.000	staff
1	2	*null*	*null*	*null*	*null*	2	2	0.333	research
1	2	*null*	*null*	*null*	*null*	3	1	0.666	research
1	2	*null*	*null*	*null*	*null*	4	4	1.000	research

(d) Matching Table

Fig. 5. Temporary Matching Tables and the Matching Table

that the *PID1* and *PID2* attributes store the parent node id of fixed matching leaf nodes in the old and new versions, respectively. The next step is to determine *matching leaf nodes groups* from *shifted matching leaf nodes*. We use the SQL query in Figure 4(c). Line 6 is to ensure that two matching leaf nodes have the same values. Lines 7–9 and 10–12 are used to filter out leaf nodes in the *old version* and *new version*, respectively, that already have been matched when the algorithm finds the fixed matching leaf nodes. Finally, the shifted matching leaf nodes are grouped by their *PID1* and *PID2* attributes.

At this point of time, we have two sets of matching leaf nodes groups, that is, one from fixed matching leaf nodes and another from shifted matching leaf nodes. The next step is to merge these sets of matching leaf nodes groups. Figure 4(d) depicts the SQL query to merge two sets of matching leaf nodes groups. We only need to use "`UNION`" operator (line 7) to merge these sets. The final step is to update the information of matching leaf nodes groups. We update the values of the *Total*, *Counter*, and *Score* attributes using the three SQL queries as depicted in Figures 4(e)–4(g). Suppose we have two set of leaf nodes, $\mathcal{G}_1$ and $\mathcal{G}_2$, whose parent nodes are i_1 and i_2, respectively, where $\mathcal{G}_1 \Leftrightarrow \mathcal{G}_2$. Then, the value of the *Total* attribute is equal to $(|t_1| + |t_2|)$, where $|t_1|$

tempTb1 (DID1, DID2, PID1, PID2, Counter, Total, Score)
tempTb2 (DID1, DID2, ID1, ID2, LO1, LO2, PID1, PID2, Counter, Total, Score, Flag)
MATCHING (DID1, DID2, ID1, ID2, LO1, LO2, PID1, PID2, Score, Name)

(a) Temporary Matching Tables

INS_INT (DID1, DID2, ID, LO, PID, Name)	UPD_LEAF (DID1, DID2, ID1, ID2, LO1, LO2, PID1, PID2, Name, Value1, Value2)
DEL_INT (DID1, DID2, ID, LO, PID, Name)	MOVE_INT (DID1, DID2, ID1, ID2, LO1, LO2, PID1, PID2, Name)
INS_LEAF (DID1, DID2, ID, LO, PID, Name, Value)	MOVE_LEAF (DID1, DID2, ID1, ID2, LO1, LO2, PID1, PID2, Name, Value)
DEL_LEAF (DID1, DID2, ID, LO, PID, Name, Value)	MOVE_LIST (DID1, DID2, ID1, ID2, LO1, LO2, PID1, PID2, Name, Type)

(b) Delta Tables

Attributes	Description
DID1	Document id of the first version
DID2	Document id of the second version
PID1	Parent node id in the first version
PID2	Parent node id in the second version
ID1	Node id in the first version
ID2	Node id in the second version
LO1	Local order in the first version
LO2	Local order in the second version

Attributes	Description
PID	Parent node id
ID	Node id
LO	Local order
Name	Node name
Value	Leaf node content
Counter	Number of matching nodes
Total	Total number of nodes
Score	Similarity score

Attributes	Description
Value1	The old value of a leaf node
Value2	The new value of a leaf node
Flag	Status for possible moved nodes
Type	Node type of the moved nodes among their siblings

(c) Attributes and Descriptions

Fig. 6. Temporary and Delta Table Descriptions

and $|t_2|$ are the numbers of leaf nodes whose parent nodes are i_1 and i_2, respectively. That is, lines 3–6 and lines 7–10 in Figure 4(e) are used to calculate the values of $|t_1|$ and $|t_2|$, respectively. The value of the *Counter* attribute is equal to $(2|A|+|B|)$, where $|A|$ and $|B|$ are the numbers of fixed and shifted matching leaf nodes in $\mathcal{G}_1$ and $\mathcal{G}_2$, respectively. Similarly, lines 3–6 and lines 8–12 in Figure 4(f) are used to calculate the values of $2|A|$ and $|B|$, respectively. Finally, the value of the *Score* attribute is equal to $\frac{2|A|+|B|}{|t_1|+|t_2|}$ as defined in the preceding section.

The results of the *findMatchingLeafNodesGroups* algorithm are a temporary table M_{c_x} in which the information of matching groups of non-inlined leaf nodes c_x are stored. The schema of the M_{c_x} table is the same as the one of the `tempTb1` table as depicted in Figure 6(a). The semantics of attributes of the `tempTb1` table are depicted in Figure 6(c). For instance, in our example, the "interest" node is a non-inlined leaf nodes. The algorithm will generate the $M_{interest}$ table as depicted in Figure 5(a).

3.2 Bottom-Up Matching Phase

The next step is to propagate the matchings in bottom-up fashion (lines 5–14, Figure 3). First, the algorithm determines the highest level of the non-inlined internal nodes in DTD U (line 5). Then, it starts to find best matching internal nodes in bottom-up fashion. There are two sub steps, that is, finding matching internal nodes (line 11) and determining best matching subtrees (line 12) by finding *best matching configurations*.

Finding Matching Internal Nodes. This phase is similar to the one discussed in [4]. Figure 7 depicts the SQL queries used to find matching internal nodes. Observe that these SQL queries are similar to the ones in [4]. The only difference is that in OXONE we include the *LocalOrder* attribute when we project the result of the SQL queries. The details on how to replace "`[moreConditions]`" (line 11, Figure 7(b)) can be found in [4]. The matching internal node i_w is stored in a temporary matching table M_{i_w}, where $i_w \in \mathbb{N}_i$. The schema of the M_{i_w} table is the same as the one of the `tempTb2` table as depicted in Figure 6(a). The semantics of attributes of the `tempTb2` table are depicted in Figure 6(c). For example, the matching "staff" node will be stored in the M_{staff} table (Figure 5(b)).

```
INSERT INTO [tempTb]
SELECT
  A1.DOC_ID AS DID1, A2.DOC_ID AS DID2,
  A1.ID AS ID1, A2.ID AS ID2,
  A1.LOCALORDER AS LO1, A2.LOCALORDER AS LO2,
  A1.PID AS PID1, A2.PID AS PID2,
  0 AS COUNTER, 0 AS TOTAL, 0 AS SCORE, 0 AS FLAG
FROM [tempMChild] AS A, [tbName] AS A1, [tbName] AS A2
WHERE
  A.DID1 = doc_id1 AND A.DID2 = doc_id2 AND
  A1.DOC_ID = doc_id1 AND A2.DOC_ID = doc_id2 AND
  A1.ID = A.PID1 AND  A2.ID = A.PID2 AND
  NOT EXISTS
    (SELECT ID1, ID2 FROM [tempTb] AS B
     WHERE B.DID1 = doc_id1 AND B.DID2 = doc_id2 AND
           B.ID1 = A.ID1 AND B.ID2 = A.ID2)
GROUP BY A1.DOC_ID, A2.DOC_ID, A1.PID, A2.PID, A1.ID, A2.ID
```

(a) Finding Matching Internal Nodes (1)

```
INSERT INTO [tempTb]
SELECT
  A1.DOC_ID AS DID1, A2.DOC_ID AS DID2,
  A1.ID AS ID1, A2.ID AS ID2,
  A1.LOCALORDER AS LO1, A2.LOCALORDER AS LO2,
  A1.PID AS PID1, A1.PID AS PID2,
  0 AS COUNTER, 0 AS TOTAL, 0 AS SCORE, 0 AS FLAG
FROM [tbName] AS A1, [tbName] AS A2
WHERE
  A1.DOC_ID = doc_id1 AND A2.DOC_ID = doc_id2 AND
  [moreConditions] AND
  NOT EXISTS
   (SELECT ID1, ID2 FROM [tempTb] AS B
    WHERE B.DID1 = doc_id1 AND
       B.DID2 = doc_id2 AND B.ID1 = A.ID1 AND B.ID2 = A.ID2)
GROUP BY A1.DOC_ID, A2.DOC_ID, A1.PID, A2.PID, A1.ID, A2.ID
```

(b) Finding Matching Internal Nodes (2)

Fig. 7. SQL Queries for Finding Matching Internal Nodes

Finding Best Matching Internal Nodes. The task in this step is to find *best matching configurations* that facilitate us to find best matching internal nodes. Recall that an internal node in T_1 can be matched to more than one internal nodes in T_2, and vice versa. The problem of finding best matching configuration is similar to the problem of finding *maximum weighted bipartite matching*. In our implementation, we use the Hungarian method [5] that addresses the problem of finding maximum weighted bipartite matching. The algorithm for finding best matching configurations is similar to the one discussed in [4] except for the following differences. After we determine the best matching configurations, the algorithm annotates the matching internal nodes whose parent nodes are not used in the best matching configuration by setting the *Flag* attribute in the M_{i_w} table to "1". The annotations mean that these subtrees may be moved to different parent nodes. Note that in [4] such matching nodes are directly deleted. Observe that we also need to update the values of the *Counter*, *Total*, and *Score* attributes accordingly as initially their values are equal to "0".

3.3 Collecting Best Matching Internal Nodes Phase

The result of the previous step is the best matching internal nodes partitioned in several relations. The objectives of this step are to merge/collect the best matching internal nodes from different relations and to determine the best matching inlined internal nodes. Observe that the moved subtree candidates are also in the temporary matching tables. The values of the *Flag* attribute of moved subtree candidates in the temporary matching tables are equal to "1". The algorithm and SQL queries for collecting best matching internal nodes are similar to the ones presented in [4] except for the following difference. In OXONE, we need to filter out the moved node candidates from being considered as best matching internal nodes. They can be filtered out by adding a condition "`FLAG =`

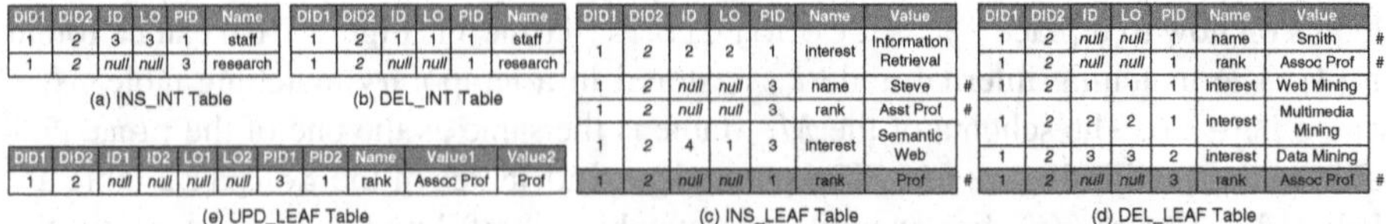

DID1	DID2	ID	LO	PID	Name
1	2	3	3	1	staff
1	2	null	null	3	research

(a) INS_INT Table

DID1	DID2	ID	LO	PID	Name
1	2	1	1	1	staff
1	2	null	null	1	research

(b) DEL_INT Table

DID1	DID2	ID	LO	PID	Name	Value	
1	2	2	2	1	interest	Information Retrieval	
1	2	null	null	3	name	Steve	#
1	2	null	null	3	rank	Asst Prof	#
1	2	4	1	3	interest	Semantic Web	
1	2	null	null	1	rank	Prof	#

(c) INS_LEAF Table

DID1	DID2	ID	LO	PID	Name	Value	
1	2	null	null	1	name	Smith	#
1	2	null	null	1	rank	Assoc Prof	#
1	2	1	1	1	interest	Web Mining	
1	2	2	2	1	interest	Multimedia Mining	
1	2	3	3	2	interest	Data Mining	
1	2	null	null	3	rank	Assoc Prof	#

(d) DEL_LEAF Table

DID1	DID2	ID1	ID2	LO1	LO2	PID1	PID2	Name	Value1	Value2
1	2	null	null	null	null	3	1	rank	Assoc Prof	Prof

(e) UPD_LEAF Table

Fig. 8. Delta Tables

```
INSERT INTO UPD_LEAF
SELECT DISTINCT doc_id1 AS DID1, doc_id2 AS DID2,
  NULL AS ID1, NULL AS ID2, NULL AS LO1, NULL AS LO2,
  I1.ID AS PID1, I2.ID AS PID2, '[nodeName]' AS NAME,
  I1.[attrName] AS VALUE1, I2.[attrName] AS VALUE2
FROM [parentTbName] AS I1, [parentTbName] AS I2
WHERE
  I1.DOC_ID = doc_id1 AND I2.DOC_ID = doc_id2 AND
  I1.[attrName] IS NOT NULL AND I2.[attrName] IS NOT NULL AND
  I1.[attrName] != I2.[attrName] AND
  EXISTS
    (SELECT * FROM MATCHING AS B
     WHERE DID1 = doc_id1 AND DID2 = doc_id2 AND
       B.NAME = '[parentNodeName]' AND
       B.ID1 = I1.ID AND B.ID2 = I2.ID )
```

(a) Update of Inlined Leaf Nodes

```
INSERT INTO UPD_LEAF
SELECT DISTINCT doc_id1 AS DID1, doc_id2 AS DID2,
  D.ID AS ID1, I.ID AS ID2, D.LO AS LO1,
  I.LO AS LO2, D.PID AS PID, I.PID AS PID2,
  D.NAME, D.VALUE AS VALUE1, I.VALUE AS VALUE2
FROM INS_LEAF AS I, DEL_LEAF AS D, MATCHING AS M
WHERE
  I.DID1 = doc_id1 AND I.DID2 = doc_id2 AND
  D.DID1 = doc_id1 AND D.DID2 = doc_id2 AND
  M.DID1 = doc_id1 AND M.DID2 = doc_id2 AND
  M.ID1 = D.PID AND M.ID2 = I.PID AND
  M.NAME = '[parentNodeName]' AND
  I.NAME = '[nodeName]' AND
  D.NAME = '[nodeName]' AND
  I.VALUE != D.VALUE AND I.LO = D.LO
```

(b) Update of Non-inlined Leaf Nodes

Fig. 9. SQL Queries for Detecting Updated Leaf Nodes

0" in the SQL queries. In addition, we need to include the *LocalOrder* attribute when we project the result of the SQL queries. The best matching internal nodes are stored in the MATCHING table. The semantics of the MATCHING table is depicted in Figure 6. For example, given the $M_{univStaff}$ and M_{staff} tables (Figures 5(b) and 5(c), respectively) and the relations containing the shredded XML documents, the MATCHING table is depicted in Figure 5(d). The MATCHING table keeps the best matching internal nodes of two XML documents that will be used to detect the changes (Phase 2).

4 Change Detection Phase

In this section, we discuss how the changes are detected by OXONE after the best matching subtrees are determined. We detect the insertion, deletion, update, and move operations as highlighted in [1]. Note that we do not elaborate on the detection of inserted and deleted nodes (subtrees) here as the SQL queries are similar to the ones presented in [4]. The only difference is that in OXONE we include the "*LocalOrder*" attribute in the projection of the result. The detected inserted and deleted internal nodes are stored in the INS_INT and DEL_INT tables, respectively. Similarly, the detected inserted and deleted leaf nodes are stored in the INS_LEAF and DEL_LEAF relations, respectively. The semantics of these relations and corresponding examples (based on XML documents in Figure 1) are given in Figures 6 and 8, respectively. Note that the updated leaf nodes are also detected during the detection of inserted and deleted nodes as they can be decomposed into pairs of deleted and inserted leaf nodes. "[param]" in the SQL queries (Figures 9 and 10) used in the later discussion will be replaced the parameter *param* that is similar to the one defined in the *findBestMatchingSubtrees* algorithm.

4.1 Content Updates of Leaf Nodes

Intuitively, the updated leaf nodes are the leaf nodes that are available in both versions and have the same node names, but have different values, and their parent nodes are best matching internal nodes. In OXONE, the updated leaf nodes are detected after the inserted and deleted leaf nodes are detected. We classify the update operations of non-inlined leaf nodes into the *absolute update operations* and the *relative update*

```
INSERT INTO MOVE_INT
SELECT
 doc_id1 AS DID1, doc_id2 AS DID2,
 M.ID1, M.ID2, M.LO1, M.LO2,
 M.PID1, M.PID2, '[nodeName]' AS NAME
FROM  INS_INT AS I, DEL_INT AS D, [tempTb] AS M
WHERE
  I.DID1 = doc_id1 AND I.DID2 = doc_id2 AND
  D.DID1 = doc_id1 AND D.DID2 = doc_id2 AND
  M.DID1 = doc_id1 AND M.DID2 = doc_id2 AND
  I.NAME = '[nodeName]' AND
  D.NAME = '[nodeName]' AND
  M.ID1 = D.ID AND M.ID2 = I.ID AND
  M.FLAG = 1 AND M.SCORE >= 0.500
```

(a) Move To Different Parent Nodes (1)

```
INSERT INTO MOVE_INT
SELECT
  doc_id1 AS DID1, doc_id2 AS DID2,
  NULL AS ID1, NULL AS ID2, NULL AS LO1, NULL AS LO2,
  M.ID1, M.ID2, '[nodeName]' AS NAME
FROM INS_INT AS I, DEL_INT AS D, [parentTempTb] AS M
WHERE
  I.DID1 = doc_id1 AND I.DID2 = doc_id2 AND
  D.DID1 = doc_id1 AND D.DID2 = doc_id2 AND
  M.DID1 = doc_id1 AND M.DID2 = doc_id2 AND
  I.NAME = '[nodeName]' AND
  D.NAME = '[nodeName]' AND
  M.ID1 = D.PID AND M.ID2 = I.PID AND
  M.FLAG = 1 AND M.SCORE >= 0.500
```

(b) Move To Different Parent Nodes (2)

```
INSERT INTO MOVE_LEAF
SELECT
  doc_id1 AS DID1, doc_id2 AS DID2, D.ID AS ID1,
  I.ID AS ID2, D.LO AS LO1, I.LO AS LO2,
  D.PID AS PID1, I.PID AS PID2, '[nodeName]' AS NAME,
  D.VALUE AS VALUE
FROM INS_LEAF AS I, DEL_LEAF AS D, MOVE_INT AS M
WHERE
  I.DID1 = doc_id1 AND I.DID2 = doc_id2 AND
  D.DID1 = doc_id1 AND D.DID2 = doc_id2 AND
  M.DID1 = doc_id1 AND M.DID2 = doc_id2 AND
  I.NAME = '[nodeName]' AND D.NAME = '[nodeName]' AND
  I.VALUE = D.VALUE AND
  M.NAME = '[parentNodeName]' AND
  M.ID1 = D.PID AND M.ID2 = I.PID
```

(c) Leaf Nodes: Move To Different Parent Nodes (1)

```
INSERT INTO MOVE_LEAF
SELECT
  doc_id1 AS DID1, doc_id2 AS DID1,
  D.ID AS ID1, I.ID AS ID2,
  D.LO AS LO1, I.LO AS LO2, D.PID AS PID1,
  I.PID AS PID2, D.NAME, D.VALUE
FROM DEL_LEAF AS D, INS_LEAF AS I
WHERE
  D.DID1 = doc_id1 AND D.DID2 = doc_id2 AND
  I.DID1 = doc_id1 AND I.DID2 = doc_id2 AND
  D.VALUE = I.VALUE AND D.NAME = I.NAME
```

(d) Leaf Nodes: Move To Different Parent Nodes (2)

Fig. 10. SQL Queries for Detecting Moved Nodes

operations. In the absolute update operation, only the content value of an updated leaf node is changed, while its position among siblings remains the same. In relative update operation, the content value and position among siblings of an updated leaf node are changed. For inlined leaf nodes, we only have absolute update operations as they occur once under the same parent nodes.

Inlined Leaf Nodes. The SQL query in Figure 9(a) is used to determine the updated inlined leaf nodes. Lines 9–10 are used to ensure that the updated inlined leaf nodes are available in both versions (line 9) and they have different values (line 10). Lines 11–15 are used to guarantee that the parent nodes of the updated inlined leaf nodes are best matching internal nodes. The result of the SQL query depicted in Figure 9(a) is stored in the UPD_LEAF table. Its schema and semantics are depicted in Figures 6. Next, we need to delete the corresponding tuples of the updated inlined leaf nodes in the DEL_LEAF and INS_LEAF relations. This is because we have detected updated leaf nodes that are previously detected as pairs of deleted and inserted leaf nodes.

Non-Inlined Leaf Nodes. To detect the absolute updated non-inlined leaf nodes, OXONE executes the SQL query depicted in Figure 9(b). Observe that we join three tables, namely, the DEL_LEAF, INS_LEAF, and MATCHING tables. Recall that an updated leaf node can be decomposed as a pair of deleted and inserted leaf nodes. Line 13 is used to guarantee that the parent nodes of the deleted and inserted leaf nodes are the best matching internal nodes. The absolute updated leaf nodes must have the same node name and the same local order, but different values (lines 13–15). The result of the SQL query depicted in Figure 9(b) is stored in the UPD_LEAF table. We also need to delete the corresponding tuples of the updated non-inlined leaf nodes in the DEL_LEAF and INS_LEAF relations.

Next, OXONE determines the *relative* updated non-inlined leaf nodes by executing the SQL query depicted in Figure 9(b) after slight modifications as follows. We replace

"I.LO = D.LO" with "I.LO ≠ D.LO". Recall that the relative updated leaf nodes must have the same node name, but different values and local orders. Note that while detecting relative updated non-inlined leaf nodes, the query may return *incorrect* results in some situations as follows. First, there is more than one relative updated non-inlined leaf node under the same parent nodes. Second, there are deletion/insertion and update of non-inlined leaf nodes occurred under the same parent nodes. Therefore, we rectify the results using the approach as discussed in [4]. The result of the SQL query depicted in Figure 9(b) (after slight modification) is also stored in the UPD_LEAF table. In our example, the UPD_LEAF table is depicted in Figure 8(e). The highlighted tuples in the INS_LEAF (Figure 8(c)) and DEL_LEAF (Figure 8(d)) tables will be deleted as they are the corresponding tuples of the updated leaf nodes.

4.2 Move Operation

The move operations are classified into *move among siblings* and *move to different parent nodes*. The algorithm for detecting the movement of nodes among their siblings is similar to the one presented in [2]. Hence, here we focus on *move to different parent nodes*.

A particular node that is moved to different parent node is detected as a pair of deletion and insertion. Hence, we are able to determine the nodes that are moved to different parent nodes by querying the DEL_INT and INS_INT tables (for moved internal nodes), and the DEL_LEAF and INS_LEAF tables (for moved leaf nodes). The moved internal nodes (leaf nodes) are best matching internal nodes (matching leaf nodes) whose parent nodes are not best matching internal nodes.

The SQL queries in Figures 10(a) and 10(b) are used to find the moved *non-inlined* and *inlined* internal nodes that are moved to different parent nodes. Note that we only consider the moved internal nodes that have similarity scores equal or greater than "0.500". Note that this "threshold" can be defined by users based on application requirements. Otherwise, they are detected as pairs of deleted and inserted internal nodes. If an internal node i is moved to different parents, then, intuitively, the subtree rooted at node i is also moved. That is, we need to detect the moved leaf nodes that are the descendants of the moved internal nodes. Figure 10(c) is used to find the moved *non-inlined* leaf nodes that are the descendants of the moved internal nodes. To find the *inlined* ones, we used the modified SQL query of the SQL query depicted in Figure 10(c). We replace "ID1" and "ID2" in line 10 with "PID1" and "PID2" respectively. Note that we need to delete the corresponding tuples of the moved nodes that are stored in the DEL_INT, INS_INT, DEL_LEAF, and INS_LEAF tables. Observe that some leaf nodes can also be moved to be the child nodes of different parent nodes. These moved leaf nodes are not the descendants of the moved internal nodes. Figure 10(d) is used to find the moved leaf nodes that are not the descendants of the moved internal nodes. Note that we also need to delete the corresponding tuples of the moved leaf nodes that are stored in the DEL_LEAF, and INS_LEAF tables.

5 Performance Study

We have implemented OXONE entirely in Java. We use Microsoft SQL Server 2000 for storing XML documents before the changes are detected. The experiments were

Dataset Code	Number of Nodes			Filesize (KB)
	Internal	Leaf	Total	
SIGMOD-01	73	258	331	13
SIGMOD-02	117	427	554	21
SIGMOD-03	187	703	890	34
SIGMOD-04	389	1,437	1,826	70
SIGMOD-05	567	2,151	2,718	104
SIGMOD-06	983	3,734	4,717	180
SIGMOD-07	1,801	6,993	8,794	337
SIGMOD-08	3,883	14,983	18,866	721

Dataset Code	Number of Nodes			Filesize (KB)
	Internal	Leaf	Total	
SIGMOD-09	7723	30,002	37,725	1,444
SIGMOD-10	18,067	71,256	89,323	3,431
SIGMOD-11	34,845	137,909	172,754	6,635
SIGMOD-12	58,587	231,952	290,539	11,167
SIGMOD-13	71,991	283,930	355,921	13,688
SIGMOD-14	91,604	361,085	452,689	17,398
SIGMOD-15	125,411	494,812	620,223	23,816

Fig. 11. Data Sets

conducted on a Microsoft Windows XP Professional machine having Pentium 4 1.7 GHz processor with 512 MB of memory. We used a set of synthetic XML data based on SIGMOD DTD (http://www.sigmod.org/record/). The characteristics of the data sets are depicted in Figure 11. The second versions of the XML documents are generated by using our XML change generator. We compared the performance of OXONE to the Java version of X-Diff [8] (downloaded from http://www.cs.wisc.edu/~yuanwang/xdiff.html), schema-oblivious relational-based approach for ordered XML change detection in [2] (called XANDY–O), and C version of XyDiff [1] (downloaded from http://pauillac.inria.fr/cdrom/www/xydiff/index-eng.htm). Note that despite our best efforts (including contacting the authors), we could not get the Java version of XyDiff. The C version of XyDiff was run in a Pentium 4 1.7 GHz processor with 512 MB of memory with Red Hat Linux 9 operating system. Note that as the Java version is in general slower than the C version, the execution times of XyDiff will differ by a constant factor in comparison with X-Diff.

Execution Time vs Number of Nodes. In this set of experiments, we analyze the performance of OXONE for different number of nodes. The percentages of change is set to "9%". Figure 12(a) depicts the performance of Phase 1 in our approaches. Observe that the performances of OXONE and XANDY–O are comparable up to data set `SIGMOD-05`. For larger data set, OXONE outperforms XANDY–O (up to 20.5 times). Note that the performance of XANDY–O is adversely affected with increase in number of nodes and for datasets larger than `SIGMOD-12`, XANDY–O fail to return results in 100,000 seconds. Hence, we do not plot the result of XANDY–O for data sets larger than `SIGMOD-12`. The performance of Phase 2 is depicted in Figure 12(b). In this case, OXONE is faster than XANDY–O (up to 81.88 times).

Figure 12(c) depicts the overall performance of our approaches. XyDiff is up to 3.5 times faster than OXONE for the first three data sets. After that the performance of XyDiff is comparable to the one of OXONE. However, our approach is more scalable as XyDiff fails to detect the changes to data sets larger than `SIGMOD-12` as its process was killed by the Linux kernel. In addition, we believe that the Java version of XyDiff will be much slower and less scalable than the C version and hence will adversely affect the response time and scalability further. X-Diff, on the other hand, is only able to detect the changes up to `SIGMOD-06` due to lack of main memory. X-Diff outperforms OXONE for the first three data sets (up to 8.15 times). For larger data sets, OXONE is up to 43.7 times faster than X-Diff. Note that the performances of XANDY–O and OXONE is slower than main memory-based approaches for smaller data sets as the database I/O cost is more expensive. Also, overall OXONE is up to 22 times faster than XANDY–O.

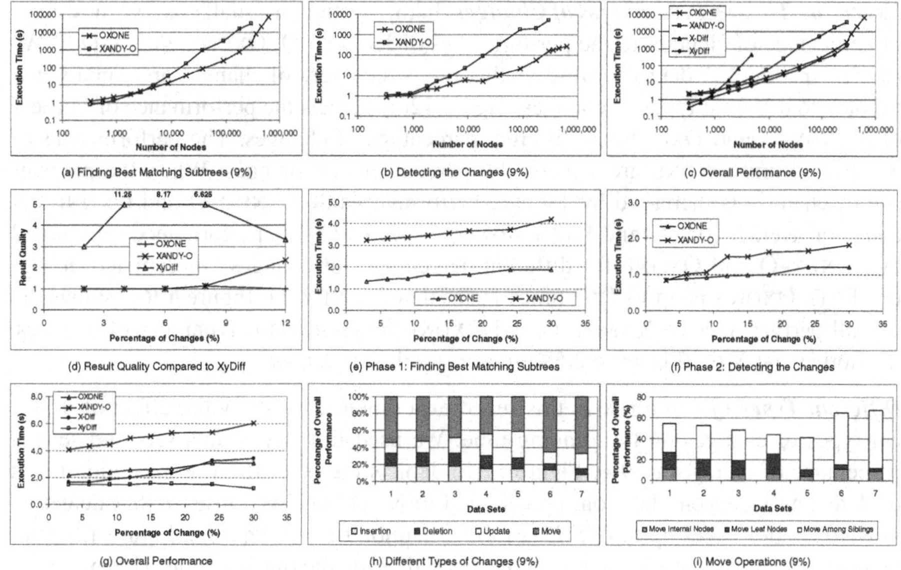

Fig. 12. Experimental Results

Result Quality. Next, we examine the result quality of OXONE, XANDY–O, and XyDiff. The result quality is defined as the ratio between the number of edit operations in the deltas detected by an approach and the one in the *optimal* deltas. Note that an optimal delta consists of minimum number of edit operations [8]. Also, we do not show the result quality of X-Diff as it is not designed for ordered change detection. We use a small data set with 100 nodes and generate the second version with various percentages of changes (2%–12%). Figure 12(d) depicts the result quality comparison results. Observe that the result quality of OXONE and of XANDY–O are comparable. Also, the result qualities of OXONE and XANDY–O are significantly better than that of XyDiff. In XyDiff's deltas, there are some unnecessary move operations, and, in some case, XyDiff mismatches the best matching subtrees. For instance, consider the example depicted in Figure 13. The delta detected by OXONE contains *delete*(1) and *update*(10, "Asst Prof", "Assoc Prof"). However, the delta generated by XyDiff contains *move*(9, 1, 2) ("move node 9 to the second child node of node 1"), *delete*(8), and *delete*(2) which is semantically incorrect.

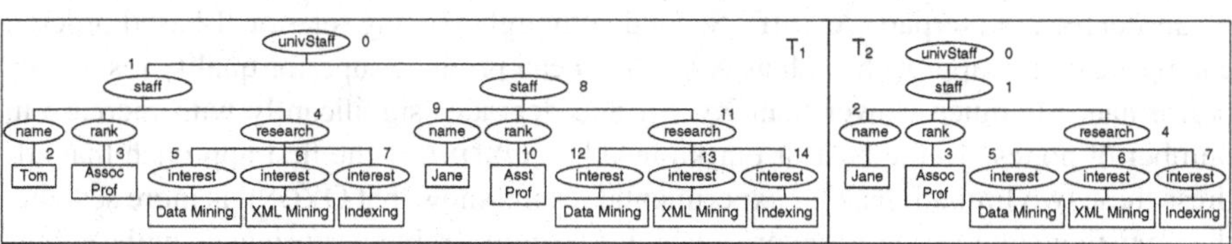

Fig. 13. Result Quality: Example

Execution Time vs Percentages of Changes. In this section, we shall observe the effects of percentage of changes to the performances of XANDY–O, OXONE, and X-Diff. We use "`Sigmod-03`" data set. Observe that the percentages of changes are equally distributed to different types of changes. Figure 12(e) depicts the performance of Phase 1 of XANDY–O and OXONE for different percentage of changes. The performances of XANDY–O and OXONE are affected by percentages of changes. When the percentage of changes is increased by 1%, the performances of XANDY–O and OXONE become, on average, 0.95% and 1.43% slower, respectively. The performances of Phase 2 of XANDY–O and OXONE for different percentages of changes are depicted in Figure 12(f). OXONE is up to 1.62 times faster than XANDY–O. Figure 12(g) shows the overall performance of XANDY–O and OXONE for different percentages of changes. We notice that XyDiff is up to 2.59 times faster than OXONE.

Different Types of Changes. In this set of experiments, we study the affect of different types of changes on the running time. We used first seven data sets and set the percentage of changes to 9%. Figure 12(h) depicts the proportion of execution times of detecting insertion, deletion, update, and move operations. Observe that detecting move operation takes up to 67.17% of the execution time of Phase 2. Figure 12(i) depicts the affect of different types of move operations on the running time. The execution time of detecting moves among siblings is significant compared to the one for detecting moved internal nodes and moved leaf nodes. It takes up to 55.68% of the execution time of Phase 2. Let us elaborate on this further. In detecting move among siblings, we compare the local order of each node. However, the local order can be changed due to the insertions/deletions of sibling nodes. Hence, we need to ensure that such local order changes are not considered in order to detect move among siblings correctly. The *adjustLocalOrder* function that is similar to the one in [2] is used to simulate the insertions/deletions of sibling nodes. Observe that an insertion/deletion of a sibling node can change more than one local orders of its sibling nodes. Hence, when there is an insertion/deletion of a sibling node, we need to adjust more than one local orders of its sibling nodes. That is, the cost of the *adjustLocalOrder* function is increased as the number of insertions/deletions is increased.

6 Conclusions and Future Work

In this paper, we present a relational-based approach (called OXONE) for detecting the changes on ordered XML documents using a schema-conscious approach. This work is motivated by the following observations. First, existing main memory-based ordered XML change detection techniques (XyDiff) produce poorer quality deltas compared to its unordered counterpart (X-Diff). Second, although existing relational-based ordered change detection approach such as XANDY–O can produce superior quality results, its performance is much slower than XyDiff and degrades significantly with increase in number of nodes. To the best of our knowledge, OXONE is the first approach that address these two limitations. Our experimental results show that OXONE is more scalable than existing state-of-the-art approaches. It has comparable performance with XyDiff and yet produce superior result quality. As parts of our future work, we would like to extend our framework so that it can handle recursive DTDs.

References

1. G. COBENA, S. ABITEBOUL, A. MARIAN. Detecting Changes in XML Documents. *In ICDE*, 2002.
2. E. LEONARDI, S. S. BHOWMICK. XANDY: A Scalable Change Detection Technique for Ordered XML Documents Using Relational Databases. To appear in DKE Journal.
3. E. LEONARDI, S. S. BHOWMICK, S. MADRIA. XANDY: Detecting Changes on Large Unordered XML Documents Using Relational Databases. *In DASFAA*, China, 2005.
4. E. LEONARDI, S. S. BHOWMICK. Detecting Changes on Unordered XML Documents Using Relational Databases: A Schema-Conscious Approach. *In CIKM*, 2005.
5. C. PAPADIMITRIOU, K. STEIGLITZ. Combinatorial Optimization: Algorithms and Complexity. Prentice-Hall, Englewood Cliffs, NJ, 1982.
6. J. SHANMUGASUNDARAM, K. TUFTE, C. ZHANG, G. HE, D. J. DEWITT, AND J. F. NAUGHTON Relational Databases for Querying XML Documents: Limitations and Opportunities. *The VLDB Journal*, 1999.
7. H. LU, H. JIANG, J. X. XU, G. YU ET AL. What Makes the Differences: Benchmarking XML Database Implementations. *In ACM TOIT*, 5(1), 2005.
8. Y. WANG, D. J. DEWITT, J. CAI. X-Diff: An Effective Change Detection Algorithm for XML Documents. *In ICDE*, Bangalore, 2003.

Schema-Mediated Exchange of Temporal XML Data

Curtis Dyreson[1], Richard T. Snodgrass[2], Faiz Currim[3], and Sabah Currim[4]

[1] Washington State University, Pullman, WA
cdyreson@eecs.wsu.edu
[2] University of Arizona, Tucson, AZ
rts@cs.arizona.edu
[3] University of Iowa, Iowa City, IA
faiz-currim@uiowa.edu
[4] University of Arizona, Tucson, AZ
scurrim@eller.arizona.edu

Abstract. When web servers publish data formatted in XML, only the current state of the data is (generally) published. But data evolves over time as it is updated. Capturing that evolution is vital to recovering past versions, tracking changes, and evaluating temporal queries. This paper presents a system to build a *temporal* data collection, which records the history of each published datum rather than just its current state. The key to exchanging temporal data is providing a *temporal schema* to mediate the interaction between the publisher and the reader. The schema describes how to construct a temporal data collection by "gluing" individual states into an integrated history.

1 Introduction

An XML schema describes the structure of XML data. The schema is used by a publisher to format the data for publication and by a reader to *validate* acquired data and add it to a data collection. Validation ensures that the data conforms to the formatting rules for XML (is well-formed) and to the types, elements, and attributes defined in the schema (is valid). A schema is also used as a guide in interpreting, editing and querying the data. Several schema languages have been proposed for XML; among them XML Schema is the most widely used.

Data formatted in XML is already available from many web servers. One example of a data provider is the National Center for Biotechnology Information (NCBI). Users can search the NCBI databases to locate data on genes and proteins. The data can then be downloaded in several formats, including as XML. In fact NCBI publishes data in three XML schemas. However, NCBI like most XML publishers only provides the current *snapshot* of the data. A snapshot is the data that is available at a single point in time, stripped of its historical context. But a data collection varies over time as new data is inserted and existing data is revised. In general, scientists want to know the *provenance* of their data: who, what, where, and *when* [3]; the evolution of the data is an important part of that provenance. Though NCBI users can download the current snapshot, they are unable to track and download changes to data. Obtaining data in an historical context is useful in many applications. For instance, scientific

D.W. Embley, A. Olivé, and S. Ram (Eds.): ER 2006, LNCS 4215, pp. 212–227, 2006.

insights gained by analyzing data often have to be revised when the data changes. To help determine whether a reanalysis is needed, especially in a large data set where manual comparison is infeasible, it is crucial to be able to ascertain whether data has been added, modified, or deleted. One might want to look at coarse changes to an entire XML document or track the evolution over time of specific elements.

Fig. 1 illustrates the process by which a user currently downloads data from a publisher like NCBI. A user requests the current snapshot, D_{now}. The data is then added to the reader's data collection, DB, typically by overwriting a previously acquired version of D in DB. A better strategy, not currently supported by NCBI, is to transmit only the changes to the data, as shown in Fig. 2. A user requests a *change summary* of updates to D from time *t*, when the user last acquired D, to *now*. The summary, which is represented as "ΔD," is used to update the local snapshot of D. A Service Data Object (SDO) is one technology that supports change summaries [28]. In contrast, Fig. 3 shows the process of acquiring *temporal data*. A user requests a thick *slice* of

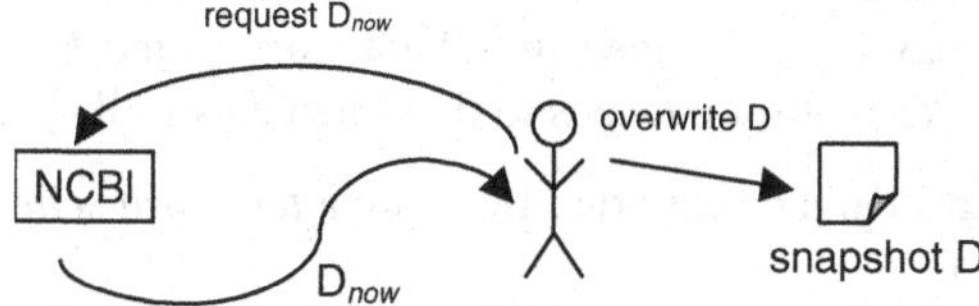

Fig. 1. Download of the current snapshot

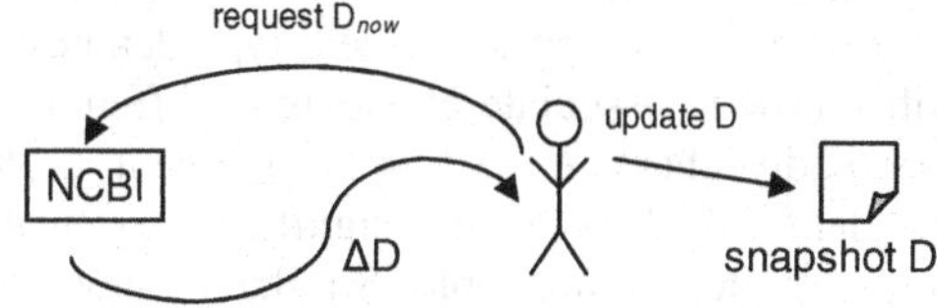

Fig. 2. Download change summary, e.g., in an SDO

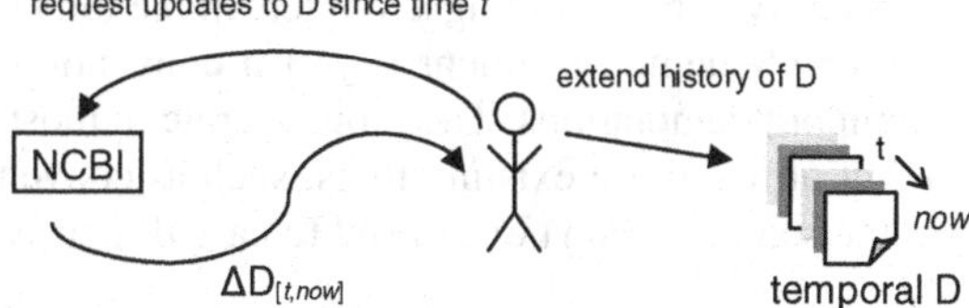

Fig. 3. A download of temporal data

data from time *t*, when the user last acquired D, to *now*. The slice as returned by the server is represented as "$\Delta D_{[t,now]}$." The temporal data is then added to DB, extending the history of D. Unlike the snapshot data in Fig. 1 and Fig. 2, temporal data records the entire version history of every data item.

Systems that support the publication of and subscription to temporal data need several novel features.

- A data publisher has to add timestamps and other markup to indicate the lifetime of versions of the data.
- The temporal data produced by a publisher has to be amenable to automatic processing on the reader's side; for instance, the reader has to be able to validate the temporal data and update a temporal data store.
- To conserve bandwidth the slice "$\Delta D_{[t\text{-}now]}$" should be compact. Ideally it will be proportional in size to the changes to D since time *t*.
- It should be possible to validate the changes to a data collection, i.e., $\Delta D_{[t\text{-}now]}$. Unfortunately an SDO's change summary cannot be validated using the data's schema, rather the changes must first be applied to the data, which must then be entirely re-validated. It would be more desirable if it were possible to validate a slice of temporal data in isolation from the rest of the data collection.
- A publisher may have changed its schema since time *t*, so each step in the process must account for changes to the schema as well.

All of the above features can be supported by using a *temporal schema* to mediate the exchange of XML data.

This paper utilizes τXSchema (Temporal XML Schema), which is an infrastructure and suite of tools for constructing and validating XML data collections as both the data [8] and schema [10] evolve, though in this paper we consider only the data evolution aspects of τXSchema. τXSchema extends XML Schema with the ability to define *temporal element types.*[1] A temporal element type denotes that an element can vary over time, describes how to associate elements in different snapshots, and provides constraints that broadly characterize how an element evolves. Biologists are reticent to learn a new data model, or even a significant extension of a data model with which they have just gotten comfortable. Similarly, they don't want to have to acquire and learn how to use a new suite of tools that comes with the new data model. Hence, an important goal in the development of τXSchema was to maximally reuse existing XML standards and technology. In τXSchema, any element type can be denoted as a temporal element type by including a single, simple temporal annotation in the type definition. So a τXSchema document is just a conventional XML Schema document with a few temporal annotations. The tools operate in most cases identically to extant tools and in fact utilize those existing tools, such as conventional validating parsers. In most cases, the scientists don't even need to care if their XML data is static or temporal.

This paper is organized as follows. The next section motivates the differences between conventional (static) XML data and temporal XML data. We then discuss how snapshots of a temporal data collection are glued to create *items* and *versions*. The extensions to XML Schema to support temporal data are presented in Section 4. Section 5 sketches the process of constructing a representational schema. The paper concludes with a discussion of related work and a summary.

---

[1] This use of "temporal element" is a generalization of "XML element," and is not related to the "temporal element" defined by Gadia [11].

2 Example

Assume that data on the gene trypsin 4 (TRY4) is described in an XML data collection called `gene.xml`. The collection has information about gene function, which is described using the Mouse Genome Institute ontology. On 2005-01-01 the function of TRY4 was unknown as shown by the XML in Fig. 4. In subsequent months, new scientific data about TRY4 became available. On 2005-02-14 it was learned that TRY4 is involved in synthesizing the trypsinogen protein. The value of the "function" attribute was updated creating a new version of the data, as shown in Fig. 5. On 2005-03-06, the gene description became more specific, relating TRY4 to β-cell receptors so an additional "desc" element was inserted as shown in Fig. 6.

Researchers that prepared a paper on TRY4 in 2005-01 would like to learn of any updates to the TRY4 data since that time, and in particular how the data has changed. Certain changes will require a new analysis of their experiments. But the data in each figure is the data at a single point in time. Instead of the current snapshot, the researchers need the *version history*, which consists of the information in each version of the data along with a timestamp indicating the version's lifetime. The version history would describe how the knowledge about a particular gene has changed over time. This is of particular interest since new genomic and proteomic data is being constantly generated, and existing data is being revised and corrected. A version history would also aid in time-related analysis such as in tracking how a disease and its symptoms evolve over time (e.g., in an epidemic like the avian flu).

```
<gene name="TRY4">
    <desc>trypsin 4</desc>
    <ontology ref="MGI" function="unknown"/>
</gene>
```

Fig. 4. `gene.xml` on 2005-01-01

```
<gene name="TRY4">
    <desc>trypsin 4</desc>
    <ontology ref="MGI" function="synthesizes trypsinogen"/>
</gene>
```

Fig. 5. TRY4 codes for a protein, as of 2005-02-14

```
<gene name="TRY4">
    <desc>trypsin 4, beta-cell receptor</desc>
    <ontology ref="MGI" function="synthesizes trypsinogen"/>
</gene>
```

Fig. 6. TRY4 is related to β-cell receptors, as of 2005-03-06

Fig. 7 shows the temporal data that captures the history of the TRY4 data. The data is largely a list of gene and ontology *items*. The concept of an item is a central contribution of this paper. An item is an element that *persists* across individual snapshots. Each item has an `itemId` attribute that uniquely numbers the item. There is one gene item in the data, and one ontology item. Each item is referenced by a *temporal element*, which places it in the context in which it appears in a snapshot of the data. For example, in Fig. 7 the element <ontology$_{Temporal}$> references the ontology item, which indicates that a version of that item appears within the context of a <gene> element for each snapshot in the range of the version's timestamp.

```
<dataTemporal>
  <data><geneTemporal itemRef="1"/></data>
  <geneItem itemId="1">
    <geneVersion><time start="2005-01-01" end="2005-03-05"/>
      <gene name="TRY4">
        <desc>trypsin 4</desc>
        <ontologyTemporal itemRef="2"/>
      </gene>
    </geneVersion>
    <geneVersion><time start="2005-03-06" end="now"/>
      <gene name="TRY4">
        <desc>trypsin 4, beta-cell receptor</desc>
        <ontologyTemporal itemRef="2"/>
      </gene>
    </geneVersion>
  </geneItem>
  <ontologyItem itemId="2">
    <ontologyVersion><time start="2005-01-01" end="2005-02-13"/>
      <ontology ref="MGI" function="unknown"/>
    </ontologyVersion>
    <ontologyVersion><time start="2005-02-14" end="now"/>
      <ontology ref="MGI" function="synthesizes trypsinogen"/>
    </ontologyVersion>
  </ontologyItem>
</dataTemporal>
```

Fig. 7. Temporal XML data

Whenever the item changes, a new *version* of the item is created. A change is defined, roughly, as a difference in an element's nontemporal content, exclusive of changes to content within the element's temporal subelements. Hence, the gene item has two versions. The second version was created on 2005-03-06 when new text content was added to the nontemporal <desc> element. The timestamp for each version indicates the version's lifetime. The end time of the second version is "*now*" indicating that the version is current. The ontology item also has two versions, because an attribute value was changed on 2005-02-14.

Note that the history of each item in a temporal data collection is more than just the current snapshot. It records not only the current state of the data, but all previous versions as well, and has timestamps to indicate when each version was current. Hence, a temporal data collection is unlike an SDO or related technology that records only a single snapshot and/or a summary of changes from the previous version.

A second contribution of this paper is a description of how to construct the temporal data (Fig. 7) by gluing the data in individual snapshots (Fig. 4, Fig. 5, and Fig. 6). The history in Fig. 7 captures the *transaction time* lifetime of each version [14]. Transaction time is the system time when the data was edited.[2]

A third contribution of this paper is explaining how to compactly represent in XML the change across a number of versions. Though the temporal data shown in Fig. 7 appears verbose in this small example, in general, it is actually *compact* in the sense that each edit results in only a localized change to the data (basically, a new version is created within an item). Fig. 8 shows the difference between the first and second versions of the data. The difference is a new version of the ontology element. The ability to represent the difference between two versions in isolation from the rest of the data is useful in both data streaming and refreshing data from a remote source, since the change is usually much smaller in size than the entire collection or even a snapshot. Note that the value of the `itemId` attribute in Fig. 8 is local to the temporal data being exchanged (the value of the attribute could be "23").

```
<dataTemporal>
  <ontologyItem itemId="1">
    <ontologyVersion><time start="2005-02-14" end="now"/>
      <ontology ref="MGI" function="synthesizes trypsinogen"/>
    </ontologyVersion>
  </ontologyItem>
</dataTemmporal>
```

Fig. 8. The difference between two versions

A fourth contribution is the description of a process to construct a schema to validate and interpret the temporal data. Although publishers can provide temporal data, there must be some means of interpreting such data. Typically, the structure of published data is described in an associated schema document. Assume that the file `gene.xsd` contains the *snapshot schema* for `gene.xml`. The snapshot schema is the schema for an individual version. The snapshot schema is a valuable guide for editing and querying individual snapshots. The snapshot schema is given (in part) in Fig. 9. Note that the schema describes the structure of the fragments shown in Fig. 4, Fig. 5, and Fig. 6. Though the individual snapshots conform to the schema, the temporal data does not. So a snapshot schema such as `gene.xsd` cannot be used (directly) to validate or interpret the temporal data of Fig. 7. Nor can the schema be used to validate version differences, such as the fragment shown in Fig. 8. In our approach a snapshot schema is annotated with additional information to create a *temporal schema*. The temporal schema describes, at a logical level, which elements can vary over time, and how those elements can change. Fig. 10 shows the temporal schema for the running example. The temporal schema includes annotations for both the gene

---

[2] Temporal data could also record the *valid time* versions (valid time is real world time) but for simplicity we consider only one kind of time in this paper, i.e., the transaction and valid times are the same (other relationships between valid and transaction time [16] can be easily modeled in our framework).

and ontology element type definitions. The annotations are shaded gray in the figure. (Section 4 describes the annotations in detail.) We present the temporal schema here to emphasize that τXSchema is fully-upwards compatible with XML Schema; that is, it extends but does not change XML Schema. A further advantage of our approach is that the temporal schema can also be used to validate the differences between versions, such as the data in Fig. 8.

```
<element name="gene">
  <complexType>
    <attribute name="name" type="text" use="required"/>
    <sequence>
      <element name="desc" type="string"/>
      <element ref="ontology" minOccurs="0" maxOccurs="unbounded"/>
    </sequence>
  </complexType>
</element>
<element name="ontology">
  <complexType>
    <attribute name="ref" type="text"/>
    <attribute name="function" type="text"/>
  </complexType>
</element>
```

Fig. 9. An extract from the gene data schema

```
<element name="gene">
  <txs:temporal>
    <txs:ItemIdentifier>
      <txs:field path="@name"/>
    </txs:ItemIdentifier>
    <txs:transactionTime kind="state" contentVarying="true"
        existenceVarying="no gaps"/>
  </txs:temporal>
    definition of gene from the snapshot schema omitted for space
</element>
<element name="ontology">
  <txs:temporal>
    <txs:ItemIdentifier>
      <txs:field path="../@name"/><txs:field path="@function"/>
    </txs:ItemIdentifier>
    <txs:transactionTime kind="state" contentVarying="true"
        existenceVarying="gaps allowed"/>
  </txs:temporal>
    definition of ontology from the snapshot schema omitted for space
</element>
```

Fig. 10. An extract from a temporal schema

3 Items and Versions

This section briefly reviews concepts related to temporal data and then discusses how to temporally associate elements in different snapshots to create temporal data.

Let D be an XML document or data collection. D is typically modeled as an ordered tree, $D = (E, V)$, where E is the set of edges and V is the set of nodes. Each edge in E is of the form (v, w, n) where v is the parent, w, is the child, and n is an ordinal representing the position of the child in the lexical ordering of the children. We will refer to XML data acquired from a (non-temporal) document as a *snapshot* indicating that it is the data at a single point in time.

Temporal data represents the history of a sequence of snapshots. Let D^T be a temporal data collection. The *snapshot operation* extracts a complete *snapshot* of D^T at a particular time. Timestamps are *not* represented in the snapshot. The *snapshot* operation is denoted as $snap(t, D^T) = D$ where D is the snapshot at time t of D^T.

Note that we haven't yet described the structure of temporal data, however it should faithfully capture entire snapshots as stated in the following definition.

Definition [Snapshot reducibility]. Let D^T be a temporal data collection. D^T is said to be *snapshot reducible* to the sequence of snapshots $D_1, \ldots, D_n$ iff for each $1 \leq k \leq n$, $D_k = snap(k, D^T)$.

To create compact temporal data it is important to identify which elements persist through changes to a data collection. We will sometimes refer to the process of associating elements that persist across various snapshots as *gluing* the elements. When a pair of elements is glued, an *item* is created. An item is an element that evolves over time through various *versions*. Only temporal elements (that is, elements of a type that has a temporal annotation as described further in Section 4) are candidates for gluing.

Determining which elements should be glued depends on two factors: the *type* of the element, and the *item identifier* for the element's type. The type of an element is the element's definition in the schema. We will denote the type of an element as $\mathcal{T}$. An element can be glued only to an element or item of the same type. An item identifier is a list of XPath expressions (much like a key in XML Schema) so we first define what it means to evaluate an XPath expression.

Definition [XPath evaluation]. Let $Eval(x, E)$ denote the result of evaluating an XPath expression E from a context node x. Given a list of XPath expressions, $L = [E_1, \ldots, E_k]$, then $Eval(x, L) = [Eval(x, E_1), \ldots, Eval(x, E_k)]$.

Since an XPath expression evaluates to a list of values, $Eval(x, L)$ evaluates to a list of lists. An item identifier is a list of XPath expressions.

Definition [Item identifier]. An *item identifier* for a temporal type, $\mathcal{T}$, is a list of XPath expressions, $L_{\mathcal{T}}$, such that for each element x of type $\mathcal{T}$, $Eval(x, L_{\mathcal{T}})$ names the *item* to which x belongs.

Each item identifier is specified by a schema designer (elsewhere we sketch a method for automatically constructing them [32]). Often an identifier will be the (snapshot) key for the element type given in the schema [4]. But an item identifier may differ from a snapshot key since the identifier should be a temporally-invariant key [22].

Example [Item identifiers]. As an example, a designer might specify the following item identifiers for the temporal elements in Fig. 7.

- `<gene>` → `[@name]`
- `<ontology>` → `[../@name, @function]`

The item identifier for a <gene> is the name of the gene, while the item identifier for an <ontology> is the gene's name (its parent's item identifier) combined with the gene's `function` attribute value.

We will further restrict item identifiers to be *unique* within a snapshot, that is, at most one element in each snapshot can belong to an item. Over time, elements that belong to different snapshots will belong to the same item. Elements that are *temporally adjacent* can be associated within an item as defined below.

Definition [Temporal adjacency]. Let x be an element of type $\mathcal{T}$ in $snap(i, D^T)$. Let y be an element of type $\mathcal{T}$ in $snap(j, D^T)$. Finally let $L_\mathcal{T}$ be the item identifier for elements of type $\mathcal{T}$. Then x is *temporally adjacent* to y if and only if $Eval(x, L_\mathcal{T}) = Eval(y, L_\mathcal{T})$ and it is not the case that there exists an element z of type $\mathcal{T}$ in a snapshot between (exclusive) the ith and j^{th} snapshots such that $Eval(z, L_\mathcal{T}) = Eval(x, L_\mathcal{T})$.

When an item is temporally adjacent to an element in a new snapshot, the element either creates a new version of the item or extends the lifetime of the latest version within the item. So an item is a sequence of versions and associated timestamps. The lifetime of each version is a set of maximal, disjoint time periods.

Definition [Item]. Let **item**(x) be the item named by Eval(x, $L_\mathcal{T}$) where x is of type $\mathcal{T}$. Then **item**(x) = $[(v_1, t_1), \ldots, (v_n, t_n)]$ where each v_i is a version of x with lifetime t_i ($1 \le i \le n$).

A version represents the content of an item in a snapshot. Basically, the version is a copy of the subtree rooted at the item, and each branch in the copy terminates at a leaf (attribute node, text node, etc.) or at the first element on that branch that is associated with an item. The element is replaced in this version with an *item reference*.

Definition [Version]. Let **item**(x) be an item of type $\mathcal{T}$ in snapshot D=(E, V). Let (E_x, V_x) be the subtree rooted at x in D. Then **version**(x, D) = (E_v, V_v) where

$$E_v = \{(a_v, b_v, n) \mid (a_x, b_x, n) \in E_x \wedge \ (b_x \text{ is an item} \Rightarrow b_v \text{ is an } \textit{item reference}) \\ \wedge (a_x \text{ is an item} \Rightarrow a_v = x) \wedge (a_x \text{ and } b_x \text{ are not items} \Rightarrow a_v = a_x \wedge b_v = b_x)\}$$

and $V_v = \{v \mid (v, \_, \_) \in E_x \vee (\_, v, \_) \in E_x\} \cup \{x\}$.

Example [Items]. Versions appear throughout the example of temporal data shown in Fig. 7. The first version of the <gene> item is a copy of the <gene> element in Fig. 4, which is the first snapshot of the data. Note that the <ontology> element is an item, so it has been replaced in Fig. 7 by an item reference whereas the <desc> element is unchanged since it is not an item.

A lifetime of a version is computed separately. The lifetime is extended when "no difference" is detected in the associated element. Differences are observed within the context of the Document Object Model (DOM).

Definition [DOM equivalence]. A pair of item versions is *DOM equivalent* if the pair meets all of the following conditions: they have the same number of children, same element tag, same set of attributes (an attribute is a name, value pair), and same text content, and for each child, the child is DOM equivalent to the corresponding child of the other (in a lexical ordering of the children).

As an aside, we observe that DOM equivalence in a temporal XML context is akin to *value equivalence* in a temporal relational database context.

DOM equivalence is used to determine versions of an item, as follows.

Definition [Versioning]. Let **item**(x) = $[(v_1, t_1), \ldots, (v_n,t_n)]$. Let **item**($y$) in snapshot D be temporally adjacent to **item**(x). Assume D is current during the period $[t, t+k]$ where t is later than any time in t_n. If v_n is DOM equivalent to **version**(y, D) then the lifetime of v_n is extended to be $t_n \cup [t, t+k]$. Otherwise, version v_{n+1}, consisting of **version**(y, D), is added to **item**(x). The lifetime of v_{n+1} is $[t, t+k]$.

A version's lifetime is extended when the version from the next snapshot (or a future snapshot) is DOM equivalent (the lifetime can have gaps or holes, although having a gap may violate a schema constraint as described in Section 4). A new version is created when temporally adjacent elements in the same item are *not* DOM equivalent.

Example [Versions]. Fig. 11 depicts the items and versions in the example in Section 2. An abstract representation of the DOM for each snapshot of the data is shown. The items in the sequence of snapshots are connected within each gray shaded region. There is one gene item and one ontology item. Each item has two versions. The transition between versions is shown as a black rectangle on the gray connection arcs. The gene item has a new version when the content of the <desc> element changes and the ontology item has a new version when its content is modified on 2005-02-14.

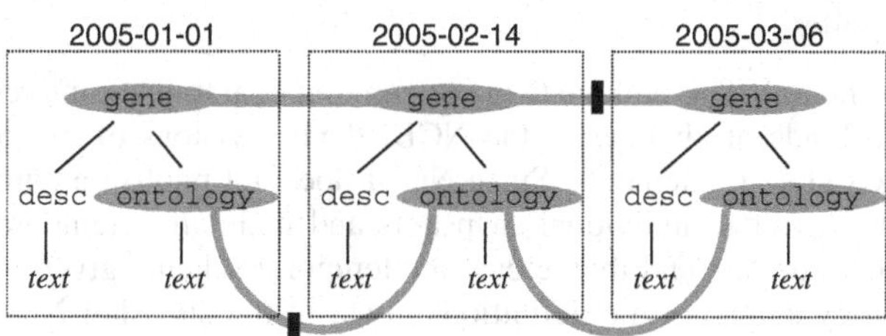

Fig. 11. Items and versions in the example

4 XML Schema Extensions

τXSchema extends XML Schema with a single annotation to denote temporal element types, but otherwise leaves XML Schema unchanged. The annotation is a `<txs:temporal>` element that can appear in the content of any element type definition. The annotation denotes that elements of that type can be time-varying. The `txs` namespace indicates that the annotation is part of τXSchema. Within a `<txs:temporal>` element there must appear an item identifier. Such an identifier has the following general form.

```
<txs:itemIdentifier
   <txs:field path="XPath expression"/>
   ...
   <txs:field path="XPath expression"/>
</txs:itemIdentifier>
```

An item identifier is list of fields, each of which is a (relative) XPath path expression.

Temporal constraints are optional. The constraints are evaluated after an item is glued. The constraints are separately specified for each kind of time, though in this paper we focus only on transaction time. The constraint specification for a `<txs:transactionTime>` element has the following general form.

```
<txs:transactionTime
    txs:kind="state (default) | event"
    txs:contentVarying="false (default) | true"
    txs:existenceVarying="false | gaps allowed (default) | no gaps" />
```

The `kind` attribute specifies whether the lifetime of an item has duration; a *state* kind of annotation implies continuity, while an *event* signifies that the lifetime is a single instant. The terminology is borrowed from temporal databases [14] where events occur at a single instant in time (e.g., a wedding on July 14, 2005), whereas a state occurs over a period of time (e.g., married from July 14, 2005 until now). The `contentVarying` attribute is used to specify whether an item's content must be constant over time, or can vary. The `existenceVarying` attribute governs whether the item can come and go in various snapshots. If the value of the attribute is *false*, then the item must be in every snapshot (or never appear). If the existence is *no gaps*, then once the item has been deleted from a snapshot, it cannot reappear in a later snapshot. Otherwise, the item's existence is unrestricted. Each attribute is optional, as is the transaction time element. If the attribute is not specified, the indicated default value applies.

Example [τXSchema]**.** The biologists in our running example are interested primarily in tracking two kinds of changes to the NCBI data: revisions of the gene itself and revisions of the ontology elements. Since NCBI does not publish a temporal schema, biologists must download individual snapshots and maintain a temporal data collection locally. Towards this end they create the temporal schema given in Fig. 10. The gene and ontology element type definitions given in the snapshot NCBI schema are annotated to indicate that they are temporal element types, and so a version history will be kept for each element of those types. While genes can be both content and existence varying, a gene's existence is slightly constrained to disallow gaps since a gene. The constraint specifies that in order for the data to be valid a gene cannot be deleted and then (later) reinserted.

Currently, τXSchema has a restricted set of temporal constraints. Richer classes of temporal constraints have been proposed [7], but for simplicity and brevity we limit the variety of constraints in the current system.

5 The Representational Schema

The representational schema is a conventional XML Schema document that is automatically generated from a τXSchema document. It is used to validate temporal data using a conventional validating parser. This section describes how to weave the temporal annotations into a snapshot schema to create the representational schema. The representational schema is transitory; it is needed only for validation, and in fact need never be seen by the user.

An XML Schema specification can be viewed as a grammar. The grammar consists of productions of the following form for each element type.

$S \rightarrow$ <s> α </s>

In the above production, α describes the content of elements of type S.

A temporal schema denotes that some of the element types are time-varying. To construct a representational schema, several new productions are added to the schema for each temporal element type; no productions are removed from the non-temporal schema though some are modified. Since only elements can be temporal, this section focuses on the element-related components of a schema. The construction process consists of several steps. We'll illustrate the process by describing what is done for a single, representative temporal element type, S.

The first step is to add a production to indicate that the element type S is temporal. The temporal production has following form:

$S_{Temporal} \rightarrow$ <s$_{Temporal}$ itemRef="m"/>

where <s$_{Temporal}$> denotes a temporal element of type S and `itemRef` is a reference to an item of type S. Next a production is added to define the S item type.

$S_{Item} \rightarrow$ <s$_{Item}$ itemId="n"> $S_{Version}+$ </s$_{Item}$>

An item has a unique `itemId` value, and consists of a list of *versions*. The third step is to add a production to specify each version of type S. The production for a version of an element of type S has the following form:

$S_{Version} \rightarrow$ <s$_{Version}$> τ S </s$_{Version}$>

where τ is the schema of the timestamp and S is the non-temporal definition of the element's type. The timestamp in a version records the lifetime of the version. We do not impose a particular schema for a timestamp, rather we assume that the schema is given separately and imported into the temporal document's schema. Without loss of generality we will assume that each timestamp has the following form.

$\tau \rightarrow$ <time start="..." end="..."/>

The next step is to modify the *context* in which a temporal element appears. For each temporal element type, S, that appears in the left-hand-side of a production, replace S with $S_{Temporal}$. For example, assume that the schema has a production of the following form:

$X \rightarrow$ <x> $\beta\, S\, \gamma$ </x>

where β and γ describe arbitrary content before and after S, respectively. The production is replaced by the following production.

$X \rightarrow$ <x> $\beta\, S_{Temporal}\, \gamma$ </x>

Only the element type is replaced, any other constraints on the element are kept (e.g., minoccurs and maxoccurs are unaffected).

This process is repeated for every temporal element type. The final step is to augment the root element type with an additional production that appends a list of items. Let the root be an element of type R. Then the new root becomes the following.

$R_{Temporal} \rightarrow$ <data$_{Temporal}$> $R?\, X_{Item}{}^{*}$ </data$_{Temporal}$>

where X_{Item} is a list of item types. The production for X_{Item} is given below, where each S^{i}_{Item} is one of k item types.

$X_{Item} \rightarrow S^{1}_{Item} \mid ... \mid S^{k}_{Item}$

An additional step is needed to recast constraints that appear in the original schema. One such constraint is the uniqueness constraint imposed by a DTD identifier or XML Schema key definition. Since the same identifiers and key values can appear in multiple versions of an element, such values are no longer unique in a temporal document, even though they are unique within each snapshot. In temporal relational databases, the concept of a *temporal key*, which combines a snapshot key with a timestamp, has been introduced. Temporal keys can be enforced by a temporal validating parser, but not by a conventional parser. So constraints that impose uniqueness within a snapshot must be relaxed or redefined as follows. The value of each `id` type attribute in a time-varying element is rewritten to be a unique value; `idRefs` are similarly rewritten. Finally, schema keys are rewritten to include `itemIds` and version start and end times, creating a temporal key.

It is important to note that the production for the root of the temporal data specifies that it is just a list of items. This enables temporal data to be incrementally validated, which is critical in data streaming applications.

Example [Representational schema construction]**.** Let's go through the construction process with an example. Assume that the productions in the schema for the example in Fig. 6 are given below.

R→ `<data>` *G*+ `</data>`
G→ `<gene>` *D*[*N* | *text*]* `</gene>`
D→ `<desc>` *text* `</desc>`
N→ `<ontology ref="`*text*`">` *text* `</ontology>`

Next, assume that the `<ontology>` element type is temporally annotated, as in Fig. 10. The schema would be transformed as follows. First, productions are added for the temporal elements.

$N_{Temporal}$ → `<ontology`$_{Temporal}$ `itemRef="`*m*`"/>`

Next, productions are added for the items of temporal elements.

N_{Item}→ `<ontology`$_{Item}$ `itemId="`*n*`">` $N_{Version}$+ `</ontology`$_{Item}$`>`

Productions are then added for each version type, and for the timestamp(s) in each version.

$N_{Version}$→ `<ontology`$_{Version}$`>` τ *N* `</ontology`$_{Version}$`>`
τ → `<time start="..." end="..."/>`

Next, the root is modified to include the new productions.

$R_{Temporal}$→ `<data`$_{Temporal}$`>`*R*? [G_{Item}|N_{Item}]* `</data`$_{Temporal}$`>`

6 Related Work

Temporal databases has been an area of intense study for the past 25 years [[29]], with Oracle now perhaps having the most mature temporal support: transaction-time, valid-time, and bitemporal tables, current modifications, and automatic support for temporal referential integrity [[25]]. Concerning the representation of temporal data and documents on the web, Grandi has created a bibliography of previous work in this area [13]. Marian et al. [20] discuss versioning to track the history of downloaded documents. Chien, Tsotras and Zaniolo [5] have researched techniques for compactly storing multiple versions of an evolving XML document. Buneman et al. [4] provide another means to store a single copy of an element that occurs in many snapshots. This paper differs from all of the above papers since our focus is on temporal schemas and validation.

It is possible to capture transaction time information for documents through change analysis, as discussed below. Cho and Garcia-Molina [6] provide evidence that some web resources change frequently (though not specifically XML resources). Nguyen et al. [23] describe how to detect changes in XML documents that are accessible via the web [30]. Dyreson et al. [9] describe how a web server can capture some of the versions of a time-varying document. Yu and Popa provide an algorithm to convert either a list of changes or just the original and altered schema to a (more semantic) evolution mapping [31].

There are various XML schemas that have been proposed in the literature and in the commercial arena. We chose to extend XML Schema because it is backed by the W3C and supports most major features available in other XML schemas [19]. It would be relatively straightforward to apply the concepts in this paper to develop time support for other XML schema languages; less straightforward but possible would be to apply our approach to other data models, such as UML [24]. As an example, we have extended the Unifying Semantic Model, a conceptual model similar to the ER Model, to utilize annotations [17] very similar to what we propose here.

Recently there has been interest in incremental validation of XML [2][26]. τXSchema takes a orthogonal approach to incremental validation in so far as the changes to documents can be validated in isolation.

Only one paper has previously addressed the issue of validating temporal data [8]. In previous work we developed the τXSchema data model and architecture. In this paper we extend the architecture with items and versions, and a different construction process for the representational schema. Also, this paper directly extends XML Schema, unlike our previous paper.

τXSchema focuses on *instance versioning* (representing a time-varying XML instance document) rather than *schema versioning* [12][27]. The schema describes which aspects of an instance document change over time. But we assume that the schema itself is fixed, with no element types, data types, or attributes being added to or removed from the schema over time. In other work we consider schema versioning [10].

One final area of related work is *intensional XML data* (also termed dynamic XML documents [1]), that is, parts of XML documents that consist of programs that generate data [21]. Incorporating intensional XML data is beyond the scope of this paper.

7 Conclusion

This paper presents τXSchema, which extends XML Schema to support temporal data. τXSchema helps schema designers easily convert existing snapshot schemas to temporal schemas for the construction, management, and validation of temporal data and documents. A temporal schema is created by adding annotations to denote that some element types are temporal. Each annotation includes an item identifier, which is used to glue elements, yielding an item. Each change in an item over time creates a new version of the item. To validate a temporal document, a temporal schema is first converted to a *representational* schema, which is a conventional XML Schema document that describes how the temporal information is represented. The representational schema is carefully constructed to ensure every snapshot of the temporal document conforms to the snapshot schema (which is the temporal schema without the temporal annotations). A conventional validating parser is then used to validate the temporal document against the representational schema. The temporal document is also checked by a temporal constraint checker.

The architectural design of the infrastructure and even of the schema language itself is driven by the critical requirement from biologists, and indeed, from data users generally, of *upward compatibility*, of data, of schemas, and even of tools and infrastructure, in the support of time-varying data. This paper has demonstrated how a schema for time-varying data can be extended very simply from a snapshot schema, and then how the data manipulation, principally gluing and validation of such data and schema, can be done, utilizing conventional, well-understood tools.

In future we plan to integrate τXSchema with an XML-based editor. By incorporating τXSchema, an editor should be able to provide improved revision control and a *change tracking* feature. We have done this for an editor for the afore-mentioned temporal USM conceptual model [18]; it turns out that the upward-compatibility of the language design extends even to design support environment. Another broad area of work is optimization and efficiency. Currently there is no separation of elements or attributes based on the relative frequency of update. In the situation that some elements (for example) vary at a significantly different rate than other elements, it may prove more efficient to split the schema into pieces such that elements with similar "rates of change" are together [15].

References

[1] S. Abiteboul et al., "Dynamic XML Documents with Distribution and Replication," in *SIGMOD*, 2003. San Diego, CA. pp. 527-538.

[2] D. Barbosa et al., "Efficient Incremental Validation of XML Documents," in *ICDE*, 2004. Boston, MA, pp. 671-682.

[3] P. Buneman, S. Khanna, and W. C. Tan, "Why and Where: A Characterization of Data Provenance," in *ICDT*, 2001. pp. 316-330.

[4] P. Buneman et al., *Keys for XML*. Computer Networks, 2002. **39**(5): 473-487.

[5] S. Chien, V. Tsotras, and C. Zaniolo, *Efficient schemes for managing multiversion XML documents*. VLDB Journal, 2002. **11**(4): pp. 332-353.

[6] J. Cho and H. Garcia-Molina, *Estimating frequency of change*. ACM Trans. on Internet Technology, 2003. **3**(3): pp. 256-290.

[7] J. Chomicki, *Efficient Checking of Temporal Integrity Constraints Using Bounded History Encoding*. ACM Transactions on Database Systems, 1995. **20**(2): pp. 149-186.

[8] F. Currim et al., "A Tale of Two Schemas: Creating a Temporal XML Schema from a Snapshot Schema with τXSchema," in *EDBT*. 2004, pp. 348-365.

[9] C. Dyreson, H.-L. Lin, and Y. Wang. "Managing Versions of Web Documents in a Transaction-time Web Server," in *WWW*, 2004. New York, NY. pp. 422-432.

[10] C. Dyreson et al., "Validating Quicksand: Schema Versioning in τXSchema," in *XSDM*, 2006. Atlanta, GA, to appear.

[11] S. K. Gadia and J. H. Vaishnav. "A Query Language for a Homogeneous Temporal Database," in *PODS*. 1985, pp. 51-56.

[12] F. Grandi, "SVMgr: A Tool for the Management of Schema Versioning," in *ER*, 2004, pp. 860-861.

[13] F. Grandi, *An Annotated Bibliography on Temporal and Evolution Aspects in the World-WideWeb*. 2003, TimeCenter Technical Report.

[14] C. S. Jensen and C. Dyreson (eds.), "The Consensus Glossary of Temporal Database Concepts – Feb. 1998 Ver.," in *Temporal Databases*, 1998. pp. 367-405.

[15] C. S. Jensen and R. T. Snodgrass, *Semantics of Time-Varying Information*. Information Systems, 1996. **21**(4): pp. 311-352.

[16] C. S. Jensen and R. T. Snodgrass, *Temporal Specialization and Generalization*. IEEE Trans. on Knowledge and Data Engineering, 1994. **6**(6): pp. 954-974.

[17] V. Khatri, S. Ram, and R. T. Snodgrass, *Augmenting a Conceptual Model with Geospatiotemporal Annotations*. IEEE Transactions on Knowledge and Data Engineering, 2004. **16**(11): pp. 1324-1338.

[18] V. Khatri, S. Ram, and R. T. Snodgrass, *On Augmenting Database Design-Support Environments to Capture the Geo-Spatio-Temporal Data Semantics*. Information Systems, 2005: pp. 1-37.

[19] D. Lee and W. Chu, *Comparative Analysis of Six XML Schema Languages*. SIGMOD Record, 2000. **29**(3): pp. 76-87.

[20] A. Marian et al., "Change-Centric Management of Versions in an XML Warehouse," in *VLDB*, 2001. Roma, Italy, pp. 581-590.

[21] T. Milo et al., "Exchanging Intensional XML Data, " in *SIGMOD*, 2003. San Diego, CA, pp. 289-300.

[22] S. B. Navathe and R. Ahmed, *Temporal Relational Model and a Query Language*. Information Sciences, 1989. **49**(1): pp. 147-175.

[23] B. Nguyen et al., "Monitoring XML Data on the Web," in *SIGMOD*. 2001. Santa Barbara, CA, pp. 437-448.

[24] OMG, Unified Modeling Language (UML), v1.5. 2003.

[25] Oracle Corporation, *Application Developer's Guide – Workspace Manager*, 10g Release 1, December 2003.

[26] Y. Papakonstantinou and V. Vianu, "Incremental Validation of XML Documents," in *ICDT*, 2003. Siena, Italy, pp. 47-63.

[27] J. Roddick, *A Survey of Schema Versioning Issues for Database Systems*. Information and Software Technology, 1995. **37**(7): pp. 383-393.

[28] *Service Data Objects for Java Specification*. http://www-128.ibm. com/dev-eloperworks/ webservices/library/specification/ws-sdo, current as of March 2006.

[29] A. Tansel, J. Clifford, S. Gadia, S. Jajodia, A. Segev, and R. T. Snodgrass, *Temporal Databases: Theory, Design, and Implementation*, Benjamin/Cummins Publishing Company, 1993

[30] L. Xyleme, *A dynamic warehouse for XML Data of the Web*. IEEE Data Engineering Bulletin, 2001. **24**(2): p. 40-47.

[31] C. Yu and L. Popa, "Semantic Adaptation of Schema Mappings when Schemas Evolve," in *VLDB*, 2005. Trondheim, Norway, pp. 1006-1017.

[32] S. Zhang, C Dyreson, and R. T. Snodgrass. "Schema-Less, Semantics-Based Change Detection for XML Documents," in *WISE*, 2004. Brisbane, pp. 279-290.

A Quantitative Summary of XML Structures

Zi Lin[1], Bingsheng He[2], and Byron Choi[1]

[1] Nanyang Technological University
{linzi, kkchoi}@ntu.edu.sg
[2] Hong Kong University of Science and Technology
saven@cs.ust.hk

Abstract. Statistical summaries in relational databases mainly focus on the distribution of data values and have been found useful for various applications, such as query evaluation and data storage. As xml has been widely used, e.g. for online data exchange, the need for (corresponding) statistical summaries in xml has been evident. While relational techniques may be applicable to the data values in xml documents, novel techniques are requried for summarizing the structures of xml documents. In this paper, we propose metrics for major structural properties, in particular, nestings of entities and one-to-many relationships, of XML documents. Our technique is different from the existing ones in that we generate a quantitative summary of an xml structure. By using our approach, we illustrate that some popular real-world and synthetic xml benchmark datasets are indeed highly skewed and hardly hierarchical and contain few recursions. We wish this preliminary finding shreds insight on improving the design of xml benchmarking and experimentations.

1 Introduction

eXtensible Markup Language (XML) is known to be a *flexible* [33] medium for online data exchange. The flexibility of XML is mainly[1] due to its capability of representing nested entities and one-to-many relationships in a tree. In comparison, the relational model is rigid and flat: neither nested entities nor one-to-many relationships are allowed in a single relation. In addition, the simplicity of the relational model has been one of its major strengths; implementations of the relational model have also been widely tested in industrial-strength applications. While XML repositories have been emerging (*e.g.* [17,12,21]), there has been an evident reservation on the advance from relational-based technology to XML-based technology. The host of work on reusing relational database systems for storing and querying XML (*e.g.* [31,30,11,3,14]) might reflect this standpoint. However, intuitively, relational systems are preferable *only when* an XML document is a mild generalization of relations. Otherwise, the impedance mismatch between the tree model and the relational model can become problematic where native XML/XML-based approaches should be adopted.

[1] For simplicity, we do not focus on the rich set of scalar data types (*e.g.* integers) in XML SCHEMAs.

D.W. Embley, A. Olivé, and S. Ram (Eds.): ER 2006, LNCS 4215, pp. 228–240, 2006.

In this paper, we define metrics for some structural properties of XML documents. We hope the metrics answer an informal question: Is an XML document "tree-like" or "relational-like"? Similar to effective techniques widely used in relational databases [24], we summarize XML structures using histograms and tree/graph structures and generate a quantitative summary from these structures, *i.e.*, our approach does not require DTDS/XML SCHEMAS. A goal of having a quantitative summary is that it may provide XML researchers (i.e. human) insights on XML documents. The advantage of quantitative approaches may be summarized by Lord Kelvin's remarks, *"When you can measure what you are speaking about, and express it in numbers, you know something about it; but when you cannot express it in numbers, your knowledge is of a meager and unsatisfactory kind; it may be the beginning of knowledge, but you have scarcely in your thoughts advanced to the state of science."* As we shall see soon, we focus on the properties that cannot be derived from DTDS/XML SCHEMAS. Specifically, we examine two important structural properties of XML: (1) entity nestings and (2) one-to-many relationships.

Knowing the structures of XML datasets, in practice, can be fruitful to XML research, *e.g.* XML storage. For example, consider a simplified DBLP dataset [17] shown in Figure 1 and the `book-author` edges in the figure. For illustration purpose, assume that `book` is an entity and `author` is another entity. The `book-author` edges represent the relationship between `book` and `author`. Since DBLP is a real-world dataset, one may expect the distribution of the number of authors per book is a Gaussian distribution. However, we discovered the skewness (see Section 3 for the definition adopted) of this distribution is large. The result is shown in Figure 6. The x-axis and y-axis are the number of authors of a book and the number of books with x authors in DBLP document, respectively. Similar highly skewed distributions of `inproceeding-author`, `proceeding-author` and `article-author` are found. The implication of this finding is that if one simply "inlines" three authors into a `book` relation, such a `book` relation covers 97% of the books in DBLP and the remaining authors of the books can be stored in a small overflow relation. This storage scheme allows retrieving the relationship between `book` and `author` by a projection on a `book` relation and a join between `book` and the small overflow relation, as opposed to a join between all `books` and all `authors`. We shall discuss some more research on XML storage in the related work section.

As a side product of our investigation, our metrics shred insights on some properties of synthetic XML datasets. For example, we report that the XMARK dataset comprises skewed distributions of structures whereas the XBENCH dataset consists of mostly Gaussian or uniform distributions of structures. While no one has asserted that XML structures are supposed to be uniform, there does not appear obvious reasons for using highly skewed data for benchmarking either. Furthermore, XML algorithms, *e.g.* DTD validation in streaming XML [29] and updates through XML views [5], for recursive XMLS are more technically challenging than their counterparts for non-recursive XMLS. Unfortunately, [9] showed that real-world DTDS are often recursive. This paper reports, in quantitative terms, that the recursive part, if any, of real-world XML documents is often tiny. Consider a simplified XMARK document shown in Figure 3 for example. The percentage of root-to-leaf paths with recursive elements is only 9.3% of the total number of all root-to-leaf paths in the XMARK document. Hence, algorithms for non-recursive XMLs may often work in practice or "survive" in experimental evaluations; but *problems may occur occasionally.*

The two main goals of this paper are (1) to define metrics for describing structural properties of an XML document, in order to study the informal concept of tree-ness of an XML document and (2) to survey a few popular XML repositories using our metrics. Applications of our metrics to specific research problems, *e.g.*, XPATH/XQUERY selectivity estimation and XML compression, are beyond the scope of this paper. For presentation simplicity, we omit the analysis on the scalar data in XML documents.

Contributions. The main contributions of this paper are listed below:

- We present metrics for describing the nestings of entities and the number of each kind of attributes of an entity in XML datasets;
- We apply the metrics on a few popular[2] real-world and synthetic XML datasets for experimentation, among other uses. We reveal that these datasets are highly skewed and hardly hierarchical and contain few recursions.

Organization. The remainder of the paper is organized as follows. Section 2 presents the background of the computation of our metrics. Section 3 presents each of our XML metrics in detail. We apply our metrics on a few popular real-world and synthetic XML datasets in Section 4. Section 5 discusses the related work on XML metrics and statistics. Conclusions and discussions on future works are presented in Section 6.

2 Preliminaries

In this section, we present some background information for the subsequent sections.

Prefix trees. The computation of our metrics of an XML document relies on the construction of the prefix tree of the document. Specifically, we associate histograms (structural information) to a prefix tree. A node in a prefix tree represents a prefix occurred in a document. First, a node in a prefix tree is associated with the support, *sup*, of the prefix in the document. Second, we define a *support ratio* between each pair of parent-child nodes (A, B) in the prefix tree, *i.e.*, sup_B/sup_A, to estimate the possible location of one-to-many relationships. There are three possible cases for the support ratio:

1. The support ratio is between 0 to 1. This implies B is probably A's optional child;
2. The support ratio is 1. This often implies a one-to-one relationship;

[2] According to Google scholars system, `http://scholar.google.com`, March 2006, the number of citations on these datasets is over 300.

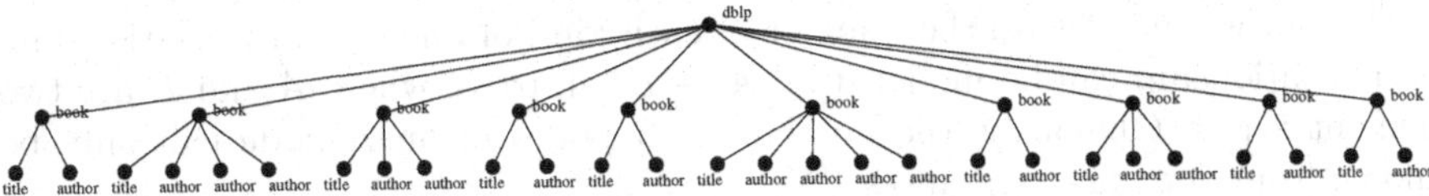

Fig. 1. Simplified DBLP document T_{dblp}

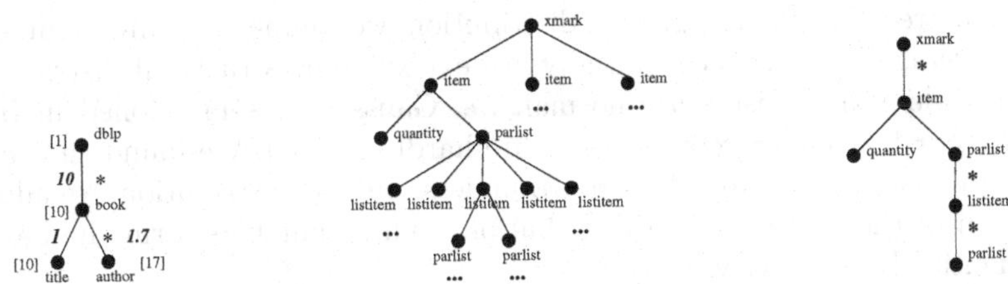

Fig. 2. Prefix tree of T_{dblp}, S_{dblp}

Fig. 3. Simplified XMARK document T_{xmark}

Fig. 4. Prefix tree of T_{xmark}, S_{xmark}

3. The support ratio is greater than one. This indicates a one-to-many relationship. We regard the edges in this class as *star edges*.

There are exceptions for these implications. Consider a pathological document in which one half of the A nodes do not have any B children and another half of the A nodes have exactly two B children. The support ratio indicates a false one-to-one relationship. However, such exceptions are rare, as we observed from our datasets.

Consider a simplified DBLP XML document shown in Figure 1 as an example. Its prefix tree is shown in Figure 2. We show the support of a node in a square bracket. Support ratios are placed next to the edges. We mark a star with an asterisk sign. Similarly, we show the stars of the prefix tree of the simplified XMARK dataset (Figure 3) in Figure 4.

Finally, for each star edge (A, B), we build a histogram for the number of B nodes of an A node.

Structural properties. In this paper, we focus on two major structural properties allowed by XML. These two properties can only be determined by the document instances, not DTDS/XML SCHEMAS.

First, we study the nestings of entities in an XML document. In the absence of user specifications, one could at best "estimate" entities in XML instances. In this paper, we assume that a star edge is an indication of a one-to-many relationship between two entities since such edges in the document instance cannot be naturally represented by a single relation. A complication here is that entities can be recursively defined in XML. Consider the XMARK dataset as an example. A `parlist` subtree may contain `parlist` subtrees. A survey [9] on DTDS shows that a large number of real-world DTDS are recursive. We investigate whether the XML documents are indeed recursive.

Second, we investigate the number of each kind of one-to-many relationship. Such relationship can be modeled by $A \rightarrow B^*$ in DTDs, where A and B are two element types. Obviously, the number of B nodes of an A node can only be known from document instances. [3]

Statistics used. Similar to the techniques developed for relational databases, we use a few statistical terms to describe the histograms (or distributions) stored in a prefix tree. Specifically, given a distribution, we compute its minimum, maximum, average and variance. Initially, we expect some structural distributions of real-world XML datasets are normal, *i.e.* Gaussian. As mentioned in Introduction, our benchmark XML datasets are hardly normal. We found that many structural distributions are skewed. To understand the distribution, we adopt a definition of the skewness of a distribution. These numbers form the basis of our quantitative summary.

3 The Metrics

In this section, we present our metrics for XML structures. Then, we describe its meaning and possible implications of each metric. For simplicity, we often refer root-to-leaf paths to as (simple) paths.

Our metrics are listed below. When applicable, we compute the minimum, maximum, variance and average of these metrics, which quantify the structure of an XML document.

1. *The number of paths;*
2. *The length of a path;*
3. *The number of star edges in the prefix tree;*
4. *The number of star edges of a path;*
5. *The number of recursive/non-recursive element types;*
6. *The number of recursive elements of a path;*
7. *The number of a particular kind of star edges of a node;*
8. *The skewness of the number of a particular kind of star edges of a node.*

The first three metrics are some (arbitrary) basic counts of an XML document. We shall discuss the next five metrics in more detail.

The number of star edges of a path. A path p in a document must also appear in the prefix tree. We count the number of edges in p that have a star edge correspondence in the prefix tree. The number of star edges in a path implies the number of nested one-to-many relationship in a tree. The larger the number of star edges is, the more the tree and a relation mismatch.

The number of recursive/non-recursive element types. This metric measures the number of recursive and non-recursive element types in a document.

[3] XML SCHEMAs allow specifying the min- and max-occurrence constraints of a repetition. However, these constraints do not accurately describe the multiplicities in a conforming document instance.

The number of recursive elements of a path. This metric attempts to quantify the recursiveness of an XML document to some extent. When elements can be recursively defined, *e.g.* `parlist` is defined in terms of `parlist`, the star hierarchy can only be known from the document. We define the number of recursive elements in a path p in a document T to be $\sum_{e \in R}$ (the count of e in p - 1), where R is the set of recursive element types in T. Algorithms for non-recursive XML may not work on documents with a large number of recursive elements in paths.

The number of a particular kind of star edges of a node. This metric measures the multiplicity of each kind of star edges of a node. Specifically, given a star edge (A, B) in a prefix tree, this metric counts the number of B children of an A node. The edges are often modeled by $A \rightarrow B^*$ in DTDs and a one-to-many relationship between A and B in ER diagrams.

The skewness of the number of a particular kind of star edges of a node. The distributions of the number of a particular kind of star edges of a node, i.e. the previous metric, of our XML benchmark datasets have a large variance. Hence, we investigate the distribution of the numbers obtained by the previous metric. In particular, we compute the skewness of the distributions, since data compression algorithms often work effectively on skewed data. The skewness is defined as $\sum_{i=1}^{n}(x_i - \bar{x})^3/(n\text{-}1)\sigma^3$, where n, x_i, $\bar{x}$ and σ are the size, an individual value, the mean and the standard derivation of a distribution, respectively.

External construction of prefix trees. When the amount of memory available is larger than the size of the prefix tree S of the input document T and the histogram N of star edges, one can easily compute S, the star edges and Metrics 1, 2, 5 and 6 in one pass of T. Metrics 3 can then be derived from S in the size of S. The remaining metrics are determined by a second pass of T followed by a scan on S and N. The overall complexity for computing all metrics is $2|T|+2|S|+|N|$.

When the prefix tree S does not fit into memory, we apply a simple divide-and-conquer method to construct S, while keeping the structure of depth first traversal. We outline the construction method as follows. (1) We traverse the document in depth first manner and maintain a root-to-current-node p as the traversal proceeds. (2) We construct a tree T_i for each M consecutive edges encountered during the traversal, where M is the amount of memory available. Initially, T_i contains p only. The edges in p are annotated as *edges in the previous subtrees*. The next M edges are added to T_i in a straightforward manner as in the internal construction of the prefix tree. (3) For each T_i, we build its prefix tree S_i. We assume that each S_i fit into memory comfortably. (4) We merge two consecutive prefix trees, S_i and S_{i+1}, by traversing the two trees "in parallel". Note that during the merge, only two edges, and their associated histograms, are needed to be stored in memory. The edges with annotations in S_{i+1} are not merged as they already appeared in the previous subtrees. This operation requires $|S_i| + |S_{i+1}|$. We obtain S of T by merging S_is iteratively. Once S is constructed, even its size may be larger than the memory size, the metrics can still be computed in two passes of S. The total number of scans on T for computing all metrics is $1 + \log(|T|/M)$.

4 A Survey on XML Benchmarks

In this section, we apply our metrics on a few popular XML datasets. The main goal of this section is to illustrate how these metrics are useful to understand XML datasets and the current state of experimentations conducted by the XML community. Hence, we present, compare and visualize numbers obtained from different XML datasets, as opposed to presenting individual summary of numbers.

XML benchmark datasets. We first describe our real-world datasets. DBLP is the XML version of DBLP Computer Science bibliography datasets [17]. It contains bibliography information of conference papers, articles, books, master and PhD theses, etc. NASA is the dataset converted from legacy flat file format by NASA XML project [21]. SP is a curated protein sequence database SWISSPROT [12]. Next, we describe the synthetic datasets used. We used two XML benchmark datasets, namely XMARK [28] and XBENCH [34], denoted as XK and XB, respectively. XMARK datasets contain synthetic auction transactions. The XMARK generator [27] allows users to vary the size of the generated dataset by providing a scaling factor. We used a few scaling factors to generate our synthetic datasets. We noted that the structural properties of these datasets remained roughly the same as the dataset size varies. Hence, we report the results from XMARK datasets with scaling factor 1. For XBENCH, we used the four example XBENCH datasets, namely TC/SD, TC/MD, DC/SD and DC/MD, shipped with the data generator [32]. (TC, DC, SD and MD stand for text-centric, data-centric, single document and multiple documents, respectively.) Note that [32] may also take templates, that describe the abstract structure of the synthetic data, as an input of data generation. When XBENCH produces multiple datasets, we concatenate them into a single dataset before checking its structural properties.

Results. We apply the first two metrics on the XML datasets. We present the numbers for these datasets in Table 1.

Table 1. Simple paths in the benchmark XML datasets

Dataset	DBLP	NASA	SP	XK	XB TC/SD	XB TC/MD	XB DC/SD	XB DC/MD
# of paths	7.5M	473K	2.0M	1.2M	250K	34K	158K	225
Minimum length	3	3	3	4	4	4	3	3
Maximum length	6	8	5	12	8	8	8	5
Average length	3.3	6.2	3.7	6.3	6.9	6.1	5.8	4.1
Variance	0.001	1.5	0.48	3.96	0.45	0.29	1.9	0.29

There has been a large body of work on storing XML as an edge table [14] in relational databases. The number of joins required for evaluating an XPATH descendant step in the absence of XML indexes, is bounded by the depth of a document. Table 1 shows that the longest path in the datasets surveyed is often small. One non-trivial fact is that the variance of the length of simple paths of our datasets is very small. Consider DBLP as an example. While the length of the longest simple path is 6, the variance of the length of paths is close to zero. This indicates that the paths in DBLP are "regular". There is one exception: The simple paths in XMARK are often lengthy (12) and the variance of their length is 3.96. This shows the paths in XMARK is rather complex.

To study the nestings of star edges, we apply the third and the fourth metrics on the benchmark XML datasets. The number of star edges in the prefix tree of DBLP, NASA, SP, XK, XB TC/SD, XB TC/MD, XB DC/SD and XB DC/MD are 52, 26, 95, 314, 12, 13, 5 and 9, respectively. Except for DBLP, SWISSPROT and XMARK, the number of star edges in the prefix tree is far fewer than 50. Recall that a star can be modeled by a one-to-many relationship in ER diagrams. When a relation is created to capture a one-to-many relationship, the number of relations required is small [31]. Therefore, most of these XML datasets can be efficiently stored and queried by using mature relational technology.

The number of star edges in a prefix tree is not sufficient for describing the hierarchy of (or the nestings in) the datasets. We apply the fourth metric – the number of star edges on paths – on the benchmark datasets. For the discussion purpose, we present the breakdown of the numbers in Table 2.

Table 2. The number of star edges in simple paths of the benchmark XML datasets

Dataset	DBLP	NASA	SP	XK	XB TC/SD	XB TC/MD	XB DC/SD	XB DC/MD
# of paths w. 1 star	3.1M	22.5K	9	521K	713	143	59.4K	160K
# of paths w. 2 stars	4.4M	102K	1.06M	452K	14K	2035	82.9K	65K
# of paths w. 3 stars	226	227K	972K	176K	224K	2623	15.2K	0
# of paths w. 4 stars	0	14.5K	0	57K	12K	24.5K	0	0
# of paths w. 5 stars	0	108K	0	4.9K	0	4113	0	0
# of paths w. 6 stars	0	0	0	0	0	341	0	0

The maximum number of star edges on paths is 6. Note also that the number of stars on a path is at least one in practice. For example, consider the `dblp` dataset again. The root node, `dblp`, of `dblp` has many `book` children and `dblp-book` is a star edge. The breakdown shows that the number of star edges on paths exhibits a Gaussian distribution. Also the average number of star edges on paths is small. That is, these datasets can be considered as a mild generalization of relations, not similar to a tall tree.

Then, we used the fifth metric to measure the number of recursive element types in the XML benchmark datasets. These datasets, including the text centric (TC) XBENCH datasets, contain only one or two recursive element types. The recursive elements in DBLP, NASA, XMARK and XBENCH TC/MD are (`sub` and `sup`), (`para`), (`listitem` and `parlist`) and (`subsec`), respectively.

Next, we used the sixth metric to illustrate the recursions in the paths of the benchmark datasets. The results are presented in Table 3. We found that

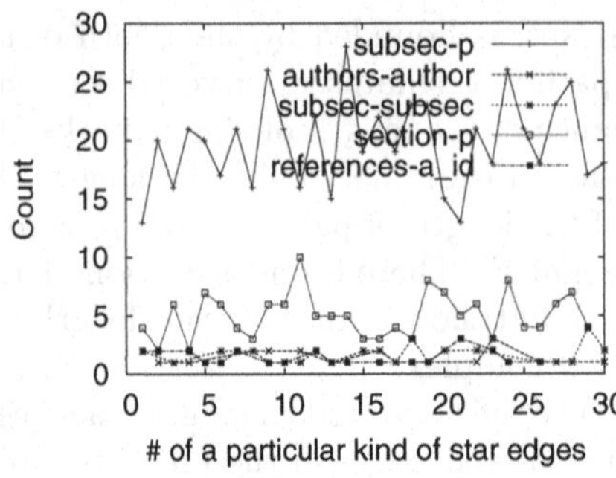

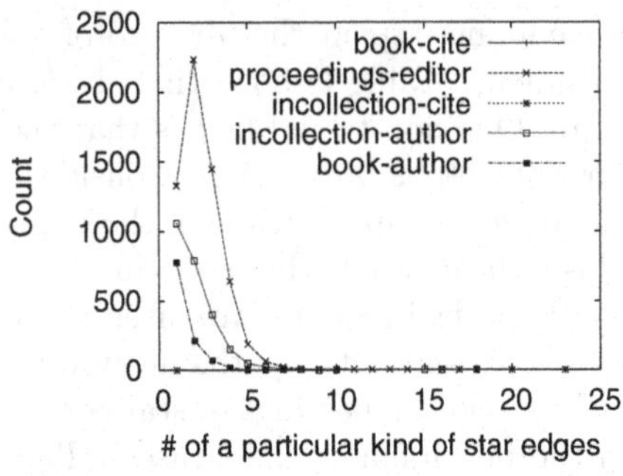

Fig. 5. The five distributions with the highest variance on the number of star edges (XBENCH TC/MD)

Fig. 6. The five distributions with the highest variance on the number of star edges (DBLP)

although DTDs may often be recursive, the recursions in the document instances are often simple. The only fairly recursive XML datasets in our benchmark datasets are XMARK and XBENCH TC/MD datasets. The number of recursions in the paths of XMARK is always 2 while that of XBENCH TC/MD is mostly 1. Due to the simplicity of the benchmark datasets, algorithms for non-recursive XML datasets may continue to work on these datasets. However, these datasets are insufficient to show the benefits of algorithms for recursive XML datasets.

Table 3. The number of recursions in simple paths in XML benchmark datasets

Dataset	DBLP	NASA	SP	XK	XB TC/SD	XB TC/MD	XB DC/SD	XB DC/MD
# of paths w. 1 recursion	15	110	0	0	0	4113	0	0
# of paths w. 2 recursions	0	0	0	112K	0	341	0	0
% of recursive paths	0%	0%	0%	9.3%	0%	13%	0%	0%

We applied the seventh metric on the XML benchmark datasets. We visualize our results for discussion purposes. For each star edge (A, B) in the prefix tree, we obtain a distribution – the number of B children of an A node. Except for the datasets generated by XBENCH, such distributions of the datasets are highly skewed. For example, we show five of such distributions with the highest variance in XBENCH in Figure 5. The figure shows that XML structures in XBENCH appear random or uniform. In comparison, as shown in Figure 6, such distributions in DBLP are highly skewed.

Another counter-intuitive finding is that while XMARK is a synthetic dataset, such distributions in XMARK are highly skewed also, shown in Figure 7. The non-zero variance of the distributions in XMARK dataset is shown in Figure 8. The x-axis is the value of variance of a distribution and the y-axis shows the number of distributions with a particular variance. The figure shows that there are many distributions with a large variance. In addition, a few distributions with a large variance are found in DBLP, NASA and SWISSPROT datasets.

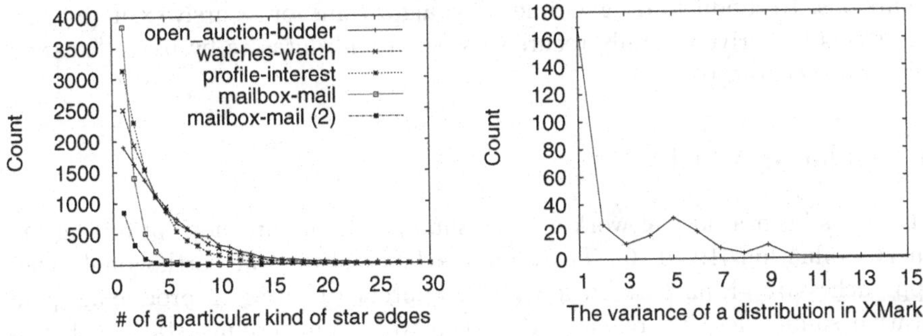

Fig. 7. The five distributions with the highest variance on the number of star edges (XMARK)

Fig. 8. The variances of the distribution of star edges in XMARK

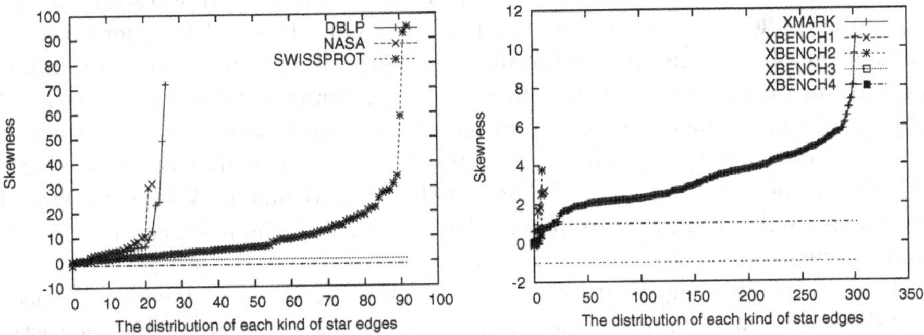

Fig. 9. Skewness of star edges in real-world dataset variance

Fig. 10. Skewness of star edges in synthetic dataset

We then apply the next metric to check the skewness of distributions of XML structures. The skewness of the distributions (with non-zero variance) of the real-world and synthetic datasets are presented in Figure 9 and Figure 10, respectively. Figure 9 shows that the number of skewed distributions (skewness > 1) is significant. We sort the distributions according to their skewness. That is, the x-axis is a canonical number of a distribution. The figure shows that the percentage of skewed distributions in DBLP, NASA and SWISSPROT are 82%, 100% and 94%, respectively. Datasets that are generated by XBENCH are not highly skewed as it is illustrated with Figure 10. When one uses highly skewed datasets for experimentations, the results are prone to be biased.

Summary and recommendations. While XMARK and DBLP datasets appear popular in the XML research community, we found that the majority of these XML datasets are mild generalization of relations - not "tree-like". Furthermore, these datasets are highly skewed. Except XBENCH TC/MD, the other three XBENCH datasets are also a mild generalization of relations. The XBENCH datasets are not skewed. All the datasets are hardly hierarchical and contain a small number of recursions. To conduct fair experiments on algorithms for recursive XML (*e.g.* [2]), one needs to derive a highly recursive schema and datasets by using "XBENCH-like" XML generator.

5 Related Work

There has been a host of work on XML summary structures for optimizing XML query evaluation [19,20,16]. These approaches and ours are orthogonal: Their approaches are graph-based whereas our approach focuses on producing quantitative summaries. There have also been works on deriving statistical summaries of XML structures [7,23,15] for estimating selectivities of a query workload. [7] counts the number of simple paths in XML documents and determines the correlation between paths for estimating the selectivity of a given query workload. In comparison, our approach does not require query workloads as our focus is not selectivity estimation. [23] proposes statistical synopses for XML for path query selectivity estimation. Such synopses are designed for query processors, as opposed to offering a structural summary for human. STATIX [15] builds histograms on entities of an XML SCHEMA and generates the optimal relational storage of an XML document for a pariticular query workload. In comparison, our approach does not require an XML SCHEMA. We derive a prefix tree from an XML document and use it as the "schema" of the XML document. While [15] stated that some real-world XMLs are highly skewed, our result is more comprehensive and informative.

In addition to query evaluation, the structure of XML documents influences the design of XML storage scheme. For example, since XML is flexible, heuristic algorithms [11,3] has been proposed to mine the optimal storage for XML. The storage subsequently affects query evaluations. Another stream of work is the XML query algorithms [4,13,25,22,6] that assume a specific physical layout or XML index structure. Although encouraging performances have been reported, it was not clear how the performance of a system may change as the structure of documents changes. Recently, [26] proposes a microbenchmark for understanding the strengths and weaknesses of an XML system. Compression can be understood as a space-efficient storage. Existing XML compression techniques [18,6,10,8] utilize properties of both scalar data and structures of an XML document. Since (real-world) XML documents are often skewed, XML compressions have been shown effective.

Finally, surveys on real-world DTDS and XML SCHEMAS are presented in [9] and [1], respectively. However, nestings of entities and the number of occurrences of star edges can only be computed from document instances.

6 Conclusions and Future Works

In this paper, we presented quantitative metrics for XML structures. We derived statistics from a prefix tree of XML structures and used simple paths and star edges as the basis of our metrics. These metrics are developed to answer our informal question stated in Introduction: whether an XML structure is tree-like or relational-like. We applied our metrics on a few popular XML datasets for experimental evaluations, among others, for XML research. Our result is that the structures of these XML documents are highly skewed, non-hierarchical and mostly non-recursive. That is, the datasets are relational-like.

In the future, we will use our metrics to aid the design of our ongoing native XML system [6,10].

Acknowledgements. We would like to thank Daxin Jiang for discussions on statistics and databases and our colleagues in CAIS at NTU for providing technical discussions. This work is supported by CoE startup grant M58020002.601001.

References

1. G. J. Bex, F. Neven, and J. V. den Bussche. DTDs versus XML Schema: A Practical Study. In *WebDB*, pages 79–84, 2004.
2. P. Bohannon, B. Choi, and W. Fan. Incremental evaluation of schema-directed XML publishing. In *SIGMOD*, 2004.
3. P. Bohannon, J. Freire, P. Roy, and J. Simeon. From XML schema to relations: A cost-based approach to XML storage. In *ICDE*, 2002.
4. P. A. Boncz, T. Grust, M. van Keulen, S. Manegold, J. Rittinger, and J. Teubner. MonetDB/XQuery: a fast XQuery processor powered by a relational engine. In *SIGMOD*, pages 479–490, 2006.
5. V. P. Braganholo, S. B. Davidson, and C. A. Heuser. From XML view updates to relational view updates: old solutions to a new problem. In *VLDB*, 2004.
6. P. Buneman, B. Choi, W. Fan, R. Hutchison, R. Mann, and S. Viglas. Vectorizing and querying large xml repositories. In *ICDE*, pages 261–272, 2005.
7. Z. Chen, H. V. Jagadish, F. Korn, N. Koudas, S. Muthukrishnan, R. Ng, and D. Srivastava. Counting twig matches in a tree. In *ICDE*, 2001.
8. J. Cheney. Compressing XML with multiplexed hierarchical PPM models. In *Data Compression Conference*, 2001.
9. B. Choi. What are real DTDs like. In *WebDB*, pages 43–48, 2002.
10. B. Choi. Document decomposition for XML compression: A heuristic approach. In *DASFAA*, pages 202–217, 2006.
11. A. Deutsch, M. F. Fernandez, and D. Suciu. Storing semistructured data with STORED. In *SIGMOD*, pages 431–442. ACM Press, Jun. 1999.
12. ExPASy. Swiss-prot and TrEMBL. Available at `http://www.expasy.ch/sprot/`.
13. T. Fiebig, S. Helmer, C.-C. Kanne, G. Moerkotte, J. Neumann, R. Schiele, and T. Westmann. Anatomy of a native XML base management system. *VLDB Journal*, 11(4):292–314, Dec. 2002.
14. D. Florescu and D. Kossmann. Storing and querying XML data using an RDMBS. *IEEE Data Engineering Bulletin*, 22(3):27–34, 1999.
15. J. Freire, J. R. Haritsa, M. Ramanath, P. Roy, and J. Siméon. StatiX: making XML count. In *SIGMOD Conference*, pages 181–191, 2002.
16. R. Kaushik, P. Shenoy, P. Bohannon, and E. Gudes. Exploiting local similarity for efficient indexing of paths in graph structured data. In *ICDE*, 2002.
17. M. Ley. DBLP Bibliography. Available at `http://www.informatik.uni-trier.de/~ley/db/`, Mar 2005.

18. H. Liefke and D. Suciu. XMILL: An efficient compressor for XML data. In *SIGMOD*, 2000.
19. J. McHugh and J. Widom. Query optimization for XML. In *VLDB*, 1999.
20. T. Milo and D. Suciu. Index structures for path expressions. In *ICDT*, 1999.
21. National Aeronautics and Space Administration. The NASA XML project. Available at `http://xml.nasa.gov/xmlwg/index.htm`.
22. S. Paparizos, S. Al-Khalifa, A. Chapman, H. V. Jagadish, L. V. S. Lakshmanan, A. Nierman, J. M. Patel, D. Srivastava, N. Wiwatwattana, Y. Wu, and C. Yu. TIMBER: A native system for querying XML. In *SIGMOD*, 2003.
23. N. Polyzotis and M. N. Garofalakis. Statistical synopses for graph-structured XML databases. In *SIGMOD*, 2002.
24. V. Poosala, Y. E. Ioannidis, P. J. Haas, and E. J. Shekita. Improved histograms for selectivity estimation of range predicates. In *SIGMOD*, pages 294–305, 1996.
25. S. Prakash, S. S. Bhowmick, and S. K. Madria. Efficient recursive XML query processing in relational database systems. In *ER*, pages 493–510, 2004.
26. K. Runapongsa, J. Patel, H. Jagadish, Y. Chen, and S. Al-Khalifa. The Michigan benchmark: Towards XML query performance diagnostics, 2003.
27. A. Schmidt. XMark – an XML benchmakr project. Available at `http://monetdb.cwi.nl/xml/generator.html`, 2003.
28. A. Schmidt, F. Waas, M. Kersten, M. J. Carey, I. Manolescu, and R. Busse. XMark: A benchmark for XML data management. In *VLDB*, pages 974–985, 2002.
29. L. Segoufin and V. Vianu. Validating streaming xml documents. In *PODS*, pages 53–64, 2002.
30. J. Shanmugasundaram, E. Shekita, and J. Kiernan. A general technique for querying XML documents using a relational database system. *SIGMOD Record*, 30(3):20–26, 2001.
31. J. Shanmugasundaram, K. Tufte, C. Zhang, G. He, D. J. DeWitt, and J. F. Naughton. Relational databases for querying XML documents: Limitations and opportunities. *VLDB Journal*, pages 302–314, 1999.
32. ToXGene. The ToX XML generator. Available at `http://www.cs.toronto.edu/tox/toxgene/`, 2005.
33. W3C. Extensible Markup Language (XML). Available at `http://www.w3.org/XML/`.
34. B. B. Yao, M. T. Ozsu, and N. Khandelwal. XBench benchmark and performance testing of XML DBMSs. In *ICDE*, pages 621–633, 2004.

Database to Semantic Web Mapping Using RDF Query Languages

Cristian Pérez de Laborda and Stefan Conrad

Institute of Computer Science
Heinrich-Heine-Universität Düsseldorf
D-40225 Düsseldorf, Germany
{perezdel, conrad}@cs.uni-duesseldorf.de

Abstract. One of the main drawbacks of the Semantic Web is the lack of semantically rich data, since most of the information is still stored in relational databases. In this paper, we present an approach to map legacy data stored in relational databases into the Semantic Web using virtually any modern RDF query language, as long as it is closed within RDF. Consequently, a Semantic Web developer does not need to learn and adopt a new mapping language, but he may perform the mapping task using his preferred RDF query language.

1 Motivation

Despite the vision of a Semantic Web [6] and many efforts helping to realize it, the actual Semantic Web still lacks of enough semantic data. Most information is still modeled and stored in relational databases and thus out of reach for many Semantic Web applications. As a consequence, such applications need to create a corresponding mapping between the relational and the semantic models by themselves for being able to access relational data. Realizing this situation, some efforts have arisen to straighten out this deplorable situation.

Most approaches translate relational data into a Semantic Web representation using a proprietary mapping language (cf. Section 2). In [19] we have introduced Relational.OWL, our technique to automatically transform relational data into a machine processable and understandable representation (cf. Section 3.1). Nevertheless, such a representation does not include *real* semantics, since it converts the schema of a database automatically into an ontology and the data items as its instances, i.e. the data is described as it was in the database. For many Semantic Web applications, this is a reasonable technique, since they are able to quickly access legacy data stored in a relational database using their own built-in functionality. However, such a representation could be inappropriate, if the data has to be processed for further reasoning tasks.

In this paper we present how to map relational data into the Semantic Web using virtually any modern RDF query language, as long as the language is closed within RDF, i.e. it returns valid RDF graphs as query results. For this purpose, data and schema components of the original relational database are

D.W. Embley, A. Olivé, and S. Ram (Eds.): ER 2006, LNCS 4215, pp. 241–254, 2006.

first translated automatically into their Semantic Web representation based on Relational.OWL. Thereupon, they may either be processed or mapped directly to a target ontology. To perform such a mapping task, a Semantic Web developer does not need to learn and adopt a new mapping language, but he may perform the mapping task using his preferred RDF query language.

The remainder of this paper is organized as follows. In the next Section we discuss some related research. In Section 3 the foundations of this paper are described. The relational database to Semantic Web mapping process is introduced in Section 4 and evaluated in Section 5. Finally, we conclude in Section 6 with a short discussion and some ideas for future work.

2 Related Work

Recently, some efforts arose in bringing together relational databases and the Semantic Web. Nevertheless, most of these approaches do not use relational databases as a data source, but to store RDF triples in tailored tables, exploting the improved query performance of current relational databases (e.g. [13], [16], or [11]). The main drawback of such approaches is, that the corresponding data has to be available in RDF, i.e. their aim is not to convert legacy data into a Semantic Web representation, but to give applications fast access to RDF triples.

Some approaches try to map legacy relational databases to the Semantic Web. Bizer [7] for example, introduces a mapping from relational databases to RDF. Unlike our approach which is based on existing query languages, this method requires a specific mapping language, which, although it is based on RDF, still has to be learned and adopted by the corresponding developers.

An et al. outline in [5] a further approach from tables to ontologies. Unlike our technique, this approach maps database schemas directly into ontological concepts, assuming that the required database was designed following several ER design principles, e.g. the database is normalized and contains meaningful table or column names.

Petrini and Risch introduce in [21] their technique to query relational databases using RDF query languages, which is closely related to the approach presented in this paper. Nevertheless, it has some drawbacks. The mapping from relational tables to the Semantic Web is defined within a custom made mapping table, where columns or tables are related to objects or attribute values. As a result, the mappings between both worlds are always 1:1. Our mapping technique is completely based on the Semantic Web and allows the mappings to be as complex as a query language can be, i.e. we would even be able to use aggregations, if they are supported by the query language used.

3 Foundations

In this section we present the foundations, this work is based on. First, we introduce Relational.OWL, an approach to automatically transform relational data and schema items into a Semantic Web representation. After this, we explain in

Section 3.2 the difficulties in querying the resulting RDF graphs using current RDF query languages.

3.1 Relational.OWL

In [19] we introduced Relational.OWL, a data and schema representation, which adopts Semantic Web techniques to the data and schema representation process of (relational) databases. Contrary to other approaches where RDF is stored in relational databases (e.g. [15]), Relational.OWL aims at bringing together the representation of both, database data and schema components with a common mediated language, based on the *Resource Description Framework* (RDF) and the *Web Ontology Language* (OWL) [14]. In this section we give a short introduction to the Relational.OWL representation technique, since it is essential for a subsequent application to the mapping process presented in this paper.

The Relational.OWL Ontology. To describe the schema of a relational database with the techniques provided by RDF and OWL, we have to define reference OWL classes centrally, to which any document describing such a database can refer. The abstract representation of classes like `Table` or `Column` becomes a central part of the knowledge representation process realized within OWL. Additionally, we have to specify possible relationships among these classes resulting in an ontology, a relational database can easily be described with. We call this central representation the Relational.OWL ontology. It contains abstract definitions of relational databases $\mathfrak{D}$, tables $\mathfrak{T}$, columns $\mathfrak{C}$, primary keys $\mathfrak{P}$, foreign keys $\mathfrak{F}$, and their corresponding relationships.

For each relational database $\mathcal{RDB}_i$, a Semantic Web correspondent $\mathcal{ROWL}_i$ $(\mathcal{S}_i, \mathcal{I}_i)$ is created, where $\mathcal{S}_i$ is the schema and $\mathcal{I}_i$ the data instance representation. $\mathcal{S}_i$ will usually contain one subclass $\mathcal{D}_i$ of $\mathfrak{D}$. Analogously, for each relation $\mathcal{R}_1, ..., \mathcal{R}_m \in \mathcal{RDB}_i$, a subclass $\mathcal{T}_1, ..., \mathcal{T}_m$ of $\mathfrak{T}$ is created and included into $\mathcal{S}_i$. The $\in$ relationship between $\mathcal{RDB}_i$ and $\mathcal{R}_j$ is then added using a corresponding *hasTable* property within the $\mathcal{D}_i$ class. The remaining components and their relationships are transformed correspondingly.

A snippet of a database representation using Relational.OWL is provided in Fig. 1. Its first element corresponds to a table containing residence information of a business contact. In this case, the `rdf:ID ADDRESS` is equivalent to the table name in the original database. Instead of exclusively using the table name as an identifier, a complete URI pointing at this specific table can be specified using an identifier, e.g. as in [17]. Each of the five columns is defined using a `owl:DatatypeProperty` class, where all the properties required are specified. The corresponding `&dbs;Table` and `&dbs;Column` objects are then linked using a `dbs:hasColumn` property.

The primary key property of the table is represented using a `dbs:isIdentifiedBy` property, whereas the `dbs:PrimaryKey` Object corresponds to the actual primary key. Since the primary key itself may consist of more than one column, they are specified with `dbs:hasColumn` entries. The second element in Fig. 1 describes the ZIP column of the address table. It contains string values with a maximum length of eight characters.

```
<...>
 <owl:Class rdf:ID="ADDRESS">
  <rdf:type rdf:resource="&dbs;Table"/>
  <dbs:hasColumn rdf:resource="#ADDRESS.ADDRESSID"/>
  <dbs:hasColumn rdf:resource="#ADDRESS.STREET"/>
  <dbs:hasColumn rdf:resource="#ADDRESS.ZIP"/>
  <dbs:hasColumn rdf:resource="#ADDRESS.CITY"/>
  <dbs:hasColumn rdf:resource="#ADDRESS.COUNTRYID"/>
  <dbs:isIdentifiedBy>
   <dbs:PrimaryKey>
    <dbs:hasColumn rdf:resource="#ADDRESS.ADDRESSID"/>
   </dbs:PrimaryKey>
  </dbs:isIdentifiedBy>
 </owl:Class>
 <owl:DatatypeProperty rdf:ID="ADDRESS.ZIP">
  <rdf:type rdf:resource="&dbs;Column"/>
  <rdfs:domain rdf:resource="#ADDRESS"/>
  <rdfs:range rdf:resource="&xsd;string"/>
  <dbs:length>8</dbs:length>
 </owl:DatatypeProperty>
</ ...>
```

Fig. 1. Schema Representation

Data Representation. After having created a schema representation of a database $\mathcal{RDB}_i$ using OWL and our Relational.OWL ontology, we can regard this representation itself as a novel ontology. With this tailored ontology-based representation of the database schema, we are able to represent the data stored in that specific database. As a result, data stored in a relational database can be represented as instances of its own OWL schema.

In order to realize this kind of data representation process, we have to ensure that all components involved (e.g. exchange partners) are able to process and understand RDF and OWL, know the Relational.OWL ontology (or a semantic equivalent), and have access to the OWL schema representation $\mathcal{S}_i$ of the database $\mathcal{RDB}_i$. As we have mentioned above, the Relational.OWL representation $\mathcal{ROWL}_i$ of a relational database $\mathcal{RDB}_i$ consists of two parts, the schema ontology $\mathcal{S}_i$ and its corresponding data instances $\mathcal{I}_i$.

Using the schema $\mathcal{S}_i$ as a novel ontology means to represent the data stored in the database $\mathcal{RDB}_i$ using a tailored data representation technique. As a result, the data can be handled using common RDF/OWL techniques for data backups, data exchanges, or any kind of data processing tasks within the Semantic Web. A sample data set of a relational database is provided in Fig. 2.

A summary of all the classes and relationships among them, together with a complete database representation can be found in [19].

3.2 Querying RDF Data

Despite the possibility to query RDF graphs in their XML representation using XML query languages like XQuery [9], their possibilities to query the graph for matching triples is rather rudimentary, ignoring the kind of information, which

```
<...>
<db:ADDRESS>
 <db:ADDRESS.ADDRESSID>6824</db:ADDRESS.ADDRESSID>
 <db:ADDRESS.STREET>Campus de Arrosadia</db:ADDRESS.STREET>
 <db:ADDRESS.ZIP>31006</db:ADDRESS.ZIP>
 <db:ADDRESS.CITY>Pamplona</db:ADDRESS.CITY>
 <db:ADDRESS.COUNTRYID>152</db:ADDRESS.COUNTRYID>
</db:ADDRESS>
<db:COUNTRY>
 <db:COUNTRY.COUNTRYID>152</db:COUNTRY.COUNTRYID>
 <db:COUNTRY.NAME>España</db:COUNTRY.NAME>
</db:COUNTRY>
</...>
```

Fig. 2. Data Representation

can be revealed using reasoning mechanisms. In fact, all queries have to be expressed as if they were treating *real* XML documents and not RDF graphs.

Hence, it soon became obvious, that tailored query languages for the Semantic Web languages (e.g. RDF) were required. Naturally, most languages were based on the SQL syntax in order to be easily understood and adopted by a broad community. As we have shown in [18], these early languages like RDQL [24] have one major drawback: they are not closed, i.e. the results of such queries are not valid RDF triples, but a list of possible variable bindings. Hence, the query results cannot be processed using ordinary reasoning mechanisms of normal Semantic Web applications.

An RDF query language has to fulfill one main characteristic for being able to describe a mapping between a relational database and the Semantic Web using our Relational.OWL [19] technique: it has to be closed. Otherwise, the queries used within the mapping process would not return valid RDF graphs but simple variable bindings. Having chosen a closed query language, the expressiveness of a mapping only depends on the query language itself.

In this paper we use the upcoming query language SPARQL [22] as an RDF query language representative, since it will hopefully be recommended soon as a de facto standard by the W3C. SPARQL is an extension of RDQL, eliminating many of its drawbacks, like lack of expressiveness and completeness [18]. Despite its novelty, the Jena Framework [2] already supports SPARQL using its ARQ extension.

Indeed, we have shown in [20], that the combination of SPARQL and Relational.OWL could replace existing interfaces for the access of relational databases out of the Semantic Web. We successfully simulated the basic operations $\{\sigma, \pi, \cup, -, \times\}$ of the relational algebra and showed how to express a join operation with SPARQL. As we will see below, it can easily be deduced from the cartesian product - just as it is done within the relational algebra.

Consider a sample database, which contains personal and contact information of e.g. business partners and contains the following two relations:

`Address(AddressID, Street, ZIP, City, CountryID)` and
`Country(CountryID, Name)`.

A typical join operation between these two relations could be as follows:

$$\sigma_{Address.CountryID=Country.CountryID}(r(Address) \times r(Country)).$$

Since SPARQL does not provide the possibility to specify nested queries, we have to express the (equi-)join operation using a combination of a cartesian product and two selections (cf. [20]). A possible SPARQL query, which holds the same constraints like the relational algebra expression above and thus may be regarded as a correspondent to the (equi-)join operation of the relational algebra can be found in Fig. 3. We again refer to [20] for a detailed and complete analysis of the basic relational operation equivalents in SPARQL.

```
PREFIX    rdf:[...]
PREFIX    db :[...]
CONSTRUCT {?a ?b ?c;
              ?e ?f}
WHERE     {{?a ?b ?c;
               rdf:type db:ADDRESS} .
           {?d ?e ?f;
               rdf:type db:COUNTRY} .
           {?a db:ADDRESS.COUNTRYID ?x} .
           {?d db:COUNTRY.COUNTRYID ?x}}
```

Fig. 3. Sample SPARQL Query

Taking into account the possibility to query the legacy data formerly stored in relational databases using a query language like SPARQL, we have achieved a reasonable alternative for Semantic Web applications to access such relational data. As a consequence, all kinds of legacy data stored in relational databases become an integral part of the Semantic Web.

4 Relational to Semantic Mapping

Despite being processable by any application understanding RDF, the data extracted using Relational.OWL still lacks *real* semantic meaning. Indeed, the information originally stored in relational tables is represented within a table object and not within an appropriate Semantic Web object, e.g. an `http://www.w3.org/2000/10/swap/pim/contact#Person` object. This drawback has to be accepted in order to achieve an automatic transformation from relational databases to the Semantic world.

Nevertheless, many applications still require the data to be represented as *real* semantic objects, for being able to perform reasoning tasks or further data processing. To meet the demands of such applications, a data mapping from the relational to the required data representation is needed.

4.1 Requirements

Common approaches like [8] introduce a special mapping language, which has to be understood and adopted by all administrators needing to perform a single mapping from a relational database to the Semantic Web. Our technique goes one step further and uses common RDF query languages for the mapping task. The following requirements have to be kept, for being able to use such query languages as a mapping language.

Relational.OWL: Contrary to a common mapping, where the relational data is directly translated into the Semantic Web, our approach passes one additional step. First, we represent the data stored in the original relational database in a semantic-rich format, i.e. in RDF. This step is either done exporting the complete data and schema sets into RDF using the Relational.OWL application [4] or using the virtual database representation provided by RDQuery [3]. Please note, that both data transformations methods are processed automatically without any human intervention. Both techniques result in a Semantic Web representation of the data and schema components of the original relational database.

Closed Query Language: We are potentially able to perform a mapping using any of the upcoming query languages, as long as it is closed within RDF and contains a construct similar to the `CONSTRUCT` clause in SPARQL (cf. [22]). Otherwise the resulting variable bindings would have to be translated again into RDF. We have chosen SPARQL as a representative query language, since it is easy to understand, its syntax is based on SQL, it is as powerful as the relational algebra in its expressiveness (cf. [20]), and will hopefully soon be recommended as a de facto standard by the W3C.

Target Ontology: Although the Relational.OWL representation (cf. Section 4.2) of the database is processable by virtually any Semantic Web application, it still lacks *real* semantics, since the data is represented as it was stored in the relational database, i.e. stored in tables and columns. Since we want to assign this data a real meaning, we require a target ontology, it can be mapped to.

4.2 Definitions

In this section we define the basic terms used for our relational database to Semantic Web mapping approach. First, we introduce the *semantic translation* of relational databases into the Semantic Web:

Definition 1 (Semantic Translation). *The semantic translation $\mathcal{ST}(\mathcal{RDB}, \mathcal{ROWL})$ of a relational database $\mathcal{RDB}$ into its Relational.OWL representation $\mathcal{ROWL}$ (see Definition 2 below) is an automatic translation process, where for each $\mathcal{RDB}$ and its schema components, a Semantic Web correspondent is created (cf. Section 3.1).*

In this context, the *Relational.OWL representation* of a database is:

Definition 2 (Relational.OWL Representation). *The Relational.OWL representation of a relational database is described by $\mathcal{ROWL}(\mathcal{S}, \mathcal{I})$, where $\mathcal{S}$ is the schema representation of the database as seen in Section 3.1 and $\mathcal{I}$ contains the corresponding data instances of the schema components described with $\mathcal{S}$.*

Having created a Relational.OWL representation of the corresponding database, we are now able to perform a *mapping*:

Definition 3 (Mapping). *A mapping $\mathcal{M}$ from a relational database to the Semantic Web is a four-tuple $\mathcal{M}(\mathcal{RDB}, \mathcal{ROWL}, \mathcal{TO}, \mathcal{Q})$, with $\mathcal{RDB}$ being the source database, $\mathcal{ROWL}$ the Relational.OWL representation of $\mathcal{RDB}$, $\mathcal{TO}$ the target ontology, and $\mathcal{Q}$ the mapping query, expressed in a (closed) query language $\mathcal{QL}$.*

Contrary to the *Relational.OWL representation* created with an automatic semantic translation, a *mapping* has to be stated manually using a query Q. The mapping is correct, iff querying $\mathcal{ROWL}$ with $\mathcal{Q}$ results in one ore multiple instances of $\mathcal{TO}$. Hence $\mathcal{Q}$ has to fulfill two main properties. First, it has to be adequate in regard to $\mathcal{ROWL}$, i.e. return the desired result and secondly, the result has to be formatted as instances of $\mathcal{TO}$.

4.3 Mapping Process

The complete relational data to RDF mapping process is illustrated in Fig. 4. It consists of two main steps, which were already introduced in the previous sections.

First, the Relational.OWL representation of the schema and the data components of the original data source are generated. The schema representation becomes thereby an instance of the Relational.OWL ontology. In turn, the data items converted become instances of the schema ontology just created. This step could either be performed using the Relational.OWL application [4], i.e. the schema and data components are translated statically in a one-time process, or using a virtual representation of that RDF model, e.g. with RDQuery [3]. The advantage of the latter is obvious, since the data stock, on which the queries are performed, is always up-to-date. This cannot be guaranteed using the Relational.OWL application. Nevertheless, if the source database does not change frequently, a static translation into the Relational.OWL representation could be enough.

Having created the Relational.OWL representation of the relational database, the second step including the actual mapping can be performed.

The RDF model just created may now be queried with an arbitrary RDF query language. As long as the query language is closed, the resulting query response is again within the Semantic Web, i.e. it is a valid RDF model or graph and may then be processed by other Semantic Web applications using their own built-in functionality for reasoning tasks.

Using the `CONSTRUCT` clause of a query language like SPARQL (cf. [22]), the resulting data items can be inserted into an arbitrary RDF skeleton. This property of the query language is vaguely comparable to an XSLT-Stylesheet [1]. If we specify an adequate RDF skeleton, we can achieve the resulting RDF model to correspond to an instance of the intended target ontology. The RDF skeleton in the `CONSTRUCT` clause of the SPARQL query becomes hereby the pivotal part of the actual mapping process. A sample mapping query is provided in Section 4.4.

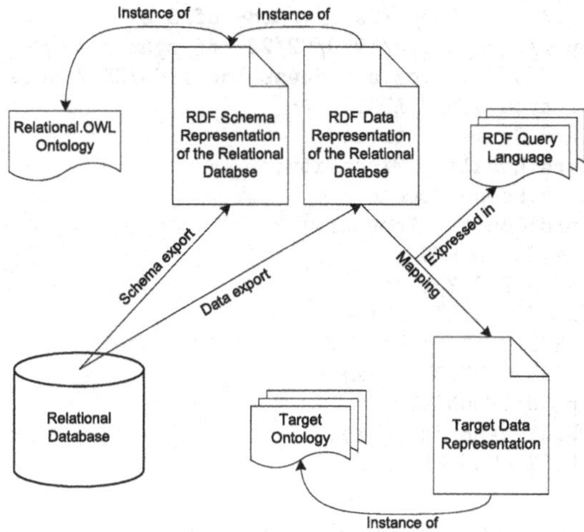

Fig. 4. Mapping Process

4.4 Sample Mapping

In this section we present a sample relational data to RDF/OWL mapping using SPARQL as our chosen mapping language, since it fulfills all of our requirements and will hopefully be recommended as a de facto standard by the W3C soon. Despite its novelty, SPARQL is already supported by the Jena Framework [2].

Consider a Semantic Web application developer, who requires access to the data stored in the database introduced in Section 3.2. Since he assumes the database schema to be quite stable, he decides to create a mapping from the relational data model to Semantic Web objets based on the `vCard` ontology [12]. A possible mapping query, which gives Semantic Web applications the possibility to access the data using its own built-in functionality and enables them to perform common reasoning operations is given in Fig. 5.

After specifying the prefix definitions for `vCard`, `rdf`, and `db` in the `PREFIX` clause, the skeleton of the resulting RDF objects is defined in the `CONSTRUCT` part of the query. At first, a new anonymous node of type `vCard:ADR` is created. This object contains the attributes `vCard:Street`, `vCard:Locality`, `vCard:Pcode`, and `vCard:Country` and could easily be extended by further attributes either specified in the `vCard` ontology or in other RDF-Schema files. The values corresponding to the given attributes are specified by free variables, bound in the following `WHERE` clause.

The actual linkage to the original database is performed in the `WHERE` clause of the SPARQL query, i.e. each of the free variables specified in the `CONSTRUCT` clause is bound to a column of the original database. To be more precise, the attributes are bound to the data instances $\mathcal{I}$ of the RDF representation $\mathcal{ROWL}$ of the relational database. Please note, that the mapping specification is identical for a *virtual* RDF model like in RDQuery [3] or a *static* data representation, e.g. with the Relational.OWL application [4]. Being stored on two different

```
PREFIX vCard:<http://www.w3.org/2001/vcard-rdf/3.0#>
PREFIX rdf:  <http://www.w3.org/1999/02/22-rdf-syntax-ns#>
PREFIX db:   <http://www.dbs.cs.uni-duesseldorf.de/RDF/address_schema.owl#>
CONSTRUCT {_:v rdf:type vCard:ADR;
               vCard:Street ?street;
               vCard:Locality ?locality;
               vCard:Pcode ?pcode;
               vCard:Country ?country}
WHERE {{?a rdf:type db:ADDRESS;
           db:ADDRESS.ZIP ?pcode;
           db:ADDRESS.STREET ?street;
           db:ADDRESS.CITY ?locality;
           db:ADDRESS.COUNTRYID ?x}.
       {?d rdf:type db:COUNTRY;
           db:COUNTRY.NAME ?country;
           db:COUNTRY.COUNTRYID ?x}}
```

Fig. 5. Sample Mapping Query

tables (ADDRESS and COUNTRY), the required data is joined using the ?x variable (cf. [20]).

Having created a suitable mapping from the Relational.OWL representation of the database to the target vCard ontology, the resulting data can be processed by any Semantic Web application as usual. In Fig. 6 a sample result set of the mapping query provided in Fig. 5 is given.

4.5 Characteristics

The major characteristics of our relational database to RDF/OWL mapping approach are discussed in this section.

Combination of Automatic and Manual Mappings: The mapping approach presented in this paper is suitable for most relational database scenarios. If we have to handle with constantly changing database schemas, an automatic mapping with Relational.OWL into the Semantic Web is the best choice. Indeed, an automatic mapping with Relational.OWL does not add real semantics to the RDF objects, but at least, the data is processable by any Semantic Web application without having to update the mapping every time the schema changes.

In many application areas, the risk of having to update the mapping is either negligible or consciously taken into account, since data with real semantics is required. For these cases, an additional, manual mapping from the Relational.OWL representation to a target ontology would be appropriate. This may easily be done using a suitable query language. Please note, that all present relational database to Semantic Web approaches require the mapping to be updated, whenever the schema of the database changes, whereas our technique provides an automatic fallback for such situations.

Mapping within the Semantic Web: The complete mapping process from the relational database to RDF objects with real semantics is performed

```
<rdf:RDF
    xmlns:rdf="http://www.w3.org/1999/02/22-rdf-syntax-ns#"
    xmlns:vCard="http://www.w3.org/2001/vcard-rdf/3.0#" >
 <rdf:Description rdf:nodeID="A0">
    <vCard:Pcode>40225</vCard:Pcode>
    <rdf:type rdf:resource="http://www.w3.org/2001/vcard-rdf/3.0#ADR"/>
    <vCard:Street>Universitätsstr. 1</vCard:Street>
    <vCard:Locality>Düsseldorf</vCard:Locality>
    <vCard:Country>Deutschland</vCard:Country>
 </rdf:Description>
 <rdf:Description rdf:nodeID="A1">
    <vCard:Pcode>31006</vCard:Pcode>
    <rdf:type rdf:resource="http://www.w3.org/2001/vcard-rdf/3.0#ADR"/>
    <vCard:Street>Campus de Arrosadia</vCard:Street>
    <vCard:Locality>Pamplona</vCard:Locality>
    <vCard:Country>España</vCard:Country>
 </rdf:Description>
</rdf:RDF>
```

Fig. 6. Sample Mapping Result

using Semantic Web applications. As a result, two different mapping architectures are possible. The first and most reliable possibility is, that such mappings are processed by small wrapper applications providing the Semantic Web applications with the required target data. Taking place within the Semantic Web, the applications may nevertheless opt to create the mapping by themselves using their own built-in functionality.

Well-known Mapping Language(s): One of the main advantages of our approach is, that it does not require a new mapping language to be adopted, since it is completely based on current RDF/OWL-techniques. Contrary to approaches like [7], Semantic Web application developers needing access to data actually stored in relational databases do not have to learn yet another mapping language, but are able to use their preferred RDF query language, as long as it fulfills the requirements mentioned in Section 4.1.

5 Evaluation

We have evaluated the performance of our relational database to Semantic Web approach using RDQuery [3]. It is a wrapper system, which enables Semantic Web applications to access and query data actually stored in relational databases using their own built-in functionality. RDQuery automatically translates SPARQL and RDQL queries into SQL and is thus able to perform the relational to semantic mapping in one step. Providing an adequate mapping query, the query is translated into SQL, the underlying relational database is queried, and the results are returned in the required format. RDQuery is thereby able to recognize the basic operations of the relational algebra within the SPARQL query (cf. [20]) and to translate them into SQL. Hence, most of the workload, including join and projection operations, is not processed directly by RDQuery, but passed to the underlying database with the generated SQL query.

Following the example shown in Section 4.4, we have created 18 different queries which map relational data to the vCard ontology (cf. `http://www.w3.org/TR/vcard-rdf`). We have categorized these queries into three different classes, depending on their complexity referring to the relational algebra (i.e. `selection`, `projection`, and `join`). Each of the categories contains six of the queries. We first measured the time required by RDQuery to translate the queries into SQL and then the time passed for the complete mapping process, including query translation, query execution via JDBC using a MySQL database, and the data translation back into RDF. The database, the queries were tested on is based on the `northwind` database and contains eight tables with a total of about 3000 tuples. Unlike the first measurement, the second depends on various factors, like network or database performance, which can hardly be influenced by RDQuery. In Table 1, the average execution time of the query translations and mapping processes for each mapping category is given.

Table 1. Average Execution Time for a SPARQL Mapping

	Execution time [s]	
SPARQL Query	Query Translation	mapping process
Selection	0.020	0.050
Projection	0.018	0.052
Join	0.023	0.067

The performance results show, that the execution time of both, the query translations and the complete mapping process are barely measurable, lying most of them far below 100 milliseconds. Even the more complex join operations were translated and executed at an average of 67 milliseconds. Consequently, our mapping relational data to Semantic Web approach enables applications to access legacy data stored in relational databases in real-time, as if that data would actually be part of the Semantic Web.

6 Discussion and Future Work

In this paper we have described how to map data from relational databases into a real RDF representation using a Semantic Web query language. To use such query languages for a mapping purpose, three main requirements have to be met. First, the relational database (i.e. its schema and data components) has to be described using the Relational.OWL ontology. This automatic semantic representation of the relational database can then be queried using any RDF query language. If the adopted query language is closed, the resulting RDF graph can be specified to match the the target ontology, the original database shall be mapped to.

The approach presented in this paper is based on mapping the Relational.OWL representation of relational databases manually into Semantic Web objects with real semantics. We are thus planning to analyze, whether existing (semi-)automatic schema and ontology matching approaches (cf. [10,23]) could provide reasonable results in matching an existing relational schema to a target ontology.

The expressiveness within the mapping process depends directly from the query language used, i.e. a more complex mapping cannot be stated with an elementary query language. For instance, we showed in [20], that all the basic operations of the relational algebra can be expressed with SPARQL. Nevertheless, its has some considerable limitations, since it does not support aggregations or nested queries. A further restriction concerns data manipulation or data updates, which is still not supported by most RDF query languages. We are currently analyzing, whether SPARQL could be extended to support such operations for enabling Semantic Web applications to manipulate the data actually stored on the relational database.

References

1. XSL Transformations (XSLT). `http://www.w3.org/TR/1999/REC-xslt-19991116`, 1999.
2. Jena - A Semantic Web Framework for Java. `http://jena.sourceforge.net/`, 2006.
3. RDQuery. `http://sourceforge.net/projects/rdquery/`, 2006.
4. Relational.OWL. `http://sourceforge.net/projects/relational-owl/`, 2006.
5. Yuan An, Alexander Borgida, and John Mylopoulos. Inferring Complex Semantic Mappings Between Relational Tables and Ontologies from Simple Correspondences. In *CoopIS, DOA, and ODBASE, OTM Confederated International Conferences, Cyprus, Part II*, volume 3761 of *LNCS*, pages 1152–1169. Springer, 2005.
6. Tim Berners-Lee, James Hendler, and Ora Lassila. The Semantic Web. *Scientific American*, May 2001.
7. Christian Bizer. D2R MAP-A Database to RDF Mapping Language. In *WWW2003, The Twelfth International World Wide Web Conference*, Budapest, Hungary, 2003. poster presentation.
8. Christian Bizer and Andy Seaborne. D2RQ -Treating Non-RDF Databases as Virtual RDF Graphs. In *The Semantic Web - ISWC 2004: Third International Semantic Web Conference*, Hiroshima, Japan, 2004. poster presentation.
9. Scott Boag, Don Chamberlin, Mary F. Fernández, Daniela Florescu, Jonathan Robie, and Jérôme Siméon. XQuery 1.0: An XML Query Language. `http://www.w3.org/TR/2005/CR-xquery-20051103/`, 2005. W3C Candidate Recommendation.
10. AnHai Doan, Jayant Madhavan, Pedro Domingos, and Alon Y. Halevy. Ontology Matching: A Machine Learning Approach. In Steffen Staab and Rudi Studer, editors, *Handbook on Ontologies*, International Handbooks on Information Systems, pages 385–404. Springer, 2004.
11. Stephen Harris and Nigel Shadbolt. SPARQL Query Processing with Conventional Relational Database Systems. In *Web Information Systems Engineering - WISE 2005 Workshops, New York, NY, USA, Proceedings*, volume 3807 of *Lecture Notes in Computer Science*, pages 235–244. Springer, 2005.

12. Renato Iannella. Representing vCard Objects in RDF/XML. `http://www.w3.org/TR/vcard-rdf`, 2001. W3C Note.
13. Gregory Karvounarakis, Vassilis Christophides, Dimitris Plexousakis, and Sofia Alexaki. Querying RDF Descriptions for Community Web Portals. In *17èmes Journées Bases de Données Avancées, BDA'2001, Agadir, Maroc*, pages 133–144, 2001.
14. Deborah L. McGuinness and Frank van Harmelen. OWL Web Ontology Language Overview. `http://www.w3.org/TR/2004/REC-owl-features-20040210/`, 2004.
15. Sergey Melnik. Storing RDF in a Relational Database. `http://www-db.stanford.edu/~melnik/rdf/db.html`, 2001.
16. Zhengxiang Pan and Jeff Heflin. DLDB: Extending Relational Databases to Support Semantic Web Queries. In *PSSS1 - Practical and Scalable Semantic Systems, Proceedings of the First International Workshop on Practical and Scalable Semantic Systems*, volume 89 of *CEUR Workshop Proceedings*, 2003.
17. Cristian Pérez de Laborda and Stefan Conrad. A Semantic Web based Identification Mechanism for Databases. In *Proceedings of the 10th International Workshop on Knowledge Representation meets Databases (KRDB 2003), Hamburg, Germany, September 15-16, 2003*, volume 79 of *CEUR*, pages 123–130. RWTH Aachen, 2003.
18. Cristian Pérez de Laborda and Stefan Conrad. Querying Relational Databases with RDQL. In Rainer Eckstein and Robert Tolksdorf, editors, *Berliner XML Tage*, pages 161–172, 2005.
19. Cristian Pérez de Laborda and Stefan Conrad. Relational.OWL - A Data and Schema Representation Format Based on OWL. In *Second Asia-Pacific Conference on Conceptual Modelling (APCCM2005)*, volume 43 of *CRPIT*, pages 89–96, Newcastle, Australia, 2005. ACS.
20. Cristian Pérez de Laborda and Stefan Conrad. Bringing Relational Data into the Semantic Web using SPARQL and Relational.OWL. In *Semantic Web and Databases, Third International Workshop, SWDB 2006, Co-located with ICDE, Atlanta, USA, April 2006*. IEEE Computer Society, 2006.
21. Johan Petrini and Tore Risch. Processing Queries over RDF views of Wrapped Relational Databases. In *1st International Workshop on Wrapper Techniques for Legacy Systems, WRAP 2004, Delft, Holland*, 2004.
22. Eric Prud'hommeaux and Andy Seaborne. SPARQL Query Language for RDF. `http://www.w3.org/TR/2006/WD-rdf-sparql-query-20060220/`, 2006. W3C Working Draft.
23. Erhard Rahm and Philip A. Bernstein. A survey of approaches to automatic schema matching. *VLDB J.*, 10(4):334–350, 2001.
24. Andy Seaborne. RDQL - A Query Language for RDF. `http://www.w3.org/Submission/2004/SUBM-RDQL-20040109/`, 2004.

Representing Transitive Propagation in OWL

Julian Seidenberg and Alan Rector

Medical Informatics Group
University of Manchester
United Kingdom
jms@cs.manchester.ac.uk, rector@cs.manchester.ac.uk

Abstract. Transitive propagation along properties can be modelled in various ways in the OWL description logic. Doing so allows existing description logic reasoners based on the tableaux algorithm to make inferences based on such transitive constructs. This is espectially useful for medical knowledge bases, where such constructs are common.

This paper compares, contrasts and evaluates a variety of different methods for simulating transitive propagation: property subsumption, classic SEP triples and adapted SEP triples. These modelling techniques remove the need to extending the OWL language with additional operators in order to express the transitive propagation. Other approaches require an extended tableaux reasoner or first-order logic prover, as well as a modification of the OWL standard.

The adapted SEP triples methodology is ultimately recommended as the most reliable modelling technique.

1 Introduction

1.1 Transitivity

A transitive relation is a relation between three elements if it holds between the first and second and it also holds between the second and third it must necessarily hold between the first and third [1].

Transitivity is one of the three intrinsic properties of part/whole relations. Winston calls this "a single sense of part" [2]: if the door is part of the car and the door-handle is part of the door, then the door-handle is also part of the car. If (A *isPartOf* B) and (B *isPartOf* C) then (A *isPartOf* C).

1.2 Transitive Propagation

However, the above does not necessarily hold true universally. Odell [3] points out that there are many different kinds of composition. When we say "part of" we often mean very different things. For example, "Iron isPartOf Car" implies a material-object relation, i.e. the car object is made of the iron material, while "Car isPartOf Traffic" implies a member-bunch relation, i.e. the car is a member of the collection of things which make up the Traffic concept.

D.W. Embley, A. Olivé, and S. Ram (Eds.): ER 2006, LNCS 4215, pp. 255–266, 2006.

$(Piston\ isPartOf\ Engine) \sqcap (Engine\ isPartOf\ Car) \rightarrow (Piston\ isPartOf\ Car)$

Fig. 1. Transitive relation because of similar semantics

$(Piston\ isPartOf\ Car) \sqcap (Car\ isPartOf\ Traffic) \nrightarrow (Piston\ isPartOf\ Traffic)$

Fig. 2. Non-transitive relation because of different semantics

While each specific type of part/whole relation is transitive along relations with the same semantics, as illustrated in Figure 1, this does not necessarily hold true across different types of relations, as shown in Figure 2.

However, as will be explained in the next section, in some cases, *transitive propagation* (sometimes also called a *role path*, or *propagates-via*) along relations with different semantics is desireable.

(Note: up to this point we referred to all relations as "partOf" in order to illustrate transitivity. However, for the purpose of more clearly distinguishing between relations with different semantics, we will proceed to name them more descriptively.)

1.3 Related Work

$Burn \sqsubseteq \exists\ isLocatedIn.Toe$
$Toe \sqsubseteq \exists\ isStructuralComponentOf.Foot$

Fig. 3. Motivating example for transitive propagation in OWL

In the example in Figure 3, one would intuitively expect a knowledge base to know that the Burn is located in the Foot, as well as the Toe (since the latter is a part of the former). However, Horrocks and Patel-Schneider point out that the description logic (DL) based Web Ontology Language (OWL) [4] currently does not support this kind of inference. Their proposed solution is to extend OWL with a rules language to, among other things, model transitive propagation [5]. Automated reasoning in such an extended OWL language requires a first-order logic or hybrid prover system. Existing tableaux algorithm based reasoners do not suffice. However, reasoning using such a system is provably undecidable [6].

Another solution, adopted by SNOMED [7] and GALEN [8] medical terminologies, is to introduce an idiom for transitive propagation into the modelling formalism. GALEN, for example, uses two special operators ("specialisedBy" and "refinedAlong") to express transitive propagation between roles [9].

In fact, the draft proposal for OWL 1.1 [10] proposes to extend the expressive power of OWL DL from $\mathcal{SHOIN}$ to the $\mathcal{SROIQ}$ description logic [11], which, among other things, allows for transitive propagation using, so called, *property chain inclusion axioms*.

However, it may be some time until the OWL 1.1 standard is ratified and implemented [12]. If and when this occurs it will be interesting to compare the reasoning performance of that implementation of transitive propagation to that of the various models which are currently available. The methods described in this paper will then, at worst, be useful for purposes of backwards compatibility and, at best, offer better performing, though less convenient, solution.

The following sections explain, compare, contrast and evaluate several ways of modelling transitive propagation, all of which avoid the need to extend the current OWL 1.0 language and are decidable using current reasoning tools.

2 Styles of Transitive Propagation

A specific illustrative example will be used throughout this paper to show the different styles of modelling transitive propagation in OWL. Assuming the knowledge base in Figure 4 is given:

$Foot \sqsubseteq \exists\ isPartOf\,.\,Leg$
$Toe \sqsubseteq \exists\ isPartOf\,.\,Foot$
$Burn \sqsubseteq \exists\ isLocatedIn\,.\,Toe$
$LegInjury \equiv \exists\ isLocatedIn\,.\,Leg$

Fig. 4. Initial example ontology

The defined class in the last line of Figure 4 serves as a query. It should subsume all possible injures to the *Leg* when the knowledge base is classified. That is, once all implicit relationships in the ontology are made explicit, and assuming transitive propagation is properly modeled, then *Burn* should be subsumed under *LegInjury*.

2.1 Property Subsumption

One way of simulating transitive propagation is to use the property hierarchy to assert one property as a subproperty of another. For example, if "*isLocatedIn* propagatesVia *isPartOf*", then "*isPartOf* subsumes *isLocatedIn*", where both *isLocatedIn* and *isPartOf* are transitive properties. This is shown more formally in Figure 5.

$r \circ s \,\dot{\sqsubseteq}\, r \;\Rightarrow\; s \sqsubseteq r \quad (\circ \textit{ indicates transitive propagation})$
$s \in R_+ \qquad (R_+ \textit{ is the set of transitive property names})$

Fig. 5. Simulating transitive propagation by using the property hierarchy

This method is easy to understand, simple to implement and, as will be shown later in section 3, provides good performance. However, it also has numerous disadvantages.

As pointed out by Rector in [13], a tangled ontology is very difficult to maintain. Tangled ontologies have subsumption hierarchies with more than one superclass per class. The maintenance difficulty is equally applicable to a hierarchy of properties. Using property subsumption to simulate transitive propagation in ontologies with large numbers of properties can therefore quickly lead to an unmaintainable knowledge base. In such cases, the information about mutual propagtion among properties is best kept externally and applied to ontology using a script. JOT [14], for example, is well suited for this purpose.

Another disadvantage of this method is that its logical meaning is inaccurate. Unexpected logical inferences are therefore sometimes possible. For example, given the knowledge bases in Figure 4 and the property subsumption method, as outlined above ($isLocatedIn \circ isPartOf \dot{\sqsubseteq} isLocatedIn \Rightarrow isPartOf \sqsubseteq isLocatedIn$), the query for *LegInjury* would result in both *Burn* and *Toe*. That is, both concepts would be inferred as subclasses of *LegInjury*, since any *isPartOf* relation is also an *isLocatedIn* relation.

Inferring *Toe* as a subclass of *LegInjury* is obviously not the intended meaning, but may be acceptable in some cases. For example, further restricting the query by adding more information, as shown in Figure 6, yields the expected result. The property subsumption technique for transitive propagation certainly requires careful analysis and should never be applied blindly.

$$Burn \sqsubseteq Injury$$
$$Burn \sqsubseteq \exists\ isLocatedIn\,.\,Toe$$
$$LegInjury \equiv \begin{pmatrix} Injury \sqcap \\ \exists\ isLocatedIn\,.\,Leg \end{pmatrix}$$

Fig. 6. Correctly behaving LegInjury query using property subsumption

2.2 Classic SEP Triples

Schulz and Hahn introduce the idea of SEP triples [15]. Their idea allows transitivity to be modeled explicitly. That is, SEP triples enable transitive relations to be expressed in formalisms that do not include transitivity by explicitly distinguishing between the whole of a concept, parts of a concept and the disjunction of the whole of a concept and its parts. Details of these triples may be found in [15].

An implementation of classic SEP triples requires extensive modification of the ontology class hierarchy. Three separate classes need to be introduced for every actual concept in the knowledge base. This results in a complex ontology structure that is difficult to maintain. Furthermore, we do not know of any algorithm for creating an ontology with SEP triples from a base ontology, given a list of transitively propagating properties. The performance of classic SEP triples was therefore not evaluated as part of this research. However, we presume their performance is inferior to that of the adapted SEP triples methodology (see below), since they do not take full advantage of OWL.

2.3 Adapted SEP Triples

Rector suggests an adapted SEP triples formalism [9] for use in description logics with transitive properties such as OWL ($\mathcal{SHOIN}(\mathcal{D})$) [16].

Similar to classic SEP triples, this methodology explicitly models transitive propagation in the knowledge base. However, unlike Schulz and Hahn's original idea, adapted SEP triples take advantage of OWL's ability to represent transitive properties. This removes the need to model transitivity explicitly in the knowledge base and therefore allows a much cleaner SEP triple-like representation to be created.

$$
\begin{array}{ll}
\textit{isLocatedIn} \in R & (R\ \textit{is the set of all property names}) \\
\textit{isPartOf} \in R_{+} & (R_{+}\ \textit{is the set of transitive properties}) \\
R_{+} \subseteq R & \\
\textit{LegInjury} \equiv \exists\ \textit{isLocatedIn}\,.\left(\begin{array}{c} \textit{Leg} \sqcup \\ \exists\ \textit{isPartOf}\,.\,\textit{Leg} \end{array}\right) &
\end{array}
$$

Fig. 7. Adapted SEP triples query

Example. Reusing the example knowledge base from Figure 4 above and classifying it together with the the query in Figure 7, results in the the expected inference: *Burn* is found to be a subclass of *LegInjury.*

Figure 8 shows how this adapted SEP triples mechanism works:

Toe, *Foot* and *Leg* are all concepts that are transitively part of each other, as indicated by the solid, upwards arcing arrows. There is also the *Burn* concept located in the *Toe.* Additionally, the model contains *LegInjury*, which is the defined class from Figure 7 that captures all things located in the *Leg*, or any of its parts.

Since *isPartOf* is a transitive property, the *Toe* concept is also part of the *Leg* concept. Therefore, anything located in the *Toe* (such as the *Burn*) matches the second part of the definition of *LegInjury.* That is, it is located in something which is part of the *Leg.* This results in *Burn* being inferred as a subclass of *LegInjury* when the knowledge base is classified by a description logic reasoner, as indicated by the dotted, straight, upwards pointing arrow.

Constraints and Assumptions. All knowledge bases used as examples in this paper are assumed to be normalised [13]. Defined classes act as queries in ontologies built using these principles. New subsumption relations are inferred only for such classes. Therefore only the defined classes in such an ontology need to be modified in order to create adapted SEP triples. However, in arbitrary ontologies SEP triples need to be applied to all classes in order to achieve a logically complete solution.

Transformations. Figure 9 shows the transformations that need to be applied to the defined classes in a knowledge base in order to create adapted SEP triples.

The last transformation rule requires some explanation: a class transformed in this way captures all classes that match the basic inverse restriction, while also being restricted to some other class in the ontology ($\top$) via the secondary property (S), where that other class must also have the same basic restriction as its superclass.

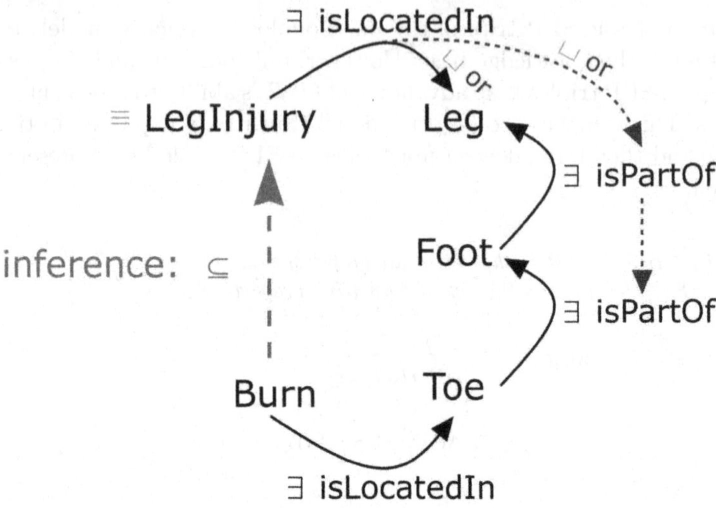

Fig. 8. Adapted SEP triples in action

for: $R \circ S \dot{\sqsubseteq} R$ (*where S is a transitive property*)

$$\exists R.C \Rightarrow \exists R.(C \sqcup \exists S.C)$$

$$\forall R.C \Rightarrow \forall R.(C \sqcup \exists S.C)$$

$$\exists R^{-}.C \Rightarrow (\exists R^{-}.C) \sqcup (\exists S^{-}.(\exists R^{-}.C))$$

$$\forall R^{-}.C \Rightarrow \begin{array}{l} \forall R^{-}.C \\ \exists S^{-}.\top \sqsubseteq \forall R^{-}.C \end{array}$$

Fig. 9. Transformations for creating adapted SEP triples

Handling Multiple Transitive Propagations. Chains of defined classes require special consideration as the rules in Figure 9 must be applied recursively. That is: when one defined class references another defined class, the transformed SEP triple restriction no longer matches the original definition. The original defined class must therefore be transformed to match the newly transformed definition of the second defined class. Chains of defined classes do not classify correctly without this additional transformation.

Figure 11 gives an example of such a case: suppose we take the ontology from Figure 8 and add a second SEP triple definition. If only the necessary and sufficient condition on the *FootComponent* class ($\equiv \exists$ *isPartOf*.(*Foot*$\sqcup\exists$ *isMultipleOf* . *Foot*)) is asserted, then the link from the *FootComponent* to the original *Foot* concept does not hold and the SEP triple inference cannot take effect; i.e. the *Burn2* concept is not classified correctly. However, if an additional transformation is applied to *LegInjury*, resulting in the new definition of that class as shown in Figure 10, then the link indicated by the striped curved upwards pointing arrow is captured and the correct inference results. That is: *Burn2* is inferred as being a kind of *LegInjury*.

$isLocatedIn \in R$
$isPartOf \in R_+$
$isMultipleOf \in R_+$

$$LegInjury \equiv \exists\ isLocatedIn.\left(\begin{array}{c} Leg \sqcup \\ \exists\ isPartOf.\left(\begin{array}{c} Leg \sqcup \\ \exists\ isMultipleOf.\ Leg \end{array}\right) \end{array}\right)$$

Fig. 10. New query for adapted SEP triples with chained definitions

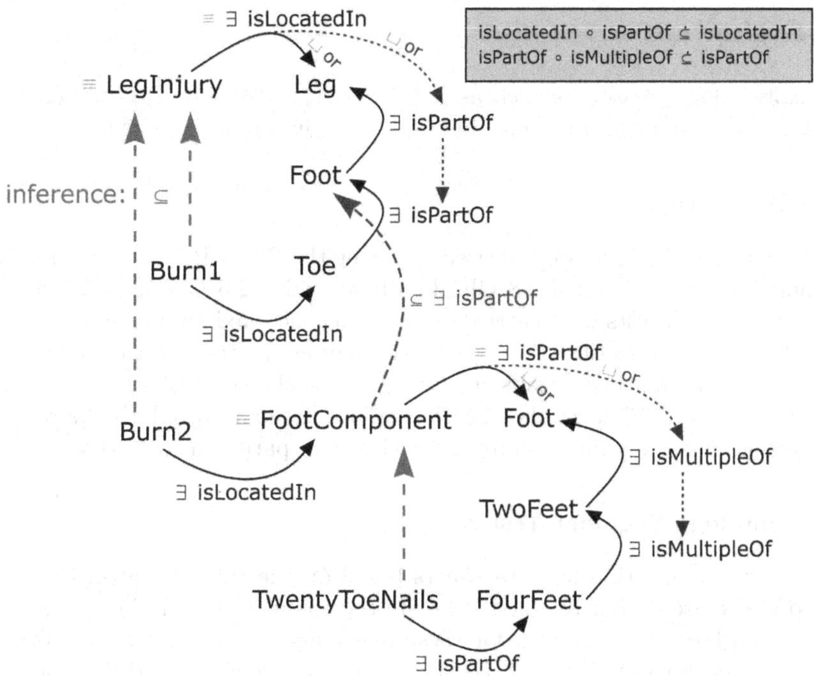

Fig. 11. Example of multiple transitive propagations

It should be noted that these kinds of chained universal restrictions may not need to be taken into account when creating SEP triples, depending on the ontology in question. However, some medical ontologies (such as GALEN) contain a substantial amounts of transitive propagation. A correct implementation is crucial in these cases.

Rector neglects to mention the need for a recursive algorithm when originally describing adapted SEP triples [9].

Discussion. Advantages of this modelling methodology are that it is logically correct and therefore, unlike the property subsumption method, will not produce any unexpected behaviour. It can also be applied selectively (unlike the potential implementation in the $\mathcal{SROIQ}$ description logic [11] based on complex property chain inclusion axioms [12]), so some concepts in an ontology can use transitive propagation, while others do not.

However, adapted SEP triples (unlike property subsumption) modify concept semantic (though not as drastically as classic SEP triples do) and may therefore be more difficult for a beginner to comprehend. They also require a somewhat complicated recursive transformation algorithm when dealing with chained transitive propagation.

3 Evaluation

Description logic reasoners such as FaCT++ [17], RACER [18], or Pellet [19] can be used to infer information that is implicit in an ontology [20].

3.1 Test Setup

Classification speed tests were carried out using the RACER 1.8 description logic reasoning system [18] on a 2.8 Ghz Pentium 4 with 2.5 GB of RAM running Windows XP. All tests were carried out utilizing the maximum memory possible in 32-bit Java applications (1.5 GB). The figures quoted are the times spent in actual reasoning. Data transfer latency is not shown. Tests were run for as long as necessary. That is, classification failure is reported only if the reasoner application crashed while attempting to classify a particular ontology.

3.2 Ontology Segment Test Sets

None of the description logic reasoners based on the tableaux algorithm mentioned above are currently able to classify the complete GALEN ontology. GALEN is too large and complex for these reasoning systems. (Note: the original classifier used for GALEN was based on different principles and did not suffer from this particular limitation [21].)

The ontology segmentation algorithm described in [22] was therefore used to create a test set of smaller, classifiable segments of the complete GALEN ontology. This test set consisted of a total of 162 ontology extracts centred around the *Heart* concept from the GALEN ontology [8]. Segments were chosen so all the base-case extracts were tractable.

The GALEN ontology employs a rich property hierarchy with over 500 distinct property types. The top-level of this hierarchy forms a meta-property structure. Using this high-level grouping it was possible to selectively include and/or exclude different ranges of properties in various segments. The following individual meta-properties and their combinations were selected for evaluation:

- **modifierAttribute:** properties which can be used to modify a given class such as "color" or "status". These are sometimes also known as "value partitions" [23]. They are not likely to adversely effect tractability, since they themselves do not contain further definitions.

- **locativeAttribute:** properties that link diseases to anatomical locations that they are in some way related to.
- **structuralAttribute:** properties linking anatomical body structures together by physical composition.
- **partitiveAttribute:** properties that link classes based on processes, divisions and other partitive relations
- **functionalAttribute:** properties that link classes by action or function.

(Note: a more detailed analysis of the GALEN property hierarchy may be found in [24].)

The GALEN ontology was filtered using four individual meta-properties (locative, structural, partitive, functional) as well as four combinations of meta-properties (functional + modifier, structural + modifier, partitive + functional + locative, structural + functional). These property sets were used to generate a various ontology segments. Additionally, the depth of the link traversal algorithm was limited in order to produce even more tightly constrained versions of these ontologies. Segments were created with maximal depths for the recursive ontology segmentation algorithm ranging from one to five, as well as without any depth limit. Finally, different styles of transitive propagation, based upon rules harvested from the original GALEN ontology, were applied to each extract (no transitive propagation, property subsumption and adapted SEP triples). This lead to a total of 144 test ontologies ($(4+4) \times 6 \times 3 = 144$).

3.3 Test Evaluation

The following observations can be made from the tests shown in Figure 12:

- Classification performance for *functional* properties is similar regardless of the method used. This is due to the relatively small amount of transitive propagation in those extracts.
- Extracts transformed to employ SEP triples using *locative* properties take an order of magnitude longer to classify than those using *partitive* segments. This is in spite of the *partitive* extracts having more actual SEP triples (388 vs. 244 triples in the case of unlimited extract depth). One can therefore conclude that classification speed is not directly correlated with the number of triples, but is more complex of an issue. Indeed, in both cases, the property subsumption technique performs very well.
- All the *structural* segments that employ property subsumption transformations crash the reasoner.
- The slowest classification performance in the test set results from an extract combining the *structural* and *functional* properties. Both of these property sets can be classified individually within about a second. However, the combination performs up to one hundred times slower. A similar pattern can be observed from the combination of *partitive* and *functional* properties.
- Extracts filtered using *structural* properties are unclassifiable when using the property subsumption technique. However when *functional* properties and

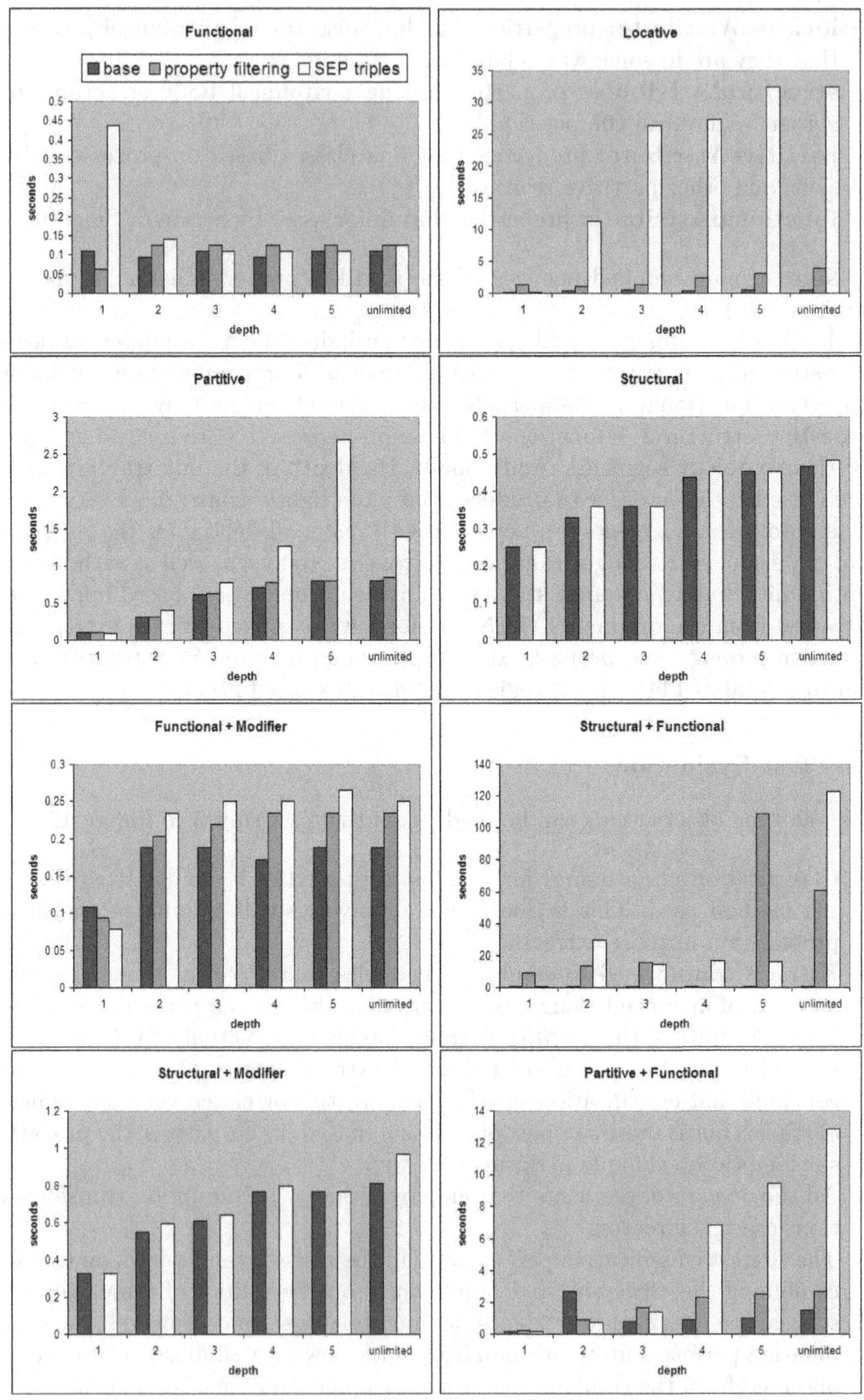

Fig. 12. Timing test results

structural properties are combined, this combination extract suddenly becomes tractable. However, classification performance suffers by almost three orders of magnitude compared to *functional* properties on their own.

In summary: *structual* properties scale extremely badly for property subsumption. *Locative* properties scale badly for SEP triples. SEP triples performance is slower than property sumbsumption and far slower than classification without transitive propagation. In rare cases, adding more information/complexity causes previously intractable knowledge bases to become classifiable.

4 Discussion and Future Work

In this paper two techniques for modelling transitive propagation in the OWL description logic have been described. Both allow an ontology engineer to express simple rule-like constructs while avoiding the use of complex first-order logic rules languages.

The property subsumption method of adding transitive propagation to an ontology results in a tangled property hierarchy, which can create complex cycles. These cycles can make classification completely intractable. This technique is also logically inaccurate and can result in incorrect/unintended inferences. However, performance is only slightly worse than the base-case.

Adapted SEP triples, on the other hand, add a large number of disjunctions in the knowledge base, thereby increasing the number of possibilities a tableaux reasoning system must explore in order to classify the ontology [25]. This can result in a significant increase in classification time. However, unlike the property subsumption mechanism, the increase in complexity does not result in intractability and is logically correct.

Adapted SEP triples are more difficult to implement and slower to classify, but we nevertheless recommend their use, as they are a much safer and more predictable modelling technique.

Future work includes evaluating the performance of a native tableaux algorithm implementation of transitive propagation. This research will be carried out if and when the $\mathcal{SROIQ}$ description logic [11] (which is due to underlie OWL 1.1) with its complex role inclusion axioms is implemented in a reasoning system. When this occurs, backwards compatibility with legacy tools and applications can be preserved, by using the methods outlined in this paper.

References

1. TheFreeDictionary.com: Transitivity definition (2004)
2. Winston, M., Chaffin, R., Herrmann, D.: A taxonomy of part-whole relations. In: Cognitive Science. Volume 11. (1987) 417–444
3. Odell, J.J.: Six different kinds of composition. Journal of Object-Oriented Programming **5**(8) (1994) 10–15
4. Smith, M.K., Welty, C., McGuinness, D.L.: OWL web ontology language guide. W3C Recommendation (10 February 2004)

5. Horrocks, I., Patel-Schneider, P.F.: A proposal for an OWL rules language. In: Proc. of the Thirteenth International World Wide Web Conference (WWW 2004), ASCM (2004) 723–731
6. Horrocks, I., Patel-Schneider, P.F., Bechhofer, S., Tsarkov, D.: OWL rules: A proposal and prototype implementation. Journal of Web Semantics **3**(1) (2005) 23–40
7. Spackman, K.: Managing clinical terminology hierarchies using algorithmic calculation of subsumption: Experience with SNOMED-RT. Journal of the American Medical Informatics Association **Fall Symposium** (2000)
8. Rector, A.L., Bechhofer, S., Goble, C., Horrocks, I., Nowlan, W.A., Solomon, W.D.: The GRAIL concept modelling language for medical terminology. Artificial Intelligence in Medicine **9**(2) (1997) 139–171
9. Rector, A.: Analysis of propagation along transitive roles: Formalisation of the GALEN experience with medical ontologies. In: DL 2002. (2002)
10. Patel-Schneider, P.: The OWL 1.1 Extension to the W3C OWL Web Ontology Language (2005)
11. Horrocks, I., Kutz, O., Sattler, U.: The Even More Irresistible SROIQ. Technical report, University of Manchester (2005)
12. Horrocks, I., Sattler, U.: Decidability of $\mathcal{SHIQ}$ with complex role inclusion axioms. Artificial Intelligence **160**(1–2) (2004) 79–104
13. Rector, A.L.: Normalisation of ontology implementations: Towards modularity, re-use, and maintainability. In: EKAW Workshop on Ontologies for Multiagent Systems. (2002)
14. Dameron, O.: JOT: a Scripting Environment for Creating and Managing Ontologies. In: 7th International Protégé Conference. (2004)
15. Schulz, S., Hahn, U., Romacher, M.: Part-Whole Reasoning in Medical Ontologies Revisited: Introducing SEP Triplets into Classification-Based Description Logics. In: AMIA Annual Fall Symposium, Hanley & Belfus (1998) 830–834
16. Horrocks, I., Patel-Schneider, P.F., van Harmelen, F.: From SHIQ and RDF to OWL: The making of a web ontology language. In: Journal of Web Semantics. Volume 1. (2003) 7–26
17. Tsarkov, D., Horrocks, I.: Reasoner prototype: Implementing new reasoner with datatypes support. WonderWeb Project Deliverable (2003)
18. Haarslev, V., Möller, R.: RACER System Description. In Gor, R., Leitsch, A., Nipkow, T., eds.: Automated Reasoning: First International Joint Conference. Volume 2083 / 2001., Springer-Verlag Heidelberg (2001) 701
19. Parsia, B., Sirin, E.: Pellet: An OWL DL reasoner. ISWC 2004 (2004) ISWC.
20. Lutz, C., Sattler, U., Tendera, L.: The complexity of finite model reasoning in description logics. In: Automated Deduction, Springer-Verlag (2003) 60 – 74
21. Horrocks, I., Rector, A.L., Goble, C.A.: A Description Logic Based Schema for the Classification of Medical Data. In: KRDB. (1996)
22. Seidenberg, J., Rector, A.: Web ontology segmentation: Analysis, classification and use. In: 15th International World Wide Web Conference. (2006)
23. Drummond, N., Horridge, M., Wang, H., Rogers, J., Knublauch, H., Stevens, R., Wroe, C., Rector, A.: Designing User Interfaces to Minimise Common Errors in Ontology Development: the CO-ODE and HyOntUse Projects. In Cox, S.J., ed.: Proceedings of the UK e-Science All Hands Meeting. (2004)
24. Rogers, J., Rector, A.: GALEN's model of parts and wholes: Experience and comparisons. Proceedings of AMIA Symposium (2000) 714–8
25. Horrocks, I.: Optimisation techniques for expressive description logics. Technical Report UMCS-97-2-1, University of Manchester, Department of Computer Science (1997)

On Generating Content and Structural Annotated Websites Using Conceptual Modeling

Sven Casteleyn, Peter Plessers, and Olga De Troyer

Vrije Universiteit Brussel
Pleinlaan 2, 1050 Elsene – Brussel
Belgium
{Sven.Casteleyn, Peter.Plessers, Olga.DeTroyer}@vub.ac.be
http://wise.vub.ac.be/

Abstract. An important milestone in the evolution of the Web is the Semantic Web: a Web in which the semantics of the available content and functionality is made explicit. Web design methods, originally aimed at offering a well-structured, systematic approach to Web design, now face new opportunities and challenges: Semantic Web technology can be used to make the semantics of the conceptual design models explicit; however a major challenge is to (semi-) automatically generate the semantic annotations, effectively enabling the Semantic Web. In this paper, we describe how WSDM, a well-known Web design method, was adapted to use Semantic Web technology for its conceptual modeling and how this can be exploited to generate semantically annotated websites. We consider two types of semantic annotations: content-related annotations and structural annotations. The first type allows to describe the semantics of the content of the website, the latter are annotations that explicitly describe the semantics of the different structural elements used in the website.

1 Introduction

Websites have evolved from a handful of statically linked pages into complex applications, serving a vast amount of rapidly changing information and functionality to a highly diversified audience. Web design methods were conceived to help the Web designer in coping with the complexity of designing and creating websites. Current Web design methods offer conceptual modeling primitives for different design concerns (i.e. most methods distinguish between data, navigation and presentation) combined with a systematic development approach.

The latest developments in the field of the Web are related to the vision of the *Semantic Web*. To allow making the semantics of the available Web content explicit, several (Semantic Web) technologies were introduced (e.g., RDF, OWL). With the arrival of the Semantic Web and its related technologies, new opportunities and challenges for Web design methods arose. A first opportunity lies in the use of Semantic Web technologies internally in the Web design method. More in particular, the use of ontologies allows to explicitly express the semantics of the different design models (meta-models), as well as the semantics of the represented data. In addition, the use of Semantic Web technology in combination with semantically rich conceptual modeling

D.W. Embley, A. Olivé, and S. Ram (Eds.): ER 2006, LNCS 4215, pp. 267 – 280, 2006.

concepts allows the generation of semantically annotated websites: websites in which the semantics of the content is made explicit by means of annotations. We call this kind of annotations *content-related annotations* to distinguish them from a second type of annotations, the so-called *structural annotations.* Indeed, it is also possible to annotate a website so that not only the semantics of its content are made explicit, but also the semantics of its structure. Dedicated ontologies describing the semantics of structural elements for a particular use (e.g., the WAfA ontology [19] is dedicated to assist visually impaired users while browsing) can be used to make the semantics of the different structural elements (e.g., a navigation menu, a logo, an advertising banner) explicit. These structural annotations can be generated by exploiting the conceptual design information captured during the design process. The more semantically rich design modeling concepts are used, the more of these semantically rich structural annotations can be generated. These structural annotations can subsequently be exploited by external applications requiring specific knowledge on the website structure: e.g., page transcoders (to transcode a webpage in a form more appropriate for screen readers used by visually impaired users) or search engine indexers.

In this paper, we explain how WSDM [4], an existing Web design method, combines Semantic Web technology and Conceptual modeling to allow the development of websites that satisfy the needs of the Semantic Web (section 2). We discuss how the adoption of Semantic Web technology is exploited to (semi-) automatically generate content-related semantic annotations (section 3), and to fully-automatically generate structural annotations (section 4). We also illustrate the benefits of structural annotations with two useful applications: facilitate accessibility for visually impaired users, and provide aid for search engines indexing websites. As the annotation process is performed on a conceptual level and the actual annotations are generated, the approach provides benefits over existing (manual) annotation approaches: (1) annotation is automatic (for structural annotations) or semi-automatic (for content-related annotations), (2) static as well as dynamic websites are supported, (3) changes in site structure or presentation do not invalidate the annotations (in contrast to manual annotation approaches) and (4) the generated annotations are more consistent. We discuss the actual implementation of the annotation generation process in section 5. Section 6 discusses related work, and finally, section 7 gives conclusions.

2 WSDM Overview and Its Ontology

WSDM (Web Semantics Design Method), developed in 1998 [4], aimed to offer a systematic, multi-phase approach to Web design. It makes a clear distinction between the conceptual design and the implementation aspects. Each design phase focuses on one specific aspect: requirements specification, task modeling, content and functionality modeling, navigational design, presentation modeling and implementation.

With the emergence of the Semantic Web, WSDM has been adapted to support the development of *semantic* websites, i.e. the method supports the semantic annotation of content and structure. To achieve this, (1) an (OWL) ontology is used to formally define the different WSDM design models, and (2) OWL is used as conceptual modeling language for the content and the functionality. The OWL ontology, which formally defines the different design models used in WSDM, is called the WSDM

Ontology. The WSDM ontology can be compared to a set of meta-models. When using the method, the WSDM ontology is populated and will contain the design models created by the designer for the website under development.

In the remainder of this section, an overview of WSDM is given (see figure 1), and the different models are formally described using Description Logic syntax[1] [1][2].

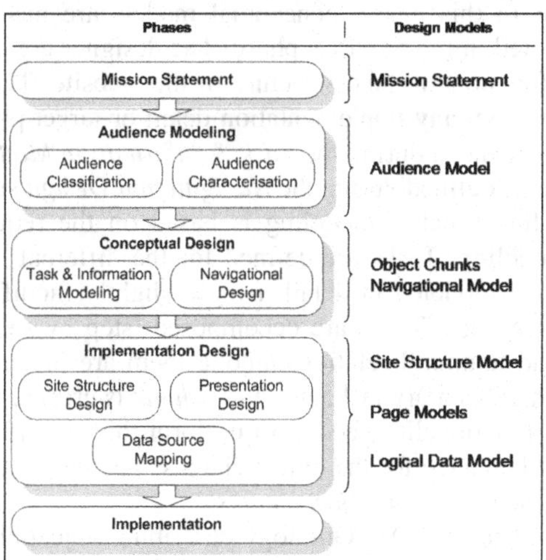

Fig. 1. WSDM Overview

Mission Statement Specification: In this first phase the *mission statement* of the website is formulated. The intention is to identify the purpose of the website, the topics and the target users. The mission statement is formulated in natural language. The WSDM Ontology fragment describing the mission statement is as follows: $\{MissionStatement \sqsubseteq (= 1\ hasValue),\ \top \sqsubseteq \forall hasValue.String\}$. Note that for the remainder of this section we will omit specification of datatype properties for reasons of clarity.

Audience Modeling: In this phase, the targeted users identified in the mission statement, are classified into so called *audience classes*. An audience class is a group of visitors that has the same information and functional requirements. An audience class that has the same and more requirements than another audience class is defined as an audience subclass. This results in an audience class hierarchy. For each audience class, the characteristics of the members of the class and their usability requirements are formulated. The output of this phase is *the audience model* consisting of the audience class hierarchy, and the characteristics and requirements of each audience class. The WSDM Ontology fragment describing the relevant concepts for the Audience Modeling phase look as follows: $\{UsabilityRequirement \sqsubseteq Requirement,\ InformationRequirement$

[1] Description Logic is the formal underlying framework for OWL(-DL).

[2] The full specification of the WSDM Ontology can be found at http://wise.vub.ac.be/ontologies/WSDMOntology.owl.

$\sqsubseteq$ *Requirement, FunctionalRequirement* $\sqsubseteq$ *Requirement,* $\exists$*hasAudienceSubclass.*$\top$ $\sqsubseteq$ *AudienceClass,* $\top$ $\sqsubseteq$ $\forall$*hasAudienceSubclass.AudienceClass,* $\exists$*hasRequirement.*$\top$ $\sqsubseteq$ *AudienceClass,* $\top$ $\sqsubseteq$ $\forall$*hasRequirement.Requirement,* $\exists$*hasCharacteristic.*$\top$ $\sqsubseteq$ *AudienceClass,* $\top$ $\sqsubseteq$ $\forall$*hasCharacteristic.Characteristic*}.

Conceptual Design: In this phase, conceptual models are made starting from the requirements formulated in the previous phase. The designer creates conceptual models for the content, functionality and structure of the website. The conceptual design makes an abstraction from any implementation detail or target platform. The content and functionality are modeled during the *Task & Information Modeling* sub phase; the navigational structure is defined during the *Navigational Design* sub phase.

Information and functionality modeling is based on the requirements identified during Audience Modeling. Tasks are defined for the different requirements. These tasks are analyzed and modeled in detail using a slightly modified version of CTT (Concurrent Task Trees) [5]. Tasks are decomposed (step by step) into a set of elementary subtasks, and temporal relations among them are indicated. The result is a *task model.* For each elementary task, an *object chunk* is created to formally describe the information and functionality needed to perform this task [5]. OWL is used as conceptual modeling language for the object chunks. The output of the Task & Information Modeling phase is a set of *object chunks.*

The relevant part of the WSDM Ontology describing object chunks is given next:

{$\exists$*isComposedOf.*$\top$ $\sqsubseteq$ *ObjectChunk,* $\top$ $\sqsubseteq$ $\forall$ *isComposedOf.*(*Class* $\sqcup$ *DatatypeProperty* $\sqcup$ *ObjectProperty*)}.

The goal of the Navigational Design is to define the conceptual structure of the website and to model how the members of the different audience classes can navigate through the website and perform their tasks (from a conceptual point of view). For each audience class, a dedicated navigation structure, called *navigation track*, is defined. A navigation track can be considered as a sub site containing all and only the information and functionality needed by the members of the associated audience class. Such a navigation track is composed of *nodes* (conceptual units of navigation) and *links* (which connect nodes). Links may be parameterized. Note that during the conceptual navigation design, no actual page structure is yet created. This is done during implementation design (see next). The output of this phase is the *navigational model.*

The WSDM Ontology fragment describing the relevant Navigation Design concepts is as follows: {$\exists$*hasChunk.*$\top$ $\sqsubseteq$ *Node,* $\top$ $\sqsubseteq$ $\forall$*hasChunk.ObjectChunk,* $\exists$*hasSource.*$\top$ $\sqsubseteq$ *Link,* $\top$ $\sqsubseteq$ $\forall$ *hasSource.Node,* $\exists$*hasTarget.*$\top$ $\sqsubseteq$ *Link,* $\top$ $\sqsubseteq$ $\forall$*hasTarget.Node,* $\exists$*hasCondition.*$\top$ $\sqsubseteq$ *Link,* $\top$ $\sqsubseteq$ $\forall$*hasCondition.Condition,* $\exists$*hasParameter.*$\top$ $\sqsubseteq$ *Link,* $\top$ $\sqsubseteq$ $\forall$*hasParameter.Parameter*}.

Implementation Design: Here, the conceptual design models are complemented with information required for the actual implementation: the distribution of nodes and links on pages (Site Structure Design), presentation issues (Presentation Design) and logical data source (Logical Data Design).

During **Site Structure Design**, the conceptual navigation structure of the website is mapped onto pages, i.e. it is decided which nodes (with associated object chunks) and links defined in the navigational model will be grouped onto Web pages. Different site structures can be defined, targeting different devices, contexts or platforms.

The output of this phase is the *site structure model*. The WSDM Ontology fragment describing the relevant Site Structure Design concepts is as follows: $\{\exists hasNode.\top \sqsubseteq Page,\ \top \sqsubseteq \forall hasNode.Node,\ \mathrm{Page} \sqsubseteq \exists hasNode.Node\}$.

The goal of the **Presentation Design** is to describe the layout of the pages, i.e., positioning and style. First, page templates are designed. Different kinds of templates may be needed, e.g., a homepage template, a title page template, leaf page templates. WSDM provides several Template Concepts (e.g., 'Footer', 'Header', 'Sidebar') to model page templates. For styles, Cascading Style Sheets are currently used. Next, it is specified how the information and functionality (modeled by means of the object chunks and grouped by means of nodes and assigned to a page) should be presented. Therefore, WSDM offers several Presentation Concepts to model the layout and presentation of a page. These Presentation Concepts vary from primitive ones (e.g., 'Grid', 'Row', 'MultimediaConcept', 'FormConcept') to high-level concepts (e.g., 'Menu', 'Section'). Also during Page Design, the designer must decide on labels and presentation styles for links. The output of this phase is the *presentation model* consisting of a set of templates, and for each page defined in the site structure model a *page model*.

The **Logical Data Design** is needed for data-intensive websites that maintain their data in a data source. In this phase, this data source must be defined and the relationship between the conceptual level (i.e. the object chunks) and the data source must be expressed. This last issue is explained into more detail in the next section.

3 Content-Related Semantic Annotations

In this section, we describe how WSDM allows designing websites of which the content is semantically annotated. Important to our approach is that this is supported at a conceptual level. The approach extends and refines our previous work as described in [15]: multiple existing domain ontology can be used, if needed, an appropriate (application) ontology can be extracted from the design, but most importantly, the use of OWL facilitates easier specification of semantic annotations.

Conceptual Design

The goal of our approach is to generate a website of which the content is automatically annotated with one or more domain ontologies which are related with the topics covered by the website. Details about the actual generation process are given in section 5. Here, we describe the principles of the approach and what must be done by the designer to obtain a semantically annotated website. In practice, three different cases may occur when designing a website:

1. *No appropriate domain ontology exists or is available.* A new ontology will be created incrementally as a result of the creation of the object chunks, i.e. by integrating all object chunks (see [6]). The object chunks are expressed as views on this ontology. Note that there is no additional effort required from the designer. Such an ontology is often called an *application ontology*.

2. *A single domain ontology exists that covers completely the domain of the website.* In this case, this ontology is taken as the basis for the conceptual design. The designer needs to express the concepts and relations used in the object chunks in terms of concepts from this domain ontology, e.g., by referring to an ontology concept instead of defining a new one. In this way, the object chunks are defined as views on this domain ontology.
3. *Multiple domain ontologies are needed to cover the domain of the website.* In this case, the different domain ontologies must be aligned first. This is done by defining a so-called *reference ontology* and by defining mappings between the domain ontologies and this reference ontology. Then, the concepts used in the object chunks can be defined in term of the concepts of this reference ontology, and the object chunks will be views on the reference ontology.

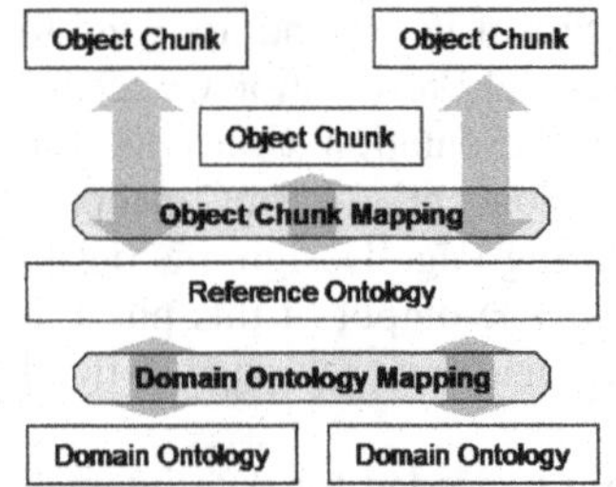

Fig. 2. General architecture illustrating the different mappings

Figure 2 shows an overview of the architecture covering these three cases. The different domain ontologies used are aligned by defining a mapping between the domain ontologies and the reference ontology (called *domain ontology mappings*). This reference ontology can also be used to define additional concepts not present in the available domain ontologies but relevant for the application. Note that in the case of just one domain ontology, the references ontology plays the role of this domain ontology (possibly also augmented with additional concepts). In the case where there is no domain ontology available, the reference ontology plays the role of application ontology that is incrementally constructed. The second type of mappings, called *object chunk mappings*, defines the object chunks as views on the reference ontology. A view mechanism is required because the conceptualization as specified by a domain ontology may not always exactly suit the requirements of the website. E.g., a domain ontology may specify an address as composed of a street, number and city, but the website may prefer to consider the address as a single entity (i.e. a single string).

To illustrate the different mappings, we give a small example. As in section 2, we use Description Logic syntax, this time to describe object chunks, reference ontology and domain ontologies. Suppose, a first (existing) domain ontology contains (besides other axioms) the following axioms: {$Man \sqsubseteq Person$, $Woman \sqsubseteq Person$, $\top \sqsubseteq \forall hasMaternityLeave.\{true, false\}$, $\exists hasMatenityLeave.\top \sqsubseteq Woman$, $Woman \sqsubseteq (= 1\ hasMaternityLeave)$} (Informally: 'Man' and 'Woman' are subtypes of 'Person', and for a 'Woman' it is specified if she is on maternity leave or not). A second (existing) domain ontology describes a partly overlapping domain, and contains the following axioms: {$\top \sqsubseteq \forall hasSex.\{M, F\}$, $\exists hasSex.\top \sqsubseteq Person$, $\exists hasStreet.\top \sqsubseteq Person$, $\top \sqsubseteq \forall hasStreet.String$, $\exists hasCity.\top \sqsubseteq Person$, $\top \sqsubseteq \forall hasCity.String$, $\exists hasCountry.\top \sqsubseteq Person$, $\top \sqsubseteq \forall hasPostalCountry.String$} (a 'Person' is either male or female, specified by the 'hasSex' property, and a 'Person' has an address which is specified by the 'hasStreet', 'hasCity' and 'hasCountry' properties). To align these two domain ontologies, it is necessary to resolve the different ways of representing a person's sex (i.e. respectively by using subtypes, and by using a hasSex property) and furthermore to merge the non-overlapping parts of both ontologies. Suppose this is done by constructing the following reference ontology:

{$Man \sqsubseteq Person$, $Woman \sqsubseteq Person$, $\top \sqsubseteq \forall hasMaternityLeave.\{true, false\}$, $\exists hasMatenityLeave.\top \sqsubseteq Woman$, $\exists hasStreet.\top \sqsubseteq Person$, $\top \sqsubseteq \forall hasStreet.String$, $\exists hasCity.\top \sqsubseteq Person$, $\top \sqsubseteq \forall hasCity.String$, $\exists hasCountry.\top \sqsubseteq Person$, $\top \sqsubseteq \forall\ hasCountry.String$}

Then, the following domain ontology mappings express the relations between the reference ontology and the two domain ontologies (trivial mappings are omitted):

Reference ontology	**Domain Ontology1**	**Domain Ontology2**
Man	Man	Person WHERE hasSex = 'M'
Woman	Woman	Person WHERE hasSex = 'F'
hasMaternityLeave	hasMaternityLeave	-

Now assume that the Web designer wants to consider an 'address' as a single string. This is expressed in the object chunk as follows: {$Man \sqsubseteq Person$, $Woman \sqsubseteq Person$, $\exists hasAddress.\top \sqsubseteq Person$, $\top \sqsubseteq \forall hasAddress.String$} ('Man' and 'Woman' are subtypes of 'Person', and a 'Person' has an address specified as a single string). Now, 'hasAddress' cannot refer in a one-to-one way to a concept in the reference ontology. Instead, the following Object Chunk Mapping is needed (trivial one-to-one mappings are again omitted). The '+'-sign indicates the concatenation of strings.

Object Chunk	**Reference ontology**
hasAddress	hasStreet + hasCity + hasCountry

Data Source Mapping

When the website is generated (from the models), the actual pages need to be filled with data. The designer may decide to use a data source (e.g., a relational database) to maintain the data. To be able to generate the actual pages a mapping is needed between the conceptual level (i.e. the object chunks) and this data source. The mapping is defined between the reference ontology and the data source. E.g., in the case of a relational database, the data source mapping indicates the tables and columns where instances of concepts of the reference ontology can be found. Note that, similar as for object chunk mappings and domain ontology mappings, no one-to-one mapping can be assumed. For example, for a relational table 'Person(ID, street, city, country, gender, hasMaternityLeave), we have the following data source mappings:

Reference ontology	Data Source
hasMaternityLeave	SELECT hasMaternityLeave FROM Person WHERE gender='F'
Woman	SELECT ID FROM Person WHERE gender='F'
Man	SELECT ID FROM Person WHERE gender='M'

The different mappings will be used to generate the actual annotations (see section 5). This approach is different from the usual annotation approaches that define mappings with the ontology directly on the implementation level (see also section 6 on related work). In our approach, the mappings are defined at the conceptual level. This has several advantages. We mention the most important ones:

1. *Implementation independent*: the basis for the annotations is made on the conceptual level, and therefore the actual website annotations can be generated along with different implementations.
2. *Consistency of annotations*: as concepts (in the object chunks) are linked to Reference Ontology concepts and only one link per concept is given, it is not possible (like in other annotation approaches) that the actual annotations (for different instances) are not consistent.
3. *Both static and dynamic websites supported*: the implementation generation process of WSDM (see section 5) does not distinguish between static and dynamic websites; annotations are effortlessly generated for both types of websites.

4 Structural Semantic Annotations

By exploiting the semantics of the modelling concepts (e.g., menu, header, node) used in the different design models (and captured in the WSDM Ontology), useful annotations concerning the structure of the website can be generated. This is realized by defining a mapping between the WSDM Ontology concepts and an external ontology describing the semantics of structural elements (tailored for a certain use). An example of such an ontology is the WAfA ontology [19]. Subsequently, these mappings can be used to annotate the actual website with concepts from this external ontology. As the mappings are dependent on the ontology used, we will illustrate the approach for two different ontologies: the WAfA ontology (developed to assist visually impaired users) and a (newly created) block-ontology (to assist search engines in more accurately indexing a website). Evidently, it is possible to annotate one website using multiple ontologies, each describing different types of structuring elements.

Structural Annotations to support Accessibility for Visually Impaired User

Currently, most visually impaired users rely on screen readers to access websites. These screen readers sequentially read a page. This is not only time-consuming for the user but in addition a lot of information that is conveyed by means of layout (e.g., white space, tables used for structuring) is lost. The Dante approach [19] allows annotating Web pages using the WAfA ontology, which defines concepts that allow indicating how objects on a page are presented and the role they fulfil in the presentation. These annotations allow (external applications) to transcode Web pages in a form more suitable for accessing pages using screen readers. However, currently it is a manual annotation process, and this is an effort that is too labour intensive to be usable in general. Moreover, the resulting annotations are typically sensitive to changes in the websites content or structure (and re-annotation is required).

By defining a mapping between the modelling concepts in the WSDM ontology and the concepts in the WAfA ontology, the WAfA annotations can be generated automatically when developing a website using WSDM. Here we give the mapping for two representative concepts. To describe the mapping rules, we use the following notational convention: first, the WAfA concept is given in bold, followed by it's meaning (in italic). Where needed an informal explanation of the mapping rule is given and finally a formal definition using Semantic Web Rule Language (SWRL)[3] which is particularly suited to handle OWL specifications and makes automatic annotation generation possible (see section 5). Some mapping rules between the WSDM and WAfA-ontology are straightforward one-to-one mappings; others are more complex and need to exploit the knowledge captured by means of several concepts, and/or the relationships between them. Two examples follow:

- **WAfA:TableOfContent:** *A list of available sections and a link to the beginning of each section*
  `wsdm:NavigationTableOfContent(?i) ⇒ WAfA:TableOfContent(?i)`[4]
- **WAfA:DropDownLinkMenu:** *A DropDownLinkMenu is a menu that appears below an item when the user clicks on it.* A linkmenu corresponds to a wsdm:Menu represented as a wsdm:List in WSDM. Furthermore, to denote it is a *dropdown* menu, it should have an associated wsdm:Behaviour defined with wsdm:Event 'onClick' and wsdm:Action 'dropDown'. Each menu with this behaviour is a DropDownLinkMenu in WSDM.

```
wsdm:Menu(?i) ∧ wsdm:representedBy(?i, ?x) ∧ wsdm:List(?x)  ∧
wsdm:hasBehavior(?x, ?y) ∧ wsdm:Behavior(?y) ∧ wsdm:onEvent(?y,
'on Click') ∧ wsdm:doAction(?y, 'dropDown')
⇒      wafa:DropDownLinkMenu(?i)
```

Other mapping rules are defined in a similar manner. Currently, we have defined mapping rules for 74% of the WAfA Ontology concepts (see [16]). Note that this mapping is a once-only activity. Thereafter, it can be used to automatically generate structural annotations for any website[5].

Structural Annotations for Search Engine Support

To improve search results, search engines apply a technique called page segmentation (see e.g. [3] for an overview). The aim of page segmentation is to distinguish meaningful "blocks" (also called "passage") in a Web page according to the logical structure, the presentation and the semantics of page objects. This information is subsequently exploited in page-rank and website indexing algorithms (e.g. [3, 10]). Extensive research has been done in devising information retrieval algorithms that are able to extract the relevant blocks from a given Web page. Unfortunately, as valuable design knowledge about the structure and semantics of page objects is not available in

[3] See http://www.daml.org/2003/11/swrl/.

[4] Both ontologies were developed independently, which explains different names for similar concepts.

[5] Compare to manual annotation approaches, where each website needs be processed by hand.

typical Web pages, output of these algorithms is unavoidably limited. Similar as in the previous case, semantics concerning structure available in the WSDM design models can be used to automatically generate semantic annotations describing the "blocks" required to sophisticate search engine's indexing algorithms. As no ontology describing these blocks and their relationships exists, we have created a prove-of-concept block-ontology describing different semantic blocks (e.g., topics, sections, units) and their relationships (both semantic, e.g., 'isSubTopicOf', and spatial, e.g., 'below'). Note that it would be possible to directly use the WSDM Ontology to make the annotations. However, this would require knowledge of the WSDM Ontology by the page segmentation algorithms. Two example mapping rules are:

- **block:Section:** *A block representing a section in a Web page*
  `wsdm:Section(?i) ⇒ block:Section(?i)`
- **block:SemanticBlock:** *A block representing a semantic unit (presented together).* In WSDM, an object chunk represents (a unit of) information needed for a single task. The wsdm:Grid representing a wsdm:ObjectChunk can be annotated as a block:SemanticBlock:
  ```
  wsdm:Grid(?i) ∧ wsdm:representsChunk(?i, ?x) ∧
  wsdm:ObjectChunk(?x) ⇒ block:SemanticBlock(?i)
  ```

5 Implementation Generation Process

To generate the actual semantically annotated website, a transformation pipeline is used. We will not explain the complete pipeline but instead focus on the generation of the annotations. The pipeline takes all the models of the conceptual and the implementation design as inputs. The transformations to generate the implementation of the website (without annotations) consists of four steps (T1, T2, T3 and T4 in Figure 3):

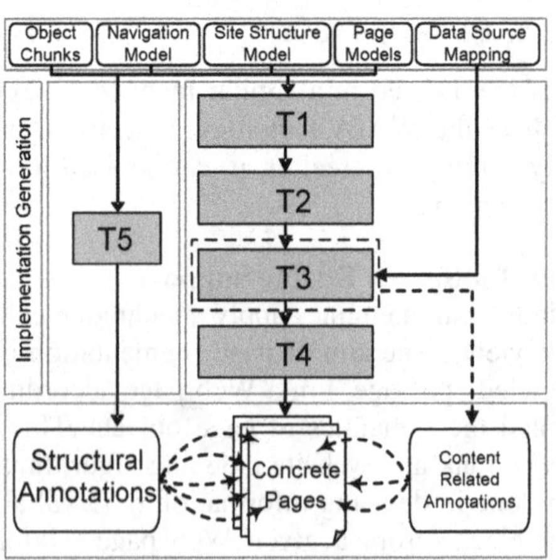

Fig. 3. Implementation Generation Overview

- *Model Integration (T1):* integrates the different input models into one single model. In principle, this transformation can be omitted, but it simplifies the following transformations.

- *Implementation Mapping (T2):* the implementation platform is chosen (e.g., HTML, XHTML, WML), and the integrated model derived in T1 is transformed towards the chosen platform. References to data (i.e., to instances in object chunks) are not yet processed; this is done in the next transformation T3.
- *Query Construction (T3):* the references to instance values in the object chunks are resolved and mapped onto queries on the data source. This is performed fully automatically because the mappings from the object chunks to the reference ontology and from the reference ontology to the data source are available (see section 5.1 for an example).
- *Query Execution (T4):* finally, the queries derived in T3 are processed, and the actual pages are generated by inserting the data at the proper places. When the query execution phase is performed offline, a static website is created; when it is performed at runtime, a dynamic website is the result.

Generating Content-Related Annotations

The content of the website is annotated by means of the OWL reference ontology (see section 3). Remember that the object chunks are defined as views (or conceptual queries) on the reference ontology. In the query construction (T3), these conceptual queries are transformed into executable queries using both the object chunk- and data source mappings. We explain by means of a small example (based on the example of section 3) how these mappings allow us to generate content-related annotations.

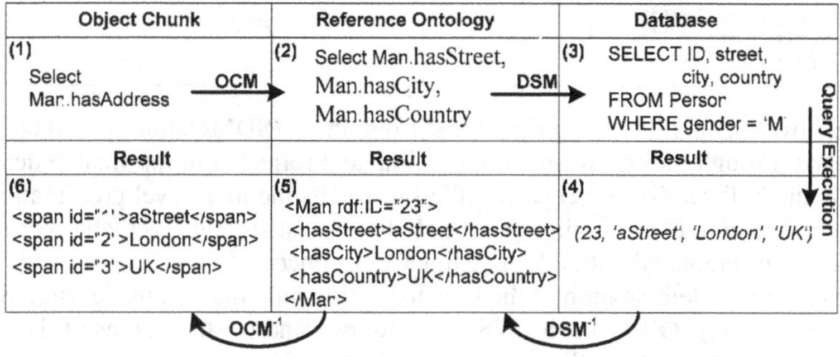

Fig. 4. Generating Content-Related Semantic Annotations

An overview of the content-related annotation generation process is illustrated in figure 4. Consider a conceptual query expressing the address of men (1). Using the object chunk mapping (OCM), this conceptual query on the original object chunk is transformed into a conceptual query on the reference ontology (2). Using the data source mapping (DSM), the resulting conceptual query is transformed into an executable (SQL) query (3) on the actual data source (here a relational database). The result of this query is a set of instances, in the form of a table, of which an example tuple is shown in (4). The data in this table is subsequently transformed into a set of instances of the reference ontology using the inverse data source mapping (DSM^{-1}) (5). Finally, the address is presented as a single string (as was specified by the object chunk), using the inverse object chunk mapping (OCM^{-1}) (6). Note that, by inserting <span>-tags surrounding the individual attributes, we are still able to refer to the individual parts of the address string on the Web page, i.e. no semantic information present in the reference ontology is lost. Finally, we link the generated HTML code (given in (6)) and the instantiation of reference ontology concepts together using XPointer expressions: page.html#xpointer(id("1"))<=>refOnt#xpointer(id("23")/hasStreet)

Generating Structural Annotations
Taking as input the design models in the WSDM Ontology and the mapping between the WSDM Ontology and an (external) ontology describing structural elements (e.g., the WAfA ontology), a transformation *T5* can be added to the transformation pipeline to generate the structural annotations. To illustrate the generation of structural annotations, consider the example in which a (WSDM) menu with menu-items is transformed to a bulleted list in HTML, including structural annotation denoting the presence of a menu for accessibility purposes (using the WAfA ontology):

(1) Result after T1

```
<wsdm:Menu rdf:id="menu1">
 <wsdm:hasItem>
  <wsdm:MenuItem rdf:id="item1">
   <wsdm:Label>item 1</wsdm:Label>
   <wsdm:hasNavRef
       rdf:resource="#ref1"/>
  </wsdm:MenuItem> </wsdm:hasItem>
 <wsdm:hasItem>
  <wsdm:MenuItem id="item2">
   ...
  </wsdm:MenuItem> </wsdm:hasItem>
 <wsdm:representedBy
    rdf:resource="#bulletedList"/>
</wsdm:Menu>
```

(2) Result after T4

```
<ul id="menu1">
 <li id="item1">
   <a href="a link">item 1</a>
 </li>
 <li id="item2">...</li>
</ul>
```

(3) Result after T5

```
http://.../wafa.owl#linkMenu
http://www.example.com/page.html
#xpointer(id("menu1"))
```

Note how the unique ids, originating from the WSDMOntology instances, are maintained through the transformation pipeline and reflected in the final code. In our example, the bulleted list in **(2)** carries the same id as the high-level presentation concept wsdm:Menu in **(1)**, denoting that the (bulleted) list structure actually represents a menu, and it is annotated with a WAfA:linkMenu concept.

A prototype implementation of the transformation pipeline was made using Semantic Web technology: OWL for the WSDM Ontology and (instantiations of the) design models and object chunks, XSLT to perform the transformation steps, and xPointer to link annotations and actual implementation (i.e. HTML).

6 Related Work

When reviewing the literature concerning semantic annotations, we can mainly distinguish three different approaches: manual, (semi-)automatic, and Web engineering approaches. The difference between manual and automatic approaches consists of the fact that the former ones require a (manual) mapping between content and semantics, while the latter attempt to extract the semantics automatically (e.g., using NLP techniques). Examples of automatic approaches include Melita [2] and KMI annotation framework [13]. Manual annotation approaches offer the user tool support to define annotations for HTML documents. The first tool in this context was the SHOE Knowledge Annotator [9], which only supports static Web pages. In course of time, other manual annotation tools arose: SMORE [18] (adding authoring support by using an embedded HTML editor), Ont-O-Mat [8] (adding support for dynamic Web pages by annotating database implementations).

Both manual and automatic approaches suffer some disadvantages. The adequacy of automatically generated annotations is generally lower compared to manual approaches; the disadvantage of manual approaches is that the annotations are defined on an implementation level (making them more vulnerable to changes) and require a substantial effort from the designer after the website is already implemented.

Recently, research has also been focused on integrating semantic Web technology into Web design methods. Examples of semantic Web design methods include SHDM [14], Hera [7], OntoWeaver [12], OntoWebber [11]. These methods use ontology languages (e.g., RDFS, OWL) as modeling language for their design models. This has the advantage that existing ontologies can be used in the design process and that a verification of the design models is feasible. Some of these approaches offer the possibility to make the data models internally constructed externally available (in the form of RDFS or OWL). However, none of these approaches actually generates websites that are annotated i.e., they rather offer the content (independently) in user- (e.g., HTML) and machine-readable form (e.g., RDF). Explicitly linking Web content with ontologies that describe the semantics (semantic annotations) is required to support for example content rating and filtering (see http://www.w3.org/TR/rdf-pics). These methods also do not provide support for structural annotations.

The only known approach similar to the one described in this paper, is WEESA [17]. However, WEESA is not a design method by itself, but can be used after the design and for design methods that specify their design models in XML. It is able to generate content-related semantic annotations by defining a mapping between the XML schemas and existing ontologies. The disadvantage of WEESA is that it cannot benefit from the Web design process itself, but instead needs to define the mapping regardless if a domain ontology was used during the design process or not. As far as we are aware of, no other Web design method generates structural annotations.

7 Conclusion

In this paper, we described how in the website design method WSDM Semantic Web technology (OWL) and conceptual modeling is used to generate two types of semantic annotations: content-related annotations and structural annotations. The use of ontologies for the conceptual modeling of information and functionality during the design process allows (semi-) automatically generation of content-related semantic annotations. Three different situations are considered 1) no existing domain ontology is available, 2) a single existing domain ontology can be used, and 3) multiple existing domain ontologies must be used. Next to content-related semantic annotations, we also discussed structural semantic annotations: annotations which (semantically) describe the structure of the website. This type of annotations is generated exploiting the semantics of the different design modeling concepts. The approach is illustrated for two types of structural annotations and their usefulness has been pointed out.

The integrating of the annotation generation in the design process of a website, as described here, has the following advantages over existing (post-website-deployment) annotation approaches: smaller effort required (i.e. content-related annotations are semi-automatically generated, structural annotations fully automatically), robustness (annotations are not invalidated when re-designing the website), higher consistency, and support for dynamic websites.

References

1. Baader, F., Calvanese, D., McGuinness, D., Nardi, D., Patel-Schneider, P.: The Description Logic Handbook (2003)
2. Ciravegna, F., Dingli, A., Petrelli, D., Wilks, Y: User-System Cooperation in Document Annotation based on Information Extraction. In Proc. of EKAW 02, Sigüenza Spain (2002)
3. Deng Cai, Shipeng Yu, Ji-Rong Wen, Wei-Ying Ma.: Block-based web search. ACM SIGIR. (2004), pp. 456-463
4. De Troyer, O. and Leune, C.: WSDM: A User-Centered Design Method for Web Sites. In Proceedings of the 7th WWW Conference, Elsevier, (1998), pp. 85-94
5. De Troyer, O., Casteleyn, S.: Modeling Complex Processes for Web Applications using WSDM. In Proceedings of the 3rd Int. IWWOST workshop (2003)
6. De Troyer, O., Plessers, P., Casteleyn, S.: Conceptual View Integration for Audience Driven Web Design. In CD-ROM Proc. of the WWW2003 Conference, Budapest Hungary (2003)
7. Frasincar, F., Houben, G.-J.: Hypermedia presentation adaptation on the semantic web. In Proceedings of AH 2002, LNCS, Springer (2002), pp. 133-142
8. Handschuh, S., Staab, S.: Authoring and annotation of web pages in CREAM. The 11th Int. World Wide Web Conference (WWW2002), Honolulu Hawaii USA (2002)
9. Heflin, J., Hendler, J.: Searching the web with SHOE. Artificial Intelligence for Web Search, Papers from the AAAI Workshop, WS-00-01, AAAI Press (2000), pp. 35-40
10. Jiang X.-M., Xue, G.-R., Song W.-G., Zeng, H.J., Chen, Z., Ma W.-Y.: Exploiting PageRank at Different Block Level. In Proceedings of the WISE 2004, (2004), pp. 241-252
11. Jin, Y., Xu, S., Decker, S., Wiederhold, G.: OntoWebber: A Novel Approach for Managing Data on the Web. In Proceedings of ICDE (2002), pp. 488-489
12. Lei, Y., Motta, E., Domingue, J.: Modelling Data-Intensive Web Sites with OntoWeaver. In proceedings of the International Workshop WISM2004, Riga Latvia (2004)
13. Kiryakov, A., Popov, B., Terziev, I., Manov, D., Ognyanoff, D.: Semantic Annotation, Indexing, and Retrieval. Elsevier's Journal of Web Semantics, Vol. 2, Issue (1) (2005)
14. Moura, S., Schwabe, D.: Interface Development for Hypermedia Applications in the Semantic Web. In Proceedings of LA Web 2004, Ribeirão Preto, Brasil. IEEE CS Press (2004)
15. Plessers, P., De Troyer, O.: Annotation for the Semamtic Web during Website Development, In Proceedings of the ICWE 2004 Conference, Munich Germany (2004), pp. 349-353
16. Plessers, P. Casteleyn, S., Yesilada, Y., De Troyer, O., Stevens, R., Harper, S., Goble, C.: Accessibility: A Web Engineering Approach, In Proceedings of the 14th Int. World Wide Web Conference, Chiba Japan (2005), pp. 353-362
17. Reif, G., Gall, H., Jazayeri, M.: WEESA - Web Engineering for Semantic Web Applications. In Proceedings of the 14th Int. World Wide Web Conference, Chiba Japan (2005)
18. Vargas-Vera, M., Motta, E., Domingue, J., Lanzoni, M., Stutt, A., Ciravegna, F.: MnM: Ontology Driven Semi-Automatic and Automatic Support for Semantic Markup. In Proc. of the 13th International Conference on Knowledge Engineering and Management (2002)
19. Yesilada, Y., Harper, S., Goble, G., Stevens, R. Screen Readers Cannot See. In ICWE 2004 Proceedings, (2004), pp 445-458

A More Expressive Softgoal Conceptualization for Quality Requirements Analysis

Ivan J. Jureta[1], Stéphane Faulkner[1], and Pierre-Yves Schobbens[2]

[1] Information Management Research Unit (IMRU), University of Namur,
8 Rempart de la Vierge, B-5000 Namur, Belgium
iju@info.fundp.ac.be, stephane.faulkner@fundp.ac.be
[2] Institut d'Informatique, University of Namur,
8 Rempart de la Vierge, B-5000 Namur, Belgium
pys@info.fundp.ac.be

Abstract. Initial software quality requirements tend to be imprecise, subjective, idealistic, and context-specific. An extended characterization of the common Softgoal concept is proposed for representing and reasoning about such requirements during the early stages of the requirements engineering process. The types of information often implicitly contained in a Softgoal instance are highlighted to allow richer requirements to be obtained. On the basis of the revisited conceptual foundations, guidelines are suggested as to the techniques that need to be present in requirements modeling approaches that aim to employ the given Softgoal conceptualization.

1 Dealing with Software Quality Requirements

Ensuring the quality of software has become a major issue in software engineering research and practice since the 1970s [5]. As increasingly complex software plays a critical role in business, comprehensive and precise methods and tools are needed to create software products and services that are safe, dependable, and efficient [26].

Software quality is defined by the International Organization for Standardization [12] as the totality of features and characteristics of a software product that bear on its ability to satisfy stated or implied needs. Ensuring the quality of software therefore amounts to making sure that software behavior is in line with stated and implied needs.

It is widely acknowledged that quality needs to be taken into account early in the software development process [8,30,19]. Quality requires specifying stated and implied needs. Approaches focusing on ensuring quality during the development process by guiding functional requirements specification decisions by quality considerations, so that the latter justify the former, are termed process-oriented. In contrast, product-oriented approaches (e.g., [11,13]) evaluate the quality of already developed software products, and are particularly relevant for, e.g., component selection [2].

D.W. Embley, A. Olivé, and S. Ram (Eds.): ER 2006, LNCS 4215, pp. 281–295, 2006.

Although a large body of work deals with quality assurance in a process-oriented manner, a non-negligible part of it relies on the usual Softgoal concept for the representation and reasoning about quality-related requirements. In doing so, procedural aspects of methods for dealing with quality during requirements engineering (RE) activities have been considerably developed, while conceptual foundations have not evolved in a notable manner. In particular, a more extensive view on the conceptualization and formalisms for representing and using quality requirements while taking into account their multi-facetted nature has not been proposed yet. We need to deal with requirements that are not only implicit, but also subjective, context-specific, imprecise, and ordered by preference.

The work presented in this paper is a step towards a more profound understanding of requirements that are expressed usually in requirements goal diagrams (such as, e.g., i^* [32]) as instances of the Softgoal concept. Overall, instances of the original Softgoal concept are seen as frequently containing information that is, not only subjective and context-specific (as assumed in the original definition), but also imprecise and involving preferences of the stakeholder who suggested the requirements modeled as the given softgoal. It is therefore suggested that the Softgoal is a multi-facetted concept that requires specialized techniques for dealing with its additional facets. This paper thus proves useful both in terms of advancing the understanding of a key concept in the RE modeling field, and in arguing that additional considerations need be taken into account when a RE method or framework that employs the Softgoal concept is being constructed and applied. Finally, the reader will undoubtedly notice that the discussion below is independent of a particular RE framework, which supports our arguments regarding the applicability of this discussion to many (at least goal-oriented) RE methods.

The paper is organized as follows. Part of the literature on the treatment of quality requirements, applicable to the discussion in this paper is first overviewed. The bulk of the paper, which discusses and revisits the original Softgoal conceptualization is then presented. A set of general guidelines on the characteristics of RE methods aiming to employ the suggested conceptualization are presented. Finally, conclusions are summarized and directions for future work are identified.

2 Related Work

To facilitate the discussion of related work, Table 1 gives a classification of process-oriented approaches. Formal approaches rely on formal notations such as temporal or fuzzy logic to specify nonfunctional requirements in a precise way, while semi-formal provide structured notations (unrelated to mathematical logic) that are used mainly to organize information about nonfunctional requirements. Qualitative approaches traditionally evaluate the degree of quality requirements satisfaction using subjective qualitative characterizations. In contrast, quantitative techniques focus on estimating the probability of failure of quality-related goals [19], or use informal measures of the degree to which software properties contribute to specific qualities [1]. Decision on placing some approaches in qualitative or quantitative category is based on the methods described in the cited papers; e.g., adapting a qualitative approach to use quantitative methods remains possible, but is not discussed in the literature.

Table 1. A classification of process-oriented approaches proposed in related work for ensuring quality during the software development process

	Qualitative	*Quantitative*
Formal	[18,20,31]	[19,23]
Informal	[8,22,27,17]	[9,1]

The NFR framework [22,8] has been the first to propose the concept of Softgoal in the RE context (the original concept that is specialized for RE in NFR has a longer history—e.g., [28]) and a process for dealing with nonfunctional requirements. In NFR, Softgoals describe quality requirements in very abstract terms. They are related with contribution links to support qualitative reasoning about the degree to which alternative software properties satisfy the desired qualities. Their intuitiveness and ease of use have led to their integration in goal-oriented RE (GORE) frameworks: $i*$ [32], Tropos [6], GRL [21], and REF [11]. However, the Softgoal concept remains informally defined and used. Many GORE frameworks that have adopted NFR suffer from the same symptoms, as few extend the NFR Softgoal conceptualization. [9] adds a probabilistic layer to study the impact of requirements change on quality satisfaction. Others [1] use multi-criteria decision techniques to select among alternative software architectures.

Formal approaches have been proposed to provide systematic support when semi-formal techniques are considered inadequate. Instead of Softgoals, [19] is focused on software goals that are precise, but cannot be completely achieved by the software (i.e., they are idealistic). Quality variables are associated with all goals that can only be partially satisfied and objective functions are defined over these variables to indicate ideal software behavior. Quality variables seem to be metrics that measure performance of the behavior specified by the goal to which the variables are associated. Based on a sample of software operation, probabilities of satisfying a goal can be estimated—these probability values indicate the degree to which the goal is satisfied. Imprecise requirements are treated with fuzzy logic in [18,20,31,23]. While fuzzy logic may be an interesting approach for formalizing imprecise requirements, it has been discussed mostly in isolation from typical RE activities, although it is not obvious how such formalisms can be integrated within existing, more extensive frameworks.

Discussion. Expressive formalisms such as fuzzy logic have unfortunately been discussed somewhat separately from confirmed GORE methodologies and frameworks, making the us of the techniques proposed in [18,20,31,23] impractical and difficult. The informed reader will also note that fuzzy logic is merely one among many approaches to imprecision. While quality requirements are indeed imprecise, they do have other characteristics that need to be accounted for during representation and reasoning. Partial satisfaction, extensively discussed in [19] is relevant, but is discussed with focus on precise goals. It should also be noted that the NFR approach and other RE frameworks using the Softgoal concept fail to address situations in which systematic and formal treatment is required, even though the growing criticality of software increases the need for rigor.

The research presented in the remainder of this paper starts from a hypothesis that the informally defined Softgoal concept, extensively used in NFR, can be more valuable if its facets: subjectivity, context-specificity, idealism, impreciseness, and preference are characterized explicitly. Such a characterization will allow both a systematic treatment of the stated facets, and a closer integration of the proposed Softgoal analysis approach and later RE activities, such as functional goal specification. In this respect, the proposed conceptualization draw on the extensive body of related work to provide a more integrative view on the representation and manipulation of software quality information.

3 The Softgoal Concept Revisited

Softgoals provided by the stakeholders at the outset of the RE process, such as "the software should be fast", can be characterized as *imprecise*, *subjective*, *context-specific*, and *ideal*. Imprecision stems essentially from the inability to specify what "fast" mean, so that they could be measured. Subjectivity results from the fact that two people can evaluate the same software as being fast to a different extent. Context-specificity further entails that "fast", or "usable", "maintainable", "adaptable" (standard qualities of software [8]) will have a different meaning for each project. Finally, implicit preference information is hidden behind terms such as "fast software": various measures can be taken, but low values will be preferred. All of the above characteristics need to be taken into account to deal systematically with quality requirements. To use the Softgoal concept to represent and reason about such requirements, it is necessary to make its traditional definition more expressive and precise. The choice of the Softgoal concept is based on the illustrated usefulness of the underlying goal concept in RE activities, such as elicitation, elaboration, structuring, specification, analysis, negotiation, documentation, and modification of requirements [29].

3.1 Functional and Nonfunctional Goals vs. Hardgoals and Softgoals

A goal can be broadly defined as a constraint on software behavior that is desired by stakeholders involved in the software development project (e.g., [10]). Among the many proposed goal taxonomies (for an overview, see [30]), two are particularly relevant for quality requirements modeling. *Functional* goals have been used to represent services that the software is expected to deliver (i.e., *what* the software does), whereas *nonfunctional* goals refer to quality requirements that the software needs to satisfy while delivering the services (i.e., *how* the software provides services; e.g., securely, safely, rapidly, etc.). While it is common to equate nonfunctional goals and softgoals (e.g., [22]), it is suggested that *softgoals* belong to another taxonomy, in which they are opposed to *hardgoals* [30]. Although softgoal satisfaction cannot be established in a clear-cut sense [22], the satisfaction of a hardgoal is objective in that it can be established using (formal) verification techniques [10]. Consequently, there are: (i) *functional hardgoals*, which are objective goals about services that software needs to deliver (e.g., "whenever an e-mail marked as important arrives, the user is informed with a pop-up window and a sound"); (ii) *nonfunctional hardgoals* which describe objective criteria for how the services are to be delivered (e.g., "the user should be informed about important e-mail arrival within 1sec"); (iii) *functional softgoals* describe imprecisely stated software services (e.g., "the user should be informed when an e-mail marked as important arrives"); and finally, (iv) *nonfunctional softgoals* characterize imprecise statements for how a service is to be delivered (e.g., "the user should be informed rapidly about the arrival of an e-mail marked as important"). It is likely that statements about the needs that the software is to satisfy will be closer to nonfunctional softgoals than to functional hardgoals at the outset of the RE phase of software development. Notice that there is a large gap in precision between nonfunctional softgoals and functional hardgoals example: the former says nothing on how the user is to be informed, while the latter gives a specific context (the e-mail reader software) and process (e-mail arrives, pop-up is displayed, and a sound is played). Having clarified the informal meaning of Softgoal in relation to goal types, we proceed to its characterization.

3.2 Characterizing Softgoals

The traditional view of softgoals [21] focuses essentially on the subjectivity facet:

> "A softgoal is similar to a (hard) goal except that the criteria for whether a softgoal is achieved are not clear-cut and a priori."

A definition proposed in the REF framework [11] adds details:

> "For a soft goal [...] it is up to the goal originator [i.e., the agent wishing goal achievement], or to an agreement between the involved agents, to decide when the goal is considered to have been achieved [...]. In comparison to hard goals, soft goals can be highly subjective and strictly related to a particular context; they enable the analysts to highlight quality issues (e.g., the concept of a 'fast computer') from the outset, making explicit the semantics assigned to them by the stakeholders."

Softgoals therefore involve subjectivity because of a lack of objective achievement criteria, and the responsibility for evaluating their achievement falls on stakeholders. Notice that it is imprecise to say that quality considerations can mainly be modeled with softgoals, since quality refers to software behavior that can be both objectively and subjectively evaluated. However, there is more to quality requirements than the current softgoal conceptualization allows representing and reasoning about. Consider a simple example of a quality requirement often encountered in practice: "the software should be fast". By examining the stated and implied information contained in this statement, a notation can be proposed to model the various softgoal facets.

Subjectivity. Since many stakeholders (i.e., parties being influenced by, or having an influence on the development project) are likely to be involved in the RE phase of software development, the specificity of each these parties' views on the software, the development process, and the environment in which the software will operate needs to be accounted for. The usefulness of separating stakeholders' concerns and the use of adapted, different notations is now widely accepted. Such multi-perspective requirements require techniques for making individual views consistent either by reconciling requirements specifications written in different specification languages (e.g., [25]), or written different styles, terminology, etc. (e.g., [14]). The resulting heterogeneous representations need to be integrated to ensure consistency [29], coordination and composition [24].

We argue that subjectivity in softgoals can be accounted for in a relatively straightforward manner by annotating the softgoal with an identifier of its stakeholder and the suggestion time. Then each stakeholder can refine his requirement (by answering, e.g.: "When is this software fast for you?") independently.

Softgoal: E-Mail reader should be fast.
Added on: 08Nov2005
Stakeholder: Mr. J. Smith
Refined into: An e-mail reader is fast if it opens quickly and creates new e-mail messages quickly.

If a similar softgoal is stated, our approach will see it as different:

Softgoal: E-Mail reader should be fast.
Added on: 08Nov2005
Stakeholder: Mr. J. Smith
Refined into: An e-mail reader is fast if it opens quickly and creates new e-mail messages quickly.

Context-Specificity. At an abstract level, information about the context to which the quality requirement refers can be specific to: the software, the software development process, and the environment in which the software will operate (which can be the hardware environment, the human environment, etc.). For example, "development cost should be low" is a softgoal related to the software development process, whereas "the throughput should be high on the production line" is specific to the human environment in which the software will operate. The combination of the software and environment compose the *information system* (IS) [34]. To specify the context of a softgoal, an attribute *applies to* (with *software*, *environment*, *process* as allowed values) is added to the softgoal template:

Softgoal: E-Mail reader should be fast.
Added on: 08Nov2005
Stakeholder: Mr. J. Smith
Refined into: An e-mail reader is fast if it opens quickly and creates

new e-mail messages quickly.

Applies To: Software

Idealism and Preferences. Quality requirements are often not clear-cut. It is thus beneficial to measure the degree to which a quality requirement, modeled as a softgoal, is satisfied. Metrics, called quality variables in [19], can be designed based on refined requirements. Consider the earlier Mr. J. Smith's Softgoal. It can be refined into two Softgoals, each having a quality variable and an objective function.

Softgoal: The E-Mail reader should open fast.

...

Preferences:

Objective Functions:

Name	Def	Type	Modal	Target	Threshold	Current
3SecOpen	P(TimeToOpen < 3sec)	Prob	Max	80%	70%	*unknown*

Quality Variables:

TimeToOpen: *Duration*

Sample space: distribution of old e-mails, size of old e-mails,...

Definition: time between the input of the request to open the software and the moment the software functionalities can be used.

Softgoal: It should be possible to create new e-mail messages quickly.

...

Preferences:

Objective Functions:

Name	Def	Type	Modal	Target	Threshold	Current
2SecCreate	E(TeToCrMail) < 2sec	Durat	Min	1Sec	2Sec	*unknown*

Quality Variables:

TimeToCrMail: *Duration*

Sample space: number of options available when writing an e-mail,...

Definition: time between the input of the request to create a new e-mail message and the moment its content can be written.

Quality variables are random variables whose distribution can be estimated using data collected by experimentation. Sample spaces can be, e.g., related to similar functionality in existing software. The estimated probability distribution functions are then used to estimate the probability of satisfying the softgoal to some desired level and questions such as, e.g., "What is the probability for the software to open in less than 2 seconds?" or "Under what time will the software open in 90% of cases?" can be answered. Objective functions are associated with quantifiable quality variables, and target levels of performance for each variable are specified. A modal (i.e., *max* or *min*) is also added to indicate the preferred direction. Because not all objective functions are stated in terms of probabilities (i.e., there are objective functions defined over quality variables), the tables used in [19] to specify objective functions are extended here with a *type* column, to give an indication on the type of variable used in the objective function. In addition, a threshold column is added to further distinguish acceptable from unacceptable degree of softgoal satisfaction.

Quality variables combined with objective functions as in [19] allow the degree of softgoal satisfaction to be measured in cases in which the degree of satisfaction is not under stakeholders' complete control (i.e., there is a probabilistic component in the events affecting softgoal satisfaction). While this is often the case, the RE phase will also involve preferences that can be perceived as deterministic. Assume that a stakeholder provides the following view of a softgoal:

Softgoal: Software should not take too much hardware resources.

...

Stakeholder's view: An e-mail reader will take little hardware resources if it does not occupy memory when not running (i.e., it does not run "in the background").

The stakeholder expresses preference in the quality requirement modeled with the above softgoal. Traditional economics preferences conceptualization (e.g., [16]) can be used to make the preference information from the stakeholders' view explicit. Implicitly, a statement of preference provides partial information about alternatives that are to be ordered using preference relations. We use the classical preference formalism to indicate strict, partial or indifference preference. Using this simple formalism, we can write:

Softgoal: Software should not take too much hardware resources.

...

Preferences:

Choice Preferences:

(run software when requested)$\succ$(software runs in background)

Modeling preferences using objective functions can refine the preference formalization given above. For example, "software should not take too much hardware resources" indicates that the degree of hardware resources used by the software would ideally be measured to determine the degree to which alternative software structures would satisfy the softgoal. Consequently, the above partial softgoal specification can be improved by adding a quality variable that can be used to quantify the "too much" term. Notice that the choice between alternatives specified in *choice preferences* influences the value of quality variables.

Imprecision. Without an accurate notion of the stated and implied needs, the degree of quality satisfaction by software cannot be measured and software properties that could satisfy quality requirements cannot be determined. The use of fuzzy logic has been suggested to formalize imprecise requirements to allow for conflicts between them to be studied ([18,20,31,23]) unfortunately outside the goal-oriented RE field. A key limitation of this approach (see, [19] for a discussion) is that the degree of imprecise requirements satisfaction, measured through a "satisfaction function" that maps software behavior to a degree (comprised between 0 and 1) to which it satisfies a fuzzy (in the sense of [33]) requirement is measure-independent. There are no specific metrics involved, and it is not obvious how the measurement could be made objective, as in [19]. It would be beneficial if objective metrics and fuzzy logic notation can be combined to express formally the information given in the softgoal template.

Imprecision is dealt with here in a procedural approach, consisting of progressively increasing the precision of initially imprecise information contained in a softgoal template. This is achieved through the application of a set of transformations that manipulate specialized formalisms defined to characterize the above discussed facets of quality requirements modeled as softgoals. The formalisms are necessary to assist stakeholders in representing and reasoning about quality requirements in a systematic manner. A softgoal formalization, based on the discussions above is as follows.

Formal Characterization of Softgoal. We make explicit the facets of softgoals described above by modeling a softgoal $\mathcal{S}$ as a tuple:

$$\mathcal{S} = \langle n, t, St, v, c, P \rangle \tag{1}$$

where n is the softgoal identifier, t is the time of softgoal statement, St is the set of stakeholders that agree on the softgoal, v is the view of the softgoal shared by members of St, c is the context of the softgoal where $c \in$ $software, process, environment)$, and P is the preference information associated with the softgoal, including utility. The utilities are evaluated over a set of alternatives for softgoal operationalization (call this set B), each including a combination of the software, environment, and development process. The softgoals are then aggregated to produce the global utility, corresponding to the top softgoal of the project.

The preference information in a softgoal can be represented with a tuple P:

$$P : Obj \times Mod \times T \times Thr \times Curr \times U \tag{2}$$

where Obj is the objective function, Mod is the modality Min, Max of the objective function, T its target value, Thr its threshold value, $Curr$ the quality variable value of the existing alternative, U indicates whether the objective function can be considered as a local utility (see the classical utility theory [15]). The definition of the objective will often make use of auxiliary quality variables. They are defined by an expression, the metric function that (implicitly) depends on the alternative $b \in B$. An objective function is thus a metric function with an associated modality: $mod(m(b))$, where $mod \in Mod$. The modality indicates in which direction the metric function will influence the global utility.

The notation defined above allows the requirements engineer to compare alternatives by:

1. Defining an order among alternatives, as a first approximation.
2. State quality variables Qv to quantitatively compare alternative behaviors, as in [19] but not limited to random variables.
3. Defining metric functions $m(b)$ to associate alternatives b_i to metric values.
4. Combining metric functions $m(b)$ with modalities mod to construct objective functions $mod(m(b)) \in Obj$ which indicate preferred metric values T.

5. Refining metrics to local utilities, and aggregating them to obtain the global utility. Tradeoffs between degrees of satisfaction can be evaluated using the marginal rate of substitution (MRS), a concept taken from economics (e.g., [15]) which, in the terminology used here, indicates the maximal amount of a metric value that a stakeholder is willing to sacrifice for a unit increase in value of another metric. Techniques described in [31] can be reused here, although with caveats noted earlier.
6. Using linguistic facilities as in fuzzy logic: a value above threshold will be deemed *acceptable*, above target *good*.

The formalisms themselves do not eliminate imprecision, but point to information to look for and a way to organize it in order to reduce imprecision.

Imprecision can further be reduced by using logic to formalize the information about alternative behaviors contained in the softgoal. This allows closer integration with later steps of software development.

3.3 Formally Specifying Softgoals

To this point, the traditional softgoal concept has been enriched with templates that allow the expression of subjective, idealist, and context-specific facets of quality requirements information. Imprecision has been indicated, and treated with a simple formal model of the enriched softgoal concept. The model, while summarizing softgoal information in a precise way, does not alleviate imprecision. However, sources of imprecision have become clearer: the fuzzy set of behaviors and time-dependency of preferences which is derived from the fuzziness of the set of behaviors (i.e., preferences change because stakeholders learn about previously unknown behaviors during the development process). Both can receive further treatment: the former through formalization of behaviors, and the latter, through the transformation activities, presented in Sect. 4.

While behavior can be represented in various ways, the goal concept, discussed earlier, proves invaluable in the RE phase (e.g., [10,19,29]). It allows more freedom in the specifications, than, e.g., pre/post condition specification of state transitions used in [18,20,31]. As precise representation of behavior is needed, and since behavior represents *what* software or stakeholders do, functional goals (see, [30]) are used as a concept to model behavior. To remain general, the choice of formal acquisition language for functional goal specification is left to the requirements engineer. It is suggested that temporal logic be used for expressivity reasons. Softgoal formalization then consists of writing formal specification of behaviors $b \in B$ using the chosen acquisition language.

Return to the "software should not take too much hardware resources" softgoal in the previous subsection. Two behaviors appear in its choice preferences attribute. Using the KAOS framework (where a goal is defined as a constraint on behavior [10]), the two behaviors can be specified as KAOS goals (i.e., precise functional goals):

Goal: Maintain [SoftwRunsInBackgr]
Definition: The e-mail reader runs constantly.
Formal Def: $os : OperatSyst; mr : MailReader; os.status = on \Rightarrow mr.status = on$

Goal: Achieve [RunSoftwWhenRequest]

Definition: When the os receives a request to start the mail reader, the mail reader should start running.

Formal Def: $os.status = on \wedge mr.status = off \wedge os.start = mr \Rightarrow mr.status = on$

The above formalization is reflected in the softgoal template by adding a keyword becomes after the imprecise preference relation and rewriting that information using the identifiers for specified behaviors. The imprecise formulation is maintained for traceability reasons.

...

Preferences:

Choice Preferences:

(run software when requested)≻(software runs in background)

becomes Achieve [RunSoftwWhenRequest] ≻ Maintain [SoftwRunsInBackgr]

In the NFR framework [22,8] terminology, the above would be represented with a softgoal, two goals, and a contribution link between each of the goals and the softgoal. The preference relation can be translated into a positive and a negative contribution. However, NFR is less expressive, since metrics and most other facets of the softgoal concept presented above are missing.

4 General Guidelines for RE Frameworks

On the basis of the revisited conceptual foundations, guidelines can be suggested as to the transformations that can be applied to softgoals and that need to be present in requirements modeling approaches that aim to employ the given Softgoal conceptualization. Any such transformation activities need to be constructed so that they can deal with all of the four Softgoal facets identified above. Ideally, the transformations would allow initially imprecise, subjective, context-specific, and idealistic softgoals to be transformed into a consistent set of hardgoals (e.g., similar to those of the KAOS acquisition language [10]). We argue that two classes of transformation activities are useful—one for dealing with individual softgoals, and another for transforming several softgoals together.

Single-Softgoal Transformations are aimed at arriving, for each softgoal, at a template in which the initially vague statement of need is made more precise, subjectivity is made explicit, objective metrics are found, and alternative behaviors influencing the degree of softgoal satisfaction are informally identified:

- *(T1) Build an initial softgoal template.* To discover softgoals, the requirements engineer will ask questions about *what* and *how* the software and the wider context should do, according to each stakeholder. The *what* and *how* questions are likely to result in informal and imprecise statements of needs that may be both related to behaviors (i.e., functional aspects) of the context, and how the behaviors need to be exhibited (i.e., nonfunctional aspects; e.g., rapidly, safely, securely, etc.). Consequently, the requirements engineer will need to fill in softgoal templates in a rather sketchy manner at first. As a result of T1, the template needs to contain information about the name of the softgoal (n), statement time (t), stakeholder identifier (St), stakeholder's view (v), and the context relevant to the softgoal (c).

- *(T2) Identify alternative behaviors that are likely to influence softgoal satisfaction.* The *what* and *how* questions will also lead stakeholders to indicate alternative behaviors whose execution will satisfy to a varying degree the softgoal. The set of identified alternative behaviors for a softgoal j (B_j) can be enlarged by looking at similar existing contexts (and observing, e.g., limitations, errors, etc.), seeking expert opinion on the specific problems, etc.
- *(T3) De-idealize the softgoal.* Stakeholders may express views which qualify or quantify behaviors in ideal ways (e.g., development cost should be lower than X—where X is simply impossible to achieve). De-idealization can be realized by further discussing alternative target values and/or behaviors, or by taking into account benchmarks, which would provide evidence on the idealistic nature of stated needs.
- *(T4-A) Construct objective measurements of softgoal satisfaction.* The aim is to find a set of quality variables (Qv), for the softgoal j. For each quality variable q_{jk}, there should be a metric function ($m_{jr}(b_i)$) to which a modal mod_{jr} is associated to form an objective function ($mod_{jr}(m_{jr}(b_i))$). A target value (t_{jr}) should be defined for the objective function. Quality variables can be derived from information contained in the stakeholders' view (as in the example in Sect. 3.2), in the parent softgoal (see transformation T7), and/or can be based on company-/industry-specific benchmarks. Metric functions can come from knowledge about the events generated by behaviors that are to be measured, from company-/industry-specific standards, and/or behavior categories (i.e., KAOS goal categories [19]). Benchmarks are an invaluable source of target values.
- *(T4-B) Establish preference relations over alternative behaviors.* Based on subjective indications of the stakeholder that has provided the information for softgoal j, alternative behaviors found by application of T2 can be related with preference relations. Preferences can also be established based on objective measurements, when, e.g., the current value for a metric is closer to the target value for a behavior over some other behavior. Notice that preference relations can be objectively constructed only when actual measurements exist (based, e.g., on similar systems) so that current values of quality variables under different behaviors can be observed.

The above transformations are likely to be given as a toolset to the requirements engineer. The order of application will probably be T1 to T4 initially, but iterations should not come as a surprise, especially when additional behaviors are suggested by the stakeholder or due to preference variability over time.

Many-Softgoal Transformations are aimed at establishing relationships between two or more softgoals, to indicate inter-softgoal contribution and refinement. Contribution and refinement are based on widely accepted conceptualizations of such relationships initially given in the NFR framework [22,8], while relying here on a formal model for argumentation of contribution and refinement choices, which itself employs the formal softgoal model proposed above.

- *(T5) Negotiate to avoid conflict.* Contribution between softgoals indicates the degree to which a softgoal supports or obstructs the satisfaction of another softgoal. Contribution is interesting mainly when negative, or conflicting contribution exists between softgoals. Conflict between softgoals may appear in the form of inconsistencies resulting from different terminology (due to subjectivity and imprecision), conflicting preferences, and/or different target values of objective functions. Because of imprecision, the requirements engineer will not be able him/herself to resolve conflicts. Instead, negotiation can be used to lead stakeholders to common understanding, consensus, and closer terminology.
- *(T6) Argument modeling decisions.* Argumentation during negotiation can be recorded using a logical model of argument (for an overview of the research specific to logical models of argument, see [7]). Rigor in recording argumentation during the early phases is relevant not only for traceability reasons, but also because it confronts stakeholders to discuss quality requirements (allowing the requirements engineer to potentially find more information about preferences and alternative behaviors)..
- *(T7) Merge softgoals.* Negotiation will ideally lead stakeholders to a shared terminology and an agreement on quality requirements that have been initially perceived differently. Merging two or more softgoals consists of selecting a subset of preference information available in all softgoals to merge, while using a shared softgoal name, view, context, etc. Objective functions from merged softgoals can be aggregated, provided that quality variables they refer to be converted into compatible types.
- *(T8) Refine a softgoal.* A softgoal is refined if there are sub-softgoals whose joint partial satisfaction is considered equivalent to partially satisfying the refined softgoal. In practical terms, refinement can consist of, e.g., decomposing a softgoal according to some taxonomy (see, e.g., [3] for a privacy and [22] for an accuracy and a performance requirements taxonomies) into sub-softgoals, or making the softgoal more specific through each sub-softgoal. For example, "software should be fast" can be refined into a set of softgoals, e.g., "operation A should be fast",..., "operation Z should be fast".

The result of these transformations can be considered as completed when all of the following conditions hold: (i) a set of behaviors is associated with each leaf softgoal; (ii) there are no conflicting softgoals; (iii) all disagreements on softgoals have been resolved through negotiation; (iv) the set of softgoals is considered sufficiently complete by the stakeholders.

5 Conclusions and Future Work

The aim of the work presented in this paper is primarily a more profound understanding of the Softgoal concept that is commonly used to model requirements in the early stages of requirements engineering. It has been argued that there is more to the information commonly represented using Softgoal instances, than currently established Softgoal definitions seem to indicate. In particular, four facets of the Softgoal concept are identified—namely: imprecision, subjectivity, context-specificity, and idealism (which involves implicit preference orderings of the stakeholders who state the information represented using Softgoal instances). A tentative formalism for this extended Softgoal conceptualization is suggested, to summarize the information that we argue the requirements engineer can and should attempt to extract from a Softgoal instance (or, in relation to it). It is also illustrated how richer requirements can be obtained when the extended conceptualization is taken into account.

Although a rather simple example has been employed to illustrate the facets we consider relevant, we believe that a powerful insight comes from this paper: a more elaborate treatment of imprecise, subjective, context-specific, and idealistic requirements, usual at the outset of a RE project, can be realized if a commonly used Softgoal concept is extended. Ultimately, this is likely to lead to richer requirements specifications and more stakeholders who are satisfied with the performance of the systems built for them.

Important directions for future work include extending the Softgoal concept further, by possibly identifying additional facets. The formalism needs to be operationalized within already common specification languages. Additional transformation techniques, more effectively exploiting the extended conceptualization remain to be explored.

References

1. Al-Naeem, T., Gorton, I., Ali Babar, M., Rabhi, F., Benatallah, B.: A Quality-Driven Systematic Approach for Architecting Distributed Software Applications. Proc. Int. Conf. Softw. Eng. (2005) 244–253.
2. Alves, C., French, X., Carvallo, J.P., Finkelstein, A.: Using Goals and Quality Models to Support the Matching Analysis During COTS Selection. In French, X., Port, D.: Proc. Int. Conf. on COTS-Based Software System (2005) 146–156.
3. Anton, A., Earp, J., Reese, A.: Analyzing Website Privacy Requirements Using a Privacy Goal Taxonomy. Proc. IEEE Int. Conf. Req. Eng. (2002) 23–31.
4. Avesani, P., Bazzanella, C., Perini, A., Susi, A.: Facing Scalability Issues in Requirements Prioritization with Machine Learning Techniques. Proc. IEEE Int. Conf. Req. Eng. (2005) 297–305.
5. Boehm, B.W., Brown, J.W., Kaspar, H., Lipow, M., MacLeod, G.J., Merritt, M.J.: Characteristics of Software Quality. North-Holland, Amsterdam (1978).
6. Castro, J., Kolp, M., and Mylopoulos, J.: Towards requirements-driven information systems engineering: the Tropos project. Info. Syst. 27, 6 (2002) 365–389.
7. Chesnevar, C.I., Maguitman, A.G., Loui R.P.: Logical Models of Argument. ACM Comput. Surv. 32, 4 (2000) 337-383.
8. Chung, L., Nixon, B., Yu, E., Mylopoulos, J.: Non-Functional Requirements in Software Engineering. Kluwer Publishing (2000).
9. Cleland-Huang, J., Settimi, R., BenKhadra, O., Berezhanskaya, E., Christina, S.: Goal-Centric Traceability for Managing Non-Functional Requirements. Proc. Int. Conf. Softw. Eng. (2005).
10. Dardenne, A., van Lamsweerde, A., Fickas S.: Goal-directed requirements acquisition. Sci. of Comput. Prog. 20 (1993) 3–50.

11. Donzelli, P.: A goal-driven and agent-based requirements engineering framework. Req. Eng. 9 (2004) 16–39.
12. ISO: Int. Standard ISO 8402. Quality – Vocabulary. Int. Org. for Standardization, Geneva (1986) (and later).
13. Issarny, V., Bidan, C., Saridakis, T.: Achieving Middleware Customization in a Configuration-based Development Environment: Experience with the Aster Prototype. Proc. Int. Conf. Config. Distrib. Syst. (1998) 207–214
14. Jackson, D.: Structuring Z Specifications with Views. ACM Trans. Softw. Eng. Method. 4, 4 (1995) 365–389.
15. Keeney, R.L., Raiffa, H.: Decisions with multiple objectives: preferences and value tradeoffs. Wiley, New York (1976).
16. Kreps, D.: Notes on the Theory of Choice. Westview Press, Boulder (1988).
17. Landes, D., Studer, R.: The Treatment of Non-Functional Requirements in MIKE. Proc. Europ. Softw. Eng. Conf. (1995).
18. Lee, J., Kuo, J-Y.: New Approach to Requirements Trade-Off Analysis for Complex Systems. IEEE Trans. Knowl. Data Eng. 10, 4 (1998) 551–562.
19. Letier, E., van Lamsweerde, A.: Reasoning about Partial Goal Satisfaction for Requirements and Design Engineering. Proc. ACM SIGSOFT Symp. Found. of Softw. Eng. (2004) 53–62.
20. Liu, X.F., Yen, J.: An Analytic Framework for Specifying and Analyzing Imprecise Requirements. Proc. Int. Conf. Softw. Eng. (1996) 60–69.
21. Liu, L., and Yu, E. Designing information systems in social context: a goal and scenario modeling approach. Info. Syst. 29 (2004) 187–203.
22. Mylopoulos, J., Chung, L., Nixon, B.: Representing and Using Nonfunctional Requirements: A Process-Oriented Approach. IEEE Trans. Softw. Eng. 18, 6 (1992).
23. Noppen, J., van der Broek, P., Aksit, M.: Dealing with Imprecise Quality Factors in Software Design. Proc. Worksh. Softw. Qual., (2005) 1–6.
24. Nuseibeh, B., Finkelstein, A., Kramer, J.: Fine-Grain Process Modelling. Proc. Int. Worksh. Softw. Spec. Des. (Dec.1993) 42–46.
25. Nuseibeh, B., Kramer, J., Finkelstein, A.: A Framework for Expressing the Relationships Between Multiple Views in Requirements Specifications. IEEE Trans. Softw. Eng. 20, 10 (1994) 760–773.
26. Osterweil, L.: Strategic Directions in Software Quality. ACM Comput. Surv. 28, 4 (1996) 738–750.
27. Rosa, N.S., Justo, G.R.R., Cunha, P.R.F.: A Framework for Building Non-Functional Software Architectures. Proc. ACM Symp. Appl. Comput. (2001).
28. Simon, A. H.: The Sciences of the Artificial. 2nd Ed. MIT Press, 1981.
29. van Lamsweerde, A.: Divergent Views in Goal-Driven Requirements Engineering. Proc. ACM SIGSOFT Worksh. Viewpoints Softw. Dev. (1996) 252–256.
30. van Lamsweerde, A.: Goal-Oriented Requirements Engineering: A Guided Tour. Proc. IEEE Int. Conf. Req. Eng. (2001) 249–263.
31. Yen, J., Tiao, W.A.: A Systematic Tradeoff Analysis for Conflicting Imprecise Requirements. Proc. IEEE Int. Conf. Req. Eng. (1997) 87–96.
32. Yu, E.: Modelling Strategic Relationships for Process Reengineering. Ph.D. Thesis, Univ. of Toronto (1995).
33. Zadeh, L.A.: Fuzzy Sets. Information and Control 8 (1965) 338–353.
34. Zave, P., Jackson, M.: Four Dark Corners of Requirements Engineering. ACM Trans. Softw. Eng. Meth. 6, 1 (1997) 1–30.

Conceptualizing the Co-evolution of Organizations and Information Systems: An Agent-Oriented Perspective

Ning Su[1] and John Mylopoulos[2]

[1] Leonard N. Stern School of Business, New York University
44 West Fourth Street, New York, NY, 10012, USA
nsu@stern.nyu.edu

[2] Department of Computer Science, University of Toronto
10 King's College Road, Toronto, ON, M5S 3G4, Canada
jm@cs.toronto.edu

Abstract. In today's ever-transforming business environment, information systems need to evolve in concert with changes in their organizational settings. In order to help system analysts conceptualize the co-evolution of organizations and information systems, we adopt an agent-oriented perspective to develop the Tropos Evolution Modeling Process for Organizations (TEMPO). Specifically, inspired by Kauffman's NKC model, we introduce the concept of goal interface into the traditional agent-oriented Tropos methodology; within this interface, evolution is conceptualized as a negotiation process between agents. TEMPO is illustrated with a case study that demonstrates how to evolve a retail website under new European e-commerce legislation. TEMPO is also evaluated with a small behavioral experiment, which offers additional evidence on the usefulness of the approach.

1 Introduction

Organizations change rapidly in the twenty-first century. Information systems, which have become an essential component of modern organizations, need to evolve in concert with changes in their organizational context. Unfortunately, the "agile" co-evolution of organizations and information systems has been impeded by a number of factors. Traditionally, information systems are modeled with programming concepts such as data structures, while organizations are understood in terms of stakeholders, competitors, customers, and their respective business objectives. The "semantic gap [2]" between the two domains constitutes a major difficulty, and so does the ever-increasing complexity of modern information systems. Complexity manifests itself in the large number of components and interconnections [12], which is approaching the limit of human analysts' capacity to absorb and manipulate information [6].

In response to these challenges, agent-orientation has emerged as a novel paradigm that aligns the modeling of organizations and information systems at the intentional level [26]. From an agent-oriented perspective, both organizations and information systems can be viewed as distributed adaptive systems consisting of coordinated agents in pursuit of their respective goals. Hence, one unified ontology can be applied

D.W. Embley, A. Olivé, and S. Ram (Eds.): ER 2006, LNCS 4215, pp. 296–310, 2006.

to model both domains. Agent is also especially appropriate for tackling the issue of complexity in information systems modeling [12]. Existing literature on agent-oriented software engineering has proposed various modeling frameworks and methodologies, e.g., [1] [5] [25]. However, the evolutionary aspects of agent-oriented information systems modeling remain unexplored.

Aimed at providing heuristics for conceptualizing the co-evolution of organizations and information systems, we draw upon agent-oriented software engineering, agent-based economics, biological evolution, and human negotiation behavior to develop the Tropos Evolution Modeling Process for Organizations (TEMPO). The rest of the paper is structured as follows. Section 2 outlines the interdisciplinary conceptual framework of TEMPO. Section 3 elaborates on TEMPO's main components. Section 4 presents a real-life based case study to illustrate how to use TEMPO to evolve an e-commerce website under new legal requirements. Section 5 reports a small behavioral study that evaluates the effectiveness of TEMPO. Section 6 concludes with discussion and future research directions.

2 An Interdisciplinary Conceptual Framework

From the perspective of complex systems [14], an enormous range of phenomena, natural and artificial, from molecular machines within cells to markets, societies and even the entire global socio-economy, can be conceptualized as evolving systems of interacting agents [11]. In the same vein, three fundamental analogies are assumed in TEMPO: information systems as socioeconomic systems, socioeconomic systems as biological systems, and information systems as biological systems.

The agent-oriented Tropos ontology [1] is adopted to provide a unified framework for modeling both organizations and information systems. Based on our fundamental analogies, Kauffman's NKC model, which was intended to simulate the co-evolution of species in an ecosystem [14], is projected into the Tropos ontology to model the co-evolution of organizations and information systems. The conceptual framework is shown in Figure 1.

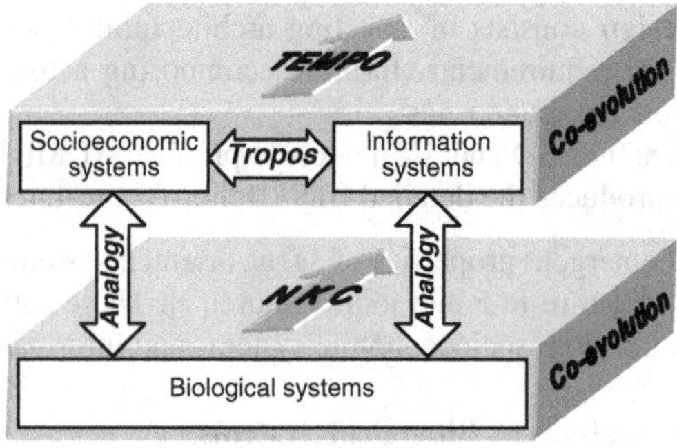

Fig. 1. The interdisciplinary conceptual framework

2.1 Information Systems as Socioeconomic Systems

Co-evolving organizations and information systems requires close alignment of business objectives and information technology. This, in turn, requires a unified framework for modeling both organizational contexts and the embedded information systems. Agent-orientation is a modeling paradigm applicable to both socioeconomic systems and information systems. According to this approach, both types of systems are viewed as distributed complex adaptive systems, consisting of large numbers of autonomous agents involved in parallel local interactions, which in turn gives rise to macro-level system behaviors [16] [21].

Tropos [1] is a state-of-the-art agent-oriented information systems development methodology. The ontology of this methodology is centered on the concept of "actor" and actors' mentalistic notions such as goals, tasks, resources, and dependencies.

1. **Actor** represents an entity that is autonomous, strategic and intentional. An actor can be a physical agent, a software component, a role, or a position.
2. **Goal** represents actors' strategic interest. Goals can be categorized into hard-goals and soft-goals.
3. **Task** represents a way of satisfying a hard-goal and/or satisficing a soft-goal.
4. **Resource** represents a physical or informational entity.
5. **Dependency** indicates that one actor depends on the other to achieve some goal, perform some task, or obtain some resource. The former actor is called depender; the latter is called dependee.

There are two types of model in Tropos: Strategic Dependency (SD) model, which captures various stakeholders, their intentions, and dependencies between one another, and Strategic Rationale (SR) model, which describes how goals are achieved through means-end analysis and contribution analysis.

The information system development process in Tropos consists of five phases.

1. **Early requirements analysis** aims at understanding the organizational context of the system-to-be. The entire development process is driven by this phase.
2. **Late requirements analysis** specifies the strategic dependencies and strategic rationales of the system-to-be. The system-to-be is added to the original models as one or several actors, and analysis is carried out to produce modified models.
3. **Architectural design** consists of selecting architectural styles that meet system-level non-functional requirements, further decomposing actors and dependencies, and assigning actors to certain roles.
4. **Detailed design** extends SD and SR models to produce AUML diagrams.
5. **Implementation** produces the detailed BDI (Belief-Desire-Intentions) architecture.

In order to model emergent properties of agent-oriented systems, Tropos includes a set of patterns, e.g., structure-in-5 and joint venture [7]. These patterns can be used as generic architectures for both socioeconomic systems and information systems.

2.2 Socioeconomic Systems as Biological Systems

Modern economics has a tradition of using biological metaphors to understand economic processes [8], giving rise to a collection of novel research paradigms such as sociobiology and bioeconomics. Biological approaches to economics rest on the ontological continuity, i.e., the construction of metaphors, between natural and socio-economic domains. Based on these metaphors, biology-based theories are extended to the economic realm. For example, the concept of self-organization has been used to account for the self-amplifying features of innovative changes in markets [24].

Similarly, TEMPO assumes an analogy between socioeconomic organizations and biological systems. The fundamental resemblance between the two domains is that both are undergoing continual evolution caused by cooperation and conflict from within, i.e., the interactions among the various comprising components, and from outside, i.e., the interactions between the systems and the environment.

2.3 Information Systems as Biological Systems

The parallel between computing and biology has inspired burgeoning research fields, such as evolutionary computation and artificial life. Recently in the face of the complexity crisis, which looms in modern software systems [11], the metaphorical use of biosciences to tackle system complexity is gaining increasing attention.

The analogy between information systems and biological systems applied in the TEMPO conceptual framework lies in the fact that both information systems and biological systems can be viewed as vast and entangled nexus of various goal-directed, self-governed agents, which constantly interact with and adapt to one another; the emergent systems consisting of these agents, in turn, demonstrate continual evolution, which helps to maintain the fitness of the systems.

2.4 Kauffman's NKC Coevolution Model

Organisms in nature continuously co-evolve both with other organisms and with a changing abiotic environment. In these processes, the fitness of one species depends upon the characteristics of other species that it interacts with. Meanwhile all species simultaneously adapt and change.

In an attempt to provide a framework for modeling the genetic interactions in the co-evolution processes and explore the structure of "fitness landscape" that underlies adaptive evolution, Kauffman [14] introduces the NKC model, which is named after the three main components that determine the behaviors of species' interaction and change with one another. Specifically, N refers to all the genes in a given genotype, each gene making a fitness contribution that depends upon the gene itself and upon a set of other genes in this genotype; this set of other genes in the same genotype are denoted as K; each of the N genes also depends on a set of genes, denoted as C, in other genotypes. By attributing the overall fitness of a composite system (a genotype) to three interacting modules (N, K, C) of the system and its embedding environment, the model provides a framework for analyzing adaptive evolution.

More generally, the NKC model can be interpreted as follows. The co-evolution of a system and its environment is the equilibrium of external coupling (i.e., the interaction between the N module and the C module) and internal coupling (i.e., the interaction between the N module and the K module).

3 Tropos Evolution Modeling Process for Organizations

By interpreting the NKC model with the Tropos ontology, i.e., modules' components as goals and the coupling between components as dependency or other relationships between goals, we construct TEMPO to conceptualize the organization-information system co-evolution. The key elements of TEMPO include the definition of goal interfaces, the taxonomy of goal relationships, the use of negotiation as a mechanism for organizational evolution, and an integrated process model that aligns the above elements.

3.1 Goal Interface

Interdependencies between the goals of interacting agents both within and beyond the original information system boundary produce a dynamic area. Specifically, some original goals might have dependency or other relationships with goals newly elicited from the business environment. These dependencies and relationships, together with the involved goals, comprise the goal interface.

Inspired by the NKC model, we partition the goal interface into three modules: C module, i.e., the newly elicited goals that have some dependency or relationship with goals in the original Tropos model; N module, i.e., goals in the original Tropos model that have direct or indirect dependency or relationship with the new goals; and K module, i.e., goals in the N module that have only indirect relationship with the new goals. Interaction between C module and N module represents the external coupling between the information system and its environment; interaction between K module and the rest of N module represent the internal coupling in the goal interface.

Goal interface is the evolution frontier of the organizational information system: C module causes immediate changes in N module; changes are then propagated through K module to the entire information system.

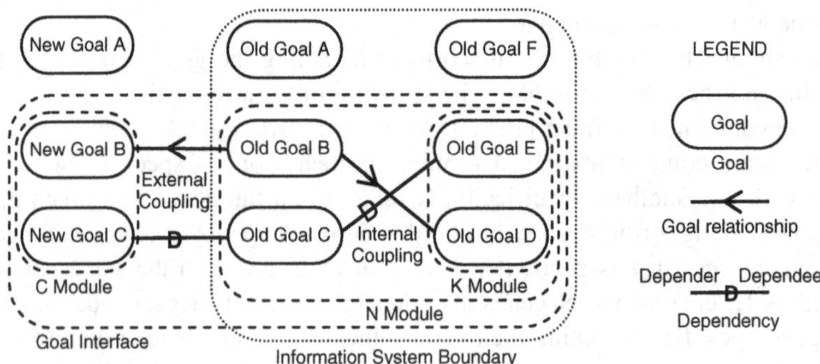

Fig. 2. Goal interface

3.2 A Taxonomy of Goal Relationships

The various cognitive elements in the goal interfaces need to be coordinated. This requires an understanding of the nature of interactions, or relationships, among goals.

Depending on whether the interactions entail favorable or adverse situations, goal relationships can be categorized into positive and negative relationships. In order to formally define the relationships, hereafter we will use the following set of notations.

$A \Rightarrow B$	:	A implies B.	Subgoal(g_1, g_2)	:	Goal g_1 is a (and-)subgoal of goal g_2.
S(g)	:	Goal g is satisfied.	D(g)	:	Goal g is denied.

3.2.1 Positive Goal Relationship

This refers to a situation where the fulfillment of one goal enhances the attainment of the other goal. Positive goal relationship might lead to cooperation between agents. According to the degree of benevolence between the two goals, positive goal relationships can be classified into three types.

1. **Equivalent.** The fulfillment of one goal implies the attainment of the other, and vice versa. One agent might be able to achieve both goals simultaneously. The specifications of equivalent goals might be, but are not necessarily, identical. The owners of equivalent goals might be different.

   Equivalent (g_1:Goal, g_2:Goal) iff $(S(g_1) \Rightarrow S(g_2)) \wedge (S(g_2) \Rightarrow S(g_1))$

2. **Subsumption.** The fulfillment of one goal implies the attainment of the other, but the achievement the latter goal can at most guarantee partial satisfaction of the former. A special case is that one goal is a (and-)subgoal of the other.

   Subsumption (g_1:Goal, g_2:Goal) iff $(S(g_1) \Rightarrow S(g_2)) \wedge \exists g$: Goal (Subgoal($g$, g_1) $\wedge \neg(S(g_2) \Rightarrow S(g))$)

3. **Overlap.** Two goals share a common subgoal. If either of the two goals is partially satisfied, so might be the other. However, the achievement of either goal can at most guarantee partial satisfaction of the other. In other words, the fulfillment of one goal contributes helpfully to the attainment of the other goal, and vice versa.

   Overlap (g_1:Goal, g_2:Goal) iff $\exists g$:Goal $((S(g_1) \Rightarrow S(g)) \wedge (S(g_2) \Rightarrow S(g)))$
   $\wedge\ \exists g'$:Goal (Subgoal(g', g_2) $\wedge \neg(S(g_1) \Rightarrow S(g'))$) $\wedge\ \exists g''$:Goal (Subgoal(g'', g_1) $\wedge \neg(S(g_2) \Rightarrow S(g''))$)

3.2.2 Negative Goal Relationship

This refers to a situation where the fulfillment of one goal conflicts with the attainment of the other goal. The antecedents, or source factors, of negative goal relationships include logic incompatibility, resource scarcity, and task interdependency [16]. Depending on the degree of incompatibility between goals, negative goal relationship can be categorized into the following three types.

1. **Negation.** The fulfillment of one goal denies the attainment of the other goal. Meanwhile, no subgoal of either goal is achievable when the other goal is satisfied.

   Negation (g_1:Goal, g_2:Goal) iff $((S(g_1) \Rightarrow D(g_2)) \wedge \forall g$:Goal (Subgoal($g$, g_2) $\Rightarrow (S(g_1) \Rightarrow D(g))$)
   $\wedge\ \forall g'$:Goal (Subgoal(g', g_1) $\Rightarrow (S(g_2) \Rightarrow D(g))$))

2. **Exclusion.** The fulfillment of one goal excludes the attainment of the other goal, as well as every subgoal of the latter goal. However, the latter goal can only partially deny the satisfaction of the former goal.

   Exclusion (g_1:Goal, g_2:Goal) iff $((S(g_1) \Rightarrow D(g_2)) \wedge \forall g$:Goal (Subgoal($g$, g_2) $\Rightarrow (S(g_1) \Rightarrow D(g))$)
   $\wedge\ \exists g'$:Goal (Subgoal(g', g_1) $\wedge \neg(S(g_2) \Rightarrow D(g'))$)

3. **Interference.** The fulfillment of one goal partially denies the attainment of the other goal, and vice versa.

   $\text{Interference}(g_1{:}\text{Goal}, g_2{:}\text{Goal}) \text{ iff } ((S(g_1) \Rightarrow D(g_2)) \wedge \exists g{:}\text{Goal}\,(\text{Subgoal}(g, g_2) \wedge \neg(S(g_1) \Rightarrow D(g))) \wedge \exists g'{:}\text{Goal}\,(\text{Subgoal}(g', g_1) \wedge \neg(S(g_2) \Rightarrow D(g'))$

3.3 Goal-Directed Negotiation Strategies

We use negotiation as a mechanism for agent-based evolution. Corresponding to the goal relationship taxonomy, a set of strategies is introduced to guide the management of goal relationships in a changing organizational information system.

3.3.1 Negotiation as a Mechanism for Organizational Evolution

From an agent-oriented perspective, evolution is the process of adaptation of the cognitive elements (e.g., goals) of a system's agents to organizational changes. In this process, the relationships between the agents' cognitive elements, especially goals, need to be identified and reconfigured such that the dysfunctional aspects of the relationships are eliminated and the functional aspects are enhanced.

This process is similar to human negotiation behavior, which is "a form of decision making where two or more parties talk with one another in an effort to resolve their opposing interests [18]". In TEMPO, we view organizational evolution as a process of negotiation on agents' goals. Human negotiation strategies provide heuristics for managing both positive and negative goal relationships in this process.

3.3.2 Negotiation on Positive Goal Relationships

Positive goal relationships can generate benefit for the overall system, and thus need to be properly utilized. Depending on the degree of benevolence among agents, a set of strategies can be applied to fully exploit the positive relationships.

1. **Redundancy elimination.** When two or more goals are equivalent, one of the equivalent goals should be preserved, while others can be removed. The preserved goal can be either assigned to the original agent, or reallocated to another agent capable of achieving it.
2. **Merge.** When one goal is subsumed by another goal, the subsumed goal can be merged into the subsuming goal. The merged goal can be either assigned to the agent of the subsuming goal, or refined into a set of subgoals, which are then allocated to a group of agents.
3. **Reconfiguration.** Overlap between goals is due to the equivalence of some of their subgoals. The equivalent subgoals can be merged with one of the overlapping goals and eliminated from the other goal. The two modified goals can continue to be possessed by their original agents.

3.3.3 Negotiation on Negative Goal Relationships

Negative goal relationships might cause difficulties in organizational evolution. Depending on the degree of cooperation that the owners of the conflicting goals may exhibit in negotiation, three strategies can be used to handle negative goal relationships.

1. **Unilateral concession.** This refers to a situation where one of the conflicting goals is relaxed, i.e., only some of its subgoals continue to be pursued, and other subgoals are dropped, while the other goal is preserved. An extreme case of unilateral concession is that one of the conflicting goals is totally abandoned.

2. **Coordination.** Both conflicting goals exchange a certain degree of relaxation in search of a mutually acceptable agreement. Coordination includes several specific forms. *Bilateral concession* is a case in which both conflicting goals selectively abandon some of their subgoals to resolve the conflict. *Bilateral reconfiguration* is a case in which the conflicting goals are refined into subgoals; some subgoals are dropped from one goal and merged with the other, until an alternative, conflict-free combination of goals is formed. *Third-party intervention* is a case in which a new agent is introduced to mediate the conflict situation.
3. **Competition.** Both conflicting goals continue to be pursued by agents. There are two types of competition: *unregulated competition*, in which the conflict is actually tolerated and preserved, and *regulated competition*, in which an external agent is introduced to mediate the conflict through certain mechanisms.

3.4 Process Model

Given the original agent-oriented model of an organizational information system, and new requirements in the form of new business goals, the process model helps analyze the impact of new requirements and evolve the original model to incorporate new goals. This process consists of three steps, each consisting of three iterative sub-steps.

Step 1: Goal interface identification. The new high-level goals emerging from the business environment could trigger a series of changes in the information system. This step is aimed at outlining the preliminary goal interface in the original model. Specifically, the three constituent modules need to be analyzed.

1. **C module elicitation.** The new goals tend to be global and abstract, and thus need to be incrementally refined into an AND goal tree. Subgoals can be elicited through asking *How* questions to high-level goals [3]. The output is one or several preliminary goal hierarchies, which constitute the C module of the goal interface.
2. **N module identification.** Through discovering external coupling, i.e., goal relationships and dependencies between goals in the C module and goals in the original model, the N module, which consists of all affected goals and associated relationships, can be identified.
3. **K module propagation.** In the original model, goals that are indirectly affected by the C module can be captured through discovering internal coupling in the goal interface. Specifically, by identifying relationships and dependencies among goals in the N module, the K module can be captured. Meanwhile, the goal interface is propagated in the original model.

During the three sub-steps, new goals and relationships might gradually emerge, and thus the sub-steps might need to be performed iteratively until no more goals or relationships can be elicited. The output of this step is the preliminary goal interface.

Step 2: Goal relationship management. The preliminary goal interface identified in Step 1 needs to be coordinated and transformed based on the goal relationships involved in the interface. The management of goal relationships contains three steps.

1. **Goal relationship diagnosis.** The various goal relationships in the interface are diagnosed according to the goal relationship taxonomy, so that appropriate strategies can be applied to negotiate on goals.
2. **Goal-directed negotiation.** Once goal relationships in the goal interface are captured, goal-directed negotiation strategies are selected according to the types of the relationships between, and the characteristics of, the involved goals. This step also includes the implementation of selected strategies, i.e., the resolution of goal relationships. The resolution usually leads to changes in the configuration of goals and agents in the original model.
3. **Resolution evaluation.** After the selected strategies are implemented, the solution is evaluated against the 'local' non-functional requirements (NFR) i.e., NFR on the agents associated with the resolution, If the NFR are not satisficed, either the specific implementation needs to be altered, or the strategies need to be changed.

The sub-steps are performed iteratively so that more goal relationships are diagnosed and resolved if needed. The output is the transformed goal interface.

Step 3: Goal interface integration. The goals in the original Tropos model that are not affected by the new business goals are integrated with the transformed goal interface. Then the architecture-level SD model is constructed from the evolved Tropos model. Specifically, this step involves three sub-steps.

1. **Strategic Rationale (SR) model composition.** The part of the original Tropos model that is outside the goal interface is integrated with the transformed goal interface. The output of the composition is a complete evolved Tropos model, the configuration of which has incorporated the new business goals.
2. **Strategic Dependency (SD) model abstraction.** Architecture, as an emergent property of organization, is abstracted from the new Tropos model, and is defined in terms of actors and the dependencies between them. Actors are individual agents or aggregations of agents. The abstraction can be based on defined organization patterns: the selected pattern is instantiated into a specific architecture [7].
3. **Architecture evaluation.** The abstracted architecture is evaluated against system-level non-functional requirements. If the NFR are not satisficed, alternative abstraction and evaluation need to be performed until a satisfactory architecture-level SD model is formed.

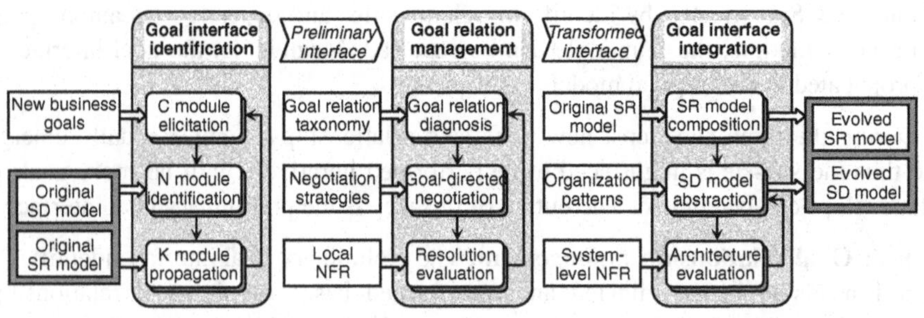

Fig. 3. Process model

4 Case Study

osCommerce [17] is an open-source e-commerce solution that helps online stores to be setup conveniently. It now supports over 1000 registered online shops worldwide. In year 2000, the European Parliament and the Council adopted the European E-Commerce Directive to regulate online market. All companies offering services to EU residents, including osCommerce, are required to comply with the Directive [4].

In this case study, we apply TEMPO to help osCommerce meet the new legal requirements. We then preliminarily evaluate TEMPO by comparing our result with the solution proposed by the osCommerce project team.

The following is a partial Tropos model of the original osCommerce website [20].

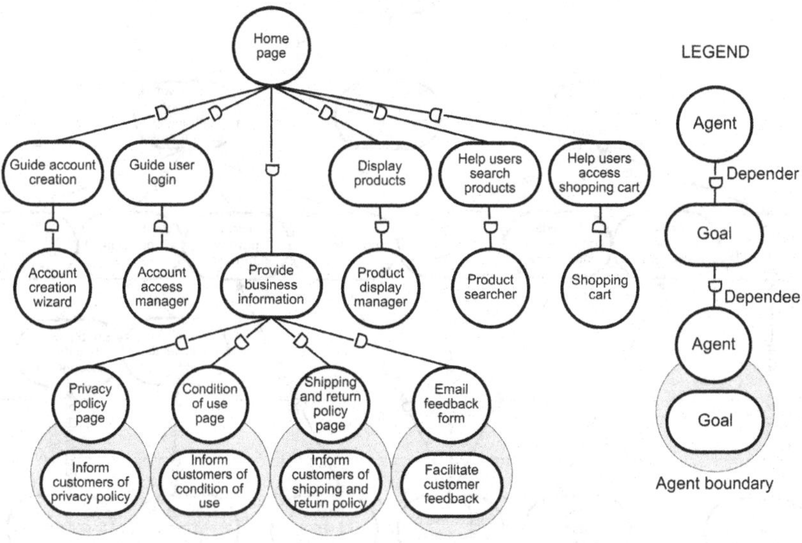

Fig. 4. Partial original Tropos model

Step 1: Goal interface identification. The new goal hierarchy is elicited through identifying clauses in the Directive that are applicable to osCommerce [22]. The new goal hierarchy constitutes the C module of the goal interface, as shown in Figure 5. Then, the N, K modules are also identified.

Step 2: Goal relationship management. Three types of goal relationships are identified: equivalent, subsumption, and overlap. According to the corresponding negotiation strategies, associated goals are removed, merged, or reconfigured. The modified goals are then assigned to responsible agents, as shown in Figure 6. The shaded goals and agents are those modified or added to the original Tropos model.

Step 3: Goal interface integration. The transformed goal interface is integrated with the remaining part the original Tropos model. Due to space constraint, the full SR and

SD models are not included here. More details can be found in [20]. Synthesizing from Figure 6, we recommend the following changes to the osCommerce solution.

1. Adding a *Help desk* page to describe the technical steps to conclude contracts.
2. Providing business contact details on the *Email feedback form (Contact)* page.
3. Indicating organization information, authorization information, and contracting languages on the *Condition of use* page.
4. Specifying privacy policy about contract on the *Privacy policy* page.

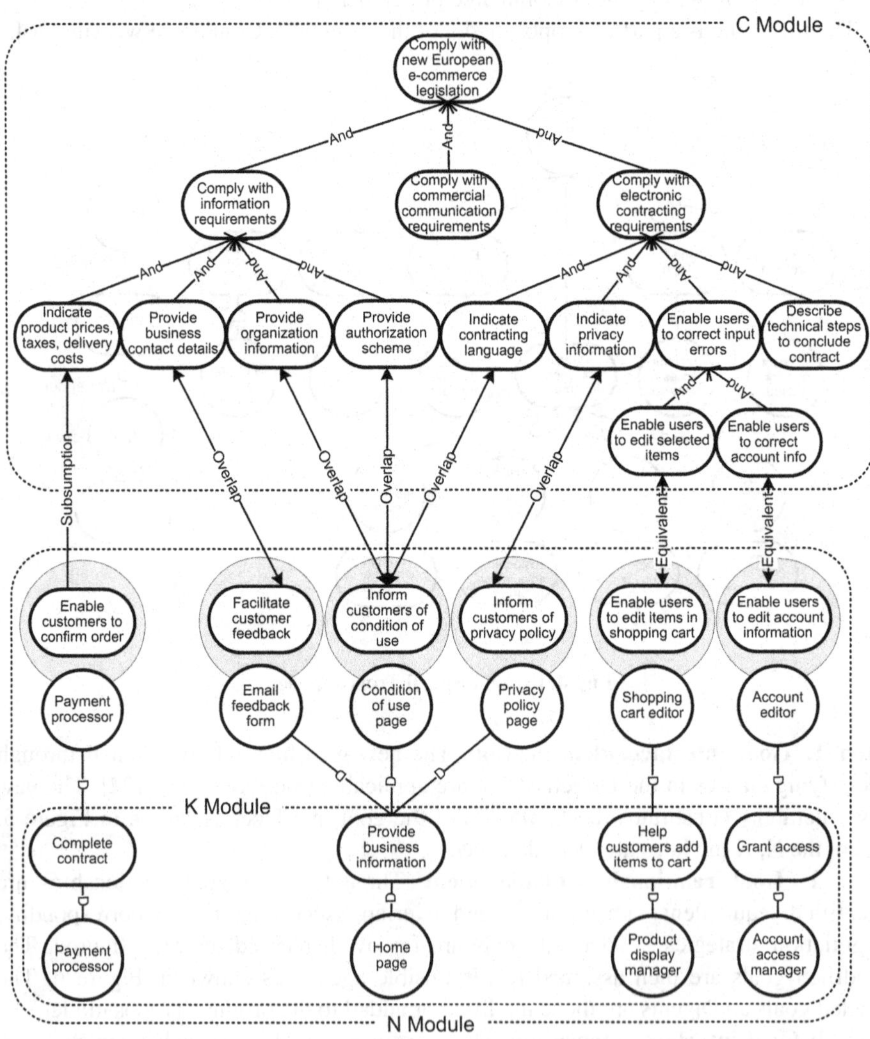

Fig. 5. Preliminary goal interface

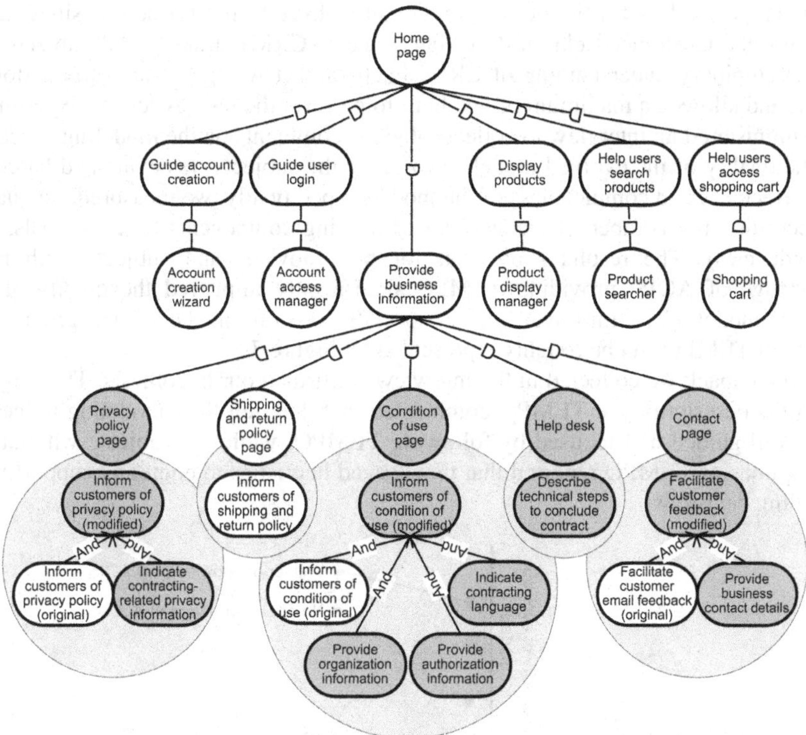

Fig. 6. Partial transformed goal interface

Comparing these recommendations with the changes proposed by the osCommerce development team (http://www.oscommerce.com/community/workboard), we find that the two sets of results are largely consistent, except that one defect is discovered in the latter: shipping charges cannot be shown in the shopping cart until the customer chooses her shipping option. The validity and effectiveness of TEMPO has been shown through this study.

5 Behavioral Evaluation

Based on the results of the case study, we propose that TEMPO can help analysts generate evolved models of higher quality. We further evaluate the proposition with a small experiment. Our subjects were four graduate students majoring in computer science or information systems. The subjects each had about two years' software development experience, either in industry or academia. Two subjects had prior knowledge of agent-oriented information systems (AOIS).

In the experiment, we first briefly introduced Tropos to the subjects, and offered to answer related questions. We then gave the descriptions of TEMPO to two subjects, including one who had learned AOIS before and one who hadn't, and let them read the TEMPO descriptions. We then assigned all subjects the same task – evolving a given Tropo model of a fictitious online retail website to meet a new business goal: realizing the Customer Relationship Management (CRM) strategy. All subjects had only preliminary understanding of CRM. Each subject was given an introduction of CRM, and allowed a maximum of one hour to perform the task. After the experiment, we administered an interview to collect subjects' comments on the modeling process.

The quality of the evolved models created by the subjects was evaluated based on the correctness and completeness of the models. Specifically, we measured the quality by recording the number of inconsistent or missing components (agents, goals, and dependencies). The results show that for both novices and subjects with prior knowledge of AOIS, providing TEMPO significantly improved the quality of the evolved models. The improvement is especially obvious in the novice group. The effects of TEMPO can be roughly represented by Figure 7.

The feedback we collected in the interview confirmed our hypothesis. The subjects given the descriptions of TEMPO commented that they felt their modeling processes were well guided and focused by following TEMPO, while the subjects without the descriptions of TEMPO reported that they lacked heuristics to elicit and support their modeling decisions.

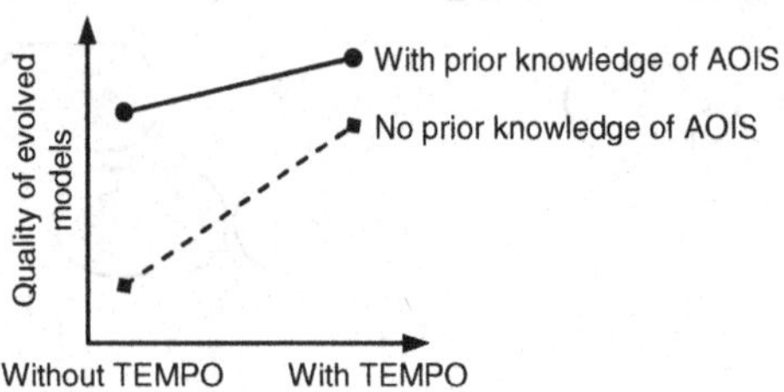

Fig. 7. Effects of TEMPO on model quality

6 Conclusions and Discussion

In order to assist analysts in conceptualizing the co-evolution of organizations and information systems, we have proposed the Tropos Evolution Modeling Process for Organizations (TEMPO). TEMPO fuses concepts and models from several areas, including agent-oriented methodologies, agent-based economics, biological evolution, and human negotiation behavior. Specifically, we define the goal interface as the evolution frontier of an information system; the interface consists of three modules, which mirror the three main components in Kauffman's NKC co-evolution model; within the goal interface, evolution is conceptualized as negotiation between agents. The metaphorical use of concepts and models from different disciplines generates heuristics that can guide the co-evolution of organizations and information systems.

We have evaluated TEMPO with a case study and a small behavioral experiment. The case study illustrates how to apply TEMPO to evolve information system models in real business scenarios; the results show that TEMPO can help construct sound and complete solutions. The behavioral experiment gives further evidence that TEMPO is able to guide analysts, both with and without prior knowledge of agent-oriented modeling, to produce evolved models of higher quality.

It is worth noting that TEMPO focuses only on modeling goals and agents, and deliberately omits other modeling constructs such as tasks and resources. The reason is that we are most interested in the intentional level of organizational information systems, and the other constructs can be derived by operationalizing goals [3].

TEMPO has its limitations. First, it requires the agent-oriented models of existing information systems. Otherwise, reengineering is needed to generate these models before TEMPO can be applied. Second, the major steps in TEMPO are performed by human analysts. Tool support is needed to further reduce the complexity of analysis in the face of large-scale models. Moreover, the validity of the behavioral evaluation is constrained by the small number of subjects and by the lack of benchmarks for measuring the quality of agent-oriented conceptual models.

This study leaves much room for further investigation. On the theoretical side, the heuristics offered by TEMPO can be applied by both human analysts and autonomous software agents. We might give automated software components a greater decision-making role by integrating TEMPO with decision-theoretic models, e.g., [9], and automated negotiation models, e.g., [13]. In an ideal scenario, information systems will be able to evolve themselves in an autonomic fashion to satisfy new requirements [11]. On the practical side, TEMPO has yet to be supported by software tools. One possibility is using existing model merging tools, e.g., [19], to merge goals in the C module into the N module, and further improve the efficiency of modeling activities.

Acknowledgement

We would like to thank Eric Yu, Yijun Yu, Steve Easterbrook, Yinghua Jia, Ou Wei, and many other participants of the "EarlyRE" seminar at the Department of Computer Science, University of Toronto for helping shape the ideas in this work.

References

1. Bresciani, P., Perini, A., Giorgini, P., Giunchiglia, F., Mylopoulos, J.: Tropos: An Agent-Oriented Software Development Methodology. Autonomous Agents and Multi-Agent Systems. Vol. 8, No. 3 (2004) 203–236
2. Castro, J., Kolp, M., Mylopoulos, J.: Towards Requirements-Driven Information Systems Engineering: The Tropos Project. Information Systems. Vol. 27, No. 6 (2002) 365–389
3. Dardenne, A., van Lamsweerde, A., Fickas, S.: Goal-Directed Requirements Acquisition. Science of Computer Programming, Vol. 20. No. 1-2 (1993) 3–50
4. European Commission Information Society: Directive 2000/31/EC of the European Parliament and of the Council of 8 June 2000 on Certain Legal Aspects of Information Society Services, in Particular Electronic Commerce, in the Internal Market. Official Journal of the European Communities (2000)
5. Ferber, J., Gutknecht, O.: A Meta-Model for the Analysis and Design of Organizations in Multiagent Systems. Proceedings of the Third International Conference on Multi-Agent Systems (1998) 128–135
6. Fox, M. S.: Organization Structuring: Designing Large Complex Software. Technical Report CMU-CS-79-155, Computer Science Department, Carnegie-Mellon University (1979)

7. Kolp, M., Giorgini, P., Mylopoulos, J.: Multi-Agent Architectures as Organizational Structures. Autonomous Agents and Multi-Agent Systems. Vol. 13, No. 1 (2006) 3–25
8. Gowdy, J. M.: Coevolutionary Economics: The Economy, Society and the Environment. Kluwer Academic Publishers (1994)
9. Haddawy, P., Hanks, S.: Utility Models for Goal-Directed Decision-Theoretic Planners. Computational Intelligence, Vol. 14, No. 3 (1998) 392–429
10. Hoyle, R. H., Harris, M. J., Judd, C. M.: Research Methods in Social Relations. 7th edn. Wadsworth (2002)
11. I.B.M.: The Vision of Autonomic Computing. www.research.ibm.com/autonomic (2004)
12. Jennings, N. R.: On Agent-Based Software Engineering. Artificial Intelligence, Vol. 117, No. 2 (2000) 277–296
13. Jennings, N. R., Faratin, P., Lomuscio, A. R., Parsons, S., Sierra, C., Wooldridge, M.: Automated Negotiation: Prospects, Methods and Challenges. International Journal of Group Decision and Negotiation, Vol. 10, No. 2 (2001) 199–215
14. Kauffman, S. A.: The Origins of Order: Self-Organization and Selection in Evolution. Oxford University Press (1993)
15. von Martial, F.: Coordinating Plans of Autonomous Agents. Springer-Verlag, Berlin (1992)
16. Miles, R. H.: Macro Organizational Behavior. Scott, Foresman and Company (1980)
17. Open Source E-Commerce Solutions. www.oscommerce.com (2004)
18. Pruitt, D. G.: Negotiation Behavior. Academic Press, Inc., New York and London (1981)
19. Sabetzadeh M., Easterbrook, S.: An Algebraic Framework for Merging Incomplete and Inconsistent Views. 13th International Requirements Engineering Conference (2005)
20. Su, N., Mylopoulos, J.: Managing the Coevolution of Organizations and Information Systems. Technical Report 516, Department of Computer Science, University of Toronto (2005)
21. Tesfatsion, L.: Agent-Based Computational Economics: Growing Economies from the Bottom Up. Artificial Life, Vol. 8, No. 1 (2002) 55–82
22. UK Department of Trade and Industry: Complying with the E-commerce Regulations 2002. http://www.dti.gov.uk (2002)
23. Wilensky, R.: Planning and Understanding: A Computational Approach to Human Reasoning. Addison-Wesley Publishing Company, Inc. (1983)
24. Witt, U.: The Evolving Economy: Essays on the Evolutionary Approach to Economics. Edward Elgar Publishing Ltd., Northampton Massachusetts (2003)
25. Wooldridge, M., Jennings, N. R., Kinny, D.: The Gaia Methodology for Agent-Oriented Analysis and Design. Journal of Autonomous Agents and Multi-Agent Systems, Vol. 3, No. 3 (2000) 285–312
26. Yu, E.: Agent Orientation as a Modelling Paradigm. Wirtschaftsinformatik, Vol. 43, No. 2 (2001) 123–132

Towards a Theory of Genericity Based on Government and Binding

Alexander Bienemann[1], Klaus-Dieter Schewe[2], and Bernhard Thalheim[1]

[1] Christian Albrechts University Kiel, Department of Computer Science
Olshausenstr. 40, D-24098 Kiel, Germany
[2] Massey University, Information Science Research Centre
Private Bag 11 222, Palmerston North, New Zealand
{binemann, thalheim}@is.informatik.uni-kiel.de, k.d.schewe@massey.ac.nz

Abstract. Conceptual modelling in the area of data-intensive systems produces database schemata and a variety of systems characteristics, which ideally could be used to facilitate the generation of an implementation. This paper proposes a framework for the development of patterns and components that will permit a direct computation of the corresponding functions, whenever all system parameters and the schemata of the application are known. For this a theory of genericity that is based on the linguistic theory of government and binding (GB), which consists of a two-step specialization of ideas or raw utterances, is developed. This theory of GB genericity is applied to obtain generic workflows and the functionality involved in them.

1 Introduction

Conceptual modelling is widely accepted as a necessity for the development of data-intensive applications. The expectations associated with it are twofold: to capture requirements of the application on a high level of abstraction that eases understanding, and the facilitation of logical and physical design. Ideally, conceptual modelling should produce database schemata and a variety of systems characteristics that could be used to generate at least partially an implementation.

One way to achieve this is to provide genericity. According to Webster's dictionary [1], the term "generic" means *relating or applied to or descriptive of all members of a genus, species, class, or group; common to or characteristic of a whole group or class; typifying or subsuming; not specific or individual.* Thus, defining a generic function should give us the advantage of a certain, universal description of what the function does, along with the possibility to make the definition more precise and/or make it comprise areas of activity not comprised by it originally.

The following challenges in specifying such *generic functions* have been identified in previous research, e.g. in [22,21]:

1. We need a general description of the demanded functionality and of the necessary data objects [26]. Depending on the individual *context* [3,5] this

D.W. Embley, A. Olivé, and S. Ram (Eds.): ER 2006, LNCS 4215, pp. 311–324, 2006.

general description has to be unfolded into a complete function specification including also imposed activities, additional data objects queried from the database, etc. Such an unfolding mechanism has to be developed in order to achieve genericity.
2. The specification method must permit the *refinement of structuring* depending on the needs of a particular user. For instance, subtyping is such a refinement operation [25]. The goal is to have general function specifications refined as well [20,6].
3. Complex generic functions are to be assembled out of other generic functions that are *instantiated* on the basis of given types and with adaptation to the refined structuring [18]. The function generation process has to be done automatically.

Generic functions can be based on software patterns. In general, patterns are an attempt to describe successful solutions to common software problems [2,11,13,14,15,19]. The research on patterns has led to a number of frameworks such as MacApp, ET++, Interviews, ACE, MFC, DCOM, RMI, and CORBA, which play an increasingly important role in contemporary software development. So far patterns have proven to be useful in reuse of successful practices.

In this paper we propose a framework for the development of patterns and components that will permit a direct computation of generic functions, whenever all system parameters and the schemata of the application are known. For this we exploit the linguistic theory of Governance and Binding (GB), which consists of a two-step specialization of ideas or raw utterances [7,9,23]. GB assumes that a universal grammar can be broken into two parts: levels of representation and a system of constraints. It assumes a derivational model and four different levels of representation. The lexicon lists the atomic units of the syntax called basic concepts. Lexical items are combined together to a D-structure, which might be a forest of concept fields [12]. D-structures are mapped into S-structures that reflect the syntactic surface order of the sentence. Examples of S-structures are query and answer forms [25], which are used for representing the general structure and functionality of a given query. S-structures are factored into phonological forms and logical forms. The former ones may be understood to be specific representations of the sentence; the latter ones combine the interface with semantics.

GB still lacks a formal foundation [8,10,24]. The idea behind it, however, summarizes one of the main approaches to generate an utterance. The subcomponents of the rule system are the lexicon, the categorical components and

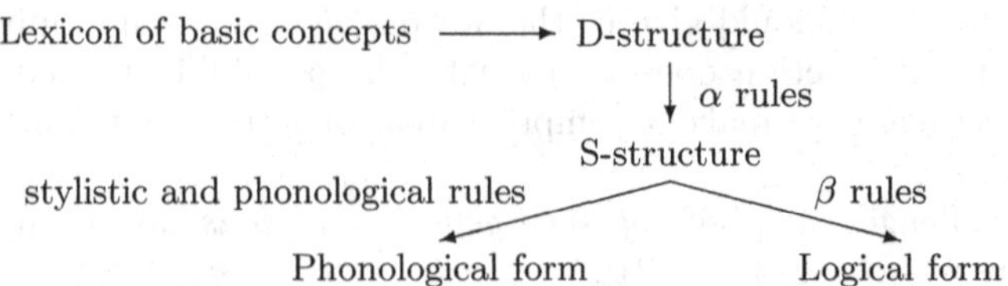

Fig. 1. The levels of representation and rules used in government and binding

the transformational components of the syntax, the LF-component and the PF-component. The systems of principles include a binding theory, a government theory, a Θ-theory, the case theory, and the control theory. The idea can be generalized to a generation framework that supports a variety of applications of generation rules. The separation into α- and β-rules permits a concentration on different aspects of concern.

We tailor GB to obtain generic workflows and the functionality involved in them. In our work the first specialisation step consists of mapping a general idea of a workflow to a particular context. Then the second specialisation step takes the special refinements and instantiations of this context into account.

We first present the concept of generic workflow in Section 2. Then we take a closer look into the generic functions appearing in such workflows in Section 3. Finally, in Section 4 we describe our approach to genericity. We conclude with in brief summary and outlook in Section 5.

To illustrate our concepts we use the relocation of a person as a running example. Here we have to consider the basic relocation data including the possible removal of data on the old location, optional relation enhancements such as the registration of pets, relocation of cars, personal specific data such as family enhancements or relationships to religious bodies, additional relocation announcements such as tax and insurance changes, and specific additional tasks such as applications for housing allowances. We observe that relocation depends on the profile of the issuer, specific tasks of the issuer, specific laws and regulations, and advanced functionality required for associating the workflow with other workflows.

2 Generic Workflows

Applications often require the adaptation of the processing context, e.g. to actual environments such as client, server, and channel currently in use, to users rights, roles, obligations, and prohibitions, to content required for the current portfolio for the current user, to preferences of actual users, to the level of task completion depending on the user, and to users completion history.

This kind of processing adaptation is not yet well supported. In our running example citizens may apply for a primary place of residence, in which case their passport must be changed. Otherwise, no change is required. Citizens with schoolboys/girls may have to complete additional documents. After completion documents may have to be decomposed into a suite of documents due to legal restrictions, e.g. the German data protection law requires that data for city officials and service offices such as the labour agency must be separated.

Depending on the role of users, workflow completion may be scheduled sequentially for some users or scheduled in parallel for others. For instance, clerks in a city office may consider documents in parallel. Citizens are completing their documents in a sequential mode.

Adaptability may be required at run-time. For instance, citizens arriving from a foreign country may be required to have a residence permit. Users may require varying support depending on the environment that is used for the completion of documents. Users should be supported whenever they are interrupted during task completion. These requirements lead directly to the task to develop a facility for *mutable, adaptable workflows* for different users, portfolios, and contexts.

A *workflow suite* consists of a set of workflows that are bundled together by an association schema, which is maintained by consistency requirements. For instance, in our running relocation example we find workflows such as *change of address data*, *change of data for associated people*, *change of registration data* for cars, pets, etc., *change of specific data*, e.g. data for public authority responsible for foreigners, *change of data for social aid*, etc. These workflows are bundled together due to their relationship to one person and to one life circumstance.

These workflows are related to different views and different functionality provided. We use the theory of media types [21] that combines views and their functions into one type. Media types may be linked to other media types. For instance, in our running example, we may distinguish input data for the workflow, retrieval data for the workflow, output data of the workflow, display data suites for each stage of the workflows, and escorting data supporting the understanding of each stage of the workflow.

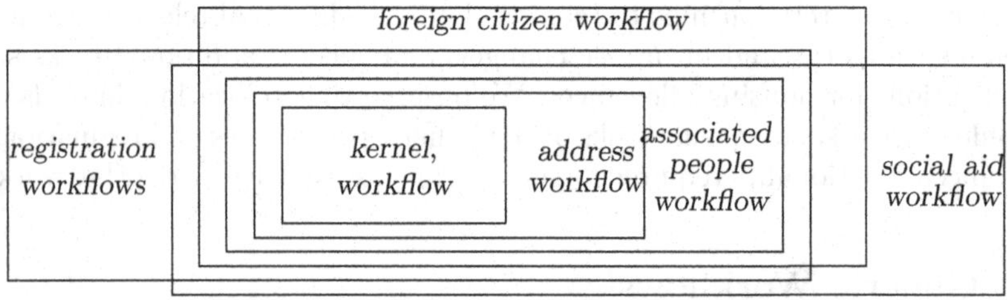

Fig. 2. Hierarchically ordered workflow suite representing the life circumstance *relocation*

The associations may be represented by adhesion between different workflows, which can be represented by a hypergraph as in Figure 2. Additionally, we may specify the adhesion of the workflows by a certain *adhesion value*. Adhesion of workflows may be used for parallel execution, generation of dependence-restricting scheduling of different workflows, and run-time adaptation of the scheduling algorithm. Additionally, we may consider transaction-based execution of workflows. These facilities provide a set of rules that may be used as β-rules for deriving the logical form of the workflow under the context that is provided during compile-time or during run-time.

We may "universalize" workflow suites. For instance, the workflow suite for *relocation* may be understood as a specific instantiation of the universal workflow *relocation*. A *generic workflow* represents the concept of a workflow suite and is specified by

Description: The workflow itself is described by a general CSP expression based on generic functions. It specifies the steps of the generic workflow.

Context: The application context discussed above is explicitly specified.

Applicability: Under certain circumstances the generic workflow may not be applicable or must be applied.

Interactions: The generic workflow requires media types for its support.

Consequences: The utilization of the generic workflow may result in non-applicability of other workflows or in specific restrictions for the context.

Strategies: The mapping to workflow suites is based on a number of α-rules; β-rules are used to map workflow suites to workflow instantiations.

Related generic workflows: A generic workflow may be substituted by or substituting other workflows.

3 Generic Functions

So far, we introduced the concept of generic workflows. This concept uses generic functions. since we are interested in generation of workflow instantiations based on a generic workflow we have to develop a theory of generic functions first. Since our approach is only practicable if the theory of generic functions has been developed in detail we introduce in more detail this concept.

3.1 Generic Functionalizations

Function Applications. Consider types $t_1, ..., t_k, t'_1, ..., t'_n$ for some $k, n \in \mathbb{N}$. Consider $Dom := Col^{t_1} \times ... \times Col^{t_k}$ and $Rng := Col^{t'_1} \times ... \times Col^{t'_n}$ to be sets of tuples of collections of objects of the corresponding types, for $k, n \in \mathbb{N}$. Consider a function $f : Dom \to Rng$ mapping a tuple of collections of types $t_1, ..., t_k$ into a tuple of collections of types $t'_1, ..., t'_n$. Consider two formulae ϕ, ψ defined over the domain and the co-domain of f, respectively. The quintuple $(Dom, \phi, f, \psi, Rng)$ is called a *function application* with precondition ϕ and postcondition ψ [4]. Function applications can be defined recursively by means of operators of the function algebra of choice, i.e. $(Dom, \phi, \theta(F_1, ..., F_m), \psi, Rng)$ is a function application, if θ is a corresponding operator of the function algebra, and $F_1, ..., F_m$ are function applications.

Machines and Genericity. Once we have chosen a computation model, e.g. JAVA, each function f has a machine realization M^f. For each function application $(Dom, \phi, f, \psi, Rng)$ there is thus a machine $M^f_{\phi,\psi}$ realizing it.

Consider function applications F and F^* having machine realizations M and M^* with a notion $\equiv$ of *equivalence of states* (selected states of interest) and of initial and final states.

The function application F is *generic* with respect to F^*, denoted by $F \succeq F^*$, iff for each M^*-run $(s^*_0, u^*_1, s^*_1, u^*_2, ...)$ there is an M-run $(s_0, u_1, s_1, u_2, ...)$ and sequences $i_0 < i_1 < ..., j_0 < j_1 < ...$ such that $i_0 = j_0 = 0$ and $s_{i_k} \equiv S^*_{j_k}$ for each k and either

- both runs terminate and their final states are the last pair of $\equiv$-equivalent states, or
- both runs and both sequences $i_0 < i_1 < \dots$ and $j_0 < j_1 < \dots$ are infinite.

The states $s_{i_k}, s^*_{j_k}$ are the corresponding *states of interest.* Note that this definition corresponds to the one of a *correct refinement* in ASMs [20,6]. We are therefore interested in obtaining a more specialized functionalization specification on the basis of a generic one, so that desired properties of the function application behaviour are still preserved. Typical properties of interest are e.g. presentation of particular data content to a specific user, or preserving the sequence of decisions met by users as imposed by legal regulations.

Functionalizations. A *functionalization* is a quadruple $(\mathcal{S}, \mathcal{F}, \Sigma, s_0)$ with

1. a specification of *structuring* denoted by $\mathcal{S} = (S, V)$ and consisting of a *database schema* $S = (T^S, \Sigma^S)$ with T^S being a set of types according to the type system as stated above, and Σ^S being a set of static integrity constraints, and a set of views V upon schema S defining collections in domains and co-domains of function applications,
2. a function application $\mathcal{F}$,
3. a set of dynamic integrity constraints Σ on $\mathcal{S}$,
4. a distinguished initial state s_0.

As we can see, a functionalization is an abstraction of an interactive information system on conceptual and logical layer [25]. The genericity of functionalizations is defined analogously to the one of function applications, and it is this notion of genericity we are interested in in the following.

3.2 Dimensions of Genericity

In order to use the advantages of a generic function specification, we need to move through the space of functionalizations that are generic to each other. In general, we make a functionalization either "more specific" (and thus "less generic"), or the other way round. However, in order to develop rules for moving throughout such functionalization space, a system of "genericity dimensions" with finer granularity is needed.

A natural choice of "dimensions" would be $\mathcal{S}$, $\mathcal{F}$, and Σ. In this case the word "dimension" is nothing but a plausible, simplified name for a more complex algebraic structure.Dimensions do not necessarily refer to totally ordered sets. Another one would be taking the three semiotic aspects of a functionalization description: syntax, semantics, and pragmatics. Also, other possibilities would be to take "aspects" or "concerns" of software systems [16].

The choice of the dimension system is thus quite arbitrary and depends on how difficult the development of a system of transformation rules for such a dimension system would be. Moreover, the dimensions should reflect typical lines of thinking during the design of a functionalization, i.e. an interactive information system [26]. This is why we introduce the dimensions *refinement of structuring, context embedding,* and *instantiation.* These dimensions are compatible with experiences gathered in the past [5] and can be briefly exemplified as follows (we abstract from functionalizations for the sake of simplicity and show only the functions themselves).

- *Refinement of structuring:*
  E.g., when decomposing a type $T(A, B, C)$ into $\{T_1(A, B), T_2(B, C)\}$, then function $f(o : T)$ can be refined to $\theta(f_1(o : T_1), f_2(o : T_2))$, with θ being an operator of the function algebra of choice.
- *Instantiation:*
  E.g., the function $insert(\cdot)$ can be instantiated with a concrete type definition $T(A, B, C, D)$. In this case a number of $insert()$ applications is necessary, joint together by operators from the function algebra of choice.
- *Context embedding:*
  E.g., if the function $purchase()$ affects not only an object of type $Item$, but also involves performing $checkFunds()$ on an object of associated type $BankAccount$, then the transformation $purchase(Item) \rightarrow \theta(purchase(o : Item), checkFunds(o : BankAccount))$ is performed. In addition, the schema needed by the function $purchase()$ is enriched with the type $BankAccount$.

It still has to be stressed that the three dimensions are arbitrary. They do not cover all aspects of software design and transformation. For instance, distribution has been left out in this paper, but might also result in imposing another dimension if considered. On the other hand, when speaking of "dimensions", we may replace one system of coordinates by another one, provided we have a mapping from one system to the other. This is also the reason for being able to look at dimensions as in Figure 3.

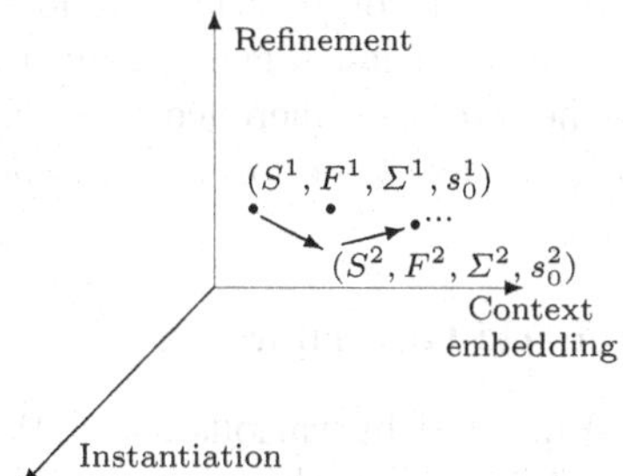

Fig. 3. Functionalization Space with Three Dimensions

3.3 Transformation Rules in Functionalization Space

Each functionalization $(\mathcal{S}, \mathcal{F}, \Sigma, s_0)$ can be transformed into either a less or a more generic one. The transformation is performed stepwise by firing rules. There is a set of rules for each of the distinguished dimensions *refinement of structuring*, *context embedding*, and *instantiation*. The rules are fired consecutively in the desired order so that the functionalization satisfies the quality criteria of the current context, as in the approach of content conditioning [22]. The quality criteria can be either heuristically or formally defined.

Let us illustrate the approach for our running example. We consider the functionalization $(\mathcal{S}, \{changeOfResidence()\}, \Sigma, s_0)$. Assume that we want to achieve a more specialised functionalization for a citizen owning a car and moving to an area where a residence parking permit must be issued. Obviously, when his/her change of residence is processed, the residence parking permit needs to be involved as well. Hence, the following context rules are fired (for schema update and for function application change):

$$\{Application\} \rightarrow \{RegistrationFile \bowtie ParkingPermit\}$$

and

$$changeOfResidence(Application) \rightarrow$$
$$updateResidence(o: RegistrationFile) \| issueParkingPermit(o: Car)$$

4 The GB Framework for Genericity

In [12] the theory of word fields has been extended to a theory of concept fields. Concept fields are governed by a verb. This verb governs

- the arguments and the logical structure of the verb,
- the semantical description with relevant and irrelevant valences, and
- the kernel semantics including a description of the semen.

We may extend this approach on the basis of the GB theory. Since we aim at the development of a framework of generic workflows we may restrict ourselves to their main specification elements. A general generation facility does not exist. We may, however, use the internal coherence of generic workflows, as some components govern the other ones. Therefore, we develop a set of governing rules and a binding mechanism.

4.1 Developing Generic Governors

Workflows may be instantiated by various rules. We assume that the core semantics of a generic workflow has a clear semantic content, but the mapping to workflow suites and the instantiation involve structural configurations refining the core semantics. At the same time, dependence provided by the core semantics must be maintained to meet the following conditions:

- conditions on the choice of governor,
- conditions on governed terms, and
- structural conditions on the relation of government.

Relating the GB theory [7] to the theory of ASM refinement [20] we conclude that the core semantics of a generic workflow is refined by the workflow suite and further refined to the instantiated workflow. A kernel element of the generic workflow governs the other components of the generic workflow, some of which may also be generic workflows. In some applications we have to assume that the dependence or government structure is irreflexive.

In our running example the kernel workflow is given by the *relocation*. *Relocation* is governed by the subject of *relocation*, i.e. in the example by people moving from one place to another one. The data structures used for representing the data of a moving person, the technical environment, the set of preferences of users, the rights and roles of users in the process of *relocation* govern the generation of the workflow suite and the instantiation of the workflow. At the same time, the generic workflow *relocation* governs the generic workflow *change_of_passport*.

A *governor* $\mathcal{G}$ is therefore defined by a function $\mathcal{G} : \mathcal{C} \times \mathcal{GW} \mapsto \mathcal{WS}$ mapping the generic workflow $\mathcal{GW}$ under consideration of the context $\mathcal{C}$ to a workflow suite $\mathcal{WS}$. For practical purposes we use term rewriting rules for the governors.

4.2 Developing Generic Bindings

The binding theory originally proposed in [7] characterizes two domains as opaque: the direct expression of a word and the rules for integrating the word into an utterance. These two binding principles may be generalized for our purposes to cover a wider range of application. There are several ways for representation of these bindings. The approach used by Chomsky is the integration into anaphorical structures. Another way we prefer to use is the expression of structural binding through attribute grammars. The latter approach allows the direct mechanism for binding to be represented in an explicit form. In our running example, the generic workflow *relocation* governs the generic workflow *change_of_passport*.

Bindings may be used for associating the parameters of the generic workflows or the workflow suites to each other. For the sake of simplicity we assume that bindings can be expressed by substitution rules σ that map parameters to expressions defined over these parameters. The expressions are based on the CSP expression that define the workflow. For instance, in the case of sequential execution the substitution rule maps some of the parameters of the second element to parameters of the first element, thus equating these parameters. In a similar form we may substitute parameters used for parallel execution.

4.3 Examples of Basic Generic Workflows

We generalize some of the patterns in [17] for access and collaboration using GB. The approach shows how generic workflows can be developed, can be mapped to workflow suites and instantiated to workflows. In the sequel, we discuss a number of basic generic workflows that might support data exchange.

The Basic Generic Workflow ACCESSOR

Description: The workflow abstracts from access details and represents the general access. It is governed by the environment, i.e. media type and the platform providing the access. It governs the generic workflow FEEDBACK that supports the error messaging after enacting the workflow. The media type may be normalized and may be based on optimized behavior. The governor incorporates these two specializations as well. The generic workflow is based on extraction of data and functionality from the source media type, transformation of the data and the functions to the target media type and an modification facility for the target database.

Context: The generic workflow uses generic contracts that provide a framework for automatic application. Typical such contracts are based on publish-subscribe, publish-trade, or publish-broker-request. The generic workflow uses a model-view-controller concept for its workflow suite.

Applicability: The generic workflow is used to hide access complexity, optimization facilities and specific semantics for data and functionality extraction and their transfer to a target database.

Structure: The structure of the generic workflow is specified by the nested structural expressions
(AccessPath.QueryExpression, TransformExpression, ResultForm)
and
ConcreteAccessor(Accessor(operationSet(Params)), MediaTypeDriver)

Interactions: The media type support collaboration of agents AnApplicat, AConcreteAccessor, AMediaTypeDriver on a protocol expression
Protocol(StartOperationA; StartOperationA;
ReturnResultFromMT; ReturnResultToSource)
which results in a data exchange between the application and the accessor and in a data exchange between the accessor and the system supporting the media type.

Consequences: The generic workflow limits application control of data access. At the same time it provides independence, optimization, and allows swapping of data sources.

Strategies: The α-rules map the generic workflow to an MVC-based workflow suite. The β-rules map the workflow suite to access programs thus supporting versatile access, incorporating enhancements and optimization points, guarding against inefficient application usage, and guarding for errors and exceptions

Related generic workflows: The generic workflow ADAPTER may be governed by the given generic workflow.

Typical examples are the JDBC or ODBC access.

The Basic Generic Workflow ACTIVE MEDIA TYPE

Description: The generic workflow abstracts from the media type structuring and functionality.

Context: The structure and the functionality of the media type constitute an element of the context. Typical functionality is based on schema matching for the media type structures, and on recharging functions such as initialize, refresh, save, and list.

Applicability: The generic workflow masks legacy, hides complexity, groups associated objects into combined objects, and is the basis for webpage containers.

Structure: The structure of the generic workflow is specified by the nested structural expression
Application(activeContainerObject (Structure,
QueryAnswerForm(MediaTypeObject)))
and may be extended by specific logging facilities.

Interactions: The protocol is based on message exchange facilities between between applications, containers and media objects. It depends on policies for data modification and bindings.

Consequences: The generic workflow spreads access across and thus limits application control. At the same time, application code becomes surveyable and maintainable. Application code independence is supported.

Strategies: α-rules inject the context (e.g. database schemata and procedures for access, matching rules,) into the workflow suite. β-rules are responsible for the connection management, the database state maintenance and the recharging process.

Related generic workflow: The generic workflow is similar to the concept of data containers [25] used for content delivery for websites.

Simple examples of the generic workflow are XML exchange facilities and EJB.

The Basic Generic Workflow MEDIA TYPE COLLABORATION

Description: The generic workflow specifies collaboration among different parties based on query-based exchange, request, and delivery of data.

Context: Collaboration is restricted by collaboration contracts [26] and by the matching of appropriate media types.

Applicability: Various schemata mappings are becoming versatile.

Structure: The structure of the generic workflow is specified by the nested structural expressions
Application(OwnMediaTypes, MediaObjectSuiteManager)
and
MediaObjectSuite(MediaObjectSuiteManager, Profiler,
CollaboratingMediaObjectSuite).

Interactions: The protocol is based on message exchange facilities such as
Protocol.read(MediaObjectSuite); mediaObjectSuite.find(Profiler);
mediaObjectSuite.collaborate(CollaboratingMediaObjectSuite);
mediaObjectSuite.create(CollaboratingObjects).

Consequences: The generic workflow limits application control of access but provides independence from the context.

Strategies: α-rules are used for profiling and suite workspace creation. β-rules provide a facility for identity matching, aggregation detection, and inheritance orchestration.

Related generic workflow: This basic generic workflow is governed by the SERVICE workflow.

A typical simple example is Java data object (JDO).

The Basic Generic Workflow SERVICE

Description: This basic generic workflow stacks orthogonal features that access issues with increasing level of abstraction.

Context: The workflow supports abstraction in terms of less abstract media objects and depends on context data such as media object mapping, data conversion, data operation mapping, resource management, distribution, caching, authorization, and logging.

Applicability: The workflow is based on separatability of features into incremental levels that might be build gradually.

Structure: The structure of the generic workflow is specified by the nested structural expressions
application(...., ImportServiceMediaType);
service(ExportMediaTypes, ImportServiceMediaTypes)
with competences such as
accessService(ExportMediaTypes).

Interactions: The workflow is based on delegation to inner services with semaphores.

Consequences: Interaction is layered and initialization complexity is increasing. At the same time the generic workflow supports functional decomposition, feature modularization, feature detail encapsulation, and layer pluggability.

Strategies: α-rules are used for top-down detailization, sequentialization, and algorithmication. β-rules support to stub layering and provide layer initializations.

Related generic workflow: The complex generic workflow ARCHITECTURE is based on the given basic generic workflow.

5 Conclusion

This paper introduces the concept of generic workflows. Similar to situations in applications, tasks may be specified on the basis of a general description of possible ways for satisfaction and completion. In traditional workflow development approaches a task may be given by a verb that represents a group of verbs with similar behavior. Each of the more special verbs is supported by its own workflow. The traditional approach will lead to a huge number of workflows with a similar behavior. Whenever a part of the context is changing the workflow must change as well.

Instead of these classical approaches we propose a different way. We associate a task with a generic workflow that accommodates all possible different ways of completing the task. The generic workflow may be unfolded to a workflow suite by consideration of the context. A workflow suite has a number of parameters that are instantiated for a given actual workflow. This approach allows to represent the "general workflow" by an activity skein displayed in Figure 4. This skein may be specialized to the workflow suite. The concrete instance of the workflow is a fiber within this skein.

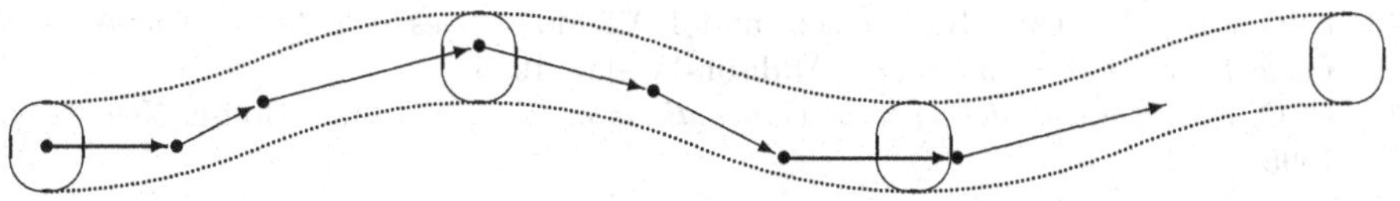

Fig. 4. Generic workflows, workflow suites and their instantiations

The paper shows that this vision can be developed on the basis of government and binding theory. The exploitation of the GB approach is our contribution to thoughtful and consistent development of applications. Our approach has already been used in some of our projects, e.g. for the citizen service portal of `www.cottbus.de` and for the e-learning portal `damit.dfki.de`. The concept is currently extended in other e-government projects.

Acknowledgement

The authors would like to thank Noam Chomsky for his helpful comments on his theory of Government and Binding.

References

1. Websters ninth new collegiate dictionary, 1991.
2. P. Aiken. *Data Reverse Engineering: Slaying the Legacy Dragon.* McGraw-Hill, 1995.
3. A. Binemann-Zdanowicz. Sitelang::edu - towards a context-driven e-learning content utilization model. In *Proc. SAC'2004 (ACM SIGAPP), Nicosia, Cyprus, March 2004*, pages 924–928. Association for Computing Machinery, 2004.
4. A. Binemann-Zdanowicz. *A Generative Approach to Functionality of Interactive Information Systems.* PhD thesis, Christian Albrecht University of Kiel, Germany, 2006 (to be submitted).
5. A. Binemann-Zdanowicz, R. Kaschek, K.-D. Schewe, and B. Thalheim. Context-aware web information systems. In *Proc. APCCM'2004, January 2004*, pages 37–48, 2004.
6. E. Börger and R. Stärk. *Abstract state machines - A method for high-level system design and analysis.* Springer, Berlin, 2003.
7. N. Chomsky. *Some concepts and consequences of the theory of government and binding.* MIT Press, 1982.
8. N. Chomsky. *Lectures on government and binding - The Pisa lectures.* Mouton, De Gryuter, 1993.
9. N. Chomsky. *The minimalist program.* MIT Press, Cambridge, 1995.
10. N. Chomsky. Personal communication, 2005, Aug., 5 and 8.
11. J. O. Coplien and D. C. Schmidt, editors. *Pattern languages for program design.* Addison-Wesley, Reading, 1995.
12. A. Düsterhöft and B. Thalheim. Integrating retrieval functionality in websites based on storyboard design and word fields. volume 2553 of *LNCS*, pages 52–63. Springer, 2002.

13. E. Gamma, R. Helm, R. Johnson, and J. Vlissides. *Design patterns: Elements of reusable software architecture.* Addison-Wesley, 1995.
14. D. C. Hay. *Data model pattern: Conventions of thought.* Dorset House, New York, 1995.
15. Taligent Inc., editor. *The power of frameworks - For windows and OS/2 developers.* Addison-Wesley, 1995.
16. P. Klint, T. van der Storm, and J.J. Vinju. Term rewriting meets aspect-oriented programming. In *Report SEN-E0421, December 2004.*
17. C. Nock. *Data Access Patterns - Database Interactions in Object Oriented Aploications.* Addison-Wesley, Boston, 2004.
18. T. Pittman and J. Peters. *The Art of Compiler Design: Theory and Practice.* Prentice Hall, 1992.
19. K. Quibeldey-Cirkel. *Design patterns.* Springer, Berlin, 1999.
20. G. Schellhorn. *Verifikation abstrakter Zustandsmaschinen.* PhD thesis, University of Ulm, Germany, 1999.
21. K.-D. Schewe and B. Thalheim. Conceptual modelling of web information systems. *Data and Knowledge Engineering*, 2005.
22. K.-D. Schewe, B. Thalheim, A. Binemann-Zdanowicz, R. Kaschek, T. Kuss, and B. Tschiedel. A conceptual view of web-based e-learning systems. *Education and Information Technologies*, 10(1-2):83–110, January 2005.
23. E. Stabler. Derivational minimalism. In C. Retore, editor, *Logical aspects of computational linguistics*, volume LNCS 1328, pages 68–95. Springer, 1998.
24. E. Stabler. Personal communication, 2005, Sept., 3.
25. B. Thalheim. *Entity-relationship modeling – Foundations of database technology.* Springer, Berlin, 2000. See also http://www.is.informatik.uni-kiel.de/~thalheim/HERM.htm.
26. B. Thalheim. Informationssystem-Entwicklung. In *BTU Cottbus, Computer Science Institute, Technical Report I-15-2003*, Cottbus, 2003.

Concept Modeling by the Masses: Folksonomy Structure and Interoperability

Csaba Veres

Department of Computer Science, Norwegian University of Science and Technology
Csaba.Veres@idi.ntnu.no

Abstract. The recent popularity of social software in the wake of the much hyped "Web2.0" has resulted in a flurry of activity around folksonomies, the emergent systems of classification that result from making public the individual users' personal classifications in the form of simple free form "tags". Several approaches have emerged in the analysis of these folksonomies including mathematical approaches for clustering and identifying affinities, social theories about cultural factors in tagging, and cognitive theories about their mental underpinnings. In this paper we argue that the most useful analysis is in terms of mental phenomena since naive classification is essentially a cognitive task. We then describe a method for extracting structural properties of free form user tags, based on the linguistic properties of the tags. This reveals some deep insights in the conceptual modeling behavior of naive users. Finally we explore the usefulness of the latent structural properties of free form "tag clouds" for interoperability between folksonomies from different services.

Keywords: Web2.0, folksonomy, interoperability, tagging, concept modeling.

1 Introduction

There is currently a great deal of activity revolving around applications and initiatives on the World Wide Web that fall under the rubric of Web2.0, the live Web, social software, or architecture of participation [1]. While there is a great deal of hype and cynicism concerning the phenomenon [2], there is nevertheless some consensus on an interesting set of properties that loosely define prototypical Web2.0 applications.

One important hallmark of Web2.0 applications is that they tend to be based around web services so that there is no requirement to install a special application on a client machine. This already introduces a new dynamic to the application space since functionality can change incrementally and with an extremely fast life cycle. It is reported that Carl Henderson, leading developer at Flickr[1] (a leading Web2.0 application) commented that "on good days, Flickr releases new versions every half an hour"[2]. This development model is complemented

[1] http://www.flickr.com/

[2] http://blogs.warwick.ac.uk/chrismay/tag/flickr/)

D.W. Embley, A. Olivé, and S. Ram (Eds.): ER 2006, LNCS 4215, pp. 325–338, 2006.

by an architecture in which constant evolution makes sense; the "architecture of participation". Such architecture is exemplified in eBay's services which are entirely dependent on the participation of its members, and increasing levels of participation can enable the gradual implementation of feature refinements. Amazon.com is another service where users add value by default: whenever they purchase multiple items, add reviews, add items to the wish list, and in general simply "use" the system, they contribute data which in aggregate can improve the service to other customers by providing recommendations and associations which would otherwise not exist. The web service is then improved to make use of the accumulating data. The architecture is designed by default to improve the service simply as a side effect of its ordinary use, and the improved service is quickly rolled out through program updates.

This participatory architecture enables the harnessing of collective intelligence by aggregating user data, which is the second hallmark of Web2.0 applications: the primacy of data over application. A hallmark achievement in this vein is WikipediA, a brave experiment in creating a collaborative encyclopedia which, ideally, anyone could contribute to. Amazingly this radical departure from the kind of authoritarian editorial style one might expect for a reference of this sort, proved to deliver a product comparable to the most venerable Encyclopedia Britannica[3]. A similar challenge is being laid to traditional news services by the activity of blogging, and services like digg. These activities aided by search tools like Technorati together with syndication and other tools like RSS and trackbacks, make it possible for news and opinions to be disseminated and discussed very rapidly.

The benefits of collective intelligence gained through social interaction have come into the popular limelight through the introduction of services like del.icio.us[4], Flickr, CiteUlike[5], Yahoo MyWeb 2.0 Beta[6] and Google Base Beta[7], in which content is contributed, aggregated, and categorized through the collective actions of its users. In some cases the content is created by users as with the photographs contributed to Flickr, but mostly they are proxied as in the case of bookmarks on del.icio.us, or scientific references in CiteUlike. In either case extra value is added through the classification and organization efforts of multiple users. All of these services employ some form of user annotation of the resources, usually referred to as *tags* (e.g. in del.icio.us, Flickr), but sometimes called *labels* and *properties* (in Google Base Beta). The primary value of these services is not simply the addition of content but organization of content in a way that allows its discovery. Crucially, the system of classification and discovery is not driven by sophisticated organizational and search strategies, but by a network of associations that emerges in the process of opportunistic user behavior.

---

[3] http://www.nature.com/nature/journal/v438/n7070/full/438900a.html
[4] http://del.icio.us/
[5] http://www.citeulike.org/
[6] http://myweb2.search.yahoo.com/
[7] http://base.google.com/

For example on the social bookmarking service del.icio.us, users mark up their favorite web sites with their chosen tags. The service requires a user account, and acts in the first instance as a web based repository for each individual user's bookmarks for their favorite web sites. The web sites are indexed by URL and described with a textual description which is typically generated from the title in the web site. As a result, most bookmarks to the same URL will have the same descriptive title, but this is not necessarily the case because users are free to insert their own descriptions. In addition, users annotate each bookmark with metadata in the form of any number of single word tags. The user interface provides access to popular tags for a given URL at the time of bookmarking, assuming of course that other users have tagged that URL. In addition, users can view other URLs annotated with a particular tag they might use. Because the aggregated "tag use" of all users is available in various forms on the service, users can derive value from each others behavior. For example popular tags for a given URL can influence a user who is also adding that URL to their bookmarks, because popular tags are, putatively, useful for other users. On the other hand, users can find new web sites by following links that were tagged with the same terms as the current one of interest. As pointed out in [3] the novel feature of services like del.icio.us is not their reliance on keywords in lieu of taxonomies for indexing – that idea has been around for years. Instead, the novelty is the immediacy of the feedback from the community of users: "Feedback is immediate. As soon as you assign a tag to an item, you see the cluster of items carrying the same tag. If that's not what you expected, you're given incentive to change the tag or add another ... you can adapt to the group norm, keep your tag in a bid to influence the group norm, or both." The benefits to indexing are that resources are grouped according to flexible category structures that are not imposed by authority. This emerging categorization activity that results from the combination of a large number of users tagging resources for their own use has been called *folksonomy* (e.g. [4]). The most fundamental unit of analysis of tagging on del.icio.us is the *tag set* that each individual assigns to an individual resource, which gives rise to a *tag cloud,* the combined set of tags all users assign to that resource weighted by frequency. A tag cloud is therefore a multiset in which order is ignored but multiplicity is significant.

Such a complex network of data lends itself to analysis in a number of different forms. One obvious approach is to use any number of mathematical techniques for the analysis of complex networks, or to find clusters in multi dimensional spaces (e.g. [5]; [6]; [7]; [8]).

In the following section we will briefly present some select observations about mathematical properties of "tag space". But we argue that such analyses are not enlightening as an explanation for the way tags are used to classify resources. Instead we argue that a cognitive perspective, which looks at the linguistic behavior of tags, can provide a useful explanatory account of tag use. Our analysis suggests that naive users produce tags which display latent properties that are typical of complex conceptual modeling activities. In section 3 we describe an approach that can uncover the latent structure in sets of tags. In section 4 we show that the explicit representation of this latent structure can facilitate interoperability. Finally we conclude in showing that we have strong evidence for sophisticated concept models in spontaneous, un solicited naive user tags, which reflect fundamental properties of the cognitive apparatus.

2 Some Mathematical Observations

[6] presents a thesis on the (by now well known) observation that the distribution of the relative popularity of tags in tag clouds approximates a power law function. Individual URLs tend to have a few popular tags (usually less than 10 in number) which are consistently used by a vast majority of users. [6] argues that there is a shift in the precise function that is approximated by the tag cloud, since the popularity of particular tags can vary due to cultural factors such as the spread of new terminologies. But, while this is undoubtedly true in some cases, [7] show on the basis of a large empirical sample that the shape of tag clouds tend to be remarkably stable. In analyzing historical trends for the most popular tags used for a given URL by an ever-increasing number of users, they make the following interesting observations:

"One might expect that individuals' varying tag collections and personal preferences, compounded by an ever-increasing number of users, would yield a chaotic pattern of tags. However, it turns out that the combined tags of many users' bookmarks give rise to a stable pattern in which the proportions of each tag are nearly fixed. Empirically, we found that, usually after the first 100 or so bookmarks, each tag's frequency is a nearly fixed proportion of the total frequency of all tags used." ([7], p. 6).

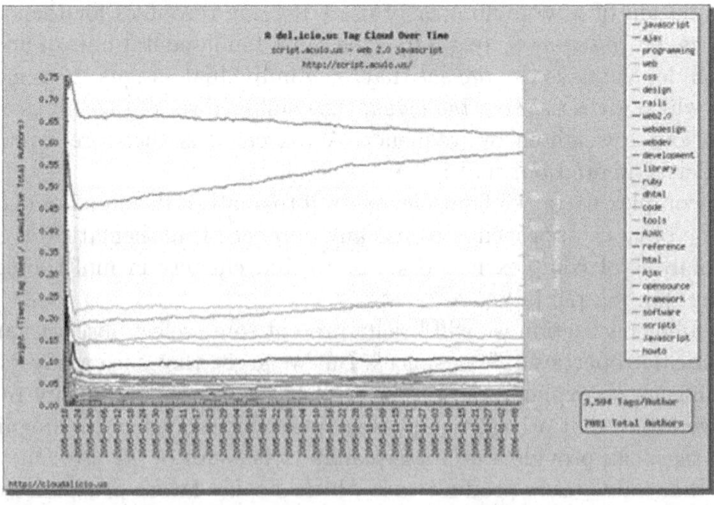

Fig. 1. Tag cloud of del.icio.us tags for the web site script.aculo.us

An example showing this stability, as well as the approximate power law curve, and some evidence for cultural influence in terms of the community uptake of the term "Ajax" is shown in figure 1. ("Ajax" is represented by the slowly ascending, second curve from the top.)

There are several possible explanations for the manifest stability, including relatively un-interesting ones concerning the user interface to del.icio.us, which suggests existing popular tags to each user who tags for their own use a site which was already bookmarked by others. But [7] make an additional observation which shows that such explanations cannot completely account for the observed stability in tag use since the less popular tags which are not shown as suggestions through the interface, display the same stability over time. They conclude that "Shared knowledge among taggers may also account for their making the same choices." Thus while the most popular tags in figure 1 evolved in full view, as it were, of the taggers, the mass of less popular tags at the bottom of the graphic evolved in private. But the two sorts of tags are indistinguishable in terms of their pattern of use, suggesting that the "shared knowledge" contributes significantly to tagging behavior. In addition, [9] suggests an interesting thought experiment. "Suppose I am a really rich guy who wants to influence tags on del.icio.us. So I pay 10000 people to tag resources according to my schema. I tell them to mark one site with 'eek', another one with 'woo hoo', a third one with 'grumpy grumpy head', and so on. With enough people, these should become the most popular tags. But how long will the dominance of these tags last? This is an experiment that does not really need doing!". The simple point, of course, is that the user interface suggestions are popular tags which somehow reflect the shared knowledge discussed in [7].

In this paper we try to find the nature of that "shared knowledge". To do so, we adopt the position that folksonomies are an abundant source of free, interesting data which can give a clue about the way humans organize knowledge, and about the extent to which the mentalistic organizational systems are shared. We subscribe to the hopefully non-controversial position that mental architecture fundamentally shapes our perceptions and organization of the world in which we live. Perhaps more controversially we argue that essential aspects of the mental architecture are fixed and therefore shared by all humans (e.g. [10]) The empirical questions then become "What are the characteristics of the shared architecture?" and "To what degree are they shared?". Clearly there are points of difference in individual conceptualizations. I say 'Library of Congress', but Clay Shirky wants to say 'LOC' [11]. Good for him. But pity the poor soul who calls it 'the square root of a banana'! The point is that the mind creates categories, because that is what minds do. These categories allow some degree of variation, but differences are tightly bounded. The mental architecture enforces the range of possible ontologies and taxonomies that we can bring to bear on the understanding of our universe. All humans share fundamental aspects of mental architecture and therefore properties of possible taxonomies and folksonomies. Folksonomy, on this view, becomes an invaluable source of data for studying the mental processes of naive human classifiers. Conversely, properties of the mental architecture as known from independent sources should give us insight into communal tagging behavior.

A second source of evidence that communal tagging is constrained by, and therefore displays properties of, deep cognitive processes comes from looking at so called *narrow folksonomies* which are to be contrasted with the *broad folksonomies* we have been considering up until now. Tim Vanderwal coined the two terms to describe the two styles of tagging that can be observed on different web applications [4]. The typical behavior on del.icio.us is that many users tag each resource, whereas on the photo sharing service Flickr the default behavior is that tags can only be added by the original contributor and their invited contacts. As a result narrow folksonomies do not display the rich collection of tags that we saw with broad folksonomies. But if we are correct in our claim that the emergent stability of tag clouds with broad folksonomies is due to cognitive facts more than to social, cultural or user interface issues, then there ought to be similar constraints on the tags observed in narrow folksonomies. Some support for this is found through the clustering feature offered by Flickr, which identifies groups of pictures which tend to be associated with overlapping tags, probably using k-means clustering methods. For example a search for clusters with the word "love" returns several distinct groups with tag groups such as {heart, red, valentine, valentinesday, nature, pink, flowers, hearts, white}, {couple, kiss, wedding, bw, people, friends, bride, groom, romance, marriage}, {dog, cat, cute, smile, happy, pet, puppy, cats, kitty, kitten}, and {family, mother, baby, child, kids, fun, daughter, christmas, children, mom}. Clearly the clusters are meant to identify overall themes in the picture collections that can be used to organize photographs. The observation that such clustering is possible suggests that people tend to tag pictures for personal use with sufficient consistency to allow aggregation in a useful way, even though each individual is tagging from their own point of view in complete ignorance of the other users. On the other hand, while clustering is a popular way to process tags for enhanced usability, they have an inherent limitation in that they conflate many dimensions simultaneously [12]. The cognitive approach will give us a way to keep these dimensions distinct.

3 A Cognitive Approach

The hypothesis that folksonomies contain hidden properties that are also observable in formal taxonomies was investigated by [13]. Inspired by the cognitive theory of Lawrence Barsalou[8] [14] and the linguistic insights of Anna Wierzbicka [15], he described a distinction between purely taxonomic concepts and a number of other categories of concepts which were not taxonomic. The idea is that taxonomic concepts are those which describe the basic entities in the world, and

[8] We realize that there is a vast literature on human categorization that we are not covering here, as kindly pointed out by an anonymous reviewer. We leave these out mainly because the theoretical underpinning as elaborated in [13] would gain little by their inclusion.

can be represented in the customary generalization hierarchies where each level in the hierarchy contains disjunctive categories whose members resemble one another more closely than they do members of other categories at the same level. Further, members of a category on a given level are also members of a category at all higher levels. Perhaps most importantly, membership in a category allows a large number of inferences to be drawn about entities. A clear example is in the domain of animals: cats resemble each other more than they resemble dogs, and all cats (and dogs) are also mammals. Cats can be further specialized as Siamese cats and Russian Blue, where Siamese cats resemble one another more than they resemble Russian Blues, and so on. There are also a very large number of inferences that can be drawn about an individual if it is known to be a cat. We know its rough dimensions, its weight, appearance, that it needs food, goes to the toilet, likes to breathe air, and so on.

On the other hand there are a large number of categories which do not display these properties. Consider as an example the class which is described by the word *weapon*. If someone tells you that their country just acquired a fantastic new weapon, what can you conclude about the acquired object? For sure, it can be used to inflict harm and destruction. But how big is it? Is it solid or gas? Is it even a substance, or is it instead a kind of psychological weapon? Does it look like a pistol? Or an inter continental ballistic missile? Or a dog? In point of fact, very little can be inferred from category membership, except its functional property. Wierzbicka [15] calls these concepts purely functional ones, because they describe heterogeneous types which can be used to fulfill a particular function. In addition, she describes three other non-taxonomic categories as follows.

A second kind of category, exemplified by *furniture*, is formed because its members are often experienced together in a *common location and serving a common function*. Furniture can refer to a very loose and heterogeneous collection of "things" which might include tables, chairs, lamps, ashtrays, stereo systems, televisions, and any number of other items with very little resemblance to one another. A third kind of category that also depends on exemplars being *collected in a common location* is exemplified by *groceries* and *dishes* (as in "go wash the dishes"). In addition to being united by a common location, exemplars of these categories share a *common explanation for their collective existence*, or a *common origin: groceries* can include anything put in a shopping basket at the supermarket including non food items, and *dishes* can refer to any food eating implement used for a meal including plates, pots, knives and forks. This latter example is also interesting because it shows that ambiguity of the word *dishes*: in its taxonomic use it can refer only to different kinds of dishes used for serving food, such as *cereal bowl*, *salad bowl*, and so on; but in its collective use it can also refer to pots and pans and forks. It is possible for elements of this sort of category to lose their collective status as long as they retain a temporal bond. For example *leftovers* can be scattered in various locations but the concept still retains its collective status by virtue of the fact that there was some time and place for their common place of origin. Finally, there is a category whose exemplars have *similar sources and similar purposes or functions*, but aren't necessarily experienced together in a common collection. This sort of category includes *vegetables*, *medicines*, and *herbs*. For example *vegetable* describes a heterogeneous collection of entities that people grow in the ground to be used for food. Members of this category acquire an unusual interpretation when used in plural form: "I had three vegetables for dinner" would seem misleading if I had three carrots, whereas "I had three birds for dinner" would be fine if I had three quails.

One important feature of these types of categories, as we have already hinted, is that they can be distinguished on their grammatical properties. This is not only theoretically interesting but also practically useful because it makes possible the automatic discovery of the appropriate type of category that a given term represents. A comprehensive set of grammatical tests for distinguishing the categories is detailed in [13]. As an example of distinguishing between two different types by their grammatical properties, consider the following sets of sentence frames. *Functional* category names display the following pattern of acceptable and unacceptable (*) frames:

- a toy/vehicle/weapon
- toys/vehicles/weapons, three toys/vehicles/weapons, many toys/vehicles/weapons
- * a lot of toy/vehicle/weapon
- a lot of toys/vehicles/weapons
- * much toy/vehicle/weapon

whereas *functional collocations* exhibit the following pattern of frames (note they are almost, but not completely identical to mass nouns in their pattern of use):

- * a furniture/cutlery/clothing
- * furnitures/cutlerys/clothings, *three furnitures/cutlerys/clothings, *many furnitures/cutlerys/clothings
- a lot of furniture/cutlery/clothing
- *a lot of furnitures/cutleries/clothings
- * much furniture/cutlery/clothing
- an item of furniture/cutlery/clothing

[13] used these categories to compare the structure of the semi formal taxonomies used in YAHOO directory and DMOZ to categorize a resource, with the set of tags assigned by users to the same resource. He found surprising similarities, indicating a similar distribution of the category structures in tags and in the directories. But an interesting difference was a disproportionately large use of taxonomic concepts in the user tags. This is sensible if we assume that the directory categories exist mainly to collect heterogeneous unknown resources according to various function related criteria. In contrast, taxonomic classifications are about single types, so the taxonomic classifiers are likely to be used more often as tags where the resource is already known and a specific view can be taken about their type. In the directories which are used for resource discovery it makes sense to commit to this sort of classification less frequently. In fact in the rare circumstance that taxonomic categories are used, they tend to be leaf nodes where the narrow categories are more appropriate.

4 Folksonomy Interoperability

The cognitive approach provides a way that latent structural information can be extracted from user tags in a given service. But if the cognitive processes are ubiquitous, then their impact should be observed in all applications that utilize user tags. We should therefore be able to achieve interoperability of tags across different applications. Tom Gruber, the author of possibly the most often cited definition of Ontology, considers two possible scenarios from a future Web2.0 where this would be beneficial; first, users might wish to interoperate different services on which they have independently tagged content, and second, search engines might be able to exploit user tags on different services to produce better search results[16]. In both scenarios the key is interoperability of tags such that no one application has precedence over another in terms of tag reference. If tags from different sources are to be compared in some way, then there must be an explicit agreement on the interpretation of the possible patterns of tag use. To solve this problem Gruber suggests an ontology of tags in which the representation of each tagging instance requires at least a four place relation: Tagging(Object1, tag1, tagger1, source1). We could then have n-tuples of the form

- Tagging(Object1, tag1, tagger1, source1)
- Tagging(Object1, tag2, tagger1, source1)
- Tagging(Object1, tag1, tagger2, source1)
- Tagging(Object1, tag3, tagger3, source2)
- Tagging(Object2, tag1, tagger4, source2)

on which a set of axioms can be defined. These axioms might address questions like tag equivalence, for example. So, tagger1 might tag Object1 as both tag1="san francisco" and tag2="sanfrancisco". Are tag1 and tag2 identical? There is obviously not an absolute right answer to this, but an explicit assumption could be stated in terms of axioms defined in the ontology. Then one could go on to ask, if tag1=tag2, does this mean tagger1 only assigned one tag to Object1? Once again assumptions made by implementations can be explicitly stated in axioms. This proposal is about establishing the relationships between individual tags, which precedes the more interesting possibilities for tag based resource discovery. While tackling the issues of syntactic equivalence, synonymy and ambiguity of tags is clearly important, the question of interoperability more broadly construed should include notions of semantic similarity.

Suppose as a concrete example that you had several web services in regular use, each annotated by a set of tags, and you wanted them to inter operate. For example you could be writing a document on Writely[9] the web based word processor, which allows users to annotate documents with tags, and you wanted to collect a set of relevant URLs from del.icio.us and a set of relevant photographs from Flickr. Suppose the document was about the impending bird flu epidemic in 2006, and you wanted relevant links and photos for the different content areas in the paper. Searching for *bird flu* on the two services gives the results in

[9] www.writely.com

figure 2. The del.icio.us tags are obtained from the list of "common tags" that are returned from a search for "bird flu". The clusters that are returned from a similar search on Flickr are shown on the left side of figure 2.

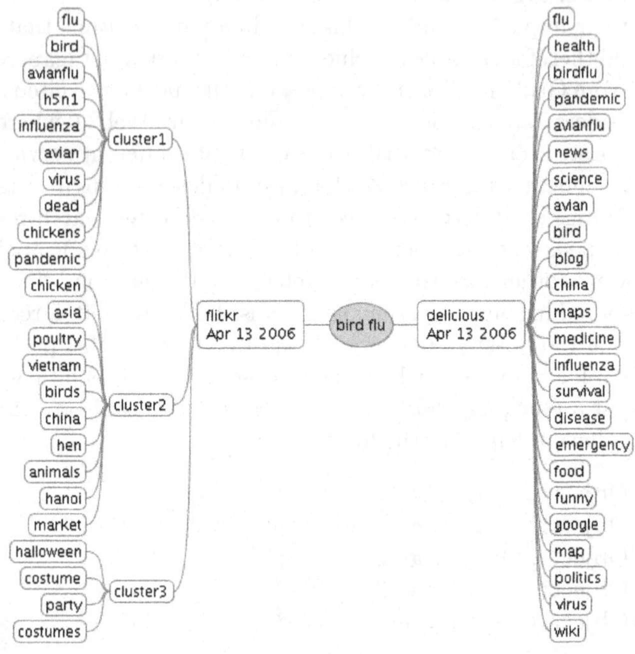

Fig. 2. Tags returned from Flickr and del.icio.us from a search on "bird flu"

It is quite apparent from looking at the set of returned tags that a wide variety of topics are related to *bird flu* in both services, and retrieving all of the resources on the basis of the single tag will give too many irrelevant results for a particular interest. The problem is in identifying the relevant resources in each service and to match them across services. The large number of tags in figure 2, mixed in terms of focus and generality, makes it difficult to find meaningful connections even for humans. The situation is obviously worse for automated processing. For example, cluster2 on Flickr appears to be more about travel, or geography, than the bird flu. How is an automated process to make sensible connections? Which cluster will contain photographs to match the content on del.icio.us?

Our claim in this paper is that tags on both services contain a latent structure which explains their cognitive associations to the various resources, and provides some semantics for the associations. Exposing this structure will clarify the ways in which various tags relate to one another across applications. The process for exposing the latent structure involves a number of steps of natural language processing, and the details are beyond the scope of this paper. (A forthcoming paper will detail this process). However, a brief summary is given here. First, tags are categorized according to a rough division according to the primary grammatical categories Noun, Proper Noun, Verb, Adjective/Adverb. This requires a number of heuristics to resolve ambiguities when they arise. Then the Nouns are further sub divided according to the categories outlined above. Currently this involves manual grammaticality decisions using the templates discussed earlier, but work is well underway toward automating the process. The outcome of the process is the division of the tags into a number of distinct grammatical/semantic categories which are shown with a human interpretable label in figure 3. For example the grammatical category of nouns which describe entities united by a common function are labeled as a category of "related things with common uses, roles". Similarly, taxonomic categories are labeled "What kind of thing is it?".

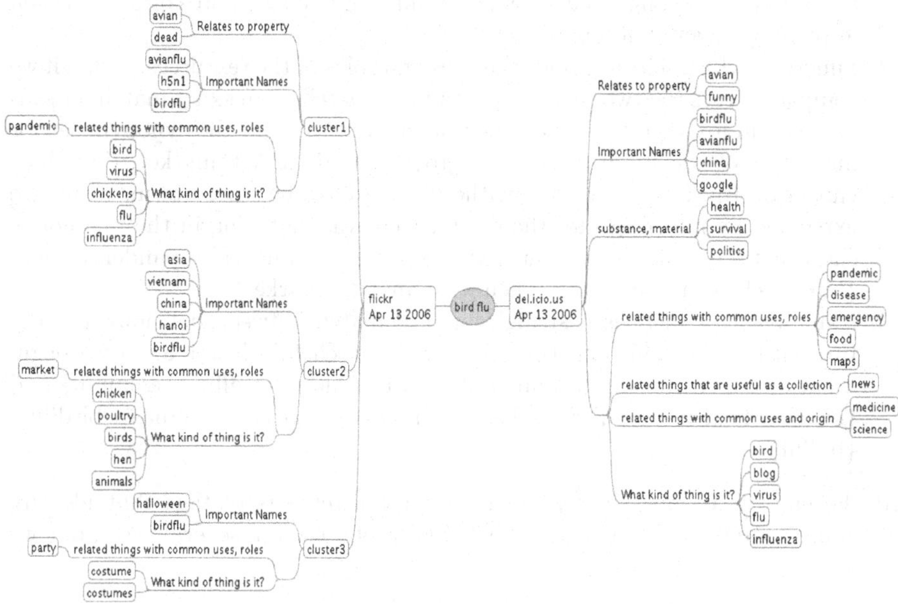

Fig. 3. Tags categorized by grammatical/semantic type

The grammatical/semantic categories tend to group the tags in sensible groups which makes their relationship to the resource, and each other, clear. For example the taxonomic tags on del.icio.us {bird, blog, virus, flu, influenza} refer to specific kinds of entities that are involved in the function/role connected events {pandemic, disease, emergency, food, maps}, and have come to be referenced with the common names {birdflu, avianflu, china, google}. The categories group tags in semantically distinguished relations to the resource. The inclusion of terms like "google" in the original tag set is odd, probably reflecting the perception that Google somehow plays an important part in our awareness of the disease. But our categories help with this, telling us that Google is not one of the things that the tag *bird flu* is about; it is about *birds*, *viruses*, and *diseases.*

Let us now compare tags across the two services by trying to match the tags in the available categories.

1. Taxonomic, which tells us specific kinds of things. Four out of five elements in the del.icio.us set match tags in cluster 1 of Flickr, only one matches cluster 2, and none match cluster 3. If we try to expand the matching process by supplementing each tag with synonyms and more/less general terms from a resource like WordNet, we discover that all of the tags in Flickr cluster 2, and *bird* in del.icio.us fall in the same hierarchy of terms. It is important to note that using WordNet in the comparison process is simplified because the linguistic categories reduce the number of terms that need to be compared. We can therefore specify more precise search phrases on both resources, based on the two matching groups of taxonomic terms, which will retrieve two sets of matching results. {virus + flu + influenza} and {bird + chicken + poultry + hen + animals}
2. Function, which tells us about the uses and roles of the resources. Again if we compare across the two services we find two matches: an exact match on *pandemic*, and a match that can easily be derived through the synonym set for market in WordNet: [grocery store, grocery, food market, market]. The third cluster on Flickr is once again without a match. The search terms again are expanded by inserting into the cluster that was matching in the taxonomic classifications. The sets become: {virus + flu + influenza + pandemic} and {bird + chicken + poultry + hen + animals + market}
3. Names. Again there is a straightforward match between delicious and the two clusters. In addition, there is now a match for cluster 3, so we begin a new set: {virus + flu + influenza + pandemic + birdflu + avianflu} and {bird + chicken + poultry + hen + animals + market + china + birdflu}, {bidflu}

At the end of the matching process we have three sets of tags that identify matching content on the two services. This can be used in several ways, but we

China closes all Beijing poultry markets (Business Week)
China Closes All Beijing Poultry Markets - Yahoo! News.

PandemicFlu.gov
CDC – Influenza (Flu) | Avian Flu
Avian Flu – What we need to know

Fig. 4. Flickr photographs and matching del.icio.us URLs for the search phrases [poultry market china bidflu] and [flu pandemic birdflu]

illustrate with simple search. Submitting all search terms as a conjunctive search yields no results because the phrase is overly specific. We therefore submitted only the most general term from each category of nouns, yielding a small number of resources in both services. Figure 4 illustrates a sample pairing of Flickr photographs and del.icio.us URLs.

The ontology helps inter operation in two ways. First, it reduces the number of nodes to be compared by introducing independent dimensions of comparison. While some correspondences between tags could be established without the linguistic categories, the search space would be much higher, as noted in point 1 above. But equally importantly the semantics of the groupings is uncovered. So, for example, if we have the need to manipulate the search terms as above, we have semantically distinct groupings that can be treated differently. We know for example that proper names do not have more general terms, so we can't exclude any of them. On the other hand we could exclude all taxonomic terms and only use functional ones, to get all markets in China, not just poultry ones.

5 Conclusion

We have argued that folksonomies which reportedly have no structure or constraint on their properties in fact do have rich structure, determined by the properties of our mental faculties. We have shown a method that can expose significant aspects of that structure, together with a semantics that can be used to construct an ontology from the folksonomy basis. This ontology, we argue, is a simple conceptual domain model built through an unconsciously mediated collaboration. Finally, we showed a way in which the ontologies can facilitate interoperability between application dependent tag sets.

The work described in this paper has lofty goals, but is described in the spirit of the emerging Web2.0. That is, the content that is needed for the complex operations is collected as a default behavior of system use. Value can be added to existing applications without first solving all the complex problems. Enhancing manual operation of tag based services is only first goal. Once the data is available, it can be used to research more complex problems addressing automation and, eventually, bootstrapped into enabling interoperability in the most complex Semantic Web applications.

Acknowledgments. This work was sponsored by the Norwegian Research Council, WISEMOD project, 160126V30 in the IKT-2010 program.

References

1. Levy, S. and Stone, B. The New Wisdom of the Web. *Newsweek,* April 3, 2006. http://www.msnbc.msn.com/id/12015774/site/newsweek/
2. Boutin, P. Web 2.0 The new Internet "boom" doesn't live up to its name. Slate. Posted Wednesday, March 29, 2006, http://www.slate.com/id/2138951/
3. Udell, Jon. Collaborative knowledge gardening. InfoWorld. August 20, (2004). http://www.infoworld.com/article/04/08/20/34OPstrategic_1.html

4. Vanderwall, T. Explaining and Showing Broad and Narrow Folksonomies, http://www.vanderwal.net/random/entrysel.php?blog=1635, February 21, (2005)
5. Shen, K. and Wu, L. Folksonomy as a Complex Network. Computer Science, abstract cs.IR/0509072. http://arxiv.org/abs/cs.IR/0509072, (2005)
6. Speroni, P. On Tag Clouds, Metric, Tag Sets and Power Laws http://blog.pietrosperoni.it/2005/05/25/tag-clouds-metric/ (2005)
7. Golder, S., and Huberman, B. A. The Structure of Collaborative Tagging Systems, http://www.citebase.org/cgi-bin/citations?id=oai:arXiv.org:cs/0508082 (2005)
8. Grigory Begelman, G. Keller, P. and Smadja, F. Automated Tag Clustering: Improving search and exploration in the tag space. Collaborative Web Tagging Workshop, 15 th International World Wide Web Conference, Edinburgh, Scotland, 2006.
9. Veres, C. Emerging Patterns. http://csabaveres.net/blog8/?p=7 February, 7, (2006)
10. Jackendoff, R. Semantics and Cognition Cambridge, Mass. MIT Press (1983)
11. Shirky, C. Matt Locke on folksonomies. March 01, 2005. http://many.corante.com/archives/2005/03/01/matt_locke_on_folksonomies.php
12. Hearst, M. Clustering versus Faceted Categories for Information Exploration, Communications of the ACM, 49 (4), April 2006
13. Veres, C. The Language of Folksonomies: What tags reveal about user classification. In Natural Language Processing and Information Systems. Proceedings of the 11th International Conference on Applications of Natural Language to Information Systems May 31 - June 2, Klagenfurt, Austria. Springer, LNCS 3999. (2006)
14. Barsalou, Lawrence W. Deriving categories to achieve goals. in Bower, G. (Ed.) The Psychology of Learning and Motivation: Advances in Research and Theory, Academic Press, 1991.
15. Wierzbicka, A Apples are not a 'kind of fruit': the semantics of human categorization. American Ethnologist 313–328 (1984)
16. Gruber, T. Ontology of Folksonomy: A Mash-up of Apples and Oranges. http://tomgruber.org/writing/ontology-of-folksonomy.htm#_edn4, Jan 19, (2006)

Method Chunks for Interoperability*

Jolita Ralyté[1], Per Backlund[2], Harald Kühn[3], and Manfred A. Jeusfeld[4]

[1] CUI, University of Geneva, Rue de Général Dufour, 24, CH-1211 Genève 4, Switzerland
Jolita.Ralyte@cui.unige.ch
[2] University of Skövde, P.O. Box 408, SE 541 28 Skövde, Sweden
Per.Backlund@his.se
[3] BOC Information Systems GmbH, Rabensteig 2, A-1010 Vienna, Austria
Harald.Kuehn@boc-eu.com
[4] Tilburg University, CRISM/Infolab, 5000 LE Tilburg, The Netherlands
Manfred.Jeusfeld@uvt.nl

Abstract. Interoperability is a key property of enterprise applications, which is hard to achieve due to the large number of interoperating components and semantic heterogeneity. Platform-based approaches such as service-oriented architectures address the technical integration of systems. However, a deep integration needs to cover the whole lifecycle of the interoperable system. We propose method engineering as a means for encoding situated knowledge about achieving interoperability in the form of method chunks. We analysed the field of interoperability for enterprise applications and propose that a tool modelling the business- and ICT-related choices in the form of method chunks is needed for a knowledge-based solution of interoperability problems. An industrial case is included to back our claims.

1 Introduction

The competitiveness and efficiency of an enterprise largely depends on its ability to interact with other enterprises and organisations. Not only large organisations set up cooperation agreements with other enterprises, also small and medium sized enterprises are combining their forces to compete jointly in the market. This evolution makes interoperability between enterprises and software systems an increasingly important issue. Interoperability is one of the key challenges for modern enterprises.

The problem of interoperability is as old as the existence of software systems. A first idea was to make enterprise applications interoperable via central databases. This approach failed in practice because not enough semantics could be covered in the database schema to understand the semantics of data. As a consequence, non-interoperable applications were created based on decentralised data management. The next attempt was to save the original vision of data independence by so-called federated databases. For the same reason as for the central databases, this approach has not passed the test in practice: it is almost impossible to create a global

* This research has been carried out within the INTEROP Network of Excellence (Contract N° IST-508011) and supported by the Swiss National Science Foundation (N° 200021-103826).

D.W. Embley, A. Olivé, and S. Ram (Eds.): ER 2006, LNCS 4215, pp. 339 – 353, 2006.

understanding of data without referring to application semantics, let alone business semantics.

Another school of interoperability has been concerned with standardising system interfaces in a way that one system can call the other system. This has led to platforms such as RPC, CORBA, J2EE and .NET, to name a few. Here, the problem of interoperability is only addressed at the technical level and fundamentally relies on information hiding. It may be perfectly feasible to call a remote service with the parameter values that are completely non-sensical.

We claim that we need a domain-dependent approach to interoperability. Rather than focusing on technical interoperability alone (which is mainly solved by industry standardisation), we propose to encode successful solutions to interoperability problems as suggested in Situational Method Engineering [13]. Some solutions deal with technical interoperability problems; others are about aligning business processes. Situational Method Engineering promotes project-specific method construction by selecting and assembling method fragments [3] or chunks [16, 20] stored in a method repository [3, 6, 16, 19] hence addressing the method requirements of the specific project. The repository then becomes the common knowledge base which can aid in interoperability solution projects. Hence, our approach can contribute in the early stages of such projects by setting up a project specific method. In this sense we envisage method engineering as a knowledge management application for projects within the interoperability domain. Instead of providing one universal method for interoperability problems solution we propose to define a knowledge base of reusable method chunks each of them addressing one or more specific interoperability problems. The latter are grouped in an extensible hierarchy of interoperability problem classes.

The remainder of this paper is organised as follows. In section 2 we characterise the field of interoperability between enterprises and systems. Section 3 presents an industrial case and identifies some associated interoperability problems. In section 4 we discuss how situational method engineering and the notion of reusable method chunks can be adopted to structure specific solutions to interoperability problems. The paper ends with a review of this work, and outlines future research.

2 Characterising the Interoperability Domain

Interoperability may be seen as "the ability for a system or a product to work with other systems or products without special effort of the part of the customer" [10]. Interoperable systems have been the goal for quite some time. However, there are some obstacles in terms of technology, organisational problems and powerful technology vendors [15, 7]. The basic infrastructure seems to be in place [15] but we have not yet achieved sufficient interoperability. The problem is well known and recurring in many domains, some examples are: database schema integration [18], interoperability between modelling techniques [5], interoperability in metamodelling platforms [14], interoperability of ERP with other systems [1], and CNC manufacturing [23].

Interoperability is not only a problem concerning software and technologies. It is also a problem that concerns knowledge and business references that must be shared in order to achieve interoperability [4]. Hence, interoperability is described in terms of a three-layered model consisting of a business layer, a knowledge layer and an ICT systems layer. In order to achieve meaningful interoperation between enterprises, interoperability must be achieved on all layers of an enterprise. This includes the business environment and business processes on the business layer, the organisational roles, skills and competencies of employees and knowledge assets on the knowledge layer, and applications, data and communication components on the ICT layer. In addition, semantic descriptions can be used to get the necessary mutual understanding between enterprises that want to collaborate.

Similarly, Mak and Ramprasad [15] point out that organisations must be able to contact each other using agreed protocols, share a common language, agree on goals and tasks, and have people assigned to complete these tasks in order to achieve interoperability. Moreover, we may not assume that interoperability concerns only the interoperability between enterprises.

We also draw on the experience of systems integration [8, 7] to further characterise the concept of interoperability. Wainwright and Waring [24] show that the term integration is open for interpretation, as is indeed the term interoperability. There are four domains of integration: technical, systems, strategic, and organisational. The technical domain corresponds to the ICT layer, which is further, refined into application, data and communication interoperability [22]. Johannesson and Perjons [12] propose three types of architectures for application integration: point-to-point, message brokers, and process brokers. We complement these views by making a distinction between development and execution with respect to the ICT layer. The development aspect concerns all parts of the systems development life cycle whereas the execution aspect focuses on runtime issues.

The business and knowledge layers are further refined in the systems, organisation and strategic domains [24]. The systems domain encompasses approaches to understand the technical, strategic and organisational behaviours from a holistic perspective. That is, organisations are complex and any effort has to handle all aspects in order to achieve interoperability between systems. Interoperability is a strategic issue; hence interoperability has to incorporate strategic planning for the entire system. Finally, the organisational domain encompasses issues such as work practices, power and knowledge sharing which are all affected if enterprises are to be interoperable. Interoperability between two organisations is a multifaceted problem since it concerns both technical and organisational issues, which are intertwined and complex to deal with. We summarise our view of interoperability in Fig. 1.

There are already various technologies to realise interoperability; some examples are TCP/IP, XML, SOAP and BPEL. However, true interoperability is not yet here since enterprises running different applications built with different designs and architectures still have difficulties talking to each other [15]. Whereas achieving interoperability also has to do with cooperative work between people from different organisations. Furthermore, we also note that interoperability in the organisational and strategic domains also remain to be achieved in many cases.

Divergence and interoperability is a well-known problem in the open source software (OSS) community. A study by van Wendel de Joode and Tineke [25] reveals a set of strategies for dealing with interoperability issues within OSS projects. In general, two types of strategies are used: committee standardisation and market coordination. We also observe that coding style guidelines and respected gatekeepers, i.e. a knowledgeable and trusted person, are two important means for coordination [25].

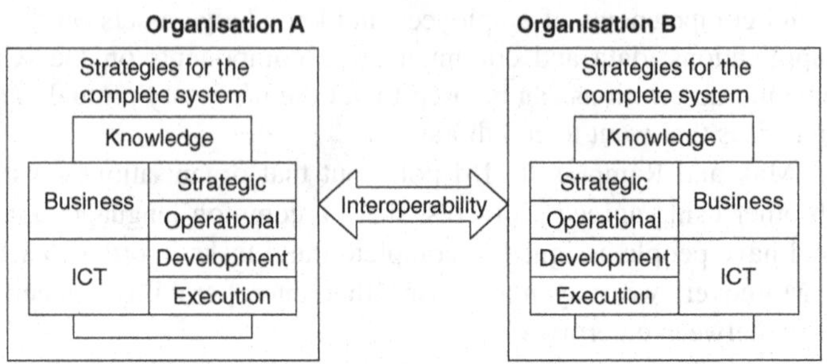

Fig. 1. Interoperability between two organisations entails interoperability in all domains

Interoperability is to be facilitated by combining knowledge concerning architectures and enabling technologies (to provide implementation frameworks), enterprise modelling (to define interoperability requirements) and ontology (to identify interoperability semantics of enterprises). The three knowledge domains identified by NoE INTEROP [10] have been further analysed to identify relevant interoperability problems [17]. From the perspective of our work we note that data integration and business process integration were identified as recurring problems. Hence, we find this issues relevant and worth pursuing from the interoperability perspective.

3 Interoperability in the Insurance Domain: A Case

In this section we analyse an industrial case of interoperability in the insurance domain and identify interoperability problems related to this case. We classify them following our characterisation framework presented in Fig. 1.

3.1 Business Model

Insurance companies develop business models based on Internet technology either to reduce administration costs or to establish new sales channels. They have to establish a well-defined strategic position in the network of their competitors - especially when they join together to establish a common Internet platform for their sales partners, e.g. agents and brokers, to share platform development and operation costs.

The following industry case describes a *B2B sales platform for insurance partners based on Internet technology* ("insurance portal"). The main objective of the insurance portal is to support independent insurance agents with a single point of access to products and services of different insurance companies. An agent is working for several competing insurance companies on a commission basis. Some advantages for the agents are a single point of access to reduce cycle times for business processes such as offer management, contract management, and portfolio management, less administration costs, and improved service quality because of a broad product and information portfolio. Some advantages for the insurance companies are reduced maintenance and operation costs for their partner systems due to cost sharing and an enlarged sales force because of potentially new agents.

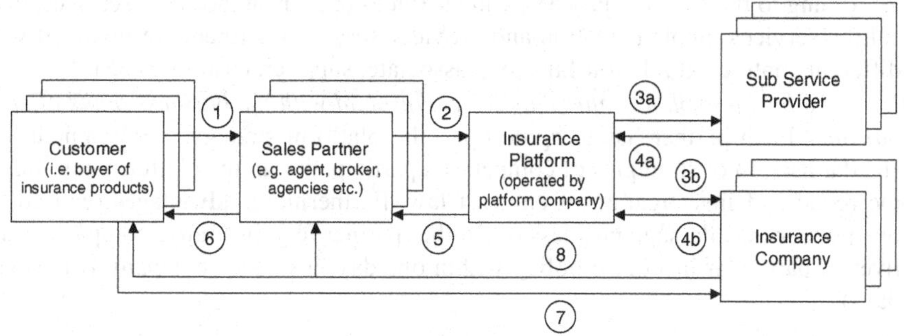

Fig. 2. Business Model from Insurance Domain based on Common Platform

Fig. 2 describes the business model of this industry case, i.e. how the different business participants interact with each other to create business value. *Customers* interact with their *sales responsibles* e.g. agents, brokers, agencies etc. (step 1). A sales responsible uses the insurance portal to execute his business processes such as offer management, order management, policy management etc. For example, a broker may request certain product offers (step 2) which are calculated and returned to him (step 5), and then sent to a customer (step 6). The insurance portal, or more precisely the company operating the platform, interacts with different *sub providers* such as application hosting companies, security companies, customer information suppliers etc. to fulfil its tasks (steps 3a and 4a). Additionally, the company operating the platform interacts with the *insurance companies* to exchange product data, customer data etc. (steps 3b and 4b). Finally, the customer signs a contract with the insurance company, which provided the best offer, and pays the insurance fee to the insurance company (step 7). The insurance company delivers the appropriate contracts, pays the commission fees, and fulfils its part of the insurance contract (step 8).

All interactions within this business model raise issues concerning interoperability. To structure these issues we use three of the interoperability domains proposed in chapter 2, namely the strategic business domain, the operational business domain, and the ICT domain including development and execution aspects.

3.2 Interoperability Issues in the Strategic Business Domain

In the *strategic business domain*, the business strategy of each participating partner has to be defined in the context of the insurance portal and interoperability questions such as the following have to be answered:

- *Which are the processes and services (products) to be realised on the platform?* Processes, services (products) and their interdependencies have to be identified. Intra-organisational business processes (e.g. user management on the platform) and inter-organisational business processes (e.g. application and claims processes) can be distinguished.
- *Which are the appropriate business partners to develop and run the platform?* According to the required processes and services (e.g. insurance core services, consulting services, implementation and provider services) partners are involved with different contractual relationships (e.g. associate, supplier, customer etc.).
- *Does the business plan of the platform correspond with the business plans of each partner?* Each partner has to agree upon the platform strategy. For example, the standardisation of strategies of competitors participating in the platform may imply the request of investigation of antitrust law. Furthermore, advantages realised by one partner may damage business of another partner (e.g. insurance company A delivers a particular insurance policy within one day, insurance company B in seven days).

3.3 Interoperability Issues in the Operational Business Domain

In the operational *business domain* the various types of processes have to be determined. The business processes have to be modelled in detail with a special focus on the products and interfaces between the business actors involved. The roles of each business actor also have to be modelled. Business processes can be divided into the following types:

- insurance *core service processes*, e.g. application processes and claims management,
- *value adding processes*, e.g. cash management processes and event management,
- *development processes*, e.g. business and software development based on the core elements: products, processes, organisational units and information technology,
- *business operations processes*, e.g. process integration of business partners and
- *additional services*, e.g. legal advisor services, training and learning.

The following list shows some areas of interoperability problems and opportunities in the business domain:

- *Product Management:* In every realisation state a set of products is integrated into the platform, which entails new requirements for the business processes. Implications for the software development and integration efforts of the insurance partners should be evaluated as early as possible.
- *Process integration of business partners:* Each actor participating in the platform realisation can be certified with respect to its business processes. Some criteria are complexity of interfaces (business operations as well as data flow), process benchmarks, availability and integrity.
- *Training and Learning:* Business processes can be documented online for learning the sequence of operations of core processes as well as administrative processes.

- *Pricing Model:* Agents pay for using the insurance portal. If insurance companies want to consolidate their customer database, the platform company can reduce the cost of the business process "Customer Data Modification" to encourage the agents to reach insurance partners objectives.
- *Test Management:* In combination with the product model, a set of test cases can be developed as a specification for testing the platform application and interoperability.

3.4 Interoperability Issues in the ICT Domain

The *ICT domain* is divided into *development issues and execution issues.* The insurance portal consists of a core service application, dynamic HTML-based user interface, complex application modules etc. During platform *development* typical interoperability problems are:

- How can the different viewpoints of requirement definition be integrated e.g. how can the metamodels of the specification models be integrated?
- Which implementation technologies and target platforms will be used and how will they be integrated?
- What are the different modules of the implementation environment and how can they be integrated?
- Which runtime libraries can be used and how can they be bound to the development environment?

The *execution* domain is influenced by short release cycles - especially driven by short term content such as news and events and by a high fluctuation of platform users. Business operation processes such as content management processes, user management, and first and second level support, are documented by exporting all required information in a process-based online operating instructions manual. Some interoperability problems in the execution domain are:

- Data conversions: Customer data, contract data, product data etc.
- Component integration: How can different components of functionality be operated within a single business service (even if they are realised with different technologies)?
- How can long lasting transactions be synchronised and consistently integrated?

3.5 Summary of the Case

The above case study is based on a real industrial project. It shows that an ICT project integrating several organisations is typically characterised by a multitude of interoperability problems, in our case totalling to about 20. It also shows that a purely ICT-based answer to the interoperability problem is not only insufficient but also misses the: first one has to solve the business-related interoperability problems before one can tackle the ICT-related issues. A consistent method that will solve all possible interoperability problems does not exist because the business and ICT domains are too diverse. Instead of a single method, an extensible and domain-specific knowledge base of method chunks shall support the development of interoperable systems.

4 Situational Method Engineering to Support Interoperability

We use the term method to denote a regular and systematic way of accomplishing a result. Methods cover a wide spectrum of industrial capabilities and services incorporated in either pragmatic or scientific working methods. Moreover, we claim that a method may be decomposed into a set of method chunks [20]. In the realm of methods there is a lack of a cohesive body of knowledge concerning interoperability issues as characterised in section 2, i.e. traditional methods have not managed to solve the interoperability problem. We argue that this is the case due to the inherent complexity and multi-facetedness of the area. In this sense, we propose method engineering as a knowledge management application. Systems development has been characterised as knowledge work [11, 9]. In this context, we view the development method as a body of knowledge. In order to make it an active body of knowledge it has to be made available for use, update and refinement, something which may be achieved by constructing a dynamic method chunk repository [2, 16, 19].

In the following we will demonstrate how Situational Method Engineering can help in solving parts of the problem of managing interoperability knowledge. More precisely, we consider specific method chunks dealing with interoperability problem solutions such as guidelines and models for data exchange, data integration, information logistics mapping, model transformation and comparison.

4.1 Method Chunk

We propose to use the notion of reusable method chunk [16, 20] to represent methodological knowledge related to interoperability. A method chunk is an autonomous, cohesive and coherent part of a method providing guidelines and related concepts to support the realisation of some specific system engineering activity. A method is viewed as a collection of loosely coupled method chunks expressed at different levels of granularity. Such a modular view of methods favours their adaptation and extension and permits to reuse chunks of a given method in the construction of new ones.

As illustrated in Fig. 3, from the engineering perspective the body of a method chunk includes two types of knowledge: the process model, also called guideline, supporting the engineer in method chunk application, and the product model defining concepts, relationships between concepts, and constraints used by the corresponding process. The structure of a guideline can be found in [16, 20]. It can be more or less rich and represented as an informal description or expressed by using different process modelling formalisms. Application *examples* can be provided in order to help the method engineer to apply the method chunk.

The context in which a method chunk is relevant is defined in its interface. It is formalised by a couple <*situation, intention*>, which characterises the situation in which the method chunk can be applied in terms of required input product(s) and the intention, i.e. the goal, that the chunk helps to achieve.

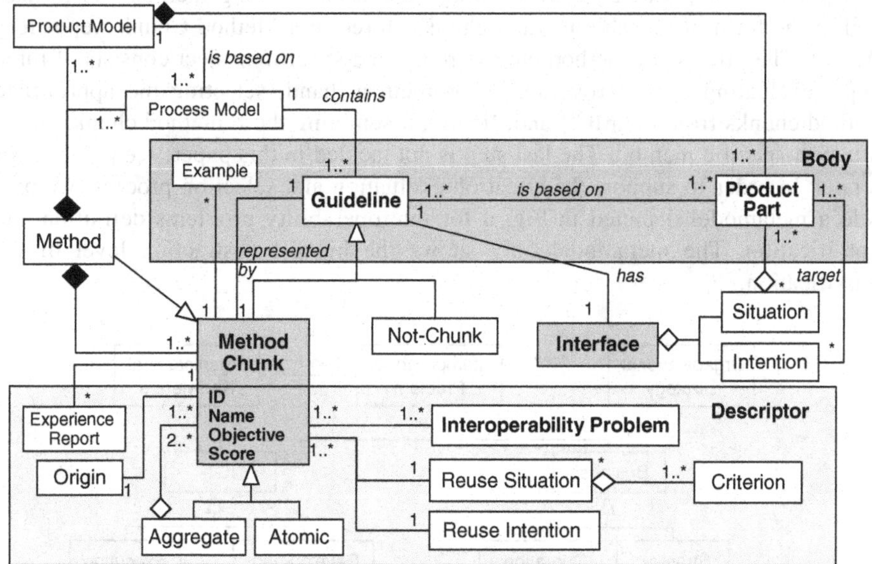

Fig. 3. Metamodel of method chunk

A set of characteristics, called a method chunk *descriptor*, is associated to each chunk in order to better situate the context in which it can be reused. The *reuse intention* expresses the generic objective that the method chunk helps to satisfy in the corresponding engineering activity. The *reuse situation* captures a set of criteria characterising the context in which the method chunk is suitable. A detailed classification of these criteria, named *Reuse Frame*, can be found in [16]. Some examples of such criteria are: system engineering activity (e.g. business modelling, requirements specification and design) in which the method chunk is relevant and characteristics of the application domain (e.g. application type, impact of legacy system and application technology). While the reuse situation and reuse intention are expressed by using keywords defined in the MCR glossary and the reuse frame, the *objective* of the method chunk provides a narrative explanation of its role.

Due to the fact that in this work we consider specific method chunks dealing with interoperability problems solution, we explicitly relate each method chunk to the corresponding *interoperability problem* identified in the interoperability classification framework illustrated in Fig. 1.

The descriptor also contains the information necessary for method chunk identification and selection such as *name, ID*, information about its structure (i.e. atomic or aggregate) and *origin* (i.e. the existing method or best practice provider). It can also include *experience reports* in order to help the method engineer to evaluate the appropriateness of the method chunk to a given situation.

4.2 Method Chunk Repository for Interoperability

In our approach, the knowledge about interoperability, based on experience and best practices or extracted from existing system engineering methods, is formalised in the form of reusable method chunks stored in a Method Chunk Repository (MCR). The process of method chunks reuse in a specific project consists of three steps: evaluating the interoperability problem at hand, selecting the appropriate method chunks from the MCR and, finally, assembling these method chunks into a situation-specific method. The last step is not tackled in this paper, see [16, 21] for details. In order to support the situation evaluation and selection process, we provide a metamodel depicted in Fig. 4 for interoperability problems definition and classification. The metamodel only shows the highest abstraction level of the classification.

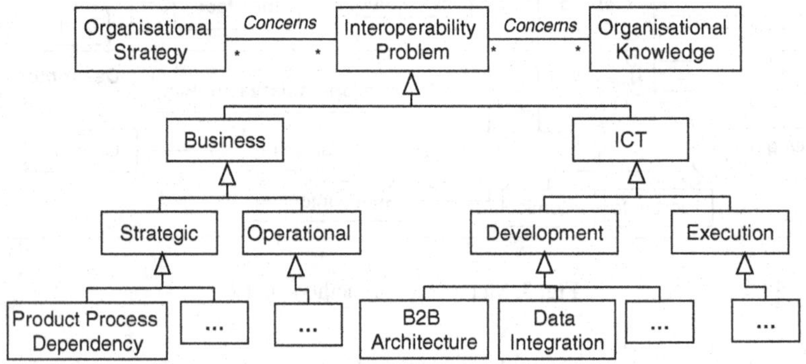

Fig. 4. Metamodel for interoperability problems classification

The interoperability problem identified is matched with those supported by method chunks stored in the MCR. Let us suppose the question: "How can we integrate the product data of several insurance companies?" We can identify that the interoperability problem that we are facing is classified as "ICT.Development.Data_Integration". The next step would be to ask the MCR to retrieve all method chunks associated to this interoperability problem.

4.3 Identifying Method Chunks for Interoperability: An Insurance Case

Based on the practical experiences in the insurance case we have identified several method chunks dealing with interoperability problems. Due to the lack of space, we present only two of them. Among the interoperability problems identified in section 3, we have selected one from the strategic and operational business domain and one from the ICT domain, which will be addressed to show how method chunks can be utilised to represent this knowledge.

Method Chunk: Product Process Dependency

Different enterprises form a supply chain and they have to align their products and their business processes. It must be defined which products and product definitions are interrelated with which processes and process interfaces. The method chunk below proposes a solution for this kind of interoperability problem.

<table>
<tr><td>Chunk ID: MC01</td><td>Name: Product Process Dependency</td></tr>
<tr><td colspan="2">Objective: Identify dependencies between products and their corresponding business processes as basis for business alignment.</td></tr>
<tr><td>Type: Aggregate</td><td>Origin: BOC Information Systems</td></tr>
<tr><td colspan="2">Interoperability problem: Business.Strategic_and_Operational.Business Alignment</td></tr>
<tr><td colspan="2">Reuse situation:
Application domain.Application type.Inter-organisation application
Application domain.Impact of legacy system.Functional domain reuse
System engineering activity.Business modelling.Business process alignment
Innovation level.Business innovation
Reuse intention: To align product definitions and business process definitions.</td></tr>
<tr><td colspan="2">Interface:
Situation: Products and business processes of partner enterprises.
Intention: To define integrated product and process modelling language.
Body:
Product Part: Integrated definition of products and business processes.
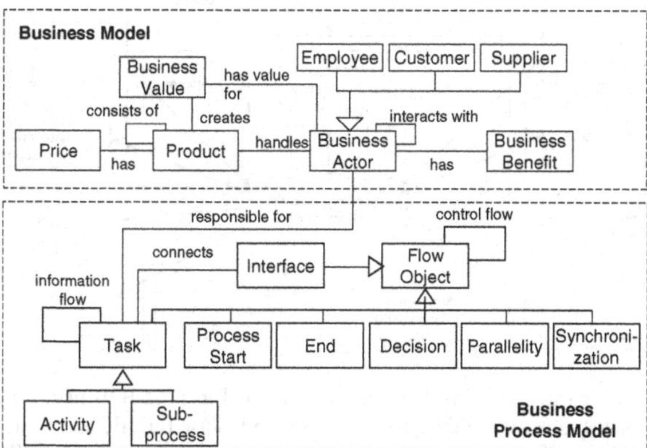

Guideline: Define the product structure in accordance with the business metamodel. Define the business process structure. Assign the responsible business actors to the activities and sub-processes of the business process. Define the interfaces which are necessary to connect the activities and sub-processes. By assigning the product responsibilities between products and business actors, the dependencies between products and business processes are defined transitively.</td></tr>
<tr><td colspan="2">Application Example:
An application example of this method chunk is the definition of insurance products and their interdependency to business processes executed in the insurance portal. A life insurance product consists of sub-products such as risk insurance and font investment. A life insurance process consists of sub-processes such as insurance application, risk check, contracting and payment. Employees of insurance companies are responsible for executing the sub-processes. These employees are also handling several insurance products. Via this, the product process dependency is defined.</td></tr>
</table>

ICT Method Chunk: B2B Architecture

Different companies want to establish a common Internet-based platform implementing parts of their e-business processes. The existing company strategies, business processes and information systems have to be interoperable with this new platform.

Chunk ID: MC02	**Name:** B2B Architecture
Objective: To provide a general architecture for a collaborative Internet-based partner platform.	
Type: Atomic	**Origin:** BOC Information Systems
Interoperability problem: ICT. Development. B2B Architecture Design	
Reuse situation: Application domain.Application type.Inter-organisation application Application domain.Impact of legacy system.Functional domain reuse System engineering activity.Design Innovation level.Technology innovation; Business innovation **Reuse intention:** To establish a common Internet-based platform.	
Interface: **Situation:** The strategies, business processes and information systems of the involved companies. **Intention:** To define building blocks for a B2B system.	
Body: **Product Part:** General software architecture of a B2B platform. The arrows depict the different places of interoperability. 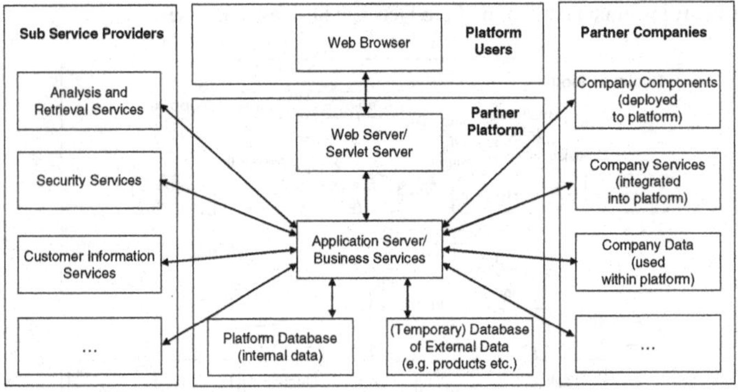 **Guideline:** Identify participants involved in operating and using a B2B platform. For each participant assign which of the generic building blocks are provided/used. Build an instance of each generic building block for the specific case. Describe the interrelationships within the B2B platform for each building block instance.	
Application Example: An insurance portal. The identification and assignment is as follows: *Platform users (sales agents, brokers etc.):* the sales partners access the portal via Internet and web browser technology. *Insurance partner platform:* The access of the business functionality and the generation of the user interface are via web server / servlet server. The business functionality runs on an application server. The application server stores platform internal data in the platform database. External (and temporary) data are stored in the database for external data. Via business services of the application server sub service providers and insurance companies interoperate with the insurance partner platform. *Insurance companies:* The insurance companies provide components (e.g. product calculators, risk check modules etc.), services (e.g. printing, mailing etc.), data (e.g. customer data, contract data, product data etc.), which have to interoperate with the insurance partner platform. *Sub service providers:* The sub service providers provide services such as analysis and retrieval services (e.g. data analysis, management reports, statistical evaluations etc.), security services (e.g. trust centres certificate management etc.), customer information services (e.g. credit agency services, market evaluation etc.), which have to interoperate with the insurance partner platform.	

The above two method chunks have to be seen as examples. A realistic method chunk repository shall contain hundreds of chunks of varying complexity. While the reusable chunks are formulated on generic type level, a specific case like the insurance case is formulated at a lower abstraction level, the instance level. By making the instance level explicit, the method chunk repository is extended to an experience based knowledge base (Fig. 5).

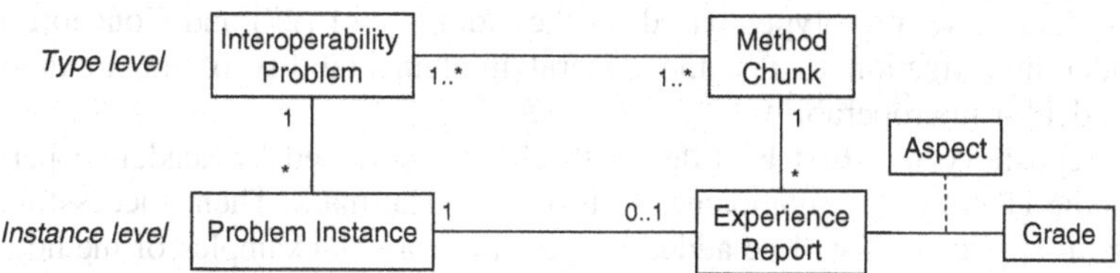

Fig. 5. Instance level in the method chunk repository

The interoperability problems from the case are formulated as a set of problem instances, which are classified into the hierarchy of interoperability problems (see also Fig. 4). When a case has been completed by executing suitable method chunks, an experience report is added to the repository that includes a critical review of the merit of the selected method chunk to solve the problem instance(s). By storing this information, subsequent cases can exploit the experience from earlier cases and select those chunks that earned high grades in the earlier cases.

5 Conclusions

Interoperability is an issue that arises when multiple organisations need to cooperate via information systems. We proposed a knowledge-based approach where solutions to common interoperability problems are encoded as method chunks. These method chunks together with experience reports and an extensible taxonomy of interoperability problems form the basis of a method chunk repository, which we are currently developing in the NoE INTEROP [10]. We see the following contributions of this paper:

- The new method chunk metamodel allows to link best practices for achieving interoperability to specific interoperability problems. It covers best practices from the business domain (e.g. aligning the business processes of enterprises) as well as from the ICT domain (e.g. integrating heterogeneous product catalogues).
- The proposed solution provides a possibility to go from generic knowledge of interoperability, via experiences of applying that knowledge, to a specific body of interoperability knowledge.
- The usefulness of the new method chunk data structure has been demonstrated by applying them to a real-world interoperability case.

A prototype for the method chunk repository is under development using the METIS tool [26] in cooperation with the METIS developers. The metamodel of Fig. 3 has been mapped to METIS meta classes. The two cases sketched in this paper have also been represented. It turned out the METIS knowledge base already had many of the business process modeling features used in the first method chunk example. For METIS, methods chunks are regarded as a substantial extension to the tool's capabilities since they are encoding procedural knowledge. The tight integration to the enterprise modelling views in METIS shall make it possible to automate parts of the method chunk execution, in particular model transformation. For non-automated parts, the system can provide assistance through the guidelines encoded in the method chunks. Additional prototypes based on the Adonis tool [27] and ConceptBase [28] are under investigation to test the general implementability of the method chunk metamodel for interoperability.

The repository will first be filled with chunks extracted by academic partners as well as the IT consulting companies to form a critical mass. Then, successful and unsuccessful applications will be added to the repository as examples of method chunks application. These examples form the experience layer of the repository. The larger the number of successful examples for a method chunk, the higher its score will be.

Future work is concerned with formalising the textual guidelines of a method chunk into a computer-interpretable process model, which allows teams from multiple collaborating enterprises to jointly execute method chunks. A related aspect is to represent the product side of method chunks, i.e. business as well as ICT models, within the repository to allow not only collaborative method chunk execution but also model sharing.

References

1. Botta-Genoulaz V., Millet P.-A. and Grabot B. (2005) A survey on the recent research literature on ERP systems. *Computers in Industry (56),* pp. 510-522.
2. Brinkkemper S. (2000) Method Engineering with Web-enabled Methods. *Information Systems Engineering: State of the Art and Research Themes.* Eds. S. Brinkkemper, E. Lindencrona, A. Sölvberg, Springer-Verlag, pp. 124-133.
3. Brinkkemper S., Saeki, M. and Harmsen, F. (1998). Assembly Techniques for Method Engineering. *10th Conference on Advanced Information Systems Engineering, CAiSE'98.* Springer, LNCS 1413, pp.381-400.
4. Chen D. and Doumeingts G. (2003) European initiatives to develop interoperability of enterprise applications — basic concepts, framework and roadmap. *Annual Reviews in Control* (27) pp. 153–162.
5. Domínguez E. and Zapata M.A. (2000) Mappings and Interoperability: A Meta-modelling Approach. *ADVIS 2000,* Ed. T. Yakhno. LNCS 1909, Springer-Verlag, pp. 352-362.
6. Firesmith D. and Henderson-Sellers B. (2001) *The OPEN Process Framework. An Introduction.* Addison-Wesley.
7. Garlan D., Allen R. and Ockerbloom J. (1995). Architectural mismatch or why it's hard to build systems out of existing parts, *Proceedings of the 17th international conference on Software engineering*, ACM Press, pp. 179-185.
8. Hasselbring W. (2000). Information system integration. *Communications of the ACM* 43 (6) pp. 32-38.
9. Hirschheim R. and Klein H. (2003) Crisis in the IS Field? A Critical Reflection on the State of the Discipline. *Journal of the Association for Information Systems,* 4, pp. 237-293.

10. INTEROP (2005) Interop Network of Excellence IST – 508011 Presentation of the Project. http://interop-noe.org/INTEROP/presentation Last accessed 2005-11-02
11. Iivari J. (2000) Information Systems Development as Knowledge Work: The body of systems development process knowledge. *In Information Modelling and Knowledge Bases XI* (Eds, Kawaguchi, E., Hamid, I. A., Jaakkola, H. and Kangassalo, H.) IOS Press, pp. 41-56.
12. Johannesson P. and Perjons E. (2000) Design principles for application integration. *Proceedings of the 12th International Conference of Advanced Information Systems Engineering, CAiSE 2000,* LNCS 1789. Eds. B. Wangler & L. Bergman. Springer.
13. Kumar, K. and Welke, R.J. (1992). Method Engineering, A Proposal for Situation-specific Methodology Construction. In *Systems Analysis and Design: A Research Agenda,* Cotterman and Senn (eds), Wiley, pp.257-268.
14. Kühn H. and Murzek, M. (2005) Interoperability in Metamodelling Platforms. In: Konstantas, D.; Bourrières, J.-P.; Léonard, M.; Boudjlida, N. (Eds.): *Interoperability of Enterprise Software and Applications.* Springer-Verlag, pp. 215-226.
15. Mak K-T. and Ramaprasad A. (2001) An Interpretation of the Changing IS/IT-Standard Game, Circa 2001. *Knowledge, Technology & Policy* (14) pp. 20-30.
16. Mirbel I. and Ralyté J. (2006) Situational Method Engineering: Combining Assembly-Based and Roadmap-Driven Approaches, *Requirements Engineering,* 11(1), pp. 58–78.
17. Ottoson A. (2005) *An Analysis of a Content of a Method Chunk Repository concerning Interoperability Problems.* Master Thesis HS-EA-DVA-2005-001, University of Skövde.
18. Rahm E. and Bernstein P. A. (2001) A survey of approaches to automatic schema matching. *The VLDB Journal,* 10, pp. 334-350.
19. Ralyté J. (1999) Reusing Scenario Based Approaches in Requirement Engineering Methods: CREWS Method Base. *10th Int. Workshop on Database and Expert Systems Applications (DEXA'99),* IEEE Computer Society, p. 305-309.
20. Ralyté J. and Rolland C. (2001). An Approach for Method Reengineering. *Proceedings of the 20th International Conference on Conceptual Modeling (ER2001),* LNCS 2224, Springer-Verlag, pp.471-484.
21. Ralyté J. and Rolland C. (2001). An Assembly Process Model for Method Engineering. *Proceedings of the 13th Conference on Advanced Information Systems Engineering (CAISE'01),* LNCS 2068, Springer-Verlag, pp. 267-283.
22. Schulz K., et al. (2003) *A Gap Analysis; Required Activities in Research, Technology and Standardisation to close the RTS Gap; Roadmaps and Recommendations on RTS activities.* Deliverables D 3.4, D 3.5, D 3.6. IDEAS Thematic Network - No.: IST-2001-37368.
23. Xu X.W. and Newman S.T. (2006) Making CNC machine tools more open, interoperable and intelligent—a review of the technologies. *Computers in Industry.* 57 (2), pp.141-152.
24. Wainwright D. and Waring T. (2004) Three domains for implementing integrated information systems: redressing the balance between technology, strategic and organisational analysis. *International Journal of Information Management,* 24 (2004) pp. 329–346.
25. van Wendel de Joode R. and Tineke E.M. (2004) Handling variety: the tension between adaptability and interoperability of open source software. *Computer Standards and Interfaces* (28), pp. 109-121.
26. Troux Technologies (2006) http://www.troux.com/products/metis/, Metis by Troux. Online. March 30, 2006.
27. BOC Information Technologies Consulting (2006) http://www.boc-eu.com/, Adonis by BOC Online. March 30, 2006.
28. ConceptBase Team (2006) http://conceptbase.cc, ConceptBase Online. March 30, 2006.

Domain Analysis for Supporting Commercial Off-the-Shelf Components Selection*

Claudia Ayala and Xavier Franch

Technical University of Catalunya
UPC-Campus Nord (Omega), 08034 Barcelona, Spain
{cayala, franch}@lsi.upc.edu

Abstract. Though new technological trends and paradigms arise for developing complex software systems, systematic reuse continues to be an elusive goal. In this context, the adoption of Commercial Off-The-Shelf (COTS) technologies introduces many challenges that still have not been fully overcome, such as the lack of comprehensive mechanisms to record and manage the required information for supporting COTS components selection. In this paper we present a domain analysis approach for gathering the information needed to describe COTS market segments as required for effective COTS components selection. Due to the diversity of the information to capture, we propose different dimensions of interest for COTS components selection that are covered by different domain models. These models are articulated by means of a single framework based on a widespread software quality standard.

1 Introduction

Systematic reuse is based on the observation that quality and productivity can be significantly increased by building an infrastructure support. The engineering discipline concerned with building these optimal reusable assets is called *domain engineering* [1]. Domain engineering supports the notion of *domain*, a set of applications that use common concepts for describing requirements, problems, capabilities and solutions. Particularly, being part of domain engineering, *domain analysis* has been identified as a major factor in the success of software reusability [2]. Domain analysis refers to the process of identifying the basic elements of the domain, organizing an understanding of the relationships among these elements, and representing this understanding in a useful way by means of different types of domain models [3]. The different existing views on domain modelling (e.g., [1], [4], [5]) share the same goal: to facilitate quality software development by reusing the knowledge of the addressed domain.

Reuse is not a context-independent activity. The type of artifact to be reused impacts on the reuse models to be adopted and the reuse processes to be undertaken;

* This research has been partially supported by the Spanish MEC project TIN2004-07461-C02-01. C. Ayala´s work has been partially supported by the Mexican Council of Science and Technology (CONACyT) and the Agència de Gestió d'Ajuts Universitaris i de Recerca (European Social Fund).

D.W. Embley, A. Olivé, and S. Ram (Eds.): ER 2006, LNCS 4215, pp. 354 – 370, 2006.

therefore, the reuse discipline has to evolve as new paradigms and artifacts emerge. In this context, we are interested in one particular case of those software artifacts, namely *Commercial Off-The-Shelf (COTS) components*. A COTS component is defined as "a product that is sold, leased or licensed to the general public, offered by a vendor trying to profit from it, supported and evolved by the vendor who retains the intellectual property rights, available in multiple identical copies and used without source code modification by a consumer" [6].

Successful COTS-based systems development requires an effective and efficient COTS selection process to deliver full potential to this technology. *COTS selection* is defined as the process of searching candidates and evaluating them with respect to the system requirements. Several COTS selection methods, processes and techniques have been formulated (see [7] for a recent survey). However, though these approaches have achieved significant results, they are mainly oriented to individual selection processes. Even in the cases in which a reuse infrastructure is suggested (e.g., OTSO, CARE, PECA), no real support or precise guidelines are offered.

To solve this problem, it seems feasible to use domain analysis for recording and structuring the informational dimensions required for selecting COTS components. This could be done by means of different domain models with the aim of supporting organizations that need continuously to carry out COTS selection processes in order to reuse their knowledge and information in a structured way (e.g., reusing criteria for COTS evaluation or reusing information of the organizational environment). However, as far as we know, COTS technology issues have not been explicitly addressed in the domain analysis discipline (although of course many concepts of domain analysis apply to this particular case).

The goal of this paper is to present a particular approach of domain analysis for supporting COTS components selection. This approach is part of our GOThIC (Goal-Oriented Taxonomy and reuse Infrastructure Construction) [8], a prescriptive goal-oriented method for building and maintaining a reliable reuse infrastructure in which COTS market segments are arranged to form a taxonomy whose nodes are decorated with domain models. In this sense, our domain analysis approach aims at producing several domain models for stating the most important aspects of a particular COTS segment in the COTS marketplace. Moreover, all these models are integrated and synchronized using a unifying framework and, widespread notations and standards.

The rest of the paper is organized as follows. Section 2 introduces the GOThIC method, the importance of domain analysis in its context and its feasibility. The informational dimensions for evaluating COTS components are identified in section 3. Section 4 discusses the most appropriate types of models to record these informational dimensions whilst section 5 explains how these models are integrated into a unified one. Section 6 illustrates our proposal with an example. Section 7 outlines the impact of domain analysis onto COTS components selection, and finally, conclusions are given in section 8.

2 The GOThIC Method

As a response to the need of organizing the knowledge of the COTS marketplace in a structured manner, we have formulated the GOThIC method [8]. Its ultimate goal is to guide the construction and maintenance of goal-oriented taxonomies that describe the contents of the COTS marketplace. The method is articulated by means of several activities, such as the exploration of information sources, the identification of goals and their hierarchization. Among these activities, we also find domain analysis of the COTS marketplace segment being addressed by the taxonomy. This activity has the mission of producing an integrated domain model (representation of important aspects of a COTS segment) that serves as the basis to gain knowledge for identifying the correct goals and to build a reuse infrastructure with several kinds of reusable assets of interest for COTS selection processes.

From an operational point of view, the goal of the GOThIC method is to populate a knowledge base with data according to the UML [9] conceptual model sketched in Fig. 1. At the heart of this model lies the taxonomy composed of two types of nodes, market segments and categories, which are characterized by their goals. Market segments are the leaves of the taxonomy, whilst categories serve to group related market segments and/or subcategories (e.g., the category of communication infrastructure systems or financial packages). From a semantic point of view, market segments stand for the basic types of COTS components available in the marketplace, i.e. atomic entities covering a significant group of functionality such that their decomposition would yield to too fine-grained domains (e.g., the domain of anti-virus tools or spreadsheet applications). As a consequence, COTS components are associated with market segments and not with categories (although an indirect relationship exists, because market segments belong to categories). Components may cover more than one market segment. Taxonomy nodes have a generic domain model bound, which is built during the domain analysis activity. Their construction is a result of the integration of diverse models which are designed from the analysis of some information sources which are gathered, analyzed and prioritized according to several characteristics of the taxonomy construction project.

The taxonomy built with GOThIC may then be browsed during COTS selection to locate the market segment (or segments) of interest. Once found, the domain model bound may be used to obtain the appropriate criteria for selecting the most suitable component.

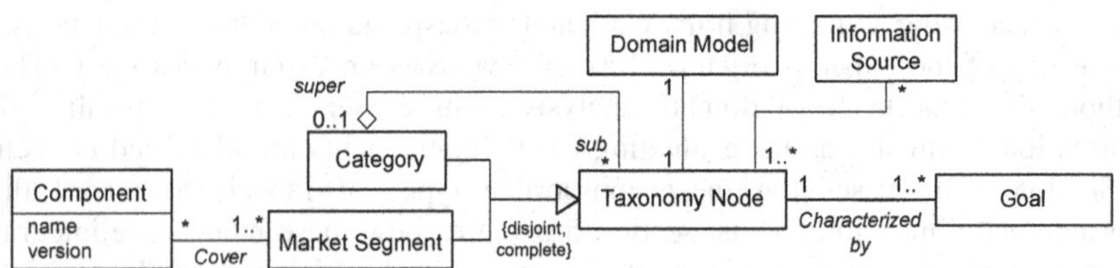

Fig. 1. Conceptual model for goal-oriented COTS taxonomies in the GOThIC method: overview

The feasibility of the GOThIC method depends on some premises:

- In general, it is mainly addressed to organizations that are carrying out subsequent COTS selection processes (e.g., a consultant company, a third-party software provider, an IT department of a big corporation, etc.). Therefore, they may find valuable to have means to transfer knowledge from one experience to another (i.e. the return on investment for building a reuse infrastructure should be justified).

- It should be applied to a COTS segment that is of general interest. This means that a great deal of organizations needs to select COTS components from this segment. Some examples are: communication infrastructure, ERP systems, security-related systems, etc. In these contexts, the number of selection processes that take place will be high and then reusability of the models likely to occur.
- It should be addressed to COTS segment that offer components of coarse-grained granularity. This makes domain understanding more difficult, time-consuming and cumbersome and so domain analysis is helpful. Market segments such as CRM and ECM systems are typical examples, whilst time or currency converters are not.

3 Domain Analysis for Supporting COTS Selection: Dimensions

In the previous sections we have justified the convenience of having domain models for describing COTS marketplace segments. In this section, informational dimensions required for selecting COTS components are identified. Each dimension will be described by a model. To guide the identification of such dimensions, we analyze the different informational needs and facts of COTS selection processes that have been reported in the literature (e.g., [10, 11, 12]) as well as our own experiences in the field (e.g., [13, 14, 15, 16]).

Fundamental Concepts

In the COTS context the same concept may be denoted by different names in different products or even worse, the same term may denote different concepts in different products. Furthermore, currently, it is not usual to find places in the COTS marketplace where fundamental concepts are stated in a clear way, making difficult to use them, customize them and make them evolve as the marketplace does [17]. On the other hand, every single COTS segment defines lots of concepts that are used over and over, e.g., anti-virus tools have "viruses", e-mail systems have "messages" and "folders", etc. These concepts may be related in many ways, e.g. "messages" are "stored" inside "folders". A poor knowledge of these fundamental concepts and semantic relationships may interfere with the efficiency and effectiveness of COTS selection processes. Therefore a model for representing all this information is needed. Its purpose is to settle the scope of a particular segment, to define its main concepts (both as a vocabulary and as a semantic model) and the relationships that facilitate the understanding of the domain as a whole. The resulting model can there be used as a reference framework for the segment. To build this model, information sources such as standards and textbooks are useful (see [8] for a set of suggested information sources). We recommend to choose one of the most trustable sources as starting point, then to synthesize the corresponding dimensions of the domain model, and last to calibrate this dimension with other informational sources.

Functionality

COTS components have their functionality already built-in, so it is a primary source of information for selecting them. Thus, instead of traditional requirements that specify "must" and "should" needs, requirements for COTS-based systems articulate broad categories of needs and possible trade-offs. A domain model must cover this dimension, but a good balance is needed. On the one hand, the most representative functionalities of a particular segment should be included (e.g., virus repair, automatic resending of messages) and described up to a level of detail that enables efficient survey and evaluation of particular COTS components. On the other hand, if too much detail is given, several obstacles, remarkably growing size and evolvability of the COTS marketplace, are harder to overcome, since a lot of information would need to be updated continuously. Also, too much detail may commit the description of the functionality to the behaviour of particular components.

Quality of Service

Quality factors are likely to break the tie when several COTS candidates provide the required functionality; consequently the role of quality information becomes utterly important for driving COTS selection [18]. Therefore, a dimension for stating quality of service is required. The resulting model needs to offer a structured description of the COTS segment addressed, organizing the different quality factors hierarchically (e.g., Throughput and Response Time as subfactors of Time Efficiency) and should also include metrics for the quality factors. This model may serve as a framework in which particular COTS components may be evaluated and compared to user requirements during selection processes.

Non-technical Description

Despite the fact that the evaluation of candidate COTS components from a technical point of view (functionality and quality of service) is necessary, experiences in COTS selection show that non-technical information (i.e., information that does not refer directly to the intrinsic quality of software, but to its context, including economic, political and managerial issues; e.g., adequacy of the procedures imposed by the COTS with respect to procedures of the organization) must be taken into account and, in fact sometimes it is even more important than the technical information [19]. As a result, we need to record this information as part of the domain model. This new dimension must distinguish several concepts and focus on the commercial nature of COTS components, stating information about licensing issues, provider reputation, post-sale supporting services, etc. One should be aware that part of the information may be difficult to obtain (e.g., provider finance information) and the corresponding factor may not be included in the model for this reason.

Interoperability

The analysis of any COTS market segment shows that some relationships among components exist. We have analyzed the types of dependencies that may exist and we have concluded that a COTS component may need another for: enabling its functionality (e.g., document management tools need workflow technology to define life cycles); complementing its functionality with an additional feature, not originally intended to be part of its suitability (e.g., a web page edition tool can complement a web browser to facilitate web page edition); enhancing its quality attributes (e.g., resource utilization can be improved significantly using compression tools). However, in the context of COTS selection, interoperability has been dealt with in a case-by-case basis. Furthermore, some of the COTS selection methods proposed so far just address single component selection, they do not even address the need to select a suite as final solution. Therefore we propose a new dimension to cover this need, otherwise COTS selection becomes not trustable. It is worth remarking that, since we are describing not a particular COTS component but a whole segment, interoperability issues must not be stated in much detail (e.g., data formats, API specificities, etc.); instead the model should include the needs and expectations that one type of component has on others in a very high-level way.

4 Domain Analysis for Supporting COTS Selection: Models

Taking into account the informational dimensions required by the COTS technology, in this section we discuss which are the most appropriated types of models for representing them. A first observation is that, due to their diversity, various types of models will be probably required.

In the domain analysis field, a variety of methods and techniques have been proposed as: FODA, DARE, ODM, DSSA and PLUS (see [20] and [21] for a survey) which use a diversity of different types of artefacts and mechanisms to record the knowledge that range from the traditional requirements models (namely models of data, behaviour, and function), as Data Flow diagrams [22], Entity-Relationship (ER) models [23], Object Oriented models [24], UML models [9] Scenarios [25], and Feature models [26], to UML metamodeling techniques and more elaborated UML extensions and stereotypes for dealing with domain structural elements, relations and domain variability [21, 27]. In practice, these proposals vary in their terms, notations, and emphases, but in general they are focused on designing product lines or product families for promoting reusability between software applications by means of an intended reuse plan [21, 27].

Furthermore, as far as we know, none of these approaches has examined in depth the special kind of relationships and information that the COTS technology requires. In this sense, we have studied whether the models proposed by the actual domain analysis practices could be suitable for recording all the COTS informational dimensions. We found that although some commonly used models could fit well enough for representing some dimensions, some other dimensions were still lacking of an adequated representation and analysis (see Table 1 for examples), for instance those relationships that enable interoperability among components, which could be partially fulfilled by establishing "Artifact Dependencies" (a special kind of variability in variability models for Software Product Lines design [21]), as well as the dimension related with stating non-technical information and quality of service (this last could also be partially addressed by test cases, but generally they are considered to be out of domain analysis).

For that reason, it is a fact that actual domain analysis approaches do not address in an optimal way all the fundamental informational dimensions required for assessing COTS components in terms of expressiveness and adequateness, structure, and compatibility. Hence, existent domain analysis strategies have to be somehow adapted and complemented to fully deal with the COTS technology characteristics [28, 29].

In the rest of this section, we propose a set of domain models for covering all the required COTS informational dimensions using widespread notations and standards. Table 1 summarizes our proposal and makes clear the gap for recording non-technical descriptions and interoperability with respect to other domain analysis approaches.

Table 1. Summary of domain analysis practices for representing COTS dimensions

COTS Dimension	Domain Analysis Practices	Our approach
Fundamental Concepts	ER Models, Feature Models, UML Diagrams, etc.	UML Class Diagrams + LEL
Functionality	Data Flow Diagrams, Scenarios, UML Diagrams, etc.	UML Use Case Diagrams + brief individual descriptions
Quality of Service	None	ISO/IEC 9126-1
Non-Technical Description	None	3 categories of non-technical factors
Interoperability	None	*i** SD Models

Fundamental Concepts

Two types of artifacts are adequate for representing fundamental concepts: conceptual data models or feature-oriented models to express the semantic meaning of the terms in the market segment together with their relationships; and a glossary to set up a vocabulary of the domain with information about synonymous and other lexical relationships. In particular, we have chosen UML class diagrams [9] for representing the semantic information due to its expressiveness and acceptance in the community. As for the glossary, the Language Extended Lexicon (LEL) [30] approach provides an adequate level of service since it allows to capture the meaning and fundamental relationships of the particular symbols (words or phrases) of the domain. The glossary includes at least the terms that appear in the rest of the models (e.g., the names of classes, attributes and associations of the UML class diagram). One could also think of the general concept of ontology [31] for capturing all the information needed.

Functionality

Any approach based on the concept of scenario seems a good option. As commented in section 3, the important point is to use the right level of detail. We propose the use of UML use case diagrams [9] for defining the functionalities of the COTS segment and a brief format of use cases [32] for describing them individually.

Quality of Service

Quality models [13] provide a measurable framework which precisely defines and consolidates the different views of quality (e.g. performance, reliability, integrity, etc.) which are required for COTS components evaluation. Among the different existing proposals, we have adopted the ISO/IEC 9126-1 standard [33] for several reasons, remarkably: it provides a two-level departing catalogue but at the same time it is highly customizable to each different COTS segment; there are some metrics already defined for this standard; and it is widespread. In the next section we give more details of this model.

Non-technical Description

Not only in the domain analysis context but in general, it is not usual to find models for representing non-technical information. Usually some categories are identified and for each of them, a list of non-technical factors identified. We have identified 3 high-level factors and 15 second-level subfactors referring to supplier information (e.g., financial information), cost information (e.g., licensing schemes) and other non-technical information about the product (e.g., history of versions). See [19] for more details.

Interoperability

Interoperability of COTS components is usually described by means of APIs or data formats. However, as already explained in section 3, we are interested in describing not particular COTS components but the general behavior of all the components belonging to a COTS segment, therefore we need more abstract descriptions. The combination of goal- and agent-oriented models provides a good response to our needs. Goals allow expressing needs and expectations in a high-level way, whilst agents are an appropriate way to model COTS segments. Then, one COTS segment may state that depends on another to attain a goal. We have chosen *i** Strategic Dependency (SD) models [34], adapting its semantic to represent COTS segments and their dependencies. See [35] for details.

5 A Unifying Model for COTS Domain Analysis

The models proposed in section 4 cover the informational dimensions that were identified in section 3. However, the primary goal of COTS segments domain analysis is to characterize COTS components for their evaluation and selection, so it is clear that having these dimensions structured in separate models hampers domain understanding and model management. For this reason, we need a unifying model which facilitates this goal. Thus, from the dimension models given, quality models seem the most appropriate type of artefact. Therefore, if we succeed in putting all the models in an ISO/IEC 9126-1 quality model we will have our goal attained.

5.1 The ISO/IEC 9126 Quality Standard

The ISO/IEC 9126-1 software quality standard proposes quality models as the artifacts that keep track of the quality factors that are of interest in a particular context. The ISO/IEC 9126-1 standard fixes 6 top level characteristics: functionality, reliability, usability, efficiency, maintainability and portability. It also fixes their further refinement into 27 subcharacteristics but does not elaborate the quality model below this level, making thus the model flexible. To carry out this refinement, subcharacteristics are, in turn, decomposed into attributes, which represent the properties that the software products belonging to the domain of interest exhibit. Intermediate hierarchies of subcharacteristics and attributes may appear making thus the model highly structured. Metrics are bound to attributes. The standard is highly customizable to different purposes and domains; e.g., in our previous work [19], we have created an extension for the particular case of quality of COTS components, and new subcharacteristics and attributes have been introduced.

5.2 Integrating All the COTS Domain Models into the ISO/IEC 9126-1

In this subsection we aim at integrating the domain models obtained so far, even considering their different nature, into an ISO/IEC 9126-1 quality model. Fig. 2 shows an overview of our proposed framework.

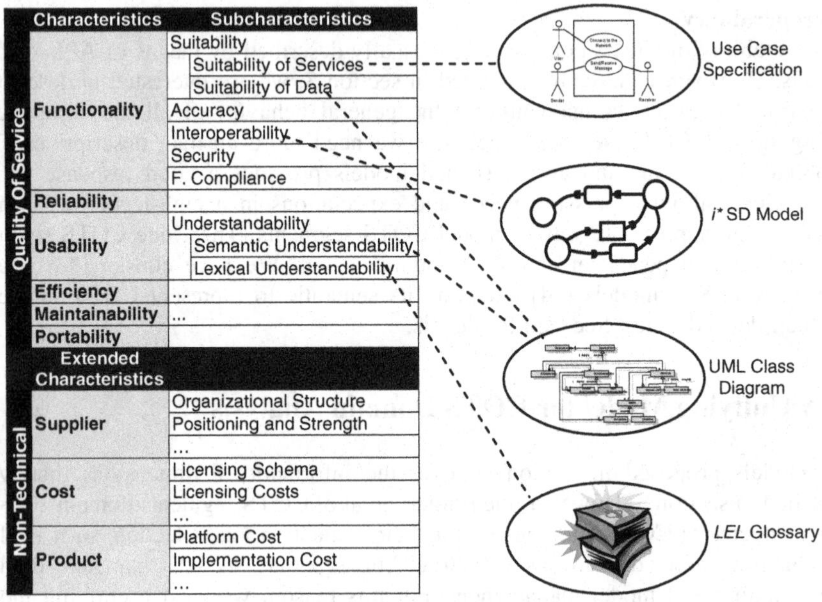

Fig. 2. An overview of the ISO/IEC 9126-1-based quality model for COTS segments

Functionality
Regardless of having the same name, the functionality of a COTS segment does not correspond with the ISO/IEC *Functionality* characteristic. Instead, it corresponds to the *Suitability* concept that is a subcharacteristic of *Functionality*. However, since functionality focuses on the services provided but not the data managed, we create a new subcharacteristic *Suitability of Services* that contains the UML Use Case diagram and the individual use case descriptions.

Fundamental Concepts
The UML class diagram is related to two ISO/IEC subcharacteristics. On the one hand, as the case before, *Suitability*, because some of the classes (and their attributes) and relationships are defining part of the suitability of the COTS segment. On the other hand, *Understandability*, which is a subcharacteristic of *Usability*, because having a UML class diagram provides a reference framework that allows testing how much a particular COTS component adheres to it. For the same reason, also the LEL

glossary supports *Understandability*. Therefore, we create 3 new subcharacteristics; *Suitability of Data*, belonging to *Suitability*, contains the class diagram; *Semantic Understandability* and *Lexical Understandability*, belonging to *Understandability*. The first one also contains the class diagram and the second one the glossary.

Non-technical Description
For arranging non-technical factors proposed in [19] in an ISO-9126-1-form, we define the 3 high-level ones as characteristics and the other 15 as subcharacteristics.

Interoperability
Interoperability is also a subcharacteristic of *Suitability* and in this case, we just consider the *i** SD model as the description of *Interoperability*.

5.3 Transforming the Models into the ISO/IEC 9126-1 Framework

Although we have achieved our primary goal, namely integrating all the dimension models under the same umbrella, there is still a question left that may be considered as a drawback when using the domain model for COTS components evaluation purposes: the fundamental concepts, functionality and interoperability models are expressed with their own formalisms which are not straightforward to evaluate. In this subsection we deal with this problem by providing rules that map the constructs in these models into ISO/IEC 9126-1 quality factors. Furthermore, we state how their metrics are defined. These rules are defined in such a way that they could generate the new, final model automatically from the former models.

Functionality
For each use case UC appearing in the Use Case diagram, a quality attribute UC belonging to the *Suitability of Services* subcharacteristic is created. The individual use case specifications are part of the description of these quality attributes.

For each obtained quality attribute, an ordinal metric which can take three values, Satisfactory, Acceptable and Poor, is created. These values express how a particular COTS component covers the service represented by the use case.

Fundamental Concepts
For each class or association C appearing in the class diagram that represents a concept provided by the COTS components in the segment, a quality attribute C belonging to the *Suitability of Data* subcharacteristic is created. The elements of the class diagram are part of the description of these quality attributes.

For each obtained quality attribute, an ordinal metric which can take three values, Satisfactory, Acceptable and Poor, is created. These values express how a particular COTS component provides the data represented by the class or association. These values will be obtained during evaluation by using different criteria (e.g., whether all the attributes are provided, whether the instances are permanent or not, etc.).

Each term of the glossary is included as part of the description of the quality attribute(s) it is related to. The same happens with the elements of the class diagram that were not tackled in the previous step. Last, two numerical metrics are bound to the *Semantic Understandability* and *Lexical Understandability* attributes. The values of these metrics will count the number of semantic and lexical discrepancies of a particular COTS component with respect to the reference models.

Interoperability
For each agent A appearing the *i** SD model, except the agent S that represents the COTS segment we are modeling, a subcharacteristic A belonging to *Interoperability* is created.

For each dependency G among S and A, an attribute G is created. For each obtained quality attribute, we create an ordinal metric whose values depend on the type of the corresponding dependency: if goal, values are Attained and Not Attained; if resource, Provided and Not Provided; if task, Executed or Failed; if softgoal, Satisfactory, Acceptable and Poor.

Once these rules are applied, evaluation of COTS component may be done in a more uniform and comfortable way. But of course, the original models should be preserved since they are easier to understand and evolve.

6 Example: The Real-Time Synchronous Communication Domain

For illustrating our proposal, we present some excerpts of the domain model obtained for the Real-Time Synchronous Communication (RTSC) market segment. This segment embraces the various tools and technologies used to enable communication and collaboration among people in a "same time-different place" mode.

Fundamental Concepts
Part of the UML class diagram is presented in Fig. 3a. Several key concepts are stated as classes. These concepts are of different nature, e.g. human roles (e.g. *Sender* and *Receiver*), artefacts of any kind (either physical or informational, e.g. *Message*), software and hardware domain-specific components (e.g. *Software Client, Software Server* and *Proxy*), etc. Inside these classes, we identify attributes but just those that

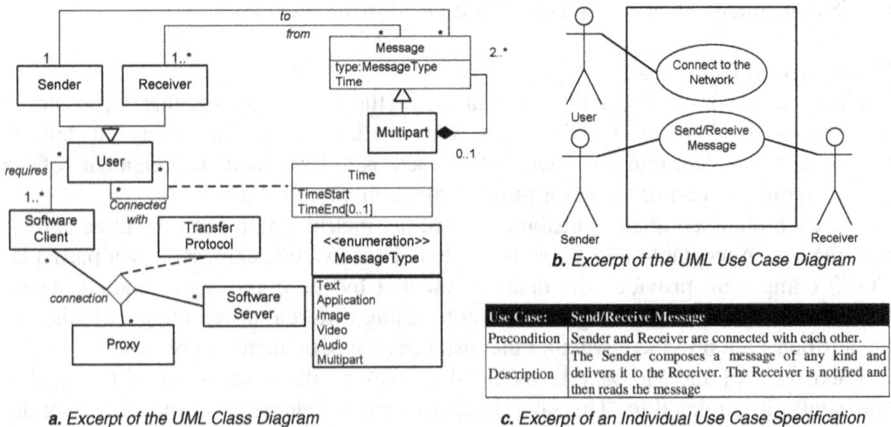

Use Case:	Send/Receive Message
Precondition	Sender and Receiver are connected with each other.
Description	The Sender composes a message of any kind and delivers it to the Receiver. The Receiver is notified and then reads the message

Fig. 3. Excerpt of some domain models constructed for the RTSC case

play a crucial part in the domain, e.g. *Message* that can be of different types. Domain relationships are also of different kinds. Thus, we can see a high-level relationship among the human roles *Sender* and *Receiver* which are generalized into a *User* class. On the other hand, associations may be of very different nature. For instance, we have permanent or at least very stable relationships (e.g., among *User* and *Software Client*) while others are highly dynamic (real-time connections that are created and destroyed dynamically). OCL restrictions may be used to decorate the model appropriately.

Functionality

As stated in section 3, the use case model for functionality focuses on the most characteristic services offered by packages in this domain. Fig. 3b shows some for the RTSC domain, namely *Connect to the Network* and *Send/Receive Message.* Others such as *Send Video Message* or *Connecting Multiuser Session* are not included either because they are not considered general enough but specific of a few COTS components, or because they are considered as secondary. In addition, we can also check that the individual use case specification of *Send/Receive Message* presented in Fig 3c follows the given recommendation of being very abridged.

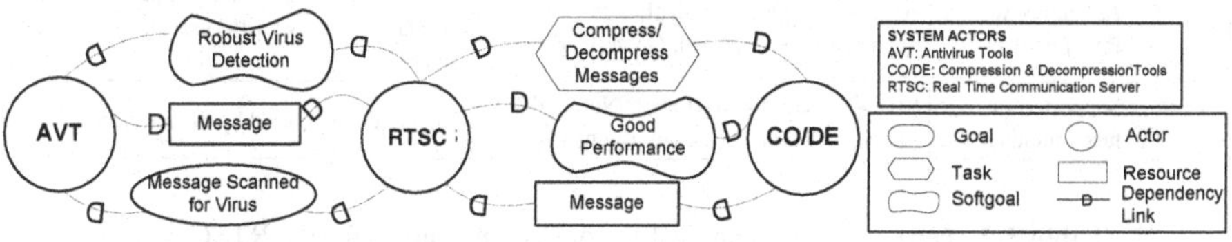

Fig. 4. Some dependencies among RTSC Tools and other types of tools

Interoperability

As it is the usual case in COTS segments that offer a lot of functionality, we may identify several relationships with other types of COTS domains. In Fig. 4 we introduce as example two COTS segments related with RTSC, AntiVirus Tools (AVT) and Compression/Decompression Tools (CO/DE), all of them modelled as *i** actors. Among their relationships, we find: a RTSC component relies on an AVT component for detecting viruses (goal dependency, since the AVT decides the best way to do it) and requires this detection to be robust (softgoal dependency, because the concept of "robust" detection is matter of negotiation); a RTSC component depends on a CO/DE one to compress/decompress messages automatically (task dependency, because the RTSC states when and how these automatic activities are done); a RTSC component may improve its performance using a CO/DE component (softgoal dependency, because the concept of "good" performance is matter of negotiation); and both related components need the message to work with from a RTSC component (resource dependency, because it is an informational entity).

Quality of Service

In table 2 we decompose a bit the *Understandability* subcharacteristic with the *Adherence to Best Practices* and *Supported Interface Languages* attributes. We include specific metrics that help to evaluate and compare user requirements. The first metric illustrate the subjective case, whilst the second one illustrates a metric that is both objective and structured (set of values). The description included in the table is in fact part of the glossary but appears for legibility purposes.

Non-technical Description
Table 3 shows an excerpt of the refinement of a non-technical factor of a product, its stability. Note the similarity compared to quality of service description, which facilitates further integration. It should be mentioned that non-technical factors are very similar among different COTS segments.

Table 2. Excerpt of the quality model for the RTSC case

Quality factor	Metric	Description
3 Usability		ISO/IEC 9126-1 Characteristic
1 Understandability		ISO/IEC 9126-1 Subcharacteristic
3 Interface Understandability		Effort to recognizing the logical concepts and its applicability by means of interfaces.
1 Adherence to Best Practices	ADP: 4valueOrder[Ordinal] 4valueOrder = (Optimal, Good, Fair, Poor)	How well events and elements of the interface comply with user interface best practices.
2 Supported Interface Languages	SIL: Languages = Set(Labels[Nominal]) Labels = (Spanish, Catalan, English, ...)	Languages supported by the interface.

Table 3. Excerpt of a non-technical factor decomposition for the RTSC case

Non-technical factor	Metric	Description
3 Product		Non-technical characteristics of a COTS product that may influence COTS selection
1 Stability		
1 Time of Product in the Market	TPM: Time[Ratio] Time = Float	Number of years the product has been in the marketplace
2 Versions Currently in the Market	VCM: List(Version[Nominal]) Version = String	Versions currently available in the marketplace
3 In-house Product	IP: Own[Nominal] Own = (Yes, Not)	Whether the product is in-house or acquired from a third party

Table 4 shows the integration of the presented excerpts in the unifying model using the mapping rules introduced in the section 5.3.

7 Domain Analysis-Based COTS Selection

Our domain analysis strategy has been integrated into the GOThIC method by considering that the ISO/IEC 9126-1-based quality model for COTS segments introduced in Fig. 2 is in fact the Domain Model that appears in Fig. 1. As stated in section 2, a GOThIC taxonomy is used to locate the taxonomy node that fulfils the

Table 4. The unifying model for the RTSC case (excerpt)

				Quality factor	Metric	Description
1				**Functionality**		See ISO/IEC 9126
	1			Suitability		See ISO/IEC 9126
		1		Suitability of Services		See 5.3
			1	Connect to Network	CN: 3ValueOrder[Ordinal] 3ValueOrder = (Satisfactory, Acceptable, Poor)	See fig. 3b
			2	Send/Receive Message	SRMsg: 3ValueOrder[Ordinal]	See fig. 3b
				…		
		2		Suitability of Data		See 5.3
			1	Message	Msg: 3ValueOrder[Ordinal]	See fig. 3a
			2	Connected with	Cw: 3ValueOrder[Ordinal]	See fig. 3a
				…		
	2			Interoperability		See ISO/IEC 9126
		1		Anti-Virus Tools		See fig. 4
			1	Robust Virus Detection	RVD: 3ValueOrder[Ordinal]	See fig. 4
			2	Message Scanned for Virus	MSV: GoalValue[Ordinal] GoalValue = (Attained, Not Attained)	See fig. 4
			3	Message	Msg: ResourceValue[Ordinal] ResourceValue = (Provided, NotProvided)	See fig. 4
		2		CO/DE Tools		See fig. 4
			1	Good Performance	GP: 3ValueOrder[Ordinal]	See fig. 4
			2	Compress/Decompress Messages	CDMsg:TaskValue[Ordinal] TaskValue = (Executed, Failed)	See fig. 4
			3	Message	Msg: ResourceValue[Ordinal]	See fig. 4
	3	..				
2				**Reliability**		See ISO/IEC 9126
3				**Usability**		See ISO/IEC 9126
	1			Understandability		See ISO/IEC 9126
		1		Semantic Understandability	SU: Number[Unit]; Number=Integer	See 5.3
		2		Lexical Understandability	LU: Number[Unit]	See 5.3
		3		Interface Understandability		See table 2
			1	Adherence to Best Practices	ADP: 4valueOrder[Ordinal] 4valueOrder = (Optimal, Good, Fair, Poor)	See table 2
			2	Supported Interface Languages	SIL: Languages = Set(Labels[Nominal]) Labels = (Spanish, Catalan, English, …)	See table 2
	2	..				
4				**…other ISO/IEC characteristics**		See ISO/IEC 9126
				Non-technical factor	**Metric**	**Description**
1				**Supplier**		See [19]
2				**Cost**		See [19]
3				**Product**		See table 3
	1			Stability		
		1		Time of Product in Market	TPM: Time[Ratio]; Time = Float	See table 3
		2		Versions Currently in Market	VCM: List(Version[Nominal]); Version = String	See table 3
		3		In-house Product	IP: Own[Nominal]; Own = (Yes, Not)	See table 3
	2	..				

needs of the user in charge of the selection process. Once located, its domain model may be used to guide the rest of the selection process by refining this model with more specific requirements. The factors in the ISO/IEC 9126-1-based quality model help to elicit and negotiate the requirements, making easier the identification of mismatches among components characteristics and the requirements. Moreover, those factors corresponding to the stated requirements are used to evaluate the capabilities of the candidate components in a uniform way, using the metrics defined in the model. For doing so, we can proceed manually, or use tool support ranging from a simple spreadsheet to a more sophisticated tool, e.g. our DesCOTS system [36].

8 Conclusions

We have detailed the domain analysis approach for building a reuse infrastructure for supporting COTS selection processes enclosed in our GOThIC method. This approach is based on the application of domain analysis principles for recording and representing all the required information for evaluating COTS. Our proposal relies on several industrial experiences that have been undertaken under action-research premises, complemented with literature survey and grounded theory.

These industrial experiences have been carried out in the field of Workflow Systems [14], Requirements Engineering Tools [15], Telephony Systems [16] and some sub-categories of Enterprise Applications (with emphasis with those related to Content Management). Industrial experiences have been complemented with academic ones (e.g. Real-Time Synchronous Communication and Message-based Communication Systems) to analyse in more depth some particular aspects.

Concerning domain analysis, we have concluded that existing approaches were not oriented to support reuse in the COTS framework, consequently the need of mechanisms to analyze and create a reuse infrastructure for COTS domains still remained. In particular, it is required to represent interoperability among COTS components and to analyze non-technical factors that may influence the selection, as well as the need of putting more emphasis to software quality issues.

With respect to COTS selection:

- We have put the emphasis on reuse, making a concrete proposal based on the domain analysis technique which allows transferring knowledge from one experience to another.
- We have explicitly identified the informational dimensions required for the effective and efficient selection of COTS components.
- We have offered guidance for representing these informational dimensions using appropriate types of domain models.
- Using some mapping rules, we have integrated all these models into a single one, based on a well-known standard, highly oriented to support the evaluation of the candidate components.
- Given this representation, we may use some existing tool-support to conduct the evaluation of candidates in the framework of the ISO/IEC 9126-1 standard.
- Domain analysis not only impacts positively on reuse, but also ameliorates some well-known obstacles for COTS selections success [8]. Remarkably, using domain analysis principles we avoid those semantic and syntactic discrepancies that are common in the COTS marketplace.

References

1. Prieto-Díaz, R., Arango, G. *Domain Analysis and Software Systems Modelling*. IEEE Computer Society Press, 1991.
2. Frakes, W., Prieto-Díaz, R., Fox, C. "DARE: Domain Analysis and Reuse Environment". *Annals of Software Engineering*, 5, pp. 125-141, 1998.
3. Software Engineering Institute (SEI). http://www.sei.cmu.edu/domain-engineering/, 2002.
4. Cornwell, P.C. "HP Domain Analysis: Producing Useful Models for Reusable Software". *Hewlett-Packard Journal*, August 1996.
5. Neighbors, J. *Software Construction Using Components*. PhD. Thesis, University of California, Irvine, 1980.
6. Meyers, C., Oberndorf, P. *Managing Software Acquisition*. Addison-Wesley, 2001.
7. Ruhe, G. "Intelligent Support for Selection of COTS Products". In *Proceedings of Web, Web-Services and Database Systems*. LNCS 2593, 2003.
8. Ayala, C. Franch, X. "A Goal-Oriented Strategy for Supporting Commercial Off-The-Shelf Components Selection". In *Proceedings of the 9th International Conference on Software Reuse* (ICSR), LNCS 4039, 2006.
9. UML Specifications. http://www.uml.org/
10. Bertoa, M.F., Troya, J.M., Vallecillo, A. "A Survey on the Quality Information Provided by Software Component Vendors". In *Proceedings of the 7th ECOOP Workshop on Quantitative Approaches in Object-Oriented Software Engineering* (QAOOSE), 2003.
11. Torchiano, M., Morisio, M. "Overlooked Aspects of COTS-Based Development". *IEEE Software*, 21(2), pp. 88-93, 2004.
12. Cechich, A., Réquilé-Romanczuk, A., Aguirre, J., Luzuriaga, J.M. "Trends on COTS Component Identification and Retrieval" In *Proceedings of 5th International Conference on COTS-Based Software Systems* (ICCBSS), IEEE Computer Society, 2006.
13. Franch, X., Carvallo, J.P. "Using Quality Models in Software Package Selection". *IEEE Software*, 20(1), 2003.
14. Carvallo, J.P., Franch, X, Quer, C., Rodríguez, N. "A Framework for Selecting Workflow Tools in the Context of Composite Information Systems". In *Proceedings of the 15th Database and Expert Systems Applications Conference* (DEXA), LNCS 3180, 2004.
15. Carvallo, J.P., Franch, X., Quer, C. "A Quality Model for Requirements Management Tools". Book chapter in *Requirements Engineering for Sociotechnical Systems*, Idea Group, 2005.
16. Carvallo, J.P. "Supporting Organizational Induction and Goals Alignment for COTS Components Selection by means of *i**". In *Proceedings of the 5th International Conference on COTS-Based Systems* (ICCBSS), IEEE Computer Society, 2006.
17. Ayala, C., Franch, X. "Transforming Software Package Classification Hierarchies into Goal-Based Taxonomies". In *Proceedings of the 16th Database and Expert Systems Applications Conference* (DEXA), LNCS 3588, 2005.
18. Maiden, N., Ncube, C. "Acquiring Requirements for COTS Selection". *IEEE Software* (15)2, 1998.
19. Carvallo, J.P., Franch, X. "Extending the ISO/IEC 9126-1 Quality Model with Non-Technical Factors for COTS Components Selection". In *Proceedings of the 4th ICSE Workshop of Software Quality* (WoSQ), ACM Digital Libray, 2006.
20. Ferré, X., Vegas, S. "An Evaluation of Domain Analysis Methods". In *Proceedings 4th CAiSE Workshop on Exploring Modelling Methods for Systems Analysis and Design* (EMMSAD), 1999.

21. Pohl, K., Böckle, G., van der Linden, F.J. *Software Product Line Engineering*. Springer-Verlag, 2005
22. McMenamin, S.M., Palmer, J.F. *Essential Systems Analysis*. Yourdon Press, 1984.
23. Chen, P. "The Entity-Relationship Model –Towards a Unified View of Data". *ACM Transactions on Database Systems*, 1(1), March 1976.
24. Cohen, S., Northrop, L. "Object-Oriented Technology and Domain Analysis". In *Proceedings of the 5th International Conference on Software Reuse* (ICSR), 1998.
25. Pohl, K., Brandenburg, M., Glich, A. "Scenario-Based Change Integration in Product Family Development". In *Procs. of the 2nd Workshop on Software Product Lines*, 2001.
26. SEI http://www.sei.cmu.edu/domain-engineering/FODA.html
27. Gomaa, H. *Designing Software Product Lines with UML: From Use Cases to Pattern-Based Software Architectures*. Addison-Wesley, 2005.
28. Almeida, E.S, *et al.* "The Domain Analysis Concept Revisited: A Practical Approach". In *Proceedings of 9th International Conference on Software Reuse* (ICSR), LNCS 4039, 2006.
29. Vitharana, P., Zahedi, F., Jain, H. "Design, Retrieval, and Assembly in Component-Based Software Development". *Communications of the ACM*, 46(11), 2003.
30. Leite, J.C.S.P. "Application Languages: A Product of Requirements Analysis". Informatics Department PUC-/RJ (1989).
31. Gruber, T.R. "Towards Principles for the Design of Ontologies Used for Knowledge Sharing". *International Journal of Human-Computer Studies*, 43(5/6), 1995.
32. Cockburn, A. *Writing Effective Use Cases*. Addison-Wesley, 2001.
33. ISO/IEC International Standard 9126-1. *Software Engineering-Product Quality-Part 1: Quality Model*, 2001.
34. Yu, E. *Modelling Strategic Relationships for Process Reengineering*. PhD Thesis, University of Toronto, 1995.
35. Ayala, C., Franch, X. "Overcoming COTS Marketplace Evolvability and Interoperability". In *Proceedings of the CAiSE'06 Forum*, 2006.
36. Grau, G., Carvallo, J.P., Franch, X., Quer, C. "DesCOTS: A Software System for Selecting COTS Components". In *Proceedings of the 30th EUROMICRO Conference*, IEEE Computer Society, 2004.

A Formal Framework for Reasoning on Metadata Based on CWM

Xiaofei Zhao and Zhiqiu Huang

Department of Computer Science and Engineering
Nanjing University of Aeronautics and Astronautics
210016 Nanjing, China
zxf-first@nuaa.edu.cn

Abstract. During the metadata creation based on Common Warehouse Metamodel(CWM), the different experiences and views of describing data of organizations involved in metadata creation bring metadata on some problems inevitably, such as inconsistencies and redundancies. However, reasoning on CWM metadata for automatically detecting these problems is difficult because CWM metamodel and metadata lack precise semantics. In this paper, we formalize and reason on CWM metamodel and metadata in terms of a logic belonging to Description Logics, which are subsets of First-Order Logic. We distinguish consistency into horizontal consistency and evolution consistency. Towards evolution consistency, we extend CWM metamodel with version capabilities so that reasoning about inconsistency caused by evolution can be done. Then reasoning engine LOOM is applied to check consistency for the above two situations, the results are encouraging.

1 Introduction

Today, as a metadata integration standard for data warehouse field proposed by Object Management Group(OMG), *Common Warehouse Metamodel*(CWM)[2,3] has been accepted as a prevailing standard. However, during the metadata creation based on CWM, for the following reasons: 1 different organizations have different experiences and expertise; 2 different organizations focus on different aspects of data; 3 metadata will evolve in use; 4 the specialities of CWM, the inconsistencies of metadata, such as: content conflicts or the violation of constraints in metamodel or inconsistencies caused by misdeletion during evolution, arise inevitably. So if CWM metadata can be reasoned, so that these inconsistencies can be detected automatically, it is possible to provide computer aided support for the development of the components of data warehouse systems, thus the reliability of metadata integration process and data warehouse system will be remarkably improved.

Unfortunately, CWM metamodel and metadata which is the instances of metamodel are rendered to users by graphs, which lack formal semantics, so how to reason on metadata with the information provided by metamodel hasn't been well solved. In this paper, we attempt to formalize and reason on CWM metadata by a logical approach. Description Logics(DLs)[1], which are subsets of First-Order Logic, provide powerful description ability and equipped with reasoning engines such as

D.W. Embley, A. Olivé, and S. Ram (Eds.): ER 2006, LNCS 4215, pp. 371 – 384, 2006.

LOOM[13], RACER[10], Fact[19], etc. which can perform various reasoning tasks, become our first choice.

In order to fully represent CWM metadata, according to the specialities of CWM metamodel and model, we propose a DL, here called DL_{id}. The DL_{id} offers highly expressive power for CWM structuring mechanisms and is equipped with decidable reasoning procedures, thus provides the description and reasoning of CWM metadata a rigorous formal and reasoning framework.

In this paper, we distinguish consistency into *horizontal consistency* and *evolution consistency* because the consistencies caused by metadata evolution are different from those caused by different views of organizations both in contributing factors and in checking approaches. Because versioning capabilities are not supported by current CWM standard, we extend CWM metamodel so that it provides the capability for recording the trace information of metadata evolution, then research on how to capture the structuring information of metamodel and model in the above two situations in terms of DL_{id}, respectively, and resort to query reasoning mechanisms of LOOM to detect inconsistency information.

2 The Description Logic DL_{id}

The basic elements of Description Logics are *concepts* and *relations*, which describe the types of objects and the relations between them in a domain, respectively. Complex concepts and complex relations can be formed from atomic concepts and atomic relations by constructors. The set of allowed constructors characterizes the expressive power of a Description Logic. Various Description Logics have been considered by the DL community. According to the specialities of CWM metamodel and model, in this paper we propose a DL which supports identification constraints on concepts, here called DL_{id}. The DL_{id} can be seen as a fragment of the Description Logic DLR presented in [9] by Diego et al.. The basic elements of DL_{id} are *concepts*(unary relations) and *roles*(binary relations). Atomic concepts and atomic roles are denoted by A and P, respectively. Arbitrary concepts, denoted by C, and arbitrary roles, denoted by R, are built according to the following syntax:

$$R ::= \top_2 \mid P \mid (i/2{:}C) \mid \neg R \mid R_1 \sqcap R_2$$

$$C ::= \top_1 \mid A \mid \neg C \mid C_1 \sqcap C_2 \mid (\leq k[i]R)$$

where i denotes the i-th component of role R, it can be 1 or 2; k denotes a non-negative integer; (i/2:C) denotes that the i-th concept associated with role R is concept C, sometimes we abbreviate (i/2:C) with (i:C); $\leq k[i]R$ is the multiplicity constraint on the participation to role R of the i-th component of R. We consider only concepts and roles that are *well-typed*, which means that $i \leq 2$ whenever i denotes a component of a role R. We also have the following equivalences in table 1:

Table 1. Equivalences in DL_{id}

$C_1 \sqcup C_2 \Leftrightarrow \neg(\neg C_1 \sqcap \neg C_2)$	$C_1 \Rightarrow C_2 \Leftrightarrow \neg C_1 \sqcup C_2$
$(\geq k[i]R) \Leftrightarrow \neg(\leq k\text{-}1[i]R)$	$\exists[i]R \Leftrightarrow (\geq 1[i]R)$
$\forall[i]R \Leftrightarrow \neg\exists[i]\neg R$	

A DL_{id} *knowledge base* (KB) is constituted by the *Tbox* and the *Abox*. The Tbox is the set of *axioms* describing domain structure and contains *inclusion assertions* of type $R_1 \sqsubseteq R_2$, $C_1 \sqsubseteq C_2$. Besides inclusion assertions, DL_{id} KBs allow for assertions expressing identification constraints.

An *identification assertion* on a concept has the form:

$$(\text{id } C\ [i_1]R_1, \ldots, [i_h]R_h)$$

where C is a concept, each R_j is a role, and each i_j denotes one component of R_j. Intuitively, such an assertion states that if two instances of concept C both participate to R_j as the i_j-th component, then they coincide.

The Abox in DL_{id} is the set of axioms describing instances, it is constituted by *concept assertions* stating whether an object belongs to a certain concept and *role assertions* stating whether two objects satisfy a certain relation.

The semantics of DL_{id} is specified through the notion of interpretation. An *interpretation* $\mathcal{I} = (\Delta^{\mathcal{I}}, \bullet^{\mathcal{I}})$ of a DL_{id} KB $\mathcal{K}$ is constituted by an *interpretation domain* $\Delta^{\mathcal{I}}$ and an *interpretation function* $\bullet^{\mathcal{I}}$ that assigns to each concept C a subset $C^{\mathcal{I}}$ of $\Delta^{\mathcal{I}}$ and to each role R a subset $R^{\mathcal{I}}$ of $(\Delta^{\mathcal{I}})^2$. More semantics are shown in table 2:

Table 2. Semantic rules for DL_{id}

$\top_2^{\mathcal{I}} \subseteq (\Delta^{\mathcal{I}})^2$	$\top_1^{\mathcal{I}} = \Delta^{\mathcal{I}}$
$P^{\mathcal{I}} \subseteq \top_2^{\mathcal{I}}$	$A^{\mathcal{I}} \subseteq \Delta^{\mathcal{I}}$
$(i/2{:}C)^{\mathcal{I}} = \{t \in \top_2^{\mathcal{I}} \mid t[i] \in C^{\mathcal{I}}\}$	$(\neg C)^{\mathcal{I}} = \Delta^{\mathcal{I}} \setminus C^{\mathcal{I}}$
$(\neg R)^{\mathcal{I}} = \top_2^{\mathcal{I}} \setminus R^{\mathcal{I}}$	$(C_1 \sqcap C_2)^{\mathcal{I}} = C_1^{\mathcal{I}} \cap C_2^{\mathcal{I}}$
$(R_1 \sqcap R_2)^{\mathcal{I}} = R_1^{\mathcal{I}} \cap R_2^{\mathcal{I}}$	$(\leq k[i]R)^{\mathcal{I}} = \{a \in \Delta^{\mathcal{I}} \mid \#\{t \in R_1^{\mathcal{I}} \mid t[i] = a\} \leq k\}$

To specify the semantics of a KB we have the following definitions:

(i) An interpretation $\mathcal{I}$ *satisfies* an inclusion assertion $R_1 \sqsubseteq R_2$ (resp. $C_1 \sqsubseteq C_2$) if $R_1^{\mathcal{I}} \subseteq R_2^{\mathcal{I}}$ (resp. $C_1^{\mathcal{I}} \subseteq C_2^{\mathcal{I}}$).

(ii) An interpretation $\mathcal{I}$ *satisfies* the assertion $(\text{id } C\ [i_1]R_1, \ldots, [i_h]R_h)$ if for all a, $b \in C^{\mathcal{I}}$ and for all $t_1, s_1 \in R_1^{\mathcal{I}}, \ldots, t_h, s_h \in R_h^{\mathcal{I}}$ we have that:

$$\begin{array}{l} a = t_1[i_1] = \ldots = t_h[i_h], \\ b = s_1[i_1] = \ldots = s_h[i_h], \qquad \text{implies } a = b \\ t_j[i] = s_j[i], j \in \{1, \ldots, h\}, i \neq i_j \end{array}$$

An interpretation that satisfies all assertions in a KB $\mathcal{K}$ is called a *model* of $\mathcal{K}$.

Several reasoning services are applicable to DL_{id} KBs. The most important ones are KB satisfiability and logical implication. A KB $\mathcal{K}$ is *satisfiable* if there exists a model of $\mathcal{K}$. A concept C is *satisfiable* in a KB $\mathcal{K}$ if there is a model $\mathcal{I}$ of $\mathcal{K}$ such that $C^{\mathcal{I}}$ is nonempty. A concept C_1 is *subsumed by* a concept C_2 in a KB $\mathcal{K}$ if $C_1^{\mathcal{I}} \subseteq C_2^{\mathcal{I}}$ for every model $\mathcal{I}$ of $\mathcal{K}$. An assertion a is *logically implied* by $\mathcal{K}$ if all models of $\mathcal{K}$ satisfy a.

Reasoning in the basic DL ALC[1] is EXPTIME-complete, on the other hand, DL_{id} can be mapped to a fragment of the Description Logic DLR[9] in which reasoning is also EXPTIME-complete, hence reasoning in DL_{id} is decidable, and is EXPTIME-complete.

3 Horizontal Consistency Checking

In this paper we distinguish two types of consistency: horizontal consistency and evolution consistency. Horizontal consistency indicates consistency within the metadata in the same version; evolution consistency indicates consistency between different versions of the metadata. The two types of consistency are shown in Figure 1: the consistency in the horizontal plane belongs to horizontal consistency, the consistency in the vertical plane belongs to evolution consistency.

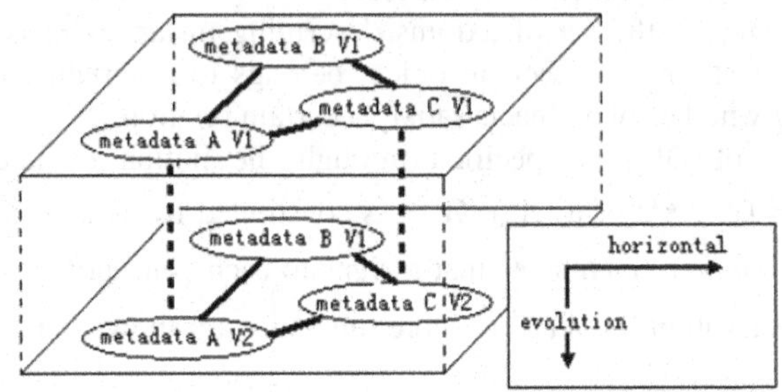

Fig. 1. Horizontal Consistency and Evolution Consistency

3.1 Formalization in Horizontal Consistency Checking

Taking advantage of the explicit information in the metamodel and the implicit information obtained by reasoning, consistency checking is the reasoning on the metadata which is the instance of metamodel, so we translate the metamodel into the Tbox and the metadata which is the instance of metamodel into the Abox. To be precise and brief, the following formalization is described in DL_{id} expressions.

3.1.1 Formalization of CWM Metamodel

(1) Metaclasses

In CWM metamodel, a *metaclass* is also a class, so in the following we don't distinguish metaclass and class. A metaclass is graphically rendered as a rectangle divided into two parts. The first part contains the *name* of the metaclass; the second part contains the *attributes* of the metaclass, each denoted by a name and with an associated class, which indicates the domain of the attribute values. For example, the attribute *namespace: Namespace* of metaclass *ModelElement* means that each namespace is an instance of *Namespace*. Each "/" indicates that the type of the attribute is the metaclass already included in the metamodel, i.e., the metaclass that the attribute belongs to is associated with the metaclass that is the type of the attribute.

A CWM metaclass is represented by a DL_{id} concept. This follows naturally from the fact that both CWM metaclasses and DL_{id} concepts denote sets of objects.

A CWM attribute a of type C' for a class C associates to each instance of C, zero, one, or more instances of a class C', so we think of an attribute a of type C' for a class C as a binary relation between instances of C and instances of C'. We capture such a binary relation by means of a role a of DL_{id}. To specify the type of the attribute we use the assertion:

$$C \sqsubseteq \forall[1](a \Rightarrow (2 : C'))$$

Such an assertion specifies precisely that, for each instance c of the concept C, all objects related to c by a, are instances of C′. It also indicates that an attribute name is not necessarily unique in the whole metadata, and hence two different metaclasses could have the same attribute, possibly of different types. Note that although the attributes after "/" denote associations between C and C′, the formalization of such attributes is necessary, because one attribute of C may has several corresponding associations between C and C′, if we only formalize the corresponding associations, the name of the attribute may be lost.

(2) Aggregation Associations
An *aggregation association* in CWM metamodel, graphically rendered as in Figure 2 (attributes are ignored), is a binary relation between the instances of two metaclasses, denoting a part-whole relationship. For example, the aggregation association between metaclass *Classifier* and *Feature* specifies that each instance of *Classifier* is made up of a set of instances of *Feature*. Observe that in CWM, names of aggregation associations (as names of metaclasses) are *unique*. In other words, there can't be two aggregation associations with the same name.

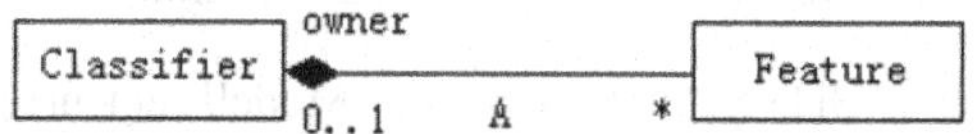

Fig. 2. Aggregation association in CWM

The general form of the formalization of aggregation association is that if instances of the metaclass C_1 have components that are instances of metaclass C_2 by aggregation association A, the multiplicity on C_1 is $m_1..m_2$, the multiplicity on C_2 is $n_1..n_2$, then A is formalized in DL_{id} by means of a role A, and the following assertions are added to the Tbox:

$$A \sqsubseteq (1 : C_1) \sqcap (2 : C_2)$$
$$C_1 \sqsubseteq (\geq n_1[1]A) \sqcap (\leq n_2[1]A)$$
$$C_2 \sqsubseteq (\geq m_1[2]A) \sqcap (\leq m_2[2]A)$$

The second assertion specifies that for each instance of C_1, there can be at least n_1 and at most n_2 instances of C_2 related to it by role A. Note that the distinction between the contained metaclass and the containing metaclass isn't lost. Indeed, we simply use the following convention: the first argument of the role is the containing class. So the aggregation association shown in Figure 2 is formalized by means of the assertions (the multiplicities 0..* on *Feature* and 0 on *Classifier* are omitted):

$$A \sqsubseteq (1 : Classifier) \sqcap (2 : Feature)$$
$$Feature \sqsubseteq (\leq 1[2]A)$$

Role names in metamodel are not formalized, such as the role name *owner* of *Classifier*, because if we want to keep track of them in the formalization, it suffices to consider them as convenient abbreviations for the components of the DL_{id} role modeling the aggregation.

(3) Ordinary Associations

Although *association class* isn't supported by CWM, each *ordinary association* has a corresponding association class for the conceptual perspective. To capture the information of an ordinary association, we formalize each ordinary association into a DL_{id} concept.

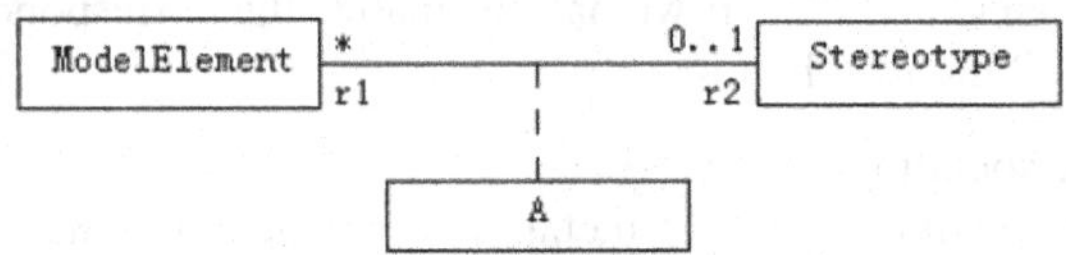

Fig. 3. Ordinary association in CWM

For example, we represent an ordinary association shown in Figure 3 by introducing a concept A and two roles r_1, r_2, one for each component of the ordinary association A. Each role has A as its first component and concept *ModelElement* or *Stereotype* as its second component. Then we enforce the following assertion:

$$A \sqsubseteq \exists[1]\, r_1 \sqcap \forall[1]\,(r_1 \Rightarrow (2 : \text{ModelElement})) \sqcap$$
$$\exists[1]\, r_2 \sqcap (\leq 1[1]\, r_2) \sqcap \forall[1]\,(r_2 \Rightarrow (2 : \text{Stereotype}))$$

Note that the presentation of r_1 and r_2 is different from that in aggregation association because the names of DL_{id} roles (which correspond to the components of an ordinary association) are unique wrt the ordinary association only, not the entire metamodel. $\exists[1]\, r_i (i \in \{1,2\})$specifies that the concept A must have all components r_1, r_2 of the ordinary association A; $\leq 1[1]\, r_2$ specifies that the corresponding component is single-valued; $\forall[1]\,(r_1 \Rightarrow (2 : \text{ModelElement}))$specifies that the second component of r_1 has to belong to *ModelElement*. Finally we use the assertion:

$$(\text{id } A\ [1]r_1,\ [1]r_2)$$

to specify that each instance of the concept A indeed represents a distinct tuple of the corresponding association. By imposing suitable number restrictions on r_1 and r_2, we can easily represent a multiplicity on an ordinary association. Differently from aggregation association, the names of DL_{id} roles (which correspond to the components of an ordinary association) may be not unique wrt the entire metamodel, so the assertions which represent the multiplicities of an ordinary association are slightly different from those of an aggregation association. The multiplicities shown in Figure 3 are captured as follows:

$$\text{ModelElement} \sqsubseteq (\geq 0\ [2]\,(r_1 \sqcap (1 : A))) \sqcap (\leq 1\ [2]\,(r_1 \sqcap (1 : A)))$$

(4) Generalization and Inheritance

In CWM metamodel, one can use *generalization* between a parent class and a child class to specify that each instance of the child class is also an instance of the parent class. Hence the instances of the child class inherit the prosperities of the parent class, but typically they satisfy additional properties that do not hold for the parent class.

Generalization is naturally supported in DL_{id}. In CWM, the metaclass *Element* generalizes *ModelElement*, we can express this by the DL_{id} assertion: ModelElement $\sqsubseteq$ Element.

Inheritance between DL_{id} concepts works exactly as inheritance between CWM metaclasses. This is an obvious consequence of the semantics of "$\sqsubseteq$" which is based on subsetting. Indeed, in DL_{id}, given an assertion $C_1 \sqsubseteq C_2$, every tuple in a role having C_2 as i-th argument type may have as i-th component an instance of C_1, which is in fact also an instance of C_2. As a consequence, in the formalization, each attribute of C_2, and each aggregation association and each ordinary association involving C_2 are correctly inherited by C_1. Observe that the formalization in DL_{id} also captures directly multiple inheritance between metaclasses.

(5) Constraints

In CWM metamodel, there are constraints expressed in the Object Constraint Language(OCL). These OCL constraints are used to express in an informal way information which can not be expressed by other constructs of CWM metamodel. Some constraints can be captured in DL_{id}, and reasoning about them is decidable. For example, the OCL constraint [C-4-4] in *Behavioral Package*: An *Interface* can only contain *Operations*, can be captured by:

$$\text{Interface} \sqsubseteq \forall \text{Classifier-Feature} \,.\, \text{Operation}$$

The other OCL constraints are essentially full first order logic formulas, hence they would make reasoning undecidable, so we don't consider these OCL constraints.

3.1.2 Formalization of CWM-Based Metadata

Each element in CWM metadata is an instance of the corresponding metaclass in metamodel. Each relation between elements is the instance of the corresponding association between metaclasses, so metadata should be formalized into the Abox in DL_{id} knowledge base. General forms are as follows:

(1) if element c in metadata is the instance of metaclass C in metamodel, then we have:

$$c : C \text{ or } C(c)$$

(2) if element c_1 in metadata aggregates c_2, the corresponding metaclsss C_1 (its ancestor) aggregates C_2 (its ancestor) by aggregation association A, aggregation association A is translated as role A in the Tbox, then we have:

$$< c_1 , c_2 > : A$$

(3) if element c_1 in metadata is related to c_2 by non-aggregation, the corresponding metaclass C_1 (its ancestor) is related to C_2 (its ancestor) by an ordinary association which is translated as concept A and roles r_1, r_2, then the relation between c_1 and c_2 can be captured by:

$$a : A$$
$$< a , c_1 > : r_1$$
$$< a , c_2 > : r_2$$

According to the rules above, the metadata shown in Figure 4 can be formalized by means of the assertions:

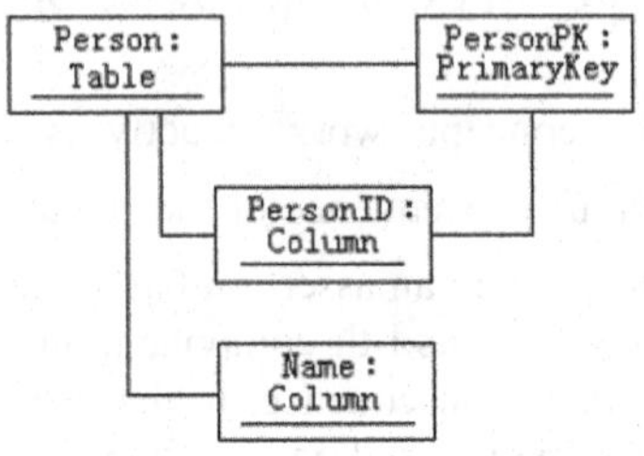

Fig. 4. Metadata for relational table

Person : Table
PersonID : Column
Name : Column
PersonPK : PrimaryKey
<Person , PersonID> : ColumnSet-Column
<Person , Name> : ColumnSet-Column
<Person , PersonPK> : Table-PrimaryKey
ColumnVUniqueConstraint : ColumnVUniqueConstraint
<ColumnVUniqueConstraint , PersonPK> : ColumnVUniqueConstraint-UniqueConstraint
<ColumnVUniqueConstraint , PersonID> : ColumnVUniqueConstraint-Column

3.2 Illustration in Horizontal Consistency Checking

After the construction of DL_{id} knowledge base, the query and reasoning mechanism of the reasoning tool will allow the query and reasoning on metadata so that various inconsistencies can be detected. After a study of each reasoning tool, we choose LOOM[13] which has a very expressive concept definition language and a powerful query and retrieval mechanism. The query facility and production rules of LOOM can be used to detect inconsistencies. Although the classification algorithm of LOOM is incomplete[18], it is complete on the knowledge base we introduce. However, although reasoning over the DL_{id} knowledge base is decidable, indeed, it is EXPTIME-complete, current LOOM is not able to deal with identification constraints which are needed to fully capture in DL_{id} the semantics of ordinary associations, so it is necessary to extend LOOM with capabilities of describing and reasoning about identification constraints. For the purpose of testing our approach, here we make proper simplification by translating each ordinary association into a role. After such simplification, LOOM can be used to check a majority of known inconsistencies although the semantics of CWM metamodel and metadata is not fully captured in DL_{id}. The following is an illustration in which LOOM is used to detect the violation of constraints:

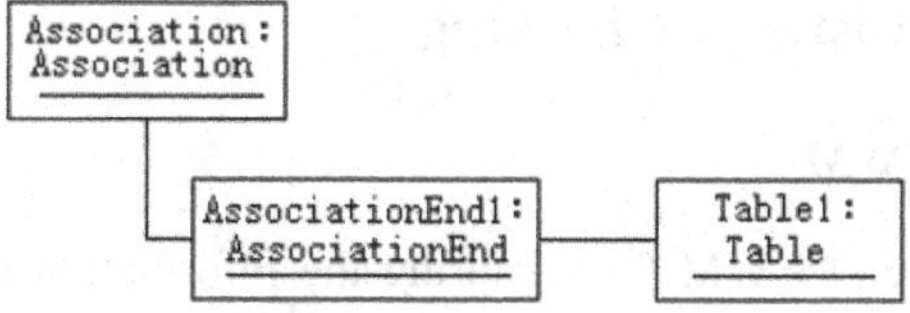

Fig. 5. Metadata: multiplicity conflict

An example of the inconsistency which arises when the multiplicity constraints are violated is shown in Figure 5, the metadata element *Association* which is an instance of metaclass *Association* aggregates *AssociationEnd1* which is an instance of *AssociationEnd*, *AssociationEnd1* is associated with *Table1* which is an instance of metaclass *Table*. According to the metamodel, an instance of *Association* should aggregate at least two instances of *AssociationEnd* by *Association-AssociationEnd*, in Figure 5, an instance of *Association* aggregates one instance of *AssociationEnd* only. In reality, what the metadata represents is probably two or more associated instances of *Table*, so the metadata is violating the multiplicity constraints imposed by metamodel, conflict arises.

The inconsistency above can be detected by the following function:

```
(defun  multiplicity (?association  ?metadata-A)
...  //the part omitted queries the knowledge base,
detects Association which is the corresponding
metaclass of ?association and Association aggregates
AssociationEnd by aggregation association Association-
AssociationEnd.
(let* ((?count1 (length (retrieve (?associationEnd)
(:and
(Association-AssociationEnd
?association  ?associationEnd)
(Namespace-ModelElement  ?associationEnd  ?metadata-
A)))))
(?count2 (get-role-min-cardinality (get-concept
'Association)(get-relation 'Association-AssociationEnd
))))
(if (<  ?count1  ?count2)
(format t "Multiplicity conflict: ~S aggregates ~S
elements, at least ~S is needed~%"  ?association
?count1  ?count2))))
```

Given the metadata context and an element, the function queries the Tbox to obtain the bottom limit of the multiplicity range of the aggregation association related to the element imposed by the metamodel, and then compares it with the result that is obtained by querying the Abox, if the constraint is disobeyed, the user is notified. The function is applied to the metadata we create intentionally with the conflict shown in Figure 5, the result is:

```
Multiplicity conflict: | I | ASSOCIATION aggregates 1
elements, at least 2 is needed
```

4 Evolution Consistency Checking

4.1 Extension for CWM

It is necessary to extend CWM for capturing the information needed for reasoning about evolving metadata. Because versioning capabilities are not supported by CWM currently, each version of metadata has to be saved to a different XML file, the information during metadata evolution is difficult to be tracked, and we have to extend CWM to enable it to support the record of evolution information, so as to make it possible to maintain consistency during metadata evolution.

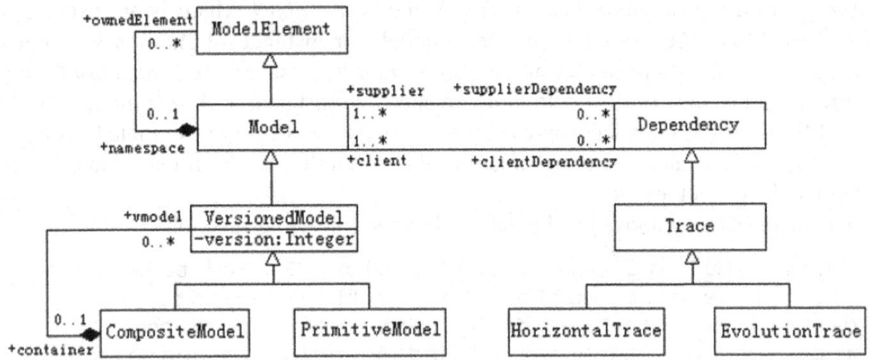

Fig. 6. Extension for CWM

We extend CWM metamodel by defining six metaclasses: *VersionedModel*, *CompositeModel*, *PrimitiveModel*, *Trace*, *HorizontalTrace*, *EvolutionTrace* as shown in Figure 6. *ModelElement*, *Model*, *Dependency* belong to the *Core Package*. The intermediate metaclasses *Namespace* and *Package* between *Model* and *ModelElement* are ignored for the sake of brief, the hierarchy has been flattened, maintaining only the subclass *Model*. The *namespace* relationship is now assumed by *Model*. Metaclass *Trace*, the subclass of *Dependency*, is used to indicate the evolution information of ModelElements. In order to record metadata versions, evolution, the *Model* metaclass is stereotyped into *VersionedModel*, so as to include a tag-value pair (version, *Integer*) that indicates the metadata version information. To specify the type of metadata that can be related by horizontal consistency or evolution consistency, *VersionedModel* is stereotyped into *PrimitiveModel* and *CompositeModel*, which indicate the metadata of the single component of data warehouse systems and the metadata which is the product of integration, respectively. *CompositeModel* is a container for all the *PrimitiveModels* that belong to the same version. In order to keep track of the metadata belonging to a *CompositeModel*, a tag-value pair (vmodel, *Set(VersionedModel)*) is introduced. For *VersionedModel*, a tag-value pair (container, *CompositeModel*) is needed. Both tag-value pairs are represented together as a bidirectional association in Figure 6. In addition, the following constraints must be specified:

(1) A *CompositeModel* contains zero or more *VersionedModels.*
(2) A *HorizontalTrace* can only be specified between the same *PrimitiveModel* belonging to the same *CompositeModel.*
(3) An *EvolutionTrace* can only be specified between different versions of the same *CompositeModel*, or between different versions of the same *PrimitiveModel.*
(4) With respect to two models participating in an *EvolutionTrace*, the version number of the *client* model must be greater than that of the *supplier* model.

In the using of extended metamodel, the metadata that is in the same version and belongs to different components is the instance of *CompositeModel*, Elements in metadata are owned by the instance of *CompositeModel* which acts as namespace, while the instance of *EvolutionTrace* is related to different versions of the same metadata by supplier association and client association, respectively.

4.2 Formalization in Evolution Consistency Checking

During the formalization in evolution consistency checking, the extension part in metamodel and the corresponding part in metadata should be added to the Tbox and the Abox, respectively. The other part is the same as that in horizontal consistency checking, here it is ignored.

4.3 Illustration in Evolution Consistency Checking

The following is an example with the evolution-induced conflict. If a relational table *Worker* has a foreign key *WorkshopID*, while the relational table *Workshop* that has the key as its primary key has been removed or may have not been included in the metadata, then the foreign key of the first table doesn't exist as the primary key of another table, the inconsistency arises.

The following function can be applied to detect the inconsistency above:

```
(defun  foreignkey (?foreignkey  ?metadata-v1)
(let* ((?count (length (retrieve (?table2)
(:and  (Column  ?column)
(Namespace-ModelElement  ?column  ?metadata-v1)
(ColumnSet-Column  ?table1  ?column)
(Namespace-ModelElement  ?table1  ?metadata-v1)
(Table-ForeignKey  ?table1  ?foreignkey)
(ForeignKey-Column  ?foreignkey  ?column)
(Table  ?table2)
(Namespace-ModelElement  ?table2  ?metadata-v1)
(Table-PrimaryKey  ?table2  ?primarykey)
(Namespace-ModelElement  ?primarykey  ?metadata-v1)
(UniqueConstraint-Column  ?primarykey  ?column))))))
(if (=  ?count  0)
(do-retrieve(?metadata-v2)
(:and  (Dependency  ?dependency)
(Model-Dependency-c  ?metadata-v1  ?dependency)
```

```
(Model-Dependency-s ?metadata-v2 ?dependency)
... //the omitted part requires that ?table2 belongs
to ?metadata-v2 and has ?column as its primary key,
?table1 belongs to ?metadata-v2 and has ?column as its
foreign key.
(format t "ForeignKey reference conflict: Foreign ~S of
the table ~S does not exist in ~S,while exists in ~S"
?column ?table1 ?metadata-v1 ?metadata-v2)))))
```

Given a foreign key and the metadata context it belongs to, the function queries the knowledge base, looking for tables that have the foreign key as their primary keys, if no table is found, the inconsistency arises. Then queries the related versions of the metadata according to evolution trace, if succeeds, the information about the inconsistency will be printed. The function is applied to the metadata we create intentionally with the conflict above, the result is:

```
ForeignKey reference conflict: Foreign | I | WORKSHOPID
of the table | I | WORKER does not exist in | I |
METADATA-A-V1,while exists in | I | METADATA-A-V2
```

5 Related Work

Until today, to the best of our knowledge, little related research on the argument in this paper is found. In what follows, we review some of the most relevant researches. Barton et al. [4] and Randall et al. [5] elaborate the inconsistencies may be encountered during metadata creation and integration, and present strategies to resolve it. Finkelstein et al. [16] elaborate a list of the technical challenges that arise when trying to build a toolset that deals with evolution and consistency. Tools dealing with these two aspects should help establish, express and reason about the relationships between formal languages and check consistency wrt these relationships and to provide diagnostic feedback. Finkelstein et al. [11] explain that consistency between partial models is not always possible, they suggest the use of temporal logic to identify and handle inconsistencies. This formalism is used to describe sequences of actions that lead to inconsistencies, unlike the approach taken in this paper that uses logic to find inconsistencies. Diego et al. [8] introduce DLR_{reg}, an expressive Description Logic with n-ary relations, for specifying database schemas and queries, they discuss whether the problem of checking query containment under the constraints is decidable. In [9], they extend DLR_{reg} so that it can be used to formalize and reason on a great variety of data models, including the relational, the entity-relational, and the object-oriented model, they also discuss the decidability problems and computational complexity of reasoning in the extended Description Logic. Simmonds [7] proposes the approach to deal with inconsistencies between UML class, statechart and sequence diagrams by means of Description Logics. Andy [6] and Andrea et al. [12] propose the approaches of formalization and reasoning on UML class diagrams, respectively, but they all don't take advantage of the information from the metamodel. In addition, Francesco et al. [17] survey the related researches on the relationship between expressive power and computational complexity of reasoning of Description Logics. Mens et al. [20] explain the extension mechanism of UML, and propose the strategies to extend the UML metamodel with support for evolution.

6 Conclusion

In this paper, we propose a new approach to formalize CWM metamodel and the metadata based on CWM in terms of a particular formal logic of the family of Description Logics, and to reason on metadata so that inconsistencies can be detected. The approach can detect automatically not only the inconsistency information irrelevant to evolution but also that caused by evolution. The approach can be favorably exploited for developing intelligent system that support automated reasoning on CWM metadata, so as to provide support for the development of the components of data warehouse systems, thus improve the reliability of metadata integration and data warehouse system. We have already started experimenting such systems, the first results are encouraging.

The future work is as follows:

(1) It is of interest to characterize interesting fragments of OCL constraints that do not lead to undecidability and study how to translate these into DL_{id}.
(2) The inconsistency information in the metadata to test our approach is artificially introduced, next work is to test our approach in practical systems, as these will provide the metadata with more natural inconsistencies and evolution steps.
(3) Current work concentrates on automatically detecting inconsistencies, automatically solving these inconsistencies will be studied in the future.

References

1. F. Baader, D. McGuinness, D. Nardi, P.F. Patel-Schneider. The Description Logic Handbook: Theory, Implementation and Applications. Cambridge University Press, 2003.
2. Object Management Group. Common Warehouse Metamodel(CWM) Specification Version 1.1. November 2001.
3. John Poole, Dan Chang, Douglas Tolbert, David Mellor. Common Warehouse Metamodel Developer's Guide. New York, John Wiley & Sons Inc, January 2003.
4. Barton Jane, Currier Sarah, Hey Jessie M. N. Building Quality Assurance into Metadata Creation: an Analysis based on the Learning Objects and e-Prints Communities of Practice. In Proceedings 2003 Dublin Core Conference: Supporting Communities of Discourse and Practice - Metadata Research and Applications(DCMI), Seattle, Washington, 2003: 39-48.
5. Randall Hauch, Alex Miller, Rob Cardwell. Information intelligence: metadata for information discovery, access, and integration. In Proceedings of the 2005 ACM SIGMOD international conference on Management of data, 2005: 793-798.
6. Andy S. Evans. Reasoning with UML class diagrams. In Second IEEE Workshop on Industrial Strength Formal Specification Techniques(WIFT98), 1998.
7. J. Simmonds. Consistency maintenance of uml models with description logic. Master's thesis, Vrije Universiteit Brussel, September 2003.
8. Diego Calvanese, Giuseppe De Giacomo, Maurizio Lenzerini. On the decidability of query containment under constraints. In Proc. of the 17th ACM SIGACT SIGMOD SIGART Symp. on Principles of Database Systems(POD'98), 1998: 149-158
9. Diego Calvanese, Giuseppe De Giacomo, Maurizio Lenzerini. Identification constraints and functional dependencies in description logics. In Proc. of the 17th Int. Joint Conf. on Artificial Intelligence(IJCAI 2001), 2001.

10. Volker Haarslev, Ralf Moller. RACER system description. In Proc. of the Int. Joint Conf. on Automated Reasoning(IJCAR 2001), 2001
11. Anthony Finkelstein, Dov M. Gabbay, Anthony Hunter, Jeff Kramer, Bashar Nuseibeh. Inconsistency handling in multi-perspective specifications. In European Software Engineering Conference, 1993: 84-99.
12. Andrea Cali, Diego Calvanese, Giuseppe De Giacomo, Maurizio Lenzerini. A formal framework for reasoning on UML class diagrams. In Proc. of the 13th Int. Sym. on Methodologies for Intelligent Systems (ISMIS'02), 2002: 503-513.
13. David Brill. LOOM reference manual, version 2.0 edition. University of Southern California, Information Sciences Institute, December 28 1993.
14. John C. Grundy, John G. Hosking, Warwick B. Mugridge. Inconsistency management for multiple-view software development environments. IEEE Transactions on Software Engineering, 1998, 24(11): 960-981.
15. Object Management Group. Unified Modeling Language specification version 1.4. September 2001.
16. Finkelstein. A Foolish Consistency: Technical Challenges in Consistency Management. In Proceedings of the 11th International Conference on Database and Expert Systems Applications(DEXA), London, UK, September 2000.
17. Francesco M. Donini, Maurizio Lenzerini, Daniele Nardi, Andrea Schaerf. Reasoning in description logics. In Principles of Knowledge Representation, Studies in Logic, Language and Information, 1996: 193-238.
18. Robert MacGregor. Inside the LOOM description classifier. SIGART Bull, 1991, 2(3): 88–92.
19. Ian Horrocks. FaCT and iFaCT. In International Workshop on Description Logics(DL99), 1999: 133-135.
20. Tom Mens, Theo D'Hondt. Automating support for software evolution in uml. Automated Software Engineering Journal, February 2000, 7(1): 39–59.
21. Joaquin Miller, Jishnu Mukerji. Model driven architecture (MDA). Draft ormsc/2001-07-01, Architecture Board ORMSC, July 2001.

A Set of QVT Relations to Assure the Correctness of Data Warehouses by Using Multidimensional Normal Forms

Jose-Norberto Mazón[1], Juan Trujillo[1], and Jens Lechtenbörger[2]

[1] Dept. of Software and Computing Systems
University of Alicante, Spain
{jnmazon, jtrujillo}@dlsi.ua.es
[2] Dept. of Information Systems
University of Münster, Germany
lechten@wi.uni-muenster.de

Abstract. It is widely accepted that a requirement analysis phase is necessary to develop data warehouses (DWs) which adequately represent the information needs of DW users. Moreover, since the DW integrates the information provided by data sources, it is also crucial to take these sources into account throughout the development process to obtain a consistent representation. In this paper, we use multidimensional normal forms to define a set of Query/View/Transformation (QVT) relations to assure that the DW designed from user requirements agrees with the available data sources that will populate the DW. Thus, we propose a hybrid approach to develop DWs, i.e., we firstly obtain the conceptual schema of the DW from user requirements and then we verify and enforce its correctness against data sources by using a set of QVT relations based on multidimensional normal forms.

1 Introduction

A data warehouse (DW) is commonly described as an integrated collection of historical data in support of decision making that structures information into facts and dimensions based on multidimensional (MD) modeling [1,2]. Since the DW integrates several data sources, the development of conceptual MD models has traditionally been guided by an analysis of these data sources [3,4,5]. Considering these data-driven approaches, MNFs (multidimensional normal forms) have been developed [6] to reason, in a rigorous manner, about the quality (faithfulness, completeness, avoidance of redundancies, summarizability) of a conceptual MD model derived from operational data sources.

Nevertheless, in these data-driven approaches the requirement analysis phase is overlooked, thus resulting in an MD model in which the user needs and expectations may not be satisfied [7]. To overcome this problem, several approaches [7,8,9,10] advocate a requirement-driven DW design process. However, hardly any of these approaches considers the data sources in the early stages of the development. Therefore, the correctness of the MD model with respect to

D.W. Embley, A. Olivé, and S. Ram (Eds.): ER 2006, LNCS 4215, pp. 385–398, 2006.

the data sources cannot be assured and the DW repository cannot be properly populated from these data sources.

In order to reconcile these two points of view (data-driven and requirement-driven), a Model Driven Architecture (MDA) [11] framework for the development of DWs has been described in [12]. Within this approach a conceptual MD model of the DW repository is developed from user requirements. This MD model must be then conformed to data sources in order to assure its correctness.

In this paper, we focus on presenting a set of Query/View/Transformation (QVT) relations in order to check the correctness of the MD conceptual model against the available data sources within our MDA framework. These QVT relations are based on MNFs proposed in [6]. The QVT language allows us to easily integrate this approach in our MDA framework from the development of DWs [12], while MNFs enable us to formalize the relationship between the data sources and the MD conceptual model of the DW repository.

The motivation of our approach is as follows: since the DW integrates the information provided by source databases, it is important to check (in early stages of the development) if the requirement-driven MD conceptual model agrees with the available data sources in order to assure that (i) the DW repository will be properly populated from data sources, (ii) the analysis potential provided by the data sources is captured by the MD conceptual model, (iii) redundancies are avoided, and (iv) optional dimension levels, i.e., levels allowing NULL values, are controlled via specialization/generalization to enable context-sensitive summarizability and to avoid inconsistent queries.

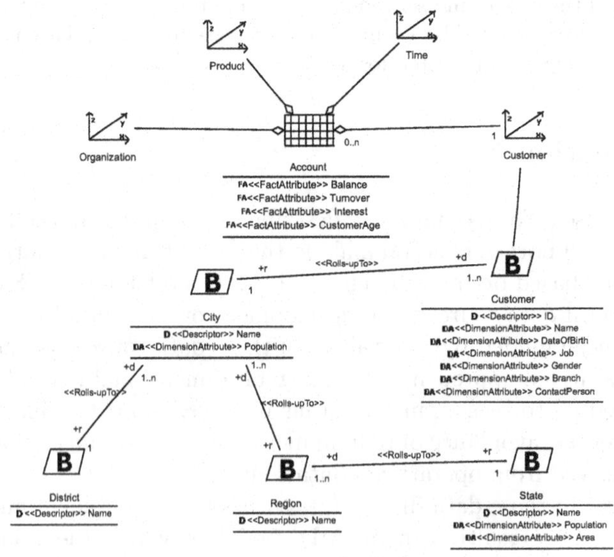

Fig. 1. MD model for banking domain

To illustrate these benefits, consider the following running example, which is inspired by an example of [6]. We assume that the MD conceptual model for the banking domain shown in Fig. 1 has been derived from analysis requirements *without* taking data sources into account, e.g., according to the guidelines presented in [9]. The notation of Fig. 1 is based on a UML profile for MD modeling presented in [13] (see Section 4.2 for details). The figure models Account facts which are composed of several measures (balance, turnover, interest, and customerAge) and described by dimensions Organization, Product, Time, and Customer. Due to space constraints, we only focus on the Customer dimension.

Every customer is described in terms of a unique identification number, a name, and a date of birth. Every customer lives in a city which is described with a name and a population. Moreover, customers may be associated with job, gender, industry branch, and contact person. Finally, a city belongs to (RollsupTo) exactly one region and exactly one district, while a region belongs to exactly one state.

This model represents a geographical classification where every region falls into exactly one state, while districts and states appear to be unrelated. From a conceptual perspective, this classification seems reasonable. However, if the data sources provide geographical information where every district falls into exactly one state, while regions and states are unrelated then (i) the source information concerning regions and states cannot be represented faithfully under the MD model and (ii) potential for roll-up queries from level district to level state is not represented, i.e., analysis potential is lost. Moreover, the MD model does not represent the structural information that industry branches and contact persons are assigned only to company customers while job and gender are only applicable to private customers, which poses challenges for summarizability and complicates querying (see [6,14]). Finally, while it certainly makes sense to analyze the age structure of customers, the measure age is not specific to accounts but only to customers. Thus, this measure should be moved to a different fact schema. To summarize, based on schema information for the data sources, the MD conceptual model shown in Fig. 1 should be improved in a number of ways to obtain the "better" model shown in Fig. 2. Indeed, in this paper we show how to apply QVT relations, which are derived from MNFs, to obtain the model shown in Fig. 2 from the model shown in Fig. 1 by taking source databases into account.

The remainder of this paper is structured as follows: Related work is put into perspective next, before necessary background concerning QVT and MNFs is collected in Section 3. Our approach is presented in Section 4 by describing data source model as well as MD conceptual model, and defining QVT relations based on MNFs. The application of sample QVT relations is illustrated in Section 5. The paper ends with conclusions and suggestions for future work in Section 6.

2 Related Work

In this section, we briefly describe the most relevant approaches for both data-driven and requirement-driven DW development.

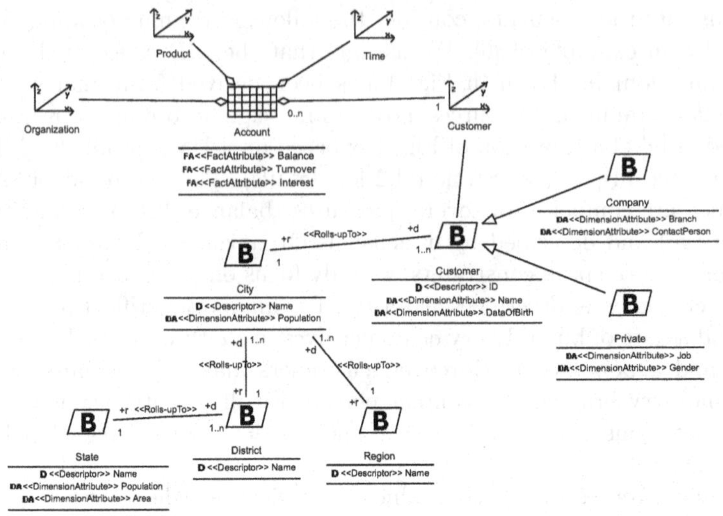

Fig. 2. Improved MD model for banking domain

Concerning data-driven approaches, in [4], the authors present the Multidimensional Model, a logical model for MD databases. The authors also propose a general design method, aimed at building an MD schema starting from an operational database described by an Entity-Relationship (ER) schema.

In [3], the authors propose the Dimensional-Fact Model (DFM), a particular notation for the DW conceptual design. Moreover, they also propose how to derive a DW schema from the data sources described by ER schemas. Also in [15], the building of a conceptual MD model of the DW repository from the conceptual schemas of the operational data sources is proposed.

In [5], the authors present a method to systematically derive a conceptual MD model from data sources. In this paper a preliminary set of multidimensional normal forms is used to assure the quality of the resulting conceptual model.

Although in each of these data-driven approaches the design steps are described in a systematic and coherent way, the DW design is only based on the operational data sources, what we consider insufficient because the final user requirements are very important in the DW design [7].

Concerning requirement-driven approaches, in [7] an approach is proposed in order to both determine information requirements of DW users and match these requirements with actual data sources. However, no formal approach is given in order to match requirements with data sources.

In [8], the authors propose a requirement elicitation process for DWs by grouping requirements in several levels of abstraction. Their process consists of identifying information that supports decision making via information scenarios. In this process, a Goal-Decision-Information (GDI) diagram is used. Although the derivation of GDI diagrams and information scenarios is described, the relationships between information scenarios and requirements are not properly specified.

Moreover, requirements are not conformed to data sources in order to obtain a conceptual MD model.

In [10], the authors present a framework to obtain a conceptual MD model from requirements. This framework uses the data sources to shape hierarchies and user requirements are used to choose facts, dimensions and measures. However, the authors do not present a formal way to conform data sources and the MD conceptual model.

As a survey, we wish to point out that these requirement-driven approaches do not formalize the relation between the data sources and the requirements to verify and enforce the correctness of the resulting DW. Therefore, we propose to use MNFs [6] in a systematic manner, thus formalizing the development of the DW repository by means of (i) obtaining a conceptual MD model from user requirements, and (ii) verifying and enforcing its correctness against the operational data sources. Details on MNFs are presented in the next section.

3 Background

In this section, we provide a brief overview of the building blocks of our approach, namely Query/View/Transformation and Multidimensional Normal Forms.

3.1 Query/View/Transformation Language

The MOF 2.0 Query/View/Transformation (QVT) language [16] is a standard approach for defining formal relations between MOF-compliant models. Furthermore QVT is an essential part of the MDA standard as a means of defining formal and automatic transformations between models.

QVT consists of two parts: declarative and imperative. The declarative part provides mechanisms to define relations that must hold between the model elements of a set of candidate models (source and target models). This declarative part can be split into two layers according to the level of abstraction: the relational layer that provides graphical and textual notation for a declarative specification of relations, and the core layer that provides a simpler, but verbose, way of defining relations. The imperative part defines operational mappings that extend the declarative part with imperative implementations when it is difficult to provide a purely declarative specification of a relation.

In this paper, we focus on the relational layer of QVT. This layer supports the specification of relationships that must hold between MOF models by means of a relations language. A relation is defined by the following elements:

- **Two or more domains**: each domain is a set of elements of a source or a target model. The kind of relation between domains must be specified: checkonly (C), i.e., it is only checked if the relation holds or not; and enforced (E), i.e., the target model can be modified to satisfy the relation.
- **When clause**: it specifies the conditions under which the relation needs to hold (i.e. precondition).

– **Where clause**: it specifies the condition that must be satisfied by all model elements participating in the relation (i.e. postcondition).

Defining relations by using the QVT language has the following advantages: (i) it is a standard language, (ii) relations are formally established and automatically performed, and (iii) relations can be easily integrated in an MDA approach.

3.2 Multidimensional Normal Forms

The formal guidelines that we are using to formulate our QVT relations in the following are the three multidimensional normal forms 1MNF, 2MNF, and 3MNF presented in [6]. Here, we recapitulate the essence of these normal forms informally. The reader is referred to [6] for formal definitions. Preliminarily we recall that within an MD conceptual model the *terminal* dimension levels of a fact are those that are attached immediately to the dimensions, i.e., those that provide the finest level of detail within each dimension.

The goal of 1MNF is to ensure that an MD conceptual model "matches" with the information provided by the source databases. More specifically, 1MNF is characterized by four conditions as follows:

1. Faithfulness. The functional dependencies (FDs) implied by the MD model must be a subset of those observed in the source databases. (Otherwise, some source data cannot be represented under the MD model.)
2. Roll-up completeness. The FDs among dimension levels contained in the source databases must be represented as roll-up arcs in the MD model. (Otherwise, analysis potential is lost.)
3. Derivation completeness. The FDs among sets of measures contained in the source databases must be represented via derivation formulas in the MD model. (Otherwise, derivation relationships are lost.)
4. Avoidance of redundancies. Each measure must be assigned to a fact in such a way that the terminal dimension levels of the fact form a key for the measure without transitive dependencies. (Otherwise, a measure is recorded redundantly at the "wrong" level of detail. E.g., in Fig. 1 in the Introduction measure customerAge was repeated for each account owned by a customer.)

In addition to 1MNF, the normal forms 2MNF and 3MNF aim to control optional dimension levels by means of so-called *contexts of validity*. Roughly, a context of validity for an optional dimension level *explains* the occurrence (and absence) of structural null values (such as NULL for industry branch of private customers in Fig. 1) based on the values of so-called *discriminating levels*. E.g., for the scenario in Fig. 1, we may assume that in the data sources there is an attribute customerType with values "private" and "company", which acts as discriminating level, such that a customerType of "private" implies NULL for Branch and ContactPerson, whereas "company" implies NULL for Job and Gender. As argued in [14] and elaborated in more detail in [6], structural NULL values can and should be avoided by suitable introduction of specialization hierarchies. In fact, in [6] it has been shown that 3MNF allows to *construct* a class hierarchy of dimension levels with an implementation as relational database that *avoids null values*. Note that such a class hierarchy is indeed part of the improved model shown in Fig. 2.

Importantly, the MD model considered in [6] does *not* provide mechanisms for specialization/generalization explicitly, which necessitates the use of context dependencies. As in this paper we consider a richer MD model that explicitly supports subclassing, we are able to explain the occurrence of NULL values directly by moving an attribute with structural NULL values into the appropriate subclass. As a result, we obtain a simplified approach.

As explained in [6,14] control over NULL values enables context-sensitive summarizability (e.g., if an analyst rolls up from individual customers to industry branches, then schema information explains that the context of analysis has changed to a subclass of all customers) and avoids inconsistent queries (e.g., a query such as "group private customers by industry branch" can be rejected based on *schema* information).

4 Checking Correctness of the MD Conceptual Model

In this section, we present our approach to check the correctness of a conceptual MD model with respect to the source databases. To this end, we present a set of QVT relations based on MNFs and obtain their inherent desirable design objectives: The resulting MD conceptual model faithfully represents the data sources and captures their analysis potential completely, redundancies are avoided, and NULL values are controlled to allow context-sensitive summarizability and avoid contradictory queries. Our approach consists of two main phases:

First, the elements of the data sources are marked as dimensional elements (fact, dimension, measure and so on). Second, a set of QVT relations between the data source model and the MD conceptual model (previously derived from user requirements) are applied, thus checking and enforcing that the MD conceptual model is aligned with data sources.

4.1 Data Source Model

We assume that the data source model is the relational representation of the data sources in third normal form. (Note that third normal form is not a restriction as well-known algorithms such as Synthesis [17] can transform any input schema into third normal form.) In particular, we use the CWM (Common Warehouse Metamodel) relational metamodel [18] in order to specify this data source model. The CWM relational metamodel is a standard to represent the structure of data resources in a relational database and allows us to represent tables, columns, primary keys, foreign keys, and so on. Since every CWM metamodel is MOF-compliant [18], it can be used as source or target for QVT relations [16].

On the other hand, this data source model must be marked before the QVT relations can be applied. Marking models is a technique that provides mechanisms to extend elements of the models in order to capture additional information [11,19]. Marks are used in MDA to prepare the models in order to guide the matching between them. A mark represents a concept from one model, which can be applied to an element of other different model. These marks indicate how every element of the source model must be matched. In our approach, the data source model is marked by appending a suffix to the name of each element according to the MD conceptual model. In particular, we assume that the data source tables corresponding to MD model elements Fact, Dimension, and Base are marked with _FACT, _DIM, and _BASE, respectively, while data source columns corresponding to FactAttribute, DimensionAttribute, and Descriptor are marked with _MEASURE, _DA, and _D, respectively. Finally, a ForeignKey representing a Rolls-upTo element is marked with _ROLLS.

4.2 MD Conceptual Model

The conceptual modeling of the DW repository is based on a UML profile for MD modeling presented in [13]. This profile contains the necessary stereotypes in order to elegantly represent main MD properties at the conceptual level by means of a UML class diagram in which the information is clearly organized into facts and dimensions. These facts and dimensions are represented by *Fact* (represented as) and *Dimension* classes (represented as), respectively. *Fact* classes are defined as composite classes in shared aggregation relationships of n *Dimension* classes. A fact is composed of measures or fact attributes (*FactAttribute* stereotype, FA). Furthermore, derived measures (and their derivation rules) can also be explicitly represented as tagged values of a *FactAttribute.*

With respect to dimensions, each level of a classification hierarchy is specified by a *Base* class (B). Every *Base* class can contain several dimension attributes (*DimensionAttribute* stereotype, DA) and must also contain a *Descriptor* attribute (*D* stereotype, D). An association with a *Rolls-UpTo* stereotype (`<<Rolls-UpTo>>`) between *Base* classes specifies the relationship between two levels of a classification hierarchy. Within this association, role *R* represents the direction in which the hierarchy rolls up, whereas role *D* represents the direction in which the hierarchy drills down. An overview of our UML profile is given in Fig. 3. Apart from these defined stereotypes the generalization/specialization relationships of UML is used for suitably representing optional dimension levels.

Other MD issues are also defined by this UML profile (degenerate dimensions, degenerate facts, non-strict hierarchies, and so on), however they are not taken into account in this paper, since only the characteristics related to MNFs are considered.

4.3 QVT Relations

In the following, each QVT relation is described: Check1MNF1_1, Check1MNF1_2, Check1MNF1_3, Check1MNF1_4, Check1MNF2, Check1MNF3, and Check1MNF4 are based on the 1MNF; Check2MNF3MNF is based on both 2MNF and 3MNF.

The relations are applied as follows: first Check1MNF1_1, Check1MNF1_2, Check1MNF1_3, and Check1MNF1_4 are applied in order to check that the FDs of the MD model are contained in those of the sources (first condition of the

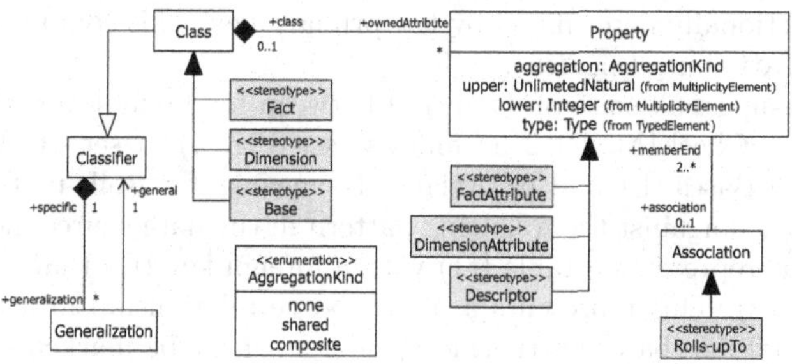

Fig. 3. Extension of the UML with the stereotypes used in this paper

1MNF); since both domains are check-only, it is only checked whether there exists a valid match that satisfies these relations without modifying any model if the domains do not match. If the check fails, there typically is no automatic solution, and the DW developer must redesign the MD conceptual model. (E.g., in our example given in Fig. 1, the user requirements express that Regions roll-up to States, whereas the data sources do not provide this information. Thus, either the conceptual model has to be modified as shown in Fig. 2 or the source data has to be aligned with the model.) Otherwise, i.e., if the check succeeds, the remaining relations can be applied to properly modify the MD conceptual model (according to the second, third, and fourth condition of 1MNF as well as according to 2MNF and 3MNF). Therefore, these QVT relations not only check the correctness of the MD conceptual model according to the data sources, but also enforce this correctness by creating the necessary elements of the MD conceptual model until each relation holds.

Throughout the checks, we assume that the names of corresponding elements in both models are equal (apart from the previously added marks) according to a linguistic approach based on name similarity [20]. This issue is captured in the *when* clause of each relation.

Verify 1MNF (first condition). According to this condition, for every FD in the MD conceptual model we have to check that there is a corresponding FD in the data source model, i.e., the FDs implied by the MD model must be a subset of those observed in the source databases. Therefore, this condition assures that the source data can be properly represented under the MD model. We have defined one QVT relation (see Fig. 4-5) for each situation in which an FD arises in the MD conceptual model in order to check if the same FD occurs in the data source model. These situations are as follows:

1. Descriptor determines DimensionAttributes. This is checked by Check-1MNF1_1 (see Fig. 4). The elements related to the MD conceptual model are the following: a Base (b), a Descriptor (d) and a DimensionAttribute (da). These elements of the MD conceptual model must be matched against a set of elements of the data source model: a table (t) with a column (c1) which is part of the primary key (pk). This table is marked as a Dimension or Base (m_n_t) and the column (c1) is marked as a Descriptor (m_n_c1). There is also a column (c2)

which is functionally determined by the primary key. This column is marked as a DimensionAttribute (m_n_c2).

2. A Rolls-upTo association is an FD between hierarchy levels (Bases). This is checked by Check1MNF1_2 as follows (see Fig. 4): a set of elements that represent two Bases (b1 and b2) related by means of a Rolls-upTo association must be checked against the following pattern in the data source model: a set of elements that represents a table (t1) with a foreign key (fk) that references the other table (t2). This represents a many-to-one relationship in a third normal form relational database. Furthermore, table t1 must be marked as Dimension or Base, t2 as Base and foreign key fk as Rolls-upTo.

3. Derived measures. This is checked by Check1MNF1_3 (see Fig. 4). It checks that if there is a derived FactAttribute (with a derivation rule) in the MD model, then in the data sources there must be a procedure which implements this derivation rule.

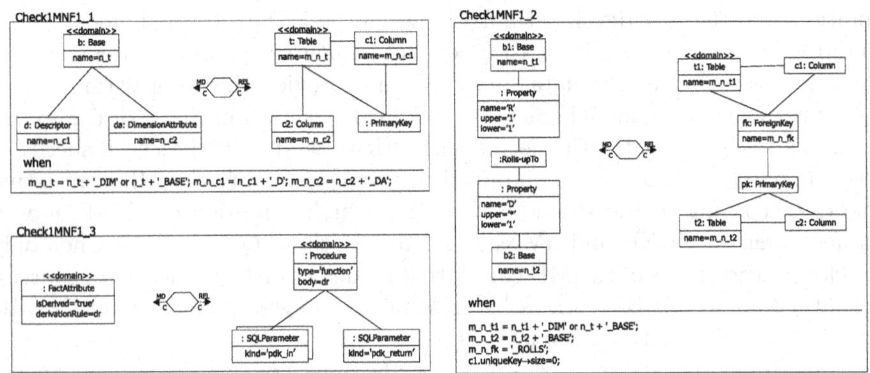

Fig. 4. QVT relations based on Multidimensional Normal Forms (1/2)

4. Dimensions (and their terminal dimension levels) functionally determine FactAttributes (i.e., measures). This is checked by Check1MNF1_4 (see Fig. 5). In this relation, a set of elements of the MD conceptual model that represent the relation between a Dimension (d), together with its terminal dimension level, i.e, Base (b) and a Fact (f) together with its attributes (fa) is matched against the following pattern of the data sources: a table (t1) with a column (c), a primary key (pk) which contains a foreign key that references another table (t2). Table t1 is marked as a Fact, while table t2 is marked as Dimension and column c is marked as FactAttribute.

Verify 1MNF (second condition). The Check1MNF2 relation checks this condition, i.e., roll-up completeness (the FDs among dimension levels contained in the source databases must be represented as roll-up arcs in the MD model). Therefore, if this relation holds then there exists a Rolls-upTo association between bases in the MD conceptual model if there is an FD between columns of different tables in the data source model. This relation is the same that the

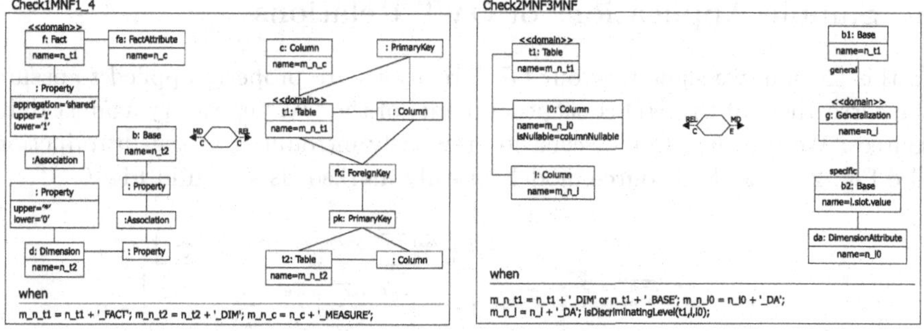

Fig. 5. QVT relations based on Multidimensional Normal Forms (2/2)

Check1MNF1_2 relation, but the kind of relation in the MD side is specified as *enforced*.

Verify 1MNF (third condition). This condition is related to derivation completeness (third condition of the 1MNF). If a certain measure can be computed from a set of other measures, then it indicates that there is an FD among measures. Therefore, the FDs among measures that appear in the data source model should be reflected as derived FactAttributes of the MD conceptual model. The relation that verifies this condition (Check1MNF3) is the same that Check1MNF1_3 (see Fig. 4), by specifying the kind of relation in the MD side as *enforced*.

Verify 1MNF (fourth condition). This condition (avoidance of redundancies) is checked by the Check1MNF4 relation. This relation is the same that the Check1MNF1_4 relation (see Fig. 5), but with an *enforced* kind in the MD side. Therefore, each measure must be assigned to a Fact (as a FactAttribute) in such a way that the terminal dimension levels of the Fact form a key for the measure without transitive dependencies.

Verify 2MNF and 3MNF. This relation is based on 2MNF and 3MNF. These normal forms control optional dimension levels by avoiding structural NULL values. The aim of this relation is check or enforce a class hierarchy of dimension levels in order to avoid these NULL values. As in this paper we consider an MD conceptual model that explicitly supports subclassing, this QVT relation covers both 2MNF and 3MNF by moving an attribute with structural NULL values into the appropriate subclass.

This relation is shown in Fig. 5. A table (t1) with two columns, an optional column (l0) and a discriminating level (l) is matched against a generalization hierarchy: a superclass is a base (b1), and a subclass is other base (b2) with a DimensionAttribute that corresponds to the optional column. Furthermore, we use context dependencies as schema level constraints to identify discriminating levels, so in the when clause there is a function (isDiscriminatingLevel) that checks whether the column l is a discriminating level according to the table t1 and the other column l0.

5 Sample Applications of QVT Relations

In this section, we show how our QVT relations are properly applied to assure the correctness of the MD conceptual model of the DW repository against data sources. We use the sample scenario previously introduced in the Introduction (see Fig. 2). The data source model (already marked) is shown in Fig. 6.

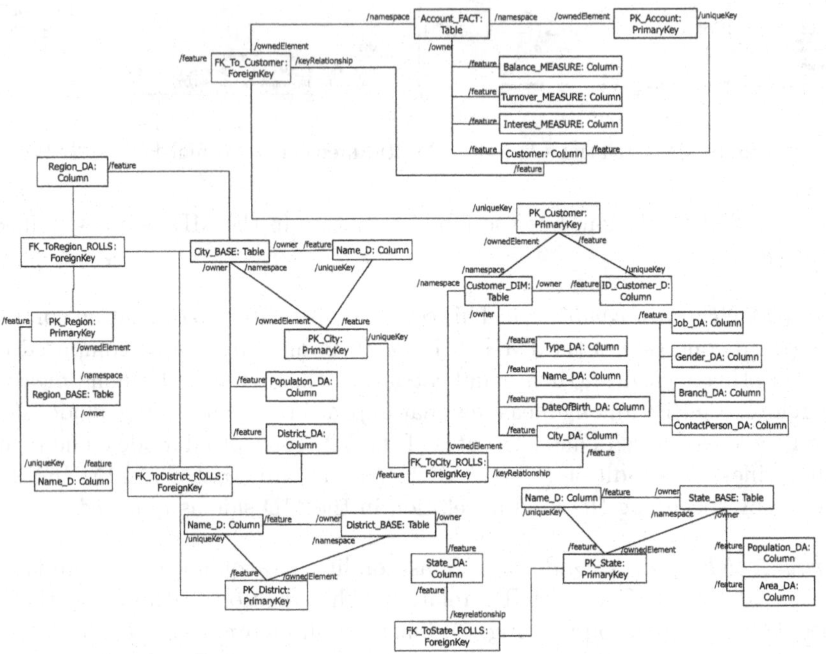

Fig. 6. Data sources model for our example

Due to space restrictions, we only describe a subset of the applied relations. These QVT relations are as follows:

Check1MNF2. This relation checks and enforces that FK_ToState_ROLLS, a foreign key in the District_BASE table referencing the State_BASE table (which embodies a many-to-one relationship between districts and states), is represented via a Rolls-upTo association between District base and State base in the MD conceptual model. We point out that this Rolls-upTo association was missing in the requirement-driven MD conceptual model (recall Fig. 1).

Check1MNF4. This relation checks that the Account_FACT table, its primary key (PK_Account), foreign key (FK_To_Customer) to the Customer_DIM table, and its columns (Balance_MEASURE, Turnover_MEASURE, and Interest_MEASURE,) correspond to the Account fact (including fact attributes) and the Customer dimension (including the terminal dimension level Customer base).

Check2MNF3MNF. The enforcement of this relation creates subclasses of the Customer base in the MD conceptual model, whose names are determined by the values of the discriminating level Type_DA: company and private. Furthermore, it enforces that the optional columns Job_DA and Gender_DA in the data source model belong to the private subclass in the MD conceptual model, while the optional columns Branch_DA and ContactPerson_DA belong to the company subclass of the Customer base.

6 Conclusions and Future Work

In this paper, we have presented an approach to assure the correctness of an MD conceptual model of the DW repository according to the data sources that will populate this repository. This approach is outlined as follows: we firstly obtain the MD conceptual schema of the DW from user requirements and then we verify and enforce its correctness against data sources by using a set of QVT relations based on MNFs. By using MNFs, we can assure that the MD conceptual model also satisfies certain desirable properties such as faithfulness, completeness, avoidance of redundancies, and context-sensitive summarizability. Furthermore, QVT relations allow us to integrate this approach into an MDA framework for the development of DWs.

Our immediate future work is to extend our approach by defining QVT relations in order to automatically transform the MD conceptual model into logical models that are closer to the relational implementation. Furthermore, non-strict hierarchies, many-to-many relationships between a fact and a dimension, degenerate facts, and other MD issues should be taken into account. Therefore, MNFs will also assure the correctness of these logical models.

Acknowledgements

This work has been partially supported by the METASIGN (TIN2004-00779) project from the Spanish Ministry of Education and Science, by the DADAS-MECA project (GV05/220) from the Valencia Ministry of Enterprise, University and Science (Spain), and by the DADS (PBC-05-012-2) project from the Castilla-La Mancha Ministry of Education and Science (Spain). Jose-Norberto Mazón is funded by the Spanish Ministry of Education and Science under a FPU grant (AP2005-1360).

References

1. Inmon, W.: Building the Data Warehouse. Wiley & Sons (2002)
2. Kimball, R., Ross, M.: The Data Warehouse Toolkit. Wiley & Sons (2002)
3. Golfarelli, M., Maio, D., Rizzi, S.: The Dimensional Fact Model: A conceptual model for data warehouses. Int. J. Cooperative Inf. Syst. **7**(2-3) (1998) 215–247
4. Cabibbo, L., Torlone, R.: A logical approach to multidimensional databases. In Schek, H.J., Saltor, F., Ramos, I., Alonso, G., eds.: EDBT. Volume 1377 of Lecture Notes in Computer Science., Springer (1998) 183–197

5. Hüsemann, B., Lechtenbörger, J., Vossen, G.: Conceptual data warehouse modeling. In Jeusfeld, M.A., Shu, H., Staudt, M., Vossen, G., eds.: DMDW. Volume 28 of CEUR Workshop Proceedings., CEUR-WS.org (2000) 6
6. Lechtenbörger, J., Vossen, G.: Multidimensional normal forms for data warehouse design. Inf. Syst. **28**(5) (2003) 415–434
7. Winter, R., Strauch, B.: A method for demand-driven information requirements analysis in data warehousing projects. In: HICSS. (2003) 231
8. Prakash, N., Singh, Y., Gosain, A.: Informational scenarios for data warehouse requirements elicitation. In Atzeni, P., et al, eds.: ER. Volume 3288 of Lecture Notes in Computer Science., Springer (2004) 205–216
9. Mazón, J.N., Trujillo, J., Serrano, M., Piattini, M.: Designing data warehouses: from business requirement analysis to multidimensional modeling. In Cox, K., Dubois, E., Pigneur, Y., Bleistein, S.J., Verner, J., Davis, A.M., Wieringa, R., eds.: REBNITA, University of New South Wales Press (2005) 44–53
10. Giorgini, P., Rizzi, S., Garzetti, M.: Goal-oriented requirement analysis for data warehouse design. In: DOLAP. (2005) 47–56
11. Object Management Group: MDA Guide 1.0.1. `http://www.omg.org/cgi-bin/doc?omg/03-06-01` (Visited January 2006)
12. Mazón, J.N., Trujillo, J., Serrano, M., Piattini, M.: Applying MDA to the development of data warehouses. In: DOLAP. (2005) 57–66
13. Luján-Mora, S., Trujillo, J., Song, I.Y.: A UML profile for multidimensional modeling in data warehouses. Data & Knowledge Engineering **In Press** (2006)
14. Lehner, W., Albrecht, J., Wedekind, H.: Normal forms for multidimensional databases. In Rafanelli, M., Jarke, M., eds.: SSDBM, IEEE Computer Society (1998) 63–72
15. Tryfona, N., Busborg, F., Christiansen, J.G.B.: starER: A conceptual model for data warehouse design. In: DOLAP, ACM (1999) 3–8
16. Object Management Group: MOF 2.0 Query/View/Transformation. `http://www.omg.org/cgi-bin/doc?ptc/2005-11-01` (Visited January 2006)
17. Bernstein, P.A.: Synthesizing third normal form relations from functional dependencies. ACM Trans. Database Syst. **1**(4) (1976) 277–298
18. Object Management Group: Common Warehouse Metamodel Specification 1.1. `http://www.omg.org/cgi-bin/doc?formal/03-03-02` (Visited January 2006)
19. Mellor, S., Scott, K., Uhl, A., Weise, D.: MDA distilled: principles of Model-Driven Architecture. Addison Wesley (2004)
20. Rahm, E., Bernstein, P.A.: A survey of approaches to automatic schema matching. VLDB J. **10**(4) (2001) 334–350

Design and Use of ER Repositories: Methodologies and Experiences in eGovernment Initiatives

Carlo Batini, Daniele Barone, Manuel F. Garasi, and Gianluigi Viscusi

Dipartimento di Informatica Sistemistica e Comunicazione (Disco)
Università degli Studi di Milano-Bicocca - Italy
batini@disco.unimib.it, daniele.barone@unimib.it,
garasima@lib.unimib.it, gianluigi.viscusi@unimib.it

Abstract. In this paper we describe the main results of a fifteen years research activity in the area of repositories of Entity-Relationship conceptual schemas. We first introduce a set of integration/abstraction primitives that are used in order to organize a large set of conceptual schemas in a repository. We describe the methodology conceived to produce the repository of schemas of central public administrations in Italy. Then we describe an heuristic methodology, applied in the production of the set of schemas of the public administrations of an italian region. We also compare the former exact methodology and the heuristic one according to their correctness, completeness, and efficiency. Finally, we show how such repositories can be used in eGovernment initiatives for planning activities and in the identification of projects. Further work highlights possible evolutions of the repositories toward enhanced semantic representations and usage.

1 Introduction

The goal of this paper is to describe several experiences of modelling, design and usage of repositories of conceptual schemas, related to central and local Italian public administration. The structure of public administration (PA) consists in many countries, of central and local agencies that together offer services to citizens and businesses. For example, in Italy, central PAs are of two types, ministries such as Internal Affairs, Revenues, and other central agencies such as Social Security, Accident insurance and the Chambers of commerce. Main types of local PAs correspond to regions (21), provinces (about 100) and municipalities (about 8.000). Each one of these administrations manages its own databases and registries. A crucial aspect in changing the relationship between PAs and citizens consists in the design of a new technological architecture (see Figure 1, where three agencies are considered) that, contrary to the past, offers the services to citizens by means of a common front office layer, on the basis of the one stop shop paradigm; furthermore, a cooperative back office layer has to be developed, that allows administrations to share information and application services, in order to reengineer the administrative procedures and reduce the burden to users. Concerning the data architecture, redundancies should be discovered and controlled, data has to be interchanged in an interoperable format, all the administrations have to assign the same meaning to the same data, achieving integration in the long term. To be able to (i) discover redundancies and heterogeneities among data bases of different administrations, (ii) reconcile the different meanings of data, (iii) reuse entities in the design of new databases achieving semantic

D.W. Embley, A. Olivé, and S. Ram (Eds.): ER 2006, LNCS 4215, pp. 399–412, 2006.

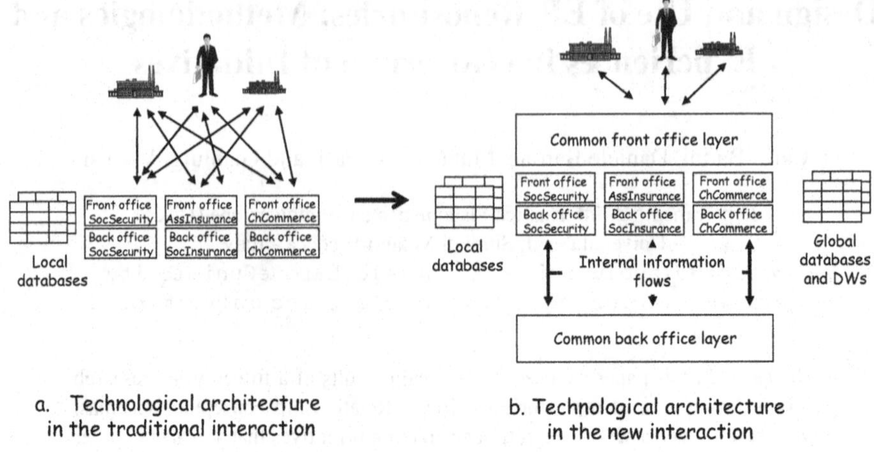

Fig. 1. New technological architecture for Government to Citizens and to Business interactions

interoperability, a unified conceptual description is needed of the different databases. This goal has been achieved building a repository of conceptual schemas (*repository* in the following) of existing databases. The repository of the main databases of Italian central PA(*central PA repository* in the following) has been produced in years 1995-1997 using a methodology for conceptual schema integration [1] and a methodology for repository structuring [2]. In 2004, one region, namely the Piedimont region, decided to build its own repository (*local PA repository*), concerning the main databases managed in its territory. Logical relational schemas were the input to the process, and limited human resources were available. As a consequence, an heuristic methodology has been conceived to allow the production of the local repository [3], [4]. In this paper we describe the experiences gained in the two activities, and compare the two methodologies. Furthermore, we show several analysis performed in years 1995-2000 on the central PA repository, that led to significant planning decisions and to the conception of innovative projects that (in some cases) improved significantly the relationships among PAs and citizens and businesses; we report also the failures. The paper is organized as follows. Section 2 discusses the basic primitives used for schema organization in the conceptual schema repositories. Section 3 outlines the methodology used in years for the construction of the central PA repository. In Section 4 we describe the heuristic methodology used to produce the local PA repository. Section 5 compares the two previous processes against criteria such as correctness, completeness and efficiency. Section 6 provides several analysis performed on the central PA repository that inspired planning activities and innovative projects. Discussion on related work (Section 7) and future research (Section 8) concludes the paper.

2 The Structure of a Repository

A repository can be defined as a set of conceptual schemas, each one describing all the information managed by an organization area within the information system

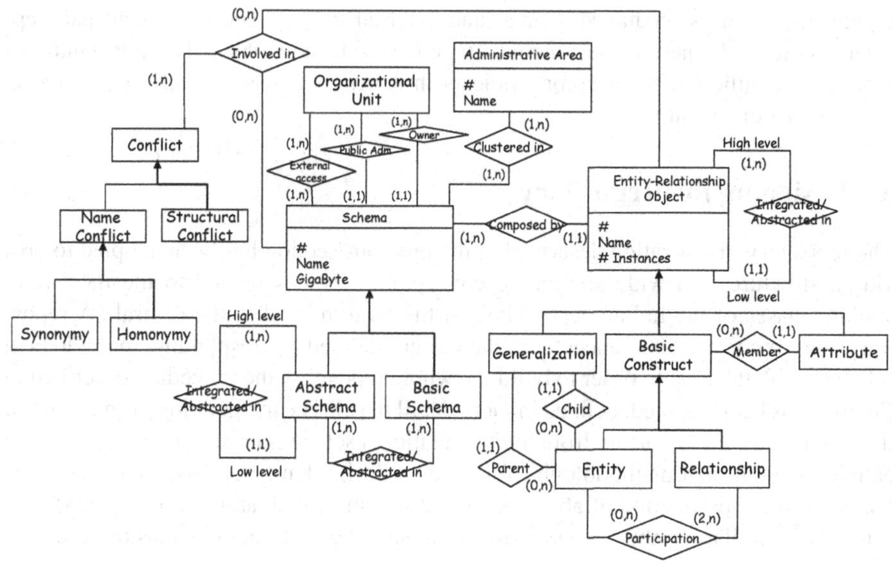

Fig. 2. Metaschema of the repository

considered. In particular, the repositories referenced in this paper use the Entity-Relationship model to represent conceptual schemas. However, a flat set of schemas does not display the relationships among concepts managed in different areas; the repository has to be organized in a more complex structure, through the use of structuring primitives. The primitives used in our approach were presented first in [2] and are: *abstraction*, *view*, and *integration*. Abstractions allow the description of the same reality at different levels, from detailed to abstract ones. We will call *refinement* the inverse primitive, that allows to proceed from abstract representations to more detailed ones. This mechanism is fundamental for a repository, since it helps the user to perceive a complex reality step by step, going from a more abstract level to a local one. Views are fragments of schemas; they allow users to focus their attention just on the part of a complex reality of interest to them. Integration is the mechanism by which a set of local schemas is merged into a unique global schema, after solving all heterogeneities present in the input schemas. By jointly using these structuring primitives we obtain a repository of schemas. In the following we name *basic schemas* the conceptual schemas defined at the bottom level of the repository, *abstract schemas* the schemas at the upper levels. In practice, when the repository is populated at the bottom level by hundreds of schemas, as in the case that we will examine in the following, it is unfeasible to manage the three structuring primitives, and the view primitive is sacrificed. Furthermore, integration and abstraction are applied together, resulting in the application of a new composed primitive, the integration/abstraction primitive. The integration/abstraction is iterated, producing schemas at several levels of abstraction. In Figure 2 we show the metaschema of the repository, where meta attributes are shown within boxes representing entities. The central part of the metaschema represents the organization of schemas, together with their classification in areas and their relationships with organizational units (managed, owner, and external to PA). The right hand part represents objects defined in the schemas, together with their types. The left hand part represents conflicts defined among objects in schemas that are involved in integration/abstraction primitives.

3 Designing the Repository

The repository organization described in the previous section has been adopted to provide a structure to a wide amount of conceptual schemas related to the most relevant databases of the Italian central PA. At the bottom level of the central PA repository, approximately 500 conceptual schemas are defined, corresponding to the logical schemas of databases. In order to build the whole repository the procedure described in Figure 3 has been adopted, defined in more detail in [2]. The methodology is made up of three steps. In step 1, starting from logical relational schemas or requirement collection activities, traditional methodologies for schema design have been used (see e.g. [5]), that lead to the production of about 500 basic schemas, with approximately 5.000 entities and a similar number of relationships. In step 2 conceptual schemas representing

1. Produce basic schemas [Batini, Ceri, Navathe 1984]
2. Cluster schemas in groups, using areas of interests
3. For each cluster of schemas, produce an integrated/abstracted schema
   3.1 Integration [Batini, Lenzerini 1984], [Batini, Lenzerini, Navathe 1984]
      3.1.1 Pairwise comparison of input schemas
      - Name conflict analysis
      - Structural conflict analysis
      3.1.2 Production of amended schemas
      3.1.3 Production of the integrated schema
      3.1.4 Inclusion of interschema properties.
   3.2. Abstraction [Batini, Di Battista, Santucci 1993]
   Until a unique abstract schema is obtained

Fig. 3. The methodology for the production of the central PA repository

the different organization areas are grouped in terms of homogeneous classes, corresponding to meaningful administrative areas of interest in central PA, such as social security, finance, cultural heritage, and education. In step 3 each group of basic schemas is first integrated and abstracted, resulting in a unique schema for each area, that populates the second level of the repository, resulting in 32 second level abstract schemas. For instance, the `Internal security` second level schema results from the integration/abstraction process, performed over 6 schemas corresponding to 130 concepts. The integration/abstraction process is iterated, producing higher level schemas, corresponding to more abstract areas, such as financial resources, human resources, social services, economic services, finally producing a unique integrated schema, that is further abstracted, resulting at the topmost level of the repository in a schema shown in Figure 4. The schema represents the most significant concepts managed in the information systems of any public administration, i.e. `Subject`, `Individual`, `Legal`

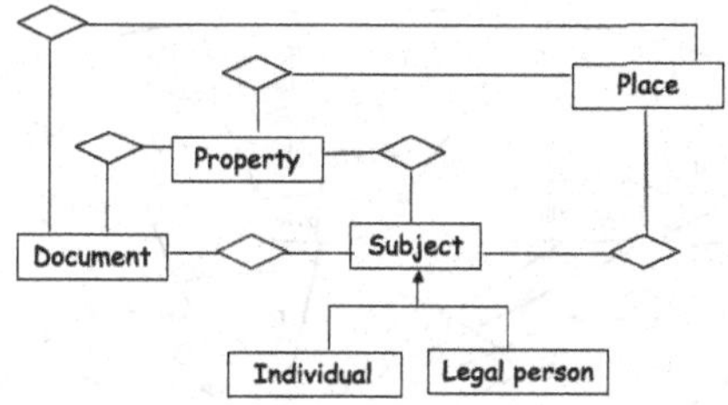

Fig. 4. The schema at the top level of repository

person, Property, Place, and Document, and their high level relationships. The resulting pyramid of schemas provides a natural representation of concepts at different abstraction levels, and, with suitable approximation, finds the common heterogeneous parts among databases pertaining to different agencies.

In order to produce the repository, about 200 person-months were needed to produce in step 1 the 500 basic conceptual schemas, while about 24 person-months were needed to produce in step 3 the 59 abstract schemas of the upper part of the repository (approximately 14 person-days per schema, both for the basic and for the abstract schemas).

4 Reusing the Repository

In this section we describe the methodology adopted in the production of the local PA repository. In this case, much less resources were available, while we could reuse as an input to the process the central PA repository. A second input concerns documentation available for the regional databases. The logical schemas of the 500 databases are documented in terms of: relational database schemas, tables, descriptions of tables, referential integrity constraints defined among tables, attributes, descriptions of attributes, identifiers. The basic sources of knowledge available for the production of the local PA repository, as results from the above discussion, are very rich, but characterized by a significant heterogeneity: the conceptual documentation concerns central PA, while the logical documentation pertains to local PAs.

A relevant condition of our activity has been budget constraints. Therefore, in conceiving the methodology for the production of the local PA repository, we made a significant assumption, and we have used heuristics and approximate reasoning, in order to reduce human intervention as much as possible. The assumption we made has been that, while basic schemas of the central PA repository and the local PA repository may probably differ, due to the different functions between the central and local administrations, the similarity should be much higher among the abstract schemas of the central PA repository and basic + abstract schemas of the local PA repository. In consequence of the above assumption and resource constraints, we decided to use a much more dense conceptual structure than the set of schemas of the central PA repository. It consists of the generalization hierarchies that have at their top level the six concepts defined in the schema of Figure 4, and having at lower levels the concepts in more refined abstract schemas and basic schemas, obtained applying top down the refinements along the integration/abstraction hierarchy. We show in Figure 5 the hierarchy of Individual. We

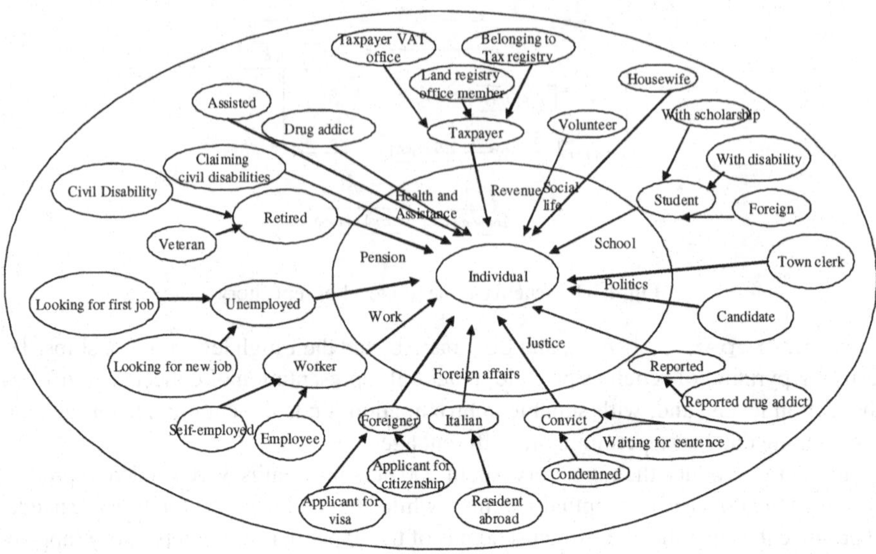

Fig. 5. The Individual generalization hierarchy

now provide the rationale of the methodology, for the details see [3], [4]. The methodology follows diverse approaches in building the basic schemas and the abstract schemas of the repository, and, consequently, can be seen as divided in two phases. For each local logical schema, available conceptual/central and logical/local knowledge is used in Phase 1 to produce a basic local conceptual schema. Then, in Phase 2, the abstract schemas are built. Phase 1 is made of five steps, shortly described in Figure 6. Concerning Phase 2 (see the details in [3]) we initially observe that the schema obtained after steps 1-3 (*draft schema* in the following) inherits high level abstract knowledge from the central PA repository and basic knowledge from the local PA logical schemas, while the enriched schema obtained in step 4 encapsulates exclusively basic knowledge from the local PA logical schemas. So, we may conjecture that the draft schema is a candidate for abstract schema for the upper levels of the repository, while the enriched schema, being a more detailed description of a logical schema, populates the basic level (see Figure 7). We have now to associate an abstraction level to the draft schema. By construction, all the entities of draft schemas belong to the central PA generalization hierarchies. So, we may associate an abstraction level to the draft schema that, intuitively, captures the relative position of its entities with regard to the five hierarchies.

1. Extract entities and attributes, looking for similar concepts between generalization hierarchies of the central PA repository and relational tables and attributes
2. Add generalizations
3. Extract relationships among entities from basic schemas of the central PA repository
4. Extract relationships from referential integrity contraints in relational schemas
5. Domain expert check

Fig. 6. Steps of phase 1 of the heuristic methodology

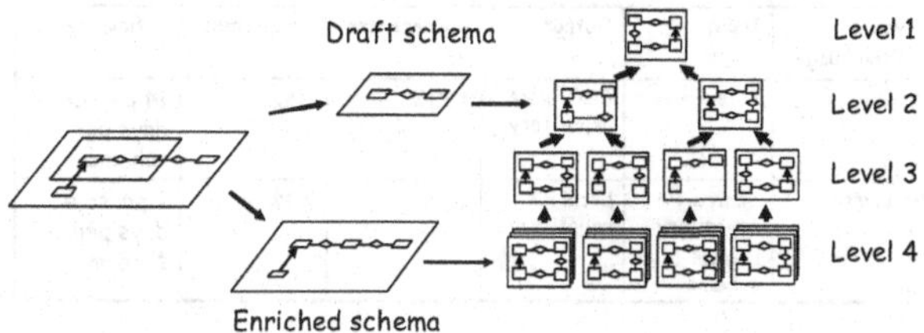

Fig. 7. Presumable locations in the repository of draft and enriched schemas

An abstraction level can be associated also to each schema in the central PA repository, defined similarly. Correspondingly, we may associate an average abstraction level to each layer in the central PA repository. The level of the draft schema in the local repository is heuristically set as the closest abstraction level among the layers in the central PA repository. We split the entities of the draft schema on the basis of their closeness to the different areas chosen to cluster schemas in the central PA repository. By iterative application to all draft schemas of the two steps discussed above, we finally obtain the complete local PA repository.

5 Comparison Among Methodologies Adopted for the Central PA Repository and the Local PA Repository

In order to compare the two methodologies used in the production of the central PA repository and the local PA repository, we performed several cases measuring three different qualities:

1. the *correctness* of the conceptual schema with respect to the "true" one, i.e. the schema that could be obtained directly by the domain expert through a traditional analysis or else a reverse engineering activity. Correctness is measured in the case of the local repository with an approximate indirect metrics, namely the percentage of new/deleted concepts in the schema produced by the expert at the end of step 5 with respect to the concepts produced in the semi automatic steps 1-4.
2. the *completeness* of the conceptual schema with respect to the corresponding logical schema. Completeness is measured by the percentage of tables that are captured in steps 1-5, in comparison with the total number of tables, after excluding tables not carrying relevant information, such as redundant tables, tables of codes, etc.
3. the *efficiency* of the process, measured by the resources needed for producing a schema.

Figure 8 summarizes main results of the comparison activity. Concerning correctness, the joint application of the central PA knowledge and local PA knowledge leads to encouraging results, considering the highly heuristic nature of the methodology. Results are more problematic for completeness. Initial values of completeness for the heuristic methodology were around 50%. As was to be expected, completeness decreases significantly when the referential integrity constraints are not documented or partially documented. Apart from the quality of the documentation, another cause of reduced completeness is the static nature of generalization hierarchies used in step 1, and the unequal

Type of methodology	Input	Output	Correctness	Completness	Efficiency
Exact	Interviews	Central PA repository	100%	100%	14 person-days per schema
Heuristic	Central PA repository Logical schemas	Local PA repository	80%	70%	2 person-days per schema

Fig. 8. Comparisons among the production process of the central PA repository and the local PA repository

semantic richness in representing related top level concepts. We have improved this step by incrementally updating hierarchies with abstract concepts generated in Phase 2. Such enriched hierarchies are progressively made more close to hierarchies characteristic of local administrations, resulting in a more effective selection mechanism. Finally, the increase in efficiency of the heuristic methodology looks really impressive, leading to a good balance between cost and quality.

Concept observed	CPA repository	LPA repository
# of basic schemas representing databases	516	567
# of basic schemas in the repository	224	168
# of attributes of basic schemas	6.916	5.464
# of abstract schemas	59	28
# of entities	2.166	1.716
# opf relationships	1.560	1.321
# of relational tables	-	18.967
# of attributes of relational tables	-	174.221

Fig. 9. General figures on the central PA and the local PA repository

6 Use of the Repositories in eGovernment Initiatives

In this section we discuss several analysis made on the repositories, that provide useful information for planning activities and for defining joint eGovernment projects in groups of administrations exploiting the new technological architecture of Figure 1. Figure 9 provides general data on schemas of the central and local repositories, and on logical tables of the regional databases. Notice that Social security and Social insurance schemas are not considered in figures related to the central repository since the two agencies were examined in a second survey. The following sections describe specific analysis on the central PA repository.

Choosing priorities and planning new initiatives. eGovernment initiatives in most countries are the result of a planning activity, whose goal is to choose the most effective projects and to establish priorities among them. The repository provides useful knowledge on the information resource for such planning. At a very high level of analysis

Area	Subarea	Min of foreign affairs	Foreign trades	De-fence	Reve-nues	Justice	Internal affairs	Cultural heritage	Com-merce and trades	Wel-fare	Edu-cation	Agri-culture	Health	Trea-sury	Transpor-tations	Re-search	Total	%
Resources	Financial	21	19	8	345		82	51		5		40		145			716	20
	Real Estate				68		59							86			213	6
	Support				25		28							3			56	2
	Human	67	16		102	6	136	12		11				127	14		491	14
Total Resources		88	35	8	540	6	305	63		16		40		361	14		1476	41
Services	Direct	78		24		203	149							93			547	15
	Economic		156				24		55	107		70		0	84		496	14
	General				66		143		27					0	84		320	9
	Social	14					40	153			120	93	204	0		116	740	21
Total Services		92	156	24	66	203	356	153	82	107	120	163	204	93	168	116	2103	59
Grand total		180	191	32	606	209	661	216	82	123	120	203	204	454	182	116	3579	100
%		5	5	1	17	6	18	6	2	3	3	6	6	13	5	3	100	

Fig. 10. Macroareas and corresponding number of entities of schemas owned by a set of selected administrations

Attributes	Chambers of Commerce	Social Security	Social Insurance
Fiscal code	X	X	X
Vat number	X	X	X
Name	X	X	X
Company deed of partnership	X		X
Activity	X		X
Legal status	X		X
Registered office	X	X	X
Code in the national registry	X		X
Registration date	X		X
Company structure	X	X	X
Administrative office	X	X	X
Address	X	X	X
Start date of activity	X	X	X
Suspension date of activity	X	X	X
End date of activity	X	X	X
Number of workers	X	X	X

Fig. 11. Common attributes of the entity Company among different administrations

we may evaluate the distribution of entities among the different areas of interest and among the different owner agencies. In Figure 10 we show such a distribution for the main areas and related macroareas, namely Services and Resources. Referring to agencies, we see that the 50% of entities is concentrated in three agencies, namely Revenues, Treasury and Internal affairs, while, referring to areas, over 40% of entities is managed for resource related support processes, while less than 60% of entities is used for service related primary processes. Similar figures can be produced for the distribution of instances. Since 1995 several projects have been conceived and set up that make an attempt to change this unequal distribution of information. A second analysis concerns the overlapping of common information related to the same entity in different schemas and administrations; in such analysis we may initially focus on macro entities defined in the high level conceptual schema of Figure 4. We represent in Figure 11 common attributes of the `Company` entity among three agencies that own national registries on businesses, namely Chambers of commerce, Social insurance and Social security. Due to such overlapping, common attributes regarding any particular business are likely to be duplicated, with no guaranteed consistency among the copies. Furthermore, high costs for agencies and for businesses are related to the multiple updates. In [6] a project set up to tackle the above issues is described, showing that in the new cooperative

Concept observed	# of instances	size of the universe
Individual	250.000.000	57.000.000
State employee	2.500.000	1.700.000
Retired person	4.900.000	10.500.000
Student	240.000	3.500.000

a. Types of individuals and number of related instances

Macroentities	% of entities
Economic issues	24
Juridical issues	52
Human resources	24

b. Macroentities of state employees and number of related entities

Fig. 12. Types of individuals, related instances and entities

architecture overall costs for agencies and businesses are reduced yearly of approximately 200 Ml euros.

Coverage analysis. Public administration, in its relationship with citizens, exercises a different "degree of attention" as to different types of individuals, such as workers, retired persons, emigrants, immigrants, etc. We show in Figure 12.a an analysis of instances of entities referring to individuals, state employees, retired persons and students compared with the corresponding size of the universe in Italy, as results from the National bureau of census statistical tables. The comparison puts in evidence uneven coverage between the four categories, e.g. students are neglected, despite a much greater availability of information (in terms of instances) for public employees. Focusing on state employees, we deepen in Figure 12.b the analysis by evaluating the number of entities of the three major areas of interest in personnel information systems, namely economic issues, juridical issues, and human resources. The low number of entities in human resources resulted in a project focused in the area, that did not produce so far significant results, due to its high unpopular objective.

Reconciliation of identifiers and knowledge potential. The knowledge represented in the information systems of public administrations is huge, but is fragmented in databases managed by different agencies. The possibility of integrating the different databases and retrieving and joining related data is enhanced by having common identifiers defined in the different databases. An analysis on the repository has shown that among all identifiers of individuals and legal persons only 25% is a standard identifier such as *fiscal code*. The interoperability of databases and the possibility to coordinate updates related to life events have been enhanced through building central databases where the different identifiers are linked in the same record; such databases have been produced through record linkage activities [6].

7 Related Work

Integration is a key issue in all information systems where several levels of cooperation have to be established between different organizations or players. As an example, [7] discusses the need for agencies to integrate their IT infrastructures, so to improve their competitiveness by integrating their systems with suppliers, or other trading partners. Methodologies for conceptual schema integration have been developed in the past, see [8] for a comprehensive comparison. A survey of the approaches to schema matching, a critical issue in schema integration, appears in [9]. Primitives for schema integration are introduced in [1], where a methodology for schema integration in the Entity-Relationship model is presented. Integration and abstraction primitives have been introduced in [2], where several properties of the repositories adopting such primitives have been formally modelled and investigated. Heuristic methodologies and tools for efficient production of service conceptual schemas are presented in [3] and in [10]. In [11] a descriptive model based on words and concepts and a set of primitives for integration of object oriented schemas that generate abstract concepts as a result of the integration process is proposed. A repository of relational schemas is described in [12] within a GLAV data integration system. In [13] the conceptual schema package is introduced as an abstraction mechanism in the ER model. Several effective techniques are proposed to group entities and relationships in packages such as dominance grouping, accumulation and abstraction absorbing.

In [14] a solution and methodology for reverse engineering of legacy databases using formal method-based techniques is presented. Similarity-based criteria are used to evaluate concept closeness and, consequently, to generate concept hierarchies. The techniques allow the analysis of conceptual schemas of databases in a federation and the definition and maintenance of concept hierarchies. In [15] and in [16] a corpus based approach is introduced, where a corpus is a collection of any kind of information related to structured data, e.g. schemas and mappings between some schema pairs. Schemas in the corpus are loosely related and belong to a single domain, but need not be mapped to each other. Repositories of conceptual schemas are proposed in several application areas; e.g. in biosciences [17], for reuse in schema design [18], [19]. A data repository is used in [20] as the core structure of a mediator-like module supporting the user-friendly integrated access to available data resources. The core of the system is the extraction and exploitation of the inter-schema knowledge (in the form of inter-schema properties) relative to the involved database schemas. In [4] and [3] methodologies are proposed for the reuse of a repository of conceptual schemas in large scale eGovernment projects.

8 Future Work

In this paper we have described several methodologies conceived and used in building and analyzing the repositories of conceptual schemas of the Italian central and local public administrations. In this section we discuss two areas of research that we aim at investigating in the future, related to (i) the enhancement of the semantic structure of the repositories, and (ii) their linkage and integration with a repository of services we have recently built.

Concerning the first issue, the two central and local repositories use a set of conceptual structures that all together represent an evolution and a semantic enrichment with respect to a flat set of conceptual schemas. Such conceptual structures correspond to (i) the *integration/abstraction primitives*, that allow to produce an integrated schema, describing a domain at different abstraction levels, and (ii) a set of *generalization hierarchies*. The recursive application of the primitives produces the entities, the relationships and the generalization hierarchies describing the core concepts of a specific domain of interest (e.g. personnel or economic services), representing, in the terminology adopted in ontologies [21], [22], the raw nucleus of a core ontology of the Italian public administration (for examples of core ontologies, see [23], [24]) . At the same time, the schemas at the top of the repositories describe the most abstract entities such as `Subject` or `Place`, not specific to a particular domain, and representing the raw nucleus of an upper ontology. Other aspects that distinguish the repositories are (iii) the name conflicts, such as synonyms and homonyms, the type conflicts and the interschema properties produced during the integration abstraction process. These semantic structures provide further contribution for possible construction of the above mentioned ontologies and of a thesaurus of terms used in public administration. Indeed, the conceptual repository offers an enriched model that goes beyond the limits of a flat set of Entity-Relationship schemas. Future work in this areas aims at exploiting such model, in order to build an enriched knowledge base. Such knowledge base could be used to support interoperability in cooperative architectures, a crucial issue for the effectiveness of eGovernment projects (see e.g. [25] and [26]). For these issues, we focus on expressing the intensional knowledge represented in the repositories through languages characterized by a richer semantics that supports reasoning activities, e.g. OWL [27], [28] or its extensions such as OWL-DL [29].

Concerning the repository of services, in [30] we have described an experience of design of a repository of services, performed in an eGovernment project related to services to businesses (S2B) provision through a cooperative architecture [6]. The S2B repository represents several characteristics of a wide number of services provided by Italian public administrations to businesses, and is used (i) to make easier, through a seamless interface, the access to services, and (ii) to characterize the relevance of the services for the value chain business processes. In future work, we focus first of all on the development of heuristic methodologies for the production of the conceptual schemas of services, on the basis of the knowledge represented both in the S2B repository and in the repositories of schemas presented in the paper. A conceptual schema of services represents the intensional knowledge needed in order to produce and deliver the service.

In the long term we conceive a framework that, starting from a high level user oriented specification of the service in terms of a set of concepts, uses conceptual schemas of services, and, by means of similarity functions, retrieves the service semantically nearest to the concepts in the specification. We argue that the advantages of such an approach rely on the user friendliness of the Entity-Relationship model and on the the explicit availability of the conceptual schema of data retrieved by the service.

References

[1] Batini, C., Lenzerini, M.: A methodology for data schema integration in the Entity Relationship model. IEEE Transaction on Software Engineering (1984)

[2] Batini, C., Battista, G.D., Santucci, G.: Structuring primitives for a dictionary of entity relationship data schemas. IEEE Trans. Software Eng. **19**(4) (1993) 344–365

[3] Batini, C., Garasi, M.F., Grosso, R.: Reuse of a repository of conceptual schemas in a large scale project. In: Advanced Topics in Database Research, Idea Book (2005)

[4] Batini, C., Grosso, R., Longobardi, G.: Design of repositories of conceptual schemas for large scale e-government projects. (Journal of Electronic Government - to be published march 2006)

[5] Elmasri, R., Navathe, S.: Foundamentals of database systems, Fifth Edition. Addison-Wesley Publishing Company (1994)

[6] Bertoletti, M., Missier, P., Scannapieco, M., Aimetti, P., Batini, C.: Improving Government-to-Business Relationships through Data Reconciliation and Process Re-engineering. In Wang, R., ed.: Information Quality - Advances in Management Information Systems-Information Quality Monograph (AMIS-IQ) Monograph. Sharpe, M.E. (2005. Shorter version also in ICIQ 2002.)

[7] Themistocleus, M., Chen, H.: Investigating the integration of smes' information systems: an exploratory case study. International Journal of Information Technology and Management **3**(2/3/4) (2004) 208–234

[8] Batini, C., Lenzerini, M., Navathe, S.: Comparison of Methodologies for Database Schema Integration. ACM Computing Surveys **18**(4) (1986)

[9] Rahm, E., Bernstein, P.A.: A survey of approaches to automatic schema matching. The VLDB Journal **10** (2001) 334–350

[10] Batini, C., Grosso, R., Longobardi, G.: Design of repositories of conceptual schemas in the small and in the large. In: Proceedings of the eGovernment Workshop '05 (eGOV05), Hosted at Brunel University, September 13, 2005, West London UB8 3PH, UK (2005)

[11] Mirbel, I.: Semantic Integration of Conceptual Schemas. In: Proceedings of the First International Workshop on Applications of Natural Language to Databases (NLDB'95), Versailles, France (1995) 57–70

[12] Motro, A., Anokhin, P.: Fusionplex: resolution of data inconsistencies in the integration of heterogeneous information systems. Information fusion (2004)

[13] Shoval, P., Danoch, R., Balaban, M.: Hierarchical entity-relationship diagrams: the model, method of creation and experimental evaluation. Requir. Eng. **9**(4) (2004) 217–228

[14] Perez, J., Ramos, I., Cubel, J., Dominguez, F., Boronat, A., Carì, J.: Data reverse engineering of Legacy Databases to object oriented conceptual schemas. Electronic Notes in Theoretical Computer Science **74**(4) (2002)

[15] Madhavan, J., Bernstein, P.A., Doan, A., Halevy, A.Y.: Corpus-based schema matching. In: ICDE, IEEE Computer Society (2005) 57–68

[16] Halevy, A.Y., Madhavan, J.: Corpus-based knowledge representation. In: In Proc. International Joint Conference on Artificial Intel ligence (IJCAI 03). Volume 18., Morgan Kaufmann (USA, 2003) 1567–1572

[17] Taxonomic Databases Working Group Annual Meeting: Taxonomic Databases Working Group on Biodiversity Informatics, University of Canterbury, Christchurch, New Zealand, Taxonomic Databases Working Group Annual Meeting (2004)

[18] Ruggia, R., Ambrosio, A.P.: A toolkit for reuse in conceptual modelling. In: CAiSE. (1997) 173–186

[19] Wohed, P.: Conceptual patterns for reuse in information systems analysis. In: CAiSE. (2000) 157–175

[20] Palopoli, L., Terracina, G., Ursino, D.: Dike: a system supporting the semi automic construction of cooperative information systems from heterogeneous databases. Software Practice and Experience **33**(9) (2003) 847–884

[21] Gruber, T.: A translation approach to portable ontology specification. Knowledge Acquisition (5) (1993)

[22] Guarino, N., ed.: Formal ontologies and information systems. In Guarino, N., ed.: Proceedings of FOIS'98, IOS Press (Amsterdam, 1998)

[23] Breuker, J., Hoekstra, R.: Epistemology and ontology in core ontologies: FOLaw and LRI-Core, two core ontologies for law. In: Proceedings of EKAW Workshop on Core ontologies. CEUR. (2004)

[24] Valente, A., Breuker, J.: Towards principled core ontologies. In: In Proceedings of the Tenth Knowledge Acquisition for Knowledge-Based Systems Workshop. (Banff, Alberta, Canada, 1996)

[25] Beneventano, D., Bergamaschi, S.: The MOMIS methodology for integrating heterogeneous data sources. In: IFIP Congress Topical Sessions, Kluwer (2004) 19–24

[26] Benetti, I., Beneventano, D., Bergamaschi, S., Guerra, F., Vincini, M.: An information integration framework for e-commerce. IEEE Intelligent Systems **17**(1) (2002) 18–25

[27] McGuinness, D., van Harmelen, F.: Owl web ontology language overview. http://www.w3.org/TR/2003/WD-owl-features-20030331/ (2003)

[28] Patel-Schneider, P., Hayes, P., Horrocks, I.: Web ontology language (owl). Technical report, http://www.w3.org/TR/owl-semantics/ (W3C, February 2003)

[29] Antoniou, G., van Harmelen, F.: Web ontology language: Owl. In: Handbook on Ontologies. Springer (2004) 67–92

[30] Barone, D., Viscusi, G., Batini, C., Naggar, P.: A Repository of Services for the Government to Businesses relationship. In Etzion, O., Kuflik, T., Motro, A., eds.: Next Generation Information Technologies and Systems. LNCS 4032, 6th International Conference, NGITS 2006 Kibbutz Shefayim, Israel, Springer (2006)

Notes for the Conceptual Design of Interfaces

Simone Santini

Universidad Autónoma de Madrid, Spain
University of California, San Diego, USA

Abstract. This paper presents a design method for user interfaces based on some ideas from conversation analysis. The method uses *interaction diagram* and it is conceived to design the overall flow of conversation between the user and the computer system in an abstract way, as an architectural prolegomenon to the designer's choice of the actual interface elements that will be used.

1 Introduction

The art of design is an art of abstraction. A design is the specification of certain structural relations between components; a specification that abstracts, on one hand, from the characteristics of the components that are not relevant for the structure of the whole and, on the other hand, from those structural relations that can be dispensed with at the level of abstraction where the designer is operating at a particular moment. For design is also a process of progressive deepening of the detail: the first sketch that Norman Foster made of his Hong Kong and Shanghai Bank building (in Hong Kong) consisted in a stack of four rectangles hanging, each one separately, from the steps of a ladder-like structure [10]. Each one of these rectangles would in the end become a block of ten stories of the bank, a transition process that required painstaking attention to a plethora of excruciatingly minute details. In the case of Norman Foster, just as in any other case of design of a complicated system, however, it is important to maintain a progressive view of the process, to possess the means to express the evolving design at different levels of detail, from a very generic one in which only the most general and most important traits of the system are represented to the most detailed one.

What is true for the design of a building is true as well for the design of an interface to a complex information system. Just as it happens for other design activities, the design of an interface needs a methodology and a notation that will allow a design to progress from its most general lines to its most minute details. The design of interfaces for information systems often fails to develop along these lines, in particular it fails to start at a suitably abstract and conceptual level. Quite paradoxically, this problem is due in part to the great success of standard computer interfaces, in particular to the interfaces based on overlapping *windows* for local programs and to those based on documents and forms for programs invoked through the web. The ubiquity of these interfaces often leads the designer to start thinking about the interface in terms of windows, buttons, data presentation options (or, in the case of web interfaces, in terms of pages, forms, and documents). This, I submit, is the interface equivalent of trying to create a program starting from the specification of its low-level functions, without an architectural design in which the overall organization of the program and the relations among its different functions are established.

D.W. Embley, A. Olivé, and S. Ram (Eds.): ER 2006, LNCS 4215, pp. 413–423, 2006.

That the design of windows or forms is a necessary step in the design of an interface doesn't entail that it should be the first, nor the most abstract. The lack of a suitably high level architectutal design of interfaces is exacerbated by the lack of a suitable design method and formalism: in many cases, interfaces are designed using the same methods and formalisms used for general programming, which these days means, more often than not, using an object oriented design method. For instance, UML, the popular object oriented graphic formalism for object oriented design, has been used in [9], and specialized for web navigation in [2]. Object oriented design has the primary purpose of designing the static structure of a program and the dynamics of the interaction among its components.

In an interface, however, the *process* of interaction is logically prior both to the static structure of the interface and to the dynamic interaction of the components, both of which depend on the more abstract process of interaction. Such a process is not well captured by program design formalisms because it is not itself a part of program design, but the description of a generalized *conversation* between the user and the system. In other words, the use of a program design method forces the designer to focus immediately on the structure of the interface rather than beginning by designing the structure of the conversation that takes place between the user and the information system. It is noteworthy, for instance, that a paper such as [9] on the use of UML for user interface design makes little of no use of the class diagram, that is, with the main conceptual tool of UML. The class diagram is of course present in this approach, but the impression is that it is by no means the main design instrument. The main graphical instrument for interface design in [9] is an interaction diagram not too dissimilar from what is presented here although, in my view, it suffers from two drawbacks. First, it is not properly grounded in a theory of interaction and, secondly, the need to resolve the interface in an object oriented design makes the specification of the interface very much oriented towards the information exchange between the user and the system, rather than on the possibilities of the conversation between the two.

In this paper, I present a method and a formalism for interface design particularly suitable for information systems interfaces, but adaptable to a considerably wider range of situations. The method abstracts from the details and the appearance of the interface to concentrate on the design of the process of conversation that takes place between the user and the system. The types of interaction that are chosen at any particular step constrain the choice of what interface elements are suitable to implement them, so that the method is also very effective as an architectural phase preliminary to the design of the appearance of an interface. The principal formal instrument of the method is the *interaction diagram*, somewhat inspired to conversation analysis [4]. Section 2 will introduce the theoretical basis of the method, which is to be sought in a form of *algebraic semiotics* [1]; section 3 illustrates the interaction diagrams and their use.

2 Semiotic Systems

The essential function of an interface is to allow an interaction between a person and a program, a communicative function that falls in the general area studied by semiotics. In this respect, however, we find ourselves in a conundrum: by its very nature and theoretical foundations, semiotics escapes any attempt at formalization while, in order to design a computer program for a given problem, we need that the problem be completely formalized. The pragmatic solution in this case is to proceed to a programme of "partial formalization," that is, of formalizing only those aspects of communication that lead themselves to formalization. It is clear that, in so doing, many of the interesting aspects of signification will be left out: in particular, all the *semantic* aspects of communication will be left out. But this is not a loss in the present situation, since if an aspect of communication can't be formalized we can't deal with it using a computer, so it can't be the object of interface design. In particular computers can't deal with semantics, unless the semantics is an *epiphenomenon* of the interaction (*episemantics,* or *emergent semantics* [5]), in which case the *syntactic* rôle of the interface is particularly important [7].

The basis for this formalization is constituted by the formal *sign system* derived, with some adaptation, from Goguen's algebraic semiotics.

Definition 1. *A* sign system *is a 5-tuple*

$$\mathfrak{S} = (T, V, \leq_T, F, A) \tag{1}$$

where:

i) *T is the set of* sorts *(or data types);*
ii) *V is a set of* parameter types*;*
iii) *$\leq_T$ is a partial order on T, called the* subsort *relation;*
iv) *F is a set of functions and relations on T and V;*
v) *A is a set of logical statements called the* axioms.

The sorts are those to which the *signs* of the system belong, that is, in the case of an interface, the types of elements and combinations of elements through which the interaction takes place. The parameters capture ancillary information about the sorts (position, color, etc.).

Definition 2. *Given two sign systems $\mathfrak{S}_1 = (T_1, V_1, \leq_{T_1}, F_1, A_1)$, and $\mathfrak{S}_2 = (T_2, V_2, \leq_{T_2}, F_2, A_2)$, a* semiotic morphism *$M : \mathfrak{S}_1 \to \mathfrak{S}_2$ is a collection of partial functions*

$$M : T_1 \to T_2$$
$$M : V_1 \to V_2$$
$$M : F_1 \to F_2$$
$$M : A_1 \to A_2$$

such that

i) *if $\tau_1 \leq_{T_1} \tau_2$, then $M(\tau_1) \leq_{T_2} M(\tau_2)$;*
ii) *if $p(s_1, \ldots, s_k) \in F_1$, and $M(p)$ is defined, then $M(p)(M(s_1), \ldots, M(s_n))$;*
iii) *if $s = f(s_1, \ldots, s_n)$ and $M(f)$ is defined, then $M(s) = M(f)(M(s_1), \ldots, M(s_n))$.*

The general idea of a semiotic morphism is to transform the system $\mathfrak{S}_1$ into $\mathfrak{S}_2$ in a way that preserves (part of) its structure. Before specifying additional properties of morphisms, I will need the following technical definition:

Definition 3. *A* selector *for a sign system $\mathfrak{S}$ is a function $f : \tau \rightarrow \nu$, with $\tau \in T$ and $\nu \in V$ for which there is a set of axioms A' such that adding A' and f to $\mathfrak{S}$ is consistent and defines a unique value $f(x)$ for each such $x : \tau$.*

The definition is a trifle involved but, essentially, it states that f attaches a parameter to each sign of sort τ and that its definition (the axioms in A', which uniquely define it) does not cause the system to become contradictory. I will clarify all this with an example in a short while, but first I need a couple more definitions.

Definition 4. *Let $\mathfrak{S}_1 = (T_1, V_1, \leq_{T_1}, F_1, A_1)$, and $\mathfrak{S}_2 = (T_2, V_2, \leq_{T_2}, F_2, A_2)$ be two sign systems and $M : \mathfrak{S}_1 \rightarrow \mathfrak{S}_2$ a semiotic morphism.*

i) *M is* axiom preserving *if, for each $a \in A_1$, $A_2 \models M(a)$;*
ii) *M* preserves a selector *f of $\mathfrak{S}_1$ if there is a selector f' of $\mathfrak{S}_2$ such that for every sign of $\mathfrak{S}_1$ for which f is defined it is $f'(M(x)) = M(f(x))$.*

Definition 5. *let $\mathfrak{S}_1$ and $\mathfrak{S}_2$ be two sign systems as in the previous definition, and $M, M' : \mathfrak{S}_1 \rightarrow \mathfrak{S}_2$ two semiotic morphisms, then*

i) *M' preserves at least as many axioms as M, written $M \leq_a M'$ if for every $a \in A_1$, if M preserves a then M' also preserves a;*
ii) *M' is at least as inclusive as M, written $M \leq_i M'$ if, for each sign x of $\mathfrak{S}_1$, $M(x) = x \rightarrow M'(x) = x$;*
iii) *M' preserves at least as much content as M, written $M \leq_c M'$, if whenever M preserves a selector of $|frakS_1$, so does M'.*

The inverse of a morphism, the definition of isomorphisms, and the various unicity and definition theorems follow pretty much the expected patterns [6,1].

2.1 An Example

As an inllustration of the principles of semiotic systems, I will present a simple interface for a fictitious image data base. As the purpose of an example is to illustrate the ideas rather than obfuscate them, I have purposedly chosen a very simple example, one for which I will reach conclusions that are, *per se*, quite obvious, and that could be obtained without the complicated machinery of algebraic semiotics. The reader is invited to consider that the purpose of the example is to illustrate the theory rather than to prove its power, and to mentally extrapolate the results to much more complicated examples.

Consider the typical interface of a system for doing content based image retrieval based on *query by example*, which displays a grid of 3×3 images, containing the images most similar to the current query image. This is a semiotic system with three sorts: *image*, *position*, and *group*. An image is composed of an identifier and the actual image data:

$$\underline{\text{type}}\ \text{image}\ \underline{\text{is}}\ (\text{id} : \text{int} \times \text{data} : \text{unit})$$

The image data are declared of the data type *unit* because, in this particular interface, there are no operations defined on them. A position is a pair of integers:

<u>type</u> pos <u>is</u> (row : int × col : int)

while the group is an array of images that is, a function that associates an image to each position:

<u>type</u> group <u>is</u> pos → image

The ordering relations of the system are

image ≤ group
pos ≤ group

Some functions defined in this system include:

img_at: group × pos → image; given a group and a position in it, returns the image in that position;
ngb : pos × pos → boolean; determines whether two positions are neighbors in the interface;
nxt : pos → pos $\cup\bot$**;** returns the next position to a given one in the textual order (left to right, top to bottom), or $\bot$ is there is no such position;
s : image → $(0,1)$**;** returns the "score" of an image.

Axioms may include:

i) structural axioms of the group, such as *ngb((1,1),(2,1)), ntx(1,3) = (2,1)*, τ : pos ⇒ $1 \le \tau.r \le 3 \wedge 1 \le \tau.c \le 3$, the symmetry of ngb, and so on;
ii) unicity axioms, such as

$$\forall p_1, p_2 : \text{pos}.(p_1 \neq p_2 \Rightarrow \text{img\_at}(p_1).\text{id} \neq \text{img\_at}(p_2).\text{id}) \qquad (2)$$

iii) scoring axioms

$$\forall p_1, p_2 : \text{pos}.(p_2 = \text{nxt}(p_1) \Rightarrow s(\text{img\_at}(p_1)) \geq s(\text{img\_at}(p_2))) \qquad (3)$$

(images are ordered by score),

$$\forall p_1, p_2 : \text{pos}.(p_2 = \text{nxt}(p_1) \Rightarrow \nexists i.s(\text{img\_at}(p_1)) \geq s(i) \geq s(\text{img\_at}(p_2))) \qquad (4)$$

(positions next to each other contains images which are next to each other in the scoring list), and

$$\forall i.(\exists p.s(i) > s(\text{img\_at}(p)) \;\; \Rightarrow \;\; \exists p'.i = \text{img\_at}(p')) \qquad (5)$$

(the interface contains the images with the highest scores).

Consider now a second interface, similar to the first with one exception: the images are laid out in a single file of 6 images. The position is now an integer number between one and six (pos′ ≡ int) and consequently the group (group′ : pos′ → image′) is now a function from integers to image′, which is isomorphic to image. A morphism between the two can be defined as a map of types M : pos ↦ pos′, M : image ↦ image′, M : group ↦ group′. The morphism maps functions M : nxt ↦ nxt′, and M : ngb ↦ ngb′, and so on. Note, however, that some of these mappings are partial functions: for instance, when mapping pos to pos′, not all the positions in the first interface are mapped to positions of the second one, since the first interface has nine position, while the second has only six. Also, only some of the axioms are translated; we have, for instance, $M(\text{ngb}((1,1),(1,2))) = \text{ngb}'(1,2)$, but an axiom such as $\text{ngb}((1,1),(1,2))$ is not translated into any axiom of the second interface, while an axiom such as $\text{ngb}'(3,4)$ of the second interface has no correspondent in the first one. These differences simply reflect the different arrangement of the two interfaces, but there are other discrepancies between the two. One, which we have already noticed, is the partiality of the function $M : \text{pos} \rightarrow \text{pos}'$ due to the fact that the first interface shows nine images, but the second only six. But, suppose the second interface as well displayed nine images: what could we say of the structural differences between the two? Note that the scoring function is a selector (considering the score as one of the parameters of the image position) and that, for each interface, axiom 4 holds: consecutive positions contain images that are consecutive in the score ordering. But for the second interface we can state the additional axiom:

$$\forall p, p'.(\text{ngb}(p, p') \Rightarrow p' = \text{nxt}(p) \vee p = \text{nxt}(p')) \tag{6}$$

(all neighbors are consecutive). With this, and defining for the sake of convenience $Q(p, p') \equiv \not\exists i.s(\text{img\_at}(p_1)) \geq s(i) \geq s(\text{img\_at}(p_2))$ one can infer for the second interface

$$\forall p, p'.(\text{ngb}(p, p') \Rightarrow Q(p, p') \vee Q(p', p) \tag{7}$$

There is no morphism from the second interface to the first that can maintain this axiom: the second interface has, in semiotic terms, a richer structure than the first.

Of course, when designing an interface, additional considerations come into play: for one thing, the order "left-to-right, top-to-bottom" is culturally so rooted in the western civilization that the "vertical" neighborhood relations are hardly perceived, so that the matrix placement is virtually equivalent to the linear one. (Things would be very different, of course, were the interface designed for a multi-cultural environment, a matter of which the blindly western-centric engineers are often blissfully oblivious: this is, however, the possible subject for a separate article.) Considerations such as this one are to be regarded as part of the designer's common sense judgment, of his *being-in-the-word*, so to speak, and, as such, they are beyond the scope of formalization, and will not be considered here. Note, however, that the model that we are using can still be useful to suggest the location of possible problems: in this case, it might suggest to the designer the opportunity to place suitable elements (lines, spacing,...) to "weaken" the vertical organization of the matrix, thereby reinforcing the horizontal order.

3 Interaction Diagrams

Consider again the query by example interface of the previous section, and the way it works. The user sees a set of images in what we might call the *display space* of the interface, a space constituted, as we have seen, by the possible instantiations of an algebraic sign system. Out of this configuration, the user operates a selection, which we'll call a member of the *composition space*, constituted by the instantiations of another sign system (in this case a very simple one whose signs are single images). A composition is then translated in a suitable request to the system that, in the case of an information system, takes the form of a query drawn from a *query space*, which can be considered, once again, a sign system: one involved in the communication between the interface and the information system. The information system executes the commands of the query space (since one can say that the query sign system belongs to an imperative *sprachspiel*, which is the active principle of the whole system), and creates a configuration in a suitable *output space*. The output space is often an abstract space and, in order to show some of its results, a further semiotic morphism translates it back in the display space. (In a query by example system, for instance, the output may consist of the whole data base organized in a high-dimensional space.) All this can be specified by a diagram constituted in this way:

$$\begin{array}{ccc} Q & \longrightarrow & O \\ \uparrow & & \downarrow \text{display} \\ C & \leftarrow\cdots & D \end{array} \tag{8}$$

The four letters are not part of the diagram *per se*, but labels used to distinguish the different semiotic systems involved. Here `Q` stands for *query (semiotic) system*, `O` for *output system*, `C` for *(query) composition system*, and `D` for *display system*; the arrows indicate semiotic morphisms (which, optionally, can be labeled), and the dotted arrow indicates a user action. It should be noted that this diagram is in many senses orthogonal to design-oriented specifications, even to very abstract ones such as the model-view-controller formalism [3,8]. In this diagram there is no *a priori* distinction between the functions performed by the user and those performed by the computer system. In this case, for instance, the semiotic morphism between query and output is implemented by a computer (specifically, by a data base) but, should we replace the data base with an archivist that does the research manually, the diagram would not change, since it describes an interaction that is the result of a certain activity, and it is logically prior to the decision of having part of that activity done by a computer. In this sense, this kind of diagram is the logical equivalent, at the interface design level, of the architectural diagrams collected during the requirement phase of a software project.

A closed loop such as this one indicates an iteratively refined query, and I call it a *context*. To make a comparison, consider querying a relational data base: here the user fills in a form, which is translated into a query and answered; the answer is suitably formatted and displayed. There is no context formation in this case and, introducing opportune symbols for the beginning and the end of the interaction, the diagram looks something like this:

$$\boxed{s} \cdots\rightarrow C \longrightarrow Q \longrightarrow O \longrightarrow D \cdots\rightarrow \boxed{e} \tag{9}$$

Where the last arrow corresponds to whatever user acknowledgment closes the query. Looking back at the query by example diagram, two things appear to be missing: a way to start a query and a way to finish it. There are typically two ways to start a query: either the user starts it from outside the loop (e.g. by providing a sample image) or the system proposes an initial configuration (e.g. a display with random images): the two alternatives (including the action that terminates the interaction) are shown in these two diagrams:

$$\begin{array}{ccccccc} & & Q & \longrightarrow & O & & \\ & & \uparrow & & \downarrow & & \\ \boxed{s} & \dashrightarrow & C & \dashleftarrow & D & \overset{}{\underset{\text{OK}}{\dashrightarrow}} & \boxed{e} \end{array} \qquad \begin{array}{cccccc} Q & \longrightarrow & O & \longleftarrow & \boxed{s} \\ \uparrow & & \downarrow & & \\ C & \dashleftarrow & D & \underset{\text{OK}}{\dashrightarrow} & \boxed{e} \end{array} \tag{10}$$

The first one assumes that the composition is exactly the same at the beginning of the interaction as it is in the context, which is seldom true: some special interface element is used to make the first image selection. The diagram is then

$$\begin{array}{ccccccc} \boxed{s} & \dashrightarrow & C' & \longrightarrow & Q & \longrightarrow & O \\ & & & & \uparrow & & \downarrow \\ & & & & C & \dashleftarrow & D & \underset{\text{OK}}{\dashrightarrow} & \boxed{e} \end{array} \tag{11}$$

The diagram can be extended to allow a more complete interaction. For instance, if the data base has some machinery to determine that the interaction is not converging towards a satisfactory solution, it can offer the user the option to disengage: the user can accept, decide to continue, or start a new context by posing a new query:

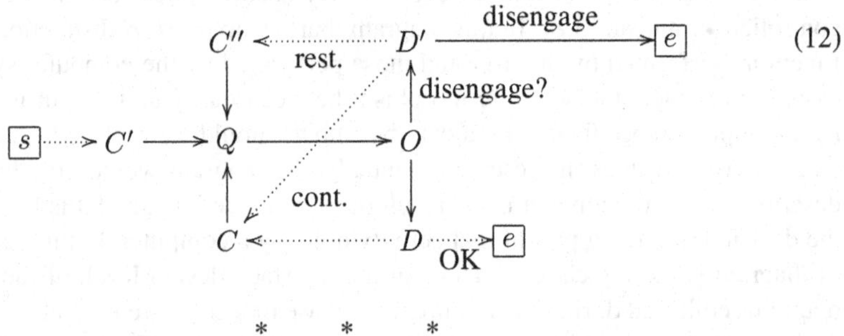

* * *

This diagrammatic notation allows one to analyze other interesting cases of interfaces. One is that of what I elsewhere called *direct manipulation* interfaces [6], in which the composition is done directly in the display space, so that the systems C and D above coincide. This situation can be represented by collapsing the two systems in a single one

$$\begin{array}{ccc} Q & \longrightarrow & O \\ & \nwarrow \;\; \swarrow & \\ & D & \\ & \circlearrowleft & \end{array} \tag{13}$$

or by joining the two symbols with a double edge (reminiscent of the "=" sign) which states that the two systems are one and the same:

$$\begin{array}{ccc} Q & \longrightarrow & O \\ \uparrow & & \downarrow \\ C & = & D \end{array} \qquad (14)$$

(The two diagrams are equivalent: the double edge is only a graphic convenience.)

In some cases we want to highlight that some of the sign systems are the union of two parts: in the previous example, for instance, it may be the case that part of the configuration comes from direct manipulation and part from some other kind of interaction. We can divide the composition space in two portions $c = c_1 \oplus c_2$ and join them with a $\cdot$ —⊕— $\cdot$ edge:

$$\begin{array}{ccc} Q & \longrightarrow & O \\ \uparrow & & \downarrow \\ C' & = & D \\ \oplus & & \\ C'' & \leftarrow\cdots & \boxed{s} \end{array} \qquad (15)$$

Note that C and C' are part of the same semiotic system: if they were two separate systems, each one to which could be used to compose a query, the diagram would have looked like

$$\begin{array}{ccccccc} \boxed{s} & \cdots\rightarrow & C'' & \longrightarrow & Q & \longrightarrow & O \\ & & & & \uparrow & & \downarrow \\ & & & & C' & = & D \end{array} \qquad (16)$$

As a final example, consider an interface that deals at the same time with two aspects of an information system—say, with the images and the text associated with them, as the interface that I discussed in [7]. Such a system consists of two separate direct manipulation interfaces that operate on the same query space, a situation corresponding to the following diagram:

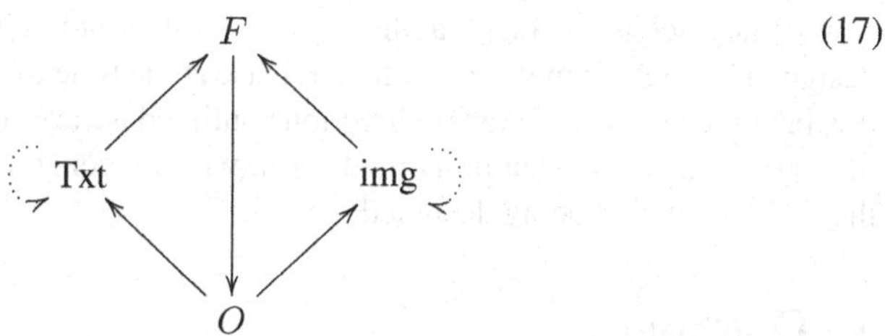

(17)

In summary, we can give the following definition:

Definition 6. *An interaction diagram is a colored graph whose nodes are either sign systems, start nodes (*$\boxed{s}$*), or end nodes (*$\boxed{e}$*), and whose edges are of four colors (types):*

$\longrightarrow$**:** *a semiotic morphism realized by the system;*
$\cdots\cdots\rightarrow$**:** *a semiotic morphism realized by the user;*

═══ : *an edge that establishes the identity of two sign systems;*
—⊕— : *an edge that composes two sign systems into one.*

Subject to the following restrictions:

i) *start nodes only have outgoing edges; end nodes only have incoming edges; all other nodes have at least one outgoing and one incoming edge;*
ii) *every cycle has at least one* ⋯⋯➤ *edge; the graph that is obtained from the original one by removing all the* ⋯⋯➤ *edges is acyclic.*

3.1 The Diagrams as a Design Instrument

In the previous examples, the diagrams were used as a semi-formal way of keeping track of the interactions between the user and the information system. In this rôle, they are useful mainly as an informal "thought instrument" to collect and organize requirement: the type of instrument that is more useful on a paper napkin or a blackboard than on a computer screen. What makes diagrams into a more complete design instrument is the presence of sign systems and semiotic morphisms. We developed a design system based on these diagrams in which each one of the nodes of the graph is associated by the designer to the formal specification of a semiotic system given in a suitable language[1]: an interface panel for query by example, for instance, can be associated to the formal specification of a system such as that briefly outlined in section 2. Some of the sign systems are chosen by the designer from a library of available interface elements (the display and the composition space are typically selected in this way), while others derive from a formalization, in semiotic terms, of the system for which the interface is designed, others yet can correspond to special modules created by the designer. Between all these elements, the designer creates the morphisms specified by the ——➤ edges of the graph.

The system tries to assist the designer by identifying the locus of possible problems (e.g. an interaction in which the user is required to add too much structure or, conversely, one in which a considerable portion of a structure is lost) and to enforce constraints (both the topological constraints of the definition of the diagram and structural constraints such as the fact that the net structural variation in a cycle must be zero). The design instrument is in its early alpha release at the time of this writing (June 2005), but it is being developed along the directions outlined here. Due to my own technical point of view, the system, even in its final form, will not generate automatically the code for the interface that is being designed.

4 Conclusions

In this paper I presented the embryo of a design method for user interfaces in visual information systems. In this area, an interface is important not only as an access to the system, but also as a way of creating the semantics of the data. The theoretical bases of the method are to be sought in conversation theory and in algebraic semiotics, and its embodiment is in the form of interaction diagrams.

[1] I am happy to report that none of the languages used by this system is based on XML.

References

1. Joseph Goguen. An introduction to algebraic semiotics, with applications to user interface design. In Chrystopher Nehaniv, editor, *Computation for metaphor, Analogy and Agents*, Springer Lecture Notes in Artificial Intelligence,. Springer-Verlag, 1999.
2. Natacha Güell, Daniel Schwabe, and Patricia Vilain. Modeling interactions and navigation in web applications. In S.W. Liddle, H.C. Mayr, and B. Thalheim, editors, *Conceptual Modeling for E-Business and the Web: ER 2000 Workshops on Conceptual Modeling Approaches for E-Business and The World Wide Web and Conceptual Modeling*, volume 1921 of *Lecture notes in computer science*. Berlin:Springer-Verlag, 2000.
3. G. Krasner and S. Pope. A description of the model-view-controller user interface paradigm in the smalltalk-80 system. *Journal of Object Oriented Programming*, 1(3):26–49, 1988.
4. Michael Norman and Peter Thomas. The very idea. In Paul Luff, Nigel Gilbert, and David Frohlich, editors, *Computers and Conversation*, pages 51–66. San Diego:Academic Press, 1990.
5. S. Santini, A. Gupta, and R. Jain. Emergent semantics through interaction in image databases. *IEEE Transactions on Knowledge and Data Engineering*, (in press).
6. Simone Santini. *Exploratory Image Databases; Content Based Retrieval*. San Diego:Academic Press, 2001.
7. Simone Santini. Image semantics without annotation. In Siegfried Handschuh and Steffen Staab, editors, *Annotation for the Semantic Web*. Amsterdam:IOS Press, 2003.
8. Matthias Veit and Stephan Herrmann. Model-view-controller and object teams: a perfect match of paradigms. In *AOSD '03: Proceedings of the 2nd international conference on Aspect-oriented software development*, pages 140–149, New York, NY, USA, 2003. ACM Press.
9. Patrcia Vilain, Daniel Schwabe, and Clarisse Sieckenius de Souza. A diagrammatic tool for representing user interaction in uml. In A. Evans, S. Kent, and B. Selic, editors, *UML 2000; The Unified Modeling Language. Advancing the Standard: Third International Conference*. Berlin:Springer-Verlag, 2000.
10. Stephanie Williams. *Hongkong Bank: The Building of Norman Foster's Masterpiece*. Boston: Little, Brown, and Company, 1989.

The User Interface Is the Conceptual Model

James F. Terwilliger[1], Lois M.L. Delcambre[1], and Judith Logan[2]

[1] Department of Computer Science
Portland State University, Portland OR 97207, USA
{jterwill, lmd}@cs.pdx.edu

[2] Department of Medical Informatics and Clinical Epidemiology
School of Medicine, Oregon Health and Science University, Portland OR 97239, USA
loganju@ohsu.edu

Abstract. Frequently, the structure and description of the data in a database bears little resemblance to the structure and description of data as it appears in the tool that captured it. This makes it difficult for users to write queries because they receive little information from the database schema regarding the precise meaning of the data. We assert that the semantics of data can be more reliably understood by viewing the data in the context of the user interface (UI) of the software tool used to enter the data rather than the bare framework of a database. GUAVA (GUi As View) presents a conceptual model that captures information about user interface components. In this paper, we describe how to model a forms-based UI using a GUAVA-tree (g-tree), which can be used to generate a natural schema against which querying is simple. We then introduce and formalize the notion of a channel of database transformation operators from the natural schema to the underlying physical schema.

1 Introduction

The user interface for a typical information system comprises various forms with controls such as radio buttons, check boxes, drop-down lists, group boxes, and text boxes that allow data to be entered. The user interface usually includes labels for each control and possibly other descriptive information that helps a user understand the data that is being entered or displayed through the user interface. More than that, one form may contain a button that allows the user to launch a second form. In short, the user interface, by design, provides a detailed description of the data (to be entered and to be displayed) in a given application.

Software development environments in common use make it quite easy to assemble a user interface, simply by selecting and placing instances of the various controls. There is typically a main-memory data structure that holds the data associated with the form. This data structure is often structured as a set of tables; we refer to this as the *natural schema* associated with the user interface. The job of the developer, then, is to write the code that provides for any special checking or handling of the data and then stores it in a database or other persistent store. The database schema may have a structure that is quite similar to the natural schema, e.g., where there is one table for each form, with one attribute for each control on a form.

D.W. Embley, A. Olivé, and S. Ram (Eds.): ER 2006, LNCS 4215, pp. 424–436, 2006.

However, our focus is on database schemas where the structure can be considerably different from the natural representation. In our experience, software tools for data entry are almost always implemented with a generic schema — where the data from the user interface is stored in attribute-value pairs, and the software can be easily extended without modifying the schema. The difference between the natural schema, where attribute names are used to indicate the field, and the underlying physical database schema, where attribute names appear as data, is referred to as *schematic heterogeneity* [5]. Although some effort has been devoted to providing an SQL-like query language that can handle schematic heterogeneity [3], the resulting language may be quite difficult for ordinary users to master.

Our research has a simple goal: use the user interface of the software tool that creates the data directly as the conceptual model for users, and allow the users to express queries against the resulting conceptual model. But we must be able to process user queries against the underlying database, as specified by the database designer. The problem, then, is how to support the natural schema for the purpose of querying, with a physical database with a significantly different structure.

This paper introduces components of the GUi As View (GUAVA) framework, as shown in Figure 1. First, the complete structure of the user interface is represented in a hierarchical structure called a GUAVA-tree (*g-tree*). GUAVA automatically generates a g-tree from the user interface controls based on our extensions to an integrated development environment. Next, GUAVA translates a g-tree into a simple relational table structure with a natural schema. Finally, a database designer can transform the natural schema into the underlying physical database schema using database operators. A collection of these operators form a *channel* that transforms the natural schema into the desired physical schema (at DB design time) and to transform simple queries from the application and the query interface from the natural schema to the physical schema (at run time).

The central purpose of this paper is to introduce the g-tree as a conceptual model and to formally define the transformation operators that can appear in the channel. The remainder of this paper is organized as follows. Section 2 provides the motivation for this work. The GUAVA framework is presented in Section 3, the main section of the paper. Section 4 describes our current work; Section 5 briefly discussed related work; and the paper concludes with a discussion of contributions and future work in Section 6.

2 Motivation

The development of GUAVA is motivated by our work with the Clinical Outcomes Research Initiative (CORI) [1] where endoscopy reports from nearly 70 sites across the US are being compiled in a data warehouse on an ongoing basis. CORI seeks to improve the practice of endoscopy by conducting retroactive studies on de-identified patient data (i.e., the endoscopy reports). CORI develops and distributes a software reporting tool that allows the clinician to enter

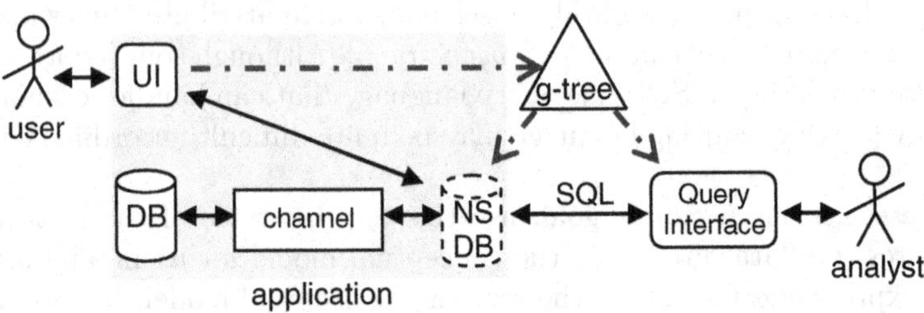

Fig. 1. The GUi As View (GUAVA) software engineering framework

data that describes the endoscopic procedure and then generates the endoscopy report, suitable for inclusion in the patient medical record.

CORI supports a number of data analysts who conduct various studies. Each study requires that the analyst select an appropriate subset of the reports in the warehouse, classify the source data into categories of interest in the study, as appropriate, and then hand-off the selected data, post-classification, for analysis in a statistical package. Given that additional vendors of endoscopic reporting tools would like to contribute to the CORI warehouse and given that the current generic schema used for the CORI warehouse is nearly unintelligible to the CORI analysts, we have defined the GUAVA framework [11] to allow the analyst to express queries directly against the user interface and an accompanying framework to support multiple classification decisions. Since we are working with report data, we have focused on source schemas with what we call a "single entity of interest" (a report, in the CORI case) with an accompanying, perhaps complex, user interface. That is, the source data has a primary entity as described in an initial form in the interface, with weak entities to provide further elaboration (corresponding to nested forms) of the primary entity.

3 Introduction to GUAVA

The GUAVA framework seeks to exploit the hierarchical nature of forms-based user interfaces (e.g., Figure 2) to provide a simple representation of its information. We define a GUAVA-tree (*g-tree*) to represent the information present on a user interface, including the relationships between forms. Also of interest are the *context elements* for the controls, such as the control's type (e.g. text box or checkbox), its default value, and its text. A control's text may be simple to find for checkboxes and group boxes, where the text is actually part of the control,

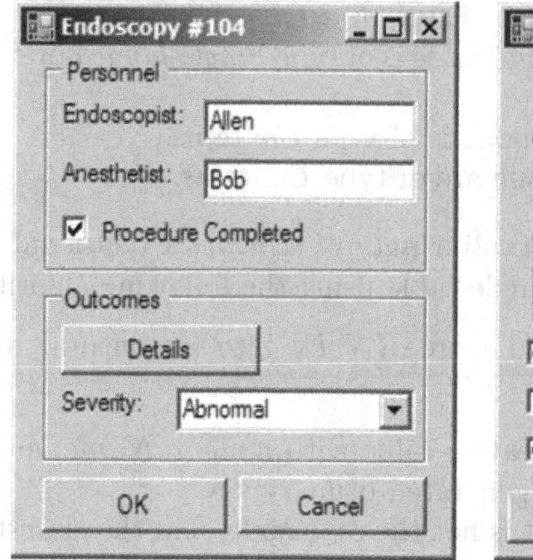

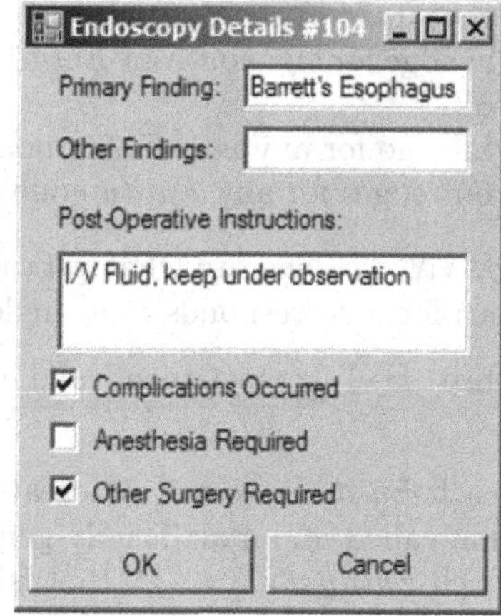

Fig. 2. A simple forms-based application with two forms. The second form provides additional details for the same person represented by the first form, and that the second form appears by clicking the first form's 'Details' button.

but harder for text boxes and drop-down lists where the text is actually in an adjacent label. These properties are important to anyone using the application, but are also informative to users that want to query the data.

Formally, a g-tree is a tree with nodes N and edges E such that:

- Each $n \in N$ is labeled with one of the values *Entity*, *Attribute*, *Container*, or *Control*.
- Each $n \in N$ has an attribute $Name$ whose value is unique in the tree.
- Each $n \in N$ has a hash function h that associates context elements with values.
- Each $e \in E$ is labeled with one of the values *Contains*, *Single-launch*, or *Multiple-launch*.

Translating a user interface into a g-tree is straightforward (Figure 3). Each form in the user interface becomes an entity node, each data-bound control becomes an attribute node, each container control (such as a group box) becomes a container node, and everything else becomes a control node. The name of each node is derived from the name of the control in code. If one form or control contains another, a *Contains* edge is drawn from one to the other. If a control launches another form, but the new form merely contains more details about the first form, a *Single-Launch* edge is drawn from the control to the form. If, instead, the new form is a new entity entirely, a *Multiple-Launch* edge is drawn.

Notice that not every g-tree corresponds to a working user interface. For instance, a single-launch edge leading to an attribute node does not make sense, because that implies clicking a button launches a text box or a checkbox, not another form. We define a g-tree to be *valid* if it satisfies these properties:

- The root node of the tree must be of type *Entity*.
- The in-edge for any non-root *Entity* node is of type *Single-launch* or *Multiple-launch*.
- The in-edge for any non-*Entity* node is of type *Contains*.
- The out-edges for any *Entity* node are of type *Contains*.

In GUAVA, we generate what we call a *natural schema*, a relational schema where each form corresponds to a single table using the following algorithm:

Algorithm 1: To translate a valid g-tree (N, E) into its natural database schema:

- For each *Entity* node $n \in N$, create a table with name $n.Name$, and add a column called *id*, an artificially-generated primary key.
- For each *Entity* node $n \in N$ that is not the root node, find the closest *Entity* node p above it in the tree. If n's in-edge is of type *Single-launch*, create a foreign key from $(n.Name).id$ to $(p.Name).id$. If n's in-edge is of type *Multiple-launch*, create a new column $(n.Name).fk$ and a foreign key from the new column to $(p.Name).id$.
- For each *Attribute* node $a \in N$, find the closest entity node p in its list of ancestors and create a column named $a.Name$ in p's table.

Figure 4 shows the result of running Algorithm 1 on the g-tree in Figure 3.

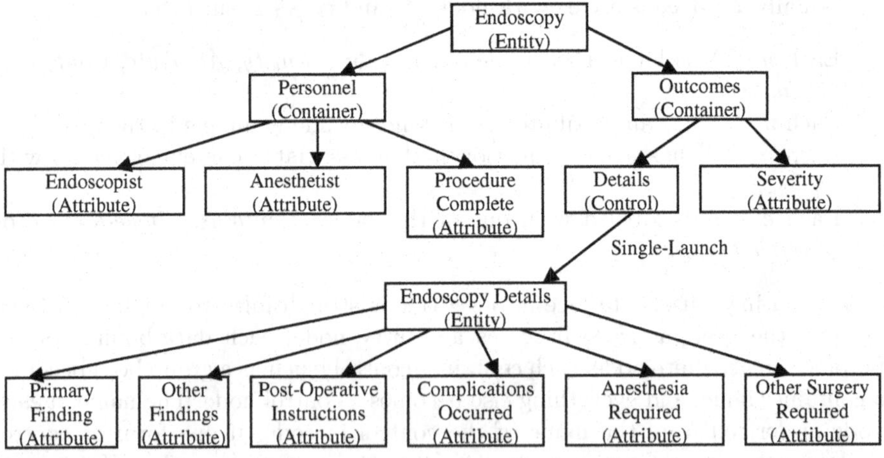

Fig. 3. An example g-tree corresponding to the application in Figure 2. Any edge that is not labeled is a *Contains* edge.

To pose a query against a g-tree, any attribute node in the tree can be marked as a "print" node or as a filter node with a boolean condition, similar to QBE. Translating a g-tree query into a query against the natural schema is straightforward. The result is a simple query language, where the following constructs are allowed:

- T for any table in the natural schema
- $Exp1 \bowtie Exp2$ only if there is a foreign key from $Exp2$ to $Exp1$
- $\pi_C(Exp)$ for any collection of columns
- $\sigma_{C=V}(Exp)$ for any column C and any atomic constant value V

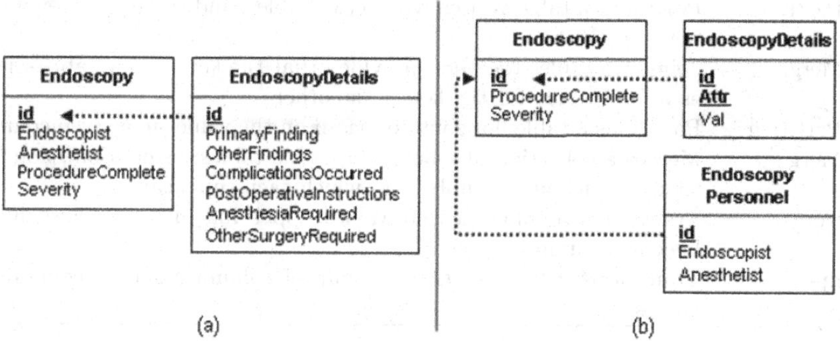

Fig. 4. The natural schema corresponding to Figure 3, before (a) and after (b) the application of a channel with operators Unpivot(EndoscopyDetails, {id}) and VPartition(Endoscopy, {id}, {ProcedureComplete, Severity}, EndoscopyPersonnel)

4 Formal Definition of Database Operators

The focus of this paper is on defining the GUAVA back-end so that queries expressed against the natural schema can be processed against an underlying physical database whose schema may be completely different. Our approach is to define invertible database transformation operators that allow a database designer the freedom to structure the physical database as he or she chooses. In the formal definition that we present here, instances of these operators provide automatic generation of the physical database schema, as well as automatic translation of the data input from the user interface for storage in the physical database. The operators are invertible, so they also describe how to translate the physical data back into the natural schema to make it available for query processing.

Table 1 lists operators that GUAVA provides, with a short description. The parameters required to instantiate each database operator are present in Table 2. Table 3 formally describes how each operator transforms a schema and an instance of a database. Each operator can take a schema or database instance as input, and produces a schema or database instance as output. The operator definitions use the following notation:

- **Tables**: The list of tables in the schema
- **Cols**(T): The list of columns in the schema for table T
- $inst(T)$: The instance of table T
- $Name(D)$: The name of the column or table D, returned as a data value
- A subscript of "in", such as $inst_{in}$, refers to the input of the operator

Table 1. Descriptions of eight database operators

Operator	Description
Apply	Uses an invertible function to transform the values in a table
Rename	Uses an invertible function to rename the tables or columns in the schema
VPartition	Partitions a table vertically into two tables, and creates a foreign key between the two
VMerge	Joins two tables together, provided that the key for one table serves as a foreign key for the key of the other
HPartition	Partitions a table horizontally based on the values in a given column
HMerge	Merges a collection of union-compatible tables, using a new column to keep track of the table from which each tuple came
Pivot	Transforms a table so that values appearing in a specific column become column headings
Unpivot	Transforms a table so that a group of column names become data values

- A subscript of "out", such as $inst_{out}$, refers to the output of the operator
- Anything in **boldface** is a set

The operators defined in Table 3 have an inverse operator, as shown in Table 4. The current focus of this work is allowing a DB designer to specify the sequence of operators necessary to transform the natural schema associated with the user interface into the stored DB. Once the sequence of transformation operators is specified, we show that the stored database instance can be transformed into an instance of the natural schema, using the sequence of inverse operators in reverse order.

Definition: A *cell* is an instantiation of a database operator with specific input parameters provided. A cell includes an instantiation of the operator's inverse. As shown in Table 4, some parameters for the inverse operator in a cell are taken from the input parameters to the operator in this cell. Thus, a cell provides a mechanism to "remember" specific details of the original transform operator. For example, the HPartition operator produces a set of new tables ($\mathbf{Ts^{result}}$) from a given table (T). The inverse operator, HMerge, within the cell uses these table names (merging $\mathbf{Ts^{result}}$ to produce T). To apply a cell *forward* is to apply the operator; to apply a cell in *reverse* is to apply the inverse operator.

Theorem 1. *Given a cell with operator O from Table 1 with specific parameters P and the inverse operator O' from Table 1 with parameters P' as shown in Table 4, $S = O'(P')(O(P)(S))$ and $D = O'(P')(O(P)(D))$ for any schema S and its instance D on which the operator O is valid. Note that $O(P)$ returns an instantiated operator that can then be applied to either a schema or an instance.*

Proof: The claim is true for Apply and Rename because the particular functions (shown as f in Table 3) are invertible and defined for all input (from the natural schema). The fact that the claim is true for the remaining operators follows from their definitions as shown in Table 3.

Table 2. Eight database operators, their parameters and restrictions

Operator	Input Parameters
Apply	T: The input table name, $T \in \mathbf{Tables_{in}}$ C^1: A column name, $\mathbf{C^1} \in \mathbf{Cols_{in}}(T)$ C^2: A column name, $\mathbf{C^2} \notin \mathbf{Cols_{in}}(T)$ f: A total, invertible function with single input and single output
Rename	f: A total, invertible function whose input and output are string values
VPartition	T: The input table name, $T \in \mathbf{Tables_{in}}$ **Ks**: The set of key column names, $\mathbf{Ks} \subset \mathbf{Cols_{in}}(T)$ **Cs**: A set of non-key column names from T, $\mathbf{Cs} \subset (\mathbf{Cols_{in}}(T) - \mathbf{Ks})$ T^{new}: The name of the new table, $T^{new} \notin \mathbf{Tables_{in}}$
VMerge	T^L: The primary input table name, $T^L \in \mathbf{Tables_{in}}$ T^R: The name of the table to merge, $T^R \in \mathbf{Tables_{in}}$ **Ks**: A set of column names where **Ks** comprises the key for both T^L and T^R and a foreign key exists from T^R.**Ks** to T^L.**Ks**
HPartition	T: The input table name, $T \in \mathbf{Tables_{in}}$ C: A column name, $C \in \mathbf{Cols_{in}}(T)$ whose values will be used to distribute the table's tuples $\mathbf{Ts^{result}}$: The set of output table names, $\mathbf{Ts^{result}} \cup \mathbf{Tables_{in}} = \oslash$
HMerge	**Ts**: A set of table names, $\mathbf{Ts} \subseteq \mathbf{Tables_{in}}$ where the tables in **T** are union-compatible T^{result}: The output table name, $T^{result} \notin \mathbf{Tables_{in}}$ C: A column name such that, $\forall T \in \mathbf{Ts}$, $C \notin \mathbf{Cols_{in}}(T)$
Pivot	T: The input table name, $T \in \mathbf{Tables_{in}}$ such that the name $Value \in \mathbf{Cols_{in}}(T)$ **Ks**: The set of key column names from T, including one column named *Attr*
Unpivot	T: The input table name, $T \in \mathbf{Tables_{in}}$ **Ks**: The set of key column names from T where the columns $(\mathbf{Cols_{in}}(T) - \mathbf{Ks})$ have the same data type

Definition: A *channel* is a sequence of cells, as shown in Figure 5. Formally, for a channel C, $C = O_n(P_n) \circ \ldots \circ O_1(P_1)$, and $C^{-1} = O_1(P_1)^{-1} \circ \ldots \circ O_n(P_n)^{-1}$. Thus, we use the notation $C(S)$ (or $C^{-1}(S)$) for a forward (reverse) application of the cells in forward (reverse) order. Similarly, we use $C(D)$ and $C^{-1}(D)$ to indicate the application of a forward or reverse data transformation. C is a *valid*

Table 3. Defining the action of eight database operators. Any table in the input schema or instance that is not explicitly referenced by the operator simply passes to the output unaffected.

Operator	Schema Transformation	Data Transformation
Apply (T, C^1, C^2, f)	$\mathbf{Cols_{out}}(T) = (\mathbf{Cols_{in}}(T) - C^1) \cup C^2$	$inst_{out}(T) = \{(d_1, d_2, \ldots, f(d_i), \ldots, d_n) \mid (d_1, d_2, \ldots, d_i, \ldots, d_n) \in inst_{in}(T)\}$ where C^1 is the ith column in T
Rename (f)	$\mathbf{Tables_{out}} = \{f(T) \mid T \in \mathbf{Tables_{in}}\}$ $\forall T \in \mathbf{Tables_{in}},\ \mathbf{Cols_{out}}(f(T)) = \{f(C) \mid C \in \mathbf{Cols_{in}}(T)\}$	None
VPartition $(T, \mathbf{Ks}, \mathbf{Cs}, T^{new})$	$\mathbf{Tables_{out}} = \mathbf{Tables_{in}} + \{T^{new}\}$ $\mathbf{Cols_{out}}(T) = \mathbf{Ks} \cup \mathbf{Cs}$ $\mathbf{Cols_{out}}(T^{new}) = \mathbf{Ks} \cup (\mathbf{Cols_{in}}(T) - \mathbf{Cs})$	$inst_{out}(T) = \pi_{\mathbf{Ks} \cup \mathbf{Cs}}(inst_{in}(T))$ $inst_{out}(T^{new}) = \pi_{\mathbf{Cols_{in}}(\mathbf{T}) - \mathbf{Cs}}(inst_{in}(T))$
VMerge $(T^L, T^R, \mathbf{Ks})$	$\mathbf{Cols}(T^L) = \mathbf{Cols}(T^L) \cup \mathbf{Cols}(T^R)$ $\mathbf{Tables_{out}} = \mathbf{Tables_{in}} - \{T^R\}$	$inst_{out}(T^L) = inst_{in}(T^L) \bowtie_{T^L.K = T^R.K \forall K \in \mathbf{KS}} inst_{in}(T^R)$
HPartition $(T, C, \mathbf{Ts^{result}})$	$\mathbf{Tables_{out}} = (\mathbf{Tables_{in}} - T) \cup \mathbf{Ts^{result}}$ $\forall T^r \in \mathbf{Ts^{result}},\ \mathbf{Cols_{out}}(T^r) = \mathbf{Cols_{in}}(T) - \{C\}$	$inst_{out}(T^r) = \pi_{\mathbf{Cols_{in}}(\mathbf{T}) - \{\mathbf{C}\}}(\sigma_{T.C = Name(T^r)}(inst_{in}(T)))$
HMerge $(\mathbf{Ts}, T^{result}, C)$	$\mathbf{Cols_{out}}(T^{result}) = \mathbf{Cols_{in}}(T) \cup \{Name(C)\}$, for any $T \in \mathbf{Ts}$	$inst_{out}(T^{result}) = \bigcup_{T \in \mathbf{Ts}}(inst_{in}(T) \times (Name(T)))$
Pivot $(T, \mathbf{Ks})$	$\mathbf{Cols_{out}}(T) = \mathbf{Ks} \cup \mathbf{Ds}$ where $\mathbf{Ds}$ = the set of values in $inst_{in}(T.Attr)$ New key for T is $\mathbf{Ks} - \{Attr\}$	$inst_{out}(T) = \pi_{\mathbf{Ks} - \{Attr\}}(inst_{in}(T)) \bowtie \rho_{Value \to D_1}\pi_{(\mathbf{Ks} - \{Attr\}) \cup \{Value\}}(\sigma_{T.Attr = D_1}(inst_{in}(T))) \bowtie \ldots \bowtie \rho_{Value \to D_n}\pi_{(\mathbf{Ks} - \{Attr\}) \cup \{Value\}}(\sigma_{T.Attr = D_n}(inst_{in}(T)))$ for $\mathbf{Ds} = \{D_1, D_2, \ldots, D_n\}$
Unpivot $(T, \mathbf{Ks})$	$\mathbf{Cols_{out}}(T) = \mathbf{Ks} \cup \{Value, Attr\}$ New key for T is $Ks \cup \{Attr\}$	$inst_{out}(T) = \bigcup_{C \in (\mathbf{Cols_{in}}(T) - \mathbf{Ks})}(\pi_{Ks \cup \{C\}}(inst_{in}(T)) \times (Name(C)))$

channel for a schema S and instance D if, when applied to S and D, none of the restrictions on the operators in C, as described in Table 2, are violated.

The following theorem guarantees that the original fully materialized natural schema is equivalent to the data returned from the physical database associated with a valid channel. This provides the foundation for query processing in GUAVA.

Theorem 2. *Given a schema S with instance D, and a channel C that is valid on S and D, $S = C^{-1}(C(S))$ and $D = C^{-1}(C(D))$.*

Proof: The proof follows from the fact that each cell in the channel represents an invertible function and the composition of invertible functions is invertible. Note, we expect that each operator in a channel to be total with respect to the input data that appear as input when using the channel in the forward direction. Thus, the function f used with the Apply operator must be defined for all values that can appear in the relevant attributes and the HPartition operator must have an input table name in $\mathbf{Ts}^{\mathbf{result}}$ for each possible value that can appear in the column upon which the HPartition is based.

In our implementation in progress, the channel does not transform an entire database instance. Rather, it transforms DML and DDL statements and SQL queries issued against the natural schema into the corresponding statements against the physical schema. The channel also transforms query results so that it appears that the query was actually executed against the natural schema.

Table 4. Defining the inverse of the eight database operators

Operator	Inverse
Apply (T, C^1, C^2, f)	Apply (T, C^2, C^1, f^{-1})
Rename (f)	Rename (f^{-1})
VPartition $(T, \mathbf{Ks}, \mathbf{Cs}, T^{new})$	VMerge $(T, T^{new}, \mathbf{Ks})$
VMerge $(T^L, T^R, \mathbf{Ks})$	VPartition $(T^L, \mathbf{Ks}, \mathbf{Cols_{in}}(T^L) - \mathbf{Ks}, T^R)$
HPartition $(T, C, \mathbf{Ts}^{\mathbf{result}})$	HMerge $(\mathbf{Ts}^{\mathbf{result}}, T, C)$
HMerge $(\mathbf{Ts}, T^{result}, C)$	HPartition (T^{result}, C)
Pivot $(T, \mathbf{Ks})$	Unpivot $(T, \mathbf{Ks} - \{Attr\})$
Unpivot $(T, \mathbf{Ks})$	Pivot $(T, \mathbf{Ks} \cup \{Attr\})$

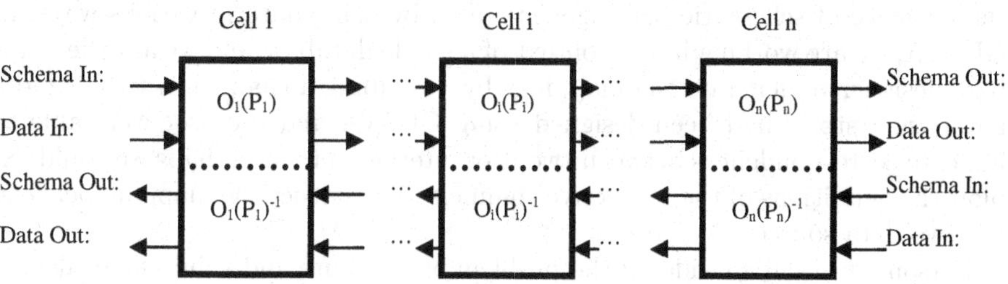

Fig. 5. Description of a channel, as used in our formal definition

5 Related Work

Our Pivot, Unpivot, HMerge, and HPartition operators are adapted from Lakshmanan, et al, [3]. Our work differs in its approach. Whereas SchemaSQL allows the user (i.e., the query writer) to express queries in the presence of schematic heterogeneity, Guava presents the user with a simple query language over a simple view of his or her data that mirrors a user interface and allows the database design to express transformations as desired, including transformations that introduce schematic heterogeneity.

There are several approaches that model a user interface as a tree structure and view the associated data as an XML document, including XAML [13] and XUL [14]. These XML-based approaches are similar in spirit to GUAVA but they are limited to describing a single form at a time; there is no automated support for describing the relationship among forms other than by using a programming language.

GUAVA allows the database designer to describe how to transform a natural relational schema (that arises from the hierarchical g-tree) to other relational schemas. So GUAVA offers an approach different from the typical XML shredding approaches [2] to choosing a relational database schema to store XML data.

Rather than starting with the UI and generating the back end as GUAVA does, a Ruby on Rails scaffold [9] starts with the database and generates a UI that performs queries and updates. That is, Ruby on Rails makes it easy to start with what we call the natural schema and then generate a user interface and provides no support for schematic heterogeneity. One approach to application development would be to start with the natural schema and use Ruby on Rails (or a similar tool) to generate a user interface and then use GUAVA to generate the back-end.

Rollinson and Roberts [8] describe how to represent the semantics of a forms-based interface in a conceptual modeling language. The applications they consider are limited to ones where the UI and the database are closely related, perhaps even where the UI is semi-automatically generated from the database.

In general, our GUAVA framework offers one approach to information transformation and is thus related to some aspects of the decades of work in information integration. We comment on a few specific efforts here. Miller, et al, [6] have considered ways to help the user identify mappings between data sources in the presence of schematic heterogeneity, e.g., by using data in various ways. In GUAVA, we are working in the context of a single database and we ask the database designer to generate the mappings by describing a channel. If two or more database systems had been designed using GUAVA and the user were able to indicate correspondences between two user interfaces, then perhaps we could exploit the definitions of the respective channels to construct the mapping between the two data sources.

Larson, et al, [4] considered the problem of attribute and values equivalences extensively. We introduce the Apply operator to handle attribute transformations. The COIN project [10] focuses on describing attributes with context elements, such as units. GUAVA captures context information about each user interface control, such as the label that appears on the screen. We do not focus specifically on the kind of context elements considered in the COIN project, such as units for a value, but such context elements could be easily incorporated in GUAVA.

GUAVA offers an alternative to the classical extract-transform-load processing associated with a data warehouse [12]. In fact, GUAVA was motivated by the difficulties experienced by CORI analysts when trying to understand the data warehouse schema well enough to extract data for their queries. The contribution of GUAVA is it allows users to express queries against the natural schema, with context elements from the user interface, rather than against the data warehouse schema.

Finally, our work is not addressing the problem of automatic schema matching [7] but perhaps suggests the possibility of trying to match user interfaces directly and then rely on the corresponding channels to determine the mappings between schemas. Also, if we succeed in extending GUAVA to propagate user interface changes to the stored database schema, we will likely have a detailed description of how one schema (from an earlier version of the software) matches new versions.

6 Conclusions and Future Work

This paper defines the initial, formal framework for supporting GUAVA, where we use the user interface, directly, as a conceptual model. The database operators, instantiated in a channel, precisely describe the transformations that take place between the natural schema and the desired, stored database schema.

Our GUAVA implementation extends a subset of the forms controls in the Microsoft Visual Studio development environment to automatically generate the g-tree and corresponding natural schema. We are currently implementing the operators shown in Tables 1-3 in the channel. Also, we are considering additiona operators besides the ones in Table 1 as necessary.

We have defined the GUAVA query language, and are developing query optimization strategies. We plan to develop a user-friendly interface that allows the user to express queries against a visual display that looks like the original user interface. Although our work was prompted by the need to describe the relationship between the user interface and the stored, generic database schemas typically used by forms-based reporting tools, we believe that the database operators introduced here can be used more generally. As one part of that work, we will define the conditions under which a channel is valid for a particular schema and instance. We would also like to consider how to modify the GUAVA framework to accommodate modifications to the UI. We hope to propagate the desired changes to the g-tree and its natural schema through the channel to the physical database. Finally, we plan to extend the set of user interface controls that can be used with GUAVA to include aggregate data structures (such as lists, tuples, and trees) over known atomic data types (such as strings, integer, and binary objects), and define appropriate translations to the natural schema.

Acknowledgements

This work is supported in part by Collins Medical Trust, by DHHS NIH National Institute of Diabetes Digestive and Kidney Diseases No. 5-R33-DK061778-03 awarded to Oregon Health & Science University (OHSU), and by NSF grant No. 0534762.

References

1. Clinical Outcomes Research Initiative. Available at http://www.cori.org/. Last accessed on April 10, 2006.
2. F. Du, S. Amir-Yahia, J. Freire. A comprehensive solution to the XML-to-relational mapping problem. In *Proceedings of the 6th Annual ACM International Workshop on Web Information and Data Management*, Washington DC, November 12-13, 2004, 31–38.
3. L. V. S. Lakshmanan, F. Sadri, and S. N. Subramanian. On efficiently implementing SchemaSQL on a SQL database system. In *Proceedings of the International Conference on Very Large Databases (VLDB 99)*, Edinburg, Scotland, September 1999, 471–482.
4. J. A. Larson, S. B. Navathe, and R. Elmasri. A Theory of Attribute Equivalence in Databases with Application to Schema Integration. *IEEE Transactions on Software Engineering*, April 1989, 15(4):449–463.
5. R. J. Miller. Using Schematically Heterogeneous Structures. In *Proceedings of ACM SIGMOD*, Seattle, WA, June 1998, 27(2):189–200.
6. R. J. Miller, M. A. Hernandez, L. M. Haas, L.-L. Yan, C. T. H. Ho, R. Fagin, and L. Popa. The Clio Project: Managing Heterogeneity. *SIGMOD Record*, 2001, 30(1):78–83.
7. E. Rahm and P.A. Bernstein. A survey of approaches to automatic schema matching. In *Proceedings of the 27th International Conferences on Very Large Databases*, 2001, 10(4):334–350.
8. S. R. Rollinson and S. A. Roberts. Formalizing the Informational Content of Database User Interfaces. In *Proceedings of the 17th International Conference on Conceptual Modeling (ER98)*, Singapore, November 16-19, 1998, 65–77.
9. Ruby on Rails. Available at http://www.rubyonrails.org/. Last accessed on April 10, 2006.
10. E. Sciore, M. Siegel, and A. Rosenthal. Using semantic values to facilitate interoperability among heterogeneous information systems. *ACM Transactions on Database Systems*, June 1994, 19(2):254–290.
11. J. F. Terwilliger, L. M. L. Delcambre, and J. Logan. Context-Sensitive Data Integration. In *Proceedings of the EDBT 2006 Workshop on Information Integration in Healthcare Applications (IIHA)*, Munich, Germany, March 26, 2006, 20–31.
12. P. Vassiliadis, A. Simitsis, P. Georgantas, M. Terrovitis, and S. Skiadopoulos. A generic and customizable framework for the design of ETL scenarios. *Information Systems*, November 2005, 30(7):492–525.
13. XAML. Available at http://www.xaml.net/. Last accessed on April 10, 2006.
14. XUL. Available at http://www.xulplanet.com/. Last accessed on April 10, 2006.

Towards a Holistic Conceptual Modelling-Based Software Development Process

Sergio España, José Ignacio Panach, Inés Pederiva, and Óscar Pastor

Department of Information Systems and Computation
Valencia University of Technology
Camino de Vera s/n, 46022 Valencia, España
Phone: +34 96 387 7000, Fax.: +34 96 3877359
{sergio.espana, jpanach, ipederiva, opastor}@dsic.upv.es

Abstract. Traditionally, the Conceptual Modelling (CM) community has been interested in defining methods to model Information Systems by specifying their data and behaviour, disregarding user interaction. On the other hand, the Human-Computer Interaction (HCI) community has defined techniques oriented to the modelling of the interaction between the user and the system, proposing a user-centred software construction, but leaving out details on system data and behaviour. This paper aspires to reconcile both visions by integrating task modelling techniques using a sound, conceptual model-based software development process in a HCI context. The system is considered on its three axis (data, functionality and interaction), as a whole. The use of CTT (Concurrent Task Trees) embedded in a model-based approach makes it possible to establish mapping rules between task structure patterns that describe interaction and the elements of the abstract interface model. By defining such structural patterns, the CTT notation is much more manageable and productive; therefore, this HCI technique can be easily integrated in a well-established conceptual modelling approach. This proposal is underpinned by the MDA-based technology OlivaNova Method Execution, which allows real automatic software generation, while still taking user interface into account at an early requirements elicitation stage.

1 Introduction

For several decades, computer science students have become aware of the Crisis of Software concept. It is related to the apparently unavoidable fact that producing an Information System is costly (it uses expensive resources over extended periods of time); it is much too slow for modern business conditions; it is very risky (it is hard to control and has a high failure rate); and it is highly unreliable (because it introduces hidden failure points).

The Conceptual Model community continues to claim that programming is still the basic task when software engineers speak in terms of the expected final software product and this fault justifies the historical failure when it is attempted to meet software system needs. From a Conceptual Modelling perspective, the development process has not changed much over the past 40 years. Even if it is strongly argued that Model-Based Code Generation can provide a reliable alternative to those

D.W. Embley, A. Olivé, and S. Ram (Eds.): ER 2006, LNCS 4215, pp. 437–450, 2006.

conventional programming-based software production environments, in most projects, the design, programming and testing activities still require substantial manual effort. Thus, the potential that modelling offers is not being taken advantage of.

After many attempts, it seems that, for the first time, the idea of transforming the model into code is an affordable dream, instead of having the code as the only real model. Many specific proposals have been presented: Extreme-Non-Programming (XNP) [18], Model Driven Architecture (MDA) [23], Conceptual-Schema Centric Development [22], Model Transformation Technologies, etc. Even tools that implement Conceptual Model Compilers have started to appear in industry.

In this challenging context, it is interesting to realize that modelling an Information System is traditionally seen as a process where there is a data-oriented component and a process-oriented component as the two basic axes. They represent the static system view and the dynamic system view, respectively. Accordingly, a lot of methods and techniques have been provided in the past to solve this specification problem, including well-known data modelling techniques (the Entity-Relationship Model [4] and its extensions) and process modelling approaches (Structured Analysis with its Data Flow Diagrams). In the nineties Object-Oriented Modelling was seen as the way to encapsulate statics (data) and dynamics (behaviour) under the common notion of object, so new methods [2][32] and languages (UML [24]) have been proposed under this unified paradigm. The focus is commonly placed on those data and functional system aspects at the modelling stage, while one very important issue is normally left aside until the design stage: the user interaction with the system.

This is the main issue that we confront in this work and several questions arise. If user interaction is a basic component of a system specification, why is interaction modelling not considered at the same level as data and behaviour modelling in the vast majority of software production methods? Isn't interaction an essential part of the world description, as system data and functionality are? Why isn't there a widely accepted model when talking about user interaction modelling, as there is when talking about data modelling (i.e. the ER model)? A possible explanation for this situation is that the interaction modelling problem has been treated separately by a parallel community, the Human Computer Interaction community (HCI), where specific techniques are proposed as potential solutions. However, these proposals normally ignore the required link of interaction modelling with data and process modelling.

In order to provide proper bridges between the Conceptual Modelling (CM) and the HCI communities, we assume that CM is considered to be strong in modelling data and functional requirements, while HCI is centred on defining user interaction at the appropriate level of abstraction. We want to define a conceptual model-based software production environment where system data, functionality and interaction are specified all together, in a precise way. We argue that if any of these aspects is not properly dealt with, the software production process will fail because, as a whole, the reality to be modelled is an inseparable mix of data, functionality and interaction.,

The purpose of this paper is to provide the basis for building a holistic software production process, with two basic principles in mind:

- To use Model Transformation as the basic strategy to automate the conversion of the Requirements Model into the Conceptual Model, and then to convert this

Conceptual Model into the final software product. A model compiler implements the corresponding mappings.
- To assume that each modelling step has to provide the appropriate methods to deal properly with the specification of structural, functional, and interaction properties.

We present an approach that introduces the following original aspects:

- The combination of two well-known techniques that come from different fields: a sound functional specification (Use Cases [10], widely used in CM contexts) that is enriched by an interaction model (CTT Model from HCI [26])
- Then a set of mappings allows the derivation of the Conceptual Schema.

The approach presented here is currently being successfully implemented in OlivaNova Model Execution (ONME)[3], an MDA-based tool which generates a software product that corresponds to the source Conceptual Schema. Without going into detail on the technical aspects of the model compilation, we intend to demonstrate that conceptual modelling is more powerful when user interaction and system behaviour are modelled within a unified view at the early stage of requirements elicitation.

The paper is structured as follows. Section 2 presents an overview of model-based user interface development environments proposed in the literature. Section 3 introduces a software production process that combines model-based and task-based approaches. This process is explained with a case study using an application generated with ONME. Finally, section 4 presents the conclusions derived from the process application, and future work.

2 Related Work

From an HCI point of view, there are a number of model-based user interface development environments (MB-UIDEs) reported in the literature. In da Silva's survey [5], several MB-UIDEs are reviewed, distinguishing two generations of tools. The aim of the first generation was to provide a run-time environment for user interface models; some examples are COUSIN [9], HUMANOID [29] and UIDE [12]. The second generation aimed to provide support for interface modelling at a high level of abstraction. Examples of these environments include ADEPT [15], FUSE [14], GENIUS [11], MASTERMIND [30], MECANO [27], MOBI-D [28], TADEUS [7], and TRIDENT [1]. Many of the second-generation MB-UIDEs rely on a domain model. This model is often a description of the domain entities and the relationships among them, which are represented as a declarative data model (as in MECANO and MOBI-D), an entity-relationship data model (as in GENIUS), or an object-oriented data model (as in FUSE). Some MB-UIDEs like ADEPT, FUSE, TADEUS, TRIDENT, and USIXML propose task models as a primary abstract interaction modelling, from which the abstract interface models (or their equivalent dialogue models) are later derived. It is important to remark that USIXML [31] is an XML-based interface description language that is supported by a suite of tools, ranging from creating User Interface (UI) sketches to generating the final UI. Therefore, we will consider USIXML as an MB-UIDE for the purposes of this review.

Moreover, there are several UML-based approaches. WISDOM [21] is a UML-based software engineering method that proposes a use-case-based and evolutive method in which the software system is iteratively developed by incremental prototypes until the final product is obtained. The UML notation has been enriched with the necessary stereotypes, labelled values, and icons to allow user-centred development and a detailed user interface design. Three of its models are concerned with interaction modelling at different stages: the Interaction Model, at the analysis stage; and the Dialog Model and the Presentation Model during the design stage, as refinements of the Interaction Model. Another important proposal is UMLi [6]. It is a set of user interface models that extends UML to provide greater support for UI design. UMLi introduces a new diagram: User Interface Diagram; it is the first reliable proposal of UML to capture the user interface formally. However, the models are so detailed that the modelling turns out to be very difficult. Middle-sized problems are very hard to specify, that maybe the reason why UMLi has not been adopted in industrial environments.

Table 1 shows a comparison between some of the reviewed MB-UIDEs. In general terms, there is poor lifecycle support, lack of integration between models to provide a full software production process, and lack of functionality specification leading to no functionality generation. In addition, some of the reviewed MB-UIDEs do not allow the automatic generation of the final UI.

Table 1. Review of several approaches

Approach	Whole life-cycle support	Model integration	Functionality specification / generation	Interface generation	Conceptual domain model
Mobi-D	Yes	Yes	No / No	Guided	Declarative
Mastermind	No	Yes	No / No	Yes	Declarative
Adept	Yes	Yes	No / No	Yes	In Task model
Genius	No	Yes	No / No	Yes	Entity relationship
Fuse	No	Yes	Partial/No	Yes	Object model
Tadeus	Yes	Yes	No / No	Yes	Object model
Trident	Yes	Yes	No / No	Yes	Enhanced data models
Usixml	No	Yes	No / No	Yes	Class diagram
Wisdom	Yes	Yes	No / No	No	UML class diagram
UMLi	No	Yes	No/No	Yes	Class diagram

The result is that the application being modelled cannot be completely generated. For example, USIXML has properly mapped the elements of a task model to the elements of domain and interface models by defining a Transformation Model and the corresponding support tools [13][17]. Although there are tools that deal with the final user interface generation, no business layer is generated due to the lack of a functional model.

From a software engineering point of view, some development methods and environments have been proposed. They normally use a class-diagram-like model to capture the system structure and a process model to fix the functionality that the system is supposed to provide. In addition, in recent years, some CASE tools (Together, Rational Rose, Poseidon, etc.) have been proposed with the objective of providing some kind of automation to manage these models. However, interaction modelling is not a key issue when requirements and conceptual modelling is represented in a software production process.

3 The Role of Conceptual Modelling in OlivaNova Model Execution

In this section, we present a complete software production process that combines functional requirements specification, analytical conceptual modelling (including user interaction design), and implementation. It is defined on the basis of OlivaNova Model Execution (ONME) [3], a model-based environment for software development that complies with the MDA paradigm [23] by defining models of a different abstraction level. Figure 1 shows the correspondence between the models proposed by MDA and the models dealt with in OO-Method [25], which is the methodology underlying ONME.

As we are about to see, the main strategy behind OO-Method is the modelling of the real world in terms of abstract concepts which are well defined. In other words, a specific syntax is given to create the models and an unambiguous semantics is conferred to the conceptual constructs. These semantically precise notations will allow us to automatically transform the Conceptual Model into the final application, thus establishing a powerful framework for software production.

At the most abstract level, a *Computation-Independent Model* (CIM) describes the Information System (IS) without considering whether or not it will be supported by any software application. In OO-Method, this description is called the *Functional Requirements Model*. As we have identified a lack of interaction requirements elicitation in these early stages of the software production process, we advocate the adoption of a task model to help to establish the user needs concerning interaction. Figure 1 gives a graphical description of the approach.

The *Platform-Independent Model* (PIM) describes the system in an abstract way, keeping in mind that the system will somehow be computerized but without determining the underlying computer platform. This is called the *Conceptual Model* in OO-Method.

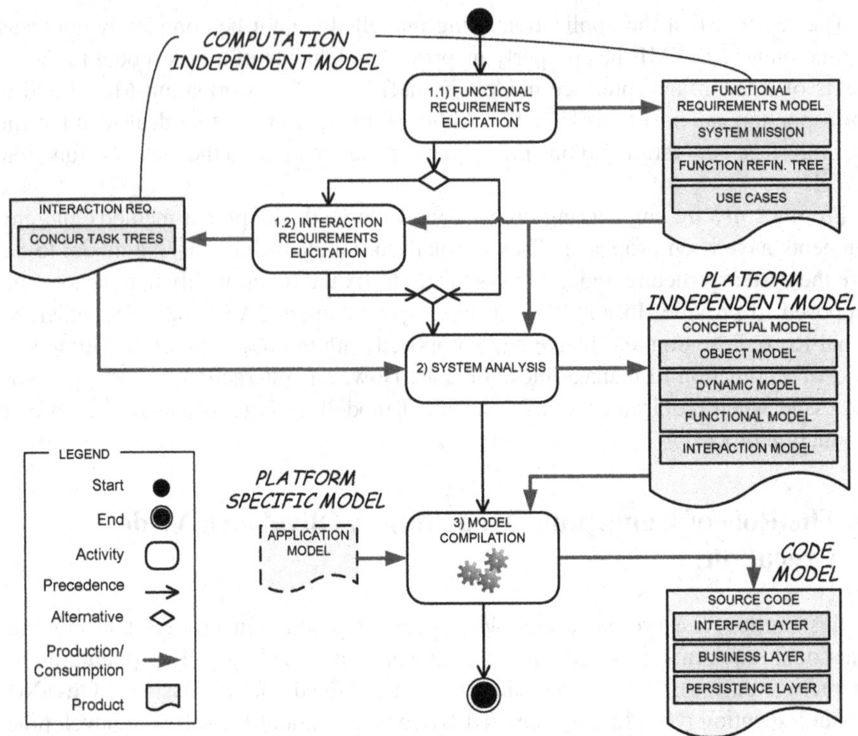

Fig. 1. OO-Method software development as an MDA-compliant process

ONME implements an automatic transformation of the *Conceptual Model* into the source code of the final user application. This is done by a *Model Compilation* process that has implicit knowledge about the target platform. This implied and tacit knowledge, which is equivalent to the *Platform Specific Model* (PSM) defined by MDA, is projected onto the mappings between the concepts of the PIM and their implementation on a specific programming language and platform (the *Code Model*, CM).

In the following, we explain the main steps of our software production process in more detail, illustrating the argumentation with examples from a real case study.

3.1 Functional Requirements Extraction

The first step in building the conceptual modelling is the capture of requirements. In our software production process, this is done through the definition of a Requirements Model [10]. This model contains a description of the objectives and the external behaviour of the system, that is, *what* the system must do without describing *how* to do it.

The Requirements Model is defined using three elements: the Mission Statement, the Functions Refinement Tree (FRT), and the Use-Case Model.

The Mission Statement is a high-level description of the nature and purpose of the system. This element describes what the system will and will not do. The FRT represents the hierarchical decomposition of the business functions of a system, independently of the current system structure. Each tree's leaf is a function of the system. The leaves are grouped into internal tree nodes that group related business functions.

Once we have defined the FRT, the next step is to create the Use-Case Model. A use case is an interaction between the system and an external entity. The leaf nodes of the FRT, which are the elemental functions, are considered to be primary use cases; they represent the most important functions of the system.

In order to explain our proposal, we use an example taken from a real system from the OlivaNova Model Execution portfolio: the Bullent Water application. This system is used in a company that delivers water to homes. The main functions of the system are: to read the customer's meter, to emit an invoice, to register the use of some material in a repair, and to maintain the stock in the warehouses. For the sake of simplicity, we have centred our attention on only one task of this system: the task to *add a meter reading* in the system.

In Figure 2, we show part of the FRT of our case study. The figure shows the functional groups, e.g. *Meter*; this group includes all the functions related to the meters, including the studied task (remarked).

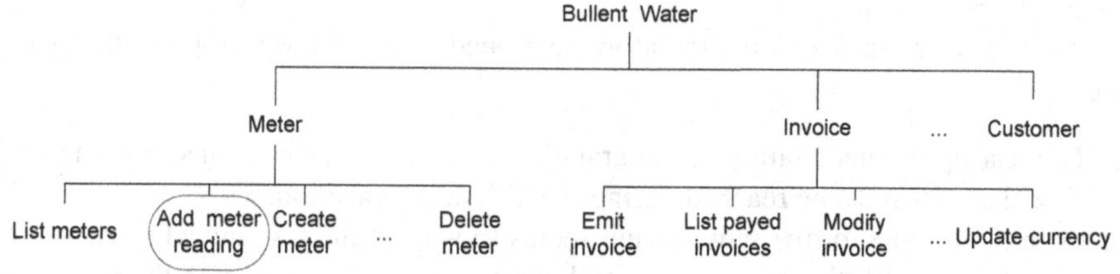

Fig. 2. Functions Refinement Tree for the Bullent Water system

Each use case is described in a template that is a specification of this use case. It consists of a use-case description, the actors who can invoke it, the conditions needed to execute it, and the list of events which compose it. Table 2 contains the specification of the studied task.

Table 2. Use-case specification

Identification:	**Add meter reading**
Description:	It creates a new meter reading in the system.
Actor:	Administrator
Precondition:	Meter must previously exist
Event flow:	1.Click on new meter reading 2.Select the meter that has been read 3.Insert the date of the reading 4.Insert the measurement (in cubic metres) 6.The entered information is saved

3.2 Modelling Interaction Requirements with CTT

We have proposed the Concur Task Trees (CTT) notation [26] in order to document interaction requirements. Although this notation from the HCI community has a formal background and is well-known among HCI practitioners, its inclusion in an industrial software production process entails some problems like:

1. The granularity of the task decomposition (when to stop refining the task model).
2. The burden of repeatedly modelling frequent and structurally similar interactions;
3. The intractability of the task models for large business management information systems, even with the aid of available tools [19][20].
4. The notorious but frequently overlooked difference between modelling an itinerary across the interface and modelling the interface itself.
5. The difficulty of defining how this task model should derive later models of the system.

Some of the problems have been addressed in the previous works that were mentioned in Section 2. That is the case of the mappings between CTT elements and elements of the abstract interface model [13]; those mappings solve problem #5 in the UsiXML framework.

In order to try to overcome the aforementioned problems, we propose the following:

1. To clear up the uncertainty of the granularity issue, we have defined that the basic data elements must be reached during the task decomposition.
2. Even though the former requirement seems to worsen the task model size, we propose the identification of structural task patterns that are common in the interaction of a user and an information system.
3. Thus, we conceive of a tool that supports this workstyle by allowing the reuse of these structural task patterns and their adjustment to each usage (that is to say, each instantiation).
4. We consider the task model to be an assemblage of task patterns, thus, by adding some recurrent-building rules, we are defining a grammar that allows both modelling user interaction in a very economic way and modelling the interface, since the task model will represent the itinerary through the whole interface.
5. Several correspondences have been defined to map elements of the Task Model (CIM) to elements of the Interaction Model (PIM), allowing a model-to-model transformation.

Our approach to the problem is similar to that taken with the use of UML notations in some of the diagrams of the Conceptual Model in OO-Method. The proposal of a pattern-oriented solution where concise semantic values are given to the elements of the model is already being applied to the definition of the business domain and the modelling of the abstract interface. This strategy simplifies the work of the analyst and makes code generation possible.

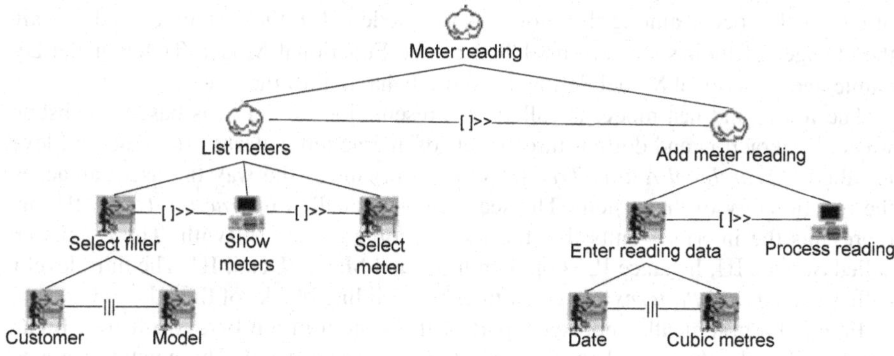

Fig. 3. CTT for the *Add meter reading* use case

To build the task model we proceed as follows. The Functional Requirements Model is taken as input and a task tree is built for each leaf of the FRT (that is, each use case). A precise mapping is defined between lines of the use case specification and elements of the task model. The steps of the use case involving elemental data manipulation appear as basic tasks of the task tree. For example, the introduction or selection of a piece of data being described in the use-case specification (i.e. step 3 of Table 2) results in an interaction task of the lowest granularity, which consists of the user introducing or selecting that data in the interface (i.e. the Date interactive task in the tree of Figure 3). Note that step 6 of the use-case description corresponds to the *Process reading* system task.

Since the task model not only reflects the interaction of use cases one-at-a-time, the interaction modelling involves the restructuring of the functional requirements represented in the FRT. Therefore, the example CTT also includes the "List meters" use case, as the selection of a meter is prior to the introduction of a new meter reading (this is stated in step 2 of the use case description).

To deal with how the initial access to the system's functionality is presented to the user, we propose building a taxonomical task tree that models this fact, taking advantage of task decomposition in order to follow the gradual approach principle.

The CIM level is fulfilled with the interaction requirements. The next section explains the Conceptual Modelling step, which is the real basis of the OO-Method approach and the cornerstone of the ONME code generation technology.

3.3 Conceptual Modelling the Three Problem Axes in ONME

In order to model what has been elicited in the Requirements Model, OO-Method [25] defines four complementary models that should be used to define the data, the behaviour, and the interaction of the system which; all together make up the Conceptual Model.

The Object Model is designed with a classic class diagram similar to UML and represents the data that the system will manipulate. The interaction and the sequences of events that occur among those objects are modelled in the Dynamic Model, while the changes of their states are modelled by the Functional Model. Together the Dynamic and Functional Model define the entire behaviour of the system.

The fourth and last model is called the Presentation Model. It is based on abstract ways of interaction and defines three levels of interaction patterns [16]. The first level is called *Hierarchical Action Tree* (HAT) and organizes the way the user can access the functionality of the system. The second level is called *Interaction Units* (IU) and represents the interface units that the user is going to interact with. These units are called Service IU, Instance IU, Population IU, and Master/Detail IU. The third level is called *Elementary Patterns* and constitutes the building blocks of the IUs.

Figure 4.a graphically represents part of the system in the first two levels. Figure 4.b describes the three levels of the case study in greater detail. These patterns are derived by applying transformation rules to the CTT and these transformations are explained elsewhere [8].

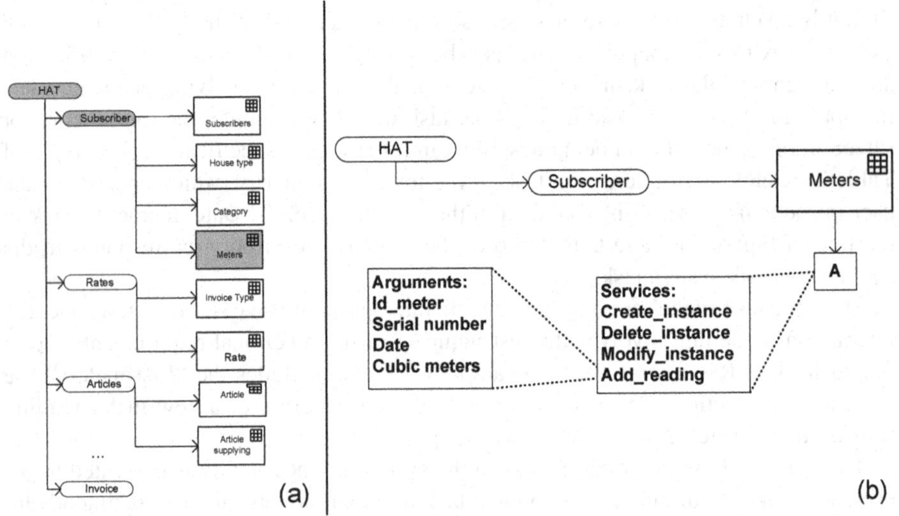

Fig. 4. Presentation Model

3.4 Automatic Code Generation

After the Functional Requirements Model and the Conceptual Model are specified, the Conceptual Model can be transformed into code by applying specific transformation rules. ONME implements these transformations for Visual Basic, C #, ASP. NET, Cold Fusion and Java, in a Model View Controller way, obtaining a full software system using SQL-Server, ORACLE, or DB2 database in the persistence tier.

As an example, Table 3 presents the transformation between the abstract patterns from the Presentation Model and the concrete widgets of the Visual Basic programming language.

Table 3. Some Transformation Patterns

Presentation model	VB component
Hierarchical action tree (HAT)	Application menu
Interaction unit	MDI child form
Service IU	MDI child form with entry controls
Simple type service argument	Entry control
Object-valued service argument	OIDSelector Generic control
Filter	Filter control
Filter variable	Entry control
Actions	Button panel
Action item	Button
Service throw	"Accept" button and code to validate and invoke the service
Cancellation	"Cancel" button and code to close the form
Services invocation	Code for linking business logical layer with service invocation
Data presentation	Code for formatting and data recovery
Navigation	Button panel
Navigation Item	Button

Figure 5 shows the generated interface. Table 4 shows the mapping used for the transformation presented in Figure 5.

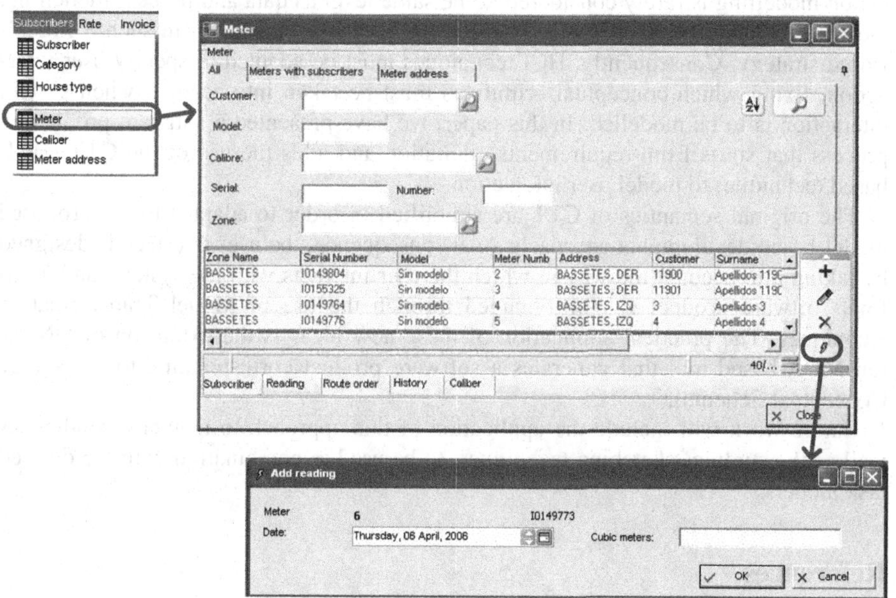

Fig. 5. *Add meter reading* window

Table 4. Mapping between Presentation Model and Final Interface

Presentation Model	Final Interface
Hierarchical action tree (HAT)	Subscribers Rate Invoice
Service IU	The whole window
Service throw and Cancellation	✓ OK ✗ Cancel
Simple type service argument	Cubic meters:
Introduction pattern for a date field	Code for validating date format
Navigation	Subscriber Reading Route order
Filter	Customer:

There is a back and forth traceability through the entire software process. The final interface was designed in the early steps of the software project and the corresponding transformation model is defined in each level of abstraction of OO-Method.

4 Conclusions and Future Work

Model-Based Software Production Methods need to integrate system functionality, behaviour, and user interaction from the early stages of the system lifecycle. As interaction modelling is rarely considered at the same level as data and process modelling, methods to model user interaction need to be properly embedded in such a Model-Based strategy. Consequently, HCI techniques must be adapted to specify user interaction, fixing which conceptual primitives must be taken into account when system interaction is to be modelled. In this paper, we have presented a software production process that starts from requirements elicitation and adds the use of the CTT (HCI-based technique) to model user interaction.

The original semantics of CTT are simplified in order to adapt it to the proposed model-based development approach. As a consequence, the user interface is designed by taking into account the way in which the user interacts with the system, and a full final software product can be obtained through the use of Model Transformation techniques. The practical application of these new ideas is the extension of ONME (an MDA-based tool that generates a software product corresponding to the source Conceptual Schema).

Future work will include the application of this approach to new case studies, as well as the study of sketching techniques, to be used in combination with the defined task models.

References

[1] Bodart, F., Hennebert, A., Leheureux, J., Provot, I., and Vanderdonckt, J.. (1994) A Model-Based Approach to Presentation: A Continuum from Task Analysis to Prototype. In Proceedings of DSV-IS'94, pp. 25-39, Bocca di Magra.

[2] Booch, G. (1993). Object-oriented Analysis and Design with Applications, 2nd ed. Redwood City: Benjamin Cummings.

[3] Care Technologies: http://www.care-t.com Last visit: June-2006

[4] Chen, P. P. (1976) The Entity Relationship Model - Toward a Unified View of Data. ACM Transactions Database Systems, 1 (1), pp. 9-36. 103

[5] da Silva, P. P. (2001) "User interface declarative models and development environments: A survey". Interactive Systems. Design, Specification, and Verification, 8th International Workshop, DSV-IS 2001, Glasgow, Scotland, Springer-Verlag Berlin.

[6] da Silva, P. P. d. and N. W. Paton (2003). "User Interface Modelling in UMLi " IEEE Softw. 20 (4). pp. 62-69

[7] Elwert, T. and Schlungbaum, E. (1995) Modelling and Generation of Graphical User Interfaces in the TADEUS Approach. In Designing, Specification and Verification of Interactive Systems, pp. 193-208, Vienna, Springer.

[8] España, S., Pederiva, I., Panach, I., Pastor, O. (2006). Integrating Model-Based and Task Based Approaches to User Interface Generation. 6th Int. Conf on Computer-Aided Design of User Interfaces (CADUI 2006). Springer.pp. 255-262.

[9] Hayes, P., Szekely, P. and Lerner, R. (1985) Design Alternatives for User Interface Management Systems Based on Experience with COUSIN. Proc. of SIGCHI'85, pp. 169-175. Addison-Wesley.

[10] Insfrán, E., Pastor, O., Wieringa, R. (2002). Requirements Engineering-Based Conceptual Modelling. Requirements Engineering, Vol. 7, Issue 2, p. 61-72. Springer-Verlag.

[11] Janssen, C., A. Weisbecker, et al. (1993). Generating user interfaces from data models and dialogue net specifications. Proceedings of the SIGCHI conference on Human factors in computing systems Amsterdam, The Netherlands ACM Press: 418-423

[12] Kim, W. and Foley, J. (1990) DON: User Interface Presentation Design Assistant. In Proceedings of UIST'90, pp. 10-20. ACM Press.

[13] Limbourg, Q. and J. Vanderdonckt (2004). Addressing the mapping problem in user interface design with UsiXML Proceedings of the 3rd annual conference on Task models and diagrams Prague, Czech Republic ACM Press: 155-163.

[14] Lonczewski, F. and Schreiber, S. (1996) The FUSE-System: an Integrated User Interface Desgin Environment. Computer-Aided Design of User Interfaces, pp. 37-56, Namur, Belgium, Namur University Press.

[15] Markopoulos, P., Pycock, J., Wilson, S. and Johnson, P. (1992) Adept - A task based design environment. Proceedings of the 25th Hawaii International Conference on System Sciences, pp. 587-596. IEEE Computer Society Press.

[16] Molina P. 2003. User interface specification: from requirements to automatic generation, , PhD Thesis, DSIC, Universidad Politécnica de Valencia. (in Spanish) .

[17] Montero, F., V. López-Jaquero, et al. (2005). Solving the mapping problem in user interface design by seamless integration in IdealXML. Proc. of DSV-IS'05, Newcastle upon Tyne, United Kingdom, Springer-Verlag.

[18] Morgan,T. "Business Rules and Information Systems – Aligning IT with Business Goals", Addison-Wesley, 2002

[19] Mori G., Paternò F., Santoro C. (2002) "CTTE: Support for Developing and Analyzing Task Models for Interactive System Design" IEEE Trans. on Software Engin.; pp.797-813

[20] Mori G., Paternò F., Santoro C. (2004) "Design and Development of Multidevice User Interfaces through Multiple LogicalDescriptions" IEEE Transactions on Software Engineering; pp.507-520

[21] Nunes, N. J. y J. F. e. Cunha (2000). "Wisdom: a software engineering method for small software development companies." Software, IEEE 17(5): 113-119.

[22] Olive, A. (2005). Conceptual Schema-Centric Development: A Grand Challenge for Information Systems Research. Proceedings of the 16th Conference on Advanced Information Systems Engineering, Oscar Pastor, João Falcão e Cunha (Ed.), Lecture Notes in Computer Science, Springer-Verlag, Porto, Portugal, Lecture Notes in Computer Science, Vol. 3520, ISBN 3-540-26095-1.pp. 1-15.

[23] OMG (2003) MDA Guide Version 1.0.1: http://www.omg.org/docs/omg/03-06-01.pdf Last visit: June-2006

[24] OMG (2003) Unified Modelling Language v1.5: http://www.omg.org/cgi-bin/doc?formal/03-03-01 Last visit: June-2006.

[25] Pastor, O., J. Gómez, et al. (2001). "The OO-method approach for information systems Modelling: from object-oriented conceptual Modelling to automated programming." Information Systems 26(7): 507-534.

[26] Paternò, F., C. Mancini, et al. (1997). ConcurTaskTrees: A Diagrammatic Notation for Specifying Task Models. Proceedings of the IFIP TC13 International Conference on Human-Computer Interaction, Chapman & Hall, Ltd.: 362-369.

[27] Puerta, A. (1996). The Mecano Project: Comprehensive and Integrated Support for Model-Based Interface Development. Computer-Aided Design of User Interfaces CADUI'96 , pp. 19-36, Namur, Belgium, Namur University Press.

[28] Puerta, A. and Maulsby, D. (1997) Management of Interface Design Knowledge with MODI-D. In Proceedings of IUI'97, pp. 249-252, Orlando, FL, USA.

[29] Szekely, P. (1990) Template-Based Mapping of Application Data to Interactive Displays. Proceedings of UIST'90, pp. 1-9. ACM Press.

[30] Szekely, P., Sukaviriya, P., Castells, P., Muthukumarasamy, J., and Salcher, E. (1996) Declarative Interface Models for User Interface Construction Tools: the MASTERMIND Approach. In Engineering for HCI, pp. 120-150, London, UK, Chapman & Hall.

[31] Vanderdonckt, J., Q. Limbourg, et al. (2004). USIXML: a User Interface Description Language for Specifying Multimodal User Interfaces. Proceedings of W3C Workshop on Multimodal Interaction WMI'2004, Sophia Antipolis, Greece.

[32] Yourdon, E. (1994). Object-Oriented Systems Design an Integrated Approach, Yourdon Press.

A Multi-perspective Framework for Organizational Patterns

Enzo Colombo[1] and John Mylopoulos[2]

[1] Politecnico di Milano – Dip. Elettr. e Informazione – via Ponzio 34/5, 20133 Milano, Italy
enzo.colombo@polimi.it
[2] Dept. of Computer Science, University of Toronto, 40 St. George Street, Toronto, Canada M5S 2H4
jm@cs.toronto.edu

Abstract. The goal of this paper is twofold. First we present a multi-perspective framework supporting the description of organizational patterns, supporting the design of business conversations among organizations within a virtual enterprise. The framework exploits three different concurrent views: an *intentional view*, a *strategic view* and a *process view*. Each view addresses a specific set of concerns of interest to different stakeholders in the system and, as a consequence, it has its own particular notation, rationale and constraints. The paper then introduces three patterns that are particularly well-suited for designing business conversations. One of these is studied in detail and validated through a non-trivial case study from an Italian industrial district.

Keywords: Requirements modeling, Perceiving and Modeling Social Reality, Organizational Patterns, Control and Coordination.

1 Introduction

An industrial district consists of a number of enterprises, often small-to-medium, that are located in the same geographic area and often collaborate through short-term projects – or, *virtual enterprises* -- to deliver products and services. Each virtual enterprise includes one or more business processes through which participating organizations collaborate. We are interested in the design of such virtual enterprises and their business processes.

The literature on information systems and workflow management systems has paid little attention to the impact of the structure of the organization on business process management. Instead, the emphasis has been on managing the execution of activities in processes, but not on their control and coordination, other than relating a sequence of activity executions to a given goal [7]. In the cooperative information systems manifesto [10], technologies are discussed for agent cooperation acting towards the fulfillment of shared goals in terms of three complementary facets: *systems*, *group collaboration*, and *organizational facets*. Flexible systems and change management are emphasized, in particular with reference to organizational change. However, the organizational facet focuses on possible changes of goals in the organization and therefore on the identification and modeling of organizational objectives and on enterprise integration.

D.W. Embley, A. Olivé, and S. Ram (Eds.): ER 2006, LNCS 4215, pp. 451 – 467, 2006.

In the workflow literature, the structure of the organization is represented only to indicate the roles of the agents executing activities. The problem of control in workflow management systems is studied from the point of view of guaranteeing a correct sequence of execution of activities. Therefore most research work focuses on methodologies for modeling workflow processes and on activity scheduling [2].

Recent work on e-services [19, 21] has focused on representing the interfaces of services provided by different organizations in a cooperative environment in terms of exchanged messages, data and control dependencies, and e-service state evolution. Little attention is paid to the problem of designing these interactions according to patterns of interactions between organizations.

However, modeling and understanding the organizational context within which cooperative relationships are deployed has been widely recognized as an important task of the requirements engineering process [14, 23]. This is especially true for cooperative and adaptive information systems where there is a need to reduce the effort for building and maintaining cross-application business conversations. [5]. Accordingly, this work presents three organizational styles and provides a multi-perspective framework to represent these patterns during requirements analysis.

In the remainder of the paper, motivations to this work are presented depending on pattern-based requirements engineering and coordination theory literature. Next, a multi-view framework for organizational patterns is presented. Three specific organizational patterns are presented in Section 4. Then one pattern, i.e. the market pattern, is studied in-depth through a non-trivial case study. Finally, conclusions are drawn and future work is discussed.

2 Related Works

Experiences with system design have shown that experts working on a particular problem tend to capture existing, well-structured solutions reusing best practices for their needs [12]. In the last decade, many researchers have stressed the importance of patterns supporting requirements engineering. Patterns are provided at different level of concerns: they support requirements elicitation, specification, analysis and validation. For example, a set of late requirements patterns for embedded software systems have been discussed in [15]. Patterns supporting goal refinement and operationalization are studied in the KAOS project, in order to support the generation of formal requirements specifications. [9]. Moreover, recurrent patterns of task, conversation, physical action and artefact usage have been observed during meetings among stakeholders aimed at establishing system requirements [17].

This work is concerned with organizational patterns supporting early requirements analysis and extends work conducted in the Tropos project. The main goal of Tropos is to provide methods, models and tools supporting the development of multi-agent information systems. In this context, researchers formalized agent-based software architectures inspired to organizational styles. These styles are based on two fundamental control and coordination mechanisms: organizational *hierarchies* and *markets*.

Within organizational hierarchies, actors are organized hierarchically, ranging from top management at the highest level to operations at the lowest level [22]. Functional specialization is usually the criterion for specialization and organizational units are built around the specific set of functional competencies that they develop. Organizations can also outsource part of their production and related decision-making activities to other organizations, such as customers, suppliers, consultants or commercial partners. A relationship between distinct organizations is implemented through the execution of economic conversations (or transactions), defined as exchanges of economic goods and services ruled by a price system [22]. Hierarchical and market coordination and control can mix and generate different organizational styles depending on the degree of *delegation* [18]. Organizational styles include market relationships [22], long-term agreements (e.g., comakership) [20], vertical quasi-integration [1], relationships based on equity exchange and vertical integration (hierarchy) [22]. The focus of this paper is on inter-organizational styles and, in particular, on networks of juridical independent agents such as *virtual enterprises*. As a consequence, organizational styles based on equity exchange and on vertical integration are not considered in this work.

In the Tropos project, organizational styles are specified through strategic relationships according to the *i** social model [3, 23] and recently formalized through the Formal Tropos language [11]. However, social specifications alone are inadequate for modeling data and control flows and message exchange typical of business conversations [5, 6]. Indeed, recently, some attempts have been conducted to embed business process semantics within *i** [14]. However, exceptional flows derived from goal violations are not considered and parallel tasks are not modeled explicitly. Moreover, this approach suffers of poor separation of concerns [16] since it is provided a single specification model that attempts to capture the overall system requirements. As a consequence, the contribution of this work is to study organizational patterns according to different views in order to address a specific set of concerns of interest to different stakeholders in the system.

3 A Multi-perspective Framework for Organizational Patterns

An organizational structure defines the way in which interrelated groups of actors manage their relationships in terms of control and coordination mechanisms [22]. Typically, organizational structures are specified according to three levels of abstraction, i.e. *strategic*, *decisional* and *operative*. Each abstraction involves different stakeholders in the organization and, as a consequence, requires its own particular notation. In particular a board of directors operates at a strategic level, a pool of decision makers operates at a decisional level and process analysts model conversations at an operative level. These actors specify organizational structures using several specification methods in well-chosen forms. In this section, these specification methods are grouped into views and the contribution of each view is singularly discussed.

Intentional View. The intentional view supports reasoning on strategic objectives. A board of directors operating at a strategic level refines high-level strategies through a set of key abstractions. These abstractions are intentional elements such as softgoals, goals, task and resources [3, 23]. *Goals* represent requirements to be fulfilled (⬭ = goal); s*oftgoals* are similar to goal but their fulfillment is not clearly defined (☁= softgoal).

A *task* is a structured sequence of decisions and actions aimed at producing an added value transformation of inputs into outputs (⬭= task) and, finally, information *resources* represent inputs to tasks (▭= resource).

An *intentional diagram* shows a set of intentional elements and their logical relationships: *decomposition* (—+), *contribution* (→) and *means-end* (➞) links. Directors define their high-level strategies and then, following a refinement process, elicit the set of tasks (and the corresponding resources) that should be performed to achieve their goals (and softgoals).

Social View. The social view concerns with the specification of social dependencies among organizations. Managers at the decision making level specify social dependencies through a model of strategic relationships [3, 23] complemented with the Formal Tropos (FT) language [11].

The *strategic relationships model* is a graph where each node is represented by an organization and each link between two actors describes a dependency in terms of intentional entities. A dependency formalizes an agreement between two organizations, i.e. a depender and a dependee (*depender* →— *int. entity* →— *dependee*). The type of dependency defines the nature of the agreement.

A goal (or softgoal) dependency represents the delegation of responsibility over the fulfillment of a goal (or softgoal) from a depender to a dependee. A task dependency represents the delegation of responsibility over the execution of a task from a depender to a dependee. With respect to goal (or softgoal), a task dependency is stronger since the depender also specifies how the task needed to fulfill a goal (or a softgoal) must be implemented. Finally, a resource dependency represents the need for an input that must be provided to a depender by a dependee. We note that actors' boundaries may embed intentional elements from the intentional view if they are involved in some way in the social relationships.

Formal Tropos (FT) is a linear-time temporal logic modeling actors, intentional entities and dependencies. It complements the strategic relationships model allowing the formalization of cardinalities and strategic policies. The formalization of cardinalities is essential to decide whether an instance of the specification is allowed or not. On the other hand, policies describe the social behavior of participating organizations depending on their strategic relationships. For example, FT is used to model policies implemented when a seller is able to provide more than one offer satisfying a delegated goal. Moreover, where possible, policies link together instances of the social model over time. Examples of FT specifications are provided in Sect. 5.

Process View. The process view takes into account some non-functional requirements such as flexibility, adaptability and controllability of business conversations. Process analysts at the lower level of our conceptual model describe the process view at several level of abstraction, each addressing a different concern.

At a highest level, the process view is a business conversation among organizations in terms of activities and control flows, resource assignments and information flows. This *process model* is a particular instance of statechart [13] enriched with (i) compensation actions derived from [5] and (ii) predicates around the correct execution of tasks and violation of goals [6]. Accordingly, the model formalizes both the standard and exceptional behavior of a business conversation where exceptions are typically triggered by goal violations and compensated at run-time.

Compensation actions are grouped into classes, i.e. delay (e.g. wait for, delay, ...), informative (e.g. notify, urge, ...), re-execute (e.g. re-execute, skip,...), re-negotiate (e.g. relax, tighten, ...) and re-transact (e.g. delegate execution,...).

At the lowest level, a specification of business conversation is complemented with a set of properties satisfied by instances of the model. Moreover, process analysts document their specification choices through a blueprint discussing rules supporting the refinement of intentional elements, the management of residual rights of control, the management of abort and the management of time-outs.

4 Organizational Patterns

In this section we describe three organizational patterns: vertical quasi-integration, comakership and market. In particular, first we provide a brief theoretical definition of these patterns as discussed in economic theories on coordination and transaction costs [1,20,22]. This theoretical introduction is necessary to recall the economic context within which a pattern can be used. Then, we present each pattern informally according to the views introduced with our framework.

Notice that our organizational patterns are grounded in data from the literature and large-scale case studies. Indeed, within the VISPO project [24], we conducted an in-depth analysis of the supply chain of a large Italian district. More precisely, within VISPO, our main goal was to study districts in order to design a service-oriented architecture supporting cooperation among organizations operating along the same value chain [5].

In this context, our interviews with managers empirically confirmed the existence of a continuum of different economic relationships between market and hierarchies as theorized by economic literature. In particular, within the district, we identified a complex network of spot relationships typical of a market system and few relationships of comakership and vertical quasi-integration. Since we note that a social model alone was not sufficient to formalize these cooperative interactions, at this stage we developed our multi-perspective framework in order to overcome this limitation and represent economic relationships unambiguously. We observe that our formalization the cooperative relationships among organizations is focused on aspects relevant for information system designers, i.e. the degree of control - either *supervised* or *distributed* - and the coordination policy in terms of *flexibility* and *adaptability* of the relationship (see Section 6).

As a second step, we used our multi-perspective framework to formalize other cases from the literature. Examples are the strategic comakership of boilers analyzed in [20] and the vertical quasi-integration between Marks & Spencer and William Baird cited in [1]. As a result we obtained schemas similar (from a structural perspective) to those formalized using data from the VISPO project. Accordingly, we abstracted these instances into the organizational patterns presented informally in the following subsections.

Finally, notice that further empirical application of our patterns have confirmed our findings but they have also highlighted some deviations from the three initial version of market, comakership and vertical quasi-integration. For example, a market pattern allows deviations in its process view since the renegotiation of price as a consequence of a failure is sometimes not enabled.

In conclusion, in Section 5 we present and formalize in detail the market pattern according our multi-perspective framework showing how this pattern can be abstracted from one of the several case studies considered in our research. Notice that due to lack of space, in this paper, vertical quasi-integration and comakership are not presented formally. However, a longer version of the present paper with the formalization of the three patterns is provided in a technical report and available on line for an in-depth exam [8]. Moreover, a detailed discussion of the possible deviations from our three patterns is presented in [4, 7].

4.1 Vertical Quasi-integration

Theoretical definition. By cooperating according to a vertical quasi-integration, organizations can benefit the advantages of hierarchical coordination without dealing with the typical risks of ownership [1, pp. 253]. Vertical quasi-integration is an organizational structure that embeds operating relationships typical of ownership and preserves juridical independence among cooperating actors.

Organizations are vertical quasi-integrated when they coordinate each other through strategic dependencies negotiated within an environment where decisional power is not symmetrically distributed among the cooperating counterparts [1]. Accordingly, in a vertical quasi-integration, a seller strongly depends from an enterprise-wide organization and it is typical required to comply with well-defined assets. Sellers are therefore unable to organize cooperation with more potential buyers because of site, physical, human and time asset specificity [18].

Intentional description. Typically, a vertical quasi-integration between a buyer and a seller is implemented when the procurement of a product/service represent a strategic activity for the buyer company. This is the case when the frequency of interactions among the counterparts is high, when specific assets (i.e., either site specificity, physical asset specificity, human asset specificity, or time asset specificity) are required to supply the product/service [18] and when the environment is uncertain [22].

Social description. In order to minimize interaction costs, the buyer controls seller's production at run-time thus reducing the period required to compensate failures. This means that the buyer company supervises the seller's primary activities while delegating the management of supporting activities (i.e., management of finance & administration, human resources, technological assets,...) [7]. In exchange, the buyer guarantees to the seller the saturation of its production capacity. On the other hand, the seller is delegated the responsibility of providing products/services which comply with buyer's strategic goals.

Process description. With respect to the traditional phases of a conversation (i.e., matchmaking, negotiation, execution and post-settlement) [22], in a vertical quasi-integration, interactions are organized into the *execution* and *post-settlement* phases only [5, 6]. This behavior is quite intuitive since here we are discussing a long-term cooperating relationship where a seller supplies a complex and strategic product. Accordingly, the buyer does not need an automatic mechanism to support discovery and negotiation since cooperation is planned and negotiated *"face-to-face"* when requirements on either physical and technological assets or service characteristics are specified. When an agreement is reached and required assets are deployed, discovery and negotiation are no more executed. Finally, notice that in a vertical quasi-integration, conversations are not isolated from each other[1]. On the contrary, as we see in Section 5, in a market, the commitment of a conversation does not depend on the previous interaction with the same supplier.

In conclusion, from a process perspective, in a vertical quasi-integration *control* is totally retained by the buyer (i.e., supervised control), a re-execution of production can be required if the product do not comply with the agreement (i.e., medium level of self-repair) and the product is always provided by the same seller (i.e., low level of adaptability to change in the environment).

4.2 Comakership

Theoretical definition. Coordination of *dissimilar* activities cannot be effectively managed according to a vertical quasi-integration (or through market mechanisms, see Section 5). Therefore, when cooperating organizations need to coordinate *dissimilar* but *complementary* activities, direct supervision is overcome by a more dynamic mechanism of mutual adjustment known as *comakership* [20]. A comakership is an organizational style grounded on a strong peer-to-peer cooperation among business partners and provides an effective solution to the problem of coordinating dissimilar activities.

Intentional description. The implementation of a comakership is based on the adoption of a policy of continuous improvement, on the reduction of process lead-time and on trust. Continuous improvement is achieved performing vendor rating, requiring information around the performance of the process, sharing knowledge (*know-how*) with the seller and requiring a continuous improvement of the product and the overall process [20]. Lead-time is reduced through a stricter integration with the business partner and implementing weekly orders on the basis of current needs.

Strategic description. From a strategic perspective, the buyer delegates to the seller the improvement of product quality and the downsizing of prices in order to pursue a continuous improvement of key performance indicators over time. The seller downsizes price improving the production process with a policy of continuous investments over time. These investments are counterbalanced by a redefinition of strategic goals with the buyer when better performance have been obtained [20]. Moreover, the improvement of product quality is achieved through the traditional quality control activities.

Process description. In a comakership, interactions are organized into *execution* and *post-settlement* as well as vertical quasi-integration. However, comakership is based on trust and, as a consequence, embeds a weaker control over the seller. Accordingly, this coordination paradigm focuses on communicating the fulfillment of goals as opposite to the communication of violations typical of market and vertical quasi-integration. Execution involves three parallel standard flows: an integrated operative

[1] We use the term *isolation* to indicate that the achievement of goals in one conversation depend on the achievement of goals in another conversation.

flow, a vendor rating flow and a flow of activities aimed at updating prices according to market trends. The integrated operative flow begins when the buyer sends a daily/weekly order to the seller. Moreover, at the end of production process, improvements around quality of production and price downsizing are notified to the buyer. Then, a quality control task (performed by the seller) receives the product and checks its compliance with the requirements specified by the buyer. If violations occur, the seller re-executes the overall production tasks. We note that, according to this pattern, the buyer is not aware of violations since control is performed by the seller. Finally, since the buyer adopts a free-pass policy, the final product is delivered directly to the seller assembly line without any other control.

In conclusion, from a process perspective, control is distributed (i.e., the seller controls the compliance with the agreement and the buyer controls the fulfillment of high-level business goals) but participative (i.e., pre-defined and agreed by the cooperating actors), production can be re-executed (i.e., medium level of flexibility) and strategic goals are refined over time by the cooperating partners (i.e., good level of adaptability to changes in the environment).

4.3 Market Pattern

Theoretical definition. A *market conversation* is defined as the exchange of economic goods and services ruled by a price system [22]. In a market system, a buyer aims at discovering a commodity minimizing its price. Coordination among cooperating actors is spontaneous and not planned beforehand [18]. In particular a market system is adopted when the frequency of conversation is low, when there is no need to deploy specific assets, when the environment is not uncertain and when the commodity is a complementary but dissimilar good for the seller (i.e., it is cheaper to outsource production than implementing its internalization).

This pattern is studied in detail and validated through a non-trivial case study in the next section.

5 Case Study

Poly Coo. Poly Coo is an organization producing polyurethane (a material derived from oil) with revenues about 4.5 mil/euro per year. When Poly Coo receives an order, it schedules production and notifies the customer whether the order can be supplied or not according to lead-time requirements. Moreover, in order to improve quality of service (QoS), Poly Coo implemented a customized information system to monitor production and obtained the ISO9002 certification. Each lot of polyurethane is therefore provided with a technical document certifying the quality of the product with respect to a set of quality parameters (e.g., granularity). This production process is organized as follows. Orders of polyurethane are received and automatically scheduled according to lead-time requirements. According to the production plan, pieces of raw polyurethane are cut either manually or with a semi-automatic machine. The polyurethane is shaped with a numerically controlled machine and glued together. Final quality control is performed according to ISO9002 norms.

Before performing an order, Poly Coo *negotiates an agreement* with its potential buyer (i.e., Sofa Coo). Negotiation on price is based on polyurethane parameters such as granularity, pressure, inflammability, toxicity and resistance to traction. Moreover also lead-time requirements and ordered quantities impact on the price of polyurethane proposed to the buyer.

Sofa Coo. Sofa Coo is part of the Comfort Group S.p.A., one of the primary organizations producing sofas worldwide. The Comfort Group exports around 92% of its production, supplying 3500 customers located in 137 countries. The success of Comfort is a consequence of a well-defined strategic plan focused on high QoS, minimization of production costs, wide variety of sofa models and a particular attention to international markets.

The quality of polyurethane needed by Sofa Coo varies according to the model of sofas. Medium quality polyurethane (e.g., medium granularity) is used to stuff cheap sofas for the U.S.A. market. On the contrary, high quality polyurethane is used for the European market. During procurement, Sofa Coo gathers offers submitted by multiple potential sellers (one is Poly Coo) that should comply with polyurethane requirements. Selection is finally ruled by the better price and the seller is committed with Sofa Coo to comply with the signed agreement. Moreover, Sofa Coo does not adopt a free-pass policy and it controls polyurethane samples for each supply. If polyurethane does not comply with the agreement, Sofa Coo is authorized either to require a new lot of polyurethane or to re-negotiate the agreement. Re-negotiation (within predefined intervals) is allowed since this polyurethane could be used to stuff sofas for the USA market anyway. Payment is therefore performed either if control activities do not show violations or if violations are successfully compensated.

5.1 Intentional View

Figure 1.(a) shows the intentional model associated with the delegated *buy polyurethane on the market* softgoal. In order to fulfill this softgoal, it is necessary to *procure polyurethane at the better price* and *satisfy customers*. The former is achieved by Sofa Coo discovering polyurethane producers, evaluating offers of

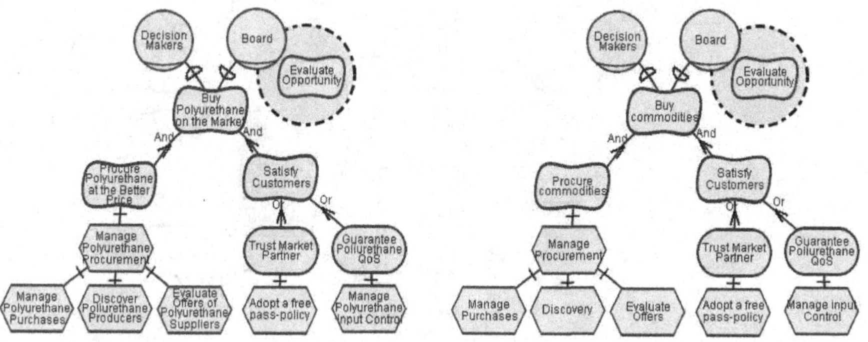

Fig. 1. (a) –Intentional reasoning of Sofa Coo in a market system

Fig. 1. (b) – Intentional view of a market pattern

polyurethane suppliers to obtain the better price and managing polyurethane purchases. The latter is fulfilled either trusting the supplier or controlling the polyurethane lot before production. Figure 1.(b) shows the intentional view of a market pattern derived from the Sofa Coo – Poly Coo scenario.

5.2 Social View

Figure 2 shows the strategic relationships between Sofa Coo and Poly Coo within a market system. Part of the intentional view in Figure 1.(a) is reported into Sofa Coo's boundaries. In particular, the task *discover polyurethane producers* requires from Poly Coo an offer complying with polyurethane requirements. We note that offers are generated in order to *fulfill Poly Coo's marketing policies* and *comply with polyurethane requirements*. Moreover, the *manage polyurethane purchases* task provides the final order to the *polyurethane production & delivery* task according to the agreement.

The *polyurethane production & delivery* task produces polyurethane in order to *comply with the current agreement on polyurethane supply*. The agreement between Poly Coo and Sofa Coo is therefore used to set the assembly line performing polyurethane production. Besides, the execution of the *polyurethane production & delivery* task over time with different buyers allows Poly Coo to improve its production process thus contributing positively to the fulfillment of the *repeat on multiple buyers* softgoal. Finally, the *manage polyurethane input control* task receives ISO9002-compliant certifications together with the polyurethane supply and performs source inspections.

Figure 3 shows the *social view* derived from the example of market relationship between Sofa Coo and Poly Coo. This view specifies an actor playing the role of

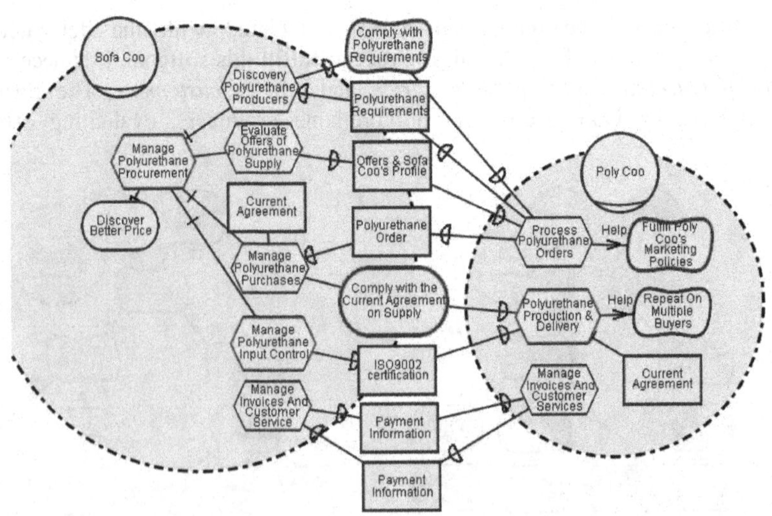

Fig. 2. Market relationship between Sofa Coo and Poly Coo

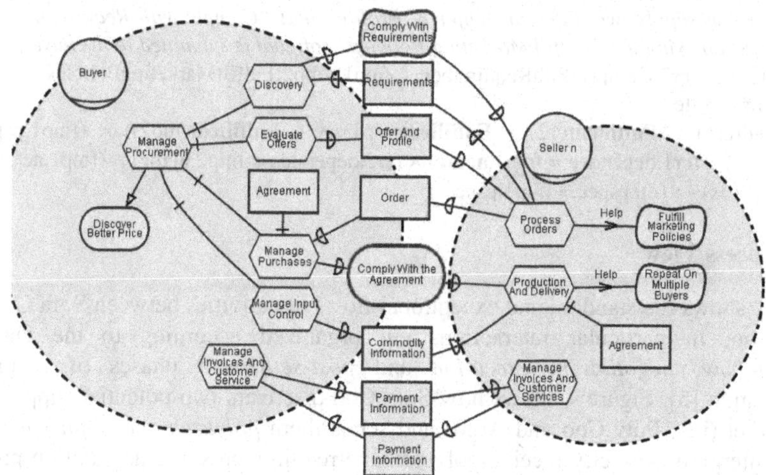

Fig. 3. Social view of a market pattern (roles and intentional elements are the parameters of this pattern)

buyer and one playing the role of seller. Moreover, the social view models an abstraction of the vertical cooperating relationships between Poly Coo and Sofa Coo obtained by generalizing the example from actors to roles and from domain dependent to domain-independent intentional elements.

Moreover, in the following, examples of structural properties constraining the representation of Figure 3 are specified with Formal Tropos (FT) [11]. The FT outer-layer of a market pattern is provided in [7]. These structural properties impose constraints on the instantiation of a pattern.

Each instance of the market relationship pattern includes exactly one Buyer actor
∃b: Buyer (b) ∧ ∀ b1, b2: Buyer (b1=b2);

Multiple instances of both the "Requirements" and the "Offer & Profile" resource (different instances have a different identification).
∀ re1, re2: Requirements (re1≠re2 ↔ re1.id ≠ re2.id)
∀ op1, op2: Offer&Profile (op1≠op2 ↔ op1.id ≠ op2.id)

The "Production & Delivery" task performed by a seller and the "Manage Purchases" task performed by the buyer share the same agreement
∀ mp: ManagePurchases, p: Production&Delivery (mp.agm=p.agm)

If more then one offer fulfills the softgoal "Comply with Requirements", the offer associated with the lower price is selected thus satisfying the "Negotiate Better Price" goal.
∀ b: Buyer, s1, s2: Seller, cr1, cr2: ComplyWithRequirements, nbp: NegotiateBetterPrice, op1, op2: Offer&Profile, or: Order
(**Fulfilled**(cr1) ∧ **Fulfilled**(cr2) ∧ (cr1.dependee = s1) ∧ (cr2.dependee = s2) ∧ (cr1.depender = b) ∧ (cr2.depender = b) ∧ (op1.dependee = s1) ∧ (op2.dependee = s2) ∧ (nbp.betterprice = op1.price) ∧ (nbp.betterprice < op2.price) → (or.depender = s1) ∧ (or.pspec = op.pspec) ∧ (or.price = op1.price) ∧ **Fulfilled**(nbp))

If a seller can supply two different "Offer & Profile" that "Comply with Requirements", the alternative satisfying the "Fulfill Marketing Policies" softgoal is submitted to the buyer.
∀ s: Seller, cr1, cr2:ComplyWithRequirements, fmp1, fmp2:FulfillMarketingPolicies, op: Offer&Profile
((**Fulfilled**(cr1) ∧ **Fulfilled**(cr2) ∧ **Fulfilled**(fmp1) ∧ (¬**Fulfilled**(fmp2)) ∧ (fmp1.pspec ≠ fmp2.pspec) ∧ (cr1.dependee = fmp1.**actor**) ∧ (cr2.dependee = fmp2.**actor**) ∧ (fmp1.actor=s) ∧ (fmp2.actor=s) → (op.pspec = fmp1.pspec))

5.3 Process View

Figure 4 shows the standard and exceptional flows of activities between Sofa Coo and Poly Coo. In particular interactions are organized according to the classical *matchmaking*, *negotiation*, *execution* and *post-settlement* phases of a market conversation [5]. Figure 4 shows how Sofa Coo discovers two potential suppliers on the market (i.e., Poly Coo and Argo) and sends them *polyurethane requirements.* If the counterparts correctly receive polyurethane requirements, the negotiation process is started. Accordingly, the transition between Matchmaking (MM) and Negotiation (NEG) is triggered through the following ECA rule.

End(MM)[**Received**($[1,7]_{days}$, Sofa Coo, Poly Coo, *"Polyur. Requirements"*) ∧
Received($[1,7]_{days}$, Sofa Coo, Argo, *"Polyur. Requirements"*)]|ξ

The potential sellers generate offers in parallel. If Sofa Coo receives at least an offer, a comparative evaluation is performed and finally, in our scenario, Poly Coo is selected as the final polyurethane supplier. Note that if at the end of the *evaluate offers of polyurethane* task (EOP), offers do not *comply with polyurethane requirements*, new offers are required, thus implementing the typical bargaining interaction of mutual adjustment of negotiation. The transition that implements this bargaining process is labeled as follows:

End(EOP)[¬**Achieved**(Poly Coo, *"Comply with Polyurethane Requirements"*) ∧
¬**Achieved**(Argo, *"Comply with Polyurethane Requirements"*)]|ξ

The negotiation process is typically time-bounded on 7 days, thus this value is specified as the maximum residence time of negotiation. Once the agreement between Poly Coo and Sofa Coo is reached, control is transferred to Sofa Coo's Purchase Office that formalizes the *polyurethane order* and then handles all supporting activities needed to terminate the purchase process. In the meantime, Poly Coo schedules, produces and delivers the polyurethane to Sofa Coo. If the *polyurethane order* is not received by the *process polyurethane order* task (PPO) within 30 days from the agreement, Poly Coo first waits for 3 days from the deadline, then urges the submission of an order.

Begin(PPO)[¬**Received**([1,30]days, Poly Coo, Sofa Coo, *"Polyurethane Order"*)]|
Sequence(**Wait-for**([1,3]days *"Polyurethane Order"*);
Urge([1,3]days, Sofa Coo, *Polyurethane Order"*)

If Sofa Coo does not acknowledge the request, the market conversation reaches a pending state that requires a manual compensation. Finally, source inspections and then payment are performed. In particular, source inspections need some information from Poly Coo about the lot of polyurethane supplied. If this information is not provided and the urge compensation fails, the transition towards the pending state is triggered. Moreover if source inspections on polyurethane discover a violation of the agreement, Sofa Coo requires Poly Coo to relax the price of the supply.

Note that the use of history here is critical to model a correct behavior. If the counterparts agree on reducing the price of polyurethane, the business conversation must evolve into the *payment* state. By marking both execution and post-settlement with history, this behavior is easily modeled since the automaton enters the execution state and immediately leaves it since history points to the final sub-state within execution. Leaving execution, the automaton enters post-settlement but since the *manage polyurethane control* state has been already visited, history points to the *payment* state as expected. On the other hand, marking post-settlement with history could generate a wrong behavior since, after the re-execution of *polyurethane production & delivery*, the automaton skips quality control. The effect is that Sofa Coo receives the second lot, does not perform source inspections and pays the full price. This behavior is corrected by specifying a *reset_history* action together with the *re-execution from component production* as follows (see also Figure 4).

End(NEG)
[(¬**Achieved**(Poly Coo, "*Comply with the Current Agreement on Supply*"))
∧ **Done**(Relax([1,3]days, Poly Coo, Current Agreement)]|
Re-execute<-, Poly Coo, Polyur. Production & Delivery> ∧ Reset_history(p-s)

Finally, if the re-execution from *polyurethane production and delivery* fails, the business conversation reaches the pending state.

Figure 5 shows the *process view* of a market pattern as a generalization of the exemplification in Figure 4. Note how the use of universal and existential quantifiers within ECA (Event-Condition-Action) rules allows the substitution of a specific actor (i.e., Poly Coo) with a general token belonging to a set modeling a role ($s \in$ Seller). Moreover, the following rules typical of a market system complement the process view shown in Figure 5.

- **Refinement.** Tasks cannot be refined since the market pattern already provides the maximum view on internal business processes (i.e., black-box view). Goals, softgoals and resources can be instead refined further. Moreover, the *requirements* resource can embed information around price, product quality, delivery time, reliability of delivery and product specification.
- **Management of residual rights of control** (*on pending*). When a market conversation reaches a pending state, the actor forcing pending has the responsibility to take control of the conversation and execute a recovery procedure.
- **Management of abort.** When a market conversation reaches an abort state, each actor has the responsibility for its recovery actions.
- **Management of time-outs.**
  A time-out violation during negotiation brings the whole transaction into abort.
  ∃t ((t>time-out) ∧ (l_q =<NEG, time-out, ->) → l_{q+1} = <abort, null, null>))
  A time-out violation during matchmaking brings the whole transaction into abort.
  ∃t ((t > time-out) ∧ (l_q =<MM, time-out, ->) → l_{q+1} = <abort, null, null>))

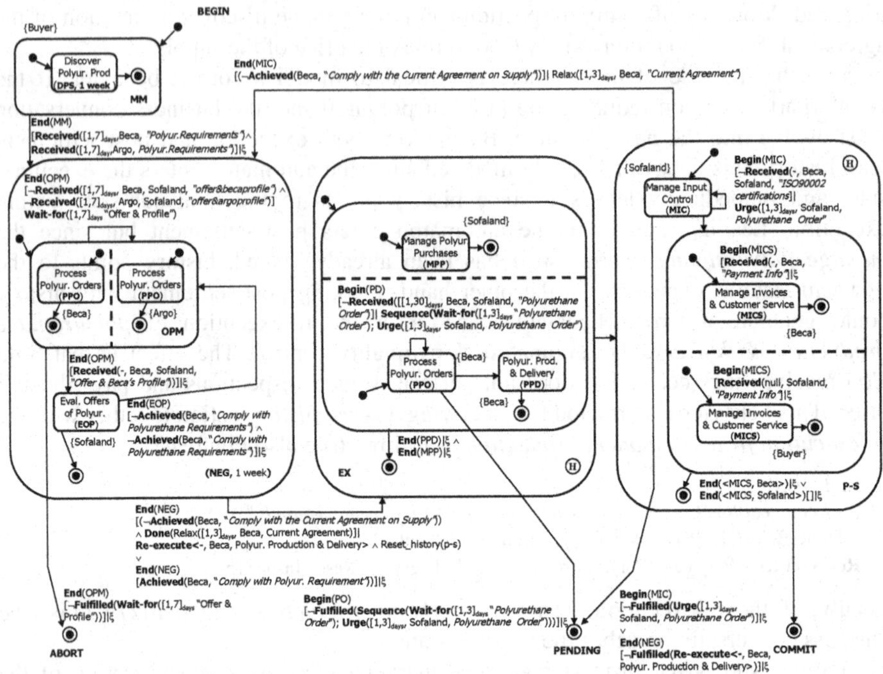

Fig. 4. Specification of standard and exceptional activity flows between Sofa Coo and Poly Coo

An example of properties satisfied by the *process view* in Figure 5 is presented in the following. Properties are formalized according to a notation that complies with FT and the process view provided in Section 3. Let *s* be an actor and *g* a goal in the social model, the following equivalence maps a goal condition of a process view into a FT formula:

Achieved(s, g) $\equiv_{def}$ (g.actor= s) ∧ **Fulfilled**(g)

The "Comply with the Agreement" softgoal can be satisfied if the "Comply with Requirements" softgoal has been satisfied in the past.
∀ s: Seller, ca:ComplyWithTheAgreement, cr: ComplyWithRequirements
((ca.actor=s) ∧ **Fulfilled**(ca)) → ((cr.actor=s) ∧ **O**(**Fulfilled**(cr))

Only the actor receiving the "Order" performs "Production & Delivery" and "Manage Invoices & Customer Services" tasks
∀ s: Seller, pd: Production&Delivery, mics: ManageInvoices&CustomerService, o: Order
((pd.actor=s) ∧ (mics.actor=s) ∧ **Received**(-, s, o) ↔ **Done**(pd) ∧ **Done**(mics))

The "Manage Purchases" task and the "Production" task are executed in parallel
∀ mp: ManagePurchases, p: Production&Delivery **And**(mp, pd)

A market transaction is always correct, i.e. each run terminates within either an abort or a commit or a pending state.
Let n be the number of transition needed to reach the final state q_n and τ our transition function, correctness is formalized as following.

$$[(\tau\,(\text{begin}, -, -)=MM) \leftrightarrow \exists\, q_{n-1}: Q\,, q_n: F\,((\tau(q_{n-1}, l_{n-1}, -)=<q_n, l_n>) \wedge$$
$$((l_n= <\text{commit, null, null}>) \vee (l_n = <\text{pending, null, null}>) \vee (l_n= <\text{abort, null, null}>)))]$$

The partial satisfaction of all delegated goals is required to commit the business transaction.

$$\exists q_n \in F\,(l_n = <\text{commit, null, null}> \rightarrow$$
$$[\exists s{:}\text{Seller}, cr{:}\ ca{:}\text{ComplyWithTheAgreement}, cr{:}\ \text{ComplyWithRequirements}$$
$$((cr.actor=s) \wedge \mathbf{Fulfilled}(cr)) \wedge (((ca.actor=s) \wedge \mathbf{Fulfilled}(ca)) \vee \mathbf{Fulfilled}(\mathbf{Re\text{-}negotiate}(s, ca))]$$

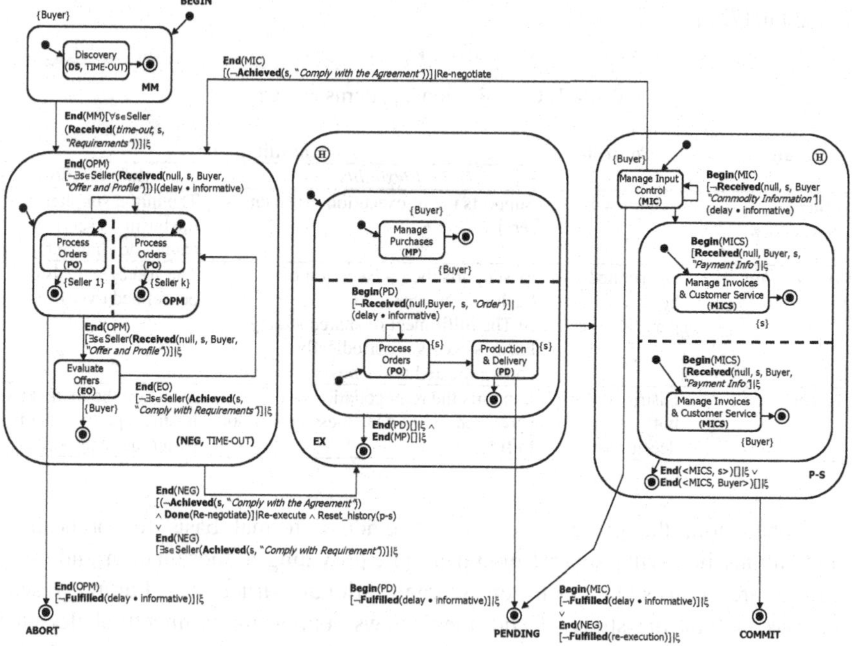

Fig. 5. Process view of a *market pattern* (state and transition labels are parameters of this pattern)

In conclusion, from a process perspective, control is distributed but decentralized (i.e., control policies are not agreed among the counterparts typically of spontaneous coordination), the agreement can be re-negotiated (i.e., high level of flexibility) and for each conversation the buyer looks for the partners that fits better its requirements (i.e., high-level of adaptability to changes in the environment).

6 Conclusion

We believe that the introduction of cooperation patterns according to a multi-perspective framework is the first step towards improving the quality of cross-organizational conversations and overcoming the limits of traditional intra-organizational workflow design. Accordingly, this paper presents three patterns for designing virtual enterprises. Each pattern has been informally discussed in terms of three complementary views: an *intentional view*, a *strategic view* and a *process view*. Moreover, these views highlight that patterns differs from each other in terms of control[2] and coordination mechanisms[3] [6]. Table 1 summarizes the main features of our three patterns in a way understandable by an IS designer. Finally, we have also presented a detailed study on the application of a market pattern in a non-trivial case study. The application of the comakership and vertical quasi-integration pattern is provided in [7, 8].

Table 1. Organizational patterns at a glance

Pattern	**Control**	**Coordination**	
		Flexibility	*Adaptability*
Vertical q.integration	Supervised	Supports the re-execution of business services.	The initial supplier of the business service cannot be changed.
Comakership	Distributed but participative	a) Supports the re-execution of business services. b) The fulfillment of shared strategic business goals is periodically communicated to the buyer.	The strategic goals can be refined over time
Market	Distributed but decentralized	Supports the re-negotiation of the agreement when a business goal is not fulfilled.	Select on the market the business partner that fits better the requirements

In conclusion, the present work can provide a formal basis for orchestrating e-applications involving several organizations, providing a coordination and control infrastructure consistent with cross-organizational structures. Future research directions include the study of additional views supporting architectural design for virtual enterprises. In particular, we are currently formalizing a *component view* that discusses how a business conversation is described as composition of multiple e-services. Moreover, a *deployment view* is under development, focusing on the service-oriented infrastructure necessary to support control and coordination according to different organizational styles. Finally, a *pattern factory* supporting pattern identification, documentation, choice and composition will be developed in order to support modelers during the requirement engineering process.

[2] *control* concerns both the level of visibility on a private business processes and the localization of control activities. In particular, supervised control is characterized by the centralization of control over cooperating activities. On the other hand, participative control is a typical peer-to-peer communication where all economic actors first define the control policies of the whole cooperation process. Finally, decentralized control means that specialized economic actors decide the control policy for their part of the global process.

[3] *coordination* concerns with the level of flexibility and adaptability of the cooperative relationship. In particular, flexibility refers to the run-time management of service self-repair intended to bring a business conversation in a consistent state at the lowest cost. Adaptability is instead concerned with modifications of the standard and exceptional behaviour of a composite process depending on the environment within which the composition is deployed.

References

[1] Blois, K. (1972). Vertical Quasi Integration, Journal of Industrial Economics, 20

[2] Casati, F., Ceri, S., Paraboschi, S. and G. Pozzi (1999), Specification and Implementation of Exceptions in Workflow Management Systems. ACM Trans. Database Syst. 24(3): 405 – 451.

[3] Castro J., Kolp M., Mylopoulos J. (2002). Towards Requirement-Driven Information Systems Enginnering: The Tropos Project. Inf. Syst. 27(6): 365 – 389.

[4] Colombo, E. (2005), A Service-Oriented Methodology for the Analysis and Specification of Business Conversation Requirements, Ph.D. Thesis, Politecnico di Milano, Italy.

[5] Colombo, E., Francalanci, C. and B. Pernici (2004), Modeling cooperation in virtual districts: a methodology for e-service design, Int. Journal of Coop. Inf. Syst., 13(4), 369 – 411.

[6] Colombo, E., Mylopoulos, J. and P. Spoletini (2005), Modeling and Analyzing Context-Aware Composition of Services, Proceedings of ICSOC'05, 198 – 213.

[7] Colombo, E. and J. Mylopoulos (2004), Organizational Patterns for Virtual Enterprises, Technical Report #2004.34, Politecnico di Milano.

[8] Colombo, E. and J. Mylopoulos (2006), A Multi-View Framework for Organizational Patterns, Technical Report #DIT-06-017 , Università degli Studi di Trento.

[9] Darimont, R. and A. van Lamsweerde (1996) Formal Refinement Patterns for Goal-Driven Requirements Elaboration. SIGSOFT FSE, 179 – 190

[10] De Michelis, G., Dubois, E., Jarke, M., Matthes, F., Mylopoulos, J., Papazoglou, M., Pohl, K., Schmidt, J., Woo, C., Yu, E. (1997), Cooperative Information Systems: A Manifesto, Cooperative Information Systems, M.P. Papazoglou, G. Schlageter (eds.)

[11] Fuxman, A., Liu, L., Mylopoulos, J., Roveri, M. and P. Traverso (2004) Specifying and analyzing early requirements in Tropos. Requir. Eng. 9(2): 132 – 150

[12] Gamma, E.. Helm, R., Johnson, R., and J. Vlissides (1995). Design Patterns: Elements of Reusable Object-oriented Software, Addison-Wesley.

[13] Harel, D. and Naamad A. (1996). The STATEMATE Semantics of Statecharts, ACM Trans. on Softw. Eng. and Meth., 5(4), 293 – 333.

[14] Kolp, M., Giorgini, P. and J. Mylopoulos (2003), Organizational Patterns for Early Requirements Analysis, Proceedings of CAiSE 2003.

[15] Konrad S. and B. Cheng (2002), Requirements Patterns for Embedded Systems, Proceeding of RE'02, Essen.

[16] Krutchen, P. (1995), The 4+1 View Model of Architecture. IEEE Software 12(6).

[17] Maiden, N. and B.P. Bright (1996), Recurrent Communication Patterns in Requirement Engineering Meetings, Proceedings of WET ICE '96

[18] Malone, T. W., Crowston, K. (1994). The Interdisciplinary Study of Coordination. ACM Computing Surveys, 26(1), 87 – 119.

[19] Mecella, M. and B. Pernici (2001), Designing wrapper components for e-services in integrating heterogeneous systems. VLDB Journal 10(1), 2 – 15

[20] Merli, G. and M. Luoni (1997), Comakership, Isedi.

[21] Papazoglou, M. P.,Yang, J. (2002), Web Component: A Substrate for Web Service Reuse and Composition. CAiSE, 21 – 36

[22] Williamson, O. E. (1996). The mechanisms of governance. Oxford University Press.

[23] Yu, E. and J. Mylopoulos (1996). Using goal, rules and methods to support reasoning in business process reengineering. Intel. Syst. and Acc., Fin. and Man., 5(1),1 – 13.

[24] Vispo Project, cube-si.elet.polimi.it/vispo.

Deriving Concepts for Modeling Business Actions

Peter Rittgen

University College of Borås, 50190 Borås, Sweden

Abstract. We outline a procedure called communicative and material functions analysis that can be used to derive business modeling concepts. It is rooted in the language-action perspective on organizations and has its point of departure in Business Action Theory, an empirically grounded framework for modeling business processes from an action perspective. We apply this procedure to enhance an existing method, the Situation-adaptable work and Information systems Modeling Method. This extended method is then used to analyze a business situation in order to follow up the commitments that are made in the course of a business process with the ultimate aim of detecting flaws in that process.

1 Introduction

According to the language-action perspective a business is understood as a network of agents that interact via language. The literature on communicative action provides a broad spectrum of frameworks to describe business processes, e.g. Business Action Theory (BAT) [7, 8, 10], Dynamic Essential Modelling of Organizations (DEMO) [5, 6, 17, 20, 21], Action Workflow [4, 13, 18], Action-Based Modeling [14] and Conversation for Action [28].

Among these frameworks BAT can, in a certain sense, be seen as the most general because

- it does not commit the modeler to any specific method,
- it provides the most comprehensive set of phases, and
- its smallest unit of discourse is not a language act but a business act.

The first two issues are discussed in the next section. The latter is unique among the language-action approaches to organizational modeling and deserves specific attention. A business act comprises both a language act and a material act, i.e. it has a broader scope. A language act is an elementary communicative activity in spoken or written form directed from one actor to another with the aim of changing the mental state of the latter. A material act is an elementary physical activity directed from an actor to the material world with the aim of changing its state.

Strictly speaking, and as observed by Goldkuhl [7], language and material acts are not so much distinct and separate acts but in many cases rather functions (or aspects) of one and the same business act. For example, the business act of delivering goods is, perhaps in the first place, a material act. i.e. transporting "stuff" from one place to another. But at the same time it has a communicative function, i.e. it implies the language act "We have fulfilled the commitment we entered by accepting the respective order."

D.W. Embley, A. Olivé, and S. Ram (Eds.): ER 2006, LNCS 4215, pp. 468 – 481, 2006.

This means that a deeper understanding of business action must be grounded in an analysis of these functions. We call this analysis 'communicative and material functions analysis' and use it as a basis for deriving concepts for modeling business actions. The objectives of such an analysis are

1. to find the communicative and material functions that are inherent in a generic or specific business act,
2. to classify the identified functions, and
3. to derive suitable concepts for business action modeling.

This procedure is applied to BAT itself to arrive at a rudimentary set of concepts that can be used as a starting point for developing a BAT method or, as in our case, to refine and extend an already existing method: the Situation-adaptable work and Information systems Modeling Method (SIMM) [7]. A case study shows that the extended method can be used successfully to analyse the commitment management within a business process and to detect flaws in that process that lead to "broken commitments".

The remaining sections are structured as follows: We first introduce the BAT framework and the generic layered patterns for business modeling. In the following section this framework is refined by combining phases and layers. We proceed by applying communicative and material functions analysis to the refined framework, followed by a classification of the resulting functions, and finally leading to the derivation of concepts for modeling business actions which are used to refine and extend SIMM. We conclude by presenting a possible application of the extended method for the purpose of commitment analysis.

2 Business Action Theory

As we already mentioned in the introduction BAT is not accompanied by its own method. On the one hand this is an advantage: The modeler can choose freely the method that is most appropriate in the actual application context. A possible choice would be that of SIMM as was suggested in the same paper that introduced BAT [7].

But on the other hand the lack of a dedicated modeling method also represents a disadvantage because choosing a method that was not tailored for BAT also implies that the modeler is not supported in applying BAT. The framework behind such a method might lack essential concepts of BAT or it might even be partially in conflict with BAT. For example, most of the frameworks mentioned above are accompanied by their own methodologies. Using them in the context of BAT might lead to conflicts. These issues have been explored in several papers comparing BAT with DEMO [22, 26] and Action Workflow [7, 26]. It can therefore be argued that the introduction of a BAT method is worthwhile as is the identification of suitable concepts for such a method.

Although the frameworks mentioned above are substantially different in many aspects they do largely agree on dividing a business process into phases. Among them BAT offers the most comprehensive phases:

1. Business prerequisites phase
2. Exposure and contact search phase

3. Contact establishment and proposal phase
4. Contractual or commitment phase
5. Fulfilment phase
6. Completion or assessment phase

The other frameworks address only a part of these phases and/or they give different names to the phases and/or they subsume several phases under one heading. As BAT is the most general framework and offers the most comprehensive phases it appears to be an ideal starting point for a business modeling method. But contrary to many others (and as already mentioned) it does not yet provide its own method. The author of BAT defends the corresponding decision with the "freedom of choice" argument [7] but this argument can be challenged as we have shown above. As a consequence we show in this paper how the existing method SIMM can be enriched with BAT concepts.

Business Action Theory (BAT) has been introduced by Goldkuhl [7] and was refined and adapted on the basis of further empirical evidence in [8, 10, 16]. It is based on Socio-Instrumental Pragmatism (SIP) [9] that combines communicative (social) and material (instrumental) aspects of actions. One of the roots of BAT is Speech Act Theory [2, 24] that views communication as action between (two) individuals, another one is the Theory of Communicative Action [12], which puts action into a social context.

According to BAT business interaction involves two principal players, i.e. the supplier and the customer, where the former sells to the latter. At the core of BAT is the so-called business transaction that consists of the six phases which we have already mentioned. Goldkuhl [7] identifies also a number of generic business actions that constitute the phases on the respective side of the transaction (i.e. supplier or customer). These actions are summarized in table 1.

Table 1. Generic Business Actions

Phase	Supplier	Customer
Prerequisites phase	Product/offer development	Identification of problems/needs
Exposure & contact search phase	Offer exposure	Contact search
Proposal phase	Offer	Inquiry
Commitment phase	Order confirmation	Order
Fulfilment phase	Delivery, Invoice, Receipt of payment	Receipt of delivery, Payment
Assessment phase	Acceptance, Claim	Acceptance, Claim

The business actions follow a certain execution logic but the whole transaction is by no means a linear, sequential procedure. In the proposal phase, for example, the supplier can make any number of offers concerning their products and/or services where each one will typically meet the customer's needs better than the preceding one. Likewise the customer can make a series of inquiries that usually become more and more "realistic". These loops terminate when offer and inquiry are sufficiently close to each other to reach an agreement whereupon we enter the contractual phase. In an ideal scenario this consists of the customer placing an order and the supplier confirming it. Both actions together constitute a contract the fulfilment of which is subject of the next phase. Here the supplier, again ideally, delivers the products/services and sends a corresponding invoice. The customer receives the delivery and makes the payment, which the supplier finally receives. In the completion phase each party decides whether they accept the receipt of the delivery/money or make a claim, i.e. request the fulfilment of that part of the contract they consider unfulfilled.

Orthogonal to the phases BAT offers another dimension, layers, that was introduced in [15]. They extend and modify the layers originally suggested by Weigand and van den Heuvel [27]. Layers refer to the granularity of an action and in BAT they are, from fine grain to coarse grain: business act, action pair, exchange, business transaction and transaction group. A business act is a communicative act (speech act, e.g. placing an order) or a material act (e.g. performing a delivery). It is directed towards somebody with the aim of changing the world, i.e. the material world or the mental world (state of mind) of the addressee. An action pair is a pair of actions where the first one is a trigger (initiative) and the second a response. Actions can have a dual function so the response of one action pair can be the initiative of another.

On the third layer an exchange consists of an arbitrary number of action pairs (but at least one). An actor gives something to another in return for something else. An exchange always concerns actions of the same type, i.e. a value is exchanged against another value (e.g. product against money) or a proposal is exchanged against another proposal (e.g. offer and inquiry). The fourth layer is called business transaction. It consists of a number of exchanges that correspond to the phases. There is an exchange of interests (contact search), an exchange of proposals (bidding), an exchange of commitments (contract), an exchange of values (e.g. products and/or services against money) and finally an exchange of assessments (claims or acceptances). A transaction starts when the (potential) customer has a need and the (potential) supplier has a corresponding ability (to satisfy the need). It ends when the need is (at least partially) satisfied or when the parties agree that this goal cannot be reached. In the latter case the actor in the customer role will search for a different supplier whereupon a new transaction begins.

On the fifth and final layer the same customer and supplier engage in a number of transactions over a longer period of time thus forming a stable business relationship [3,11]. In the next section we elaborate the generic business actions with the help of communicative and material functions analysis. We use the results of that analysis to develop a set of essential functions of business acts that can be basic concepts of a language for BAT.

3 Refining the Framework

A method for BAT would have to take into account both dimensions, phases and layers. Strictly speaking, the phases are only a refinement of one particular layer, namely the transaction layer. On the way towards concepts for such a method we also need a refinement of the other layers. Such a refinement is suggested in fig. 1 with the exception of the transaction group layer. The transaction layer is divided into the exchanges (or phases) that have already been mentioned. An exchange consists of two handover actions: One is directed from the supplier to the customer and the other vice versa. These handovers usually happen one after the other where the second happens in return for the first but the order is not predefined, i.e. in some cases the supplier hands over first and in others the customer. In certain cases, e.g. if the parties do not trust each other, the handovers can be near-simultaneous as for example in "delivery versus payment".

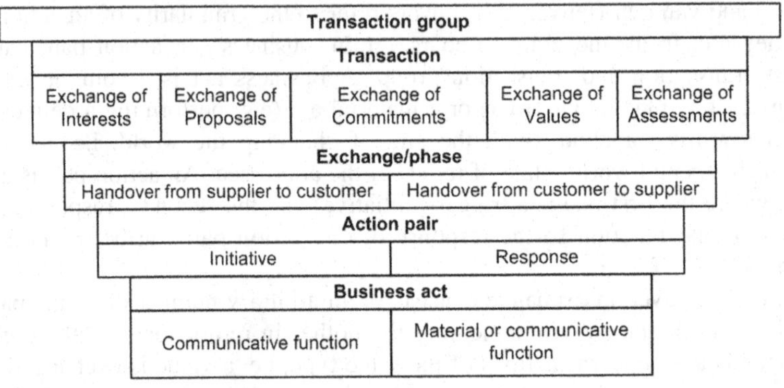

Fig. 1. Structure of the Layers

4 Communicative and Material Functions Analysis

An action pair consists of two business acts, an initiative and a response. They have already been introduced as trigger and response in [15]. On the lowest layer a business act consists of one or more functions. The importance of these functions was already recognized in [7] where they were named mixed communicative actions. This suggests that a business act can be further divided into distinct, separate acts. But the mixed actions are rather different functions of the same act than different acts. We therefore prefer to call them the communicative and/or material functions of a business act as outlined in the introduction. Goldkuhl [7] gives the examples of (commercial) offer and order. A commercial offer can be a single business act that has two communicative functions,

1. that of requesting the potential customer to buy (i.e. to place an order),
2. that of committing the potential supplier to sell (i.e. to deliver) under certain conditions.

These are two communicative functions that are often part of the same business act rather than two separate steps (i.e. distinct actions). The same holds for the order which has the functions of

1. requesting the supplier to sell (i.e. to deliver),
2. and committing the customer to buy under certain conditions.

If we apply the same kind of analysis, which we call communicative and material functions analysis, to the remaining generic business actions we get the results shown in table 2.

Table 2. Material and Communicative Functions of the Generic Business Actions

Business Action	**Material and/or communicative function**	**Business Action**
Offer exposure	*State* general offer	Offer exposure
Contact search	*Express* interest	Contact search
Inquiry	*Request* commercial offer + *Express* interest	Inquiry
Commercial offer	*Offer* delivery + *Request* order	Commercial offer
Order	*Request* delivery + *Offer* payment	Order
Order confirmation	*Promise* delivery	Order confirmation
Delivery	*Transfer* merchandise/*Perform* service + *State* delivery	Delivery
Invoice	*Request* payment + *State* contract fulfilment [supplier]	Invoice
Receipt of delivery	*Accept* delivery + (*Accept* contract fulfilment [supplier])	Receipt of delivery
Payment	*Transfer* money + *State* contract fulfilment [customer]	Payment
Receipt of payment	*Accept* payment + (*Accept* contract fulfilment [customer])	Receipt of payment
Acceptance	*Accept* contract fulfilment [supplier or customer]	Acceptance
Claim	*Request* contract fulfilment [supplier or customer]	Claim

These results show that a business act typically has one or two functions. The communicative function is always present (even in the case of material acts) but there might also be another function that is either communicative or material. This is reflected in the model of fig. 1. The generic business action "receipt of delivery or payment" can in some cases imply the acceptance of the contract fulfilment of supplier or customer, respectively. In other cases the acceptance is stated explicitly (i.e. separately in the assessment phase) or a claim is made (also in the assessment phase).

We are aware of the fact that such a list of generic actions and their functions can only serve as a recommendation that covers some typical or common situations. It is not meant to be a prescriptive template for all business interactions. The main purposes of it are rather as follows: First it should give an example of how communicative and material functions analysis can be used to identify material and communicative functions. Using that analysis in a different context might yield different actions and even different functions concerning the same actions. But the results can nevertheless be useful, and that is the second purpose, to find a set of recurring material and communicative functions that can be used as a pattern for a modeling language.

5 Classifying Functions

If we compile the identified material and communicative functions and sort them according to the illocutionary points introduced in [25], adding a column for material functions, we arrive at the structure show in table 3.

Table 3. Classification of material and communicative functions

material	communicative				
	expressives	**declaratives**	**Assertives**	**commissives**	**directives**
Transfer	Express	Accept	State	Promise	Request
Apply			Reply	Offer	Ask
Transform					
			Perform		

The material functions are transfering and object (i.e. moving it in space), applying an object as an instrument and transforming and object (i.e. changing some of its properties) possibly with the help of an instrument (this is in accordance with SIP). The function "express" is used to show an emotion or an attitude (e.g. interest in a product). A directive is usually a request in a business context. A less formal and less compelling directive would be to ask a question. The reply is the corresponding assertive. There is another assertive, state, that carries a higher illocutionary force. It is a unilateral establishment of a fact, whereas the declarative "accept" is a confirmation of a stated fact, i.e. a mutual agreement on that fact. An "accept" must therefore always be preceeded by a "state" because one party alone cannot declare agreement. The commissives are divided into promise and offer. The former is an unconditional commitment, the latter is subject to some conditions. If these conditions are fulfilled (typically by the other party) the offer becomes a promise. To avoid confusion of the communicative function "offer" with the same term as used in a business context we have called the latter a commercial offer. The function "perform" refers to a business act that is elementary at the current level of abstraction (i.e. with respect to the model under consideration) but a complex action on some lower, more detailed level.

The development of a set of material and communicative functions was motivated by [7, 15]. Both stress the importance of this issue (in the latter paper it was called multi-functional business acts, in the former mixed communicative actions). We agree with Goldkuhl [7] that the illocutionary points of Searle [25] are too coarse for business modeling and have therefore developed the set of functions in table 3 which is somewhat more elaborate and more adapted to business interaction. But nevertheless such a classification should be seen as a suggestion rather than a fixed template. Such a set might require adaptation to a particular modeling scenario.

A classification of speech acts has also been done by Reijswoud et al. [23]. They employed a purely theoretical method that consisted in viewing the one-dimensional classifications of Searle and Habermas, respectively, as two dimensions of a matrix. As a result they got the six speech acts question, answer, request, promise, state and accept. These are also found in table 3. Our classification can therefore be seen as an extension of that of Reijswoud et al. [23].

Based on the suggested refinements, the next section derives a set of concepts that are fundamental for modeling business actions.

6 Deriving Business Action Concepts

The development of a full-blown language or even a method is a huge project. Such a project is only justified if the new language or method really offers something substantially new. As we have mentioned earlier, there is already a number of methods that "implement" language-action concepts to some extent. We do therefore not propose a comprehensive new language but rather a set of concepts that can, for example, be used to extend existing languages. In this context we refer to these concepts as language elements. The techniques for such an extension are offered by (situational) method engineering [19]. The idea behind method engineering is to design methods in such a way that they fit the particular modeling situation. This can be done in different ways. One way is to extend an existing method. Another one is to create a new one from chunks of existing methods by performing method chunk selection and assembly. The third way is to construct a new method from scratch with the help of a suitable meta-model or paradigm. Using the first approach, method extension, we enrich and refine the language of SIMM with the concepts introduced in this section.

We propose that a business action language requires at least three basic categories: actors, actions and (action) objects. As SIMM has the most elaborate concept of an action object, we borrow both the notion and the notation of an object from SIMM. Examples of information and material objects are shown in fig. 2 but SIMM offers many additional types. Actors are denoted by a rectangle containing the name of the actor as is common in many approaches. The actions themselves are divided into two categories according to the layer: business acts (layer 1) and the other layers. Actions on layers 2 to 5 are represented by a rounded rectangle with a double line. An additional classification symbol can be used to identify the particular layer: two intersecting circles for an action pair, two arrows pointing towards each other for an exchange, a "T" for a transaction and a "G" for a transaction group. For business acts in general we also use the rounded rectangle, for material acts the octagon. Both shapes have only one line to show that the act is elementary. The box can either contain the name of the business act or the respective material or communicative function where the function header is italicized. In the case of multiple functions the box can be divided into horizontal compartments, one for each function. If material and communicative functions are mixed we can also mix the respective shapes. Fig. 2 shows an overview of the business action concepts and their notational representation.

Among the notational elements there are also four types of arcs. Two undirected arcs that represent an information flow (thin arc) or a material flow (thick arc). These have been borrowed from the SIMM Action Diagram where the direction of the flow is coincides with the drawing direction (from top to bottom). The condition arc allows us to show that one action is a condition for another action. The end with the black

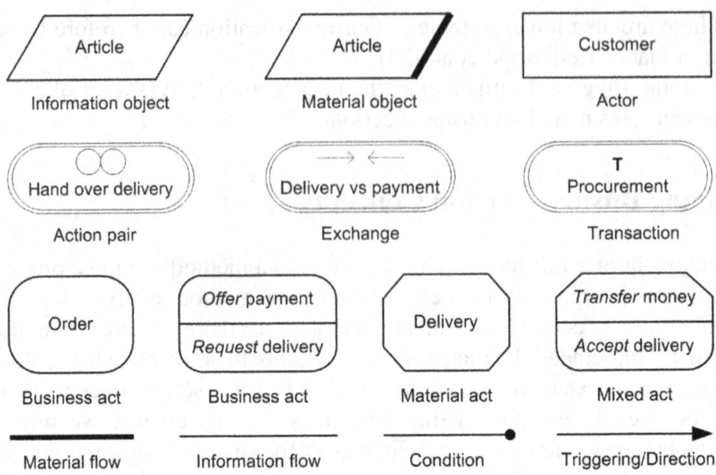

Fig. 2. Concepts for business action modeling and their notation

dot is attached to the latter action. The arrow serves two purposes. If it points from one action to another, the former triggers the latter. If it points from one actor to another, it represents an action that is directed from the first actor to the second. In this case the name of the action is written along the arrow. It can be accompanied by a symbol denoting the layer. For layers 2 to 5 we use the classification symbols introduced above. For communicative or material acts we use a small rounded rectangle (or circle) or a small octagon (or diamond), respectively. As an alternative to the arrow form of the action the boxed form of the action can be interlaced with the arrow.

In the next section we apply the extended method for the analysis of commitments.

7 Applying the Extended Method: A Case Study

Commitment analysis in terms of language action was introduced by Auramäki et al. [1]. They used discourse analysis to develop a discourse graph, a conversation graph and finally a network graph of actions and commitments that shows in which way the actions influence the commitments. This helped them to discover flaws in the way that commitments are handled. As the main objective in our case project was business process re-engineering we used the existing business process analysis as the point of departure instead. The project involved two companies that have a very close business relationship. One of them is the headquarters of a retail chain in the home textiles and decoration industry. The other is a third-party logistics provider, let us call them LogPro, that performs all inbound and outbound logistics for the retailer.

Our goal was to discover the major problems in their relationship and to suggest appropriate solutions. For this purpose we carried out a thorough analysis of the relevant business process, order processing and delivery, that involved, apart from Headquarters and LogPro, also the shops of the chain which are organizations in their own right although they do maintain a very close, franchise-like relation with

Headquarters. For the analysis of the interaction between these players we first used the Interaction Diagrams of SIMM. But then we discovered that we also need information on the type and level of an action so we enriched the Interaction Diagram with the features introduced above. The resulting diagram is shown in fig. 3.

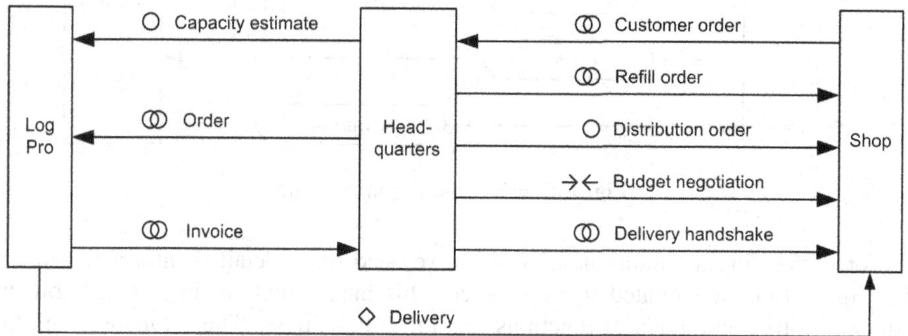

Fig. 3. Enriched Interaction Diagram

The process starts when Headquarters send an estimate regarding the capacity required for executing future orders. Such estimates are send six months, two months and two weeks in advance of the time of delivery. Shortly before that time the Shop can place different kinds of orders. A customer order is iniated by the Shop on behalf of a customer who wishes to buy an article that is not currently available in the Shop. The refill order is triggered by Headquarters whenever the Shop's stock is running low on articles of the basic assortment. Both actions are on the action-pair level because they require some kind of confirmation from the partner. The third type of order is called a distribution order. It is based on the budget that was negotiated before and the shop has to accept it as part of its franchise obligations. The distribution order is therefore only a single speech act that has a more informative character. The negotiation of the budget on the other hand is a bilateral process that is initiated by Headquarters but consists of an exchange of budget proposals.

Orders of all types are combined into one order by Headquarters and forwarded to LogPro. As a consequence LogPro will perform the delivery to the Shop. Headquarters inform the Shop about the upcoming delivery and receive a confirmation that is has arrived (delivery handshake). In regular intervals LogPro bill their services to Headquarters.

On the basis of this overview we developed detailed Interaction Diagrams for the interactions between Headquarters and Shop as well as between LogPro and Headquarters. The latter is shown in fig. 4. This diagram is on the business-act level, i.e. all actions in it are business acts. It shows that Headquarters send a capacity estimate first. On the day of delivery a pick file is transferred to LogPro that contains the order data. This is used by LogPro to pick the appropriate articles from the shelves and to pack them for delivery. As soon as the articles are on their way, LogPro reports the delivery to Headquarters. At the next billing occasion LogPro send an invoice and Headquarters makes the respective payment.

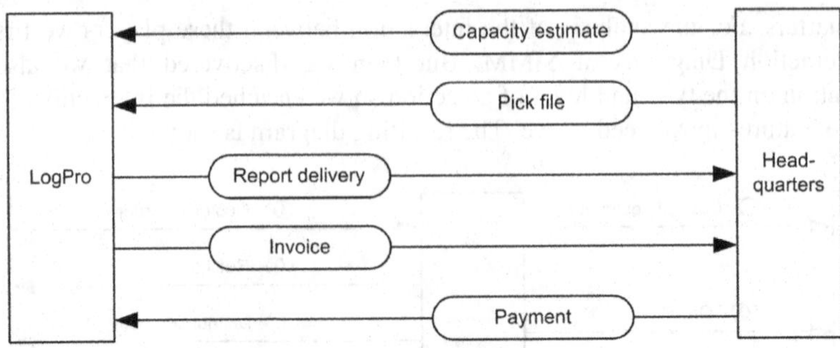

Fig. 4. Detailed Interaction Diagram

For performing a commitment analysis we need more detailed information about how the actions are related to each other. This means that we have to exhibit the communicative and material functions that the actions have. These functions are the ones that lead to the establishment or fulfilment of commitments. When they have been made explicit we can show the conditional and causal relationships between the functions. This in turn helps us to uncover broken commitments. For this purpose we have created a new type af diagram, the Business Act Diagram. A diagram of this type for the relation between LogPro and Headquarters is shown in fig. 5.

Each actor box covers the actions that are performed by this actor. The capacity estimate is an action that implies both a request to provide this capacity and a promise to place an order that requires approximately the requested capacity. LogPro makes an offer to provide this capacity subject to Headquarters' order in general and their offer of payment in particular. This offer is implicit (i.e. not communicated) because LogPro is required to provide the respective capacity by the terms of the frame

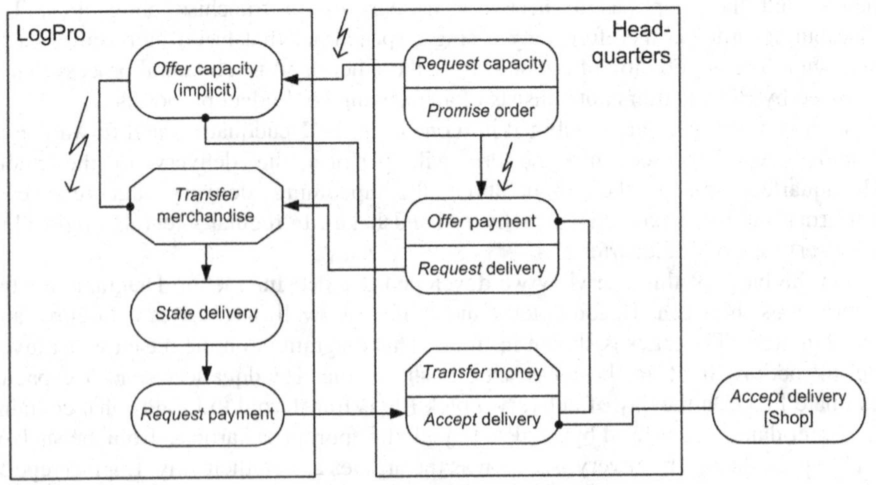

Fig. 5. Business Act Diagram

contract. The provision of the capacity is a condition for the ability to perform the delivery that is triggered by the respective request from Headquarters that is a function of the order. The other function, offer payment, is subject to an accepted delivery. The performed delivery triggers a respective report (state delivery) which in turn triggers the invoice (request payment). The latter triggers the payment (transfer money) but only if the Shop has confirmed the arrival of the delivery. Headquarters does not explicitly accept the delivery towards LogPro but does so implicitly by paying the invoice. Therefore "Transfer money" and "Accept delivery" are functions of the same business act.

The Business Act Diagram has shown us that the commitment concerning capacity is broken in three different places (see the flash symbols in fig. 5):

1. Headquarters promise that the order will require the capacity that was requested. But in reality the orders often deviate substantially from the estimates.
2. The request for the capacity is not in a for LogPro suitable format so that they can hardly plan for providing this capacity. But Headquarters assume that the capacity is provided.
3. As a consequence of 1 and 2 the condition for performing the delivery are not given in many cases. This leads to higher costs and sometimes failure to meet the deadlines for delivery.

We have used this approach for other parts of the business process where we also succeeded in finding mistakes in commitment management. Among the problems we have identified this way are:

1. Indistinct communication structures: It is often unclear who communicates with whom regarding which issue.
2. Lack of trust: Different interpretations of the frame contract by the parties lead to expectations that are not fulfilled.
3. Lack of information: LogPro is not provided with suitable information for reliable capacity planning, This is not specified clearly in the existing frame contract.
4. Excessive communication: A considerable amount of personal communication between organizations is spent on handling everyday work. This is only necessary because of insufficient specification of routine procedures in the frame contract.
5. High transaction costs due to ad-hoc solutions.

8 Conclusion

Business Action Theory is a stable framework for analysing business processes. It can guide the modeler in finding appropriate abstractions of the studied process and in relating different parts of the model to each other. These features are achieved by rooting the theory solidly in an ontology, i.e. Socio-Instrumental Pragmatism, that describes all important aspects of social behaviour in general and business behaviour in particular. Other cornerstone of BAT are the existence of different dimensions, layers and phases, and the multi-functionality of business acts. All these features contribute to better business process models. But the support of the modeler can be strengthened by providing a modeling language that reflects these features of BAT. We have suggested a number of concepts of such a language and we have shown two ways in which they can be used: to refine the exisiting modeling methods SIMM and to define new diagram types that are adapted to a particular modeling situation.

As an example for such a situation we have used the analysis of commitments that are created and fulfilled (or broken) in the course of a business process. An enriched Interaction Diagram and a Business Act Diagram, two examples of newly defined diagram types, have proved useful in this context. But the concepts are only potential language elements. How they can be introduced into existing languages and whether they can contribute to the development of new languages depends on the context of use of such languages. This is subject to future research.

References

1. Auramäki, E., Lehtinen, E., Lyytinen, K. (1988). A Speech-Act-Based Office Modeling Approach. ACM Transactions on Office Information Systems 6(2), pp. 126-152.
2. Austin, J. L. (1962). How to Do Things with Words. Oxford University Press.
3. Axelsson, K., Goldkuhl, G., Melin, U. (2000). Using Business Action Theory for Dyadic Analysis. 10th Nordic Workshop on Interorganisational Research, 18-20 August, 2000, Trondheim.
4. Denning, P. J., Medina-Mora, R. (1995). Completing the Loops. Interfaces, 25 (3), 42-57.
5. Dietz, J. L. G. (1999). Understanding and modeling business processes with DEMO. In Akoka, J., Bouzeghoub, M., Comyn-Wattiau, I., Métais, E. (eds.): Conceptual modeling - ER '99: proceedings (Lecture notes in computer science 1728). Berlin: Springer, 188-202.
6. Dietz, J. L. G., Habing, N. (2004). The Notion of Business Process Revisited. In Proceedings of the OTM Confederated International Conferences, CoopIS, DOA, and ODBASE (Meersman, R., Tari, Z., Eds), pp. 85-100, Springer, Berlin, Germany.
7. Goldkuhl, G. (1996). Generic business frameworks and action modelling. In Dignum, F., Dietz, J., Verharen, E. and Weigand, H. (eds.): Communication Modeling – The Language/Action Perspective, Proceedings of the First International Workshop on Communication Modeling, Electronic Workshops in Computing, Berlin: Springer.
8. Goldkuhl G. (1998). The six phases of business processes - business communication and the exchange of value. 12th biennial ITS conference "Beyond convergence" (ITS´98), Stockholm.
9. Goldkuhl G. (2002). Anchoring scientific abstractions – ontological and linguistic determination following socio-instrumental pragmatism. European Conference on Research Methods in Business and Management (ECRM 2002), Reading, 29-30 April, 2002.
10. Goldkuhl G., Lind M. (2004). Developing e-interactions – A framework for business capabilities and exchanges. 12th European Conference on Information Systems, June 14-16, 2004, Turku, Finland
11. Goldkuhl, G., Melin, U. (2001). Relationship Management vs Business Transactions: Business Interaction as Design of Business Interaction. 10th International Annual IPSERA Conference, 9-11 April, 2001, Jönköping International Business School.
12. Habermas, J. (1984). The Theory of Communicative Action 1, Reason and the Rationalization of Society. Boston: Beacon Press.
13. Kethers, S., Schoop, M. (2000). Reassessment of the Action Workflow Approach: Empirical Results. In Proceedings of the Fifth International Workshop on the Language-Action Perspective on Communication Modelling LAP 2000 (Schoop, M., Quix, C., Eds), pp. 151-169, RWTH Aachen University, Germany.

14. Lehtinen, E., & Lyytinen, K. (1986). An Action Based Model of Information Systems. Information Systems 11 (4), pp. 299-317.
15. Lind, M., Goldkuhl, G. (2001). Generic Layered Patterns for Business Modelling. In Proceedings of the Sixth International Workshop on the Language-Action Perspective on Communication Modelling (LAP 2001) Montreal, Canada, July 21-22, 2001.
16. Lind M., Goldkuhl, G. (2005). Designing business process variants. Business Process Design Workshop at the Third International Conference on Business Process Management, September 5-8 2005, Nancy, France.
17. Liu, K., Sun, L., Barjis. J., Dietz, J. L. G. (2003). Modelling dynamic behaviour of business organisations - extension of DEMO from a semiotic perspective. Knowledge-Based Systems 16(2), pp. 101-111.
18. Medina-Mora, R., Winograd, T., Flores, R., Flores, F. (1992). The Action Workflow Approach to Workflow Management Technology. In Turner, J. and Kraut, R. (eds.): Proceedings of the Conference on Computer-Supported Cooperative Work, CSCW'92. New York: ACM Press.
19. Ralyté, J., Deneckère, R., Rolland, C. (2003). Towards a Generic Model for Situational Method Engineering, In Proceedings of 15th International Conference on Advanced Information Systems Engineering (Caise 2003), Klagenfurt, Austria, June 16-18, 2003, (Eds, Eder J, et al.) Heidelberg, Germany: Springer-Verlag, pp. 95-110.
20. Reijswoud, V. E. van (1996). The Structure of Business Communication: Theory, Model and Application. PhD Thesis. Delft, The Netherlands: Delft University of Technology.
21. Reijswoud, V. E. van, Dietz, J. L. G. (1999). DEMO Modelling Handbook, Volume 1. TU Delft. Online version available at http://www.demo.nl/documents/handbook.pdf.
22. Reijswoud, V. E. van, Lind, M. (1998). Comparing two business modelling approaches in the language action perspective. In Proceedings of Language Action Perspective (LAP'98), Stockholm.
23. Reijswoud, V. E. van, Mulder, H. B. F., Dietz, J. L. G. (1999). Communicative action-based business process and information systems modelling with DEMO. Information Systems Journal 9(2), pp. 117-138.
24. Searle, J. R. (1969). Speech Acts, An Essay in the Philosophy of Language. London: Cambridge University Press.
25. Searle, J. R. (1979). Expression and meaning. Studies in the theory of speech acts, Cambridge University Press, London.
26. Verharen, E. (1997). A language-action perspective on the design of cooperative information agents. PhD thesis, KUB, Tilburg.
27. Weigand, H., van den Heuvel, W.J. (1998). Meta-Patterns for Electronic Commerce Transactions based on FLBC. Hawaii International Conference on System Sciences (HICSS '98), IEEE Press.
28. Winograd, T., Flores, F. (1986). Understanding Computers and Cognition: A New Foundation for Design. Norwood, NJ: Ablex.

Towards a Reference Ontology for Business Models*

Birger Andersson[1], Maria Bergholtz[1], Ananda Edirisuriya[1], Tharaka Ilayperuma[1], Paul Johannesson[1], Jaap Gordijn[2], Bertrand Grégoire[3], Michael Schmitt[3], Eric Dubois[3], Sven Abels[4], Axel Hahn[4], Benkt Wangler[5], and Hans Weigand[6]

[1] Royal Institute of Technology
Department of Computer and Systems Sciences, Sweden
{ba, maria, si-ana, si-tsi, pajo}@dsv.su.se

[2] Department of Computer Science
Vrije Universiteit, Amsterdam
gordijn@cs.vu.nl

[3] Public Research Centre Henri Tudor
Luxembourg
{bertrand.gregoire, michael.schmitt, eric.dubois}@tudor.lu

[4] University of Oldenburg,
Business Information Systems
Department of Computing Science, Germany
{abels, hahn}@wi-ol.de

[5] University of Skövde,
School of Humanities and Informatics, Sweden
benkt.wangler@his.se

[6] Tilburg University, P.O. Box 90153,
5000 LE Tilburg, Netherlands
H.Weigand@uvt.nl

Abstract. Ontologies are viewed as increasingly important tools for structuring domains of interests. In this paper we propose a reference ontology of business models using concepts from three established business model ontologies; the REA, BMO, and e3-value. The basic concepts in the reference ontology concern actors, resources, and the transfer of resources between actors. Most of the concepts in the reference ontology are taken from one of the original ontologies, but we have also introduced a number of additional concepts, primarily related to resource transfers between business actors. The purpose of the proposed ontology is to increase the understanding of the original ontologies as well as the relationships between them, and also to seek opportunities to complement and improve on them.

1 Introduction

It is increasingly recognized that when modelling enterprises and the ways they do business, a starting point could be to identify the main actors and the values transferred between them. This can be expressed in terms of business models. A

* This paper represents a community effort coordinated by KTH within the Interop, a NoE in EU 6th FP. The author order starts with authors from KTH and continues with authors in affiliation order.

D.W. Embley, A. Olivé, and S. Ram (Eds.): ER 2006, LNCS 4215, pp. 482–496, 2006.

business model is created in order to make clear who the actors are in a business case and explain their relations, which are formulated in terms of values exchanged between the actors.

In this paper, we propose a reference ontology for business models. The purpose is not to present an all encompassing ontology of the business domain. Neither is the purpose to question the design of the ontologies that are analysed. The purpose is to identify, analyse, and compare the basic notions of business models by constructing a reference ontology based on three established business model ontologies: REA, e^3-value, and BMO.

A reference ontology will be richer and wider in scope than any of the ontologies it is based on. One benefit from widening the scope is the increased applicability of the reference ontology. Another benefit is that opportunities for extensions and revisions of the component ontologies are discovered and can be considered. Finally, the main benefit of the reference ontology is that it provides a clear understanding of the relationships between the original ontologies. A characteristic of business models is the focus on concepts related to value transfers between actors. This makes their scope different from enterprise model ontologies (e.g. TOVE [Fox92] or EO [Uschold96]) that are more focused on organisational activities, structures, and management.

The work presented in this paper represents a continuation of the effort reported in [Andersson06a] but has also a bearing on work presented in [Weigand06, Bergholtz05, Schmitt05, Andersson06b]. The main purpose of those works was to investigate methods for going from business models to process models in structured ways. Such methods need a clear understanding of the business domain, and ontologies are useful as tools for getting this understanding.

The paper is structured as follows. Section 2 provides a brief overview of the three ontologies used as a basis for the reference ontology. In section 3, the reference ontology is presented. Mappings between concepts in the original ontologies and the reference ontology are presented in section 4. Section 5 concludes the paper with a summary and directions for further work.

2 Features of REA, e^3-Value and BMO

The reference ontology presented in this paper is based on three established business model ontologies: REA, e^3-value, and BMO. As these are the most comprehensive and well defined ontologies for business models, they provide an adequate basis for a reference ontology. These three ontologies were originally developed for different and specific purposes, but there has also been recent work on expanding their applicability. REA was originally intended as a basis for accounting information systems [McCarthy82] and focused on representing increases and decreases of value in an organisation. REA has been extended to form a foundation for enterprise information systems architectures [Hruby06], and it has also been applied to e-commerce frameworks [UMM03]. e^3-value focuses on modelling value networks of cooperating business partners and provides instruments for profitability analysis that help in determining whether a certain value network is sustainable [Gordijn04]. Extensions of e^3-value have been suggested that incorporate process related aspects as well as risk management [Bergholtz05] and [Weigand06]. BMO differs from the two other ontologies by being much wider in scope. In addition to modelling exchanges of resources, BMO also addresses internal capabilities and resource planning. Furthermore, BMO incorporates marketing aspects describing value propositions as well as marketing channels [Osterwalder05].

2.1 The Resource-Event-Actor Ontology

The Resource-Event-Actor (REA) ontology was formulated originally in [McCarthy82] and has been developed further, e.g. [Geerts99, UMM03]. Its conceptual origins can be traced back to business accounting where the needs are to manage businesses through a technique called double-entry bookkeeping. This technique records every business transaction as a double entry (a credit and a debit) in a balanced ledger.

The core concepts in the REA ontology are Resource, Event, and Actor and the intuition behind the ontology is that every business transaction can be described as an event where two actors exchange resources. To get a resource, an agent has to give up some other resource. For example, in a purchase a buying agent has to give up money to receive some goods. The amount of money available to the agent is decreased, while the amount of goods is increased. There are two events taking place here: one where the amount of money is decreased and another where the amount of goods is increased. This combination of events is called a duality. A corresponding change of control of resources takes place at the seller's side. Here the amount of money is increased while the amount of goods is decreased. An exchange occurs when an agent receives economic resources from another agent and gives resources back to that agent; and vice versa. A conversion occurs when an agent consumes resources to produce other resources [Hruby06]. Events often occur as consequences of existing obligations of an actor; in other words, events fulfill the commitments of actors. A commitment is defined as being "an agreement to execute an event in a well-defined future that will result in either an increase or a decrease of resources" available to an agent. Thus, events "happen" because commitments exist between actors, and the duality relation between events exists because of a relation called reciprocity between commitments. Which commitment is related to which is established through an agreement.

2.2 The e^3-Value Ontology

The e^3-value ontology [Gordijn00] aims at identifying exchanges of value objects between the actors in a business case. It also supports profitability analysis of business cases. The ontology was designed to contain a minimal set of concepts and relations to make it easy to grasp for the intended users. The basic concepts in e^3-value are actors, value objects, value ports, value interfaces, value activities and value exchanges. An actor is an economically independent entity. An actor is often, but not necessarily, a legal entity, such as enterprises and end-consumers. A value object is something that is of economic value for at least one actor, e.g. cars, Internet access, and stream of music. A value port is used by an actor to provide or receive value objects to or from other actors. A value port has a direction, in (e.g., receive goods) or out (e.g., make a payment) indicating whether a value object flows into or out of the actor. A value interface consists of in and out ports that belong to the same actor.

Value interfaces are used to model economic reciprocity. In the case of e^3-value models without actor compositions a value exchange is a pair of value ports of opposite directions belonging to different actors. It represents one or more potential trades of value objects between these value ports. A value activity is an operation that can be carried out in an economically profitable way for at least one actor.

2.3 The Business Model Ontology

The Business Model Ontology (BMO) as proposed in [Osterwalder04] provides an ontology that allows describing the business model of a firm accurately and in detail. The BMO takes the perspective of a single enterprise, highlighting its environment and concerns for facing a particular customer's demands. It consists of nine core concepts in four categories (or "pillars" as they are called). The categories are Product, Customer Interface, Infrastructure Management, and Financial Aspects.

The single concept in Product is Value Proposition. A value proposition is an overall view of a company's bundle of products and services that are of value to the customer.

Customer Interface contains three concepts; Target Customer, Distribution Channel, and Relationship. A target customer is a segment of customers to which a company wants to offer value. A distribution channel is a means of getting in touch with the customer. A relationship is the kind of link a company establishes between itself and the customer.

Infrastructure Management contains three concepts; Value Configuration, Capability, and Partnership. A value configuration describes the arrangement of activities and resources that are necessary to create value for the customer. A capability is the ability to execute a repeatable pattern of actions that is necessary in order to create value for the customer. A partnership is a voluntarily initiated cooperative agreement between two or more companies in order to create value for the customer.

Financial Aspects contains two concepts; Cost Structure and Revenue Model. Cost structure is the representation in money of all the means employed in the business model. Revenue Model describes the way a company makes money through a variety of revenue flows.

3 A Reference Ontology

In this section, we introduce the reference ontology for business models. It is constructed using the concepts of REA, e^3-value, and BMO as inputs to an analysis and subsequent synthesis. The approach used in constructing the reference ontology has been to survey all concepts from all the established ontologies and analyse similarities and differences.

As the three original ontologies include concepts on the operational level as well as the knowledge level, the reference ontology has to include both these levels. As described in [Fowler97], the operational level models concrete, tangible individuals in a domain. The knowledge level, on the other hand, models information structures that characterise categories of individuals at the operational level. For example, the ontology distinguishes between Resource Types (categories of resources like car models) and Resources (specific, tangible things like concrete cars).

We have aimed at including all of the concepts in REA and e[3]-value except for a small number of peripheral concepts, i.e. concepts that occur in only one of the ontologies and are not central for transfers of values. For BMO, we have not aimed at including all its concepts. In particular, some concepts from Customer Interface and all concepts from Financial Aspects are excluded from this work. The reasons are that the Distribution Channel and Link from Customer Interface concerns technical distribution issues. The reason for omitting the Financial Aspects category is that this category goes into issues of internal capabilities and resource planning, and has little to do with transfers of values between actors.

We have also introduced a small number of concepts that do not have any direct correspondences in the original ontologies. This has been done mainly in order to facilitate the analysis of value transfers and resources. The introduction of those additional concepts represents an extension of the reference ontology with respect to the combination of the originals.

The concepts are described in the following paragraphs and the correspondences to an original ontology are discussed and motivated in section 4.

Actor

An *Actor* is someone who is able to participate in events (event defined below).

Resource, Feature, and Right

A *Resource* is an object that is regarded as valuable by some actors. An actor views a resource as valuable because she can use it for producing other resources, for trading it with other actors, or for deriving some consumer experience. Essentially any object can be a resource. However, it is possible to identify some typical categories of resources like goods, information, and services. A resource may have properties and associations to other objects, like the weight of a pizza or the number of shops accepting a credit card. Such properties and associations are modelled by means of the class *Feature*.

Resources are furthermore related to rights. A *Right* on a resource means that an actor is entitled to use that resource in some way. An example is the ownership of a book, which means that an actor is entitled to read the book, give it to someone else, or even destroy it. Another example of a right is borrowing a book, which gives the actor the right to read it, but not to give it away or destroy it or use it in any other way. Figure 1 shows the main concepts: Resource, Feature and Rights that are described in this section together with their relationships to other concepts.

Event, Transfer, and Conversion

An *Event* changes a feature or a right of a resource. An event is associated to exactly one actor representing the perspective from which the event is viewed. This means that each event can be seen as either an increment or decrement event from that actor's perspective. An increment event changes a feature or a right of a resource in such a way that the resource becomes more valuable for the actor, while a decrement event causes a change that decreases the value of the resource. In order to model increments and decrements, an attribute *stockflow* of the class Event is introduced that can take one of the values in {use, consume, produce, give, take}. This corresponds to the stockflow relationship in REA [McCarthy82].

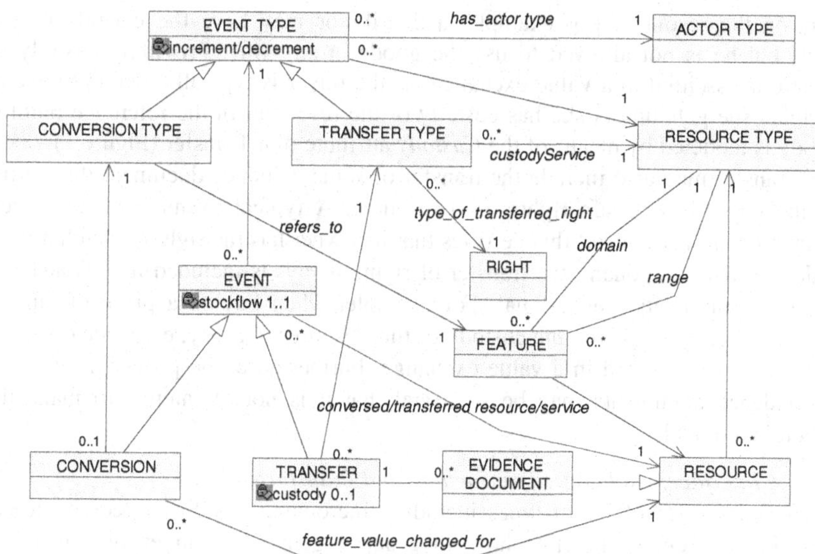

Fig. 1. Resource, Feature, and Right, and their respective relationships

The class Event has two subclasses, *Transfer* and *Conversion* [Hruby06]. A transfer means that a right is transferred from one actor to another (for a more detailed analysis, see the next subsection). If the actor of the event receives the right to the resource, the event is a take event (represented by the stockflow attribute). If the actor gives up the right to the resource, the event is a give event. Similarly, a conversion event changes some feature of a resource. If this change means that a new resource is created or the value of an existing resource is increased, the event is a produce event. If the resource is completely consumed and no longer exists after the event, it is called a consume event. If the resource is used but continues to exist also after the event, it is called a use event. Use, consume, and give are decrement events, while produce and take are increment events. Figure 2 shows the events, transfers, conversions and their relationships to other concepts such as exchanges, interfaces, and transactions.

Rights, Custody and Evidence Documents - Three components of a transfer

A Transfer from A to B can be viewed as consisting of three components:

- transferring rights on a resource from A to B
- giving custody of the resource to B
- transferring an evidence document (documenting the transferred right) from A to B

The second component of a Transfer is transferring the custody of the resource being exchanged from one actor to another. An actor has the *Custody* of a resource if he has immediate charge and control of the resource, typically physical access of the resource. If an actor has the custody of a resource, this does not mean that she has any rights on the resource. For example, a distributor may have the custody of some goods, but he is not allowed to use the goods in any way. Providing custody of a resource is essential in a value exchange, as the buyer is typically unable to exercise the rights she gets unless she has custody of the resource. In the reference ontology, custody is modeled by means of the *Custody* attribute of a Transfer (Figure 1).

A Transfer may also include the transfer of some evidence document that certifies that the buyer has certain rights on a resource. A typical example of an evidence document is a movie ticket that certifies that its owner has the right to watch a movie. While the first component, the transfer of right, always is included in a Transfer, the last two components are optional. For example, when buying a piece of land, the buyer is typically not given the custody of that resource. Clearly, evidence documents are not always provided in a value exchange. Furthermore, the provision of custody and evidence documents may be so trivial that it is not of interest to make them explicit in a model.

Process, Interface, Exchange, Transaction, and Transformation

A *Process* is a set of Event types including increment as well as decrement event types, i.e. a process specifies how to group together a number of transfer and conversion events. This means that a process, as defined here, only describes the changes of rights and features of resources; it does not specify temporal or communicative aspects. These aspects are certainly relevant for processes in general, but they are outside the scope of business models. The notion of a process is quite general, as it may contain any event types. It is, therefore, useful to identify a number of specialised processes, and the ontology distinguishes between interfaces, exchanges, transactions, and transformations. An *Interface* is a process consisting of transfer event types all associated to the same actor type. An interface specifies that an actor (type) is prepared to trade according to the transfer event types of the interface. An *Exchange* is a process consisting of a pair of one give transfer event type and one take transfer event type associated to two different actor types. An exchange specifies that one actor (type) is prepared to give a resource to another actor (type) who takes it. A *Transaction* is a process consisting of a number of exchanges, or more precisely, the transfer event types included in the exchanges. A transaction specifies that two actor (types) are prepared to trade with each other according to the transfer event types of the exchange. A *Transformation* is a set of conversion event types all associated to the same actor type. A transformation specifies that some resource is produced while other resources are consumed or used.

Commitment, Claim, Contract, and Agreement

A *Commitment* is an obligation to carry out a give Transfer within an Exchange in the future. A *Contract* is a collection of Commitments. An *Agreement* is an arrangement between two Actors that specifies in advance the conditions under which they will trade. A Claim comes into existence when one business partner has fulfilled an Economic Commitment while the other partner has yet to fulfill the reciprocal Economic Commitment.

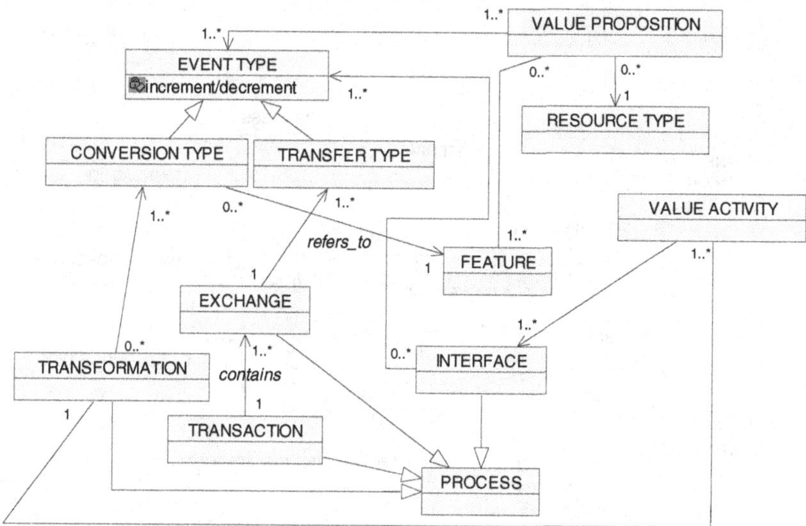

Fig. 2. Events, Transfer, Conversion and their respective relationships

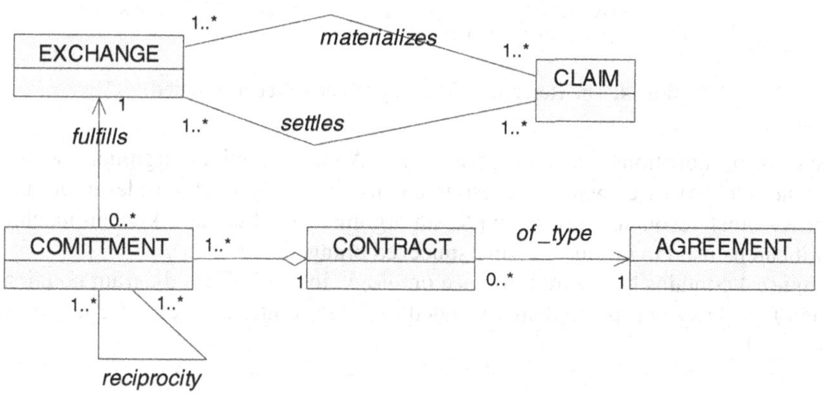

Fig. 3. Commitment, Claim, Contract and Agreement and their respective relationships

Value Activity
A *Value Activity* consists of a number of interfaces associated to one actor. A value activity is a set of related processes carried out by one actor, but that could potentially be performed by another actor.

Value Proposition
A *Value proposition* consists of a resource type and a number of features and processes containing decrement event types associated to that resource type. Intuitively, a value proposition does not only specify a resource type offered by an organisation but also arguments why the customer should buy that resource type. These arguments could consist of references to features of the resource, such as the

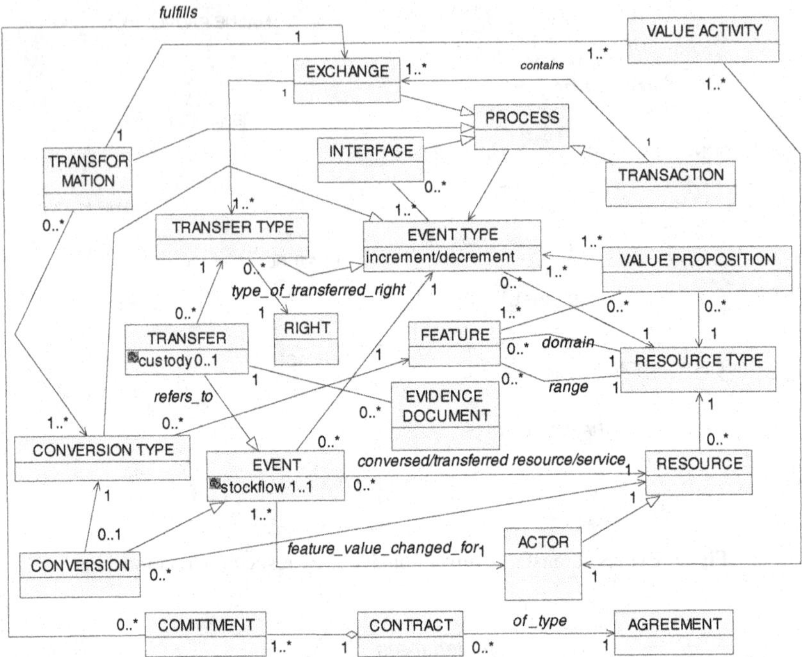

Fig. 4. The Reference Ontology (some concepts omitted)

freshness or nutritional content of a pizza. Another kind of argument would be references to processes where the resource is used or consumed in order to produce or improve other resources. For example, an argument for buying a kitchen machine is that it can be used to produce freshly squeezed orange juice.

Figure 4 contains the entire reference ontology, in UML Class diagram notation, except for a few concepts that are excluded to reduce clutter. Figures 1-3 are views of this model.

4 Mappings of Business Model Ontologies to the Reference Ontology

In this section, we map each of the business model ontologies REA, e^3-value, and BMO to the Reference ontology. For reasons of space, the mappings are presented informally in tables as relationships between concepts of the ontologies.

4.1 REA-Reference Ontology Mappings

The version of REA used in this analysis is based on UMM [UMM03]. This version does not explicitly distinguish between the notions of conversion and transfer described in [Hruby06], as it focuses on electronic commerce. In fact, only transfers of resources are modeled in UMM.

REA	Reference ontology
Partner	Actor
Partner type	Actor type
Economic Event	A pair of Transfers (1)
Economic Resource	Resource
Economic Event Type	Exchange (2)
Economic Resource Type	Resource Type
Duality	Transaction (3)
Economic Commitment	Commitment (4)
Claim	Claim (5)
Economic Contract	Contract (6)
Agreement	Agreement (6)
Reciprocity	Reciprocity (7)

(1) In REA, an Economic Event represents the transfer of an Economic Resource from one partner to another. In the reference ontology, this is mapped to two Transfers. One Transfer represents that one Actor gives up a Resource, while the other Transfer represents that the other Actor receives that Resource. It can be noted that REA does not model the right being transferred but only the Resource.

(2) In REA, an Economic Event Type resides on the knowledge level, while an Economic Event is on the operational level. As Economic Events are mapped to pairs of Transfers, an Economic Event Type will be mapped to a pair of Transfer Types – one give and one take Transfer Type. In other words, an Economic Event Type is mapped to an Exchange.

(3) In REA, Economic Events can be related to each other by means of the duality association, which means that one Economic Event is carried out as a compensation for another, see Section 2. In the reference ontology, a number of Economic Events that are related by duality will, therefore, belong to the same Transaction. Note that while the reference ontology differentiates between Economic Events in terms of Conversions and Transfers of Resources from one Actor to another, REA does not make this distinction.

(4) In REA, an Economic Commitment is an obligation to perform an Economic Event in the future. An Economic Commitment can be fulfilled by an Economic Event. Hence, in the reference ontology, an Economic Commitment is mapped to a Commitment.

(5) A Claim in REA materializes when one business partner has fulfilled an Economic Commitment, while the other partner has yet to fulfill the reciprocal Economic Commitment. Thus a Claim in REA is mapped to a Claim in the reference ontology.

(6) An REA Economic Contract is an aggregation of Economic Commitments. In REA, an Economic Contract is a subtype of an Economic Agreement. In the reference ontology, however, the concept of Agreement is an arrangement between two actors that specifies in advance the conditions under which they will trade, i.e. a concept defined on the knowledge level. Economic Contract is mapped to Contract in the reference ontology.

(7) Reciprocity is a relationship between two or more Economic Commitments that expresses that the corresponding Economic Events are related through one and the same duality. The REA Reciprocity relationship is mapped to the equally named relationship in the reference ontology.

4.2 e^3-Value -Reference Ontology Mappings

e3value	Reference ontology
Actor	Actor
Market segment	Actor type
Value object	Resource type and Right (1)
Value port	Transfer type (2)
Value exchange	Exchange (3)
Value offering	Set of Transfer types (4)
Value interface	Interface (5)
Value activity	Transformation (6)
Value transaction	Transaction (7)

(1) When a Value Exchange occurs in e^3-value, some (instance of a) Value Object is transferred from one agent to another. However, it is not sufficient to specify only which resource that is transferred; the right that the receiving actor obtains also has to be given. For example, buying a car is different from renting a car. In the first case, the recipient gets an ownership right on the car, while in the second case, the recipient gets a time limited use right on the car. Thus, there are two different value objects though only one Resource Type. For this reason, a Value Object is mapped to the combination of a Resource Type and a Right.

(2) A Value Port in e^3-value represents that an Actor Type is prepared to provide or receive some Value Object. Thus, a Value Port is mapped to a Transfer Type. The direction of the Value Port, in or out, is represented by means of the Transfer Type being an increase or a decrease of value for the actor.

(3) A Value Exchange in e^3-value is a pair of Value Ports belonging to different actors or market segments. It represents one or more potential trades of Value Objects between these Value Ports. A Value Exchange is, therefore, mapped to two Transfer Types of different Actor Types, where one is an *increase* Event Type and the other a *decrease* Event Type. In other words, a Value Exchange in e^3-value is mapped to an Exchange.

(4) A Value Offering in e^3-value is a set of Value Ports with the same direction. Thus, it is mapped to a set of Transfer Types, either all decrease or increase.

(5) A Value Interface is either one Value Offering or one in-going and one out-going Value Offering that belong to the same Actor. Value Interfaces are used for modeling economic reciprocity and are hence mapped to Interface, i.e. a Process consisting of Transfer Event types all associated to the same Actor Type.

(6) A Value Activity in e^3-value corresponds closely to a Transformation. However, a Transformation tells what resources that are used or consumed in order to produce some other resource, while a Value Activity tells what activities carried out by an actor and what value objects are used as inputs to produce value objects that are

tradable. In the reference ontology the Transformation specifies that some resource is produced while other resources are used or consumed. Therefore the Value Activity in e^3-value is mapped to the Transformation in the reference ontology.

(7) A Value Transaction in e^3-value is defined as a set of Value Exchanges. The Value Exchanges in a Value Transaction are performed according to the Value Interfaces connected to the Value Exchanges. This means that if a Value Object is exchanged through a particular port of a value interface, then Value Exchanges must occur via all the other ports of that value interface. In the reference ontology a Transaction is defined as process containing a set of Exchanges. We also mapped the Value Exchange in e^3-value to the Exchange in the reference ontology. Therefore the Value Transaction in e^3-value is mapped to the Transaction in the reference ontology.

As can be seen from the mappings above, there are close relationships between the concepts in REA and e^3-value, but also some differences:

Resource, Right, and Value Object

Economic Resource in REA and Value Object in e^3-value models similar, but not identical concepts. In an Economic Event, something is transferred from one agent to another agent, but what is transferred is not an only an Economic Resource, but the control of an Economic Resource and in some cases also the custody of the same resource. For example, one Economic Event may transfer the ownership of a car, while another Economic Event lends the car. These Economic Events concern the same Economic Resource but transfer different rights on that resource. This motivates the introduction of Rights in the reference ontology. In e^3-value, a Value Exchange transfers a Value Object from one agent to another. Therefore, Value Object can be mapped to both Right and Resource in the reference ontology.

A recent analysis on Value Objects, [Weigand06], points out that a Value Object has a dual character combining both a right and transformations, i.e. how the value object can be used to modify some object of interest to an actor. The reference ontology is able to capture this through Conversions that use or consume the Value Object.

4.3 BMO-Reference Ontology Mappings

BMO	Reference ontology
Target Customer	Actor Type (1)
Value Proposition	A set of Value propositions (2)
Offering	Value Proposition (3)
Agreement	Agreement (4)
Actor	Actor OR Actor Type (1)
Activity	Value Activity (5)
Value Configuration	Process, in particular Transformation, and Transaction OR the corresponding classes defined on the knowledge level (6)
Resource	Resource
Capability	A relationship between Value Proposition, Resource and Value Configuration (7)

(1) A Target Customer is mapped to the class Actor of the reference ontology, while the class Actor is mapped to Actor or Actor type. In BMO actors are viewed from an internal perspective. This means that the ontology is designed from one particular actor's viewpoint making this actor implicit. In contrast, the reference ontology views actors from an external perspective. Therefore, an Actor in BMO does not exactly correspond to an Actor of the reference ontology. The class Actor in the reference ontology represents all actors, whereas the class Actor in BMO represents all actors except the one from whose perspective the ontology is constructed. Furthermore, an Actor in BMO (as opposed to a Target Customer) should be understood as being defined on the operational level, whereas a Target customer (segment) is defined as the type of customers a company intends to address, i.e. a definition on the knowledge level.

(2) In BMO, a Value Proposition represents value for one or several Target Customers, i.e. how a firm differentiates what it offers from its competitors. A Value Proposition may be decomposed into a set of Offerings (2), and hence is mapped to a set of reference ontology Value Propositions, see (3).

(3) An Offering in BMO is part of an overall Value Proposition (which in turn may be decomposed into a set of Offerings). Each BMO Offering describes an elementary product or service, offered (directed) towards the target customers. In the reference ontology it is mapped to a Value Proposition related to (set of) decrement Event type(s).

(4) In BMO an Agreement specifies functions, terms and conditions of a partnership with an (external) actor. It is mapped to the concept of Agreement in the reference ontology, where an agreement is an arrangement between two actors that specifies *in advance* the conditions under which they will trade, i.e. a concept defined on the knowledge level.

(5) An Activity in BMO is an action relative to one company, performed in order to do business and achieve the company goals. It is mapped to the concept of Value Activity in the reference ontology, since value activities in the reference ontology are defined as activities that can be profitably performed by some Actor.

(6) BMO Value Configuration describes the arrangements of activities and resources that are necessary to create value for the customer (a Value proposition), which is mapped to the reference ontology class Process. In the reference ontology Process is a set of increment and decrement Event Types that have to happen in order to fulfill transfers of value. The reference ontology further distinguishes between a number of specializations of processes: Interfaces, Exchanges, Transactions and Transformations. In mapping Value Configuration to Processes it should be noted that the sub types Transformation and Transaction are probably most similar to Value configuration. A Transformation tells what resources are used or consumed in order to produce some other resource of value for some actor. A Transaction groups a number of Exchanges.

(7) A BMO Capability describes the ability to execute a repeatable pattern of actions. A Capability hence describes whether or not a particular needed Value Configuration can be applied by a particular company to provide the value proposition and if the appropriate resources (i.e. services and resources) are available. This concept of capability has no immediate correspondence in the reference ontology. Capability is mapped to a relationship between a particular Value

Proposition, a Value Configuration and the needed services and resources, where the capability relationship signals that the offering partner can deliver its value proposition.

5 Concluding Remarks

In this paper we have presented a reference ontology based on three business ontologies – the REA, e^3-value, and BMO. We constructed the reference ontology primarily in order to gain a better understanding of the original ontologies. An additional use of such an ontology is that it may serve as a mapping tool where models can be transformed from one formalism to another.

The work has shown that there is a considerable overlap between the ontologies but that there are also differences, some obvious and some subtle. An example is that Economic resource in REA and Value object in e^3-value might seem identical to each other. However, they are different as can be seen by analysing what is happening in an Economic event. In an Economic event, something is transferred from one agent to another agent, but what is transferred is not an Economic resource, but the control of an Economic resource. For example, one Economic event may transfer the ownership of a car, while another Economic event lends the car. These Economic events concern the same Economic resource but transfer different rights on that resource. This motivates the introduction of Rights in the reference ontology – in a Transfer, the right to a resource is transferred from one agent to another. In e^3-value, a Value exchange transfers a Value object from one agent to another. Therefore, Value object is mapped to the combination of Right and Resource in the reference ontology Similarly, the concept of a Transfer gave rise to the issue of what is transferred. To address this question, i.e. what is actually transferred in a value transfer, we analysed the concept into three sub-concepts; Custody, Documentary Evidence and Right transfer and thereby extended the reference ontology with concepts not present in the originals.

Future research includes validation of the reference ontology. One way of doing this is to implement the original ontologies as well as the reference ontology using an ontology management tool such as Protégé [Protégé06]. Formalized mappings between the ontologies could then be formulated using an ontology mapping language.

References

[Andersson05] Andersson, B., Bergholtz, M., Edirisuriya, A., Ilayperuma, T., Johannesson, P., *A Declarative Foundation of Process Models*. Proceedings of Advanced Information Systems Engineering: 18th International Conference (CAiSE05), Porto. Springer-Verlag, LNCS, 2005.

[Andersson06a] Andersson, B., Bergholtz, M., Edirisuriya, A., Ilayperuma, T., Johannesson, P., Bertrand G., Michael S., Dubois E.,, Abels S., Hahn A., Gordijn J., Weigand H., Wangler B., *Towards a Common Business Ontology*. Proceedings of the 3rd Open Interop Workshop on Enterprise Modelling and Ontologies for Interoperability (Interop-EMOI'06). Luxembourg, 2006.

[Andersson06b] Andersson, B., Bergholtz, M., Grégoire B., Johannesson, P Michael Schmitt, M., Zdravkovic, J., *From Business to Process Models – a Chaining Methodology.* In proceedings of BUSITAL (a workshop on Business/IT Alignment and Interoperability), co-located with CAISE'06, Luxembourg, 2006.

[BPMN03] *Business Process Modelling Notation (BPMN)*, http://www.bpmn.org/ Accessed November, 2005.

[Bergholtz05] Bergholtz M., Bertrand G., Johannesson P., Schmitt M., Wohed P. and Zdravkovic J., *Integrated Methodology for linking business and process models with risk mitigation.* In proceedings of the 1st International Workshop on Requirements Engineering for Business Need and IT Alignment (REBNITA05). Paris, 2005.

[Fowler97] Fowler M., *Analysis Patterns. Reusable Object Models.* ISBN: 0-201-89542-0. Addison-Wesley, 1997.

[Geerts99] Geerts, G., McCarthy, W. E., *An Accounting Object Infrastructure For Knowledge-Based Enterprise Models.* IEEE Intelligent Systems & Their Applications, pp. 89-94, 1999.

[Gordijn00] Gordijn J., Akkermans J.M., Vliet J.C. van, *Business Modeling is not Process Modeling.* Conceptual Modeling for E-Business and the Web, LNCS 1921, Springer-Verlag pp. 40-51, 2000.

[Gordijn04] Gordijn, J., *e-Business Model Ontologies.* Book chapter contribution to "e-Business Modelling Using the e^3*value* Ontology", Wendy Curry (ed.), pp. 98-128, Elsevier Butterworth-Heinemann, UK, 2004.

[Hruby06] Hruby, P., *Model-Driven Design Using Business Patterns.* Forthcoming book. ISBN: 3-540-30154-2. Springer Verlag, 2006.

[McCarthy82] McCarthy W. E., *The REA Accounting Model: A Generalized Framework for Accounting Systems in a Shared Data Environment.* The Accounting Review, 1982.

[Osterwalder04] Osterwalder, A., *The Business Model Ontology. A Proposition in a Design Science Approach.* PhD-Thesis. University of Lausanne, 2004.

[Osterwalder05] Osterwalder, A., Pigneur, Y., Tucci, C., *Clarifying Business Models: Origins, present and Future of the Concept.* In Communications of the Association for Information Science (CAIS), Vol. 15, 2005, p. 751-775

[Protégé06] *Protégé Open Source Ontology Editor and Knowledgebase Framework.* Protégé Beta 3.2, 2006, http://protege.stanford.edu.

[Schmitt05] Schmitt M., Grégoire, B., *Risk Mitigation Instruments for Business Models and Process Models.* Proceedings of the 1st International Workshop on Requirements Engineering for Business Need and IT Alignment (REBNITA05). Paris, 2005

[UMM03] *UN/CEFACT Modeling Methodology (UMM) User Guide.* Accessed November, 2005, http://www.unece.org/cefact/umm/.

[Fox92] Fox, M.S., (1992), *The TOVE Project: Towards A Common-sense Model of the Enterprise.* Enterprise Integration Laboratory Technical Report. Available at http://www.eil.utoronto.ca/enterprise-modelling/papers/fox-tove-uofttr92.pdf

[Uschold96] Uschold M., Gruninger M., *Ontologies: principles, methods, and applications.* Knowledge Engineering Review, 11(2), pp.93-155, 1996.

[Weigand06] Weigand H., Johannesson P., Andersson B., Bergholtz M., Edirisuriya A., Ilayperuma T., *On the Notion of Value Object.* Proceedings of Advanced Information Systems Engineering: 18th International Conference (CAiSE06), Luxembourg, 2006.

Reasoning on UML Class Diagrams with OCL Constraints

Anna Queralt and Ernest Teniente

Universitat Politècnica de Catalunya
Dept. de Llenguatges i Sistemes Informàtics
c/ Jordi Girona 1-3, 08034 Barcelona (Catalonia, Spain)
{aqueralt, teniente}@lsi.upc.edu

Abstract. We propose a new approach to check whether a given UML class diagram with its OCL integrity constraints satisfies a set of desirable properties such as schema satisfiability, class liveliness, redundancy of integrity constraints or reachability of partially specified states. Our approach is based on translating both the class diagram and the OCL constraints into a logic representation. Then, we use the CQC Method to verify whether these properties hold for the given diagram and constraints.

1 Introduction

The quality of an information system is largely determined early in the development cycle, i.e. during requirements specification and conceptual modeling. Moreover, errors introduced at these stages are usually much more expensive to correct than those of design or implementation. Thus, it is desirable to prevent, detect and correct errors as early as possible in the development process.

The quality of a conceptual schema (CS) can be seen from two different points of view. From an external point of view, quality refers to the correctness of the schema regarding the user requirements. This can be validated, for instance, through checking whether the schema specifies the relevant knowledge of the domain. From an internal point of view, quality can be determined by reasoning on the definition of the CS, without taking requirements into account. In this sense, there are some typical reasoning tasks that can be performed on a CS like satisfiability checking or class consistency, among others.

As a simple example, consider the schema in Figure 1 which contains information about employees (distinguishing among rich and average employees) and their departments. The schema contains also five integrity constraints stating conditions that each state of the information base should satisfy.

At first glance, it may seem that the schema is perfectly right. It allows instances of *Employee* (like John with a salary of 7000), *Department* (like Sales with a minimum salary of 6000) and *WorksIn* (like John works in Sales). However, a deeper analysis allows determining that *AverageEmp* will never have any instance since constraint 5 requires the salary of average employees to be lower than 5000 while constraints 2 and 3 assert that it must be higher than 5000. This means that *AverageEmp* is ill specified. Moreover, constraint 4 is redundant (and it should not be defined) since constraints 2 and 3 already guarantee that the salary of a rich employee is higher than 5000.

D.W. Embley, A. Olivé, and S. Ram (Eds.): ER 2006, LNCS 4215, pp. 497–512, 2006.

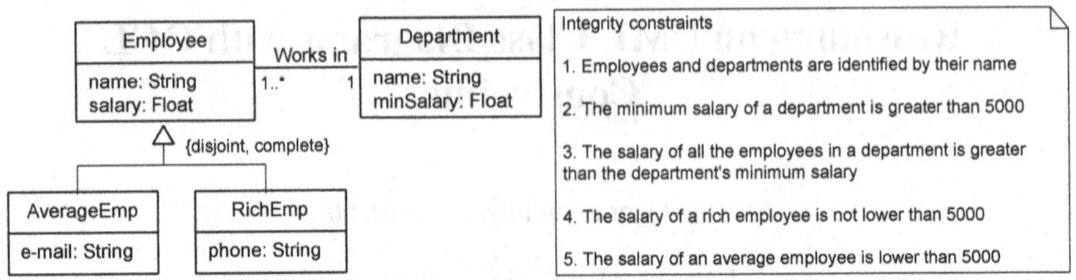

Fig. 1. Conceptual schema about employees and their departments

The previous example illustrates the need to be able to reason on CSs to improve information systems quality. In fact, this has been identified as one of the key problems to be solved to achieve the goal of automating information systems building [13].

Several efforts have already been devoted to this problem. There are automatic procedures for the verification of some properties of CSs in Description Logics [2], to check whether a given CS accepts particular system states at a given time point [9] or to reason about cardinality constraints of the CS [10-12]. However, there are still several open problems in reasoning on CSs. Probably, the most important one is the lack of methods able to reason about general-purpose integrity constraints like the ones in Figure 1. This is indeed the main goal of this paper.

Hence, the main contribution of our work is to propose a new approach to reason on the structural part of UML conceptual schemas, defined by means of the corresponding UML class diagram with its OCL integrity constraints. Two different kinds of reasoning are provided by our method. On the one hand, it automatically verifies whether the CS satisfies a set of desirable properties such as schema satisfiability, class liveliness (in the example above it would determine that *AverageEmp* is not lively) or redundancy of integrity constraints (like constraint 4 in Figure 1). On the other hand, it provides the designer with the ability to ask questions to check whether certain goals may be satisfied according to the CS. For instance, if he or she wants to know whether the CS in Figure 1 accepts a department Marketing with a salary of 8000, our method would answer positively, specifying that there must also be at least one employee working in it (required to satisfy the cardinaltiy constraint of the association *WorksIn*), with a salary higher than 8000 (entailed by constraint 3) and who is a *RichEmp* (because of the complete constraint of the generalization).

This paper is organized as follows. Section 2 presents an overview of our method. Section 3 defines how to translate an UML CS into a logical representation. Section 4 describes how to use the CQC Method to reason on UML CSs. Section 5 reviews related work. Finally, section 6 presents our conclusions and points out future work.

2 Overview of the Method

The structural part of a CS consists of a taxonomy of classes together with their attributes, a taxonomy of associations among classes, and a set of integrity constraints over the state of the domain, which define conditions that each state of the information base must satisfy. Those constraints may have a graphical representation or can be defined by means of a particular general-purpose language.

In UML, a structural schema is represented by means of a class diagram, with its graphical constraints, together with a set of user-defined constraints, which can be specified in any language. According to [15], we assume they are specified in OCL.

The subset of the OCL language we consider consists of those OCL expressions that are used in integrity constraints, not those operations that can only be used in pre or postconditions, such as *@pre* and *oclIsNew*. Moreover, we only deal with OCL operations that result in a boolean value. Exceptions are *select* and *size* that, despite returning a collection and an integer, can also be handled by our method.

In Figure 2 we show the structural schema we will use throughout the paper. It consists of a UML class diagram with three classes, three associations and seven OCL constraints. It states that several employees work in a department, which is managed by one employee. Some employees have a superior, and some employees are bosses.

The OCL constraints provide the class diagram with additional semantics. There are two key constraints (*UniqueEmp* and *UniqueDep*), one for each class. The constraint *ManagerIsWorker* states that the manager of a department must be one of its workers. Constraint *ManagerHasNoSuperior* guarantees that the manager of a department does not work for any other employee. The constraint *BossIsManager* guarantees that a boss is the manager of some department. The next constraint, *BossHasNoSuperior,* states that a boss does not work for any other employee. Finally, *SuperiorOfAllWorkers* states that the workers of a deparmtent managed by a boss must work for that boss.

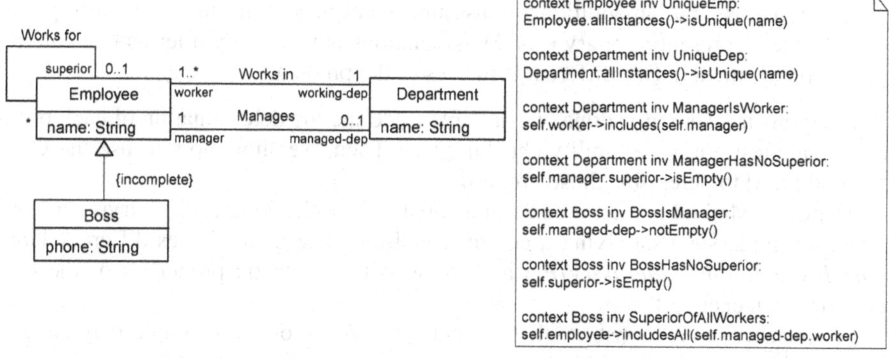

Fig. 2. UML class diagram and OCL integrity constraints for Employees and Departments

Given a structural schema such as the one in Figure 2, our method determines a number of properties, namely satisfiability, liveliness, constraint redundancy and state reachability, taking both the UML class diagram and the OCL constraints into account. This is achieved by means of two different steps.

First, we automatically translate the UML class diagram and the OCL constraints into a logical representation. Classes, attributes and associations are represented by means of basic predicates. For instance, in the example of Figure 2, classes *Employee* and *Deparmtent* become *Employee(e), EmployeeName(e,n)* and *Deparmtent(d), DepartmentName(d,n)*, and the association *WorksIn* is represented by *WorksIn(e,d)*.

The OCL constraints of the schema are translated into formulas in denial form, which represent conditions that must not be satisfied by any state of the information base. For instance, the constraint *BossHasNoSuperior* is translated into:

$\leftarrow Boss(e) \wedge Superior(s,e)$

The graphical constraints of the schema, such as cardinality and taxonomic constraints, also need to be translated into this kind of conditions.

A class diagram has also a set of implicit constraints that need to be taken into account in the logical representation of the schema to preserve the semantics of the original one. For example, since UML is an object-oriented language, each instance has an internal object identifier (OID) which uniquely differentiates two instances, even though they are externally equivalent. Thus, additional constraints are needed in the logical representation to guarantee that two instances of the schema do not have the same OID. In the example of Figure 2 we need to specify the following constraint:

$\leftarrow Employee(x) \wedge Department(x)$

As well as OIDs, the implicit constraints we can find in a class diagram are:

- In class hierarchies, an instance of a subclass must also be an instance of the superclass.
- In associations or association classes, an instance of the association must link instances of the classes that define the association.
- In association classes, there cannot exist several instances linking exactly the same instances. Note that this is also true for associations without an association class, but an additional constraint is not needed in this case, since predicates representing n-ary (n>=2) associations have exactly n terms that can not be identical in two different instances of the predicate.

Once this translation is done, we are able to define the determination of each property as a constraint-satisfiability checking test. Then, we show how to use the CQC Method [7, 8] to determine those properties.

The CQC Method performs constraint-satisfiability checking tests by trying to construct a sample state satisfying a certain condition. The method uses different *Variable Instantiation Patterns (VIPs)* according to the syntactic properties of the CSs considered in each test.

For instance, to demonstrate that the class *Employee* of our example may have at least one instance, the CQC Method constructs the following state:

```
[employyee(0), employeeName(0,0), worksIn(0,1),
department(1), departmentName(1,0), manages(0,1)]
```

This means that it is possible to have an instance of *Employee* satisfying all the graphical, implicit and OCL constraints. The values of the instantiation correspond to a representative state of the information base. That is, this solution given by the CQC Method means that an instance of employee can exist if he works in a department (since all employees must work in a department) and is the manager of that department (since every department must have a manager and he must be one of its workers).

3 Translating a UML Structural Schema into Logic

In this section we propose a set of rules that, applied to a UML class diagram and a set of OCL constraints, result in a set of first-order formulas that represent the structural schema. The subset of first-order logic considered does not provide functions; and rules and conditions are required to be safe, that is, every variable occuring in their head or in atoms of their body that are negated or use comparison operators must also occur in an ordinary positive literal of the same body.

We will explain first how to obtain the formulas for the class diagram, taking into account its implicit and predefined constraints. Later, we propose a translation for user-defined OCL constraints. The complete logic representation of the schema can be found in [14].

3.1 Translation of a UML Class Diagram

A UML class diagram is translated into a set of first-order formulas according to the following rules.

3.1.1 Translation of classes

For each class C not being an association class we define a unary predicate C, where its term represents the internal object identifier (OID).

For example, the class *Employee* is translated into a predicate *Employee(e)*.

3.1.2 Translation of Attributes, Associations and Association Classes

Let R be an association between classes $C_1,...,C_n$. If R is not an association class, we define a base predicate $R(c_1,...,c_n)$. Otherwise, if R is an association class we define a base predicate $R(r,c_1,...,c_n)$. Although it is not strictly necessary, we also include an OID *r* so that all classes can be treated uniformly.

For example, the association *WorksIn* that relates *Employees* and *Departments* is translated into the predicate *WorksIn(e,d)*.

Attributes can be regarded as binary associations between a class C and a datatype. Then, for each attribute a_i in C we define a binary predicate $CA_i(c,a_i)$. Note that, since several classes can have an attribute with the same name, we need to use the class name in the definition of the predicates representing attributes.

For example, the attribute *name* of *Employee* is translated into *EmployeeName(e,n)*.

3.1.3 Translation of Implicit and Graphical Constraints

First of all, we must guarantee that there cannot exist two instances with the same OID. This is already guaranteed for instances of the same class, since they are represented by unary predicates. Then, we must define rules to prevent the existence of two literals of different predicates with the same OID, defining the following constraint for each pair of predicates not representing classes in the same hierarchy:

$$\leftarrow C_1(x) \wedge C_2(x)$$

According to this rule, we must define the following constraint in our example:

$\leftarrow Employee(x) \land Department(x)$

Class hierarchies also require the definition of a set of constraints to guarantee that an instance of each subclass C_{subi} is also an instance of its superclass C_{super}. This is done by means of the rule:

$\leftarrow C_{subi}(c) \land \neg C_{super}(c)$

In the example, the hierarchy of employees requires the following constraint:

$\leftarrow Boss(e) \land \neg Employee(e)$

Moreover, additional rules are sometimes required to guarantee that an instance of the superclass is not an instance of several subclasses simultaneously (*disjoint* constraint), or that an instance of the superclass is an instance of at least one of its subclasses (*complete* constraint). Then, for each pair of subclasses C_{subi}, C_{subj} we define a constraint stating that an instance cannot belong to both of them simultaneously:

$\leftarrow C_{subi}(c) \land C_{subj}(c)$

and another one stating that an instance of C_{super} must belong to at least one of the C_{subi}. To do this we need a derived predicate $isKindOfC_{super}$, with a rule for each C_{subi}:

$\leftarrow C_{super}(c) \land \neg IsKindOfC_{super}(c)$
$IsKindOfC_{super}(c) \leftarrow C_{subi}(c)$

Another set of constraints is needed to guarantee the implicit constraint that an instance of an association can only relate existing instances of the classes that define it. Then, for each association R, being or not an association class with OID r, represented by the predicate $R([r,],c_1,...,c_n)$, we define the following constraint for each c_i:

$\leftarrow R([r,],c_1,...,c_n) \land \neg C_i(c_i)$

In our example, the association *WorksIn* requires the addition of the rules:

$\leftarrow WorksIn(e,d) \land \neg Employee(e)$
$\leftarrow WorksIn(e,d) \land \neg Department(d)$

Similarly, we must define constraints to guarantee that the first term of a predicate representing an attribute corresponds to an instance of the class to which the attribute belongs. In our example:

$\leftarrow EmployeeName(e,n) \land \neg Employee(e)$
$\leftarrow BossPhone(e,p) \land \neg Boss(e)$
$\leftarrow DepartmentName(d,n) \land \neg Department\ (d)$

Additionally, for the definition of association classes, we must guarantee that there are not several instances of an association class having the same value in the terms defining the instance. Then, if R is an association class, defined by classes $C_1,...,C_m$, we define the following constraint:

$\leftarrow R(r1,c_1...c_m) \land R(r2,c_1...c_m) \land r1<>r2$

Finally, let *min..max* be a cardinality constraint attached to an attribute or to a class C_i in an association R defined by classes $C_1,...,C_n$. If *min*>0 we must add the following constraint:

$$\leftarrow C_1(c_1) \wedge ... \wedge C_{i-1}(c_{i-1}) \wedge C_{i+1}(c_{i+1}) \wedge ... \wedge C_n(c_n) \wedge \neg MinR(c_1,...,c_{i-1},c_{i+1},...,c_n)$$
$$MinR(c_1,...,c_{i-1},c_{i+1},...,c_n) \leftarrow R([r1,]c_1,...,c_{i-1},c_i1,c_{i+1},...,c_n) \wedge ...$$
$$\wedge R([rmin,]c_1,...,c_{i-1},c_imin,c_{i+1},...,c_n) \wedge$$
$$\wedge c_i1 <> c_i2 \wedge ... \wedge c_i1 <> c_imin \wedge ... \wedge c_imin\text{-}1 <> c_imin$$

And if $max < *$, the following constraint is needed:

$$\leftarrow R([r1,]c_1,...,c_{i-1},c_i1,c_{i+1},...,c_n) \wedge ... \wedge$$
$$R([rmax+1,]c_1,...,c_{i-1},c_imax+1,c_{i+1},...,c_n) \wedge c_i1 <> c_i2 \wedge ... \wedge c_i1 <> c_imax+1 \wedge ...$$
$$\wedge c_imax <> c_imax+1$$

As an example, we must define the following constraint to guarantee the lower multiplicity of class *Employee* in the association *WorksIn*:

$$\leftarrow Department(d) \wedge \neg OneWorker(d)$$
$$OneWorker(d) \leftarrow WorksIn(e,d)$$

And we also have to define the following one due to the upper multiplicity of *Department* in the same association:

$$\leftarrow WorksIn(e, d1) \wedge WorksIn(e, d2) \wedge d1 <> d2$$

For attributes, if no multiplicity is specified in the class diagram, it is assumed that they are single-valued and not optional. Then, in our example we need the constraints:

$$\leftarrow Employee \wedge \neg OneEmployeeName(e)$$
$$OneEmployeeName(e) \leftarrow EmployeeName(e,n)$$
$$\leftarrow EmployeeName(e,n1) \wedge EmployeeName(e,n2) \wedge n1 <> n2$$

Analogous constraints are needed for *phone* in *Boss* and *name* in *Department.*

3.2 Translation of OCL Integrity Constraints

We perform the translation of OCL integrity constraints into first-order logic in two steps. First, we transform each OCL expression into an equivalent one expressed in terms of the operations *select* and *size.* Both *select* and *size* are OCL operations that apply to collections of elements, *select* returns the subset of the collection that satisfies a condition, and *size* returns the number of elements in the collection. The aim of this transformation is to reduce the number of OCL constructs to be translated, so that a uniform treatment can be applied to all constraints in order to obtain the corresponding logic formulas.

3.2.1 Simplification of OCL Operations

The first step in the translation process consists in the reduction of the number of OCL operations that appear in the constraints. Table 1 shows the OCL operations we consider, and gives their equivalent simplified expressions. These translations are iteratively applied until the only OCL operations that appear in the expression are *select* and *size.*

Table 1. Equivalences of OCL operations

Original expression	Equivalent expression with *select* and *size*
source->includes(obj)	source->select(e I e=obj)->size()>0
source->excludes(obj)	source->select(e I e=obj)->size()=0
source->includesAll(c)	c->forall(eI source->includes(e))
source->excludesAll(c)	c->forall(eI source->excludes(e))
source->isEmpty()	source->size()=0
source->notEmpty()	source->size()>0
source->exists(e I body)	source->select(e I body)->size()>0
source->forall(e I body)	source->select(e I not body)->size()=0
source->isUnique(e I body)	source->select(e Isource->select(e2 I e <>e2 and e2.body = e.body))->size()=0
source->one(e I body)	source->select(e I body)->size()=1
source->reject(e I body)	source->select(e I not body)

As an example we give the simplified form of *ManagerIsWorker* in our example:

context Department **inv** ManagerIsWorker:
self.worker->select(e Ie = self.manager)-> size() > 0

Notice that if a department could have many managers (and we still wanted all of them to be workers of the same department) the expression obtained from the simplification would have been different, since the operation *includesAll* would appear instead of *includes* in the original OCL expression.

3.2.2 Translation of OCL Invariants into Logic

Once simplified, an OCL invariant has the following form:

context *C* **inv:** *path-exp*->select(eI body)->size() *opComp k*

where *C* is a class of the CS, *path-exp* is a sequence of navigations through associations, *opComp* is a comparison operator <, >, = or <> and *k* is an integer not lower than zero[1].

The translation of the simplified OCL invariants into logic depends on the specific operator after *size()*. We are going to see first how to translate the navigation defined by *path-exp* and the translation of the *select* operation. The select expression does not necessarily appear in the simplified OCL invariant, in which case it is not translated.

Tr-path(path-exp). Let *path-exp* = $obj.r_1...r_n[.att]$ be a path starting from an instance *obj* of a class *C*, or from a call to the *allInstances* operation on *C*, navigating through roles r_1 to r_n and, optionally, ending with the access to an attribute. Let *C(obj)* be the literal resulting from the translation of the class to which *obj* belongs, and $R_i(obj_{i-1}, obj_i,...)$ be the literals corresponding to the association between roles r_{i-1} and r_i, and C_2 be the class where the attribute *att* is defined. Then, this navigation path is translated into logic by means of the clause:

$$C(obj) \wedge R_1(obj,obj_1,...) \wedge ... \wedge R_n(obj_{n-1}, obj_n,...) \; [\wedge C_2(obj_n) \wedge C_2Att(obj_n, att)]$$

[1] When <=k or >=k appear in the original invariant and k is an integer greater than 0, they are translated into <k+1 and >k-1. Those cases in which k is equal to 0 do not represent valid constraints and, thus, they are not taken into account.

For instance, the navigation *self.worker* appearing in constraint *ManagerIsWorker* will be translated into *Department(d)* $\wedge$ *WorksIn(e,d)*.

Tr-select(e| body). We provide here the translation of a select expression in its most simplified and usual form, where *body = path1 opComp path2*. In this case, the select operation is translated into:

$$Tr\text{-}path(path1) \wedge Tr\text{-}path(path2) \wedge obj1\ opComp\ obj2$$

where *obj1* and *obj2* are the objects obtained as a result of the navigation paths *path1* and *path2*, respectively. Note that if any of the paths is a constant or *e*, then it must not be translated. The details of the translation for the rest of cases may be found in [14].

For instance, the translation of the expression *select(e| e=self.manager)* appearing in the simplified OCL invariant of the constraint *ManagerIsWorker* will be translated into *Department(d)* $\wedge$ *Manages(e2,d)* $\wedge$ *e=e2*.

Translation of an OCL invariant. Let $path\text{-}exp=obj.r_1...r_{n-1}.r_n$. Depending on the comparison operator, we define the translation of an OCL invariant in terms of the translation of the path expression (*Tr-path*) and the select (*Tr-select*) as follows:

a) **context C inv:** obj.r_1... r_{n-1}.r_n -> select(e| body)-> size() < k becomes

$$\leftarrow C(c) \wedge Tr\text{-}path(obj.r_1...\ r_{n-1}) \wedge Tr\text{-}path_1(r_n) \wedge Tr\text{-}select_1(e|\ body)$$
$$\wedge \ldots \wedge Tr\text{-}path_k(r_n) \wedge Tr\text{-}select_k(e|\ body)$$

b) **context C inv:** obj.r_1... r_{n-1}.r_n -> select(e| body)-> size() > k becomes

$$\leftarrow C(c) \wedge \neg Aux(c)$$
$$Aux(c) \leftarrow Tr\text{-}path(obj.r_1...\ r_{n-1}) \wedge Tr\text{-}path_1(r_n) \wedge Tr\text{-}select_1(e|\ body)$$
$$\wedge \ldots \wedge Tr\text{-}path_{k+1}(r_n) \wedge Tr\text{-}select_{k+1}(e|\ body)$$

c) **context C inv:** obj.r_1... r_{n-1}.r_n -> select(e| body)-> size() = k becomes

$$\leftarrow C(c) \wedge \neg Aux(c)$$
$$Aux(c) \leftarrow Tr\text{-}path(obj.r_1...\ r_{n-1}) \wedge Tr\text{-}path_1(r_n) \wedge Tr\text{-}select_1(e|\ body)$$
$$\wedge \ldots \wedge Tr\text{-}path_k(r_n) \wedge Tr\text{-}select_k(e|\ body)$$
$$\leftarrow C(c) \wedge Tr\text{-}path(obj.r_1...\ r_{n-1}) \wedge Tr\text{-}path_1(r_n) \wedge Tr\text{-}select_1(e|\ body)$$
$$\wedge \ldots \wedge Tr\text{-}path_{k+1}(r_n) \wedge Tr\text{-}select_{k+1}(e|\ body)$$

d) **context C inv:** obj.r_1... r_{n-1}.r_n -> select(e| body)-> size() <> k becomes

$$\leftarrow C(c) \wedge Tr\text{-}path(obj.r_1...\ r_{n-1}) \wedge Tr\text{-}path_1(r_n) \wedge Tr\text{-}select_1(e|\ body)$$
$$\wedge \ldots \wedge Tr\text{-}path_k(r_n) \wedge Tr\text{-}select_k(e|\ body) \wedge \neg Aux(c)$$
$$Aux(c) \leftarrow Tr\text{-}path(obj.r_1...\ r_{n-1}) \wedge Tr\text{-}path_1(r_n) \wedge Tr\text{-}select_1(e|\ body)$$
$$\wedge \ldots \wedge Tr\text{-}path_{k+1}(r_n) \wedge Tr\text{-}select_{k+1}(e|\ body)$$

Each translation *Tr-path* or *Tr-select* may be performed several times depending on the constant *k*. Each $Tr\text{-}path_i$ or $Tr\text{-}select_i$ expressions refer to the same translations but with different variables for those attributes not coming from $obj.r_1...\ r_{n-1}$. Clearly, the previous formalization becomes much simpler in the usual cases where *k* is 0 or 1.

Intuitively, we may see that the translation of each OCL invariant defines a denial stating that a given situation cannot hold. The first part of each denial includes the logic representation of the path leading to the collection of instances to which the select and the size operations are applied. The second part, the one defined by the subindexes 1 to k, is required to guarantee that the cardinality of the set of elements that fulfill the select condition satisfies also the required comparison.

As an example, consider the simplified invariant of constraint *ManagerIsWorker*:

context Department **inv:** self.worker -> select(e| e=self.manager)-> size() > 0

applying the translation b) above we obtain[2]:

$\leftarrow Department(d) \wedge \neg Aux(d)$

$Aux(d) \leftarrow Tr\text{-}path(self) \wedge Tr\text{-}path(worker) \wedge Tr\text{-}select(e|\ e=self.manager)$

and, after translating paths and selects, we get the following formulas which force all departments to have at least one worker who is also a manager.

$\leftarrow Department(d) \wedge \neg Aux(d)$

$Aux(d) \leftarrow Department(d) \wedge WorksIn(e,d) \wedge Manages(e2,d) \wedge e=e2$

It may also happen that the original expression does not include any OCL operation. Then the constraint has not been simplified and has the form:

context C **inv:** *path-exp opComp value*

where *value* is either a constant or another navigation path. The translation of these invariants into logic is:

$\leftarrow C(c) \wedge Tr\text{-}path(path\text{-}exp) \wedge Tr\text{-}path(value) \wedge obj1\ opComp\ obj2$

where *obj1* and *obj2* are the objects obtained as a result of the navigation path(s) *path-exp* and *value*. Note that if *value* is a constant then it must not be translated.

4 Reasoning on UML Structural Schemas Using the CQC Method

4.1 The CQC Method in a Nutshell

The CQC Method performs query containment tests on deductive database schemas. Moreover, it is able to determine several properties on a database schema: satisfiability, predicate liveliness, constraint redundancy and reachability [7, 8]. It is a semidecidable procedure for finite satisfiability and unsatisfiability, i.e. it always terminates when there is a finite consistent state satisfying the property, or when it is unsatisfiable.

Roughly, the CQC Method is aimed at constructing a state that fulfills a goal and satisfies all the constraints in the schema. As we will see, the goal to attain is formulated depending on the specific reasoning task to perform.

In this way, the CQC Method requires two main inputs besides the database schema definition itself. The first one is the definition of the *goal to attain*, which the method will try to obtain by constructing an information base. The second input is the set of *constraints to enforce*, which must not be violated by the constructed information base.

Then, in order to check if a certain property holds in a schema, it has to be expressed in terms of an initial goal to attain (G_0) and the set of integrity constraints to enforce (F_0), and then ask the CQC Method Engine to construct a sample information base to prove that the initial goal G_0 is satisfied without violating any integrity constraint in F_0.

---

[2] Note that, since k=0, the translation of the select and the path must be performed only once.

4.2 Using the CQC Method to Reason on UML and OCL Class Diagrams

In this subsection we show how to use the CQC Method to reason on UML class diagrams with OCL constraints. There are two kinds of reasoning tasks we can perform. The first ones consist in verifying, without the designer's intervention, that the schema satisfies a set of properties, namely satisfiability of the schema, liveliness of classes or associations and redundancy of constraints. On the other hand, state reachability requires the designer to ask questions and see if the answers given according to the conceptual schema correspond to what he expected.

We give the initial goal (G_0) and the set of constraints to enforce (F_0) in order to perform each reasoning task with the CQC Method. In most cases, F_0 coincides with the set of constraints of the schema (IC). The results of each reasoning task applied to Figure 2 have been proved by a Prolog implementation of the method.

4.2.1 Satisfiability

A schema is satisfiable if there is a non-empty state of the information base in which all its integrity constraints are satisfied.

To check this property with the CQC Method, G_0 is to have any instance of any class or association, and F_0 = IC. If the CQC Method engine succeeds in this task, i.e. if it finds a sample information base, then the schema is satisfiable. Otherwise, it is not.

The schema of Figure 2 is satisfiable, since it accepts at least a non-empty state. For instance, it may have an employee, which has to work in a department. Since each department must have a manager that is one of its workers, a sample state (obtained by the CQC Mehtod) proving satisfiability is {Employee(John), WorksIn(John,Sales), Department(Sales), Manages(John,Sales)}.

4.2.2 Liveliness of a Class or Association

Even if a schema is satisfiable, it may turn out that some class or association is empty in every valid state. Liveliness of classes or associations determines if a certain class or association can have at least one instance.

In this case, G_0 is to have any instance of the predicate representing the class or association to be checked, and F_0 = IC. If the CQC Method engine succeeds in this task then the class or association is lively.

Class *Department* of the schema in Figure 2 is lively, since there exists at least a state satisfying all the constraints in which *Department* has an instance. If we want to have a department, we also need at least one employee that works in it, and another one that is its manager. Besides, the manager must be one of the workers, so a valid state (obtained by the CQC Method) is {Department(Sales), WorksIn(John, Sales), Manages(John, Sales), Employee(John)}. At the same time, this state proves that class *Employee* and associations *Manages* and *WorksIn* are lively as well.

Let us see then if the association *Superior* and the class *Boss* are lively too. We have that there is at least a state in which *Superior* is not empty, which consists in an employee that works for another one, both of them working in the same department and the superior employee being the manager of the department. For example {Superior(Mary, John), Employee(Mary), Employee(John), WorksIn(Mary, Sales), WorksIn(John, Sales), Department(Sales), Manages(Mary, Sales)}.

In contrast, if we reason on the liveliness of *Boss*, we see that to have an instance of *Boss* we need that he or she is the superior of all the workers of the department managed by that boss (constraint *SuperiorOfAllWorkers*). A state satisfying this condition would be one in which a boss does not manage any department, but this is prevented by the constraint *BossIsManager*. Another way of satisfying this condition would be a state in which the department managed by the boss does not have workers, but the constraint *ManagerIsWorker* forces each department to have at least a worker, its manager. Then, the only option is to have a boss that manages a department and that all the workers of that department (including the boss himself) are subordinates of that boss. But this is impossible according to the constraint *BossHasNoSuperior* and, therefore, the class *Boss* is not lively.

When eliminating either of these constraints, a state fulfilling the rest of conditions can be found and *Boss* becomes lively. For instance, if we remove *BossIsManager* we obtain the following state, in which the boss works in a department but is not a manager. Since every department must have a manager, it is another employee the one who manages the department: {Boss(John), Employee(John), WorksIn(John,Sales), Department(Sales), Manages(Mary,Sales), WorksIn(Mary,Sales), Employee(Mary)}.

4.2.3 Redundancy of an Integrity Constraint

An integrity constraint is redundant if integrity does not depend on it, that is, if the states it does not allow are already not allowed by the rest of constraints.

Let Ic1 be one of the integrity constraints defined in the schema. In order to check if it is redundant, G_0 = Ic1, and F_0 = IC – {Ic1}. If the CQC Method engine is not capable of constructing such a state, then Ic1 is redundant.

If we analyze the constraints of the schema in Figure 2 we can see, for instance, that the constraint *BossHasNoSuperior* is redundant. We can try to build a state in which this constraint is violated while the rest are not, but it is not possible since a boss must be the manager of some department (constraint *BossIsManager*). Additionally, the constraint *ManagerHasNoSuperior* prevents the manager of a department from having a superior and thus, the constraint *BossHasNoSuperior* can never be violated.

There are other redundancies in this example, for instance between a graphical and an OCL constraint. In particular, *ManagerIsWorker* implies that a department must have at least a worker, since it must have a manager and he must be one of its workers. At the same time, the cardinality constraint 1..* of *Employee* in the association *WorksIn* already forces the existence of at least a worker in each department. Both redundancies are confirmed by the execution of the CQC Method.

4.2.4 Reachability of a Partially Specified State

We may also be interested in more general properties of the schema, like checking whether it accepts certain states. This is usually known as checking reachability of partially specified states.

Let S be a partially specified state of the information base, that is, a set of instances probably inconsistent. If the CQC Method engine is capable of building a state with G_0 = S and F_0 = IC, then S is reachable.

We can do this in two ways, either by giving specific instances of some classes or associations, or by specifying a condition, that is, a state not fully instantiated.

For instance, taking the example in Figure 2, we may wonder whether it is possible to have a manager that is not a boss. Assuming that the initial partially specified state is {Manages(John, Sales) ∧ ¬Boss(John)}, a solution given by the CQC Method is {Manages(John,Sales), Employee(John), Department (Sales), WorksIn(John, Sales)}. This means that the state is reachable, as long as there exist the corresponding instances of *Employee* and *Department* and the employee works in the department he manages.

Another question we could ask is whether there can be a boss who is not the superior of any employee, which may not be clear at first sight. If we try to construct a state satisfying {Boss(x) ∧ ¬isSuperior(x)} with isSuperior(x) ← Superior(x,e) we can see that this is not possible. The constraint *BossIsManager* forces a boss to be the manager of some department while the constraint *SuperiorOfAllWorkers* guarantees that all employees that work in the department managed by a boss are his subordinates. In this case, the CQC Method determines that the goal can not be attained.

5 Related Work

We review how reasoning on CSs has been addressed so far. We will start in ER conceptual schemas and later we will deal with UML conceptual schemas. As will be seen, the main contribution of our approach is to deal with more expressive conceptual schemas than previous methods. We must state however that those methods are in general more efficient than ours for the particular cases they handle.

5.1 Reasoning on ER Conceptual Schemas

The most popular task addressed in ER schemas is strong satisfiability, in particular regarding cardinality constraints. Strong satisfiability was introduced in [12] and their approach consists in reducing the problem to solving a linear inequality system. This system is defined from the relationships and cardinality constraints of the schema. Then, a schema is strongly satisfiable if and only if there are solutions for its corresponding inequality system.

On the other hand, [10] determines strong satisfiability of a schema by means of a graph-theoretic approach. This work deals with int-cardinality constraints, which are more general than traditional ones since they allow gaps in the sets of cardinalities.

The same method is used in [11], but this time it serves more specific purposes. Given a cardinality constraint set S, the method can find superfluous entities, i.e. entities whose population is empty in every instance of the schema satisfying S determine which is the minimal subset of constraints that causes a schema not to be satisfiable suggest strategies to resolve inconsistency.

Another problem is approached in [5], which is the detection of potentially redundant associations in an ER schema. The method is based this time in adjacency matrixes, but it is incomplete since some types of redundancy involving more than one relationship between two entities cannot be detected.

Summarizing, we may see that several methods have approached reasoning on ER schemas, mainly through cardinality constraints. Nevertheless, none of them takes general-purpose integrity constraints into account, while we do.

5.2 Reasoning on UML Conceptual Schemas

Description Logics (DL) is a family of formalisms for knowledge representation, based on first-order logic [1]. In the last years, DL has gone beyond its traditional scope in the Artificial Intelligence area to provide new alternatives and solutions to many topics in the database and conceptual modeling areas [3, 4, 6].

DL allows inferring represented knowledge from the knowledge explicitly contained in the knowledge base. Such an inference mechanism can be used to determine some properties of the schema, such as schema consistency (satisfiability), class consistency, class equivalence or class subsumption. DL assumes that the system should always check these properties in reasonable time and, thus, it restricts the expressive power of each specific DL to guarantee that the problem to be solved remains decidable.

An interesting approach to reasoning on UML specifications (i.e. class diagrams) is to translate them to DL and then use current standard DL-based reasoning systems on them [2] to automatically verify properties like the ones stated above. However, this approach does not deal with general-purpose OCL constraints since they may not be taken into account to guarantee decidability of the problem being handled.

An important exception on the treatment of OCL integrity constraints is the system USE [9], which allows to validate UML and OCL models by constructing snapshots representing system states with objects, attribute values and links (something similar to our reachability of partially specified states). With this feature USE allows to validate whether the schema specifies the relevant knowledge of the domain, as perceived by the designer. Nevertheless, USE is not able to automatically verify whether the schema satisfies desirable properties like satisfiability, liveliness or redundancy.

Moreover, we see two important differences between USE and the work reported here. Firstly, in USE the designer must define by hand an operation to build each of the states of the CS to be validated, while we allow defining them declaratively by stating (the subset of) the information they should contain.

Secondly, and most important one, in USE the generated snapshots are checked against the constraints and then rejected if some of them is violated. On the contrary, in our approach the partially specified states that violate some constraint are repaired by assuming additional information that allows repairing the violations. In this way, we obtain solutions that may not be generated in USE. For instance, in the example of the introduction, USE would conclude that a *Department* named Marketing with a minimum salary of 8000 is not a valid snapshot, while we draw that it is possible to have such a department if the state contains also an *Employee* named Mary with a salary of 9000, who is a *RichEmp* and *WorksIn* Marketing.

6 Conclusions and Further Work

We have proposed a new approach to reason on structural schemas specified in UML with OCL constraints, both regarding the correctness of their structure and the states of the domain they accept. In this sense, we have provided a set of automatic tests that can be performed on a schema, namely satisfiability, liveliness or redundancy, and also facilities to check if the schema represents the information expected by the designer.

Our approach consists of two main steps. First, we translate the UML class diagram and the OCL constraints into a first-order logic representation, and then we use the CQC Method, which performs constraint-satisfiability checking tests, in order to perform the reasoning and validation tasks stated above. The CQC Method is a semidecidable procedure for finite satisfiability and unsatisfiability. This means that it always terminates when there exists a finite consistent state satisfying the property, or when the property is unsatisfiable (finitely or infinitely).

We have illustrated the usefulness of our results by applying our approach to a simple conceptual schema. We have translated the whole schema into its logic representation following our proposal and we have determined all properties pointed up in the paper by means of an implementation of the CQC Method.

The main contribution of our approach is to be able to deal with general-purpose OCL constraints. In particular, we may reason about OCL invariants defined by means of OCL operations that result in a boolean value plus *select* and *size* operations.

There are some interesting directions for further work to take from this point. First, we plan to provide an implementation of the first step of our method, that is, the translation of UML and OCL into logic. Also, we plan to extend the subset of the OCL language considered in order to improve the expressiveness of the constraints treated. Moreover, we would like also to extend the kind of reasoning we may perform on UML conceptual schemas by considering also their behavioral part.

Acknowledgments. We would like to thank J. Cabot, J. Conesa, D. Costal, C. Gómez, A. Olivé, R. Raventós and M.R. Sancho for helpful discussions on previous drafts of this paper. This work has been partially supported by the Ministerio de Ciencia y Tecnología under project TIN2005-06053.

References

1. Baader, F., Calvanese, D., McGuiness, D., Nardi, D., Patel-Schneider, P., (Eds.): The Description Logic Handbook: Theory, Implementation and Applications. Cambridge University Press (2003)
2. Berardi, D., Calvanese, D., De Giacomo, G.: Reasoning on UML Class Diagrams. Artificial Intelligence 168(1-2) (2005) 70-118
3. Borgida, A.: Description Logics in Data Management. IEEE Transactions on Knowledge and Data Engineering 7(5) (1995) 671-682
4. Borgida, A., Lenzerini, M., Rosati, R.: Description Logics for Data Bases. In: F. Baader, D. Calvanese, D. McGuiness, D. Nardi, and P. Patel-Schneider, (eds.): The Description Logic Handbook: Theory, Implementation and Applications. Cambridge University Press (2003) 472-494
5. Bowers, D. S.: Detection of Redundant Arcs in Entity Relationship Conceptual Models. ER 2003 Ws LNCS 2784 (2003) 275-287
6. Calvanese, D., Lenzerini, M., Nardi, D.: Description Logics for Conceptual Data Modeling. In: J. Chomicki and G. Saake, (eds.): Logics for Databases and Information Systems. Kluwer (1998) 229-263
7. Farré, C., Teniente, E., Urpí, T.: A New Approach for Checking Schema Validation Properties. In: Proc. 15th International Conference on Database and Expert Systems Applications (DEXA'04) (2004) 77-86

8. Farré, C., Teniente, E., Urpí, T.: Checking Query Containment with the CQC Method. Data and Knowledge Engineering 53(2) (2005) 163-223
9. Gogolla, M., Bohling, J., Richters, M.: Validation of UML and OCL Models by Automatic Snapshot Generation. «UML» 2003 LNCS 2863 (2003) 265-279
10. Hartmann, S.: On the Consistency of Int-cardinality Constraints. 17th International Conference on Conceptual Modeling - ER'98 LNCS 1507 (1998) 150-163
11. Hartmann, S.: Coping with Inconsistent Constraint Specifications. 20th International Conference on Conceptual Modeling - ER 2001 LNCS 2224 (2001) 241-255
12. Lenzerini, M., Nobili, P.: On the Satisfiability of Dependency Constraints in Entity-Relationship Schemata. In: Proc. 13th International Conference on Very Large Databases - VLDB'87 (1987) 147-154
13. Olivé, A.: Conceptual Schema-Centric Development: A Grand Challenge for Information Systems Research. 17th Int. Conf. on Advanced Information Systems Engineering (CAISE'05) LNCS 3520 (2005) 1-15
14. Queralt, A., Teniente, E.: Reasoning on UML Class Diagrams with OCL Constraints. Departament de LSI, UPC, Technical Report LSI-06-15-R (2006)
15. Warmer, J., Kleppe, A.: The Object Constraint Language: Getting Your Models Ready for MDA. 2nd edn. Addison-Wesley Professional (2003)

On the Use of Association Redefinition in UML Class Diagrams

Dolors Costal and Cristina Gómez

Universitat Politècnica de Catalunya
Departament de Llenguatges i Sistemes Informàtics
Jordi Girona 1-3 E08034 Barcelona (Catalonia)
{dolors, cristina}@lsi.upc.edu

Abstract. Association redefinition is a new concept in UML 2.0 that makes it possible to impose additional constraints on some instances of associations. In this paper, we describe how to use association redefinition to declare additional referential integrity and cardinality constraints for associations. We also analyze the interactions between taxonomic constraints and association redefinitions and their impact on the satisfaction of taxonomic constraints. Finally, we establish several conditions that are necessary to guarantee well-formed association redefinitions.

1 Introduction

Association redefinition is a new concept in UML 2.0 [11] that makes it possible to define association ends more specifically. This paper focuses on association redefinitions that allow designers to specify additional constraints on associations. Figure 1.1 shows an example in which the association *Enrols* connects students to the courses they take. There are two generalizations representing that there are two types of students (degree students and foreign students) and two types of courses (degree courses and master courses) respectively.

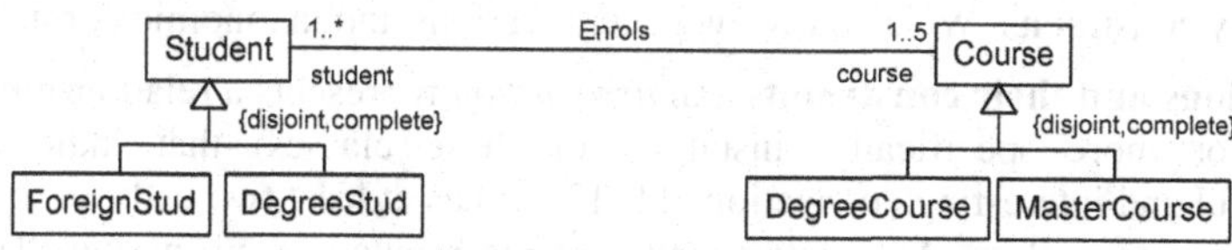

Fig. 1.1. Examples of association and generalization

Association redefinitions facilitate the specification of constraints that apply only to instances that belong to a particular descendant of one of the associated classes. In the previous example, we can specify that foreign students can take up to two courses (although the maximum for the rest of the students is five) and that degree students can only take degree courses (and not courses of other types). Both examples establish constraints that do not affect the whole set of students but rather only students that belong to a particular descendant subclass, i.e. students who are foreign students or students who are degree students.

D.W. Embley, A. Olivé, and S. Ram (Eds.): ER 2006, LNCS 4215, pp. 513 – 527, 2006.

These examples show that both associations and generalizations are involved in association redefinitions. As a consequence, interactions may appear between constraints specified by association redefinitions and taxonomic constraints of generalizations such as disjoint or complete constraints.

The analysis of association redefinitions to specify additional constraints is important for several reasons:

(1) To facilitate their use in conceptual schemas.
(2) To allow the development of specialized procedures for reasoning about them.
(3) To develop efficient patterns of implementation for their enforcement.

Our work has the aim to contribute to objectives (1) and (2). We analyze the use of association redefinitions to specify additional constraints on associations and we introduce a classification of association redefinitions according to the kinds of constraints they specify with the objective of clarifying their use.

We also study the interactions between taxonomic constraints and association redefinitions. Based on those interactions, we identify conditions that guarantee the satisfaction of taxonomic constraints, which contributes to objective (2). Additionally, we establish several rules that are necessary to guarantee well-formed association redefinitions. These results can be used by designers to help guarantee the validity of their specifications.

This paper is structured as follows. Section 2 reviews some basic concepts. Section 3 analyzes the use of association redefinitions to specify additional constraints on associations and compares the expressiveness of association redefinitions with previous proposals. Section 4 discusses the satisfaction of taxonomic constraints in the presence of association redefinitions. Section 5 presents several rules that are necessary to define well-formed association redefinitions. Section 6 discusses related work. Finally, in Section 7 we present our conclusions and suggest future work.

2 Basic Concepts for UML Association Redefinitions

In this section, we review the concept of association and their referential integrity and cardinality constraints. We also review generalizations and taxonomic constraints.

Associations and their constraints. An *association* represents a relationship between classes (or more specifically, instances of those classes) that indicates some meaningful and interesting connection [11, 13]. It has at least two ends, each of which is connected to a class. Association ends are represented by *properties*. This paper deals with non-recursive binary associations (two ends). In Figure 1.1, for instance, the association *Enrols* relates students to the courses they take.

Two kinds of integrity constraints that are relevant to associations are *referential integrity constraints* and the *cardinality constraints* specified by multiplicities. Referential integrity constraints are inherent to associations, since an instance of an association is a tuple with one value for each end of the association, where each value must necessarily be an instance of the class at its corresponding end. Multiplicity is almost always specified for association ends. In binary associations, it restricts the possible number of values of the association end that can simultaneously be related to an object at the opposite end. For example, in the association *Enrols* shown in Figure

1.1, the multiplicity *1..5* specified for the end *course* indicates that each student must be enrolled in at least one and at most five courses.

Generalizations and taxonomic constraints. *Generalization* is a directed relationship that can be specified between two classes [11, 13]. It relates a more general class (*superclass*) to a more specific class (*subclass*). *Specialization* is the same relationship viewed from the subclass. It implies a taxonomic *specialization* constraint that states that all instances of the subclass are also instances of the superclass.

A set of subclasses that share a common superclass may be grouped into a *generalization set*. Other taxonomic constraints may be applied to a generalization set. These are *disjoint constraints* and *complete constraints*. Disjoint constraints indicate that an object can be an instance of at most one subclass of the corresponding generalization set. Complete constraints indicate that each object of the superclass must be an instance of at least one subclass of the corresponding generalization set. Generalization sets labelled as *overlapping* (*incomplete*) indicate the absence of a disjoint (complete) constraint. Figure 1.1 shows a generalization set in which *Course* is the superclass and *DegreeCourse* and *MasterCourse* are the subclasses. Disjoint and complete taxonomic constraints are specified for this generalization set.

This paper focuses on redefinitions that only involve direct subclasses of classes connected by the redefined associations. Thus, we only deal with one level of generalization or specialization hierarchies.

3 UML Association Redefinitions for Specifying Additional Constraints on Associations

The concept of association redefinition introduced in UML 2.0 is complex, since it involves not only associations but also generalizations. In fact, the description of redefinition in the UML metamodel is scattered over more than 20 locations, as remarked in [3]. Therefore, in order to clarify its use to specify additional constraints on associations, it is necessary both to analyze in detail this concept and to introduce a classification of different kinds of redefinitions based on the types of constraints they specify.

A redefinition of a binary association allows us to define an association end more specifically [11, 13]. Several redefinitions may be specified for each association end. The notation {redefines <end-name>} is applied to an association end (the *redefining end*) to indicate that this end redefines the one named <end-name> (the *redefined end*). For instance, in the example in Figure 3.1, the ends *dCourse* and *mCourse* redefine the end *course*.

Association ends are represented by properties. The redefinition of association ends is a particular case of property redefinition. In general, the characteristics of a property that can be redefined are name, type (which may be specialized), default value, derivation status, visibility, multiplicity and constraints on values. For properties corresponding to association ends in particular, we can redefine name, type, derivation status, visibility and multiplicity.

In this paper, we deal with property redefinitions that apply to name, type and multiplicity, since we focus on using redefinitions to specify new types of constraints that are relevant at a conceptual level. Type and multiplicity redefinitions impose additional referential and cardinality constraints on an association respectively.

To analyze in detail the additional constraints that a property redefinition may imply for an association, we will consider three separate cases: a property redefinition that redefines type, a property redefinition that redefines multiplicity and a property redefinition that redefines both type and multiplicity.

In all three cases, the redefinition of an end property applies to instances connected by the association that are instances of a class that specializes the class used at the opposite end. We call this set of instances the *affected instances* of the redefinition. Consider, for example, the end *dCourse*, which redefines the end *course* of the association *Enrols*, shown in Figure 3.1. Since the class at the opposite end of the redefinition is *DegreeStud*, the instances affected by the redefinition are the instances of the class *Student* that are also instances of *DegreeStud*.

This implies that the following condition must hold in all three cases of property redefinition: (C1) in a redefining association, the end opposite the redefining end is always connected to a class that is a descendant of the class connected by the end opposite the redefined end.

In our example, condition C1 holds because the class *DegreeStud* is a descendant of the class *Student*. The UML 2.0 metamodel [11] establishes that condition C1 must hold for any association end redefinition.

According to C1, when we have a redefinition of an association end, we always have a specialization (or generalization) of the class opposite the redefined end and consequently a taxonomic specialization constraint. In cases in which there are two or more redefinitions of an association end with affected instances from different subclasses, it is possible to have a generalization set for those subclasses with a disjoint and/or complete taxonomic constraint.

3.1 Type Redefinition

A *type redefinition* establishes an additional referential integrity constraint that states that the affected instances of the redefinition are connected by the association to instances that must belong to the class of the redefining end.

Figure 3.1 shows two type redefinitions. The end *dCourse* redefines the type of the end *course* by establishing that all courses in which a degree student is enrolled must be degree courses. Similarly, the end *mCourse* redefines the end *course* by establishing that all courses in which foreign students are enrolled must be master courses. In this example, only the end *course* is redefined. However, in general, both ends of an association can be redefined.

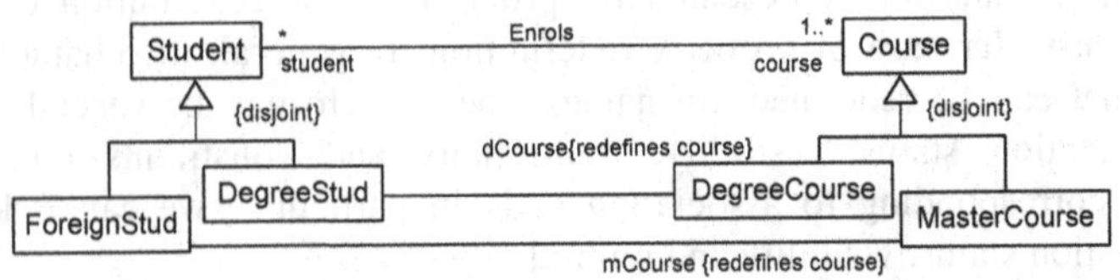

Fig. 3.1. Examples of type redefinition

When designers specify a type redefinition, they must fulfil the following conditions (in addition to condition C1): (C2) the redefining end must be connected to a class that is a descendant of the class connected by the redefined end, and (C3) the redefining end must not specify a multiplicity.

Conditions C2 and C3 hold for the redefinitions depicted in Figure 3.1. Both *DegreeCourse* and *MasterCourse* are descendants of *Course*. The UML 2.0 metamodel [11] imposes that either condition C2 must hold or the redefining end must be connected to the same class connected by the redefined end. The latter case would not be a type redefinition (see Section 3.2).

3.2 Multiplicity Redefinition

A *multiplicity redefinition* restricts the multiplicity allowed for the affected instances of the redefinition to the redefining multiplicity.

Figure 3.2 shows two multiplicity redefinitions. The end *dCourse* restricts the number of courses that degree students take to between three and five. The end *fCourse* restricts the courses that foreign students take to one or two.

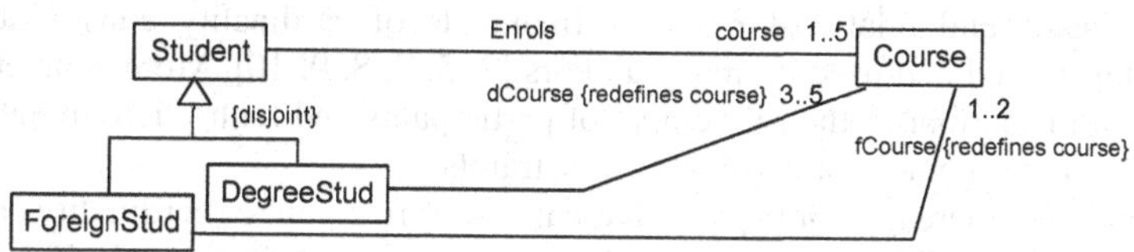

Fig. 3.2. Examples of multiplicity redefinition

In order to specify a multiplicity redefinition (not combined with a type redefinition), designers must fulfil the following conditions (in addition to condition C1): (C4) the redefining end is connected to the same class as the redefined end, and (C5) the redefining end has an associated multiplicity, that we call *redefining multiplicity*, which is more restrictive than the multiplicity of the redefined end.

In Figure 3.2, the redefining ends are connected to the class *Course*, which is the class that corresponds to the redefined end (condition C4), and the redefining multiplicities are more restrictive than the redefined multiplicity (condition C5). If the redefining end specifies multiplicity, the UML 2.0 metamodel [11] ensures that C5 holds. UML 2.0 also imposes that either condition C4 or condition C2 (from Section 3.1) must hold. The case in which C2 and C5 are both true corresponds to a type and multiplicity redefinition as we will see in Section 3.3.

3.3 Type and Multiplicity Redefinition

A *type and multiplicity redefinition* establishes that the affected instances of the redefinition are connected by the association to instances that must belong to the class of the redefining end. Additionally, the multiplicity allowed for those affected instances is restricted to the redefining multiplicity.

Figure 3.3 depicts two type and multiplicity redefinitions. The end *dCourse* establishes that degree students may only be enrolled in degree courses and that they may take between three and five of them. Similarly, the end *mCourse* establishes that foreign students may only be enrolled in master courses and that they may take one or two of them.

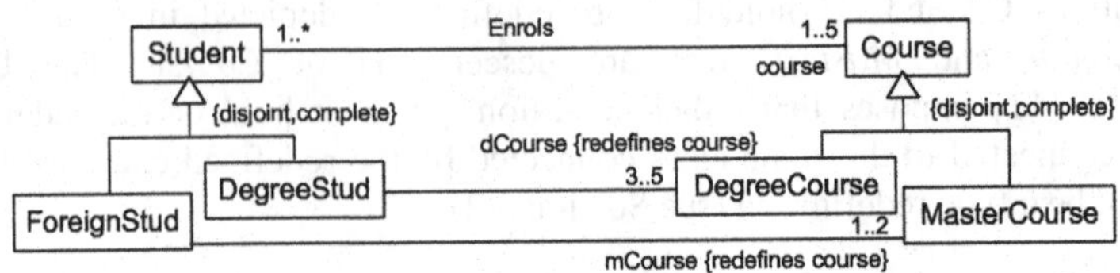

Fig. 3.3. Examples of type and multiplicity redefinition

In type and multiplicity redefinitions, conditions C1, C2 and C5 hold.

3.4 Relationship Between Association Redefinition and Previous Proposals

Type and multiplicity redefinitions are closely related to relationship type refinements of participants and relationship type refinements of cardinality constraints, which have been studied and used by many authors [2, 5, 7, 8, 9, 10]. More concretely, type redefinition is similar to the refinement of participants and multiplicity redefinition is similar to the refinement of cardinality constraints.

Despite this, there are some particular cases of refinement of cardinality constraints that are not expressible by means of UML association redefinitions. In Figure 1.1 we could specify, using a cardinality constraint refinement, that a foreign student can take up to three degree courses without disabling the possibility that foreign students take other types of courses as well. A UML association redefinition can not express this case because, when the multiplicity is redefined in a subclass, the type is implicitly redefined (and is a type and multiplicity redefinition).

Additionally, the proposal of [8] allows sets of subclasses to be in the antecedents and consequents of refinements, while a UML association redefinition allows a single subclass both in the redefining end and in the opposite end of the redefinition.

4 Interactions Between Taxonomic Constraints and Association Redefinitions

Constraints defined in a class diagram must be satisfied in the information base (IB). An IB satisfies a constraint if the constraint is true in the IB.

We say that a constraint is satisfied by a class diagram when the diagram entails this constraint. This means that other constraints defined in the diagram imply the former. In other words, the constraint is a logical consequence of the conceptual schema represented by the diagram. In this case no particular action needs to be taken at runtime to ensure the constraint is satisfied, but it may be important to keep it in the class diagram for verification, validation, implementation or evolution purposes. If a constraint is not satisfied by means of the class diagram, it must be enforced.

We will show that, in some cases, taxonomic constraints may be entailed by constraints on association redefinitions and, as a consequence, their enforcement is not necessary.

We will illustrate some of our results based on the example shown in Figure 4.1, which refers to a fragment of an example shown in [13]. The class diagram defines account products and legal entities in a bank. Accounts have at least one legal entity owner and may have several agents. Legal entities own at least one account and may act as agents of various accounts. Accounts are specialized into personal and corporate accounts. Legal entities are specialized into person and company entities. Each generalization set is disjoint and complete. Three type and multiplicity redefinitions are defined, which establish that personal accounts must have at most one *trustee* (a person who acts as agent), corporate accounts must have between two and five *signers* (companies that act as agents) and corporate accounts must have just one *owner*, which must be a company.

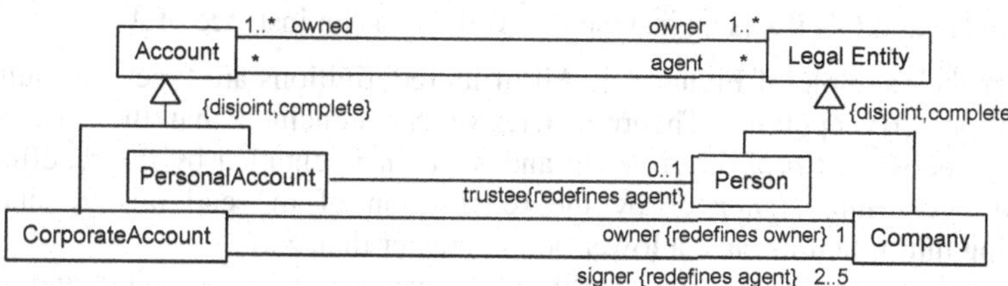

Fig. 4.1. Examples of type and multiplicity redefinition of an association end

This diagram includes eight taxonomic constraints. Four of them are specialization constraints. They define that personal accounts are accounts, corporate accounts are accounts, people are legal entities and companies are legal entities. Two of them are disjointness constraints, which define that an account cannot be corporate and personal at the same time and that a legal entity cannot be a person and a company at the same time. Finally, two complete constraints define that an account must be corporate or personal and a legal entity must be a person or a company.

We discuss, in the following, how each kind of taxonomic constraint can be satisfied by association redefinitions.

4.1 Specialization Constraints Entailed by Association Redefinitions

This section presents a theorem that establishes the conditions in which specialization constraints are entailed by redefinitions. Figure 4.2 illustrates the situations it describes.

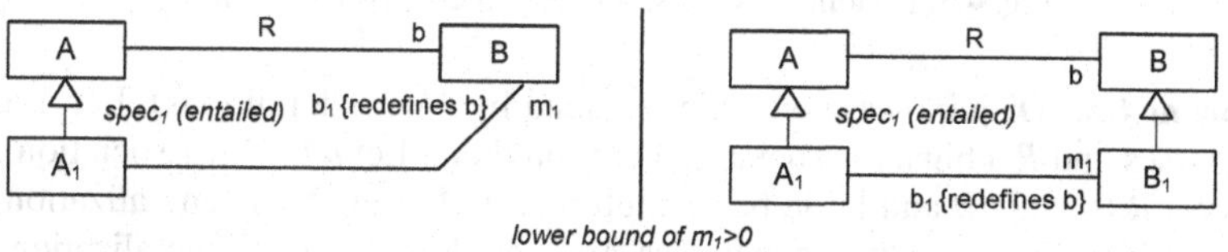

Fig. 4.2. Specialization constraint entailed by a multiplicity or a type and multiplicity redefinition

Theorem 4.1. (Specialization constraint entailed by a multiplicity or a type and multiplicity redefinition). Let A and B be two classes and R a binary association between them. Let b be the association end that connects R to class B. Let $spec_1$ be the specialization of A into subclass A_1. Assume that b_1 is a multiplicity redefinition (resp. type and multiplicity redefinition) of end b with multiplicity m_1, that b_1 is connected to B (resp. to B_1) and that the opposite end of b_1 is connected to class A_1. Then, if the lower bound of m_1 is greater than zero, the specialization constraint of $spec_1$ is entailed by the redefinition.

Proof. (1) Assume that x is any instance of A_1. We say that R_1 represents a subset of R that contains the instances involved by the redefinition. There must be an instance y of B (resp. B_1) such that x is R_1*-related* to y since the lower bound of m_1 is greater than zero.

(2) If x is R_1*-related* to y, then x is R*-related* to y since b_1 is a redefinition of b.
(3) If x is R*-related* to y, then x is an instance of A due to the referential integrity of R.
(4) From (1) and (3), if x is an instance of A_1 then x is an instance of A. □

Consider the example of Figure 4.1. All of its redefinitions are type and multiplicity redefinitions. By applying Theorem 4.1, we can conclude that the specialization constraint between *CorporateAccount* and *Account* is entailed by the redefinition of the end *agent* into *signer* or by the redefinition of the end *owner*, since both redefining multiplicities have a lower bound greater than zero.

However, the specialization constraint between *PersonalAccount* and *Account* must be enforced because the redefinition of the end *agent* into *trustee* has a redefining multiplicity with a lower bound equal to zero. There may be instances of *PersonalAccount* that do not have a *trustee* person and, consequently, type and multiplicity redefinitions do not apply to those instances.

4.2 Disjointness Constraints Entailed by Association Redefinitions

This section presents four theorems that establish the conditions in which disjointness constraints are entailed by redefinitions. The first one corresponds to the case of type redefinition, which is illustrated in Figure 4.3.

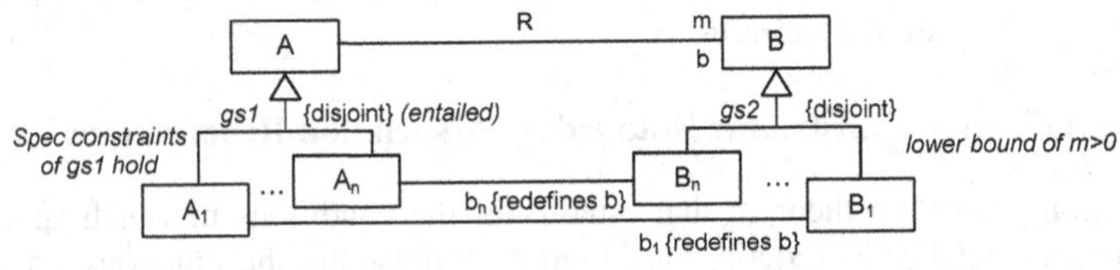

Fig. 4.3. Disjointness constraint entailed by type redefinitions

Theorem 4.2. (Disjointness constraint entailed by type redefinitions). Let A and B be two classes and R a binary association between them. Let b be the association end that connects R to class B and let m be its multiplicity. Let gs_1 be a generalization set that specializes superclass A into subclasses $A_1,\ldots,A_n$. Let gs_2 be a generalization set that specializes superclass B into subclasses $B_1,\ldots,B_n$. Assume that all specialization constraints of *gs1* hold. Assume that $b_1,\ldots,b_n$ are type redefinitions of the end *b*, that each b_i is connected to B_i and that the opposite end of b_i is connected to class A_i. Then, if the lower bound of *m* is greater than zero and gs_2 is disjoint, the disjointness constraint of gs_1 is entailed by the type redefinitions.

Proof. (1) Assume that *x* is an instance of A_i and A_j, where $1 \leq i \leq n$ and $1 \leq j \leq n$ and $i \neq j$. We say that R_i (R_j) represents a subset of *R* that contains the instances involved by the redefinition b_i (b_j).
(2) If *x* is an instance of A_i, then *x* is also an instance of *A* by the specialization constraint of *gs1* involving A_i.
(3) If *x* is an instance of *A*, there must be an instance *y* of *B* such that *x* is *R-related* to *y* since the lower bound of *m* is greater than zero.
(4) From (1) and (3), as *x* is an instance of A_i and *x* is *R-related* to *y* then *x* is R_i-*related* to *y* and *y* is an instance of B_i because b_i is a type redefinition of *b*.
(5) From (1) and (3) as *x* is an instance of A_j and *x* is *R-related* to *y* then *x* is R_j-*related* to *y* and *y* is an instance of B_j because b_j is a type redefinition of *b*.
(6) (4) and (5) are contradictory because they state that *y* is an instance of B_i and B_j and gs_2 is disjoint. □

In Figure 3.1, the disjointness constraint between *DegreeStud* and *ForeignStud* is entailed by the type redefinitions of the end *course*, since the lower bound of its multiplicity is equal to one and *DegreeCourse* and *MasterCourse* are disjoint.

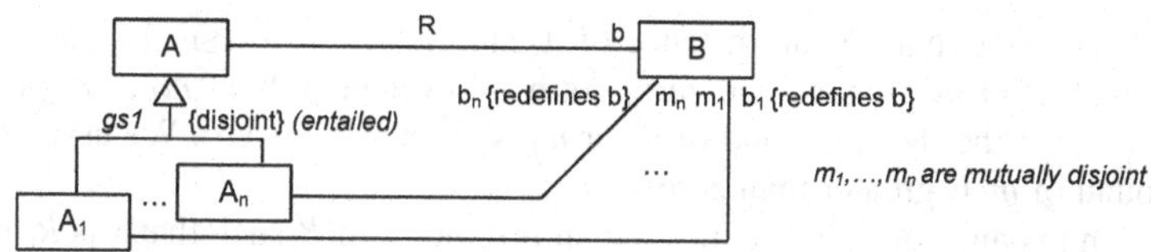

Fig. 4.4. Disjointness constraint entailed by disjoint multiplicity redefinitions

Theorem 4.3. (Disjointness constraint entailed by disjoint multiplicity redefinitions). Let *A* and *B* be two classes and *R* a binary association between them. Let *b* be the association end that connects *R* to class *B*. Let gs_1 be a generalization set that specializes superclass *A* into subclasses $A_1,\ldots,A_n$. Assume that $b_1,\ldots,b_n$ are multiplicity redefinitions of the end *b* with their corresponding multiplicities $m_1,\ldots,m_n$, that each b_i is connected to *B* and that the opposite end of b_i is connected to class A_i. Then, if each pair of multiplicities m_i and m_j, where $1 \leq i \leq n$ and $1 \leq j \leq n$ and $i \neq j$, are mutually disjoint (i.e. each intersection is empty), the disjointness constraint of gs_1 is entailed by the multiplicity redefinitions (see Figure 4.4).

Proof. (1) Assume that *x* is an instance of A_i and A_j, where $1 \leq i \leq n$ and $1 \leq j \leq n$ and $i \neq j$.
(2) If *x* is an instance of A_i, there must be a number of instances (between the minimum and the maximum of m_i) of *B* such that *x* is R_i-*related* to them. Consequently, by the redefinition b_i, *x* is *R-related* to them.
(3) If *x* is an instance of A_j, there must be a number of instances (between the minimum and the maximum of m_j) of *B* such that *x* is R_j-*related* to them. Consequently, by the redefinition b_j, *x* is *R-related* to them.
(4) Because m_i and m_j are mutually disjoint, (2) and (3) are inconsistent. □

In Figure 3.2, the disjointness constraint between *DegreeStud* and *ForeignStud* is entailed by the multiplicity redefinitions of the end *course*, since the multiplicities of *dCourse* and *fCourse* are disjoint intervals.

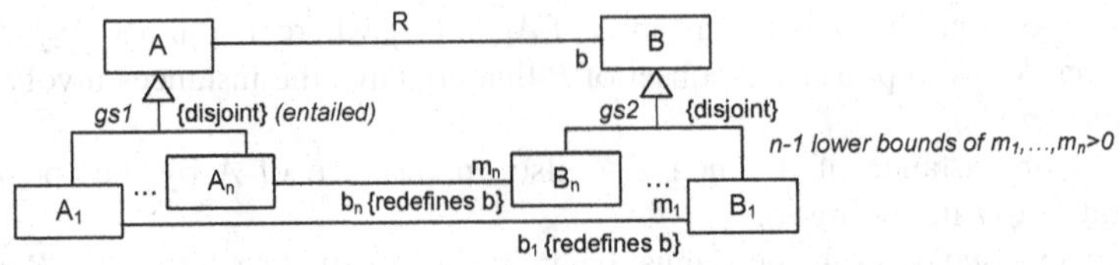

Fig. 4.5. Disjointness constraint entailed by type and multiplicity redefinitions

Theorem 4.4. (Disjointness constraint entailed by type and multiplicity redefinitions). Let *A* and *B* be two classes and *R* a binary association between them. Let *b* be the association end that connects *R* to class *B*. Let gs_1 be a generalization set that specializes superclass *A* into subclasses $A_1,...,A_n$. Let gs_2 be a generalization set that specializes superclass *B* into subclasses $B_1,...,B_n$. Assume that $b_1,...,b_n$ are multiplicity redefinitions of the end *b* with their corresponding multiplicities $m_1,...,m_n$, that each b_i is connected to B_i and that the opposite end of b_i is connected to class A_i. Then, if *n-1* lower bounds of $m_1,...,m_n$ are greater than zero and gs_2 is disjoint, the disjointness constraint of gs_1 is entailed by the type and multiplicity redefinitions (see Figure 4.5).

Proof. (1) Assume that *x* is an instance of A_i and A_j, where $1 \leq i \leq n$, $1 \leq j \leq n$, $i \neq j$ and the lower bound of m_i is greater than zero. As n-1 lower bounds of $m_1,...,m_n$ are greater than zero then either lower bound of m_i or m_j is greater than zero. We assume that the lower bound of m_i is greater than zero.
(2) If *x* is an instance of A_i, there must be an instance *y* of B_i such that *x* is R_i*-related* to *y* by the lower bound of m_i.
(3) If *x* is R_i*-related* to y, then *x* is *R-related* to y, since b_i is a redefinition of *b*.
(4) If *x* is an instance of A_j and *x* is *R-related* to y, then *x* is R_j*-related* to *y* and *y* is an instance of B_j, since b_j is a redefinition of *b*.
(5) Because *y* is an instance of B_i and B_j and gs_2 is disjoint, (2) and (4) are contradictory. □

In Figure 3.3, the disjointness constraint between *DegreeStud* and *ForeignStud* is entailed by the type and multiplicity redefinitions of the end *course*, since the lower bound of the multiplicity of *dCourse* is greater than zero and *DegreeCourse* and *MasterCourse* are disjoint.

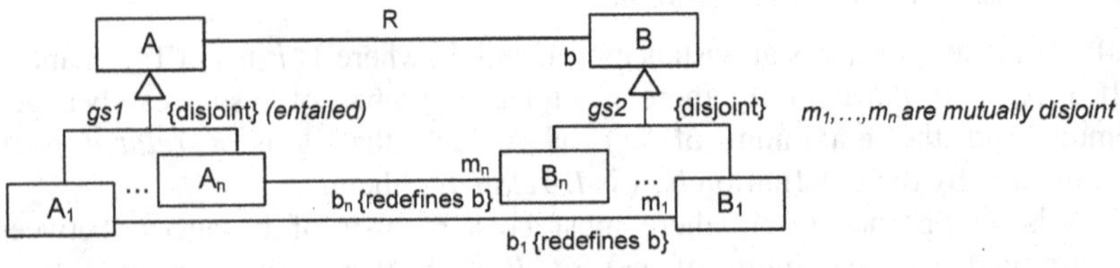

Fig. 4.6. Disjointness constraint entailed by type and disjoint multiplicity redefinitions

Theorem 4.5. (Disjointness constraint entailed by type and disjoint multiplicity redefinitions). Let A and B be two classes and R a binary association between them. Let b be the association end that connects R to class B. Let gs_1 be a generalization set that specializes superclass A into subclasses $A_1,\ldots,A_n$. Let gs_2 be a generalization set that specializes superclass B into subclasses $B_1,\ldots,B_n$. Assume that $b_1,\ldots,b_n$ are multiplicity redefinitions of the end b with their corresponding multiplicities $m_1,\ldots,m_n$, that each b_i is connected to B_i and that the opposite end of b_i is connected to class A_i. Then, if each pair of multiplicities m_i and m_j, where $1 \leq i \leq n$, $1 \leq j \leq n$ and $i \neq j$, are mutually disjoint (i.e. each intersection is empty), the disjointness constraint of gs_1 is entailed by the type and multiplicity redefinitions (see Figure 4.6).

Proof. (1) Assume that x is an instance of A_i and A_j, where $1 \leq i \leq n$, $1 \leq j \leq n$ and $i \neq j$.
(2) If x is an instance of A_i, there must be a number of instances (between the minimum and maximum of m_i) of B_i such that x is R_i-*related* to them. Consequently, by the redefinition b_i, x is R-*related* to them.
(3) If x is an instance of A_j, there must be a number of instances (between the minimum and maximum of m_j) of B_j such that x is R_j-*related* to them. Consequently, by the redefinition b_j, x is R-*related* to them.
(4) Because m_i and m_j are mutually disjoint, (2) and (3) are inconsistent. □

Consider the example given in Figure 4.1. By applying Theorem 4.5, the disjointness constraint between *CorporateAccount* and *PersonalAccount* is entailed by the type and multiplicity redefinitions of the end *agent*, since the redefining multiplicities are mutually disjoint and *Person* and *Company* are also disjoint.

4.3 Complete Constraints Entailed by Association Redefinitions

For complete constraints, we only consider the case presented in Figure 4.7.

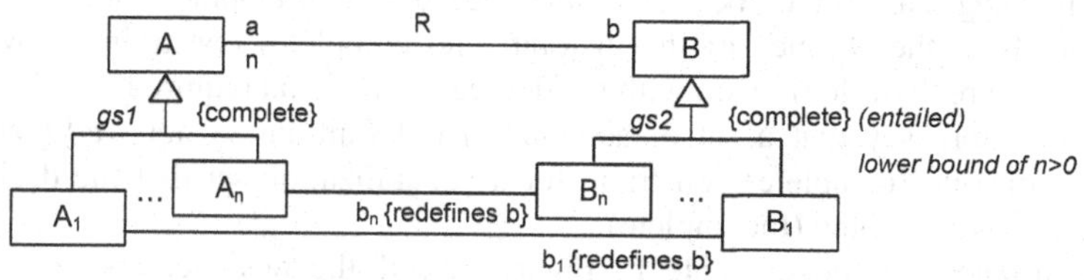

Fig. 4.7. Complete constraint entailed by type or type and multiplicity redefinitions

Theorem 4.6. (Complete constraint entailed by type or type and multiplicity redefinitions). Let A and B be two classes and R a binary association between them. Let b be the association end that connects R to class B and a the opposite end that connects R to class A with multiplicity n. Let gs_1 be a generalization set that specializes superclass A into subclasses $A_1,\ldots,A_n$. Let gs_2 be a generalization set that specializes superclass B into subclasses $B_1,\ldots,B_n$. Assume that $b_1,\ldots,b_n$ are type or type and multiplicity redefinitions of the end b with their corresponding multiplicities, that each b_i is connected to B_i and that the opposite end of b_i is connected to class A_i. Then, if the lower bound of n is greater than zero and gs_1 is complete, the complete constraint of gs_2 is entailed by the type or type and multiplicity redefinitions.

Proof. (1) Assume that y is an instance of B. There must be an instance x of A such that x is *R-related* to y, since the lower bound of n is greater than zero.
(2) If x is an instance of A, then x is an instance of at least one A_i, where $1 \le i \le n$, since gs_l is complete.
(3) If x is an instance of at least one A_i and x is *R-related* to y, then y is an instance of the corresponding B_i since b_i is a type or type and multiplicity redefinition of b.
(4) As a consequence of (1), (2) and (3), if y is an instance of B, then y is an instance of at least one B_i where $1 \le i \le n$. □

In Figure 4.1, the complete constraint of the generalization of *Person* and *Company* into *LegalEntity* must be enforced because the multiplicity of *owned* is *1..**, but *owner* is not redefined for *PersonalAccount*. Moreover, the end *agent* is redefined for all subclasses of *Account*, but the lower bound of the multiplicity of *account* is equal to zero. In Figure 3.3, by applying Theorem 4.6, the complete constraint of the generalization of *DegreeCourse* and *MasterCourse* into *Course* is entailed by the type and multiplicity redefinitions.

5 Well-Formed Association Redefinitions in UML

The previous section showed that constraints imposed by association redefinitions may ensure that several taxonomic constraints of the generalization sets involved are satisfied. As mentioned above, those constraints, although redundant, should be specified in the diagram for verification, validation, implementation and evolution purposes.

In the case of a generalization set with a disjoint (or complete) taxonomic constraint entailed by association redefinitions, the designer might accidentally specify that the generalization set is overlapping (or incomplete). Although the resulting diagram would be satisfiable because overlapping (and incomplete) corresponds to the absence of the disjoint (and complete) constraint, it would not represent the real-world domain with the degree of precision required.

We therefore say that a set of association redefinitions is not *well-formed* if it entails a disjoint (complete) constraint for a generalization set that the designer has specified as overlapping (incomplete).

For instance, in the example in Figure 3.1, if the designer specifies that the generalization of *ForeignStud* and *DegreeStud* into *Student* is overlapping, it will nevertheless be impossible for a student to belong to the foreign and degree types at the same time. This is because the type redefinitions of the association end *course* entail a disjoint constraint for that generalization.

To help designers avoid this situation and more accurately describe the real-world domain, we formulated five rules that define conditions necessary to guarantee well-formed association redefinitions. These rules are based on the results for satisfying disjoint and complete constraints presented in Section 4.

Rule 1. A generalization set with a superclass connected to the opposite end of a redefined end with type redefinitions in each direct descendant subclass must be disjoint if the lower bound of the redefined end multiplicity is greater than zero and the generalization set with a superclass connected to the redefined end and subclasses connected to the redefining ends is disjoint. This rule is extracted from Theorem 4.2.

Rule 2. A generalization set with a superclass connected to the opposite end of a redefined end with multiplicity redefinitions in each direct descendant subclass must be disjoint if the multiplicities of the redefining ends connected to the same class as the redefined end are mutually disjoint (from Theorem 4.3).

Rule 3. A generalization set with a superclass connected to the opposite end of a redefined end with type and multiplicity redefinitions in each direct descendant subclass must be disjoint if *n-1* lower bounds of the redefining end multiplicities are greater than zero and the generalization set with a superclass connected to the redefined end and subclasses connected to the redefining ends is disjoint (from Theorem 4.4).

Rule 4. A generalization set with a superclass connected to the opposite end of a redefined end with type and multiplicity redefinitions in each direct descendant subclass must be disjoint if the generalization set with a superclass connected to the redefined end and subclasses connected to the redefining ends is disjoint and the multiplicities of the redefining ends are mutually disjoint (from Theorem 4.5).

Rule 5. A generalization set with a superclass connected to a redefined end and subclasses connected to the redefining ends must be complete if the generalization set with a superclass connected to the opposite end of the redefined end with type and multiplicity redefinitions in each direct descendant subclass is complete and the lower bound of multiplicity of the opposite end of the redefined end is greater than zero (from Theorem 4.6).

All the redefinitions shown in the examples given in this paper are well-formed because they follow the rules presented above.

As seen in Section 3, a single association redefinition in UML must fulfil a set of conditions in order to be a well-formed redefinition. These conditions are expressed in the UML metamodel as constraints attached to the metaclass *RedefinableElement.* In order to define well-formed redefinitions, a constraint representing each rule presented above must be attached to the metaclass *RedefinableElement* in the UML metamodel.

6 Related Work

Relationship type refinements, which are closely related to association redefinitions (see Section 3.4), have received much attention in the literature. Relationship type refinements were defined in [9] and they have been studied and used by many authors [2, 5, 7, 8, 9, 10]. All of these studies focus exclusively on the definition and use of refinements for conceptual models. However, a few works such as [6, 8] focus on reasoning about relationship type refinements.

[6] presents a method that makes it possible to verify the satisfiability of a schema that may have refinements of participants and cardinality constraints and also check whether the schema implies specialization and cardinality constraints. However, this work does not deal with disjoint and complete constraints.

[8] establishes a set of necessary conditions to guarantee that a given set of refinements is valid, assuming multiple classification. However, this work is restricted to the case of generalization sets that are partitions.

Other works have dealt with satisfaction of constraints. Specifically, [12] studies the satisfaction of taxonomic constraints and is complementary to our work, although [12] considers the impact of derived classes while ours deals with the impact of association redefinitions. [1] proposes to reason about interesting properties of UML class diagrams using DL-based reasoning systems. From those properties, satisfaction of several kinds of constraints may be deduced. The authors show that this reasoning task is decidable for UML class diagrams including elements such as object classes, associations, aggregations and generalizations. However, association redefinitions are not included in their decidability analysis.

7 Conclusions and Further Work

We have analyzed and explained the concept of association redefinition in detail to make it easier to use in class diagrams. Moreover, we have introduced a classification of different kinds of redefinitions according to the different types of constraints they specify.

Additionally, we have studied the interactions between association redefinitions and taxonomic constraints and the impact that association redefinitions have on the satisfaction of related taxonomic constraints.

Finally, in order to help designers more accurately describe the real-world domain, we have provided a set of rules that establish several necessary conditions to guarantee that association redefinitions are well-formed.

Future work may involve the interaction of association redefinitions with other types of constraints that can be defined in a class diagram and the analysis of other kinds of redefinitions. We also plan to incorporate the results of this work into a CASE tool.

Acknowledgments. We would like to thank Jordi Cabot, Jordi Conesa, Antoni Olivé, Anna Queralt, Ruth Raventós, Maria Ribera Sancho and Ernest Teniente for helpful discussions on previous drafts of this paper. We also thank the anonymous referees for their useful comments. This work has been partially supported by the Ministerio de Ciencia y Tecnologia under project TIN2005-06053.

References

1. Berardi, D., Calvanese, D., De Giacomo, G., Reasoning on UML class diagrams. Artificial Intelligence 168 (2005) 70-118.
2. Brachman, R.J., Schmolze, J.G., An Overview of the KL-ONE Knowledge Representation System. Cognitive Science 9 (2) (1995) 171-216.
3. Büttner, F., Gogolla, M., On Generalization and Overriding in UML 2.0, UML Workshop on OCL and Model Driven Engineering, Lisbon (Portugal), 2004.

4. Bratsberg, S.E., Odberg, E., Relation Refinement in Object-Relation Data Models. Nordic Workshop on Programming and Software Development Research, Tampere (Finland), 1992.
5. Cook, S., Daniels, J., Designing Object Systems: Object-Oriented Modeling with Syntropy. Prentice-Hall, 1994.
6. Calvanese, D., Lenzerini, M., On the Interaction Between ISA and Cardinality Constraints, 10th Int. Conference on Data Engineering. (ICDE'94), pp. 204-213.
7. de Champeaux, D., Lea, D., Faure, P., Object-Oriented System Development. Addison-Wesley, 1994.
8. Costal, D., Olivé, A., Teniente, E., Relationship Type Refinement in Conceptual Models with Multiple Classification, 20th International Conference on Conceptual Modeling. (ER'01), LNCS 2224, pp. 397-411.
9. Mylopoulos, J., Bernstein, P.A., Wong, H.K.T, A Language Facility for Designing Database-Intensive Applications, TODS 5 (2) (1980) 185-207.
10. Martin, J., Odell, J., Objects-Oriented Methods: a Foundation. Prentice-Hall, 1995.
11. OMG. UML 2.0 Superstructure Specification, OMG Adopted Specification, 2005. Available online at http://www.omg.org/cgi-bin/doc?formal/05-07-04.
12. Olivé, A., Teniente, E., Derived types and taxonomic constraints in conceptual modeling. Information Systems 27 (2002) 391-409.
13. Rumbaugh, J., Jacobson, I., Booch, G., The Unified Modeling Language Reference Manual, Second Edition, Addison-Wesley, 2005.

Optimising Abstract Object-Oriented Database Schemas

Joachim Biskup and Ralf Menzel

Universität Dortmund, 44221 Dortmund, Germany
{biskup, menzel}@ls6.cs.uni-dortmund.de

Abstract. Conceptual design is one step on the way from requirements analysis to implementation. During conceptual design of a database application we work with conceptual database schemas, which are based on a formal model. Because of this formal model it is possible to investigate equivalence of schemas and consequently to examine schema transformations. In an earlier work we presented a cost model that allows us to estimate time costs for machine programs of an abstract database machine. In this paper we show how this cost model can be employed to evaluate cost effects of schema transformations. This enables us to steer schema transformations to meet given time requirements of critical database queries and updates. In particular, we analyse the schema transformation pivoting. As a result of such an analysis we can characterise high-level queries and updates and tell how the time required for their execution is affected by the schema transformation.

1 Introduction

A major part of the design of a database application is the design of a database schema. Typically, there are several candidate schemas to choose from. By the choice the designer tries to meet given design goals. One important goal is to minimise the time required to execute given queries and updates.

It is common practice to put a conceptual design step before the implementation. Typically, there is no formal model for the implementation, while the conceptual design of our interest is based on a formal model. With this formal model the designer can make sure that the different schema alternatives are formally equivalent or that one alternative can be embedded into another. In particular it is possible to use schema transformations that guarantee an equivalence or an embedding when they transform a given schema into another.

In this paper we want to show how our cost model [2], which is based on an abstract oriented database machine [1], can be used to analyse the cost effects of schema transformations. Such an analysis not only tells us when it is desirable to transform a schema because given critical queries and updates take less time, but also provides an estimate of the expected savings. With this information we can systematically optimise conceptual object-oriented database schemas.

As an example we analyse the schema transformation we call pivoting [4,5]. We did a case study of pivoting [3,6] without using a formal model. Now, we employ the cost model to examine the cost effects of pivoting.

D.W. Embley, A. Olivé, and S. Ram (Eds.): ER 2006, LNCS 4215, pp. 528–543, 2006.

We see the contribution of this paper as an elaboration of the steps 3 to 5 of a generic model-based method instantiated for database schema design as follows:

1. Choose a model: our abstract database machine and cost model.
2. Judge suitability: preparatory inspection underlying our contribution.
3. Apply model to problem: cost effects of schema transformations.
4. Get results: cost differences for characteristics of high-level operations.
5. Look for model-caused artifacts: discussion in conclusion.
6. If not happy, use knowledge gained in Step 5 to reiterate from Step 1.

It has been a research topic for quite some time to account for the need of optimisation at conceptual design level already. There are several investigations considering costs while designing databases [17,18,20,21]. The field of software performance engineering researches how to develop software that satisfies given performance requirements. There is an especially noteworthy approach by Nixon [15,16] who describes a Performance Requirements Framework that illustrates how to consider time costs requirements while designing a database application. We base our analysis of the time cost effects of schema transformations on an abstract object-oriented database machine. In this way we compose high-level queries and updates from the different machine operations. In a similar way Yao [22] analyses different query evaluation algorithms for relational databases by breaking them into simple access operations. The maintenance of semantic constraints takes time. One way to check constraints is by globally querying the database after each update or at least before committing a transaction. But it is typically more cost effective to take care of constraint maintenance during the execution of updates incrementally [10,12,13,14]. Gupta and Widom [8] with their approach for local verification of global integrity constraints even show how to handle this task in an distributed environment.

2 Abstract Database Machine and Cost Model

For the purpose of this paper we only sketch a simplified version of our cost model and its underlying abstract object-oriented database machine. You can find a formal definition of the complete versions in our earlier publications [1,2].

Object Model. We base our database machine on a simple object model that is inspired by the object-oriented models of the ODMG [7] and F-logic [11].

The basic values in our object model are *literals* like integers or strings. Complex structures must be represented through *objects*. Each object has a unique *object identifier*. Furthermore it can give values for any number of *attributes*. In our object model, these attribute values can only be literals, object identifiers, sets of literals, or sets of object identifiers. We collectively call the corresponding types *value types*.

The *conceptual (database) schema* declares the *classes* and their *object types*. It declares a *class hierarchy* and for all object types it declares the valid *attribute types*. While the full version of our object model employs an explicit class type

Table 1. Operations of the abstract database machine

name	number of input streams	number of output streams	access to persistent database state	may generate duplicates	sorted input required	needs entire input stream for operation
const	—	1	—	yes	n/a	n/a
duplicate	1	2	—	—	—	—
scan	—	1	read	—	n/a	n/a
activate	1	1	read	—	—	—
unnest	1	1	—	yes	—	—
nest$_{\mathrm{O}}$	1	1	—	—	yes	—
project	1	1	—	yes	—	—
unique$_{\mathrm{O}}$	1	1	—	—	yes	—
select	1	1	—	—	—	—
sort	1	1	—	—	—	yes
product	2	1	—	—	—	yes
unionall	2	1	—	yes	—	—
create	1	1	—	—	—	—
write	1	—	write	n/a	—	—
delete	1	—	write	n/a	—	—
union$_{\mathrm{O}}$	2	1	—	—	yes	—
join$_{\mathrm{O}}$	2	1	—	—	yes	—
access	1	1	read	—	—	—

assignment to set up the relation between classes and their object types, for the simplified version we consider in this paper we assume that there is an implicit one-to-one correspondence between classes and object types. We will therefore henceforth use the same name for a class and its object type. A further simplification is to assume that attribute names are unique and don't need to be qualified by class names. We will often use the same identifier for an attribute name, the attribute type name, and the name of the corresponding class.

The *internal (database) schema* declares access structures. An *access structure declaration* consists of a class and one of its attributes. It tells that the database system shall set up an access structure for the class on the attribute.

Abstract Database Machine. The state of our abstract database machine consists of a *persistent* and a *transient* part. The persistent database state is an instance for a conceptual database schema as described above.

The transient data in the abstract database machine is represented through *streams.* In this form data is passed from one machine operation to another. Streams are typed. A *stream type* is a list of value types. A stream itself is a sequence of *value lists* (i.e., lists of values). The values in the value lists are numbered by their *positions.* All the value lists in a stream must adhere to the stream type. Additionally a stream can be lexicographically sorted, which is described by a position list $(k_1, \ldots, k_n)$.

Table 1 gives an overview of the operations of the abstract database machine.

A *machine program* consists of one or more *steps.* Each step designates one operation and describes the input and output of the operation. For this purpose, streams are represented by program variables of the form x_i, called *channels.* Every input stream for an operation is given as a channel that stands for the output stream of an earlier step.

Depending on the number of output streams, a machine program step is denoted as either $op(args)$, or $x_k := op(args)$, or $(x_k, x_l) := op(args)$. Here x_k and x_l denote channels, *op* is an operator, and *args* is a comma separated list of suitable arguments. An argument that stands for an input stream is in turn given as a channel x_i. A machine program is a sequence of machine program steps that satisfies the following requirements:

- The preconditions of the operators in all steps are satisfied. All arguments are of valid types in particular.
- Each channel is used as output by exactly one step. (The two outputs of 'duplicate' must be two different channels.)
- Each channel is used as input by at most one step.
- Each channel that is used as input by a machine program step is used as output by an earlier step.

Note, that every program can be represented by an ordered directed acyclic graph, where the vertices stand for program steps and the edges for channels.

Cost Model. For the purpose of this paper we will only sketch how the time cost estimation works. Time costs are estimated for a given machine program. The estimation works by successively assigning a *step cost statement* to every step of the machine program and a *channel cost statement* to every channel of the program. These cost statements result from evaluating *cost functions* that are provided by the cost model for every type of operation. Finally, all step cost statements are combined by an *aggregation function* into a *total cost statement.*

The cost functions model the underlying database system. Table 2 contains the simple cost functions that we employ in the context of the present paper. They use cost parameters, which are given in Tables 3 and 4. The cost functions work with channel cost statements that describe the *stream length.* The step cost statements consist of *block accesses* (I/O) and *value accesses* (CPU). The aggregation function is just an addition of the individual step cost statements.

3 Schema Transformations and Pivoting

A schema transformation has two input parameters: the original schema and the part of the schema to be transformed. A schema transformation can be extended to transform instances and queries for the schema. While a schema transformation is a syntactic operation, it must exhibit certain semantic properties to be of interest. Common schema transformations warrant that the original schema can be embedded into the transformed schema, or, if achievable and desirable, that the two schemas are even equivalent.

Usually, during the design process, schema transformations are considered at the conceptual level. At this level a formal model is available that can be used to specify the desired semantic properties of schema transformations. Our abstract database machine reaches to the internal level. When we investigate pivoting we must therefore supplement the usual transformation of the conceptual schema with a matching transformation of the internal schema.

Table 2. Simple cost functions for the operations used in the paper

operation	block accesses	value accesses	stream length
$(x', x'') :=$ duplicate(x)	$2 \cdot \|x\| \cdot n_{\text{type}_x}$	0	$\|x\|, \|x\|$
$x' :=$ scan(c)	$\lceil N_c / n_{\text{OID}} / \theta_{\text{s}:\,c} \rceil$	0	N_c
$x' :=$ activate(x, pos_c)	$\|x\| \cdot (\theta_{\text{a}:c} + n_{\text{type}_c})$	$\|x\|$	$\|x\|$
$x' :=$ project$(x, \ldots)$	0	0	$\|x\|$
$x' :=$ unique$_0(x)$	0	$(\|x\| - 1) \cdot n_{\text{q}:\,\text{type}_x}$	$f_{\text{q}:\,\text{type}_x}(\|x\|)$
$x' :=$ sort$(x, (\text{pos}_1, \ldots))$	$2 \cdot n_{\text{type}_x} \cdot \|x\| \cdot \lceil \log_q(k) \rceil$	$\|x\| \cdot \log_2(\|x\|/k) \cdot n$	$\|x\|$
write(x, c, pos_c, f)	$\|x\| \cdot (n_{\gamma(c)} + \eta(N_{0,c}) + \sum_{(c',A) \in X_c} \eta(N_{c'}) \cdot n_{\text{A}:\,c',A})$	0	—
delete(x, c, pos_c)	$\|x\| \cdot \left(\theta_{\text{d}:\,c} \cdot n_{\gamma(c)} + \theta_{\text{D}:\,c} \cdot (\eta(N_{0,c}) + \sum_{(c',A) \in X_c} \eta(N_{c'}) \cdot n_{\text{A}:\,c',A})\right)$	0	—
$x' :=$ access$(x, (c, A), \text{pos}_A)$	$\|x\| \cdot (\eta(N_c) + n_{\text{X}:\,c,A} \cdot (\theta_{\text{a}:c} + n_{\text{type}_c}))$	$\|x\|$	$\|x\| \cdot n_{\text{X}:\,c,A}$

where $k = \lceil \|x\| \cdot n_{(t_1,\ldots,t_n)} / n_{\text{mem}} \rceil$, $q = \min(\lceil n_{\text{mem}} / n_{(t_1,\ldots,t_n)} \rceil, n_{\text{files}})$, n is the number of positions in the input stream, and $X_c = \{(c', A) \mid (c', A) \in X \wedge c \trianglelefteq c'\}$.

Table 3. Application dependent cost parameters

parameter	description	relevant for
N_c:	number of objects in the extension of class c.	scan, write, delete, access, *space*
$N_{0,c}$:	number of objects in the direct extension of class c.	write, delete, *space*
n_t:	average number of blocks for an object of type t.	activate, write, delete, access, *space*
$n_{(t_1,\ldots,t_n)}$:	average number of blocks for a value list of type $(t_1, \ldots, t_n)$.	duplicate, sort, product, join$_0$
$n_{\text{u}:\,t}$:	average number of elements in a set of type t.	unnest, nest$_0$
$n_{\text{A}:\,c,A}$:	average number of values for attribute A of class c.	write, delete, *space*
$n_{\text{X}:\,c,A}$:	average number of objects of class c per value of attribute A.	access
$n_{\text{q}:\,(t_1,\ldots,t_n)}$:	average number of value accesses necessary to decide whether two value lists of type $(t_1, \ldots, t_n)$ are identical or not.	nest, unique$_0$, union$_0$
n_p:	the number of values that must be accessed to evaluate the predicate p.	select, join$_0$
$\theta_{\text{s}:\,c}$:	average filling level of the object identifier access structure for class c.	scan, *space*
$\theta_{\text{a}:\,c}$:	portion of objects of class c that have been moved from their original second memory location.	activate, access
θ_p:	selectivity of predicate p.	select
$\theta_{\text{d}:\,c}$:	fraction of objects in class c that are only members of c or any subclasses of c.	delete
$\theta_{\text{D}:\,c}$:	correction factor for deletion of objects of class c to model additional costs to delete the given objects from all subclasses of c.	delete
$f_{\text{q}:\,(t_1,\ldots,t_n)}(l)$:	average number of unique elements in a stream of type $(t_1, \ldots, t_n)$ of length l.	unique$_0$

Table 4. System dependent cost parameters

parameter	description	relevant for
n_a:	fraction of a block that is needed for the non-data part of an access structure per element of the stored set.	*space*
n_{OID}:	number of object identifiers that fit into one block.	scan, *space*
n_{mem}:	size of memory that is reserved for sorting and similar operations.	sort, product, $join_0$
n_{files}:	maximum number of open files for sorting.	sort
$\eta(n)$:	number of block accesses required to locate an element using an access structure for a set with n elements.	write, delete, access

3.1 Pivoting

Pivoting is a schema transformation that tries to reduce the redundancy of a schema by effecting that values are stored with the values they functionally depend on. That way, we avoid storing the values multiple times and ease the maintenance of the functional dependency involved.

Pivoting moves attributes from one class to another, new class. A precondition for applying pivoting is that there exists a functional dependency among the attributes of a *basic* class, b, such that one attribute, p, (that is of an object identifier type) functionally determines some other attributes, D. In this case we can pivot the basic class using the attribute on the left-hand side of the functional dependency, p, as the so-called *pivot attribute.* The class of the pivot attribute is called *pivot class.* The attributes on the right-hand side of the functional dependency, D, are called *pivoted attributes* or *dependent attributes.* In the standard case pivoting does the following things:

1. It introduces a new class, p', as a sub-class of the pivot class, p.
2. The new class, p', becomes the class of the pivot attribute, p.
3. The pivoted attributes, D, are moved from the basic class, b, to the new class, p'.

In Fig. 1 we use a UML style presentation to show a generic schema and its pivoted alternative for the functional dependency $p \to D$. We simplified the diagram by assuming that all attributes are of object identifier types and therefore correspond to object classes. Furthermore, though there is only one attribute D and only one attribute A shown, they should be seen as representing a set of attributes. We will concentrate on a standard case, neglecting further options while pivoting or more general situations as presented by Hartmann [9].

3.2 Pivoting the Internal Schema

Since pivoting changes the schema, we must adjust the internal schema accordingly. This is mostly straightforward. Each access structure on one of the pivoted attributes is moved along with the attribute from the basic class to the new class. This may lead to the loss of an 'access path' from the pivoted attributes to the basic class. To avoid this, we add an access structure on the basic class for the pivot attribute if such an access structure is not already there.

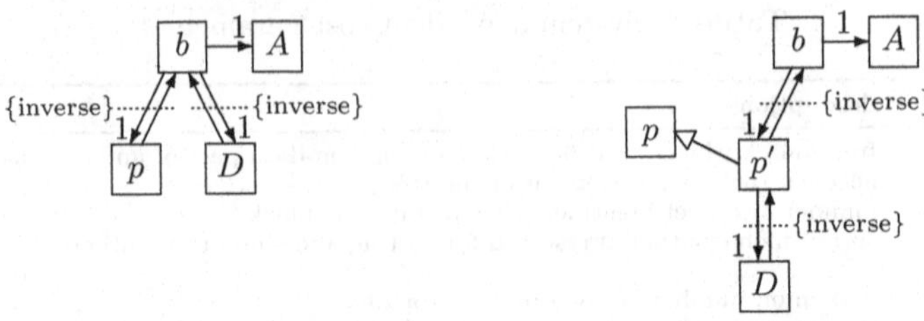

Fig. 1. A pattern for pivoting a schema with the functional dependency $p \to D$ and moving access structure while pivoting

In Fig. 1 the access structures are shown as additional associations. Their role as access structures is signified by the 'inverse' constraints. The figure pictures the case were there is an access structure in the original schema for the pivot attribute and for the pivoted attributes.

4 Cost Analysis of Schema Transformations

The cost model allows us to calculate cost statements for programs of the abstract database machine. How can we use this to estimate the effect of schema transformations on the time requirements of an application? We would like to be able to tell how a transformation might change the execution time of queries or updates that are given in a high-level language. To do this we must bridge the gap between high-level queries and updates on the one side and low-level machine programs on the other side.

In a database management system it is the task of the optimiser to translate statements of a high-level data manipulation language into low-level execution plans. Since we can hardly incorporate the complete design of an optimiser into our analysis, we need to find another way to relate the conceptual and the internal level. First, we make some observations:

1. The total cost statement is a sum of step cost statements. This allows us to use a compositional approach, where we examine the effects of the transformation on single operations or short sequences of operations.
2. As we can see in Table 1 only a few of the available machine operations access the persistent database state. These are the only operations that are affected by a schema transformation. This allows us to divide the machine operations into schema-dependent and schema-independent machine operations.
3. Schema-dependent machine operations and high-level queries and updates work on common aspects given by the schema like classes, types, attributes etc. Additionally, there are only one or two possible machine operations that can access the particular information required for a high-level query or update. Thus, when we identify a machine operation where there is a significant difference between the costs for the original schema and the transformed schema, we can give a meaningful description of characteristics of high-level queries and updates that are affected by the schema transformation.

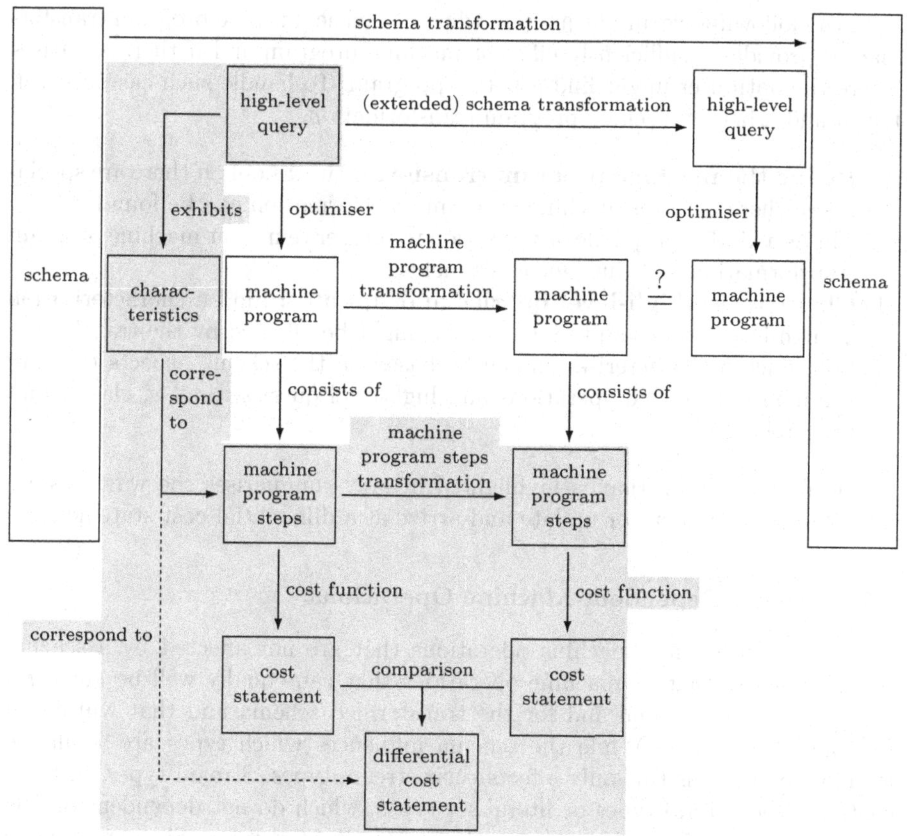

Fig. 2. The transformations and the affected time costs

We can use these observations to approach the cost analysis of schema transformations according to the following plan:

1. **Determine all schema-dependent machine operations:** This complete enumeration serves to cover all possible queries. Note, that most operations are schema-independent.
2. **Define basic machine program transformation:** For each schema-dependent operation, find an equivalent sequence of machine operations for the other schema and evaluate the costs. With that we can provide a machine program transformation that matches our schema transformation.

To keep our investigation manageable, we only look at the effect of the schema transformation on single steps and not on complete programs. This leads to the problem that the optimiser might find a better machine program for the transformed schema than we get by using our machine program transformation on the machine program of the original schema. The upper half of Fig. 2 shows the two paths to arrive at a machine program for the transformed schema.

In the following we aim at judging when our basic machine program transformation provides a sufficiently efficient machine program and if there are cases where the optimiser might find a better program. To handle such cases we will try to find a better machine program transformation.

3. **Refine the machine program transformation:** Look, if there are special cases where a better machine program transformation can be found.
   This is a kind of peep hole optimisation to further refine our machine program transformation and thus our assessment.
4. **Characterise high-level queries and updates:** Find a characterisation of high-level queries and updates that might be affected by the transformation. Such a characterisation can be based on the schema aspects that are common to machine operations and high-level queries, that is, classes and their relations.

The part of Fig. 2 that is highlighted in grey summarises the way to start from a high-level query or update and arrive at a differential cost statement.

4.1 Schema-Dependent Machine Operations

There are quite a few machine operations that are not affected by a schema transformation, that is, machine operations that can equally well be part of a program for the original and for the transformed schema and that will entail the same time costs. While the schema influences which types are available, for most operations this only affects their stream types. Stream types, in turn, contain either literal types or literal set types, which do not dependent on the schema, or object identifier types or object identifier set types. Since we assume that object identifiers have a fixed size, in our analysis of time costs we can disregard operations that are only affected through their stream types by a schema transformation.

Therefore, in our time cost analysis we regard the following machine operations as *schema-independent*: const, duplicate, unnest, nest_O, project, unique_O, select, sort, product, unionall, create, union_O, join_O.

We must pay special attention to the select operation. This operation works using a predicate. The description of the abstract database machine does hardly limit the type of this predicate. It is therefore conceivable that there may be a predicate that tests for schema-dependent properties. For this paper we assume that the predicate of the select operation is schema-independent.

What remains are the five *schema-dependent* operations, which are used to access the persistent database state: scan, activate, write, delete, access.

4.2 Basic Machine Program Transformation

The schema-dependent machine operations are affected by changes to the class hierarchy, extensions, types, and access structures (cf. Table 2). Figure 3 shows which of these schema elements are changed by pivoting by marking them grey.

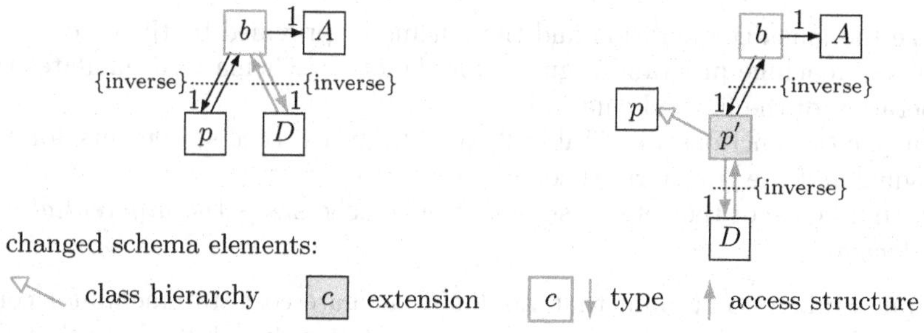

Fig. 3. Highlighting the differences caused by pivoting

Table 5. Cases to investigate

class	operation			
	scan	activate	write	delete
b	—	o⇄t	o⇄t	o⇄t
p	—	—	—	o⇄t
D	—	—	—	—
A	—	—	—	—
p'	o←t	o←t	o←t	o←t

class	attribute	operation
		access
b	p	o→t
b	D	o→t
b	A	o⇄t
b	p'	o←t
p'	D	o←t

scan: For scan changes to extensions are relevant. The only interesting case is the scan of the new class p' in the transformed schema.

activate: For activate changes to types are relevant. There are two classes for which the types differ between the schemas. These are the class b in both schemas and p' in the transformed schema.

write: For write changes to types and extensions and changed access structures for a class or any of its super-classes are relevant.

delete: For delete changes to types and extensions and changed access structures for a class or any of its super-classes as well as changes to a class's sub-classes are relevant.

access: For access changes to types and access structures are relevant. Pivoting the internal schema moves the access structures for the pivoted classes, $d \in D$, from the basic class, b, to the new class, p'.

Table 5 gives an overview of the interesting cases, which we are going to investigate. The entries in the table indicate whether the cases must be respected when moving from the original schema to the transformed schema, o→t, from the transformed schema to the original schema, o←t, or in both directions, o⇄t.

How to Create the Basic Cost Tables: We can now construct what we call *cost tables.* These cost tables contain the information about how to perform the machine program steps transformation and the corresponding differential cost statements. For each case we get a table through the following procedure:

- Take the machine operation and the schema as provided by the case.
- Write a machine program fragment for the other schema that emulates the operation of the first schema.
- Apply cost functions (see Table 2) and calculate cost statements for the original and the transformed schema.
- The difference of the total costs for the two schemas is the *differential cost statement.*

We must take into account that we don't calculate cost statements for complete machine programs but for program fragments only. This effects that the resultant differential cost statements do not only depend on the cost parameters belonging to the relevant schema but also on the properties of the input stream for the fragment. The essential property of an input stream is its size, that is, the number of value lists in the stream. When we associate high-level characteristics to these low-level cost statements, we can see that a value list on the low level corresponds to an object (in an extension) or a relationship between an object and its attribute value on the high level. Due to the space restrictions we cannot provide the cost tables for all cases and only give two examples in Appendix A.

Summary of the basic cost tables: As shown in Table 5 there are seven cases for the transformation from the original schema to the pivoted schema. Out of these seven the case of write of b has the biggest increase in costs, because its emulation requires two write, one duplicate and one sort operation. For the other six cases there are only slight changes to the costs. The costs for activate of b and access of b from D increase, while the costs for delete from b or p and access of b from p or A decrease. Depending on the cost parameters involved, the difference could even become negligible.

For the transformation from the pivoted schema to the original schema there are eleven cases given in Table 5. As there is no class p' in the original schema the five cases for operations on this class require a complex emulation with consequentially increased costs. Only the transformation of the delete operation is simpler, but it still entails slightly increased costs. The costs for the five cases of operation on class b increase mostly due to the bigger size of b objects in the original schema. For the case of write of b there is a further cost increase, because its emulation requires an additional activation to access the required values of the moved D attributes. The costs for delete from p increase slightly.

4.3 Refined Machine Program Transformation

There are cases where a given machine operation does more than necessary to implement a high-level statement. Then, part of the transformation given in the basic machine program transformation might be unnecessary. In essence, this happens for the operations activate and write. These operations access the complete type, even if only some of the attributes are accessed by the high-level query or update. Here we can define special sub-cases for the appropriate cases from Table 5 by adding pre- or postconditions. In Appendix B you can find an example of a cost table for the refined machine transformation.

Table 6. Accessing the Entity and Relationship Sets

Reading Entity Sets:	1. scan: to read the complete extension of a class.
	2. activate/access: to read a subset of an extension, that is restricted through a relationship.
Reading Relationship Sets:	1. activate: to read the attribute values for given objects.
	2. access: to read the objects for given attribute values.
Writing Entity Sets:	1. write: to add objects to an extension.
	2. delete: to remove objects from an extension.
Writing Relationship Sets:	1. write: to add a relationship.
	2. write: to change a relationship.
	3. write: to remove a relationship.

Cases where we can refine the machine program transformation: The transformation from the original schema to the pivoted schema for the activation of b can be simplified when the D attributes are not needed. A cost table for this special case shows that the costs decrease with the transformation. For write on b we can add two special cases. The first one when no D attribute is accessed, and the second one when only D attributes are accessed. For the first case we now get a decrease in costs, while in the second case we have a smaller increase in costs than for the basic transformation. Similarly, for the transformation from the pivoted schema to the original schema we can refine the case of write on p'. When no D attributes are accessed the costs increase only slightly, while when only D attributes are accessed, there is still a non-negligible increase in costs that yet improves on the basic transformation.

4.4 Characterisation of High-Level Queries

Envision a declarative high-level query and manipulation language in the style of an object domain calculus that uses the following features to query a database instance:

- Entity Sets: Variables are used to access class extensions.
- Relationship Sets: Object/attribute relationships can be used to restrict variables.

We employ these two features to set high-level queries in relation with our machine program operations.

In a concrete database management system an optimiser translates high-level queries and updates into low-level execution plans. Similarly, our abstract database machine uses machine programs to implement high-level queries and updates. In general we can not predict the complete resulting machine programs without knowing the workings of an optimiser. But for the task of reading and writing the instance information that represents entity and relationship sets, we can find crucial operations that must be part of an eligible machine program. The relevant cases are shown in Table 6.

Analysing these cases, we can find characteristics of high-level queries and updates that enable us to predict operations that must be part of a corresponding machine program:

[Unrestricted Scan of c**]** Reading the extension of a class c not restricted through any relationships: scan of class c.

[Relational Read for $c \to a$**]** Reading the extension of a class c restricted by a relationship $c \to a$: either activate of objects of class c or (if the appropriate access structure exists) access of class c from attribute a.

[Insert into c**]** Adding objects to the extension of a class c: write of class c.

[Delete from c**]** Removing objects from the extension of a class c: delete from class c.

[Update of $c \to a$**]** Modifying a relationship $c \to a$: write of class c.

See Appendix C for an example high-level query and its characteristics.

5 Conclusion

The execution of queries and updates can take different amounts of time for a schema and its transformed alternative. We presented a method to find out characteristics of high-level queries and updates for which schema transformations change the time required for the execution of these operations. This method employs the cost model for an abstract object-oriented database machine that we introduced in an earlier work.

In particular we determined the quantitative effects of pivoting on the execution time. The basic effects of pivoting on query execution time were already addressed in a qualitative manner in earlier publications. This contribution expands on the earlier publications by providing quantitative results in the form of differential cost statements. This is an essential step on the way to an interactive design tool that helps to find database schemas that meet specific time requirements for given use cases.

During the application of our cost model for conceptual schema design as described in this paper we encountered some cost statements whose validity could be questioned. These statements indicate points where our cost model could be refined. One point shows in Table 7: For the pivoted schema the costs of the second activate statement disregard any possible caching effects arising when the same object is activated more than once. Another point shows for some more complex emulations. Here we could sometimes reduce the costs if slight variations of the current operations were available. For example, we wouldn't need to use a duplicate operation for the emulation of write of b, as mentioned in Sect. 4.2, if the available write operation passed its input through as output instead of throwing it away.

Accordingly, there remain possibilities for future research and development: The experiences gained could be exploited to improve our existing abstract database machine and the corresponding cost model. In particular, we devise to build an experimental design tool to validate the method of this contribution and the underlying cost model. In this context we plan an empirical evaluation based on the Oracle database management system. It is a nice fiction to dream of one day finding the functionality suggested in this paper in future versions of tools like Oracle JDeveloper or Sybase PowerDesigner®.

References

1. J. Biskup and R. Menzel. An abstract database machine for cost driven design of object-oriented database schemas. In *Adv. in Databases and Inf. Syst., Fifth East European Conference, ADBIS 2001*, number 2151 in LNCS, pages 366–380, Vilnius, Lithuania, Sept. 25–28, 2001. Springer.
2. J. Biskup and R. Menzel. A flexible cost model for abstract object-oriented database schemas. In *ER 2002, Proc. 21th Int. Conf. on Conceptual Modeling*, number 2503 in LNCS, pages 444–462, Tampere, Finland, Oct. 7–11, 2002. Springer.
3. J. Biskup, R. Menzel, T. Polle, and Y. Sagiv. A case study on object-oriented database schema design. In *Int. Baltic Workshop on Databases and Inf. Syst.*, Tallinn, Estonia, 1996.
4. J. Biskup, R. Menzel, T. Polle, and Y. Sagiv. Decomposition of relationships through pivoting. In Thalheim [19], pages 28–41.
5. J. Biskup and T. Polle. Decomposition of object-oriented database schemas. *Annals of Mathematics and Artificial Intelligence*, 33:119–155, 2001.
6. J. Biskup, Y. Sagiv, R. Menzel, and T. Polle. A case study on object-oriented database schema design. TR 27/95, Univ. Hildesheim, Inst. f. Informatik, 1995.
7. R. G. G. Cattell and D. K. Barry, editors. *The Object Data Standard: ODMG 3.0.* Morgan Kaufmann, San Francisco, CA, 2000.
8. A. Gupta and J. Widom. Local verification of global integrity constraints in distributed databases. In *Proc. 1993 ACM SIGMOD Conf.*, pages 49–58, 1993.
9. S. Hartmann. Decomposing relationship types by pivoting and schema equivalence. *Data & Knowledge Eng.*, 39(1):75–99, 2001.
10. H. V. Jagadish and X. Qian. Integrity maintenance in an object-oriented database. In *Proc. 18th Int. Conf. on VLDB*, pages 469–480, Vancouver, Canada, 1992.
11. M. Kifer, G. Lausen, and J. Wu. Logical foundations of object-oriented and frame-based languages. *J. ACM*, 42(4):741–843, 1995.
12. U. Lipeck. Transformation of dynamic integrity constraints into transaction specifications. *Theoretical Comput. Sci.*, 76:115–142, 1990.
13. W. W. McCune and L. J. Henschen. Maintaining state constraints in relational databases: A proof theoretic basis. *J. ACM*, 36(1):46–68, 1989.
14. J.-M. Nicolas. Logic for improving integrity checking in relational databases. *Acta Inf.*, 18(3):227–253, 1982.
15. B. A. Nixon. Representing and using performance requirements during the development of information systems. In *Adv. in Database Technology – EDBT '94*, number 779 in LNCS, pages 187–200. Springer, 1994.
16. B. A. Nixon. Management of performance requirements for information systems. *IEEE Trans. Softw. Eng.*, 26(12):1122–1146, Dec. 2000.
17. M. Steeg. The conceptual database design optimizer CoDO – Concepts, implementation, application. In Thalheim [19], pages 105–120.
18. M. Steeg and B. Thalheim. A computational approach to conceptual database optimization. Technical report, BTU Cottbus, May 1995.
19. B. Thalheim, editor. *Proc. 15th Int. Conf. on Conceptual Modeling*, number 1157 in LNCS, Cottbus, Germany, Oct. 7–10, 1996. Springer.
20. P. van Bommel. Experiences with EDO: An evolutionary database optimizer. *Data & Knowledge Eng.*, 13(1994):243–263, 1994.
21. P. van Bommel and T. P. van der Weide. Reducing the search space for conceptual schema transformation. *Data & Knowledge Eng.*, 8(1992):269–292, 1992.
22. S. B. Yao. Optimization of query evaluation algorithms. *ACM Trans. Database Syst.*, 4(2):133–155, June 1979.

A Basic Machine Program Transformation for Activate of b

In this section we show example cost tables constructed as described in Sect. 4.2 using the cost functions from Table 2 on page 532. As cost parameters change through pivoting, we use a tilde to mark cost parameters of the pivoted schema that might have a different value than for the original schema. Furthermore, we need additional parameters for class p'.

Table 7 is the cost table for activate of b for the transformation from the original schema to the pivoted schema. Here the main costs are the block accesses. For simplicity, let's assume that no objects have been moved from their secondary memory location, that is, all the parameters of the form $\theta_{\mathrm{a}:\,c}$ (according to Table 3 on page 532, line 11) are zero. Then we have n_b block accesses per value list for the original schema and $\widetilde{n_b} + n_{p'}$ block accesses for the pivoted schema. While pivoting decreases the size of b objects, in the average case p' objects are large than p objects by about the same amount. Thus we can infer that the emulating program fragment is slightly more costly than the activate operation on the original schema.

Table 7. $\langle \mathrm{act}\, b\rangle^{\mathrm{o}\to\mathrm{t}}$: Transformation for activate of b on the original schema

original schema

program fragment	block accesses/ $\lVert x_{\mathrm{O}} \rVert$	value accesses/ $\lVert x_{\mathrm{O}} \rVert$	stream length/ $\lVert x_{\mathrm{O}} \rVert$
$x_{\mathrm{f}} :=$ activate$(x_{\mathrm{O}}, \mathrm{pos}_b)$	$\theta_{\mathrm{a}:\,b} + n_b$	1	1

pivoted schema

program fragment	block accesses/ $\lVert x_{\mathrm{O}} \rVert$	value accesses/ $\lVert x_{\mathrm{O}} \rVert$	stream length/ $\lVert x_{\mathrm{O}} \rVert$
$x_1 :=$ activate$(x_{\mathrm{O}}, \mathrm{pos}_d)$	$\widetilde{\theta_{\mathrm{a}:\,b}} + \widetilde{n_b}$	1	1
$x_2 :=$ activate$(x_{\mathrm{O}}, \mathrm{pos}_p)$	$\theta_{\mathrm{a}:\,p'} + n_{p'}$	1	1
$x_{\mathrm{f}} :=$ project$(x_2, \ldots)$	0	0	1

Table 8. $\langle \mathrm{act}\, b\rangle^{\mathrm{t}\to\mathrm{o}}$: Transformation for activate of b on the transformed schema

pivoted schema

program fragment	block accesses/ $\lVert x_{\mathrm{O}} \rVert$	value accesses/ $\lVert x_{\mathrm{O}} \rVert$	stream length/ $\lVert x_{\mathrm{O}} \rVert$
$x_{\mathrm{f}} :=$ activate$(x_{\mathrm{O}}, \mathrm{pos}_b)$	$\widetilde{\theta_{\mathrm{a}:\,b}} + \widetilde{n_b}$	1	1

original schema

program fragment	block accesses/ $\lVert x_{\mathrm{O}} \rVert$	value accesses/ $\lVert x_{\mathrm{O}} \rVert$	stream length/ $\lVert x_{\mathrm{O}} \rVert$
$x_1 :=$ activate$(x_{\mathrm{O}}, \mathrm{pos}_b)$	$\theta_{\mathrm{a}:\,b} + n_b$	1	1
$x_{\mathrm{f}} :=$ project$(x_1, \ldots)$	0	0	1

Table 8 shows the respective transformation for the opposite direction. Using the same assumptions as above, we see that the operation on the pivoted schema is cheaper, because of the smaller size of the b objects.

B Refined Machine Program Transformation from the Original to the Pivoted Schema for Activate of b

Table 9 shows the special case of activate of b where no D attribute is used in the subsequent program. In the cost table we show this constraint by a pseudo project statement. Using the assumptions from Appendix A we can see that the costs decrease with the size of the b objects.

Table 9. $\langle \text{act}\, b \rangle^{\text{o}\rightarrow\text{t}}_{\neg D}$: Transformation for activate of b on the original schema with no attribute out of D getting used

original schema

program fragment	block accesses/ $\lVert x_0 \rVert$	value accesses/ $\lVert x_0 \rVert$	stream length/ $\lVert x_0 \rVert$
$x_1 :=$ activate(x_0, pos_b)	$\theta_{\text{a}:\,b} + n_b$	1	1
$x_f :=$ project(x_1, L)	0	0	1

where no $d \in D$ appears in L.

pivoted schema

program fragment	block accesses/ $\lVert x_0 \rVert$	value accesses/ $\lVert x_0 \rVert$	stream length/ $\lVert x_0 \rVert$
$x_1 :=$ activate(x_0, pos_d)	$\widetilde{\theta_{\text{a}:\,b}} + \widetilde{n_b}$	1	1
$x_f :=$ project(x_1, L)	0	0	1

C Example Characterisation

Regard the following example OQL query (a_p is some attribute of p):

```
select p.a_p
from b in class_b, p in class_p
where b.attr_p = p
```

The example exhibits relational read characteristics for $b \rightarrow p$ and $p \rightarrow a\_p$. Of these only the relational read for $b \rightarrow p$ is affected by pivoting. The corresponding differential cost statements are those for activate of b and access from p to b. For activate of b we have the special case where we don't access any D attributes. For both cases pivoting promises a decrease of costs. (Table 9 provides the differential cost statement for this special case of activate of b.)

Experimental Research on Conceptual Modeling: What Should We Be Doing and Why?

Geert Poels[1], Andrew Burton-Jones[2], Andrew Gemino[3], Jeffrey Parsons[4], and V. Ramesh[5]

[1] Faculty of Economics and Business Administration, Ghent University, Gent, Belgium
[2] Sauder School of Business, University of British Columbia, Vancouver, Canada
[3] Faculty of Business Administration, Simon Fraser University, Burnaby, BC, Canada.
[4] Faculty of Business Administration, Memorial University of Newfoundland, St. John's, NL, Canada
[5] Kelley School of Business, Indiana University, Bloomington, IN, USA

Geert.Poels@ugent.be, Andrew.Burton-Jones@sauder.ubc.ca, gemino@sfu.ca, jeffreyp@mun.ca, venkat@indiana.edu

Abstract. This panel considers a number of contentious issues in the conduct of experimental research on conceptual modeling. The panelists will present a range of perspectives on the issues to encourage audience input and discussion.

1 Panel Summary

Recently, there has been a growing interest in experimental research on conceptual modeling. A key objective of such research is to demonstrate the influence of one or more independent variables (such as modeling grammar, modeling process, domain familiarity) on one or more dependent variables (such as comprehension, understanding, recall, perceived difficulty, confidence). However, there is considerable uncertainty and some disagreement about the theoretical underpinnings of conceptual modeling techniques, the appropriateness or usefulness of certain independent and dependent variables, and the balance between rigor and relevance of such research. Recently, several papers have examined some of these questions explicitly (e.g., [3][5]), while a range of other research has examined aspects of evaluating conceptual modeling techniques (e.g., [1][2][4]).

This panel will present a range of opposing perspectives on important issues regarding theoretical foundations, choosing independent and dependent variables, and the balance between rigor and relevance, from researchers who have conducted experiments in this area and struggled over some of the issues involved. The main issues for debate in the panel include:

- What are the purposes of a conceptual model, and should these purposes influence the design of empirical studies?
- Is theory necessary or useful in the design of experimental studies?

D.W. Embley, A. Olivé, and S. Ram (Eds.): ER 2006, LNCS 4215, pp. 544–547, 2006.

- What measurements are most appropriate in evaluating conceptual modeling techniques?
- Is experimental research relevant to the practice of conceptual modeling?
- What can experimental research on conceptual modeling teach us that other research approaches can't?
- Is experimental research a necessary component in the process of developing new or improved conceptual modeling constructs, models, methods or implementations?

2 Position Statements

2.1 Andrew Burton-Jones

In the ideal research cycle, knowledge of practice informs theoretical and empirical work, which informs observations of and perhaps even change in practice, and the cycle continues. Over the last 20 years, conceptual modeling researchers have undertaken a great deal of theoretical work and have carried out experiments to test these theories. Although more of this work is needed, we sorely need to improve our understanding of and impact on practice. At present, our theories and empirical tests have a tenuous relationship with conceptual modeling practice. For example, a key reason for using conceptual models in practice is to help analysts and users to reach a shared understanding of a domain, but no experimental studies to my knowledge have ever examined this issue. Likewise, several case studies show that social factors influence how conceptual models are used in practice. However, most theories and experimental tests of conceptual modeling "assume away" such factors. I will discuss recent exemplar studies that show how researchers can improve experimental research on conceptual modeling through insights from practice.

2.2 Andrew Gemino

If the objective of comparing alternative conceptual modeling techniques is to find which modeling technique performs better, then empirical tests and comparative results fulfill this objective. This phenomenon-based approach to comparison is based on inductive principles. While this may be one of the objectives of evaluating alternatives, I will argue that relative performance should not be the ultimate objective. Instead, the objective should be to understand why these performance differences occur. To explain "why" requires theory that enables us to reason deductively. I will suggest that we evaluate techniques in order to test theories of how characteristics of modeling techniques affect the eventual understanding of individuals viewing or creating models. A focus on theory rather than phenomena will improve our area's ability to design and refine effective conceptual modeling techniques.

2.3 Jeffrey Parsons

Conceptual modeling grammars and processes should be evaluated in ways that deem their 'fitness for purpose.' In other words, when evaluating grammars and/or processes, we should focus on tasks and measures that are relevant to how they are used in practice. I will argue that the primary purpose of conceptual modeling techniques is to represent domain semantics in order to promote a shared understanding of domain semantics among clients, analysts, and systems developers, and that other uses are built on this purpose. Furthermore, our knowledge of the capacity of modeling grammars to express domain semantics remains primitive. I will argue for the need for more basic studies focusing on representation fidelity as a prerequisite for studies that examine other purposes of conceptual modeling, such as integrating semantics expressed in a conceptual schema with existing knowledge.

2.4 V. Ramesh

Experimental research on data modeling has been a topic of interest for at least 15 years. This area has gone through a transformation over the past few years with an increasing emphasis on academic rigor and theory as evidenced by publications in top IS journals (e.g., [1][2][4]). However, this has also resulted in research that is very deep and narrow. In this panel, I will highlight some of the key areas that are still ripe for the plucking and that might allow us to broaden the focus of our research questions. These include:

Examining the impact of multiple conceptual models: Experimental research has typically examined performance on various tasks using a single conceptual model and compared it with another model. However, in practice a single model is unlikely to be used in isolation for communicating with various stakeholders. I will present some thoughts how to bridge this gap between theory and practice.

Understanding the fit between the intended target of the conceptual model and its inherent characteristics: Conceptual models have been designed and used with a one-size fits all mentality, i.e., the same model and its constructs are used irrespective of whether they are intended to be a tool for communication between users-analysts, analysts-designers or any other stakeholder combination. I will present some arguments for why there is a need to better understand the needs of each dyad and how cognitive principles can be used to guide the design and/or use of conceptual models in each situation.

Role of application domain knowledge: [4] and [5] describe two of very few attempts at examining the role that application domain knowledge plays in conceptual schema comprehension. I will present some fertile areas for future study in this area.

References

1. Bodart, F., Sim, M., Patel, A., Weber, R.: Should Optional Properties be Used in Conceptual Modeling? A Theory and Three Empirical Tests. Information Systems Research. 12(4) (2001) 384-405
2. Burton-Jones, A. and Meso, P.: Conceptualizing Systems for Understanding: An Empirical Test of Decomposition Principles in Object-Oriented Analysis. Information Systems Research, 17(1) (2006), 38-60.

3. Gemino, A., Wand, Y.: A Framework for Empirical Evaluation of Conceptual Modeling Techniques. Requirements Engineering. 9 (2004) 248-260
4. Khatri, V., Vessey, I., Ramesh, V., Clay, P., Park, S.-J.: Understanding Conceptual Schemas: Exploring the Role of Application and IS Domain Knowledge. Information Systems Research. 17(1) (2006) 81-99
5. Parsons, J., Cole, L. What Do the Pictures Mean? Guidelines for Experimental Evaluation of Representational Fidelity in Diagrammatical Conceptual Modeling Techniques. Data and Knowledge Engineering. 55(3) (2005) 327-342

Eliciting Data Semantics Via Top-Down and Bottom-Up Approaches: Challenges and Opportunities

Lois Delcambre, Vijay Khatri, Yair Wand, Barbara Williams, Carson Woo, and Mark Zozulia

Portland State University, USA; Indiana University, USA
University of British Columbia, Canada; Hill-Rom Company, USA
University of British Columbia, Canada; Deloitte Consulting, USA
lmd@cs.pdx.edu, vkhatri@indiana.edu, yair.wand@ubc.ca, Barb_Williams@Hill-Rom.Com, carson.woo@ubc.ca, mzozulia@deloitte.com

1 Introduction

Data semantics can be defined as the meaning and use of data [2]. In the context of databases, data semantics refers to the set of mappings from a representation language to agreed-upon concepts in the real world [1]. Eliciting and capturing data semantics can enable better management of the enterprise data. Additionally, elicitation of data semantics can enhance understanding of applications and result in reduced maintenance and testing costs along with improved administration of applications. "Bad" data, or data whose semantics are not known or are not clear, is considered a major cause of failures such as "botched marketing campaigns, failed CRM[1] and data warehouse projects, angry customers, and lunkhead decisions" [3]. To investigate the practical challenges and to propose future research opportunities, this discussion panel, moderated by Vijay Khatri and Carson Woo, will present: 1) views from Management Information Systems (MIS) and Computer Science (CS) research as well as 2) methods, tools and approaches employed in practice.

The current regulatory and competitive environment necessitates organizations to understand and leverage their enterprise-wide data assets. Two main approaches to understand the meaning of data assets can be differentiated as: 1) *top-down* and 2) *bottom-up*. The top-down approach seeks theoretical guidance, via an ontology, to help articulate *explicit* data semantics. In contrast, bottom-up approaches help articulate *implicit* data semantics, for example, those based on data source and context, which can help explain the meaning of data. While both approaches have merit for practitioners who seek to manage data quality while developing enterprise-wide data models, each has inherent drawbacks. The four panelists from MIS, CS and industry will present three distinct perspectives. In the context of business intelligence (BI), the industry panelists, Barbara Williams and Mark Zozulia, will provide background for eliciting data semantics. The panelists from MIS (Yair Wand) and CS (Lois Delcambre) will present the top-down and bottom-up approaches, respectively, and will discuss how one approach can complement/supplement the other. In presenting different perspectives, this panel will explore *how* the two

[1] Customer Relationship Management.

D.W. Embley, A. Olivé, and S. Ram (Eds.): ER 2006, LNCS 4215, pp. 548 – 551, 2006.

approaches can dove-tail with each other, thus, ultimately helping address challenges faced by the industry.

In the following, we describe three aspects that will be included in this panel discussion: 1) background for eliciting data semantics in the context of enterprise-wide modeling and data quality program; and two approaches for eliciting data semantics, that is, 2) top-down and 3) bottom-up.

2 Background

Competitive and regulatory pressures are requiring organizations to take a fresh look at the value of their information assets. These organizations are taking an enterprise-wide, business-focused approach to developing or re-engineering their enterprise data warehouses, data marts and analytical applications. Central to this approach is: 1) enterprise data models referred to as business information models (BIM); and 2) a well-defined data quality program. Mark Zozulia will discuss BIM and how eliciting data semantics via BIM supports source-to-report transparency. Barbara Williams will discuss the importance of a data quality program and how such a program is dependent on data semantics elicitation.

2.1 BIM

Panelist: Mark Zozulia (mzozulia@deloitte.com), Senior Manager, Deloitte Consulting, LLP, Chicago, Illinois, USA.

My position is that BIM provides the bridge between the usage of business information and the storage of data in technical repositories. It establishes a consistent language and definitions within a framework that links metrics to information assets to underlying information sources and business processes. The practical aspects of BIM include increased business understanding, agreement and adoption of technical data models through the use of more simplified contextual and conceptual models. The process followed to develop and validate the model and the artifacts created also supports the implementation of an enterprise information governance and stewardship program.

2.2 Data Quality Program

Panelist: Barbara Williams (Barb_Williams@Hill-Rom.Com), Director of Enterprise Business Intelligence Solutions, Hill-Rom Company, Inc., Batesville, Indiana, USA.

Faced with plethora of data quality issues that result in conflicting answers to basic business questions, inconsistent approach to data management, no mandatory data retirement practice and inability to drive informed and insightful decisions have caused organizations to reassess their enterprise BI solution. The key to BI success is a vision and a roadmap to that vision that enables an enterprise-wide use of data to drive insightful decisions. I will argue that a fundamental part of the enterprise BI solution is the introduction of a data quality program, which enables greater business ownership and accountability for comprehensive, consistent, relevant and timely enterprise BI reporting. This is achieved through the use of a data quality architecture linked with the metadata architecture, business rule integration into ETL mappings, data quality metrics management and a closed loop data quality reports for data stewards.

3 Top-Down Approach

Panelist: Yair Wand (yair.wand@ubc.ca), CANFOR Professor of MIS, Sauder School of Business, University of British Columbia, Canada.

My position is related to the role of ontology in data semantics. Data semantics is viewed as a mapping from representation (data) to concepts in the real world. Hence, the question of what representational concepts can be used to define the meaning of data is germane to the analysis and determination of data semantics. My position is that since ontology (in the philosophical meaning) deals with beliefs of what exists in the world, the use of ontology can provide an important theoretical guidance for analyzing data semantics. However, ontology-based analysis has three potential drawbacks. First, it is unclear how a set of ontological concepts can be determined and agreed upon by a "community." This can be viewed as a "social" issue. Second, even if a set of ontological constructs can be agreed upon, it is not guaranteed they would match the way users of the data perceive application domains. This can be considered a cognitive issue. Third, as ample work about formalized ontologies exists with the intention to make such ontologies software-accessible a danger of confounding meaning issues with processing aspects exists. This can be considered an implementation risk. The use of ontological guidance to data semantics has to address these three issues.

4 Bottom-Up Approach

Panelist: Lois Delcambre (lmd@cs.pdx.edu), Professor, Computer Science, Portland State University, Portland, Oregon, USA.

The value of using a standard or otherwise agreed-upon representation of data semantics is undisputed, regardless of whether the representation is considered to be a standard schema, XML DTD, thesaurus or a classification scheme. If the schema for two or more systems is mapped to the same thesaurus, then we can expect that the corresponding data from the systems have the same meaning or semantics. In this panel, I will consider other issues beyond this type of mapping. First, I will discuss the problem of implicit semantics of a data source. Sometimes, part of the semantics of particular data is implied (solely) by its membership in a data source. For example, one dataset might be limited to students in the honors program in the College of Engineering and another dataset might consist of students from the College who, at some point in the past four years, were placed on academic probation. Such information, that is often implicit, is also part of the semantics of the data. Second, I will discuss the importance of retaining links to the original source data. Seeing information in its original context can provide important documentation of the original semantics of the data. In one of our current research projects that seeks to integrate clinical endoscopy reports, for example, the analysts attempting to analyze trends in the data want to see the text of the question or label on the original user interface in order to understand the meaning of the data. In another of our research projects, in collaboration with David Maier, we are developing generic mechanisms to support *superimposed information* that allow one to easily connect information used in a new application, to support some new perhaps unanticipated purpose, to the underlying, original information in context.

References

[1] Sheth, A. (1995). *Data semantics: What, where and how?* Paper presented at the 6th IFIP Working Conference on Data Semantics (DS-6), Atlanta, Georgia.

[2] Woods, W. A. (1975). What's in a link: Foundations for semantic networks. In D. G. Bobrow & A. Collins (Eds.), *Representation and understanding: Studies in cognitive science* (pp. 35-82). New York: Academic Press.

[3] Whiting, R. (2006). Aawww, rubbish, *Information Week*, pp. 37-44, May 8.

The ADO.NET Entity Framework: Making the Conceptual Level Real

José A. Blakeley, S. Muralidhar, and Anil Nori

Microsoft Corporation, One Microsoft Way, Redmond, WA 98052-6399, USA
{joseb, smurali, anilnori}@microsoft.com

Abstract. This paper describes the ADO.NET Entity Framework, a platform for programming against data that raises the level of abstraction from the logical (relational) level to the conceptual (entity) level, and thereby significantly reduces the impedance mismatch for applications and data services such as reporting, analysis, and replication. The conceptual data model is made real by a runtime that implements an extended relational model (the Entity Data Model aka the EDM), that embraces entities and relationships as first class concepts; a query language for the EDM; a comprehensive mapping engine that translates from the conceptual to the logical (relational) level, and a set of model-driven tools that help create entity-object, object-xml, and entity-xml transformers.

1 Introduction

Modern applications require data management services in all tiers. They need to handle increasingly richer forms of data which includes not only structured business data (customers, orders) but also XML, email, calendar, files, and documents. These applications need to integrate data residing in multiple data sources and enable end-to-end business insight by collecting, cleaning, storing, and preparing business data in forms suitable for an agile decision making process. Developers of these applications need data access, programming and development tools to increase their productivity.

This paper describes the ADO.NET Entity Framework, a platform for programming against data that significantly reduces the impedance mismatch for applications and data services such as reporting, analysis, and replication. We argue that modern applications and data services need to target a higher-level conceptual model based on entities and relationships rather than the relational model and that such conceptual model needs to be implemented concretely in a data platform. The Entity Framework makes the conceptual data model concrete by a runtime that implements an extended relational model – the Entity Data Model, or the EDM -, that embraces entities and relationships as first class concepts, a query language for the EDM, a comprehensive mapping engine that translates from the conceptual to the logical (relational) level, and a set of model-driven tools that help create entity-object, object-xml, and entity-xml transformers. The Entity Framework is part of a broader Microsoft Data Access vision supporting a family of *products and services so customers derive value from all data, birth through archival.*

D.W. Embley, A. Olivé, and S. Ram (Eds.): ER 2006, LNCS 4215, pp. 552 – 565, 2006.

Section 2 describes the physical, logical, conceptual and programming levels as well as other terms used throughout the paper. Section 3 describes the evolution of applications and data services and motivates the need for making the conceptual level central to application and data services design. Section 4 introduces the Entity Data Model and the concrete manifestation of this model in the Entity Framework. Section 5 presents a summary and conclusions.

2 Database Modeling Layers

Today's dominant information modeling methodology for producing database designs factors an information model into four main levels: Physical, Logical (Relational), Conceptual, and Programming/Presentation.

The ***physical*** model describes how data is *represented* in physical resources such as memory, wire or disk. The vocabulary of concepts discussed at this layer include record formats, file partitions and groups, heaps, and indexes. The physical model is typically invisible to the application - applications usually target the logical or relational data model described in the next section. Changes to the physical model should not impact application logic, but may impact application performance.

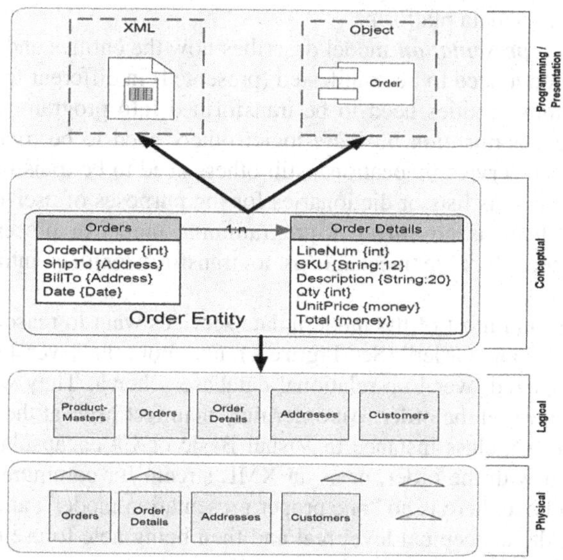

Fig. 1. Physical, logical, conceptual and multiple programming and presentation views of an Order

A ***logical*** data model is a complete and precise information model of the target domain. The relational model is the representation of choice for most logical data models. The concepts discussed at the logical level include tables, rows, and primary key-foreign key constraints, and normalization. While normalization helps to satisfy important application requirements such as data consistency and increased concurrency with respect to updates and OLTP performance, it also introduces significant challenges for applications. (Normalized) Data at the logical level is too fragmented and application logic needs to aggregate rows from multiple tables into higher level entities that more closely resemble the artifacts of the application domain. The conceptual level introduced in the next section is designed to overcome these challenges.

The ***conceptual*** model captures the core information entities from the problem domain and their relationships. A well-known conceptual model is the Entity-Relationship Model introduced by Peter Chen in 1976 [1]. UML is a more recent example of a conceptual model [2].

Most significant applications involve a conceptual design phase early in the application development lifecycle. Unfortunately, however, the conceptual data model is captured inside a database design tool that has little or no connection with the code and the relational schema used to implement the application. The database design diagrams created in the early phases of the application life cycle usually stay "pinned to a wall" growing increasingly disjoint from the reality of the application implementation with time. However, a conceptual data model can be as real, precise, and focused on the concrete "concepts" of the application domain as a logical relational model. A goal of the Microsoft Data Access vision is to make the conceptual data model (embodied by the Entity Data Model, described in Section 4.2) a concrete feature of the data platform.

The ***programming/presentation*** model describes how the entities and relationships of the conceptual model need to be manifested (presented) in different forms based on the task at hand. Some entities need to be transformed into programming language objects to implement application business logic; others need to be transformed into XML streams for web service invocations; still others need to be transformed into in-memory structures such as lists or dictionaries for the purposes of user-interface data binding. Naturally, there is no universal programming model or presentation form; thus applications need flexible mechanisms to transform entities into the various presentation forms.

Most developers, and most of the modern data services want to reason about high-level concepts such as an "Order" (See **Figure 1**), not about the several tables that an order may be normalized over in a relational database schema. They want to query, secure, program, report on the order. An order may manifest itself at the presentation/ programming level as a class instance in Visual Basic or C# encapsulating the state and logic associated with the order, or as an XML stream for communicating with a web service. We believe there is no "one proper presentation model"; and that the real value is in making the conceptual level real and then being able to use that model as the basis for flexible mappings to and from various presentation models and other higher level services.

3 Application and Data Services Evolution

This section describes the platform shift that motivates the need for a higher level data model and data platform. We will look at this through two perspectives: application evolution and SQL Server's evolution as a product. A key point we make in this section is that the need for rich data model is motivated not just for developing application logic but also for supporting building higher-level data services such as reporting and replication.

3.1 Application Evolution

Data-based applications 10-20 years ago were typically structured as data monoliths; closed systems with logic factored by verb-object functions that interacted with a database system at the logical schema (e.g. relational) level. A typical order entry system built around a relational database management system (RDBMS) 20 years ago would have logic partitioned around verb-object functions associated with how users interacted with the system. In fact, the user interaction model via "screens" or "forms" became the primary factoring for logic – there would be a new-order screen, and update-customer screen. The system may have also supported batch updates of SKU's, inventory, etc. The application logic was tightly bound to the logical relational schema.

Much of the data-centric logic (e.g. validation logic) is embedded within the application logic. People typically wrote batch programs to interact directly with the logical schema to perform updates. Programming languages did not support representation of high-level abstractions directly – objects did not exist. These applications can be characterized as being closed systems whose logical data consistency was maintained by application logic implemented at the logical schema level. An order was an order because the new-order logic ensured that it was.

A key reason for custom data-centric logic by applications is the well-known ***application impedance mismatch problem***. The logical schema does not match the level of abstraction of the application. Applications address this problem by developing at the data abstraction (e.g. relational) and by writing custom mapping code to bridge the gap between the application and the data abstractions. This not only leads to duplication of effort but also reduces application development productivity. In the next sections we will show how the Entity Framework and the Language Integrated Query innovations in .NET languages help to minimize this impedance mismatch.

Several significant trends have shaped the way that modern data-based applications are factored and deployed today. Chief among these are object oriented factoring, service level application composition, and higher level data services. When we think about the factoring, composition, and services from above, we can see that the conceptual entities are an important part of today's applications. It is also easy to see how these entities must be mapped to a variety of representations and bound to a variety of services. There is no one correct representation or service binding. XML, Relational and Object representations are all important but no single one will suffice.

Consider a "StockNotifications" application which deals with concepts like Customer Order, Product, and Stock. How do we make them real and use our conceptual understanding of them throughout the system whether they are stored in a multi-dimensional database for analytics, in a durable queue between systems, in a mid-tier cache; a business object, etc. **Figure 2** captures the essence of this issue by focusing on several entities in our order entry system. Note that conceptual level

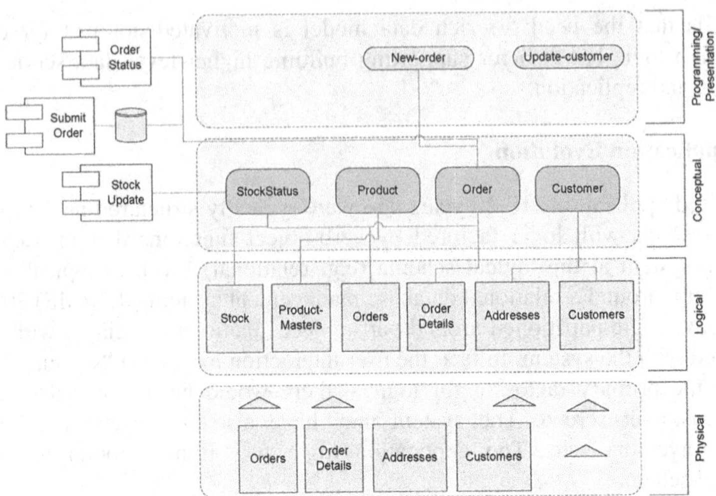

Fig. 2. Order Entry System circa 2005

entities have become real. Also note that the conceptual entities are communicating with and mapping to various logical schema formats, e.g. relational for the persistent storage, messages for the durable message queue on the Submit Order service, and perhaps XML for the Stock Update and Order Status web services.

3.2 SQL Server Evolution

The data services provided by a "data platform" 20 years ago were minimal and focused around the logical schema in an RDBMS. These services included query & update, atomic transactions, and bulk operations such as backup and load/extract.

SQL Server itself is evolving from a traditional RDBMS to a *complete data platform* that provides a number of high value data services over entities realized at the conceptual schema level. While providing services such as reporting, analysis, and data integration in a single product and realizing synergy among them was a conscious business strategy, the means to achieve these services and the resultant ways of describing the entities they operate over happened more organically – many times in response to problems recognized in trying to provide higher level data services over the logical schema level. There are two good examples of the need for concrete entity representation for services now provided within SQL Server: *logical records* for merge replication, and the *semantic model* for report builder.

Early versions of merge **replication** in SQL Server provided for multi-master replication of individual rows. In this early mode, rows can be updated independently by multiple agents; changes can conflict; and various conflict resolution mechanisms are provided with the model. This row-centric service had a fundamental flaw – it did not capture the fact that there is an implicit consistency guarantee around entities as they flow between systems. To address this flaw, the replication service introduced "logical records" as a way to describe and define consistency boundaries across entities comprised of multiple related rows at the logical schema level. "Logical records" are defined in the part of the SQL catalog associated with merge replication. There is no proper design-time tool experience to define a "logical record" such as an Order that includes its Order Details – applications do it through a series of stored procedure invocations.

Report Builder (RB) is another example of SQL Server providing a data service at the conceptual entity level. Since it operates at the logical schema level though, writing reports requires knowing how to compose queries at the logical schema level – e.g. creating an order status report requires knowing how to write the join across the several tables that make up an order. End users and analysts, however, want to write reports directly over Customers, Orders, Sales, etc. Thus, the SQL Server team created a means to describe and map conceptual entities to the logical schema layer we call the Semantic Model Definition Language (SMDL).

These are just two of a number of mapping services provided within SQL Server – the Unified Dimensional Model (UDM) provides a multi-dimensional view abstraction over several logical data models. A Data Source View (DSV), on which the BI tools work, also provides conceptual view mapping technology.

A key observation is that several higher-level data services in the SQL Server product are increasingly delivering their services at the conceptual schema level. Currently, each of these services has a separate tool to describe conceptual entities and map them down to the underlying logical schema level. **Figure 3** illustrates the evolution of SQL Server into a data platform with many high value data services and multiple means to map conceptual entities to their underlying logical schemata.

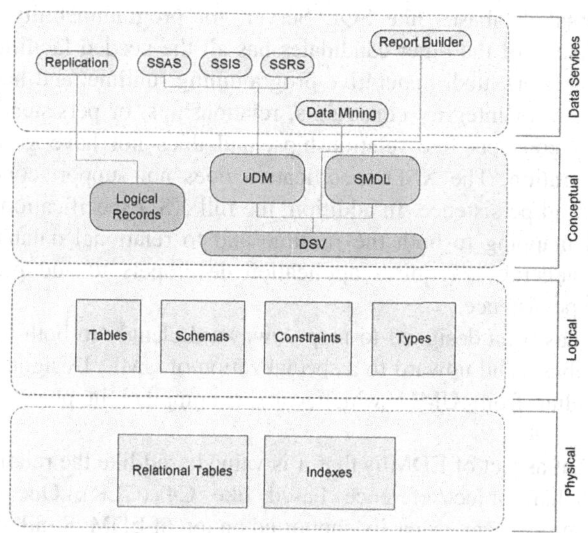

Fig. 3. SQL Server 2005

4 Entity Framework

This section describes the ADO.NET Entity Framework that makes the conceptual level real. We start with the rationale that led us to the development of an Entity Data Model (EDM) followed by an overview of the EDM. We present an architectural description of the entity framework implementing a runtime supporting the EDM, a query language, and mapping. We conclude the section with a description of the development process around the EDM.

4.1 Why a New Model?

The Entity Data Model (EDM) is intended for developing rich data-centric applications. The obvious question that arises is: "why not use (or extend) one of these established data models? There are at least four other modern candidates for such a data model:

- The SQL data model (tables, columns, keys, referential integrity constraints...). SQL99 extends this core model to include object relational features (user defined-, structured-, and distinct-types, methods, typed tables, refs…).
- The CLR data model (classes, fields, methods, properties, value, and Ref types, collections…)
- The XSD model based on XML Infoset (Atomic-, list-, and union-types, primitive- and derived-types, token, ID, IDREF, ENTITY…)
- The UML data model (classes, objects, associations, generalizations, attributes, operations, aggregations…)

The overall reason is that we need something that maps cleanly to both the CLR and to relational databases like SQL Server, for programmability and persistence respectively. None of the other candidates has all the needed facilities for both. The CLR is an object-oriented, imperative-programming runtime, and has no native data model or notions of integrity constraints, relationships, or persistence. SQL99 lacks data modeling concepts like relationships, and does not have good programming language integration. The XSD specification does not support concepts like keys, relationships, and persistence. In addition, the full XSD specification is complex and has awkward mapping to both the runtime and to relational database models. The UML is too general: it requires application developers to add precise semantics, especially for persistence.

The EDM has been designed to map downward cleanly to both the CLR and to a relational database, and upward to a specialization of UML. Designers can work with concepts familiar from UML, which can be compiled in phases to XML, CLR programs, and SQL.

An important aspect of EDM is that it is value based like the relational model (and SQL) rather than object/reference based like C# (CLR). One or more object programming models can be easily supported on top of EDM. Similarly, the EDM can mapped to one or more relational DBMS implementations for persistence.

4.2 EDM Overview

The EDM extends the classic relational model with concepts from E-R modeling. The central concepts in the EDM are entities and relationships. *Entities* represent top-level objects with independent existence and identity, while *Relationships* are used to *relate* (or, describe relationships between) two or more entities.

4.2.1 Types

An ***EntityType*** describes the definition of an entity. An entity typically is a top-level object with independent existence. An entity has a *payload* - zero or more properties that describe the structure of the entity. Additionally, an entity type must define a *key* – a set of properties whose values uniquely identify the entity instance within its container. EntityTypes may derive from (or subtype) other entity types. EDM supports a single inheritance model.

The properties of an entity may be simple or complex types. A ***SimpleType*** (or a PrimitiveType) represents scalar (or atomic) types (e.g. integer, string), while a ***ComplexType*** can be used to represent structured properties (e.g. an Address). A ComplexType is composed of zero or more properties, which may themselves be scalar or complex type properties.

A ***Relationship*** type is a specialized entity type that describes relationships between two (or more) entity types. The EDM supports two kinds of Relationships. ***Containment*** relationships model parent-child relationships (e.g. Order-Line), and are binary relationships, while ***Associations*** model peer-to-peer relationships (Supplier-Part). The key for a relationship type is usually, but not necessarily, the concatenated keys of the entity types participating in the relationship. Relationships – especially many-to-many relationships - may optionally include a payload.

EDM ***Schemas*** provide a grouping mechanism for types – types must be defined in a schema.

In addition to the types above, the EDM supports *transient* types in the form of RowTypes and CollectionTypes. These occur mostly in the context of query operations (e.g., projections, joins). A *RowType* is an anonymous type that is structurally similar to a *ComplexType*. A RowType's structure depends on the sequence of typed and named members that it is comprised of. A rowtype has no identity and cannot be inherited from. Instances of the same row type are equivalent if the corresponding members (in order) are respectively equivalent. Rows have no behavior beyond their structure. A *CollectionType* represents a homogenous collection of objects.

4.2.2 Primitive Types

The EDM is a data model, not a type system. The EDM defines shaping constructs (entity types etc.), but the actual types (and their semantics) are defined by the hosting environment. The EDM does define a set of abstract (or template) primitive types, and a set of associated facets, that enable the abstract primitive types to represent primitive types of the hosting environment (SqlServer databases, the CLR, etc.). These abstract types are proxies for the real primitive types defined by the host, and the semantics of operations over these types are entirely governed by the host.

4.2.3 Instances

Entity instances (or just entities) are logically contained within an ***EntitySet***. An EntitySet is a homogenoous collection of entities (i.e.) all entities in an EntitySet must be of the same (or derived) EntityType. An entity instance must belong to exactly one entity set. In a similar fashion, relationship instances are logically contained within a ***RelationshipSet***. The definition of a RelationshipSet scopes the relationship, that is, it identifies the EntitySets that hold instances of the entity types that participate in the relationship. SimpleTypes and ComplexTypes can only be instantiated as properties of entity instances.

An ***EntityContainer*** is a logical grouping of EntitySets and RelationshipSets – akin to how a Schema is a grouping mechanism for EDM types.

4.2.4 Examples

```
<?xml version="1.0"?>
<Schema Namespace="CNorthwindSchema"
     xmlns="urn:schemas-microsoft-com:windows:storage">
<!—
Typical Entity definition, has identity (via the key) and some members
-->
  <EntityType Name="Product" Key="ProductID">
    <Property Name="ProductID" Type="System.Int32" />
    <Property Name="ProductName" Type="System.String" Size="max" />
    ...
  </EntityType>

<!—
A derived product
-->
  <EntityType Name="DiscontinuedProduct" BaseType="Product">
    <Property Name="DiscReason" Type="System.String" Size="max" />
  </EntityType>

<!—
A complex type defines structure but no identity. It can be used inline
in 0 or more Entity definitions
-->
   <ComplexType Name="CtAddress" >
      <Property Name="Address" Type="System.String" Size="max" />
      <Property Name="City" Type="System.String" Size="max" />
      <Property Name="PostalCode" Type="System.String" Size="max" />
      ...
   </ComplexType>
<!—
A Customer Entity
-->
   <EntityType Name="Customer" Key="CustomerID">
       <!— Address is a member which references a complextype -->
      <Property Name="Address" Type="CNorthwind.CtAddress" />
      <Property Name="CustomerID" Type="System.String" Size="max" />
   </EntityType>
<!—
An example of an association between Product [defined above] and
OrderDetails [not shown for sake of brevity]
-->
  <Association Name="Order_DetailsProducts">
    <End Name="Product" Type="Product" Multiplicity="1" />
    <End Name="Order_Details" Type="OrderDetail" Multiplicity="*" />
  </Association>
</Schema>

<!—
The Entity Container defines the logical encapsulation of
EntitySets (sets of (possibly) polymorphic instances of a type) and
AssociationSets (logical link tables for relating two or more entity instances)
-->
  <EntityContainer Name="CNorthwind">
    <Using Namespace="CNorthwindSchema" />

    <EntitySet Name="Products" EntityType="Product" />
```

```
    <EntitySet Name="Customers" EntityType="Customer" />
    <EntitySet Name="Order_Details" EntityType="OrderDetail" />
    <EntitySet Name="Orders" EntityType="Order" />

    <AssociationSet Name="Order_DetailsProductsSet"
                    Association="Order_DetailsProducts">
      <End Name="Product" EntitySet="Products" />
      <End Name="Order_Details" EntitySet="Order_Details"/>
    </AssociationSet>

  </EntityContainer>
```

4.3 Entity Framework Architecture

This section briefly describes the architecture of the Entity Framework being built as part of ADO.NET. The main functional components of the ADO.NET Entity Framework (see **Figure 4**) are:

Data source-specific providers. The Entity Framework builds on the ADO.NET data provider model. There are specific providers for several relational, non-relational, and Web services sources.

Map provider. The Entity Framework includes a new data provider, the Map provider. This provider houses the services implementing the mapping transformation from conceptual to logical constructs. The Map provider is a value-based, outside-the-store view runtime where data is accessed in terms of EDM entities and relationships and queried/updated using an entity-based SQL language (eSQL). The Map provider includoes the following services:

- **EDpM/eSQL.** The Map provider processes and exposes data in terms of the EDM values. Queries and updates are formulated using eSQL. They are processed through the query and update pipeline engines which incorporate mapping transformations and knowledge about the specific capabilities of the data sources.
- **Mapping.** View mapping, one of the key services of the Map provider, is the subsystem that implements bidirectional (read and write) views that allow applications to manipulate data in terms of entities and relationships rather than rows and tables. The mapping from tables to entities is specified declaratively through a mapping definition language.
- **Store-specific bridge.** The bridge component is a service that supports the query execution capabilities of the query pipeline and coordinates the generation of queries using provider specific syntax.
- **Metadata services.** The metadata service supports all metadata discovery activities of the components running inside the Map provider. All metadata associated with EDM concepts (entities, relationships, entitysets, relationshipsets), store concepts (tables, columns, constraints), and mapping concepts are exposed via metadata interfaces. The metadata services component also serves as a link between the domain modeling tools which support model-driven application design.
- **Transactions.** The Map provider integrates with the transactional capabilities of the underlying stores.
- **API.** The API of the Map provider follows the ADO.NET provider model based on Connection, Command, and DataReader objects. The Map provider accepts

commands in the form of eSQL text or canonical trees and produces DataReader objects as results.

Occasionally Connected Components. The Entity Framework enhances the well established disconnected programming model of the ADO.NET DataSet. In addition to enhancing the programming experiences around the typed and un-typed DataSets, the Entity Framework embraces the EDM to provide rich disconnected experiences around cached collections of entities and entitysets.

Embedded Database. The Entity Framework encompasses the capabilities of a low-memory footprint, embeddable database engine to enrich the services for applications that need rich middle-tier caching and disconnected programming experiences.

Design and Metadata Tools. The Entity Frameowkr integrates with domain designers to enable model-driven application development. The tools include EDM, mapping, and query modelers.

Programming Layers. ADO.NET allows multiple programming layers to be plugged onto the value-based entity data services layer exposed by the Map provider. The object services component is one such programming layer that surfaces CLR objects. There are multiple mechanisms by which a programming layer may interact with the entity framework. One of the important mechanisms is LINQ expression trees.

Services. Rich SQL data services such as reporting, replication, business analysis will be built on top of the Entity Framework.

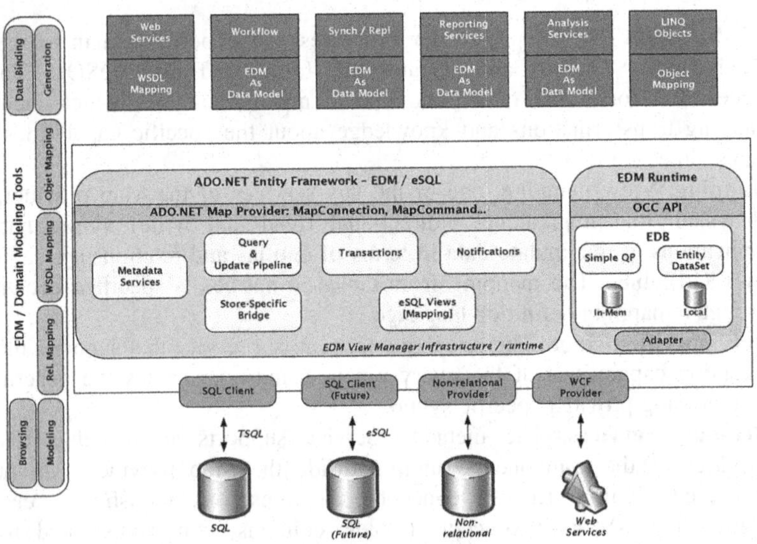

Fig. 4. Entity Framework Architecture

4.4 Making the Conceptual Level Real

This section outlines how one may define a conceptual model and work against it. We use a modified version of the Northwind database for familiarity.

4.4.1 Build the Conceptual Model

The first step is to define one's conceptual model. The EDM allows you to describe the model in terms of entities and relationships. The model may be defined explicitly by hand writing the XML serialized form of the model as shown above. Alternately, a graphical EDM designer tool may be used.

4.4.2 Apply the Mapping

After we define the EDM conceptual model, we identify a target store, and then map the conceptual model to the target store's logical schema model. As with the conceptual EDM, one can hand write an explicit mapping or use a mapping tool. For example, the Northwind store may stripe data across multiple tables (the vertical partitioning strategy); however, applications would want to reason about the data as a single entity without the need for joins or knowledge of the relational model. The mapping layers isolate the application from knowledge of the store's schemas.

4.4.3 Automatically Generated Classes

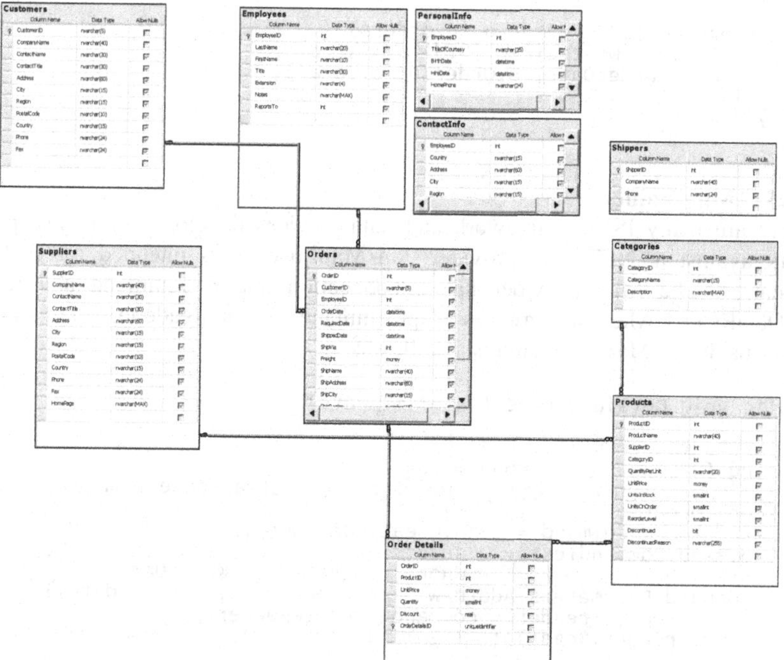

Fig. 5. Entity Data Model for Northwind

Having the conceptual level is indeed sufficient for many applications as it provides a domain model that is live within the context of a comfortable pattern (ADO.NET commands, connections and data readers) and allows for late bound scenarios. Many applications, however, prefer an object programming layer. This can be facilitated through code generation driven from the EDM description. For increased flexibility and data independence between the object and conceptual level, a mapping may be defined between classes and the conceptual model. The mapping between classes and the conceptual model is a straightforward member-wise mapping. This enables applications built against these classes to be reused against other versions of the conceptual model, provided a legal map can be defined.

4.4.4 Using Objects

One can interact with objects and perform regular Create, Read, Update and Delete (CRUD) operations on the objects. The example below demonstrates the use of Language Integrated Query (LINQ) to identify all orders that are newer than a given date

```
class DataAccess
{
  static void GetNewOrders(DateTime date) {
    using (NorthWindDB nw = new NorthWindDB ()) {
      var orders = from o in nw.Orders
               where o.OrderDate > date
               select new { o.orderID, o.OrderDate,
                            Total = o.OrderLines.Sum(
                                    l => l.Quantity);

      foreach (SalesOrder o in orders) {
        Console.WriteLine("{0:d}\t{1}\t{2}",
           o.OrderDate, o.OrderId, o.Total);
      }
    }
  }
```

4.4.5 Using Values

There are many ISVs, framework and data services developers who just prefer to work against a .NET data provider; the MapProvider is intended for such usage scenarios. The Map Provider has a connection and a command and returns a DbDataReader when one invokes MapCommand.ExecuteReader(). An example of a query using the MapCommand is as follows:

```
public void DoValueQueries(DateTime date)
{
  //--- get a connection
  using (MapConnection conn =
             new MapConnectionFactory().GetMapConnection()){
    conn.Open();
    MapCommand command = conn.CreateCommand();
    command.CommandText = @"select value e from Employees as e
                            where e.HireDate > @HireDate";
     command.Parameters.Add(new MapParameter("HireDate",date));
     DbDataReader reader = command.ExecuteReader();
     while(reader.Read()){
        //--- process record
     }
   }
  }
```

5 Summary and Conclusion

Significant application and database technology trends require richer services at the conceptual rather than at the logical schema level. The Entity Framework provides a broad data platform with a rich and concrete conceptual schema to enable new applications and data services. The data platform includes the following components:

1. Entity Framework. A value-based runtime that implements an extended relational model - EDM - that embraces entities and relationships as first class concepts, a query language for the EDM, and a comprehensive mapping engine from the conceptual to the logical (relational) level.
2. Comprehensive programming model. We need programming model innovations that bridge the gap between different data representations (XML, relational, objects). In fact, by developing programming languages and APIs at the conceptual level, we will be able to liberate the programmer from the impedance mismatches that exist among different logical models. Programming language extensions such as Linq [5] provide richer, declarative programming models across different data representations.
3. Data services targeting the conceptual level. Examples include Synchronization/Replication, Reporting, and Security.
4. Design-time tools. Data modeling tools today produce models that are largely abstract. They are used sometimes to produce a logical or physical design for a relational database implementation. We envision design-time tools that are used to: (a) build EDM models, (b) map EDM models to logical (relational) as well as other programming and presentation representations, and (c) semantics tools where you may introduce synonyms, aliases, translation and other semantic adornments for natural language and end user query.

References

1. Chen, P. *The Entity-Relationship Model—toward a unified view of data*, ACM Transactions on Database Systems, Vol. 1, Issue 1, March 1976, pp. 9-36.
2. Unified Modeling Language. http://www.uml.org/.
3. Microsoft. The ADO.Net Entity Framework Overview. http://msdn.microsoft.com/ data/ default.aspx?pull=/library/en-us/dnvs05/html/ADONETEnFrmOvw.asp, June 2006.
4. Blakeley, J.A., Campbell, D., Gray, J., Muralidhar, S., Nori, A.. Next-Generation Data Access: Making the Conceptual Level Real. http://msdn.microsoft.com/data/ default. aspx?pull=/library/ en-us/dnvs05/ html/nxtgenda.asp, June 2006.
5. Microsoft. The Linq Project. http://msdn.microsoft.com/data/ref/linq/default.aspx.

XMeta Repository and Services

Lee Scheffler

IBM Distinguished Engineer
Chief Architect, WebSphere Information Integration Services
IBM Corporation, 50 Washington Street, Westboro, MA 01581, USA
lscheffl@us.ibm.com

Abstract. The XMeta repository is an emerging industrial-strength model and instance persistence, management, access, query, update, upgrade and mapping facility based on EMF modelling technology. It is actively used as the foundation of several commercial metadata intensive products within IBM as well as several research efforts involving conceptual modeling. This talk covers both the features of XMeta and its services, and some of its current uses. It is expected that a version of XMeta will be made more widely available in some external form in the future.

Keywords: EMF, metadata, repository.

Part 1 - XMeta Repository and Services

This part of the talk covers the features and design of the XMeta repository and services, including:

- EMF model development and maintenance
- Repository interfaces (query, access, concrete Java and reflective)
- Object-relational binding
- Model packages and model extension
- Repository services
- Import/export/backup/restore/upgrade
- Dynamic cross-model mapping
- Versioning, concurrency, identity, instance reconciliation
- Analysis services
- Future directions

Part 2 - Uses and Usage Models

This part of the talk surveys several current uses of these repository facilities, including:

- The WebSphere Information Integration Services product family including data profiling, data integration, data quality enhancement, information integration services
- The WebSphere enterprise services directory
- Several IBM current and anticipated research uses
- Usage issues and tradeoffs

D.W. Embley, A. Olivé, and S. Ram (Eds.): ER 2006, LNCS 4215, p. 566, 2006.

IBM Industry Models: Experience, Management and Challenges

Pat G. O'Sullivan and Dan Wolfson

IBM Enterprise Master Data Management Solutions

Abstract. IBM's Industry Models for Banking and Insurance continue to evolve to encompass our accumulated experience with our customers, the changing needs of the industry, and the changing directions in technologies. With over 15 years of use, these models represent a wealth of information about the information models, process models and integration models for these industries. The models are in use today by more than 300 leading Banks and Insurance companies, where they serve in a variety of capacities - from supporting Data Consolidation initiatives and Business Process Re-Design to addressing Risk & Compliance issues such as Anti-Money Laundering, Sarbanes-Oxley, or Basel II.

As successful as these models have been, technical challenges remain. Such challenges include:

- the extension of the models to formally incorporate (and relate) additional dimensions (ontologies, states, KPIs, rules, etc)
- how to establish both inter-model relationships as well as traceability (and per-haps round-tripping) from models to runtime
- how to better identify and reuse common model snippets across domains
- how to facilitate better understanding of complex models
- automating the deployment of run-time artifacts based on models

While the IBM Industry Models represent a significant body of content, the management of this content and more broadly the management of metadata are also key concerns. In this talk, we will review the IBM Industry Models, discuss how this work is evolving, the metadata management roadmap and discuss some of these key ongoing technical challenges to be addressed by both research and development communities.

Keywords: IBM Industry Models, Financial Industry, Metadata Management.

D.W. Embley, A. Olivé, and S. Ram (Eds.): ER 2006, LNCS 4215, p. 567, 2006.

Community Semantics for Ultra-Scale Information Management

Scott Renner

Principal Engineer, Command and Control Center
The MITRE Corporation, 202 Burlington Road, Bedford, MA 01730, USA
sar@mitre.org

Abstract. The U.S. Department of Defense (DoD) presents an instance of an ultra-scale information management problem: thousands of information systems, millions of users, billions of dollars for procurement and operations. Military organizations are often viewed as the ultimate in rigid hierarchical control. In fact, authority over users and developers is widely distributed, and centralized control is quite difficult – or even impossible, as many of the DoD core functions involve an extended enterprise that includes completely independent entities, such as allied military forces, for-profit corporations, and non-governmental organizations. For this reason, information management within the DoD must take place in an environment of limited autonomy, one in which influence and negotiation are as necessary as top-down direction and control.

This presentation examines the DoD's information management problems in the context of its transformation to network-centric warfare The key tenent of NCW holds that "seamless" information sharing leads to increased combat power. We examine several implications of the net-centric transformation and show how each depends upon shared semantic understanding within communities of interest. Opportunities for research and for commercial tool development in the area of conceptual modeling will be apparent as we go along.

D.W. Embley, A. Olivé, and S. Ram (Eds.): ER 2006, LNCS 4215, p. 568 , 2006.

Managing Data in High Throughput Laboratories: An Experience Report from Proteomics*

Thodoros Topaloglou

Information Engineering, Department of Mechanical and Industrial Engineering, University of Toronto, 5 King's College Circle, Toronto, Ontario
thodoros@mie.utoronto.ca

Abstract. Scientific laboratories are rich in data management challenges. This paper describes an end-to-end information management infrastructure for a high throughput proteomics industrial laboratory. A unique feature of the platform is a data and applications integration framework that is employed for the integration of heterogeneous data, applications and processes across the entire laboratory production workflow. We also define a reference architecture for implementing similar solutions organized according to the laboratory data lifecycle phases. Each phase is modeled by a set of workflows integrating programs and databases in sequences of steps and associated communication and data transfers. We discuss the issues associated with each phase, and describe how these issues were approached in the proteomics implementation.

1 Introduction

A key problem in building systems to manage data and processes in biological laboratories is the lack of a reference framework. A reference framework provides a blueprint for the main system components and their functionality, methodologies for modeling, building and testing such systems, and domain specific best practices that include data standards for representation and data exchange that enhance interoperability.

The majority of the relevant work on scientific data focuses on representation of data results (MIAME [1], MAGE-ML [2], MIAPE [3]), infrastructures for data analysis (myGRID [4]), integration of data from public databases (Alladin [5], SRS [6]), and assembling and managing of large community databases (IMG [7], UCSC Browser [78]). Management of experiment designs, protocols, protocol execution and of laboratory data is less systematic and not well integrated with the result datasets. This fragmented and bottom up approach to biological data management is rooted in the organizational separation of data production from data consumption and the fact that laboratory information management systems are tied to specific instrument platforms. It is well documented [9, 10, 11] that the characteristics of samples,

* The proteomics experience section of this paper draws from the following manuscript: An End-to-End Bioinformatics Platform for High Throughput Proteomics. T. Topaloglou, M. Dharsee, M. Li, R.M. Ewing, Y.V. Bukhman, P. Chu, P. Economopoulos, S. Huynh, D. Lee, A. Pasculescu, A.-M. Salter, H. Wang.

D.W. Embley, A. Olivé, and S. Ram (Eds.): ER 2006, LNCS 4215, pp. 569–580, 2006.

experiment designs, and details of experiment execution, such as protocol parameter values, are important in the interpretation or integration of experimental datasets. Recognizing this, industrial and high throughput laboratories opt for an integrated data management strategy that spans the entire data production life cycle; we call it the top-down approach. The goal in top-down is to model and document both the processes and the data starting from the requisition of an experimental study and up to the publishing of analyzed results. It essentially captures the purpose, provenance, and additional technical context metadata that enrich the generated data with additional semantics.

The contributions of this paper are include (a) the description of an implemented, end-to-end information management platform that is deployed in an industrial laboratory, (b) the definition of a reference framework that can guide the development of similar scientific data management solutions, (c) an account of the various types or heterogeneity that is present in scientific data operations, (d) a summary of comprehensive application and data integration strategy that we put together proven to address these heterogeneities, (e) a report on productivity gains that were realized using the system, and (f) experience drawn from this project and a list of ongoing challenges in scientific data management.

2 Proteomics Data Management: Background

2.1 Proteomics 101

The goal of proteomics is to identify and characterize proteins in biological samples [12]. In order to achieve this goal, proteomics combines three main components: laboratory techniques for protein separation from biological samples, advanced instrumentation for proteomics measurements, and computational tools for translating measurements to biologically relevant entities. Currently, the de-facto proteomics measurement platform is mass spectrometry [13]. Its ability to interrogate proteins in complex biological samples makes proteomics a valuable discovery and diagnostics tool for studying disease processes or the effects of drugs in biological systems.

Mass spectrometry based proteomics generates large volumes of complex data. As laboratory techniques and instruments improve, and demand for higher throughput experiments increases, the interpretation and management of proteomics data needs to move to the next level. Before we explain what this means, we will provide a taste of what proteomics data and analysis looks like.

A protein identification experiment starts with a laboratory phase where proteins are separated from samples, using one of many techniques, and then are cleaved into smaller fragments that are called peptides. Intuitively, a protein is a long string of elements, and a peptide is a smaller substring. The peptide mix goes to the mass spectrometer for mass analysis. Peptides are electrically charged and introduced to the instrument in a slow flow. The mass spectrometer measures masses. By analogy, we can think the mass spectrometer as a camera the periodically "takes pictures" of all the peptides in view, sorted by weight – each picture is an MS spectrum. The instrument can also select and zoom in at certain peptides and take a second picture of its ion fragmentation pattern, i.e., its prefix and suffix substrings – this is an MS/MS spectrum. MS/MS spectra can reveal the sequence string of a peptide. MS/MS sequence assignment is assisted by programs called search engines. A search engine takes as input a protein sequence database and MS/MS spectra, and produces as an output sequence assignments. The search engine performs two operations: first, it calculates theoretical spectra for the peptide substrings derived from the sequences in the database, and second, it matches the MSMS spectra to the computed ones thus producing sequence assignments. At a next step, the mapping of peptides to protein sequences reveals the identity of the proteins present in the sample.

There are several ambiguities with respect to data meaning in the above described process. First, the result of peptide assignment depends on the search engine used, and there are many of them, and the input database including its size. Capture of experimental provenance [13] is essential in order to be able to trust, repeat, or verify the peptide sequence assignments. The same holds for all upstream processing steps. Second, the different vendor instruments produce proprietary output formats and measurements in non-matching scales. This introduces heterogeneity that is both syntactic (the format) and semantic (the measurements). Third, the search engines produce outputs that are also syntactically and semantically heterogeneous. Although there are ongoing effort to define proteomic data standards (PSI [3], mzXML [15]), these issues have to be dealt with by rigorous data and provenance modeling until agreement on, and compliance with, the standards is achieved.

Another important point is that of data volume. A typical proteomics study results in hundreds of acquisitions (experiments). An acquisition of a complex biological sample using a high resolution instrument produces tens of megabytes of binary data containing thousands mass spectra. Mass spectra and other associated experimental information are saved in electronic storage including relational databases. Each acquisition requires significant amounts of both relational and file storage space. Production laboratories collect terabytes of data leading to a multitude of data management and integration challenges. In research/discovery mode the bulk of these data can be dropped, but in industrial/drug development context these data need to remain accessible and not tampered according to regulatory requirements (21CFRpart11 [16]).

2.2 Laboratory Data Lifecycle

The lifecycle of proteomics data involves the following discrete phases: sample processing, data acquisition, data processing and biological interpretation.

2.2.1 Study Design / Sample Processing

Management of samples and sample processing steps is a tedious task. A laboratory information management system (LIMS) is required to keep track of samples, study structure, grouping of samples by disease state or treatment, and other auxiliary sample parameters. Such parameters include but are not limited to sample donor attributes, clinical tests, sample amount and concentration, and sample preparation measurements. These attributes differ from study to study, requiring a database design that enables schema evolution. Furthermore, complex biological samples are fractionated in order to derive low complexity protein mixtures that are amenable to mass analysis. Documentation of fractionation as well as replication information is important not only for interpretation but also for tracking experiments in the laboratory pipeline. It is very common for a single sample in a study to result in tens or hundreds of MS acquisitions, requiring the creation and maintenance of an acquisition plan for tracking and logistics purposes.

2.2.2 Data Acquisition

Mass spectrometry acquisitions are performed and documented using vendor-supplied software running on the computer that controls the mass spectrometer. Data files are first saved on the local machine. There are several good reasons for not storing data files on instrument attached computers including physical limitations and data security requirements. Data files are therefore need to be copied to a centralized file store using custom scripts, where their location is presumably recorded in a database. Maintaining integrity and coordination between heterogeneous sources (file store and databases) with administrative autonomy is not an easy problem. Furthermore, acquisition protocol parameters such as instrument identifier, operator, settings, etc. also need to be recorded in a database.

2.2.3 Data Processing

Spectral data are extracted from the raw data files and undergo analysis that follows typically two workflows: identification and quantitation. In identification analysis each MS/MS spectrum is searched against a protein sequence database with the help of a search engine. The results of the search are reported as files but commonly are parsed and loaded into some sort of an experiments database. Quantitation analysis addresses the MS portion of the signal. Specialized applications perform recognition and integration of peaks into tuples of the form <mass, time, intensity> that represent peptides. The use of a relational store for proteomics data analyses has several advantages, including the integration of separate analysis steps and scalability of data processing. Conceptually, a join on <mass, time> between samples reports the differentially expressed peptides between samples. A join on <mass, time> between an identification and quantitation object reports the identities of the quantitated peptides. This simplified example suppressed some interesting "entity-matching" problems the solution of which involves deeper understanding of the scientific semantics of the entities.

2.2.4 Analysis and Interpretation

One goal of proteomics is to determine which proteins are present in a sample based on the (limited) peptide evidence collected in the experiment. If multiple acquisitions are available, assignment of peptides to proteins is strengthened by pulling evidence and clustering peptide hits across multiple acquisitions [17]. Visualization of the peptide and protein clusters is very important for evaluating quality of the clusters. A second goal is to translate peptide level measurements to protein level measurements, report statistically significant differential proteins, and evaluate the biological relevance of significant hits using available annotation and literature. The later requires integration of experimental, analyzed, and bioinformatics annotation data. Public databases are valuable resources of sequence and function based annotations. Integration of annotation from public sources is a very well studied problem [5,6,7,8]. Yet, a decision that organizations face is to build yet another bioinformatics database or access data directly from primary or integrated public data sources. Control over versions, content data integrity, data security, reconciling the heterogeneity of public sources, and the lack of a COTS solution, are some of the factors that influence this decision. The challenges of building a bioinformatics database are outlined in [18] and include heterogeneity, data granularity and redundancy of the public data sources.

2.3 Data and Workflow Management

The data management and bioinformatics platform for a laboratory has to satisfy two major requirements: (a) enable high throughput data acquisition, and (b) facilitate analysis, interpretation and dissemination of laboratory results. The applications and databases needed to support each of these requirements are to a large extent different [19]. Databases supporting data acquisition are designed to optimize update performance. Databases in support of data analysis are tuned for rapid exploration of massive datasets. In some cases, both requirements are present at the same time. In the proteomics example, the database of experimental data is bulk-loaded periodically, while at the same time it serves as the backend of spectral analysis programs. However, after the completion of spectral analysis, it becomes a reference warehouse of peptide and protein analyses and is extensively used for statistical reporting and data mining.

The systems supporting the laboratory workflow are both distributed and vastly heterogeneous. For example, mass spectrometry data files are acquired using vendor supplied applications running on remote machines that controls the mass spectrometer and then are copied to central file storage where an appropriate analysis workflow extracts the MS/MS data, performs database searches, and parses the results in the experiments database, and so on. Coordinating such data transfers, applications invocations and analytical data processing workflows requires the deployment of a comprehensive workflow management framework.

The metadata of laboratory data goes beyond the how, when and by whom the data were collected. Each technology platform is associated with a deep body of technical knowledge, explicit and implicit, which somehow needs to be captured in the conceptual model of the data, in order to be meaningful. For instance, the reproducibility of the measurement platform, availability and use of error models, or quality control parameters that are used for normalization are important for enabling reliable comparisons between experiments or methods. Even if the modeling methodology exists, we lack guidelines for its consistent application thus producing semantically heterogeneous data. Efforts such as MAGE-ML for microarray experiments try to alleviate this issue, but the problem sometimes is that the model, built by non-data modelers, has weak semantics and often introduce ambiguities instead of removing them [20].

3 The Proteomics Data Management System: Experience Report

In this section we highlight the components of a proteomics data management and bioinformatics platform intended for high-throughput and scalable proteomics analysis. The design objective was to do everything close to the database server including data management, application and data integration, workflow management, and implementation of proteomic analysis algorithms. The platform was developed at MDS Proteomics / Protana (now Transition Therapeutics).

The data management system encompasses databases, file management, workflow management, the database integration strategy, and data dissemination applications.

3.1 Databases

In the proteomics application there are three data spaces that need to be modeled: the sample space, the protein space and the experiment (measurement) space. Each data space is implemented as a separate database. The separation is driven by practical considerations related to maintenance and control of data entry applications. In our system, the three databases are the sample tracking database (SATS), the protein index and annotations database (AIDA), and the repository for mass spectrometry experiments and results (MSdb).. A fourth database, the analysis database, is introduced in order to (a) streamline and improve efficiency of statistical analysis, and (b) serve as persistent storage of statistical analysis results. The analysis database heavily depends on the other three and is essentially a special purpose data warehouse. All four databases form a federation which is viewed as a single database to read-only, user-facing tools

SATS (Sample and Acquisition Tracking System) is the sample database and backend of the sample tracking system. An important feature of SATS is that samples are organized in studies that consist of groups of samples and each group represents a treatment or disease condition. Studies belong to programs and programs are linked to customers. The program tag is used to control access to samples and their experimental results. In SATS, a sample can be transformed many times, producing new samples. Transformations include splitting (fractionation) and merging (pooling). Each sample keeps a reference to its root sample. Depending on the sample or study type, the descriptive attributes of the sample may differ. Modeling these attributes as (property, value) pairs solves the schema evolution problem. When a sample is transferred to the lab for MS acquisition, an acquisition name is assigned to the sample. The acquisition name serves as the join attribute between the sample, the acquisition data file, and the acquisition record that is created in the experiments database (MSdb).

MSdb is the database of MS experiments. In addition to metadata of experiments, MSdb stores the results of the identification, quantitation and differential analyses, as well as intermediate data generated by these processes. MSdb possesses properties of an operational system and a warehouse system. After the completion of the spectral analysis, a fraction of the MSdb data forms a conceptual matrix where one dimension is defined by acquisitions and the other dimension by peptides. This representation is the basis of statistical analysis and data mining and matches the structure analysis database.

AIDA (Automated Integration of Datasets and Applications) integrates protein-centric information from many internal and external sources and provides a uniform view across protein-space. A central feature is the assignment of an institutional protein-identifiers (PI) to all sequences. Each PI represents a unique combination of protein sequence and species, so that identical sequences from a given species will be grouped as a single PI (identical sequences are required to be identical in both sequence and length). The PI has the following properties: (a) The PI is persistent, i.e., the identity of a unique sequence, in a given species, will never change. Oftentimes, a unique sequence changes identity or has multiple identities (e.g. GenBank identifiers or GIs) in the public sources. Using a PI, a sequence is immune from public ID changes, yet all these changing GIs are linked to the PI. If a GI based database is used for protein searching, the comparison of identification results becomes more difficult, since the same sequence may be referenced by multiple GIs. (b) The PI maintains provenance of protein sequences, since any name changes of the sequence in the public sources is recorded in the PI record. (c) The PI functions as the cross-database link between AIDA, MSdb, and the analysis database.

AIDA is also a protein annotation system. Annotations are imported from public sources or computed. An in-house developed ETL application, called the data feeder, is responsible to maintain the database up to date. The data feeder selectively extracts information from external data sources, it transforms it to local schema, performs the necessary entity matching operations, and loads this information into AIDA. In addition, each protein entry in AIDA has several fields that hold pre-computed annotations that are calculated using a number of computational annotation tools, such as sequence feature prediction programs. These pre-computed predictions are stored in the database for rapid access.

The analysis database stores the results of statistical analyses. Since high-throughput LC-MS technology enables simultaneous analysis of hundreds of proteins represented by thousands of peptides, statistical analyses generate sizable datasets consisting of average intensities, differential effects, p-values and summary statistics on peptides and proteins. The structure of the results of these analyses is related to the methods e.g., choice of statistical tests, and necessitates a database design with built-in support for evolution. Finally, a dataset may be analyzed multiple times using different methods or decisions. The analysis database enables the persistent storage and provenance of statistical results by storing both the computed results of statistical analyses and the information necessary to document and re-compute them, including the input data, information about the software used in the analysis and various procedural choices and settings.

3.2 Integration

There are both technical and non-technical reasons for maintaining several component databases. For example, AIDA is a reference database with a complicated content building and update policy, whereas SATS is a classic LIMS database. Then again, useful scientific and operational queries often cross the boundaries of a single component. A frequent multi-database query is to find all the extra-cellular proteins that were identified with more than N peptide hits with Mascot score greater than K in all studies done for a given customer M. Such a query requires access to AIDA for sub-cellular localization, to the analysis database for protein and peptide hits, to MSdb for peptide scores and linkage to acquisitions, and to SATS for connecting acquisitions to the customer.

Multi-database queries are difficult both to specify and to compute [21]. In certain cases we try to avoid such queries by reorganizing, summarizing and materializing study data in the analysis database. As everywhere else, our team has debated the quick and dirty versus the elegant data access arguments – and there was no winner. Some user applications opted to implement scripts as an alternative for processing cross-database queries. Some others opted for federated queries assisted by the DB2 Information Integrator. The component databases are by design complementary and have minimal overlap. The overlap is limited to common fields (foreign database keys) that are used for cross-linking (joins). For example, the sample acquisition name links SATS, MSdb and the analysis databases. The PI is the cross link between AIDA, MSdb and analysis database, and so on.

Several data analysis programs run outside of the database. In production mode these programs runs either one after the other or iterate over sets of similar inputs. They may also contain side effects, i.e., update the databases or interact with users. Such programs include raw data extraction utilities, implementations of spectral analysis algorithms (not described here), and data viewers. For reasons of conceptual simplicity, maintainability and scalability, these programs are wrapped in workflows the execution of which was coordinated using a commercial workflow management engine (www.turboworx.com). The result is a simplified process, as many steps are now under the control of the workflow engine, resulting in better resource utilization and overhead reduction.

3.3 Dissemination

The Discovery Portal (DP) is a web application and collaboration environment that allows scientists to access information on proteins, maintain their projects, access proteomics analysis applications, map proteins to scientific literature and explore

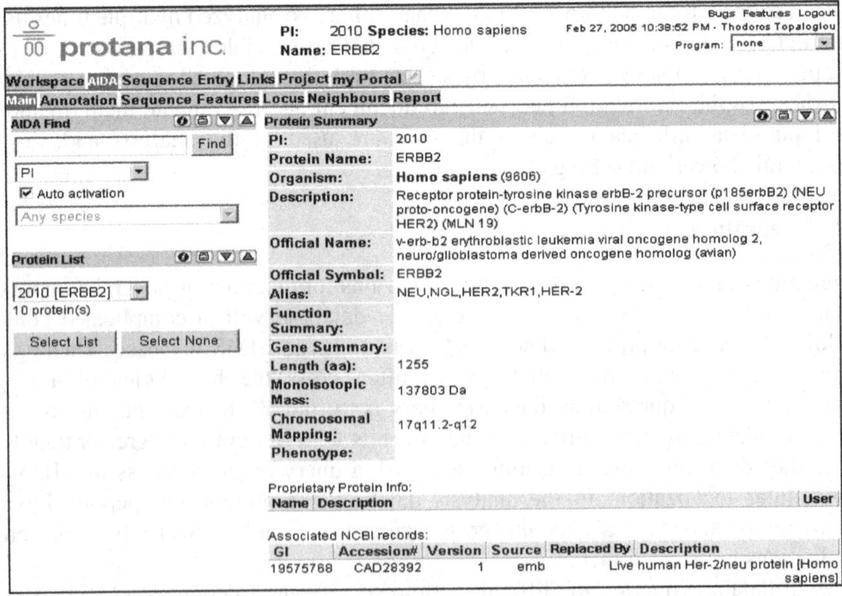

Fig. 1. The Discovery Portal showing the AIDA find, Protein list and Protein summary portlets

external databases. The Discovery Portal was designed to be the single point of access for all internal and external applications and data in the bioinformatics area. It creates a hub of information based on the family of databases mentioned earlier and provides an access interface to them.

The Discovery Portal is built using the Jetspeed portal application builder with the goal to enable aggregation of multiple Web applications is a single page as portlets, and allows users to customize and personalize the content of the page. Important portlets include the AIDA query, AIDA annotation (Fig. 1), custom reports, and a literature mining portlet, among others. The Discovery Portal is easily extendable and enables economic and rapid development of interfaces for bioinformatics applications and data sources.

The portal supports a variety of ways to integrate applications. Specifically it implements a container framework with standardized navigation features and style sheets, and a specification of a general method for deploying applications inside the framework. It also provides a common user authentication component for controlling data access and ownership. The portal maintains a runtime data object holding the data/information to be rendered, and a publisher/subscriber pattern to facilitate acting on modifications to the data object. This allows for results (proteins) of an operation, to be available for use in another application, making it really easy to run multiple applications on the same data without copying, pasting and opening of new applications.

The Workspace is another key portlet that further aids user collaboration and application interoperability. The motivating principle behind the Workspace is that experiments and bioinformatics analyses produce lists of proteins that scientists may want to store, share, modify or compare. Within the Portal, the scientific user can create protein lists as workspace objects and open them in some other application or promote them to the Portal's runtime object. The Workspace facilitates both persistent storage of user selected data and data exchange between portal applications. The latter reduces the proliferation of disparate spreadsheets and promotes interoperability. Workspace protein lists may also be associated with an open-ended set of attributes, both user-defined and derived from underlying databases. An XML database is employed to tackle the representation and storage of Workspace objects.

4 Discussion

Scientific laboratories are data rich environments that need advanced data modeling and information management technologies, but primarily need an integrated data management strategy that spans the entire data production life cycle. Traditional database management systems and data integration methodologies help greatly but are not enough to address the laboratory data lifecycle. Organizations support their needs through point solutions based on conventional technology. Principled approaches to scientific data management are still to come, although some promising proposals have emerged recently [22, 23, 24]. These proposals emphasize data semantics, data provenance, development of standards and better utilization of domain ontologies, "best-effort" integration strategies, integration of powerful analysis tools into databases, active data, notification, and workflows to enhance access to, and interpretation of, data by multiple experts.

Here we presented a particular problem instance of laboratory data management and an experience report from implementing a solution for proteomics. We claim that our problem requirements and solution can serve as a template for implementing similar solutions for laboratories following a similar data lifecycle. An important part of our solution is the integration of components through an underlying infrastructure for data and workflow management, enabling us to connect otherwise disparate information and processes, including sample preparation, mass spectrometry, protein identification, spectral analysis, and biological interpretation. This integration is proven beneficial in discovery studies. Our experience with the system shows the following benefits. First, the time it takes to do data analysis has been significantly reduced. Second, the size of the data analysis project has increased. Third, results from intermediate analysis steps are available in well-designed databases and are accessible through queries. Finally, the integrated and automated platform frees the bioinformatics scientists from manual tasks, such as running software applications and locating and connecting diverse data, and enables them to focus on data exploration and method development.

The implementation of the data management and bioinformatics platform for proteomics and high throughput laboratories in general, can not be completely supported by commercial of-the-self (COTS) tools yet. The wide set of requirements, and the fact that proteomics is a new scientific application that has not been specifically addressed by the data management vendors, are two reasons that restrict the availability of COTS tools. The commercial tools that we used in our work are limited to tools of generic functionality such as a workflow management system and data management systems, leaving plenty of application development and customization work to be done "on site". Emerging data standards are expected to pave the ground for new tools for proteomics. MzXML and PSI/MIAPE have begun to gain support of proteomics software vendors and are expected to simplify aspects of proteomics software.

The proteomics data management system that we described has been successfully deployed in production at Protana. Over a period of 12 months, the system processed nearly 20,000 acquisitions that have undergone quantitation and/or identification analysis. The performance and utility of the system have been tested in several biomarker discovery studies where we realized significant throughput gains (20-50 fold improvement) over the non-automated and manual way of processing and managing spectral data. In addition the end-to-end platform allowed for faster, more comprehensive reporting and traceability of analysis results.

Acknowledgements

I express my gratitude to my former colleagues at former MDS Proteomics/Protana and MDS Denmark who contributed to the design and implementation of the proteomics data management platform, especially to Soeren Schandorff, Soren Larsen, Brian Ramsgaard, Peder Ruhoff, Moyez Dharsee, Yury Buckman, Rob Ewing, Mike Li, Adel Shrufi, John Sulja, Panos Economopoulos, Sum Huynh, Derek Lee, Adrian Pasculescu, Anne-Marie Salter, Huicheng Wang, Kevin Mok, and all the members of the Scientific Computing team. Special thanks to Shane Climie,

Nancy Ng, Daniel Figeys and the scientists in MDSP/Protana for expressing the requirements of the proteomics data management platform.

References

[1] Brazma A., P. Hingamp, et al. Minimum information about a microarray experiment (MIAME)—toward standards for microarray data. Nature Genetics, vol 29, pp 365 - 371. 2001

[2] Spellman P, M. Miller, et al. Design and implementation of microarray gene expression markup language (MAGE-ML)., Genome Biology, 3(9), 2002.

[3] Orchard S, Hermjakob H, Binz PA, Hoogland C, Taylor CF, Zhu W, Julian RK Jr, Apweiler R. Further steps towards data standardisation: the Proteomic Standards Initiative. Proteomics, 5(2):337-9. 2005.

[4] C. Goble, C. Wroe, R. Stevens, and the myGrid consortium. The myGrid Project: Services, Architecture and Demonstrator. In Proc UK e-Science programme All Hands Conference, pages 595-603, 2003

[5] U. Leser, F. Naumann. (Almost) Hands-Off Information Integration for the Life Sciences. CIDR. 2005.

[6] T. Etzold, H. Harris, and S. Beaulah SRS: An Integration Platform for Databanks and Analysis Tools in Bioinformatics. In Bioinformatics: Managing scientific data. Edited by Z. Lacroix and T. Chrichlow. Morgan Kaufmann, 2003.

[7] Markowitz, V. M., Korzeniewski, F., Palaniappan, K., Szeto, E., Ivanova, N., and Kyrpides, N. C. 2005. The integrated microbial genomes (IMG) system: a case study in biological data management. VLDB 2005.

[8] Hsu, F., et al., *The UCSC Proteome Browser.* Nucleic Acids Res, vol. 33 (Database issue): p. D454-8. 2005

[9] Boguski, M.S. and McIntosh, M.W. Biomedical informatics for proteomics. *Nature* 422, 233–237 (2003).

[10] David Searls. Data Integration challenges in drug discovery. Nature Reviews. Drug Discovery, 2005. 4(1): p. 45-58

[11] V. Markowitz, J. Campbell, A. Chen, A. Kosky, K. Palaniapan, and T. Topaloglou. Integration Challenges in Gene Expression Data Management. In Bioinformatics: Managing Scientific Data, Edited by Z. Lacroix and T. Chrichlow. Morgan Kaufmann, 2003

[12] Tyers, M. and M. Mann, *From genomics to proteomics.* Nature, 2003. 422(6928): p. 193-7

[13] Aebersold. R. and M. Mann "Mass spectromentry-based proteomics." Nature 422: 198-207, 2003.

[14] M. Greenwood, C. Goble, R. Stevens, J. Zhao, M. Addis, D. Marvin, L. Moreau, and T. Oinn, "Provenance of e-Science Experiments --experience from Bioinformatics," in Proceedings of the UK e-Science 2nd All Hands Meeting, 2003

[15] Pedrioli, P.G., J.K. Eng, et al., *A common open representation of mass spectrometry data and its application to proteomics research.* Nature Biotechnology. **22**(11): p. 1459-66, 2004.

[16] FDA. Guidance for Industry: Part 11, Electronic Records; Electronic Signatures: Scope and Application. *http://www.fda.gov/cder/guidance/index.htm,* 2003.

[17] Yang, X., Dondeti, V., et al., *DBParser: web-based software for shotgun proteomic data analyses.* J Proteome Research. 3(5): p. 1002-8, 2004

[18] Topaloglou, T. Biological Data Management: Research, Practice and Opportunities. VLDB, 2004.
[19] Markowitz, V. and T. Topaloglou Applying Data Warehouse Concepts to Gene Expression Data Management. 2nd IEEE International Synposium in Bioinformatics and Bioengineering (BIBE), 2001.
[20] L. N. Soldatova and R. D. King. Are the current ontologies in biology good ontologies? *Nature Biotechnology* 23, 1095 - 1098 (2005)
[21] Topaloglou, T., A. Kosky, and V. Markowitz. Seamless Intergation of Biological Applications within a Database Framework. ISMB, 1999.
[22] M. Franklin, A. Halevy, D. Maier. From Databases to Dataspaces: A new abstraction for information management. SIGMOD Record 34(4). 2005
[23] J. Gray, D.T. Liu, M. Nieto-Santisteban, A. Szalay, D. DeWitt and G. Heber. Scientific Data Management in the Coming Decade. SIGMOD Record 34(4). 2005.
[24] H. V. Jagadish and F. Olken. Database management for life sciences research. SIGMOD Record 33(2), 2004

Policy Models for Data Sharing

Ken Smith

Principal Database Scientist
The MITRE Corporation, Mail Stop H317
7515 Colshire Drive, McLean, Virginia 22102-7508
kps@mitre.org

Abstract. Data sharing has become an enabler of a diverse and important set of activities in areas such as science, law enforcement, and commerce. Data sharing scenarios frequently involve issues such as personal confidentiality, data misinterpretation, the potential for malicious exploitation of shared data, data with proprietary or first-use value, secret data, and governmental regulation. For these reasons, the need to state and enforce data sharing policy has grown increasingly significant. In this talk, we discuss models for data sharing policy and their key concepts.

Keywords: Data sharing, policy model, access, community, agreement.

1 Introduction

Data sharing has recently come to the forefront as an enabler of a diverse and important set of activities including the development of brain atlases, monitoring disease outbreaks (whether naturally occurring or the result of bioterrorism), and cooperative counter-narcotics efforts. In this talk, we first describe several motivating examples which require widespread data sharing. For example, many human populations have characteristic features of brain anatomy and patterns of brain development. This is not only true for disease populations, but also for those determined by demographic measures like handedness and gender. However, due to high intersubject variability, these population-specific features and patterns may not be visible in a given individual, and may only emerge when studying a large-N composite brain atlas for that population. Since it may be beyond the resources of a single laboratory to obtain a sufficiently large N, data sharing acts as an enabler of this important type of neuroscientific research.

The topic of data sharing is also subject to the *blind men and the elephant* effect. Data sharing draws on many fields, and each specialty involved can tend see it as an extension of their own field, without seeing the full bigger picture. In the second part of this talk, I will briefly provide an overview of five perspectives which make a major contribution to data sharing. These include: delivery services, understanding (e.g., annotation, integration), discovery, incentivization (i.e., the reward perspective), and policy. Although our focus is policy, this places policy in its appropriate context.

Finally, I will conclude with a discussion of models for data sharing policy. In the case of unrestricted access, policy does not play a large role in data sharing. However

D.W. Embley, A. Olivé, and S. Ram (Eds.): ER 2006, LNCS 4215, pp. 581 – 582, 2006.

many realistic data sharing scenarios require data owners to control access to shared data. Shared information requiring special protection includes: confidential personal information, information which may be misinterpreted, information which could be maliciously exploited, secret or classified information, information subject to federal or local regulation (e.g., HIPAA), and information with a proprietary or first-use value (e.g., copyrighted songs, pre-publication scientific data). This confluence of the need to share and the need to protect information requires well-designed policy models and tools. Policy models must be human-interpretable so policies are easily and correctly formulated, and tool-interpretable so policies can be automatically enforced. It is also useful to provide gradations of data visibility, and to address concepts such as *obligation* and policy evolution. We will present several such models including community-based sharing [1], and data sharing agreements [2].

References

1. Smith, K., Jajodia, S., Swarup, V., Hoyt, J., Hamilton, G., Cornett, T., and Faatz, D. Enabling the sharing of neuroimaging data through well-defined intermediate levels of visibility. *NeuroImage* 22 (2004), 1646-1656.
2. Swarup, V., Seligman, L., and Rosenthal, A. Specifying Data Sharing Agreements, *Proceedings of Policy 2006: IEEE Workshop on Policies for Distributed Systems and Networks,* London, Ontario, June 2006

Protocol Analysis for Exploring the Role of Application Domain in Conceptual Schema Understanding

Vijay Khatri and Iris Vessey

Indiana University, USA; UQ and QUT, Australia
vkhatri@indiana.edu, i.vessey@qut.edu.au

In keeping with prior research [1] that suggests that the objective of empirical research in conceptual modeling is to understand the cognitive model created by viewing conceptual schemas (e.g., ER diagrams), this research contributes to the foundation for developing a cognitive model of conceptual modelers. The aspect on which we focus in our research is the role of the application domain in conceptual schema understanding.

Although Information Systems (IS) development can be viewed as application domain problem solving using a software solution, research in the field of IS development has investigated the role of the *IS domain* almost to the total exclusion of the *application domain*. Additionally, most of the empirical research in conceptual modeling has focused primarily on observing the effects of certain stimuli and has, thereby, treated IS problem solving as a "black box." Studies that address *how* problem solving occurs focus on "opening up the black box" that lies between problem-solving inputs and outputs; that is, they investigate what happens during individual problem solving (*isomorphic approach*) rather than simply observing the effects of certain stimuli averaged over a number of cases, as in traditional studies (*paramorphic approach*). The most common approach to opening up the black box is to examine the characteristics of the problem-solving process using protocol analysis.

Because both the theory and prior exploratory findings [2] suggest that application domain knowledge is important on just those problem-solving tasks that require transformation of knowledge in the conceptual schema, so-called *schema-based problem-solving tasks*, we explored how problem solvers address such tasks by examining participants' problem-solving processes using protocol analysis.

We found that knowledge of the application and IS domains result in similar search behavior: both familiarity with the application domain and high IS knowledge result in more focused, that is, deeper search, while unfamiliarity with the application domain and low IS knowledge result in broader, and therefore shallower search.

References

Gemino, A. and Wand, Y. "A Framework for Empirical Evaluation of Conceptual Modeling Techniques," *Requirements Engineering*, 9, 2004, pp. 248-260.

Khatri, V., Vessey, I., Ramesh, V., Clay, P., and Park, S.J., "Understanding Conceptual Schemas: Exploring the Role of Application and IS Domain Knowledge," *Information Systems Research*, (17:1), March 2006, pp. 81-99.

D.W. Embley, A. Olivé, and S. Ram (Eds.): ER 2006, LNCS 4215, p. 583, 2006.

Auto-completion of Underspecified SQL Queries

Terrence Mason[1] and Ramon Lawrence[2]

[1] University of Wisconsin-Stout, Menomonie, WI, USA
[2] University of British Columbia Okanagan, Kelowna, BC, Canada

Formulating SQL queries involving joins is tedious, error-prone, and requires in-depth schema knowledge. We demonstrate a modified version of SQL [2] that does not require specification of table references and joins. The Schema-Free SQL system can expresses queries not supported in keyword-based searches [1]. Unlike Universal Relation approaches, the system is scaleable to large schemas, and it has built-in mechanisms for handling ambiguity and ranking interpretations for the user. The auto-completion feature is not intended to remove all of the complexity in building SQL queries, just like auto-completion of code fragments does not remove the challenges of programming. However, it *does* make it easier to build SQL queries. Thus, the system provides a value-added feature to SQL querying that increases its flexibility and usability with no sacrifice in expressiveness or performance. The amount of the final SQL code that is auto-completed depends on the number of joins and the complexity of the rest of the SQL expression. The time to complete a query takes around 5 milliseconds [3].

This demonstration also illustrates the value of identifying semantically equivalent join paths (shortcut joins) [3]. If not handled properly, a query with a single unique interpretation may have multiple equivalent SQL interpretations. Removing this false ambiguity results in fewer queries being identified as ambiguous and reduces user confusion. In the demonstration we:

- Show pre-entered queries on the TPC-H schema and their auto-completion.
- Allow users to enter queries and have them completed by the system.
- Demonstrate how removal of shortcut joins greatly reduces the amount of ambiguity and number of query interpretations. For TPC-H the number of unambiguous queries is increased by a factor of three [3].

Overall, the contribution is a very usable system for auto-completion of SQL, and a general technique (shortcut joins) for reducing query ambiguity that can be also applied to other interfaces such as keyword search.

References

1. Hristidis, V., Gravano, L., Papakonstantinou, Y.: Efficient IR-Style Keyword Search over Relational Databases. VLDB (2003) 850–861
2. Mason, T., Lawrence, R.: INFER: A Relational Query Language Without the Complexity of SQL. ACM CIKM (2005) 241–242
3. Mason, T., Wang, L., Lawrence, R.: AutoJoin: Providing Freedom from Specifying Joins. ICEIS (2005) 31–38

D.W. Embley, A. Olivé, and S. Ram (Eds.): ER 2006, LNCS 4215, p. 584, 2006.

iQL: A Query Language for the Instance-Based Data Model

Jeffrey Parsons[1] and Jianmin Su[2]

[1] Faculty of Business Administration,
[2] Department of Computer Science,
[1,2] Memorial University of Newfoundland,
St. John's, NL, Canada
{jeffreyp@mun.ca, jianmin@cs.mun.ca}

1 Summary

Unlike class-based models, such as the relational model and object-oriented models, the instance-based data model (IBDM) [1] separates data stored about individual things (instances) from how those instances are classified, resulting in a 'two-layered' approach (instance and class layers). In this poster and system demonstration, we illustrate the use of iQL (instance-based query language) for the IBDM. This language supports unique query capabilities that exploit the separation of data about instances from their classification. The tool has been implemented in conjunction with a prototype DBMS to support the IBDM [2]. The basic structure of an iQL query is:

```
Select < attribute and function list >
    [from <class list>]
    [sharing <mutual property condition list>]
    [where < intrinsic property condition list>].
```

We show that iQL is compatible with SQL for class-based queries, and further demonstrate its additional query capabilities. A prototype implementation of a DBMS based on IBDM, including an implementation of iQL, has been developed [2], and will be demonstrated at the conference.

Note two structural differences between iQL and SQL: (1) the `from` clause is optional in iQL; (2) the `sharing` clause is new to iQL. These two differences give iQL more powerful capabilities than SQL. In the instance-based model, it is possible to query the whole instance layer to find which instances possess some properties (e.g., to find which instances possess 'age', the iQL command is: `Select age`).

References

1. Parsons, J. and Y. Wand. 2000. Emancipating Instances from the Tyranny of Classes in Information Modeling. ACM Transactions on Database Systems. 25, 2, 228-268.
2. Su, J. 2003. A Database Management System to Support the Instance-based Data Model: Design, Implementation, and Evaluation. Master's Thesis, Department of Computer Science, Memorial University of Newfoundland.

D.W. Embley, A. Olivé, and S. Ram (Eds.): ER 2006, LNCS 4215, p. 585, 2006.

Designing Under the Influence of Speech Acts: A Strategy for Composing Enterprise Integration Solutions

Karthikeyan Umapathy and Sandeep Purao

College of Information Sciences and Technology, Penn State University
{kumapathy, spurao}@ist.psu.edu

Designing enterprise-wide integration solutions remains a difficult task. Enterprise Integration Patterns (EIP) [1] provide possible design solutions that may be used to compose enterprise-wide integration solutions. Because of the multitude of platforms on which legacy systems are implemented, these composed solutions must ensure platform-independent implementation, e.g. with web services. A promising mechanism that allows this path is conversation models [2] that may be used to implement interactions among web services that represent different legacy systems. For this translation to occur, though, EIPs must be converted into a representation that is amenable to a conversation models.

For example, consider the pattern publish/ subscribe channel [1]. This pattern will need to be defined in terms of speech acts [3] (e.g. informative). A precondition to this informative message exchange would be an agreement on part of publishers to publish such information. Further, the roles played may include: Publisher as Initiator and Sender, and Subscribers as Receiver. A knowledge base that captures the EIPs would, thus, need to capture all, the pre-conditions, the post-conditions, the roles, and the speech acts that comprise the integration pattern.

We are developing a research prototype, IDAssist (Integration Designer Assistant), which would include such a knowledge base, and present the designers with the functionality to decide appropriate EIPs for their integration task. This research prototype is being developed using Java^{TM} with an interface that allows drag and drop capability using Java Swing. This interface would allow designers to develop business process diagrams using BPMN [4] and guide them in identifying appropriate pattern for each connections in the business processes. It contains knowledge base that stores integration patterns in an XML specification, called Enterprise Integration Pattern XML (eipXML). Outputs from the tool can be used to design enterprise integration solutions based on EIPs and network of speech acts, converted into appropriate conversation policy specifications [2] that govern interactions among web services.

References

1. Hohpe, G., Woolf, B.: Enterprise Integration Patterns. Addison-Wesley (2004)
2. Hanson, J.E., Nandi, P., Kumaran, S.: Conversation support for Business Process Integration. IEEE International Enterprise Distributed Object Computing Conference (EDOC) (2002) 65-74
3. Searle, J.R.: Speech acts: An essay in the philosophy of language. Cambridge University, Cambridge, England (1969)
4. BPMN: Business Process Modeling Notation Specification. Vol. 2006. Object Management Group, Inc. (OMG) (2006)

D.W. Embley, A. Olivé, and S. Ram (Eds.): ER 2006, LNCS 4215, p. 586, 2006.

Geometry of Concepts

Olga Brazhnik

Center for Information Technology
National Institutes of Health,
10401 Fernwood Rd, Bethesda, MD 20897
brazhnik@nih.gov

Every study organizes data according to a specific conceptualization scheme, which is defined by the purpose and method of exploration. Co-processing data from diverse studies requires concept mapping. The model presented in this work places all elements of knowledge into a topological space. Conceptualization schemes subdivide this space into subspaces of lower dimensionality where every element has well-defined coordinates. Allocating semantics to the conceptualization scheme enables the use of abstract mathematical approaches, such as category theory and geometry, for concept and data mapping. Relative coordinates of concepts, models and data are defined via morphisms that represent complex relationships among these elements. Data models for implementing morphisms in a database are presented here. This work provides a framework for data and knowledge integration illustrated with practical examples. It addresses several important challenges in interdisciplinary data integration and ontology building, such as defining complex relationships and unambiguous data interpretation. The geometrical interpretation enables visualization of the intangible world of data and knowledge and facilitates interactive and meaningful discussions of the subject.

D.W. Embley, A. Olivé, and S. Ram (Eds.): ER 2006, LNCS 4215, p. 587, 2006.

Geometry of Concepts

Author Index

Lecture Notes in Computer Science

For information about Vols. 1–4169

please contact your bookseller or Springer

Vol. 4270: H. Zha, Z. Pan, H. Thwaites, A.C. Addison, M. Forte (Eds.), Interactive Technologies and Sociotechnical Systems. XVI, 547 pages. 2006.

Vol. 4265: N. Lavrač, L. Todorovski, K.P. Jantke (Eds.), Discovery Science. XIV, 384 pages. 2006. (Sublibrary LNAI).

Vol. 4264: J.L. Balcázar, P.M. Long, F. Stephan (Eds.), Algorithmic Learning Theory. XIII, 393 pages. 2006. (Sublibrary LNAI).

Vol. 4254: T. Grust, H. Höpfner, A. Illarramendi, S. Jablonski, M. Mesiti, S. Müller, P.-L. Patranjan, K.-U. Sattler, M. Spiliopoulou (Eds.), Current Trends in Database Technology – EDBT 2006. XXXI, 932 pages. 2006.

Vol. 4253: B. Gabrys, R.J. Howlett, L.C. Jain (Eds.), Knowledge-Based Intelligent Information and Engineering Systems, Part III. XXXII, 1301 pages. 2006. (Sublibrary LNAI).

Vol. 4252: B. Gabrys, R.J. Howlett, L.C. Jain (Eds.), Knowledge-Based Intelligent Information and Engineering Systems, Part II. XXXIII, 1335 pages. 2006. (Sublibrary LNAI).

Vol. 4251: B. Gabrys, R.J. Howlett, L.C. Jain (Eds.), Knowledge-Based Intelligent Information and Engineering Systems, Part I. LXVI, 1297 pages. 2006. (Sublibrary LNAI).

Vol. 4249: L. Goubin, M. Matsui (Eds.), Cryptographic Hardware and Embedded Systems - CHES 2006. XII, 462 pages. 2006.

Vol. 4248: S. Staab, V. Svátek (Eds.), Engineering Knowledge in the Age of the Semantic Web. XIV, 400 pages. 2006. (Sublibrary LNAI).

Vol. 4247: T.-D. Wang, X. Li, S.-H. Chen, X. Wang, H. Abbass, H. Iba, G. Chen, X. Yao (Eds.), Simulated Evolution and Learning. XXI, 940 pages. 2006.

Vol. 4243: T. Yakhno, E.J. Neuhold (Eds.), Advances in Information Systems. XIII, 420 pages. 2006.

Vol. 4241: R.R. Beichel, M. Sonka (Eds.), Computer Vision Approaches to Medical Image Analysis. XI, 262 pages. 2006.

Vol. 4239: H.Y. Youn, M. Kim, H. Morikawa (Eds.), Ubiquitous Computing Systems. XVI, 548 pages. 2006.

Vol. 4238: Y.-T. Kim, M. Takano (Eds.), Management of Convergence Networks and Services. XVIII, 605 pages. 2006.

Vol. 4236: L. Breveglieri, I. Koren, D. Naccache, J.-P. Seifert (Eds.), Fault Diagnosis and Tolerance in Cryptography. XIII, 253 pages. 2006.

Vol. 4234: I. King, J. Wang, L. Chan, D. Wang (Eds.), Neural Information Processing, Part III. XXII, 1227 pages. 2006.

Vol. 4233: I. King, J. Wang, L. Chan, D. Wang (Eds.), Neural Information Processing, Part II. XXII, 1203 pages. 2006.

Vol. 4232: I. King, J. Wang, L. Chan, D. Wang (Eds.), Neural Information Processing, Part I. XLVI, 1153 pages. 2006.

Vol. 4229: E. Najm, J.F. Pradat-Peyre, V.V. Donzeau-Gouge (Eds.), Formal Techniques for Networked and Distributed Systems - FORTE 2006. X, 486 pages. 2006.

Vol. 4228: D.E. Lightfoot, C.A. Szyperski (Eds.), Modular Programming Languages. X, 415 pages. 2006.

Vol. 4227: W. Nejdl, K. Tochtermann (Eds.), Innovative Approaches for Learning and Knowledge Sharing. XVII, 721 pages. 2006.

Vol. 4225: J.F. Martínez-Trinidad, J.A. Carrasco Ochoa, J. Kittler (Eds.), Progress in Pattern Recognition, Image Analysis and Applications. XIX, 995 pages. 2006.

Vol. 4224: E. Corchado, H. Yin, V. Botti, C. Fyfe (Eds.), Intelligent Data Engineering and Automated Learning – IDEAL 2006. XXVII, 1447 pages. 2006.

Vol. 4223: L. Wang, L. Jiao, G. Shi, X. Li, J. Liu (Eds.), Fuzzy Systems and Knowledge Discovery. XXVIII, 1335 pages. 2006. (Sublibrary LNAI).

Vol. 4222: L. Jiao, L. Wang, X. Gao, J. Liu, F. Wu (Eds.), Advances in Natural Computation, Part II. XLII, 998 pages. 2006.

Vol. 4221: L. Jiao, L. Wang, X. Gao, J. Liu, F. Wu (Eds.), Advances in Natural Computation, Part I. XLI, 992 pages. 2006.

Vol. 4219: D. Zamboni, C. Kruegel (Eds.), Recent Advances in Intrusion Detection. XII, 331 pages. 2006.

Vol. 4218: S. Graf, W. Zhang (Eds.), Automated Technology for Verification and Analysis. XIV, 540 pages. 2006.

Vol. 4217: P. Cuenca, L. Orozco-Barbosa (Eds.), Personal Wireless Communications. XV, 532 pages. 2006.

Vol. 4216: M.R. Berthold, R. Glen, I. Fischer (Eds.), Computational Life Sciences II. XIII, 269 pages. 2006. (Sublibrary LNBI).

Vol. 4215: D.W. Embley, A. Olivé, S. Ram (Eds.), Conceptual Modeling - ER 2006. XVI, 590 pages. 2006.

Vol. 4213: J. Fürnkranz, T. Scheffer, M. Spiliopoulou (Eds.), Knowledge Discovery in Databases: PKDD 2006. XXII, 660 pages. 2006. (Sublibrary LNAI).

Vol. 4212: J. Fürnkranz, T. Scheffer, M. Spiliopoulou (Eds.), Machine Learning: ECML 2006. XXIII, 851 pages. 2006. (Sublibrary LNAI).

Vol. 4211: P. Vogt, Y. Sugita, E. Tuci, C. Nehaniv (Eds.), Symbol Grounding and Beyond. VIII, 237 pages. 2006. (Sublibrary LNAI).

Vol. 4210: C. Priami (Ed.), Computational Methods in Systems Biology. X, 323 pages. 2006. (Sublibrary LNBI).

Vol. 4209: F. Crestani, P. Ferragina, M. Sanderson (Eds.), String Processing and Information Retrieval. XIV, 367 pages. 2006.

Vol. 4208: M. Gerndt, D. Kranzlmüller (Eds.), High Performance Computing and Communications. XXII, 938 pages. 2006.

Vol. 4207: Z. Ésik (Ed.), Computer Science Logic. XII, 627 pages. 2006.

Vol. 4206: P. Dourish, A. Friday (Eds.), UbiComp 2006: Ubiquitous Computing. XIX, 526 pages. 2006.

Vol. 4205: G. Bourque, N. El-Mabrouk (Eds.), Comparative Genomics. X, 231 pages. 2006. (Sublibrary LNBI).

Vol. 4204: F. Benhamou (Ed.), Principles and Practice of Constraint Programming - CP 2006. XVIII, 774 pages. 2006.

Vol. 4203: F. Esposito, Z.W. Raś, D. Malerba, G. Semeraro (Eds.), Foundations of Intelligent Systems. XVIII, 767 pages. 2006. (Sublibrary LNAI).

Vol. 4202: E. Asarin, P. Bouyer (Eds.), Formal Modeling and Analysis of Timed Systems. XI, 369 pages. 2006.

Vol. 4201: Y. Sakakibara, S. Kobayashi, K. Sato, T. Nishino, E. Tomita (Eds.), Grammatical Inference: Algorithms and Applications. XII, 359 pages. 2006. (Sublibrary LNAI).

Vol. 4200: I.F.C. Smith (Ed.), Intelligent Computing in Engineering and Architecture. XIII, 692 pages. 2006. (Sublibrary LNAI).

Vol. 4199: O. Nierstrasz, J. Whittle, D. Harel, G. Reggio (Eds.), Model Driven Engineering Languages and Systems. XVI, 798 pages. 2006.

Vol. 4198: O. Nasraoui, O. Zaiane, M. Spiliopoulou, B. Mobasher, B. Masand, P. Yu (Eds.), Advances in Web Minding and Web Usage Analysis. IX, 177 pages. 2006. (Sublibrary LNAI).

Vol. 4197: M. Raubal, H.J. Miller, A.U. Frank, M.F. Goodchild (Eds.), Geographic, Information Science. XIII, 419 pages. 2006.

Vol. 4196: K. Fischer, I.J. Timm, E. André, N. Zhong (Eds.), Multiagent System Technologies. X, 185 pages. 2006. (Sublibrary LNAI).

Vol. 4195: D. Gaiti, G. Pujolle, E. Al-Shaer, K. Calvert, S. Dobson, G. Leduc, O. Martikainen (Eds.), Autonomic Networking. IX, 316 pages. 2006.

Vol. 4194: V.G. Ganzha, E.W. Mayr, E.V. Vorozhtsov (Eds.), Computer Algebra in Scientific Computing. XI, 313 pages. 2006.

Vol. 4193: T.P. Runarsson, H.-G. Beyer, E. Burke, J.J. Merelo-Guervós, L.D. Whitley, X. Yao (Eds.), Parallel Problem Solving from Nature - PPSN IX. XIX, 1061 pages. 2006.

Vol. 4192: B. Mohr, J.L. Träff, J. Worringen, J. Dongarra (Eds.), Recent Advances in Parallel Virtual Machine and Message Passing Interface. XVI, 414 pages. 2006.

Vol. 4191: R. Larsen, M. Nielsen, J. Sporring (Eds.), Medical Image Computing and Computer-Assisted Intervention – MICCAI 2006, Part II. XXXVIII, 981 pages. 2006.

Vol. 4190: R. Larsen, M. Nielsen, J. Sporring (Eds.), Medical Image Computing and Computer-Assisted Intervention – MICCAI 2006, Part I. XXXVVIII, 949 pages. 2006.

Vol. 4189: D. Gollmann, J. Meier, A. Sabelfeld (Eds.), Computer Security – ESORICS 2006. XI, 548 pages. 2006.

Vol. 4188: P. Sojka, I. Kopeček, K. Pala (Eds.), Text, Speech and Dialogue. XV, 721 pages. 2006. (Sublibrary LNAI).

Vol. 4187: J.J. Alferes, J. Bailey, W. May, U. Schwertel (Eds.), Principles and Practice of Semantic Web Reasoning. XI, 277 pages. 2006.

Vol. 4186: C. Jesshope, C. Egan (Eds.), Advances in Computer Systems Architecture. XIV, 605 pages. 2006.

Vol. 4185: R. Mizoguchi, Z. Shi, F. Giunchiglia (Eds.), The Semantic Web – ASWC 2006. XX, 778 pages. 2006.

Vol. 4184: M. Bravetti, M. Núñez, G. Zavattaro (Eds.), Web Services and Formal Methods. X, 289 pages. 2006.

Vol. 4183: J. Euzenat, J. Domingue (Eds.), Artificial Intelligence: Methodology, Systems, and Applications. XIII, 291 pages. 2006. (Sublibrary LNAI).

Vol. 4182: H.T. Ng, M.-K. Leong, M.-Y. Kan, D. Ji (Eds.), Information Retrieval Technology. XVI, 684 pages. 2006.

Vol. 4180: M. Kohlhase, OMDoc – An Open Markup Format for Mathematical Documents [version 1.2]. XIX, 428 pages. 2006. (Sublibrary LNAI).

Vol. 4179: J. Blanc-Talon, W. Philips, D. Popescu, P. Scheunders (Eds.), Advanced Concepts for Intelligent Vision Systems. XXIV, 1224 pages. 2006.

Vol. 4178: A. Corradini, H. Ehrig, U. Montanari, L. Ribeiro, G. Rozenberg (Eds.), Graph Transformations. XII, 473 pages. 2006.

Vol. 4177: R. Marín, E. Onaindía, A. Bugarín, J. Santos (Eds.), Current Topics in Artificial Intelligence. XV, 482 pages. 2006. (Sublibrary LNAI).

Vol. 4176: S.K. Katsikas, J. Lopez, M. Backes, S. Gritzalis, B. Preneel (Eds.), Information Security. XIV, 548 pages. 2006.

Vol. 4175: P. Bücher, B.M.E. Moret (Eds.), Algorithms in Bioinformatics. XII, 402 pages. 2006. (Sublibrary LNBI).

Vol. 4174: K. Franke, K.-R. Müller, B. Nickolay, R. Schäfer (Eds.), Pattern Recognition. XX, 773 pages. 2006.

Vol. 4173: S. El Yacoubi, B. Chopard, S. Bandini (Eds.), Cellular Automata. XV, 734 pages. 2006.

Vol. 4172: J. Gonzalo, C. Thanos, M.F. Verdejo, R.C. Carrasco (Eds.), Research and Advanced Technology for Digital Libraries. XVII, 569 pages. 2006.